# American
# democracy

St. Martin's Press
New York

# Lewis Lipsitz

University
of North Carolina
at Chapel Hill

# American democracy

For Max Blatt, who first taught me to love political debate

For Lucho Quiros, Chilean democrat, who chose exile over compliance with tyranny

For my friends from the struggles of the sixties— when comradeship was part of democracy

Library of Congress Catalog Card Number: 85-61292

Copyright © 1986 by St. Martin's Press, Inc.

All rights reserved.

Manufactured in the United States of America.

09876

fedcba

ISBN: 0-312-02780-X

**Book design:** Betty Binns Graphics/Betty Binns
**Cover:** Darby Downey
**Cover photo:** Mark Antman/The Image Works
**Photo researcher:** R. Lynn Goldberg, Visual Impact

## ACKNOWLEDGMENTS

Acknowledgments and copyrights continue at the back of the book on pages 596 ff., which constitute an extension of the copyright page.

Willy Martinussen: *The Distant Democracy* (London: John Wiley and Sons, Ltd., 1977). Reprinted by permission.

Johann Wolfgang von Goethe: "The United States," translation reprinted from Robert Bly (ed.): *Forty Poems on Recent American History* (Madison, Minn.: Sixties Press). Copyright © by Robert Bly. Reprinted with his permission.

Richard F. Tomasson: *Sweden: The Prototype of Modern Society* (New York: Random House, 1970). Reprinted by permission of the author.

Jess Stein (ed.): *The Random House Dictionary*. Copyright © 1978 by Random House, Inc. Reprinted by permission of the publisher.

Table 4.1 from Advisory Commission on Intergovernmental Relations: *Significant Features of Fiscal Federalism*, 1980–81, p. 62.

Figure 4.1 from U.S. Bureau of the Census: "Federal Aid to State and Local Government 1965–1981"; *Statistical Abstracts of the United States, 1981*, p. 282.

Figure 4.3 from John J. Harrigan: *Politics and Policy in States and Communities*, 2nd ed. Copyright © 1984 by John J. Harrigan. Reprinted by permission of Little, Brown and Company.

Figure 4.4 data from Andrew Hacker: *U/S: A Statistical Portrait of the American People* (New York: Viking Penguin, 1983).

Figure 4.5 from Martha V. Grotton (ed.): *Congressional Districts in the 1980s* (Washington, D.C.: Congressional Quarterly Press, 1983). Reprinted by permission.

Table 5.1 reprinted by permission from *1980 Supplement to Constitutional Interpretation: Cases, Essays, Materials* by H.W. Chase and C. Ducat. Copyright © 1980 by West

# Preface

I WAS never a person who placed much faith in textbooks. When I began my career as a university professor, I tended, like many of my fellow political scientists, to scorn the entire genre. Textbooks, it seemed to us, were typically dull, overloaded with irrelevant information, and eminently forgettable. A textbook with opinions and interpretations was almost a contradiction in terms: punches had to be pulled, values and commitments disguised, issues evaded or drained of real controversy. There were, of course, a small number of exceptions, but they seemed only to illuminate how general the problem was.

It is therefore with a considerable sense of irony that I write this preface to my own U.S. politics text. What excuses can I find now that I have committed the deed and fathered one of those hardcover behemoths!

*American Democracy*, I tell myself, is different. Although it covers the nuts and bolts of U.S. politics in full detail, it is something more. It is a book about democracy, about what that concept means, about how democratic politics operate, especially how they operate in the U.S. It is a book that attempts to link theory and practice, to describe the workings of American politics within a framework that helps us to form judgments about how successful our democracy has been.

It is a book I hope will stimulate and provoke both student and professor. It is a skeptical book. I am not satisfied, by a long shot, with the current state of democratic politics in the United States. We have come a long way in two hundred years toward remedying many obviously undemocratic aspects of our system, but many difficulties remain in distributions of economic and political power, in foreign policy confusions, in the way political influence is exercised, in the workings of presidency and Congress, in vast gaps in public information and understanding. I am not inclined to dampen my concerns by agreeing with the claim that real world democracies can never live up to a supposedly utopian democratic ideal—and that therefore we just have to be satisfied with what we've got, more or less. Such "realism," in my opinion, is a bad compromise with history. It fails to recognize how much effort must continually be activated if democratic politics, in this or any other nation, are to survive, and more important, to grow and prosper. Therefore, my book is a critical one, designed to entice the reader to ask some difficult and perhaps sometimes uncomfortable questions—but I hope always interesting ones—about our polity.

Most important, I hope *American Democracy* will not bore its users. Inevitably, there are some dry moments. Very few, if any, authors have yet succeeded in making the legalities of American federalism or the organization of the bureaucracy as hot a set of topics as sex, drugs, and rock-and-roll (though I like to think that both of these important topics receive here a questioning treatment that highlights their relevance to democratic concerns). Such dry spots will not come along too often, I hope, and when they do will be part of a larger discussion that should carry the text along. It has been my aim to have the reader remain aware throughout the book of its underlying purpose—understanding and judging democratic politics. If this text is to have a meaning more enduring than its service in a one-semester required course, then this is it.

I don't mind telling the reader that I care very deeply about the subjects discussed here. Having lived in the United States and having participated in the turmoils of the sixties, having spent my adult life teaching about politics, I readily acknowledge that many of these subjects are ones that I have wondered about, fought about, and tried to influence. It is my caring, I hope, rather than my particular political positions, that have shaped this book. Not that I have disguised my views; they should be evident to the reader. But it is not so much agreement that is important as thought, concern, and a struggle to understand.

## Acknowledgments

Professor Ronald Claunch of Stephen F. Austin University has prepared a Study Guide to assist students in learning the concepts covered in the book. Professors Thomas Yautek and Trudy Steuernagel of Kent State University and Professor Priscilla Southwell of the University of Oregon have prepared the Instructor's Manual. A Test Item File is available in both printed format and on floppy disks, compatible with the IBM-PC and Apple 2II.

I would like to express thanks to the Institute for Social Science Research, University of North Carolina—Chapel Hill, and to Betsy Taylor for help in preparing the manuscript; to Paul Price, Sandy Milroy, Rick Hall, Rich Forgette, John Haskell, and Scott Kessler for assistance and suggestion; to Carolyn Watkins and David Garrow for their willingness to pause in their own demanding tasks in order to prepare small pieces for this book; to Al Wurth for constructive encouragement; to my sister, Barbara Geller, for help in obtaining information about and making sense of Congress; to Mike Lienesch, Jeff Obler, Jurg Steiner and Thad Beyle for general helpfulness.

Lewis Lipsitz

# Contents

# American
democracy

# Part one

# Foundations

# Chapter one

# Democracy

## The ideal
## and
## the real

MOST Americans are used to thinking of their country as a "democracy." In fact, public opinion research has shown that Americans are particularly proud of the fact that they live in a democratic country. There is no point in debating whether or not the United States is a democracy—as if there were only two categories that nations could fit into, the democratic and the undemocratic. In the ordinary sense in which the term is used, the United States clearly is a democratic nation. However, a more difficult, more intricate, more interesting question is, Just *how democratic* are we?

To put this question into perspective, imagine a society with a written constitution that grants everyone the right to vote, holds free elections, proclaims its belief in free speech, free press, the rights of political parties to organize and put forward their views, and so on. Superficially, such a nation might seem democratic. But we would have to look beyond the constitution to find out if that was in fact the case. For example, we might, upon closer examination, discover that this nation was actually ruled by a small group of wealthy landowners who ignored the constitutional provisions whenever it was convenient to do so. Most of the inhabitants might be relatively poor peasants who depended on the land-owners for employment. Anyone voicing serious dissent might be jailed or otherwise intimidated.

We learn several things from this hypothetical case. To begin with, the written word is not enough: democratic provisions in a constitution may or may not be honored in practice. Second, we see that great differences in wealth and power can undermine the possibility of achieving democracy. Where very few control most of the wealth and have inordinate access to power, democracy will probably be drained of its meaning.

Consider another case: a country that gradually moves toward greater degrees of democracy. Early in this nation's history, only some citizens were allowed the right to vote. Over decades, after considerable agitation and struggle, others are permitted to join the suffrage. Finally, after almost two hundred years, the suffrage is opened to all. Nonetheless, many citizens remain ignorant about politics, and almost half of those who could vote simply do not bother to do so, even in the most important elections. How democratic would we say such a nation was?

The nation just described, of course, is the United States—in which women and blacks were excluded from the suffrage for many years, and full legal protections for voting rights were not achieved by these

3

groups until 1920 and 1965, respectively. In our society today, many citizens remain politically uninformed and inactive, with only 50 percent of eligible voters likely to turn out even in presidential elections.

Democracy is a matter of degree and quality. The question of whether or not a country is democratic can be looked at from many perspectives:

Are the political rights of every citizen effectively protected (and used)?

Is the level of public knowledge high? Is public discussion informed and useful?

Do most people, and especially most leaders, support the democratic idea?

Do some people or groups have far more influence than others, because of wealth, power, prestige, or other factors? Do small groups have power and influence in great disproportion to their numbers?

Does the government keep its trust with the people? Does it violate its own laws?

Are politics honest, leaders trustworthy?

Does the government often use violence against citizens? Is political life characterized by a high level of coercion?

Does each citizen have a realistic chance of attaining and maintaining a decent life—including basic security, a reasonable standard of living, and opportunities for education and some amenities?

Are some groups discriminated against and/or excluded from full participation in social and political life?

Do groups conflict with each other violently outside the political arena?

Do nongovernmental institutions, such as churches, unions, and social organizations, encourage democratic attitudes and practices?

Some of these questions are fairly easy to answer. For example, it is not hard to see that the degree of democracy in the United States was once sharply diminished by the systematic exclusion of blacks from basic political rights. Other questions are tougher to handle. Exactly how much "influence" is too much influence? Just how great a degree of equality can we reasonably aim for in the power and political leverage exercised by various groups? After all, won't it always be true that some individuals and some groups will wield greater power than others in even the most democratic polity?

These are the basic issues addressed in this book. Because this is a text in U.S. politics, it covers many topics, from constitutional history to current debate about nuclear weapons. But the connecting thread running through the text, knitting the chapters loosely together, is the idea of "democracy": we will try to understand the strengths and weaknesses of U.S. politics from a democratic perspective. In each chapter, the reader will be asked to weigh the democratic issues involved, to decide just how democratic our society is, or might be.

Before discussing specific issues, however, we must decide just what democracy is. To do so, we will now look at the various ways one can view democracy and then try to come up with an overall definition to be used as a yardstick as we examine the U.S. political system. Along the way we must inevitably make distinctions between democratic ideals and the way democracy is practiced.

## Various definitions of democracy

Discussions about democracy often become confusing because different people have different things in mind when they use the term, and because people often fail to specify exactly what is involved in their particular definition. As a result, we import into the idea of democracy various elements that may or may not belong. To avoid such problems, we must sort out the main ideas about democracy, and then clarify exactly how the term will be used in this book.

### Majoritarian democracy

The most basic and straightforward notion of democracy is that of simple majority rule. This means that a majority of the people give their consent to specific policies or leaders. They can do so either directly or through representatives selected to rule in the name of the people. But what about the content of **majoritarian democracy**? Will a majority, for example, decide to outlaw certain religions or political views? Will it take away the property of those few who hold great wealth? Will it be able to run the government in a coherent and sensible fashion? These are questions that a simple definition of majoritarian democracy cannot answer. Yet they are the very questions that have been asked about majoritarian democracy ever since its beginnings.

It was in Athens, in ancient Greece, that the issues associated with majority rule first became highly charged political questions. Democracy in ancient Athens took the form of a legislative assembly selected by lot, which meant that any citizen might be called upon to serve. In addition, there were popular courts, whose members also were selected by lot. Basic issues of public policy were debated in the assembly, with the citizens listening, participating, and finally voting to decide the issues. The defenders of majority rule in Athens saw this system as a device for allowing the populace to have a voice in political decision making. Any other arrangement, they argued, would tend to place the rich or the well-born into power—as had often been the case in Athens prior to the democratic reforms. For democrats* the Athenian political system demonstrated that a random selection of the people could assemble and attend to the public's business in a reasonable fashion. Some also argued that the Athenian experience showed that people who participate in making and enforcing the laws are likely to be more law-abiding. Democracy, that is, made for a more committed citizenry.

The critics of majoritarian democracy had no shortage of arguments either. They maintained that democracy could degenerate into sheer mob rule under which no one is safe. Property could be seized by the majority. Unpopular ideas could be suppressed. A popular assembly or jury might be easily swayed by emotion. Worst of all, the critics stated, majoritarianism recognized no moral limits to its au-

*The term *democrat*, with a small "d," refers to those who support "democratic" ideas and practices. The term *Democrat*, with a capital "D," refers to supporters of the Democratic party of the United States.

thority. A majority was empowered to do *anything*. The democrats replied that despite these problems, the majority was likely to rule more wisely than would any self-selected group of rich or powerful individuals.

Many of these same arguments have surfaced again and again throughout Western history. Can the people make decisions? Are experts needed to rule? Will majorities violate the rights of minorities? Or is it more likely that a ruling minority will violate the rights of a majority? It is important to note, however, that the debate about democracy in Athens took place in a political context in which many people were arbitrarily excluded from citizenship (as was, of course, still the case in the United States in the eighteeenth century). Women were not citizens, and the many foreigners who lived in Athens were not permitted to attain citizenship. In addition, during some periods of Athenian history a certain level of property ownership was required to participate in political decisions (a limitation also found in many eighteenth- and nineteenth-century democracies).

## Liberal democracy

A second, somewhat more complex idea of democracy, and the one most familiar to Americans, is what has become known as **liberal democracy**. This concept combines majority rule with respect for civil liberties and protection of individual rights. Generally, when people in the Western world today speak of democratic government, this is what they have in mind.

The concept of liberal democracy first came into political thought about three hundred years ago, when a great debate raged in Europe over the powers of kings and the rights of citizens. The monarchs of the seventeenth and eighteenth centuries claimed they ruled by "divine right," but the early liberal democrats formulated a vision of a different kind of political society. As well as arguing for a society based on the consent of those governed, they also began to talk about basic human rights, equality among citizens, and the right to protest and rebel against oppressive governments.

These critics of monarchy were in no sense egalitarians, however. Many of them wanted a government based only on the consent of a small, prosperous middle class; very few were willing to advocate a society based on the consent of *all*. The notion that every person should have a voice in shaping the destiny of political life was so radical then it was barely conceivable. As we shall see, many of the struggles over democracy in the last two centuries have focused on exactly this issue: Whose consent is to be included?

We should note briefly here that these modern democratic ideas developed in concert with a new socioeconomic system knows as **capitalism**. The rising middle classes of the seventeenth and eighteenth centuries wanted to free themselves from constraints on their freedom to buy and sell, to accumulate wealth, and generally to conduct business free of government interference. Many commentators have argued that democracy became possible only because of the rise of capitalism, which naturally emphasized the individual. Capitalists struggled to limit governmental power, defending the individual's rights in an effort to carve out a sphere of private life exempt from government interference. It must be noted, however, that though these efforts surely contributed to an atmosphere in which democratic ideas could take root, the simultaneous development of a capitalist economic system and a democratic political system also created problems and tensions that persist to this day (and form the basis of a third view of democracy, to be discussed shortly).

Although most of the critics of the divine right of kings were not, by current standards, true democrats (in that they did not advocate universal suffrage), they did lay the groundwork for American ideas of democracy. Out of their concern for consent, equality, and basic human rights grew such documents as the Declaration of Independence, in which Thomas Jefferson claimed as "self-evident truths" the ideas that all people were endowed with the rights to life, liberty, and the pursuit of happiness; and the Bill of Rights, which added to the Constitution important rights and protections for all American citizens.

Today the two tenets basic to the practice of democracy are **majority rule** and the protection of **basic rights** for all citizens (sometimes referred to as "minority rights"). Majority rule is expressed mainly through regular elections, though the exact type and timing of elections vary considerably from one nation to another. In the United States the timing of elections is fixed by law—every four years, for example, for the presidency. In Great Britain, a prime minister can call an election at any time within a five-year term.

Sometimes majorities are easy to recognize, as when a referendum (a specific issue on the ballot) must be voted up or down. But in democratic elections, the clarity of majority rule varies according to how clearly the issues are drawn between the competing parties and candidates. On occasion, the numerical majority is actually made up of a series of minorities, each of which supports a particular candidate or party for somewhat different reasons. Sometimes parties and candidates deliberately blur the issues in an attempt to gain more votes. It is difficult, in other words, to be sure just what majority rule means in any one case. But the general fact of rule by majorities is a crucial element in democratic life today.

Equally crucial is the protection of basic rights. Citizens must have the right to organize groups, to form and join political parties, to acquire information, to protest in various ways, and to enjoy many other freedoms that allow for the expression and exchange of opinion. Without such rights, public opinion could be easily manipulated, authority abused, and elections made meaningless. And though elections are usually the most significant means of shaping public policy, they are not the only means. U.S. citizens, for instance, can try to influence political parties to nominate certain kinds of candidates and they can place referenda on the ballot, and they can also seek change in the courts. They can protest in the streets. They can lobby in Washington. They can peacefully refuse to obey certain laws.

There is another set of basic rights that democracy must protect: the rights fundamental to a decent social and political order. In most democratic countries such protections include prohibitions against the arbitrary use of government authority. In the United

States, for example, the government is required to employ **due process of law** in dealing with its citizens: people cannot be arrested without reason or confined indefinitely without trial, property cannot be confiscated without cause, cruel and unusual punishments cannot be used. Such protections against arbitrary government action were the principal issues in the struggle against the monarchies of the late eighteenth century.

Finally, the concept of equal protection of the laws is critical to democratic life. Equal protection means that no individual or group can be denied the rights and privileges granted to others. As we will see, the question of exactly who should be given equal protection has been one of the crucial issues fought out in democratic nations over the last two centuries.

The early adherents of democracy focused most of their attention on the problem of arbitrary governmental power, and tended to ignore, for the most part, the power exercised by nongovernmental institutions such as churches, businesses, and private groups. Also, their conception of rights was relatively negative: they sought mainly to protect rights they regarded as already in existence. Later proponents of democratic rights viewed the issue in a more positive light, one in which the government played a far more creative role. For example, many of us would argue that every citizen has the right to an education. Such a right involves positive government action and community decision-making, rather than simply the protection of a right already possessed by the citizen. In other words, the ideas about civil liberties and rights held by our ancestors were significantly more limited than those held widely today.

## Egalitarian democracy

A third view of democracy holds that it is not enough to specify and protect liberties and rights; an attempt must also be made to provide for basic social and economic equality. **Egalitarian democracy** finds the spirit of democracy violated in societies in which a few enjoy lives of affluence while many live in poverty. Such a democrat advocates a significant redistribution of wealth and calls for the equalization of educational opportunities and vigorous enforcement of social rights to protect people from exploitation. The basic premise of the egalitarian democrat is that democracy attains its full meaning only in a society of relative equality.

Such views were first set forth about one hundred years ago by critics of the capitalist system, who maintained that real democracy could not work as long as large social and economic inequalities persisted in society. Giving each person a vote would hardly provide for genuine equality of influence, they argued. How could an average person hope to compete politically with a wealthy and powerful industrialist? It might take an organization of thousands of workers to wield as much real political clout as a single steel company owner. These critics called for radical changes in the patterns of ownership in democratic societies, assuming greater social and economic equality to be a precondition for real rule by the people. Otherwise, they contended, there would be only partial rule by the people and partial rule by those with great economic power.

## A more comprehensive view of democracy

One can see immediately the kinds of arguments that might spring up among majoritarian, liberal, and egalitarian democrats, but that is a matter for another book. The concept of **democracy** explored in this book incorporates the basic elements of all three interpretations: that is, that democracy must be founded on majority rule (expressed through meaningful, competitive elections), must include effective protections for individual rights and liberties, and must strive to achieve a significant degree of equality among citizens. Beyond these elements, however, the idea of democracy presented in the pages to follow includes several other factors: citizen participation that is extensive and informed, government that is honest and does not use unwarranted force to create order,

# Comparative perspective
# The consociational model of democracy

In recent years, some political scientists have come to the conclusion that many democratic nations in Western Europe do not really operate according to the norms of majoritarian democracy, but have evolved into a somewhat different kind of system. Austria, Belgium, the Netherlands, and Switzerland all seem to have developed systems based on compromise and coalition rather than on the majoritarian winner-take-all pattern followed in the United States. Known as *consociational* democracy, this system seems to follow certain unwritten rules developed to preserve stability and avoid conflict.

Each of these nations has clearly identifiable subgroups that have existed for long periods of time. Austria has long been divided politically and culturally between socialists and Catholics; Belgium has the French-speaking and Flemish-speaking; the Netherlands has several religious and social-class subcultures, including Catholics and labor; and Switzerland is made up of French, German, and Italian speakers.

In each of these nations, political patterns have developed to accommodate the interests of each subgroup. Leaders of the various groups engage in extensive negotiations in order to avoid the kinds of disagreements and outright splits that might lead to serious social conflict. Rather than settling issues by majority rule, they seek compromise.

The Swiss, for example, created the Federal Council, a seven-member executive office that is the equivalent to the American presidency. Elected by the national parliament, the council allows all major political parties a share in the government: each of the three major parties is allocated two seats and one important smaller party has one. In addition, each of the three linguistic groups is guaranteed representation. Naturally, such a spirit of compromise carries over into the making of public policy.

To take another example, the Netherlands has institutionalized a special form of coalition government. Rather than each party seeking a narrow majority of votes in order to win power, they seek to be members of one large governing coalition. This pattern of politics has been characterized as "accommodationist" for its effort to allocate a reasonable share of resources to each important group.

Of course, all democratic politics involves some compromise and accommodation. The significant point to be drawn about consociational systems is that they have established certain norms of accommodation as a regular part of their political processes, thus depending less on majority rule than is the case in American politics today.

Sources: Arend Lijphart, *The Politics of Accommodation: Pluralism and Democracy in the Netherlands* (Berkeley, Cal.: University of California, 1968); Val R. Lorwin, "Segmented Pluralism: Ideological Cleavages and Political Cohesion in the Smaller European Democracies," *Comparative Politics*, January 1971, pp. 141–75; Jeffrey Obler, "Assimilation and the Moderation of Linguistic Conflict in Brussels," *Administration*, Winter 1974, pp. 400–432; Jeffrey Obler, Jurg Steiner and Guido Diereckx, "Decision-making in Smaller Democracies: The Consociational Burden," *Comparative Politics Series*, vol. 6 (Beverly Hills, Cal.: Sage, 1977), pp. 13–14, 21–33.

and foreign policies that serve democratic purposes as much as possible.

With this rather detailed conception of democracy we will be examining the government, politics, and policies of the United States today. As a yardstick definition it sets a high standard, and in this text we will be looking at democracy for the many possibilities it offers. To be sure, many of them have *not* been achieved, in the United States or anywhere else; some may not even be within reach. Of course, this definition, like the others just described, is itself controversial and subject to many interpretations— but then, that is what political discourse is all about. And it is one of our purposes here to identify and illuminate the tensions, problems, and possibilities inherent in the democratic approach to politics.

## Ideal and real democracies

We can construct the ideal circumstances for a democratic society. To begin, imagine a rather small, homogeneous community, with limited and generally acceptable inequalities. The citizens are active, informed participants in the political process. They attend town meetings. They talk and debate, weighing important issues with genuine inquisitiveness. They are fiercely committed to the democratic process and to the ideals of a democratic life. They are fair-minded and tolerant, accepting and even encouraging dissent. Children are reared in families that stress equality among parents and respect for the young, and they learn early in life that they are personally secure.

No gross differences in wealth, power, and respect separate the citizens. There are no juxtapositions of conspicuous wealth and acute deprivation, no slums located two blocks from expensive condominiums. There are no color or sex barriers, prejudice and group hatred having long since dissolved in the soothing waters of common citizenship. These democratic citizens take their social and political responsibilities seriously; they inculcate respect for the law, but a respect that is not idolatrous. They recognize that democratic commitments sometimes allow for disobedience to law.

The government of this ideal democracy is highly responsive. Citizens' views are frequently consulted. Political debate, as in campaigns, is reasonable and civil. Candidates do not make personal assaults on each other, or attempt to obscure the issues, or pander to the baser emotions of the public; a democratic public would reject such tactics quickly and thoroughly. Political leaders are selected from among the most qualified citizens. Leaders and those led relate to each other in an atmosphere of mutual instruction. Leaders attempt to put the difficult issues of political life before the electorate as clearly and fully as they can. The public, on its part, tries to comprehend these matters, and its response helps to inform the directions of future policy. When disputes occasionally go beyond the usual bounds of public discussion and threaten to burst into bitter controversy, the disputants either find ways of compromising their differences or take their disputes before a court system that aids them in finding a reconciliation.

Such an ideal democracy was imagined by early democratic theorists such as the French-Swiss political philosopher Jean-Jacques Rousseau (1712–1778), who felt that political democracy was possible *only* in a small and homogeneous society. This ideal world is of course very far from the reality of contemporary life. It now is apparent, however, that a minimum level of political democracy can exist under many different conditions, some of them very different from the ideal scenario just described. We know, for example, that most citizens are not very well-informed about political matters, and that large numbers never participate in political life even in the most minimal ways. We know that great differences of wealth, power, and respect obtain in democratic societies, and that these differences sharply affect the functioning of democracy. We know that political debate is often deliberately confusing, that leaders often mislead or fail to lead, that politicians are frequently dishonest, that many of the best potential political leaders never seek or attain office. We also know that many of the people who live in democratic societies are not particularly democratic. Some hold deep-seated prejudices toward certain groups, others would prefer a political system that aided only themselves and their groups and that even caused harm to others. Many people in democratic societies, in other words, do not really hold democratic attitudes.

What conclusion can we draw from this failure of reality to approximate the ideal? On the one hand, we could be amazed that political democracy exists at all, and even prospers, despite many adverse conditions. On the other hand, we could react with concern about just how successful contemporary democracies really are.

Many students of politics have adopted the first of these alternative positions, taking what might be characterized as a **minimalist view of democracy.** This view was summed up by Winston Churchill, the late British prime minister, who stated that democracy was the worst political system, except for all the rest. Churchill, like many others, saw the democratic process as a way of avoiding the greater evils possible with other political forms. At least in a democracy, minimalists argue, it is possible to get rid of a bad government through periodic competitive elections.

What about the low level of public information in the average electorate? Although this may be unfortunate, they argue, it is probably unrealistic for believers in democracy to think that most citizens can take an active, informed interest in politics. Perhaps it is even to the good that most people do not take such an interest, for too many citizens participating too actively might cause too much political conflict. In this view, our hopes for democracy must be scaled down quite a bit. All in all, minimalists tell us, current democracies are doing rather well.

Under the minimalist approach, then, a democracy is any government that has relatively open political debate and competition and also holds periodic elections. Under a maximalist perspective, however, democracy brings the possibilities of achieving far more, as indicated earlier. It is the **maximalist view of democracy** that informs the organization and approach of this text. We will assume that democracy encompasses far more than open elections, that elections are a necessary, but not sufficient, condition for democratic life. In examining U.S. democratic institutions we will hold maximalist

Voters wait in long lines to cast their ballots in the 1982 elections in El Salvador. The turnout was high, and a government elected. The U.S. government hailed the elections as a sign of El Salvador's developing democratic character. Others, however, worried about the meaningfulness of elections in a nation where violence and intimidation were everyday facts of life. Elections are of course a necessary element in democracy, but they should not be seen as sufficient evidence that democracy exists.

# Which nations are democracies?

Political scientists have never entirely agreed on the definition of a democratic political process, but there has been enough agreement to establish some general criteria with which to evalute political systems. Usually, democracies are defined as nations in which

The government states that it derives its mandate to govern from the people.

Leaders are chosen through competitive elections, in which at least two political parties have a meaningful chance to win.

Alternative sources of information are available.

Balloting is secret, and votes are not coerced.

Citizens and leaders enjoy freedom of speech, press, assembly, and organization.

Majorities win elections and can carry through their public policy choices.

Of course, each of these criteria is subject to various interpretations, and some investigators also include additional requirements, for example, that each vote counts equally, or that force is not employed against any political group.

There seems to be agreement, based on criteria such as these, that between twenty and thirty nations fall in the category of democracies. The exact number varies according to which criteria are used and which years are looked at, since some normally democratic nations have experienced periods of undemocratic rule. The following chart offers one example of how contemporary nations can be classified.

*Nations with democratic regimes for at least five years, 1958–1976*
Australia
Austria
Belgium
Canada
Costa Rica
Denmark
Finland
West Germany
Iceland
Israel
Italy
Japan
Luxembourg
Netherlands
New Zealand
Norway
Sweden
Switzerland
United Kingdom
United States
Venezuela[a]

*Democratic regime temporarily limited or suspended*
France (1958)
India (1975–76)
Jamaica[b] (1976)
Sri Lanka[c] (1971–76)
Turkey (1960–61, 1971–72)

*Democratic regime definitely replaced*
Chile (1973–     ) —u.s.A. caused
Greece (1967–74) .....
Philippines (1972–     )
Uruguay (1973–85)

To the top list we could now add the new nation of Trinidad-Tobago, and some today would also add Colombia, the Dominican Republic, Malaysia, and Cyprus. Sources: Bingham Powell, *Contemporary Democracies: Participation, Stability, and Violence* (Cambridge, Mass: 1982) and Robert Dahl, *Polyarchy: Participation and Opposition* (New Haven: Yale University Press, 1971).

[a]A democratic regime was established in Venezuela in 1959, although periodic emergencies and terrorism limited democratic freedoms in the early 1960s.
[b]Jamaica became independent in 1962. A state of emergency was declared in 1976, but elections were subsequently held late that year, and the emergency later was lifted.
[c]Following massive guerrilla attacks in 1971, the government of Sri Lanka (formerly Ceylon) imposed restrictions on freedom of press and assembly that made the country's status as a democracy doubtful until 1977, although elections continued to be held.

standards, to see where the problems lie and what possibilities for improvement can be found.

Efforts to discuss levels of democratic achievement lead to another difficult and complex issue: Are there cut-off points or plateaus that tell us whether or not a nation is democratic? Although we can specify various criteria for deciding whether a country is a democracy, there is no definitive, agreed-upon way to go about this. Political scientists have tried various ways of defining "democratic" nations (for one example, see the box above). But in the end, democracy is always a matter of degree, and judgments about the degree of democracy are inherently controversial. In the next section of this chapter, we will explore some of the typical problems and struggles of democratic life, so as to see more clearly what kinds of issues are involved before we plunge directly into the murky, crowded sea of American politics.

## Problems inherent in democratic life

To get a feeling of the sorts of issues that plague efforts to create a more democratic society, we will look in this section at some of the most common and fundamental problems in contemporary democracies, including our own. These include the uneven distribution of power, failures to respect democratic rights, and citizen-government conflict of a sort that threatens the democratic process.

### Uneven distribution of power

In *Animal Farm*, the celebrated satirical novel by George Orwell, the farm animals, after revolting and taking control of the farm, proclaim that "all animals are equal." Somewhat later, one faction (the pigs) takes increasing control. The rest of the animals wake up one morning to find their slogan, printed on the barnyard wall, altered to "all animals are created equal, but some are more equal than others." That, in fact, is what we find when we look closely at democratic politics: some individuals and groups enjoy great advantages in political life. Certain of these advantages can pose serious threats to the idea of democratic politics. Here we will look briefly at three such advantages: those generated by concentrations of wealth and economic power; those accruing from ease of political influence; and, finally, those that develop out of oligarchy, when democratic competition for leadership is actually curtailed.

**Economic power:**  Some socialists are fond of saying that economic power more or less equals political

power. Although this may not always be true, it is a good approximation. In every democratic society, those who are financially better off usually have political access and influence far out of proportion to their numbers. For one thing, they can use their money for political purposes. A wealthy campaign contributor is likely to excercise a level of influence hundreds and perhaps thousands of times greater than the average voter. Although money is not everything in politics, it *is* a vital element; the unequal distribution of financial resources tends to skew democracy in the direction of the more affluent.

At another level, many of the major social decisions made in democratic societies are not really under democratic control. Important economic decisions made by corporations affect the lives of tens of thousands and yet are rarely based on democratic consultation. Generally speaking, business decisions are made with business calculations in mind. Decisions made by a few individuals can shut down plants, alter work processes, pour new products onto the market. That is, of course, how capitalism is supposed to work; but it also means that a relatively small number of people wield great economic power and make significant economic decisions, and yet are usually far removed from any sort of democratic control. Inevitably, those in politics are highly attentive to the interests and ideas of the business community, since business decisions affect the entire economic climate and may be a major source of trouble or success for political leaders.

In the latter part of the nineteenth century, popular movements fought pitched political battles against economically powerful interests. Small farmers organized to battle the railroads. Factory workers organized to fight for better wages and decent working conditions. Much of U.S. politics around the turn of the century focused on the issue of economic power, which was then growing more and more concentrated in the hands of a few. Increasingly, government sought to limit and regulate concentrations of private economic power through legislation such as the Sherman Antitrust Act, which was enacted in 1890 to limit monopolies. Social movements also stirred governmental action on such matters as child labor, the purity of food and drugs, and a whole range of other economic areas.

Our political system provides for one person/one vote, but our economic system leads to a world in which some command far more resources than others. Such resources can be put to political use, and can even enhance the economic positions of their possessors. An egalitarian democrat would ask, How much inequality can democracy tolerate and still remain meaningful?

Political decisions, especially during and after the Great Depression of the 1930s, began to play a larger and larger role in economic life. Nowadays there is a balance of sorts between economic power on the one side and political power on the other. The key issue for us to consider here is whether democratic politics prosper—are political decision makers free to focus on enhancing the lives of the majority, or are they hemmed in by the concentration of economic decision making in the hands of a few?

Great inequalities of wealth affect democratic life in yet another way. Often, money can help purchase the sorts of basic rights that should be open to all. We can say, for example, that in the United States every person is entitled to a fair trial and to decent legal assistance. But in practice, we know that money helps a great deal in getting the best legal representation. The same situation obtains in the areas of education and health care. It is still true in our society that money makes many important options available, and may even make the difference between having real choices and having no choices.

To return to the fundamental point: great inequalities of wealth and great concentrations of economic power both pose serious threats to the relative equality that is one of the basic premises of democratic life. Of course, there are countervailing tendencies that limit the powers of wealth. Sometimes sheer numbers can prevail over the power of money; sometimes powerful organizations such as trade unions can weigh in on the other side of the scale; sometimes the wealthy are divided among themselves. But as long as some have a great deal more than others, democrats will have to worry that politics may serve moneyed rather than majority interests.

**Special interests:** In democratic societies, many groups organize and lobby for favorable policies from the government. Oil companies, for example, hire professional lobbyists to influence Congress, and the American Medical Association makes heavy campaign contributions to candidates it feels will advance its interests in matters of health policy. The more powerful and well-organized such interest groups are, the greater the influence they exert over governmental affairs. Over the years, interest groups often develop very friendly relationships with the legislators and with bureaucrats responsible for overseeing their particular interests, and as a result, seem to be systematically favored by government policy. Once established, such strong alliances are very difficult to dislodge. One after another, particular well-organized segments of society come to enjoy subsidies, protective tariffs, or other benefits. Truckers benefit from one sort of special arrangement, airlines another, tobacco growers another, and sugar producers yet another.

Amid all this special-interest policy making, who is looking out for the public interest, for the needs and long-term good of the larger public? When it happens that no one is watching out for such interests, democracy suffers, and political life becomes a way of gaining wealth, power, and advantage at the expense of the general public. Government comes to serve the knowledgeable and the organized few, not the generally unorganized and uninformed many. Just how serious a problem this can be we will see in Chapter 11, which discusses the role of interest groups in American politics.

**Oligarchy:** We can define **oligarchy** as "rule by the few." By definition, oligarchy and democracy are incompatible. When leadership becomes entrenched and unresponsive, democracy suffers. The problems posed by oligarchies within democracies were first discussed extensively in Robert Michels' 1915 study

*Political Parties.* Michels saw a tension between the democratic impulses that originally lead to the formation of political parties and the pressures toward bureaucratization that seem inevitably to remove initiative from the rank-and-file and place it in the hands of a governing elite better situated to exercise continuous power.

Accusations of oligarchy have been made many times in U.S. history. In the late nineteenth century, for example, popular movements decried economic oligarchy, maintaining that industrialists were able to manipulate the economic and political systems to their advantage at the expense of the ordinary person. President Franklin Roosevelt joined in a similar attack on vested economic interests during the 1930s. In 1968, many Democratic party members complained that oligarchy in the party limited the role of popular sentiment in the nominating process. Finally, both trade unions and corporations have been justly accused of oligarchic practices by which leaders are able to perpetuate themselves. (It is interesting that, even in a democracy, certain institutions are not usually expected to be organized in a democratic manner. Corporations, for example, are not run by majority rule except in very exceptional circumstances, when stockholders organize to press their interests. Churches, too, are often oligarchical. When nondemocratic forms of decision making are justified, and why, are interesting questions that can only be touched on peripherally in this book.)

Unresponsive political or economic oligarchies often find themselves locked in bitter and protracted conflicts with those they seek to lead or control. These conflicts are costly and often fruitless. The challenge for democracies is to reach some balance between effective leadership and mass influence.

Failure to exercise
democratic rights

The quality of democratic life in large part depends, many have believed, on the quality of the people who make up the polity. If the masses have undemocratic sentiments, if there is a strong animus against democratic institutions, if many are attracted by authoritarian movements, then democracy will be severely challenged.

The same is true if large numbers of people are hostile to the major political institutions, if they feel turned off or alienated by politics as it is usually conducted. Finally, if the mass of the population is uninformed, if the average person cannot or does not understand what political life and political issues are all about, decisions will be made by the few, without reference to the ideas, such as they are, of the real majority. Let us look more closely at each of these matters.

**Antidemocratic attitudes:** We cannot be sure exactly what most German citizens were thinking in 1933, when the National Socialist German Workers party (the Nazis) received 40 percent of the vote in the last relatively open election held in that country before World War II. No Gallup or Harris polls were conducted; the opinions of the "average" person were not tapped for posterity. Yet it does not seem too far-fetched a guess that large numbers of Germans no longer had very strong ties to democratic politics, if they had ever had such ties. Democratic politics were new in the Germany of that day: only after World War I was a fully democratic political process installed. At a time when German democracy was just beginning to set down roots, many aspects of German society remained resolutely undemocratic. Many prevalent ideas and practices were hostile to democracy. Strong patterns of military tradition and inherited aristocracy persisted. The Nazis represented perhaps the most extreme of the antidemocratic elements: their ideology was not just critical of democracy, but entirely alien to it.

Many factors conspired to give the Nazis their

chance at political power in 1933, including a worldwide economic crisis, but there seems little doubt that many Germans had a shaky allegiance, at best, to democratic institutions and practices. The great majority of them embraced authoritarian leadership and were willing to accept violence and prejudice as an integral part of political and social life.

It seems wise not to be too smug about this, to think that our country could never be like Germany in the early 1930s. Fascist movements, in fact, arose in almost every European country, as well as in the United States, between the wars. The sorts of attitudes we associate with Nazism, such as anti-Semitism and racism, were common attitudes throughout the West. Perhaps we were simply lucky to avoid our own version of fascism, or perhaps the strength of our democratic attitudes and institutions served to protect us. Nonetheless, we have had our own share of antidemocratic movements and attitudes. In the 1920s, for example, the Ku Klux Klan numbered its membership in the millions.

Why do such attitudes matter? Why does it matter if millions of Americans are anti-Semitic or racist, or have very weak allegiance to democratic ideas? It

Joseph Goebbels, Hitler's minister of propaganda, emerges from a polling station in the 1933 German elections. The Nazi Party won a plurality of the vote that year; then, their power secure, they permitted no further political competition in Germany.

matters because experience shows that the sort of equal treatment in social and political life that democracy requires is impossible where prejudice is widespread. And in a time of crisis and conflict, such antidemocratic attitudes may surface and lead to widespread violations of civil liberties or violence against certain groups. This too threatens democratic life, as we will see in Chapter 2.

**Alienation:** There have been many definitions of **alienation.** Some commentators have equated it with the sense of being an outsider. Others have associated it with powerlessness, futility, or meaninglessness. But even though a vast literature in sociology is devoted to discussing and understanding the phenomenon, it is usually not hard to spot alienation when one sees it. Alienated people are turned off; they've given up on something. Alienated people feel that nobody cares, that things have turned against them, that the world is dishonest, that they and people like them are too weak to change things. The extremes of alienation are either total hostility and cynicism or passive withdrawal, complete apathy.

In recent years many Americans have suffered from fairly serious bouts of political alienation (as we will see in greater detail in Chapter 8). How does this concern democratic politics? At one level, that question is easy to answer. If large numbers of people are alienated, then politics suffers in two ways. First of all, many people withdraw from political life, and to that extent the effectiveness and breadth of democracy are reduced. These alienated people may also pose a threat to democracy, because of the hostility they have built up toward current politics. In either case the circle of meaningful participants in political life is narrowed.

At another level, alienation poses a more complicated problem. A skeptical commentator might suggest that some degree of alienation is to be expected in any political process, even the most democratic. Some people will always be put off because the political situation is not going their way. Many white Southerners, for example, were alienated by legislation in the 1960s that fostered greater racial equality. Perhaps this type of alienation is the price we have to pay for democratic change. The questions

we need to ask are, Who is alienated? Why are they alienated? and How widespread and deep is the alienation? The answers to these questions will give us a better idea of whether to see alienation as a sign of a defective democracy or as a price of change.

**Ignorance:** Ignorance is a different matter. Here we rejoin the debate between the optimistic and the pessimistic democratic thinkers. Just how much can we expect the public to understand about political life? Isn't large-scale public ignorance to be expected in any large, complicated modern society? Can most Americans really understand the issues debated in political life? How many of us are prepared to put in the time and energy required to master the intricacies of the SALT II arms-control agreements, to perceive the alternatives in the energy crisis, to assess the results of school busing, or to grasp the consequences that would flow from passage of the proposed equal rights amendment to the Constitution? Clearly, many such matters are beyond the grasp of the average citizen. What, then, can a reasonable democrat hope for?

The minimum, it would seem, is that the public have a rough sense of the major alternatives available on the main questions of the day. Even if the average person may not be able to argue at length about the arms race or about supply-side economics, he or she usually can grasp the basic issues involved, provided that (1) plentiful, accurate, and many-sided information about the issues is available and (2) the person cares enough to seek that information. When one of these factors is lacking, widespread public ignorance results and the quality of democratic life suffers. Some of the dimensions of these issues will be examined more fully in Chapters 7 and 9.

The relationship between government and citizen

The democratic ideal requires a relatively open, honest, and responsive relationship between citizens and government. But this relationship is often precarious. The power exercised by the citizenry might not be sufficient to keep the government responsive and under control. Abuses of power by governments are always possible, and perhaps even likely. The power of political office might lead to corruption or even to the development of imperial attitudes more appropriate to a monarchy. Citizens might also abuse the relationship, for example, by evading their responsibilities as voters or by disobeying reasonable and necessary laws.

Then there is the problem of how to deal with conflict. Every society must cope with forms of conflict among the citizenry and between citizens and government. Every society is faced with problems of crime, disorder, and open social and political combat. In a democratic society, such conflicts should be dealt with in a manner consistent with democratic norms. Let us now look a bit more closely at the issues of honesty and conflict and at the problems contemporary societies face in living up to democratic standards.

**Honesty and trust:** In our society, citizens and governments relate at many levels. In elections, candidates appeal to citizens for votes. Once in office, legislators and executives make and enforce laws that affect the lives of citizens. The most common way in which citizens encounter governmental authority in our society, however, is in the form of the school board official, the social worker, the police officer, the social security bureaucrat, the mine inspector—that is, at the local level. Though we are usually taught to trust and respect such authority figures as teachers and police officers, encounters with these figures all too often breed a sense of grievance. In the ghetto, police are frequently feared or hated. Bureaucrats tend to be loathed for their tiresome attention to routine, or for their insensitivity. And yet these and other government employees play essential roles in our lives.

The citizen-government encounter, then, is many-sided. Consider, for example, just one of the levels at which citizen and government relate: that of executive leadership. Political executives, such as the U.S. president, play a critical role in modern societies. What presidents say and don't say, what they

decide and how they make decisions, and how they communicate their ideas to the public at large, have significant consequences for democratic life. At this level of political life, democratic ideals furnish us with rather straightforward standards for judgment. Most obviously, we should expect a high level of integrity in a chief executive, as well as a determined effort to be honest and open with the public. Where such honesty and integrity are lacking, democratic practice is jeopardized. We have seen glaring examples of lack of integrity in some presidents of recent times. Both Lyndon Johnson and Richard Nixon departed at times from any sensible idea of democratic behavior. By corrupting the dialogue between leaders and citizens, they helped to erode public confidence in political institutions.

**Handling conflicts:** In May 1970, at the height of political protest over the Vietnam War, four students were shot to death and many others wounded at Kent State University by National Guard troops, most of whom were no older than the students they shot. The Kent State tragedy underlined an issue that was to come up again and again in the 1960s and early 1970s: how governmental authority should be used to deal with conflict and protest.

The Kent State affair was an especially grievous and unnecessary event. It was made worse by the inaction of the Nixon administration, which refused to pursue a broad investigation into the killing of four unarmed youths. Wasn't anyone to blame? It was many years before some compensation was ordered for the parents of the slain students. But Kent State was just one of many such incidents in the Vietnam War era. Throughout much of our history, in fact, deadly force has been used both by citizens and governments to settle disputes. But ours is no longer a frontier society; we are a long way from the Wild West. Democratic ideals require that we show sensitivity to the problems of force and coercion.

Again, the sense of democratic norms is quite clear: we cannot use force, especially deadly force, easily and often, if we are to continue to view our society as one that values individual life. A democrat wants to see such coercion reduced to a minimum. Wide-

17

spread use of police power inevitably indicates a failure for democratic life. And if force is absolutely necessary, it should be used with considerable care. A troubled conscience over the use of police power is a good sign in a democratic society. Anytime democratic leaders find the killing or coercing of some citizens easily acceptable, that nation's democratic ideals are in deep trouble.

This does not mean that there are simple answers to social conflict, only that we must be sensitive to the way we settle disputes and the degree of respect we accord individual life.

## Struggles to realize democratic ideals

The preceding discussion of democratic ideals and practices may have seemed somewhat abstract. It is now time to infuse the words with life, by looking at a few exemplary cases of the struggle to realize democratic ideals in the highly imperfect real world. These cases will be presented very briefly, but their significance and the lessons to be drawn from them ought to be very clear. They are lessons that will serve us well in looking at the operation of American government today.

### Restricting democracy

We will look first at two cases where democracy was curtailed. Case one concerns the failure of Reconstruction after the Civil War and the growth of segregation in the American South. Case two concerns American involvement in overthrowing the democratically elected socialist government in Chile in 1973.

### Segregation in the United States:

I will say then that I am not, nor ever have been in favor of bringing about in any way the social and political equality of the white and black races—that I am not

nor ever have been in favor of making voters or jurors of negroes, nor of qualifying them to hold office, nor to intermarry with white people, and I will say in addition to this that there is a physical difference between the black and white races which I believe will forever forbid the two races living together on terms of social and political equality. And inasmuch as they cannot so live, while they do remain together there must be the position of superior and inferior, and I as much as any man I am in favor of having the superior position assigned to the white race. *Abraham Lincoln, 1858*

We should not be too surprised that our sixteenth president, the man commonly known as the Great Emancipator, would make such remarks. In them, Lincoln was just expressing views that represented the majority sentiment not only in the South, but in the North as well. Northern blacks were not slaves in the pre–Civil War period, but they did have to live with a *de facto* pattern of segregation in housing, schools, and transportation, much of which remains in force today.

Still, Lincoln's statement, and the realization that "equality" was not actually supported by most Northern whites of the day, may come as something of a shock. Most of us were taught at a young age that the Civil War was fought to free the slaves and to realize the democratic ideal of equality for all. Perhaps a bit later we learned that the situation was more complicated, that democratic ideals were only a part of the story. In any event, the North won, and in the Thirteenth, Fourteenth, and Fifteenth amendments to the Constitution (the Civil War amendments), slavery was abolished and, seemingly, all U.S. citizens guaranteed equal rights and equal protection under the law.

For over a decade after the Civil War, Northern troops occupied the South, and lengthy and intense political struggles were waged over how government in the South was to be reconstructed. Some people favored radical measures to secure full equality for freed slaves, and for a time in the 1870s there was some progress toward racial equality. Many blacks were elected to state and local offices, and whites and blacks mixed together on public transportation, in schools, and on juries. But others wished to turn back the clock and return as far as possible to a situation in which whites held the upper hand. In the end, it was the latter view that prevailed. What a bloody and terrible war had seemed to accomplish in gaining at least some equality for blacks was substantially wiped out and a new system of white supremacy restored by the 1880s.

A series of United States Supreme Court decisions also helped to restrict the meaning of the constitutional amendments passed after the Civil War. In 1877 the Court found that a state could not prohibit segregation in transportation, and in 1883 it sharply limited the application of the clause in the Fourteenth Amendment mandating equal protection of the laws for all citizens. And in 1890 it upheld a Mississippi state law that *required* segregation in transportation.

Then, in the famous case of ***Plessy v. Ferguson*** (1896), the Court established a constitutional standard for segregation that was not finally overturned until 1954, declaring that "separate but equal" treatment of the races was legitimate under the Constitution. Being treated as a separate group, the court majority argued, did not imply inferiority. Such doctrine was of course a blatant and deliberate avoidance of the real facts: *separate* did, in fact, mean "inferior."

As the rest of the country acquiesced, one Southern state after another established remarkably complete systems of separation of the races. First, blacks were gradually denied the right to vote through various subterfuges, including the white primary (nominating elections restricted to white voters), literacy tests, and the "grandfather" test (one could not vote unless one's grandfather had voted, which effectively excluded all blacks). Social segregation followed— on street cars, in theatres, at water fountains, in boarding houses, toilets, and waiting rooms, at sporting and other recreational events, in mental institutions, orphanages, prisons, and hospitals, on jobs, in housing, in churches, and finally in funeral homes, morgues, and cemeteries. The breadth of the new

Oklahoma City, 1939. Segregated drinking fountains were but one part of an elaborate system of racial separation imposed and maintained by law and custom throughout the American South. The races were supposedly accorded separate but equal treatment, but in fact black facilities were generally far inferior to those provided for whites.

# Plessy v. Ferguson

In 1890 the Louisiana legislature passed a law for the "comfort of passengers" that "all railway companies . . . carrying passengers in their coaches in this State, shall provide equal but separate accommodations for the white and colored races." Until this time the races had traveled together in second-class railway cars, though it was generally "whites only" in first-class cars.

The law evoked a strong protest from the large and vocal black community in New Orleans, leading to a deliberate test of its constitutionality. On June 7, 1892, Homer Adolph Plessy, a man seven-eighths white and one-eighth black, boarded an East Louisiana Railway train in New Orleans and took a seat in a car reserved for whites. When he refused to move to the colored car, he was arrested and brought before Judge John H. Ferguson of the Criminal District Court of the Parish in New Orleans, who ruled against him. The case was appealed to the State Supreme Court, and then to the U. S. Supreme Court, which handed down its decision in 1896.

The issue was whether Plessy had been denied his privileges, immunities, and equal protection of the law under the Fourteenth Amendment. Writing for the Court majority, Justice Henry Brown declared that the Louisiana statute did *not* deprive blacks of equal protection of the laws, provided they were given accommodations equal to whites, thus establishing the precedent for "separate but equal." He also stated that the Fourteenth Amendment was not intended to abolish distinctions based upon color, or to enforce social equality, citing many examples of already established segregation in support of his argument. In a complicated, convoluted, and, subsequently, much denigrated opinion, Brown declared: "If the civil and political rights of both races be equal one cannot be inferior to the other civilly or politically. If one race be inferior to the other socially, the Constitution of the United States cannot put them upon the same plane."

In his famous and eloquent dissent Justice John Marshall Harlan spoke for the deeper conscience and ideals of the country, writing: "In view of the Constitution, in the eye of the law, there is in this country no superior, dominant, ruling class of citizens. There is no caste here. Our Constitution is color-blind, and neither knows nor tolerates classes among its citizens. In respect of civil rights, all citizens are equal before the law."

system of segregation can be judged by the extremes to which it sometimes went: a 1909 curfew law in Mobile, Alabama, required blacks to be off the streets by 10:00 P.M.; a 1915 Oklahoma law required segregated telephone booths; laws in North Carolina and Florida required the separate storage of school textbooks.

A racist ideology elaborated on the new system. Many psychologists and biologists at the turn of the century held that the black race was inherently inferior to the white race in intelligence and morals. In the meantime, white violence against blacks increased, with the Ku Klux Klan picking up activity. What evolved out of the Civil War and Reconstruction periods turned out to be, from the standpoint of the democratic spirit, about the worst possible outcome short of a return to slavery. This despite the fact that many voices were raised, even among Southern whites, in favor of other options. Many Southern conservatives, while taking a paternalistic view of race relations, did not intend to create a system of total separation of the races. Unfortunately, the view that prevailed over the final twenty years of the nineteenth century in the South was one that precluded any hope of respect for the full humanity of black people. That formal segregation did happen, and that once installed, the system of segregation lasted so long, testifies to the depth of racial fears in our society and to the failure of democratic leadership to live up to its own ideals.

**Undermining democracy in Chile:** Our failure to live up to democratic ideals often has consequences outside our own country. Such was the case in Chile in the early 1970s. Salvador Allende, elected president of Chile in 1970, was a socialist and the leader of a coalition of various left-wing political groups. He had run for president several times before and was a familiar figure in Chilean politics. The 1970 race for the presidency was a three-way affair, and Allende was able to win with only 36 percent of the total vote. By Chilean tradition, an absolute majority of the votes cast was not necessary for election; the candidate with a plurality could be declared the winner by the Chilean Senate.

President Richard Nixon and presidential advisor (and later secretary of state) Henry Kissinger regarded Allende's election as a serious threat to U.S. influence in the hemisphere. The United States had some important interests in Chile. Several major U.S.

corporations—including the International Telephone and Telegraph Company and the Anaconda and Kennicott copper-mining companies—had significant holdings there. Also, U.S. political leaders feared the spread of communism into Chile. They were not prepared to tolerate another Cuba, which under Fidel Castro had embraced communism in the early 1960s.

Even before Allende took office, the U.S. government apparently was thinking about ways of undermining his regime. Then, during his three years in power, Allende faced several serious threats from the U.S. government. Not only did it supply money and other resources to political groups in Chile that were hostile to the Allende government, but it made it difficult for Chile to obtain needed financial assistance from international funding agencies; and, it now seems probable, Americans aided the Chilean military forces who overthrew the Allende government in 1973. In the midst of that military coup Allende lost his life. (The ruling junta said that he committed suicide.)

It may be that domestic opposition would have led to Allende's overthrow in any case, but we cannot

Salvador Allende waves the Chilean flag at a political rally. Allende, a socialist party leader, was a well-established figure in Chilean politics when he won the presidency in 1970 on his third try for the office. A nationalist and democrat as well as a Marxist, he took office committed both to radical reforms of Chilean society and to the maintenance of political liberties. The military coup that overthrew and killed him in 1973 established an authoritarian regime that continues today.

be sure. Chile had a strong democratic tradition, and so if the United States had not thrown its weight so strongly against Allende, his experiment in democracy and socialism might well have survived, at least until the next presidential election, in 1976. Although U.S. policy was not the only factor involved, it may well have been a critical one in determining the fate of Chilean democracy. After the coup, there was virtually no remnant of democratic politics in Chile, and the next decade saw the military regime of that nation became one of the world's major violators of human rights.

Why did U.S. policy makers act as they did? What accounts for their single-minded opposition to the Allende regime? The key factors seem to have been a mistaken understanding of anticommunism and strong pressure from U.S. economic interests in Chile. Because Allende was a socialist, Nixon and Kissinger regarded him as a threat to U.S. interests. They saw him as a revolutionary, someone who would turn Chile toward communism, as Castro had done in Cuba, and ally himself with the Soviet Union. Once Chile had gone communist, perhaps such influence would spread to other nations in South America.

It is true that Allende was friendly with Cuba in particular and more friendly to communist countries in general than previous Chilean governments had been. He was also intent upon nationalizing (seizing and turning into state-run enterprises) large U.S. corporate holdings in Chile. At the same time, however, he and his coalition had won the presidency fairly in an open election, and there was every reason to believe that another fair election would have been held in 1976. Allende was a socialist who was also a democrat; in the minds of U.S. leaders, however, those two qualities simply didn't go together.

Some U.S. leaders are quick to see a threat to U.S. interests whenever a self-proclaimed socialist advocates rapid or radical social change, an attitude that confuses the issue of defending democracy with that of defending capitalism and watching out for our economic interests. This problem is especially acute when it comes to South America, our geographic backyard, where the U.S. government's big brother attitude and intention of imposing its will on other societies seems especially prevalent.

The bitter irony of the Chilean situation is that after the military seized power, imprisoned or killed tens of thousands (the exact figures are in dispute), and abolished all democratic politics and basic civil liberties, many U.S. leaders still talked of our role in Chile as "defenders of democracy." Both Henry Kissinger and President Gerald Ford declared that we had helped save the Chileans from a communist fate. But instead of saving Chileans from a communist fate, it seems, we helped to fashion a fascist fate that doomed democratic life, perhaps for decades to come.

The lessons here are clear: (1) that indiscriminate anticommunism can lead the United States to destroy democratic political movements, and (2) that we must learn to distinguish democracy from capitalism, and the interests of U.S. society from the interests of particular U.S. corporations. Otherwise, we may mistakenly come to view all radical change as anti-American.

## Extending democracy

Two examples of democracy expanded are the movement to gain female suffrage and the protest to stop the war in Vietnam.

**The fight for women's suffrage:** The Grimke sisters of Charleston, South Carolina, were quite a formidable pair. Long before the issues of women's suffrage or women's rights made a significant impact on the public agenda in the United States, they were articulating concepts very close to those we have become familiar with in recent decades:

Human beings have *rights*, because they are *moral* beings: the rights of all men grow out of the moral nature, and as all men have the same moral nature, they have essentially the same rights . . . Now, if rights are founded in the nature of our moral being, then the mere circumstance of sex does not give to man higher rights and responsibilities, than to a woman. *Angelina Grimke, 1836*

Arizona, 1906. A priest
casts his vote. Universal
suffrage for white males was
achieved very early in the
United States (around 1830)
though it was many more
years before female suffrage
was even considered.

In most families it is considered a matter of far more
consequence to call a girl off from making a pie, or
a pudding, than to interrupt her whilst engaged in her
studies.  *Sarah Grimke, 1838*

The Grimkes were among the more radical and for-
ward-looking of the early advocates of women's rights.
Like many other campaigners for women's equality,
they participated in the antislavery movement. To
many women the position of black slaves paralleled
the position of women: both were excluded from full
participation in democratic society because of physical attributes.

The Grimkes began their campaigning against
slavery and for women's suffrage in the 1830s. More
than eighty years of prolonged political and social
struggle were to pass before the basic democratic
right to vote was granted to American women. The
story of the battle for the suffrage testifies to the
tenacity of opposition to democratic rights and, even
more, to the tenacity required to overcome such opposition. It seems remarkable, looking back, that the

issue was so controversial at all. Why, after all,
shouldn't women have the right to vote? But in asking
the question in this way, we fail to understand how
deeply rooted were the sentiments that stood in the
way of female equality.

Until the late nineteenth century, most men—and
most women, as well—believed that women had a
proper "place" in society, and that that place did
not include full-fledged participation as a citizen.
Former president Grover Cleveland stated in 1905
that "sensible and responsible women do not want
to vote"; in his view "a higher intelligence" had assigned the relative positions of men and women. Political life was not entirely out of bounds to women—
for example, some women participated in political
campaigns in the early part of the nineteenth century—but equal participation was regarded as a violation of the natural order of things. Women were to
play a domestic role, maintaining the home and rearing children.

By roughly 1830, universal suffrage for white males

had been achieved in the United States—the first
such achievement in the world. A few men and a
few women spoke of the need to extend voting rights
to women, but the dominant view of the day was that
women could not be equal participants. In 1848 the
first feminist convention was held in Seneca Falls,
New York, and many date the struggle for the suffrage from that meeting. The convention issued a
"Declaration of Sentiments," one of the most significant documents in the history of feminism, that
pointed not just toward suffrage but also toward an
entire women's-rights ideology of the sort that emerged
fully only in the twentieth century. It was clear to
some women even then that the struggle for equality
between the sexes involved considerably more than
the right to vote.

But that right itself proved difficult to obtain. The
passage of the Civil War amendments raised some
hopes, but then Supreme Court rulings narrowed the
scope of these amendments. In 1878, a constitutional amendment to give women the right to vote
was introduced for the first time in the Senate. Eleven
years later, it reached the floor of the Senate for a
vote. It was turned down. Meanwhile, the suffrage
movement split into moderate and radical branches,
and for a time the movement fell into decline. Yet
as social attitudes began to change, some states moved
to grant women the vote. The first to do so were in
the West—Wyoming, Utah, Colorado, and Idaho.
And by the turn of the century, more women had the
time and energy necessary to join the movement.
Families had grown smaller, and child rearing took
up less time. Women were graduating from universities in larger numbers, considerably swelling the
pool of leadership for a women's movement.

Women began to organize on a state-by-state basis
and to campaign for suffrage reform within the states.
Between 1910 and 1913, they succeeded in Washington and California. Then Illinois granted women
the right to vote in presidential elections. At the
same time, however, the opposition to women's suffrage also increased. A formal association was formed
in 1911 to defeat the suffrage effort. This opposition
came from many sources: textile manufacturers, who
feared that women would favor stricter child labor
legislation and thus limit the use of children in their
factories; brewers and distillers, who feared that
women would help pass laws prohibiting the sale of
alcohol; and many Southerners, who felt women's
suffrage would endanger white supremacy. And the

traditional arguments continued about the appropriate "place" for women. For a long time political leaders played almost no role in the voting rights struggle. In 1912 the Progressive Party became the first major political party to endorse the vote for women, but the opposition was still strong enough to bring about the overwhelming defeat of a constitutional amendment in the Senate in 1914.

Women's organizations kept the pressure on at both state and national levels. In 1916, both the Democratic and Republican parties endorsed the idea of the individual states granting suffrage to women. Two years later, women's votes contributed significantly to President Woodrow Wilson's reelection in those states in which they could vote for president. Wilson then advised a delegation of Democrats to support the constitutional amendment. In January 1918, the House did so, 274–136, but the Senate rejected the measure, by two votes. A new Congress passed the amendment in June 1919, and after fierce battles in state legislatures, the necessary three-fourths of the states ratified it by August 1920. It had been 72 years since the Seneca Falls convention, and 84 since Angelina Grimke had spoken of rights growing out of our status as equal moral beings.

The ideals on which U.S. political life was founded pointed toward women's suffrage from the start. But cultural assumptions pointed in the other direction—toward a subordinate and unequal role for women in politics and society. To extend democratic rights to half the population required decades of gradual social change plus the determined efforts of women's-rights advocates. And the struggles over women's rights continue, as recent political battles over the proposed equal rights amendment, abortion, and many other issues indicate. How equal are women in our society? Should equality extend to every area of life? If so, how should it be extended? We will look further at these questions in Chapters 5 and 21. Meanwhile, it is instructive to keep in mind how long it took to provide the most basic democratic right to 50 percent of the people.

**The protest movement during the Vietnam War:** One of the most useful roles a minority can play in democratic politics is that of critic, gadfly, questioner. The minority can keep alive debate and discussion that the majority would rather not hear. Such was the constructive role of political protest during the Vietnam War. Thanks to the determined democratic activities of millions of Americans, debate on the war deepened, and real communication among citizens increased. This was debate that our government did not wish to hear, and did much in its power to avoid.

In 1964 the overwhelming majority of Americans knew little about Vietnam. That small southeast Asian nation became something of an issue in the presidential campaign that year, however. Lyndon Johnson, who was subsequently elected by a wide margin, pledged during the campaign that he had no intention of sending American troops to Vietnam. As we now know, the decision to send troops had already been made during the presidential campaign, but Johnson did not care to argue the issue before the public. Moreover, the Johnson administration misled congressional leaders about attacks on U.S. naval vessels in Vietnam, in order to gain congressional approval for sending U.S. forces there. Soon U.S. planes were bombing North Vietnam and the first of five hundred thousand U.S. combat troops were embroiled in a jungle guerrilla war.

Most Americans were willing to take the president's word for the fact that we had to fight in Vietnam. The chief executive is usually granted the benefit of the doubt, especially when it comes to foreign policy emergencies. But a few were not so willing. Particularly in universities and among the young, a spirit of questioning and rebellion arose. Protests were held on college campuses, antiwar rallies were staged in Washington, D.C. The government was challenged to defend its case. The dissenters claimed that they were supplying the sort of public debate that was needed to clarify the real meaning of U.S. involvement in Vietnam. This was the sort of debate that the Congress should have engaged in, but had not, that the president himself should have listened to, but instead sought to avoid at every turn.

The dissenters did not have an immediate effect, and the war lasted ten years, during which millions were killed and wounded (over 50,000 Americans died), two other countries (Laos and Cambodia) were

drawn into the fighting, and there were consequences both in the United States and elsewhere that no one could possibly have anticipated. But as more and more citizens expressed opposition to the war, government leaders began to feel the pressure. In 1968 an astounding grass-roots presidential campaign for peace candidate Eugene McCarthy helped persuade Lyndon Johnson to bow out of the presidential race altogether.

If the Vietnam War taught us many bitter lessons, it also gave rise to encouraging signs for democracy. Many Americans proved to be willing to raise difficult and painful questions about the behavior of their own government, and some risked jail or exile in order to express the conviction that the war was immoral. These were notable victories for the democratic spirit, regardless of what one might conclude about the wisdom of our involvement in Vietnam.

It should also be noted that some of those who attacked American policies in Vietnam employed undemocratic practices in the process. These practices varied from the shouting down of public speakers to the destruction of property to the planting of bombs. The issue of violence and disruption that these tactics raise is one that we address more fully in Chapter 12.

## The plan of this book

This text is built around the questions and problems of democratic theory as outlined in this introductory chapter. In each subsequent chapter we will take up a different basic aspect of U.S. politics and relate it

One of many rallies held to protest the Vietnam War. As the war continued, more and more Americans of all backgrounds voiced their opposition to U.S. involvement. The antiwar move-ment raised many moral questions about American goals in Vietnam, the means employed to reach them, and the price paid to do so.

to one or another of the elements of democratic theory. For example, Chapter 2 focuses on U.S. political culture. The key questions informing that chapter are, Just how democratic is our political culture? and Which aspects of that culture point in a democratic direction and which aspects do not? (Of course, it is not possible to reduce all interesting political issues to questions of democracy; occasionally, we will take detours into other territory.)

Chapters 3 and 4 discuss basic political arrangements in the United States: specifically, the Constitution and the federal system. Do these particular political arrangements facilitate or thwart democracy? Does the Constitution, for example, frustrate or enhance majority rule? Do the states do enough to protect democratic rights? Is a government "closer to the people" (such as local government) likely to be more democratic?

Chapter 5 turns to basic questions of civil rights and liberties. How has U.S. society fared in these areas? We have already briefly glimpsed the problems of realizing democracy in connection with blacks and women, but what about other questions: free speech, freedom of religion, due process of law, and so on?

Chapter 6 takes up a thorny but very important question: the shape of the U.S. political economy. Here we return to the issues of democracy's relationship to capitalism and socialism, but in a more specific vein, exploring the distribution of wealth and income, the distribution of poverty, the way government affects the distribution of material goods. Is there excessive influence on the part of the rich? Is democracy thwarted by a highly unequal distribution of resources?

The first five chapters, comprising Part I, lay the foundation for all that comes later in the book. They explore the most basic aspects of political and social life. In Part II we dig more deeply into political *processes*. Here we explore political attitudes (Chapter 7), voting and political participation (Chapter 8), political parties (Chapter 9), campaigns and the media (Chapter 10), interest groups (Chapter 11), and mass political action (Chapter 12). All these chapters relate to the issues of democratic representation. In each of them, the fundamental question posed is, How are opinions shaped and acted upon in our political life? How effective is the democratic process? For example, are the political parties clearly related to popular attitudes? Do the media generate enlightenment? Is mass action constructive and sensible?

In Part III (Chapters 13–17), we turn to the fundamental political *institutions* of American national government—the Congress, the presidency, the federal bureaucracy, and the court system. How well do each of these institutions meet the needs of democratic politics? More specifically, are they responsive to popular sentiment, honest, protective of democratic rights and liberties, concerned in word *and* deed with creating a more decent society? These general questions break down into particular ones addressed to each institution. For example, we will ask whether presidential power has grown too great in some areas, or, conversely, whether presidential power is great enough to allow the chief executive to function properly in U.S. politics. In the case of Congress, we will be especially concerned with the power of "special interests" in the legislative process. Is Congress really a democratic body, or is it too heavily under the influence of the well-organized few?

Finally, Part IV (Chapters 18–23) is concerned with the four major areas of public *policy-making*—economic policy, policies concerning civil rights and civil liberties, foreign and defense policies, and energy and environmental policies. The questions arising from democratic politics are somewhat different in each area. The discussion of economic policy is divided into two parts. First we take up the overall management of the economy, including such issues as the relationship between government and business, the handling of inflation and unemployment, and the structure of the tax system. *In whose interest*, we will ask, is the economy managed? The second chapter on economic policy concerns the development of the welfare state—that series of social programs designed to deal with the stresses and insecurities of economic life, such as Social Security, Medicare, and Aid to Families with Dependent Children. The welfare state is one of the most controversial aspects of U.S. politics. What should a democrat ask of the welfare state? And how well does the U.S. welfare state meet these democratic demands?

The chapter concerned with civil liberties and civil rights considers several contemporary controversies, such as equality for women, affirmative action, and abortion. We will look at the arguments revolving around each of these (and other) issues and evaluate the patterns of governmental action in these areas. The thrust of the chapter is a consideration of how well civil rights and civil liberties are being protected. What does democratic theory have to tell us about ways of handling these current controversies?

In the treatment of foreign and defense policy, our main concern is to examine the democratic issues involved: What forces shape foreign and defense policy? Who has the most influence over policy making? What role does public opinion play, and how is public opinion shaped? Does the United States further democratic goals through its foreign policy activities? Here we will consider recent wars, the arms race, Soviet-American relations, and other issues.

Finally, in the chapter on energy and environment we focus on the dilemmas posed for U.S. society by the problems of energy shortages and environmental damage. From the standpoint of democratic theory, several issues are significant: How are key decisions made in the energy and environment areas? Who benefits most from these decisions? Can the common citizen understand the complex trade-offs involved in dealing with energy/environment problems?

## Conclusions

This is a book that asks questions. I have my own opinions on many of these questions, and I'm sure my opinions will show, both in the way the material is selected and in specific comments I make. At the same time, I hope to be able to discuss other views with enough fairness so that the reader will understand what others think even when I disagree with them. Most important, I hope that the reader will come away from this book with a deeper sense of the meaning, the problems, and the possibilities of democratic life, U.S. brand. I will be satisfied with that.

## SELECTED READINGS

### Various definitions of democracy

Discussions of Greek political ideas and practices can be found in Walter Agard, *What Democracy Meant to the Greeks* (Madison, Wis.: University of Wisconsin Press, 1960); T. R. Glover, *Democracy in the Ancient World* (New York: Cooper Square Publishers, 1966).

There are many commentaries on the epic seventeenth and eighteenth century political struggles. See G. P. Gooch, *English Democratic Ideas in the Seventeenth Century* (New York: Harper, 1959); Carl Becker, *The Heavenly City of the Eighteenth Century Philosophers* (New Haven, Conn.: Yale University Press, 1932); Harry K. Girvetz, *The Evolution of Liberalism* (New York: Collier Books, 1963).

Certain definitions of democracy are quite broad, whereas some include many detailed sets of requirements. For discussion and examples, see Carl Cohen, *Democracy* (Athens, Ga.: University of Georgia Press, 1971), and H. B. Mayo, *An Introduction to Democratic Theory* (New York: Oxford, 1960). S. M. Lipset emphasizes the significance of competitive elections in *Political Man* (Garden City, N.Y.: Doubleday & Co., 1960).

There have been three centuries of discussion on the subject of egalitarian democracy. For a sampling of interesting approaches, see C. B. MacPherson, *The Political Theory of Possessive Individualism: Hobbes to Locke* (Oxford: Clarendon Press, 1962) and *Democratic Theory* (Oxford: Clarendon Press, 1973); R. H. Tawney, *Equality* (London: G. Allen & Unwin, 1964); G. B. Shaw, *The Intelligent Woman's Guide to Socialism and Capitalism* (Garden City, N.Y.: Garden City Publishing Co., 1928).

### Ideal and real democracies

The political philosophy of Rousseau has been interpreted in several ways. See, for example, J. L. Talmon, *The Origins of Totalitarian Democracy* (New York: Praeger, 1960), and Maurice Cranston, "Rousseau and the Ideology of Liberation," *Wilson Quarterly*, January 1, 1983.

For a description of a modern "utopian" democracy, see Melford E. Spiro, *Kibbutz: Venture in Utopia* (New York: Schocken, 1971).

For discussions of democratic theory from several perspectives, see J. Cohen and J. Rogers, *On Democracy* (Middlesex, England: Penguin, 1983); Amy Gutmann, *Liberal Equality* (Cambridge, England: Cambridge University Press, 1980); Elaine Spitz, *Majority Rule* (Chatham, N.J.: Chatham House, 1984); Giovanni Sartori, *Democratic Theory* (New York: Praeger, 1965); Elias Berg, *Democracy and the Majority Principle* (Stockholm: Scandinavian University Books, 1965).

### Problems inherent in democratic life

Oligarchy and the problems of influence are among the most discussed topics in modern politics. For a sampling, see Robert Michels, *Political Parties* (New York: Hearst's International Library, 1915); Michael Parenti, *Democracy for the Few* (New York: St. Martin's, 1983); John Plamenatz, *Democracy and Illusion* (New York: Longman's, 1978), Chapter 3.

The literature on alienation is vast. A good starting point is R. S. Gilmour and R. B. Lamb, *Political Alienation in Contemporary America* (New York: St. Martin's, 1975).

### Struggles to realize democratic ideals

Among the more interesting sources on women's suffrage are Aileen S. Kraditor, ed., *Up from the Pedestal* (Chicago: Quadrangle Books, 1968); William L. O'Neill, *Everyone Was Brave* (Chicago: Quadrangle Books, 1969); Eleanor Flexner, *Century of Struggle* (New York: Atheneum, 1973).

There are many views about the protest movements of the 1960s. For a sampling of different perspectives see Milton Viorst, *Fire in the Streets* (New York: Simon and Schuster, 1979); David Dellinger, *More Power Than We Knew: The People's Movement Towards Democracy* (New York: Doubleday, 1975); Lewis Feuer, *The Conflict of Generations* (New York: Basic Books, 1969); Stanley Rothman and Robert Lichter, *Roots of Radicalism* (New York: Oxford, 1982).

For more-extensive discussion of the U.S. role in Chile, see Seymour Hersh, *The Price of Power: Kissinger in the Nixon White House* (New York: Summit, 1983); Jorge Valacion, *Chile: An Attempt at Historic Compromise* (Chicago: Banner Press, 1979); Paul Sigmund, *The Overthrow of Allende and the Politics of Chile, 1964–1976* (Pittsburgh: University of Pittsburgh Press, 1977).

# Chapter two

# American political culture

# Liberty and its limits

THE American political experience seems at first glance simple and straightforward enough. The traditional view of grammar school textbooks was that the United States was created as a full-fledged democracy, born in a revolution that rallied around the call for liberty and equality. Since that time, according to this version of history, the nation has gone on to greater and greater heights as a democratic society and as a defender of democracy elsewhere in the world. A closer look at our political history, however, reveals a far more ambiguous and troubling picture. The American experiment with government by the people was an innovative and world-significant effort. But there have been many rough moments in the evolution of U.S. democracy, from its beginnings up to the present day. The very meaning of democracy has sometimes been called into question, and many battles have been waged over the concept of making democracy more meaningful for more people.

Before investigating the complexities of democratic politics in the United States, however, we must first ask the basic question, What factors make it likely that a society will develop a democratic political system? It seems that affluence helps, by soothing the sores of social conflicts. High levels of education make a difference. The presence of a large middle class also helps, in preventing the polarization of conflict between the rich and poor. Political and social beliefs also are important: when both political elites and ordinary citizens subscribe to democratic values, democracy is far easier to institute and sustain. The sum of these beliefs comprise a political culture.

## What is political culture?

A society's **political culture** arises from its members' attitudes toward the processes and institutions of politics. Such attitudes reflect conceptions about how politics works or ought to work, about the proper role of government, about one's fellow citizens and their place in the political process, about the rules of the political game. Political culture usually includes deeply rooted preconceptions about political life, which, in turn, shape political attitudes and behavior.[1]

31

## Political culture and democratic values

Is it possible to characterize the kind of political culture that is compatible with democracy? It is easy, after all, to point to attitudes hostile to democratic government. If, for example, citizens feel they play no legitimate role in their nation's politics; if a nation's leaders distrust its citizens and one another; if force is accepted as a necessary method of political action; if dissent and opposition are considered unacceptable—such feelings are unlikely to spawn a democratic form of goverment. As easy as it may be to point out undemocratic aspects of political culture, however, it is not so simple to describe the sort of political milieu likely to support democracy. The best we can do is to specify certain minima that any democratic policy would have to include in its cultural repertoire. These would be such things as belief in citizen participation, in the legitimacy of dissent and opposition, and in the meaningfulness of public debate and elections; reasonable respect for law and democratic principles; tolerance toward other social groups; and so on.[2]

We might try to describe the kind of society likely to develop and maintain a democratic political culture. Some political scientists have cited high levels of education, affluence, and a large middle class as crucial elements.[3] Yet it is difficult to argue that democracy is promoted by any or all of these factors. Democracies have developed under many conditions, and the vagaries of history have sometimes helped to shape political life in ways that could never have been anticipated. At the end of World War II, for example, democracy was actually imposed on West Germany and Japan, two rabidly antidemocratic, fascist societies. Many commentators argued, not surprisingly, that the cultures of these nations were inherently inhospitable to democratic practices. Yet democracy has not only survived, but even thrived, in both nations.

## Cohesiveness
in political culture

One factor critical to the stability of a nation's political culture is the degree of consensus present in the society. Where political culture lacks a consensus, political life is likely to be conflict-ridden, marked by disagreement over fundamentals.[4] In U.S. society, certain basic elements of the political culture, such as the near-sacred status of the Constitution, are virtually unchallengeable. Other elements of U.S. political culture, such as the interplay between religion and politics, have long been matters of intense controversy. Our political culture, like most others, includes contradictory values, as well as conflicts between the values people proclaim and the values reflected in the ways they actually behave.

But if conflicts and contradictions are important facets of the style and dynamics of U.S. politics, so too are the areas of basic agreement, or consensus, in U.S. political culture. Many observers of U.S. history have remarked on the strong consensus on political attitudes achieved in a society made up of so many disparate ethnic and racial groups. Ethnic diversity alone, obviously, does not rule out the development of a cohesive political culture. British colonists, who comprised 60 percent of the original colonial population, established the political processes, dominant language, and social and economic norms of interaction to which subsequent immigrant groups adjusted.

There has been one occasion in U.S. history when the political consensus broke down and the issue was settled by war. This was, of course, the Civil War, which erupted out of the clash of differing concepts of citizenship and basic rights, as well as disagreements over how political power should be exercised. The heritage of that conflict remains with us in our political life today.

Overall, U.S. political culture has remained sufficiently cohesive to permit orderly government to carry on in spite of the many conflicts and contradictions in our society and political life. In fact, looking back over the last twenty-five years, it may seem remarkable that our political processes have been able to survive, relatively unchanged, in the face of assassinations, domestic violence, a bitterly opposed and costly war, and the resignation of a president. Whether this is a testimony to the resilience of our political culture, or to its irrelevance, is a question we will consider at the conclusion of this text.

## U.S. political culture
and democratic values

If we assume that our government is a democracy, does it follow that our political culture must therefore be democratic? As we saw in Chapter 1, things are not that simple. It is true that many of our democratic practices have been supported by our political culture, but it is also true that we have often proclaimed our belief in democracy without practicing what we preached. Is it possible to pinpoint the contradictions and tensions in U.S. political culture and in the larger culture of which it is a part? And would doing so help us understand some of the failings of our democracy? In the pages that follow we will look at the pattern of our political culture with an eye to recognizing the many ways it has supported and strengthened our democratic behavior. We will examine the fundamental values that have shaped U.S. political life, beginning with the liberal democratic tradition that informs much of our political culure. Then we will turn to the limitations of that same political culture, and to an analysis of some cultural and political patterns that have contradicted and thwarted the evolution of democracy in the United States.

July 4, 1961. One of the chief bonds in any political culture is the spirit of belonging to the nation. In many American communities, this spirit remains a powerful force. This picture shows citizens of a neighborhood on Chicago's west side.

## The liberal tradition

The United States was conceived in the tradition of eighteenth-century **liberalism, a social and political set of values that decisively shaped our democratic politics.**[5] The cornerstones of this political value system were a belief in government based on the consent of the governed and a belief that certain rights are guaranteed to all persons simply by virtue of the fact that they are human beings. These rights, as enunciated so eloquently by Thomas Jefferson in the Declaration of Independence, included "life, liberty and the pursuit of happiness." Government, according to eighteenth-century liberals, derives its right to govern from the fact that it protects these rights. And when a government violates the rights of its citizens, those citizens have a right to rebel—which is exactly what some of the colonists did.

Liberals placed great emphasis on the liberty of the individual. The concept of the free individual actually evolved over the course of several centuries. In the Renaissance era (roughly, 1350–1600), as the tenets of classical humanism were revived and reinterpreted, intellectuals and artists celebrated what they saw as the uniqueness of human potential and the virtually unlimited possibilities of human creativity.[6] To the Renaissance celebration of humanism was added, beginning in the early 1500s, the Protestant Reformation's emphasis on the primacy of the individual conscience and the solitary relation of the individual to God.[7] At the same time, the development of the capitalistic form of economic life, based on private property and individual initiative, gave rise to the notion that every individual should be free to buy and sell, to invest and gamble, to work and to relocate, as that person saw fit. Finally, seventeenth-century political philosophers such as John Locke applied the concept of the free individual to the political realm, arguing that government existed only in order to safeguard the **natural rights** of individuals.[8]

The ideal society of free individuals envisioned by the liberal thinkers of the seventeenth and eighteenth centuries was a society open to all and based entirely on merit, in which each person was free to pursue any course of action desired, so long as it did not impinge on the freedom or rights of others. In such an open society, you had only yourself to blame if you failed to take advantage of life's opportunities. In the infant United States, a nation that consisted primarily of small individually owned farms and was located on the edge of a vast, unexplored continent, these liberal ideas set down particularly tenacious roots.

## Economic, social, and political values

Given the tenets of the liberal creed, it is easy to see why the United States acted as a magnet for immigrants. Although some immigrants were refugees from political or religious persecution, most came to the United States in order to find a better life, lured by the liberal promise that even the lowest-born person could, through hard work, climb the ladder of success. The United States, with no hereditary nobility and seemingly no social or political restrictions on individual initiative, drew great waves of immigrants looking for a chance to better themselves.[9]

Along with this faith in individual responsibility and success went a belief in the small business or individually owned farm as the appropriate vehicle for economic success. Throughout the nation's history, Americans generally have believed that although bigger may be better in some matters, too much bigness is a dangerous thing. Recurrently in U.S. political history, **populist** movements have arisen to defend the interests of the common citizen against institutions or power elites perceived as too big and oppressive. In the 1890s the Populist Party attacked the big corporations and the railroads. More recently, populist movements have focused their attacks on so-called big government.[10]

Populist agitation, however, has rarely been directed against the capitalistic system itself—only against perceived abuses of it. True to their liberal democratic heritage, most Americans have continued to believe that capitalism is the best economic system. Private ownership has remained popular, although most people now accept the idea that sometimes business must be regulated for the public good.

Along with these economic values, eighteeenth-century liberalism included political and social values predicated on a considerable degree of equality among citizens. Because all individuals are born with certain rights, all are entitled to have those rights protected by society and government. Each person should be equal before the law—a person cannot claim superiority before a judge, for example, simply by virtue of belonging to a richer or more privileged class. Wealth, accidents of birth, social position— these should not matter when it comes to the legal rights of each individual. In addition, each person is entitled to basic political rights, starting with the right to participate meaningfully in political life.

Such, at any rate, were the theoretical tenets of eighteenth-century liberalism. Application of those tenets to a concrete situation proved to be another matter entirely. In applying theory to practice, for example, early liberals were highly ambiguous about whether everyone ought to have the right to vote. Both in England and America many liberals were wary of the potential power of "the many" that political equality might create. They feared what was sometimes called the tyranny of the majority, or, less politely, mob rule. As a result, eighteenth-century liberals had trouble creating a political process that would actually live up to liberal principles. The U.S. Constitution, significantly, left the issue of voting rights up to the individual states, many of which stipulated that only those who owned a certain amount of property could vote. Still, for white males the right to vote was achieved earlier in the United States (by 1830) than it was anywhere else in the world.

Liberals were also suspicious of the power of governments in general. Governmental power, they felt, could all too easily be abused and turned against the rights of the individual—through excessive taxation, for example. As a safeguard, liberals argued for a contractual arrangement between government and governed. Government, they said, should be limited to specific functions, and the governed should be guaranteed certain rights; if any of those rights are violated, moreover, individuals have cause for disobedience or even rebellion.

The liberal values on which the United States was founded actually made it a purer liberal society than those European societies that gave birth to liberalism. In Europe, liberals were forced to do combat with the defenders of monarchy, of which there were few in the new United States. Of course, there was (and remains) tremendous disagreement over what "democratic liberalism" actually means, but the United States has never experienced the struggles over the very *form* of government that have been fairly commonplace in European history.[11] Compared with Europe, then, the United States was from the start more egalitarian, despite the vast differences in wealth that have always existed here.

To summarize, the values that eighteenth-century liberalism contributed to the U.S. democratic tradition included

*Individualism:* A belief in the central value of the individual, whose rights government is created to defend. Each individual is responsible for his (or, by logical extension, her) own fate.

*Liberty:* Each person should have the maximum freedom possible, compatible with equal freedom for others.

*Equality:* All are entitled to equal legal and political rights.

*An Open Society:* Each person should be judged on individual merits and be free to enter various occupations and pursuits.

*Rule of Law:* Government must be nonarbitrary, exercising power through equitable laws that are fairly administered.

*Limits on Government:* Since power cas easily corrupt, governments must be watched closely and hedged with restrictions lest they infringe on citizens' rights. A written Constitution helps to set such limits.

Of course, many Americans throughout history have neither supported nor acted upon these values, preferring beliefs and practices that have often been at great variance with the liberal tradition. Nevertheless, liberalism is the American creed. We may not honor it, but it haunts our consciences. It represents our collective ideal, even if it is not always reflected in our collective practice.

### The legacy of liberalism in the United States

The strength of the liberal tradition in the United States has helped democratic government survive here for two centuries. Apart from the Civil War crisis, there has been no serious challenge to the legitimacy of democratic government and constitutional authority in our political history. As the nation's conscience, the liberal tradition has kept alive the hope of equal treatment and basic civil rights for all. Despite long periods of religious, racial, and political intolerance, respect for civil liberties has gradually increased throughout our history. Legal equality for American blacks, long believed to be a virtual im-

possibility, was achieved after a long struggle. The fundamental liberal commitment to political equality served as a goad in that struggle.[12]

Liberalism has also sustained a considerable distrust of government, which continues to show itself in grass-roots resistance to governmental intrusions, in tax revolts, and in attacks on the growth of government budgets at all levels. The liberal belief in equality before the law also served as the basis of the Watergate investigations of the early 1970s, leading to the first resignation of a president in U.S. history.

Finally, the individualist thrust of liberalism has been reflected in the continuing commitment of most Americans to the capitalistic economic system, the central concept of which is private ownership of the means of production. Despite many modifications in

One person, one yacht, one personal onboard computer. Is this the ultimate realization of the American dream? How are the Yuppies of the 1980s connected to the aspirations of frontier days—was it just material wealth, personal comfort, and convenience that we sought?

this economic system and much greater government involvement in economic life, capitalism is still viewed by most Americans as essential to what often has been called the American way of life.

## Two types of liberalism

U.S. political debate today revolves around two seemingly opposed viewpoints, usually labeled liberalism and conservatism. But both views actually are structured by eighteenth-century liberal ideas and assumptions. Regardless of the labels "liberal" and "conservative," U.S. political life basically operates within the framework and norms established at the founding of the nation.

## Conservatism: traditional liberalism

By and large, most U.S. "conservatives" are traditional liberals who have kept faith with liberalism as it was propounded two hundred years ago.[13] Conservative politicians such as President Ronald Reagan and Senator Jesse Helms emphasize the individualist, antigovernment portions of the liberal tradition. They continue to believe in the strength of U.S. capitalism, as represented by what conservatives like to call free enterprise. Out of a belief in individual responsibility, they generally disapprove of government programs to aid the disadvantaged. Because of their commitment to capitalism, they prefer to leave dollars in private hands, rather than to redistribute wealth through social programs. They want less economic regulation by government and see virtue in what President Reagan has called the "magic of the marketplace"—that is, the creation of wealth through

# The United States

America, you are luckier
Than this old continent of ours;
You have no ruined castles
And no volcanic earth.
You do not suffer
In hours of intensity
From futile memories
And pointless battles.
Concentrate on the present joyfully!
And when your children write books
May a good destiny keep them
From knight, robber, and ghost-stories.

JOHANN WOLFGANG VON GOETHE (1749–1832)
*translated by Robert Bly*

Early in the nineteenth century, the German poet Goethe expressed this poignant hope for the newly created United States. Unlike Europe, Goethe proclaims, America will not have to live under the shadow of a long and painful history. Note that Goethe's char- acterization of European history draws on the imagery of feudalism (knights and castles). Like many other observ- ers before and since, he believed that it was the absence of a feudal his- tory that made America different.

individual initiative and free enterprise in business and finance, unfettered by governmental restrictions.

Occasionally, powerful forces on the political right (the Ku Klux Klan, for instance) have championed ideals contrary to the liberal creed, but such fringe elements have not been in the mainstream of con- servatism. Today's conservatives usually think of themselves as upholding the truest traditions of the nation, and they are fond of citing the words of the Founders on such issues as the danger of too much government power and the importance of the indi- vidual. Unlike most conservatives in Europe, U.S.

conservatives are not usually comfortable with pa- ternalistic government—with using the power of the state to protect or assist individuals.

## The new liberalism

The Great Depression of the 1930s prompted a major shift in U.S. politics. At that time millions were out of work, banks were failing, many stocks were prac- tically worthless, much of the population was afraid and in want. President Franklin D. Roosevelt said he saw "one third of the nation ill-housed, ill-clothed and ill-fed." The U.S. economic system had failed, and there was widespread agreement on the need for a restructuring of the economy, in which government would gain far more power over economic affairs and make a firm commitment to the well-being of the common person. President Roosevelt's solution was a wide range of social and economic initiatives called the **New Deal**, which involved government regula- tions and subsidies in the economic sphere and wel- fare programs in the social sector.

FDR's New Deal was the crystallization of the "new" liberalism, an activist creed committed to the im- provement of the average person's conditions of life, and particularly to elimination of the worst forms of poverty and deprivation.[14] Politicians committed to the new liberalism, such as former vice-president Walter Mondale and Senator Edward Kennedy, are not satisfied to let the economy run according to its own laws, preferring instead to direct economic ac- tivity toward larger social interests. In general, this means the initiation of social programs aimed at aid- ing the unemployed, improving health care and housing for low-income people, raising educational opportunities for all, and so on.

The new liberals, like the conservatives, are not entirely consistent in their views and policies. De- spite their commitment to social change, liberals often favor balanced budgets and reduced government spending. Conservatives, on their part, frequently defend government subsidies to groups such as farm- ers, while maintaining a general opposition to government spending. Conservatives also are the chief champions of government involvement in matters of personal morality such as abortion, pornography, and homosexuality.

When it comes to an activist government, then, conservatives usually prefer action in the realm of personal life, while opposing regulation of business. Liberals tend to take the opposite view: that morals are a matter of personal choice, whereas economic matters have general social significance and therefore are legitimately within the areas that government may regulate.

## The failure of radicalism in U.S. politics

One consequence of the strength of the U.S. liberal tradition has been the relative failure of radical movements to gain national power. The United States is, in fact, the only industrial democracy without a significant **socialist** political party. By comparison, socialists have played a key part in the national politics of European democracies since the nineteenth century, and in recent years **democratic socialist parties** have held power in France, Spain, Great Britain, West Germany, Sweden, Denmark, Norway, Finland, Austria, Greece, the Netherlands, and Portugal. Even in Canada, where the political left has never been a major force nationally, the socialist New Democratic Party has elected provincial governments in British Columbia, Saskatchewan, and Manitoba.

Many arguments have been put forward to explain this weakness of the American left.[15] Some have argued that the United States is simply too rich a country: that is, that general affluence has made socialism less appealing to the masses. Others have argued that the country's many ethnic, racial, religious, and regional divisions have made organizing a party based on social class very difficult. Most observers believe, however, that one of the central factors has been the strength of the liberal tradition. The American emphasis on individualism, with its

ideology of opportunity and success, together with this nation's relative equality and lack of feudal heritage, have prevented radical ideas from catching on. European socialists, on the other hand, have benefited from the greater class consciousness and solidarity of the working class, as well as a more closed social system than in the United States. It has even proved more difficult to organize trade unions here, and union membership today is much lower in the U.S. than in most other democratic nations.

This is not to say, however, that socialists have seen no success at all in the United States. Many socialist mayors and legislators were elected during the period around World War I, for example, and California came close to electing a socialist governor during the Depression. More recently, we saw something of a left-wing revival in the 1960s. It is also important to note that many programs advocated by socialists have, in fact, become accepted U.S. policies, from social security and unemployment insurance to the many efforts to protect consumers or the very idea of governmental responsibility for the performance of the economy. Nonetheless, one of the overwhelming political facts of American history has been the failure of a socialist party to become a significant part of the political spectrum. This fact has had many important political consequences, among them the relative weakness of the American **welfare state** (a point we will return to in Chapters 6 and 20).

Looking to the other side of the American political spectrum, we see that the far right, including such antidemocratic groups as the Ku Klux Klan, has also failed to gain national power. Outright racist groups have had much greater success at the state and local levels. The Klan, for example, (as we describe more fully in Chapter 12) exerted some influence in several states during the 1920s, but never actually succeeded at anything more than a march in the nation's capital.

Both the far left and the far right, then, have played a less significant role in our history than they have in many other democratic nations. Shaped by our own brand of liberalism, the American political spectrum has remained narrower than that of most other democratic nations.

## Limits
## of liberalism

As we have seen, our nation's liberal heritage has in many ways been supportive of democratic values and practices. Yet, we have often failed to live up to the standards of this heritage. Americans are proud of reciting the tenets of the liberal faith, but sometimes find it difficult to put those beliefs into practice. Too often, the doors of the "open society" have been shut to some citizens. Respect for law has not prevented bouts of violence. Our attempts to spread democracy to the world have become ensnared in national self-interest. Religious beliefs, supposedly matters of individual concern, have occasionally been thrust into the political arena.

This is not to imply that liberal values are not upheld much of the time. The United States justly

deserves its reputation as the "land of opportunity," and many Americans are respectful of the rights of others and generous in sharing their resources. This section focuses on our lapses simply to indicate where we need to apply our ideals more strictly to political reality.

## Intolerance
## and discrimination

"Fellow immigrants," President Franklin Roosevelt once began an address to the Daughters of the American Revolution, a group sometimes noted for its snobbish celebration of special hereditary connections. Roosevelt's irony was well placed. Except for the American Indians, whose journey here came cen-

Albert Einstein becoming a U.S. citizen, Trenton, N.J., 1940. Inspection of arriving aliens, Ellis Island, 1923. Laotian refugees grocery shopping, Albuquerque, N.M., 1980. The story of U.S. immigration is long and complex. The doors of our nation have opened repeatedly to admit vast numbers of immigrants. In the first fifteen years of this century almost a million people a year arrived. The 1920s saw a sharp reduction in the number of immigrants allowed, which remained true for decades. In that period, the U.S. established quotas favoring Western Europeans and people with certain skills. In recent years immigration is up again, partly because of our overseas involvements, with Cubans, Vietnamese, and Laotians arriving in large numbers. U.S. immigration policy is now highly controversial, with much debate over illegal aliens and those seeking political asylum. The vastness of diversity of U.S. immigration has always been a unique and significant factor in our political culture.

turies earlier, we are *all* immigrants. Social and economic distinctions often boil down to who got here first and made the most of it.

While certainly not the only immigrant society, the United States stands alone in the number, size, and diversity of its immigrant groups (see Figure 2.1 and box). Yet, most immigrants have understood that a certain degree of assimilation into the dominant Anglo-Saxon pattern is necessary in order to succeed in this society. To remain too ethnic, too closely identified with the Old World and old ways, has often meant being left behind in the New World. In their understandable efforts to "Americanize" themselves, however, immigrants at times have lost touch with deep and important traditions, languages, and styles that might have enriched the dominant culture.

Enough lumps have remained in the so-called melting pot that politicians frequently find it advantageous to pitch their campaigns to various ethnic groups.[16] Particular ethnic groups have even taken firm hold on local politics in certain areas. Still, only in recent years have the members of some ethnic groups been able to attain high elective office. The first Catholic president, John F. Kennedy, was elected in 1960, and it will probably be quite some time before a black or Hispanic president is elected.

Foreigners, minority groups, and many who just seemed different have been subject to both personal intolerance and official discrimination. Discrimination has run the gamut from highly personal prejudices to the actions of organizations and of government itself. Discrimination has taken many forms: in employment, in college quotas established to limit the entrance of certain groups, in restrictions on where people can live. Social humiliation, harassment, and even murder have sometimes greeted new Ameri-

Hayward, California, 1942. The Mochida family awaits evacuation to an internment camp. Almost 100,000 Japanese-Americans were confined to camps in remote areas during World War II. Though the courts upheld the Japanese internment as a justifiable wartime measure, many concluded after the war that it was a policy based more on panic and racism than reason. In the 1980s, Congress has been considering restitution to the victims of the internment.

cans. In the middle of the nineteenth century the Nativist Party accused newly arrived Catholic immigrants of plotting to take over the nation in the name of the papacy. This was to be the first of many such accusations and efforts to restrict the entry of "foreigners" to the United States. Again and again religious, ethnic, and racial hatreds have flared, necessitating a continuous struggle to keep our society open.

Many immigrant groups have had to contend with blatant discrimination by fellow Americans. In early 1942, close to one hundred thousand U.S. citizens were rounded up, forced to leave their homes, and taken to detention camps in remote areas, where they were confined for three years. The only "crime" committed by these people was being of Japanese descent at at time when hatred of the Japanese, who had just attacked Pearl Harbor, was at fever pitch. The government justified its actions on the grounds that Japanese-Americans posed a security threat to the country, even though there was no specific evi-

dence that more than a very few had offered or intended to offer aid to the Japanese cause. The vast majority of Japanese-Americans were loyal to U.S. institutions, and yet the U.S. government, with the blessing of the Supreme Court, interned them without trial.[18]

Looking back from the vantage point of forty years, we can only be ashamed of what was done. Although the internment camps were not the concentration camps of the Nazis, Japanese-Americans nonetheless were innocent victims of hysteria and prejudice.

Governmental intolerance has also been displayed toward those whose political views deviated from the mainstream, particularly in times of crisis and tension. In the 1920s[19] and again in the 1950s,[20] for example, real or imagined fears of communist subversion led the U.S. government to violate the rights of thousands of citizens, in many cases merely because they held (or were thought to hold) "un-American" political views. And during the Vietnam War, President Lyndon Johnson and other high government officials refused for years to believe that critics of the war were actually loyal citizens who simply disagreed with the government's policies. Certain that antiwar groups must be financed by communist sources, Johnson instructed government agencies to investigate such groups.[21] In such ways, the legitimacy of dissent is undermined.

## Violence and the rule of law

Americans historically have displayed considerable respect for law and legal procedures. The existence of a written constitution provides for a legal basis on which to settle fundamental political questions. Faith in the Constitution, in the Supreme Court, and in the court system in general has helped to keep social and political conflicts within accepted boundaries. Many observers have noted, in fact, that Americans seem overly fond of legal procedures and tend to litigate endlessly about all sorts of matters. Even one hundred years ago, foreign commentators observed that Americans would take each other to court at the drop of a hat. Respect for law and the use of law to settle disputes seems an ingrained part of our heritage, and one that fits the liberal tradition's preference for an agreed-on legal framework as the basis of government.

Yet there is also a contrary tradition in the United States—the tradition of the gun. The use of force, by both government and individuals, has played a central role in the nation's growth and in the shaping of our folkways. Settlers fought with Indians, waged a war of independence, feuded over land. The Wild West remains legendary, its heroic figures still popularized in books, on television, and in films.[22] To survive in much of the United States in the nineteenth century, the gun was as necessary as the plow, the ax, or the Bible. The frontier often had no enforceable legal authority, so individuals relied on themselves and their friends to maintain social stability. Americans were also wary of granting to the

Most immigrant groups have accepted a certain degree of assimilation into the dominant Anglo-Saxon pattern in order to succeed in American society. The American Indian, whose journey here began centuries before the migrations from Europe, was in many respects the first victim of a type of discrimination that would be applied to other minority groups in the nineteenth and twentieth centuries.

FIGURE 2.1
Historical and
recent patterns
of immigration: During the
1970s, the U.S. Spanish-origin
population increased by 60
percent, to 14.6 million. The
black population, meanwhile,
grew by only 17 percent, to 26.5
million. The number of Asians
and Pacific Islanders rose from
1.5 million to 3.5 million, one-
third living in California.

# The melting pot today

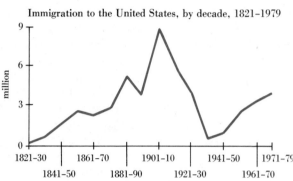

Immigration to the United States, by decade, 1821–1979

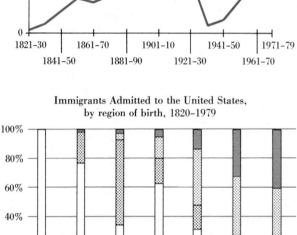

Immigrants Admitted to the United States,
by region of birth, 1820–1979

Canada

Northern and Western Europe

Southern and Eastern Europe

Latin America

Asia

Other

Source: W.P. Adams, "A Dubious Host," *Wilson Quarterly*, January 1, 1983, p.114.

Of the over 226 million Americans counted in the 1980 census, more than 118 million traced their origins to a single foreign nation, and almost 70 million others listed multiple foreign origins. Those of English ancestry led the list, with those of German origin a very close second and Irish-Americans a relatively close third. Some experts have speculated that the figures on English ances-try may be low because the English were thor-oughly assimilated so long ago. About 38 million people polled by the census classified them-selves as "Americans."

central government the exclusive right to police. Even today, policing remains a predominantly local func-tion in our country. The Constitution expressly pro-vides for the citizen's right to bear arms, which, as the colonists considered it, was necessary for a cit-izen militia.

Private violence has taken many forms in the United States. Between 1885 and 1916, for example, more than 3,000 blacks were lynched and thousands of others brutalized.[23] Throughout the late nineteenth and early twentieth centuries, industrialists often hired private armies to combat strikes by workers. And

there is a long tradition of vigilantes pursuing crim-inals and others who were thought to threaten com-munities. Examples of *public* violence are not lack-ing, either. Police forces, the army, and the National Guard have frequently been used against various perceived threats—Indians, union organizers, pro-testors, and others.

We do not have to go back very far in history to find striking evidence of the persistence of the vio-lent streak in U.S. society. Five of the last nine presidents have been targets for assassins. The two most prominent black leaders of the 1960s, Martin

The ancestry groups reported by 100,000 or more Americans included:
English, 49,598,035
German, 49,224,146
Irish, 40,165,702
Afro-American, 20,964,729
French, 12,892,246
Italian, 12,183,692
Scottish, 10,048,816
Polish, 8,228,037
Mexican, 7,692,619
American Indian, 6,715,819
Dutch, 6,304,499
Swedish, 4,345,392
Norwegian, 3,453,839
Russian, 2,781,432
Spanish-Hispanic, 2,686,680
Czech, 1,892,456
Hungarian, 1,776,902
Welsh, 1,664,598
Danish, 1,518,273
Puerto Rican, 1,443,862
Portuguese, 1,024,351
Swiss, 981,543
Greek, 959,856
Austrian, 948,558
Chinese, 894,453
Filipino, 795,255
Japanese, 791,275
French-Canadian, 780,488
Slovak, 776,806
Lithuanian, 742,776
Ukrainian, 730,056
Finnish, 615,872
Cuban, 597,702
Canadian, 456,212
Korean, 376,676
Belgian, 360,277
Yugoslavian, 360,174
Romanian, 315,258
Asian Indian, 311,953
Lebanese, 294,895
Jamaican, 253,268
Croatian, 252,970
Vietnamese, 215,184
Armenian, 212,621
African, 203,791
Hawaiian, 202,052
Dominican, 170,698
Colombian, 156,276
Slovene, 126,663
Iranian, 122,890
Syrian, 106,638
Serbian, 100,941.

Source: *The New York Times*, June 5, 1983.

Luther King, Jr., and Malcolm X, were assassinated. Senator Robert Kennedy was killed and Governor George Wallace crippled by assailants. Also in the 1960s, rioting and arson erupted in black ghettoes throughout the country, and police and National Guard units often met this violence with deadly force. Fatalities were common.

Compared with contemporary Europe, the United States is a particularly violent country. Police are far more likely to kill citizens in this country, both in normal times and in times of disorder, than they are in the European democracies.[24] Perhaps because

Europeans have experienced the violence of which totalitarian governments are capable, they are more sensitive about governmental use of force. A more important factor, however, may be that far more Americans are armed. Because tens of millions of guns circulate rather freely in U.S. society, the police here constantly face the possibility of deadly threat—something that European police rarely have to confront. The large number of guns available has helped make U.S. homicide rates the highest among democratic countries (see Table 2.1). It is important to note, however, that various European nations have shown their own particular sorts of violent tendencies. Organized terrorism has become all too common in Italy and West Germany, as has violence among soccer fans in England.

Many issues connected with the problem of violence have not been solved in our society. Gun ownership is one: Who should be permitted to own guns? And what kind of guns should be allowed? Relations between police and citizens have also been controversial matters in some communities: How can such relations be made cooperative rather than confrontational? Finally, a penchant for violence has often found its way into foreign and military policymaking.[25] It has been argued that an excessive reliance on firepower in Vietnam deepened the disaster of U.S. involvement there.

TABLE 2.1
## Violent crime rates in selected nations*

| | Murder | Rape | Serious Assault |
|---|---|---|---|
| United States | 9.60 | 29.1 | 241.5 |
| Netherlands | 7.15 | — | — |
| Finland | 4.88 | 6.4 | 196.9 |
| West Germany | 4.47 | — | — |
| Sweden | 3.36 | 10.3 | 15.9 |
| France | 2.70 | 3.1 | 58.0 |
| England | 2.24 | — | — |
| Denmark | 2.03 | 9.5 | 85.5 |
| Japan | 1.74 | 2.5 | 25.2 |
| Spain | 0.67 | — | — |
| Norway | 0.50 | 3.4 | 12.3 |

*per 100,000 population
Sources: Interpol Crime Statistics, 1977–78; *The New Book of World Rankings* (New York: Facts on File, 1984).

The subway vigilante. For a brief period in 1985, Bernhard Goetz occupied the national spotlight. Threatened by four black teenagers on a New York subway, Goetz (who had been mugged previously) pulled a gun and shot each one. Some hailed him as a citizen defending his rights, but others regarded his act and its positive reception as a revival of American vigilantism. Dissatisfied with the forces of law and order, people sometimes decide to take both law enforcement and punishment into their own hands.

| Making the world
safe for democracy—
or for us?

I have always believed that this anointed land was set apart in an uncommon way, that a divine plan placed this great continent here between the oceans to be found by people from every corner of the earth who had a special love of faith and freedom. *President Ronald Reagan, 1982*

It would be hard to find a more extreme statement of the allegedly special place in the world occupied by the United States. Although many U.S. leaders have been hard-headed, practical men who understood that the United States is very much like other nations, there has also been a strong missionary element in U.S. government policy throughout history.

Every country occasionally demonstrates a well-developed self-appreciation, but Americans early on displayed an especially lofty view of their role in the world and of the purity of their motives. From the founding of the nation to the present day, Americans have tended to decry other nations for seeking power or imperial domination, while asserting that their country was seeking only to spread democracy throughout the world. According to the Founders, we were to act as an example for mankind. As George Washington put it in his first inaugural address, "The preservation of the sacred fire of liberty and the destiny of the republican model of government are justly considered . . . staked on the experiment intrusted to the hands of the American people."

The American example did spread. One Latin American country after another modeled its constitution on our own. And as recently as 1946, a radical nationalist quoted Thomas Jefferson when making a plea for his country's independence. That leader was Ho Chi Minh, the Vietnamese communist.

The United States has also been famous for its altruism and its generosity toward others. We opened our doors to the refugees of the world. Our magazines are filled with ads asking us to "save the children" in some faraway land, or to send food to drought-stricken countries. When a disaster strikes, U.S. aid is often the first to be sent. We train Peace Corps volunteers to assist in development efforts across the globe. We like to think of ourselves as an idealistic people trying to spread the gospel of democracy and capitalism to the rest of the world. Along with Washington and Jefferson, we want the United States to light the way for others, to help make the world, in President Woodrow Wilson's phrase, "safe for democracy."[26]

But there is another side to U.S. relations with

the world—that of an expanding participant on the world scene. Throughout most of the nineteenth century the United States steered clear of entanglements abroad, largely because there was more than enough to do at home. The nation expanded internally, spreading across the continent, fighting constant battles against Indian tribes, as well as waging a war with Mexico. Our treatment of the Indian tribes certainly provided no model of democratic (or ethical) practice. The American Indians, by and large, were mistreated, betrayed, and often virtually exterminated.[27] Some U.S. leaders of the time proclaimed that it was our "manifest destiny," our God-given task, to expand across the continent, to put to use the vast resources available in North America. In their view, the Indians were too uncivilized to really matter.

By the end of the nineteenth century, the United States was ready to emerge as a world power. After

intervening in Cuba and in the Philippines during the Spanish-American War (1898), purportedly to help end unjust Spanish rule, U.S. military forces actually helped to suppress the independence movements they were supposedly assisting.[28] And throughout the twentieth century, our government repeatedly stepped in in Latin America to support U.S. interests and to stop radical social movements regarded as threats to our security.

After fighting World War II against the antidemocratic forces of Nazism and fascism, many Americans expected the postwar world to be one in which democratic forces would generally prevail. But the onset of the global rivalry, or **Cold War**, between the United States and the Soviet Union rapidly led to the division of the world into communist and Western spheres of influence. One of the chief dilemmas of U.S. foreign policy since 1945 has been to decide whether we are chiefly an anticommunist or a pro-

1945. It was two for two for the United States—two world wars, and two victories. Throughout Europe, Americans were welcomed as liberators: we had fought against tyranny, and we'd won. The political consequences, however, proved difficult to handle and to predict.

democratic power. As anticommunists, our policy makers could justify suporting many undemocratic regimes, such as those of Francisco Franco in Spain, Anastasio Somoza in Nicaragua, and Fulgencio Batista in Cuba. A foreign policy oriented more toward democratic values would have led us to keep our distance from such dictators.

The debate over the direction of our foreign policy continues today. The key questions are: What role should a U.S. commitment to democratic values play in shaping our foreign policy? Should the United States be primarily committed to the protection of its own security and power, or to the protection of democratic values? If the latter, how are those values best protected?

### Religion and morality in politics

In recent years many influential political leaders, including President Reagan, have advocated a vigorous injection of religion into public life. The most evident example of this trend has been the widespread support for a constitutional amendment allowing prayer in public schools. To supporters of this amendment and of similar measures, religious values can help define and shape public policies.

Controversy over the proper place of religion in political life is not new in U.S. politics. From the founding of the nation, many people have argued that a democratic society must be based on strong religious values. The adherents of various secular crusades, such as efforts to outlaw the sale of alcohol and to regulate matters of personal morality ranging from forms of marriage to sexual tastes and conduct, have frequently solicited the support of religious groups. And religious values have been invoked by our leaders in support of U.S. foreign policies. Some students of U.S. political life have argued that we have fashioned a "civic religion," in which church-related values are combined with a reverence for secular political forms and practices.[29]

Of course, the United States is not the only nation to mix religion and politics in various ways. Struggles over the appropriate political role of organized religion have played a very significant part in political conflict in most democratic nations over the last two centuries. The role of the Roman Catholic church in nations like France and Italy has also been politi-

America the imperial? We are not accustomed to thinking of ourselves as an overbearing nation, pointing to our anticolonial heritage and noting that we have never created colonies as many European nations have. The United States has, however, flexed its political and military muscles a great deal, especially in our own hemisphere. Our presence in such nations as Nicaragua, Mexico, Guatemala, and the Philippines has not always been completely welcomed.

# Comparative perspective

# A look at the national characteristics of Sweden and the U.S.

In *Sweden: Prototype of Modern Society* the social scientist Richard Tomasson compares Swedish and American values. In his comparison he considers many values, including democracy, freedom, progress, achievement, work, material comfort, efficiency. Tomasson concludes that Swedish and American values are very similar in many ways, but he also notes some important differences. The selection that follows focuses on some of the differences.

*Abhorrence of violence*
There are extremely strong inhibitions on violence and the manifestation of aggression in Swedish culture. While it is now almost commonplace to see nudity and sexual intercourse in Swedish films, it is not usual to see violence. Most of the violence in the mass media (and much is censored) is in American films and television programs. . . .

Even when Swedes have been drinking heavily at parties, it is rare for any physical aggressiveness to be shown. It may be that the abhorrence of violence is greater in Sweden than in other Scandinavian countries, though in all of them it is clearly greater than in America. . . . In any case, if data on willful murder and sex offenses can be used as indicators of how much violence is inhibited in a society, then Sweden is certainly an extreme case. The disdain for violence in Sweden might be likened to the abhorrence of pornography in a puritanical society.

*Democracy* Democracy is ideologically the most absolute of all modern values in Sweden. It is an ultimate appeal. That is ipso facto good which is democratic. In Sweden, democracy means the right of individuals to choose their leaders in the nation and in organizations, but, at the ideological level, it is frequently confounded with egalitarianism and equality of opportunity. While this is also the case in America, democracy seems to be a more pervasive value in Swedish than American culture. In Sweden it is believed that all organizations should be "democratic," and anything that is "not democratic" is liable to suspicion. In recent years there has been much concern with industrial democracy, the bringing of workers into the decision-making process. A common viewpoint is that democracy has been achieved in the political realm, in education, in most of the great organizations, but still not yet in the realm of work. It is clear that there is greater democracy in organizations in Sweden, notably in unions and in political parties, than in America.

*Equality* This is a most complex value area and one with many ramifications. Yet in the aggregate it is probably as strong and pervasive a Swedish value as it is an American value, although it takes different forms than in American culture. Swedish egalitarianism is shaped by opposition to the traditions of the old hierarchical society, vestiges of which remain in the form of differential terms of address and titles. There is greater respect for authority and for expert opinion and less celebration of the views of "the common man" than one finds in American culture. Yet there is a greater concern in Sweden with economic equality, with the greater privileges of salaried as compared with wage workers, with realizing equality of opportunity in education, as well as with the greater emphasis on sexual equality.

Source: Richard F. Tomasson, *Sweden: Prototype of Modern Society* (New York: Random House, 1970).

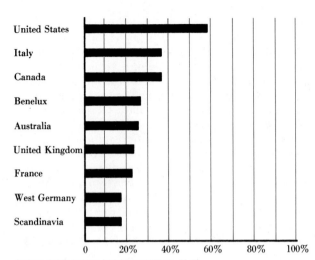

United States
Italy
Canada
Benelux
Australia
United Kingdom
France
West Germany
Scandinavia

0    20%   40%   60%   80%   100%

Source: *Public Opinion*, March/May 1979, pp. 38–39.

FIGURE 2.2
The importance of religious beliefs at home and abroad: The chart illustrates the percentage of respondents in each country who answered "very important" to the question, "How important to you are your religious beliefs?"

"That government is best which governs least." The impression such sentiments give, of course, is that the ideal government would be a very limited arrangement, providing for national defense plus a few public works.

We are, however, no longer living in the eighteenth century. Twentieth-century life is marked by great complexity in economic and social life. Huge organizations, particularly the modern corporation, dominate the landscape of our society. We have come a long way from the yeoman farmer and small-town life that fostered Thomas Jefferson's democratic vision. We are an urban people, a nation of 250 million with an enormously intricate, highly vulnerable economy. We are a nation which the Founders could not have imagined.

In response to the problems and opportunities created by this complex, urban, twentieth-century life, government has grown, in both size and power. Many Americans see this growth as a sign of our decline as a nation and react almost automatically against "too much government." We can quote the radical of American revolutionary days, Tom Paine, who said: "Society is created by our wants and government by our wickedness." The bigger the government, the more problems we must be having.

But Paine was wrong. Government is not just a negative enforcer of law and order, a maker of rules. The point sorely overlooked by our liberal heritage is that government can perform as a positive institution, contributing to society things that society cannot do for itself. It can enhance the quality of life. At its best, government can represent the collective will of the community and put plans into action that no other element in the community could manage on

cally controversial, especially on such issues as divorce, abortion, or aid to church-related schools.

Throughout U.S. history, Americans have divided over the question of whether or not religion should be a part of our politics. Although, on the whole, the nation has tended to move in a more secular direction, Americans have remained overwhelmingly prorelition in attitude (see Figure 2.2). Thus, many significant conflicts and questions in this area remain unresolved. Where should religious values end and public policy begin? Our liberal tradition calls for tolerance and acceptance of a diversity of values and approaches. To the liberal, morality and taste are personal matters. Yet it also has been argued that morality can and should be enforced, that public authorities ought to legislate what is good and right for us all. As a predominantly religious people and, at the same time, a liberal society, how do we decide?

## Government and the individual

One of the limitations of the U.S. variant of liberalism is its basically antigovernment stance. We are all familiar with the eighteenth-century statement,

District of Columbia, 1923. 749 cases of illegally produced beer are being destroyed. Prohibition was a failure in that many citizens continued to drink alcohol and an underground trade flourished. It was perhaps America's greatest effort to suppress a practice that some found not just dangerous or destructive, but immoral.

its own. We can see this, for example, in space exploration, in public education, in environmental planning, in collective efforts toward economic security.

Because of this blindspot from our liberal tradition, we often distrust government unnecessarily, and turn instead to an almost magical belief in the individual. In many areas, Americans tend to be deeply distrustful of government involvement, fearful that such involvement will mean a loss of rights and liberties. We can see such pervasive fears in regard to governmental efforts in gun control, in taxation and economic regulation, and in racial integration.

This is, of course, one of many struggles between the old and new forms of liberalism. But all forms of liberalism place heavy emphasis on individual rights and tend to denigrate governmental possibilities. Such distrust is far less pervasive in many other democracies. This is not to say that government is a panacea, or even that it is the appropriate instrument for many

of our efforts. The important point is that our distrust often limits the uses we might make of government on our own behalf.

## Conclusions

Many of our values are supportive of democratic practices. As a predominantly "liberal" society, we officially and unequivocally favor individual rights, tolerance, equal opportunity, the rule of law, and democratic political institutions. On the other hand, Americans have experienced great difficulties in measuring up to the norms of democracy. Many groups have been the objects of discrimination and exploitation. We have often been prone to reach for the gun in settling disputes, forgetting, in the process, the rule of law. In foreign relations, the United States

51

has acted both as a defender of democracy and as an imperial world power. Playing both of these roles has often left Americans and their leaders confused about just what the nation is supposed to stand for. Finally, some Americans have wished to enforce their ideas of morality on others, in the name of preserving values essential to democracy. Others have maintained that enforcing one person's morality on another violates the basic spirit of liberalism.

In short, U.S. political culture is a mix, some parts of which tend to support democratic practices, other portions of which are hostile to them. The conflicts evident in U.S. history over equal treatment, tolerance, rule of law, and the direction of foreign policy are still with us, as subsequent chapters will demonstrate.

## NOTES

1 Jarol B. Mannheim, *The Politics Within: A Primer in Attitudes and Behavior*, 2nd Edition (New York: Longman, 1982), Chapter 4.

2 William F. Stone, *The Psychology of Politics* (New York: Free Press, 1974), Chapter 7; and Seymour Martin Lipset, "Values, Social Character and the Democratic Polity," in *The First New Nation: The United States in Comparative and Historical Perspective* (New York: Basic Books, 1963), pp. 274–85.

3 Seymour Martin Lipset, *Political Man* (Garden City, N.Y.: Doubleday, 1970), Chapter 2.

4 Mannheim, pp. 61–64.

5 Louis Hartz, *The Liberal Tradition in America* (New York: HBJ, 1964); and Alexis de Tocqueville, *Democracy in America* (New York: Harper and Row, 1966).

6 Erich Fromm, *Escape from Freedom* (New York: Avon, 1965), Chapter 2.

7 *Ibid.*, Chapter 3; and Erik H. Erikson, *Young Man Luther* (New York: Norton, 1958).

8 John Locke, *Second Treatise of Civil Government* (New York: Appleton Century Crofts, 1937), Chapters 1–7; and Harry K. Girvetz, *The Evolution of Liberalism* (New York: Collier, 1963), Chapters 4 and 5.

9 Thomas Archdeacon, *Becoming American: An Ethnic History* (New York: Macmillan, 1983).

10 Lawrence Goodwyn, *The Populist Movement: A Short History of the Agrarian Revolt in America* (New York: Oxford University Press, 1978).

11 Seymour Martin Lipset, "Values and Democratic Stability," in *The First New Nation*, op. cit., pp. 207–47.

12 Gunnar Myrdal, *An American Dilemma* (New York: Harper and Row, 1962).

13 Girvetz, Chapter 15.

14 John Dewey, *Liberalism and Social Action* (New York: Capricorn Books, 1963).

15 John H. M. Laslett and Seymour M. Lipset, eds., *Failure of a Dream: Essays on the History of American Socialism* (Garden City, N.Y.: Doubleday, 1974).

16 Daniel P. Moynihan and Nathan Glazer, *Beyond the Melting Pot* (Cambridge, Mass.: MIT Press, 1963).

17 Terry Eastland and William J. Bennett, *Counting by Race: Equality from the Founding Fathers to Baake and Weber* (New York: Basic Books, 1979); Stanley Feldstein, *The Poisoned Tongue: A Documentary History of American Racism and Prejudice* (New York: Morrow, 1972).

18 Peter Irons, *Justice at War* (New York: Oxford University Press, 1983).

19 Robert K. Murray, *Red Scare: A Study in National Hysteria, 1919–20* (Minneapolis, Minn.: University of Minnesota Press, 1955).

20 Robert Griffity and Athan Theoharis, eds., *The Spectre: Original Essays on the Cold War and the Origins of McCarthyism* (New York: Franklin Watts, 1974).

21 Arthur M. Schlesinger, Jr., *Robert Kennedy and His Times* (New York: Ballantine, 1978, pp. 798–800.

22 J. F. Kirkham, S. Levy and W. J. Crotty, eds., *Assassination and Political Violence: Staff Report to the National Commission on the Causes and Prevention of Violence* (U.S. Government Printing Office, 1969), pp. 171–77.

23 Joe B. Frantz, "The Frontier Tradition: An Invitation to Violence," in Hugh David Graham and Ted Robert Gurr, eds., *The History of Violence in America* (New York: Praeger, 1969), pp. 127–53.

24 George E. Berkley, *The Democratic Policeman* (New York: Ballantine, 1976).

25 Theodore Draper, *Abuse of Power* (New York: Viking, 1967), Chapter 8.

26 Reinhold Niebuhr and Alan Heimert, *A Nation So Conceived* (New York: Scribners, 1963).

27 Richard Drinnon, *Facing West: The Metaphysics of Indian-Hating and Empire-Building* (New York: New American Library, 1980).

28 Frederick Merk, *Manifest Destiny in American History* (New York: Vintage, 1966); Albert K. Weinberg, *Manifest Destiny* (Baltimore, Md.: Johns Hopkins University Press, 1970).

29 Robert Bellah, *The Broken Covenant: American Civil Religion in a Time of Crisis* (New York: Seabury, 1975); and Ernest Tuveson, *Redeemer Nation: The Idea of America's Millenial Role* (Chicago, Ill.: University of Chicago Press, 1968).

## SELECTED READINGS

For general discussions of democracy and its preconditions, see Robert Dahl, *Polyarchy* (New Haven: Yale University Press, 1971); Peter Berger, *Pyramids of Sacrifice: Political Ethics and Social Change* (New York: Basic Books, 1974).

### What is political culture?

Insights into political culture can be found in Donald Devine, *The Political Culture of the United States* (Boston: Little Brown, 1972); Walter Rosenbaum, *Political Culture* (New York: Praeger, 1975); Gabriel Almond and G. Bingham Powell, *Comparative Politics: A Developmental Approach* (Boston: Little Brown, 1966).

### The liberal tradition

For illuminating discussions of the liberal tradition in the United States, see Louis Hartz, *The Founding of New Societies* (New York: Harcourt, Brace and World, 1964); Vernon Parrington, *Main Currents in American Thought* (New York: Harcourt, Brace, 1954); E. Fawcett and T. Thomas, *The American Condition* (New York: Harper & Row, 1982); John Patrick Diggins, *The Lost Soul of American Politics: Virtue, Self-Interest, and the Foundations of American Liberalism* (New York: Basic Books, 1984).

### Two types of liberalism

The economic values of liberalism are treated in Max Weber, *The Protestant Ethic and the Spirit of Capitalism* (New York, Scribner, 1958); R. H. Tawney, *Religion and the Rise of Capitalism* (New York: New American Library,

1947); Michael Novak, *The American Vision* (Washington, D.C.: ABI, 1982).

U.S. conservatism has been a notoriously difficult subject to pin down. For an assortment of approaches, see Russell Kirk, ed., *The Portable Conservative Reader* (New York: Viking Press, 1982); George Will, *The Pursuit of Happiness and Other Sobering Thoughts* (New York: Harper & Row, 1978); Garry Wills, *Confessions of a Conservative* (Garden City, N.Y.: Doubleday, 1979).

There are many interpretations of the failure of socialism in the United States. For one recent interpretation see Michael Harrington, *Socialism* (New York: Saturday Review Press, 1972), Chapter 6.

### Limits of liberalism

For one general treatment of intolerance in the United States, see Richard Hofstadter, *The Paranoid Style in American Politics and Other Essays* (New York: Random House, 1965). On current immigration issues, see Nathan Glazer, ed., *Clamor at the Gates* (San Francisco, Cal.: ICS Press, 1985).

For discussions of violence in the United States, see especially Richard M. Brown, *Strain of Violence* (New York: Oxford University Press, 1975); Monica D. Blumenthal et al., *Justifying Violence* (Ann Arbor, Mich.: Institute for Social Research, 1972); Charles E. Silberman, *Criminal Violence, Criminal Justice* (New York: Random House, 1978), and H. D. Graham and T. R. Gurr, eds., *Violence in America* (Beverly Hills, Cal.: Sage Publications, 1979).

Among the more provocative discussions of U.S. foreign policy are William Appleman Williams, *The Tragedy of American Diplomacy* (New York: Dell, 1972); Robert Dallek, *The American Style of Foreign Policy* (New York: Knopf, 1983); William Blanchard, *Aggression: American Style* (Santa Monica, Cal.: Goodyear, 1978); Lester D. Langley, *The United States and the Caribbean in the Twentieth Century* (Athens, Ga.: University of Georgia Press, 1985).

For perspectives on morality and politics, see Joseph R. Gusfield, *Symbolic Crusade* (Urbana, Ill.: University of Illinois Press, 1963); Alan Crawford, *Thunder on the Right* (New York: Pantheon Books, 1980); Martin Marty, *Righteous Empire* (New York: Dial Press, 1970); Richard Pierard, *The Unequal Yoke: Evangelical Christianity and Political Conservatism* (Philadelphia: J. P. Lippincott, 1970); Jerry Falwell, *Listen, America* (Garden City, N.Y.: Doubleday, 1970).

# Chapter three

# Revolution and Constitution

# The American way

NOWADAYS the U.S. Constitution is often viewed as if it were of heavenly manufacture. We tend to forget the struggles embodied in it, the compromises made to create it. Often, we also forget that many of the integral figures in the American Revolution were not very happy with the Constitution, and that the battles over its ratification were bitter and very closely contested.

What did the American Revolution and the Constitution have to do with democracy? Did the revolutionaries espouse truly democratic ideals? Were they thinking of a government by consent, a society of equal rights and liberties? Why do some scholars claim that the American Revolution was not really a revolution? What political and social realities did the Constitution reflect? As we come to understand the colonial situation and mentality of the American revolutionaries, we will gain a clearer view of the implications of our constitutional heritage for contemporary politics. We will then be in a position to address the question of whether the Constitution still responds to the demands of modern democratic life.

## Background of the American Revolution

What kind of society was colonial America? How was its economy structured, its wealth distributed? What political ideals were widely shared, and what role did those ideals play in conflicts between the colonies and Great Britain? These questions and others must be addressed before we examine the Revolutionary War itself and the system of government that grew out of it.

## The socioeconomic environment

In the 1770s the thirteen American colonies comprised a rapidly growing society of some 2.5 million inhabitants, 60 percent of whom were English in origin. The principal ethnic minorities were Scots, Irish, Welsh, and Germans, plus a significant number of black slaves (28 percent of the Southern population). Americans were a young people: half the population was under 16, and much of the rest under 40. The population was doubling every twenty years.

Trading was a vital component of the colonial economy. The southern colonies carried on a large volume of direct trade with England, exporting tobacco, rice, and indigo. (This despite the fact that British taxes on American tobacco consumed an estimated 75 percent of all profits.) The middle, or "bread," colonies, including New York, New Jersey, Pennsylvania, and Delaware, traded principally in grain and flour. Pennsylvania was the fastest-growing colony, and Philadelphia, with a population of 40,000, was America's largest town. Only four urban centers apart from Philadelphia could properly be called cities: New York; Charlestown, S.C.; Boston; and Newport, R.I. Notably, all of these cities were Atlantic ports, where news and traffic from abroad arrived first. Apart from these few urban centers, the colonies were overwhelmingly rural. Only 10 percent of the population lived in towns of more than 2,000 inhabitants. Whatever the importance of trading activities, America was mainly a society of farmers and farm workers.

As many students of early American history have pointed out, colonial society was not fundamentally egalitarian. In many colonies, a small number of aristocratic families exercised great political and social power; this was particularly true in Virginia, perhaps the most aristocratic of the colonies. Throughout America, too, property ownership had grown increasingly concentrated in the hands of a few. In 1771, 5 percent of Boston families held almost half the total taxable wealth, and in Philadelphia 10 percent held 46 percent.[1]

In contrast, an estimated 20 to 30 percent of the colonial population, excluding slaves, was impoverished. In major cities, food shortages occasionally sparked riots; in rural areas, discontent with the conditions under which tenant farmers labored led to popular upheavals. Some of the poverty-stricken formed the core of urban mobs that helped foment revolutionary agitation, and many served in the Continental Army.

Between these extremes of wealth and poverty, however, was a fairly prosperous middle class comprising 50 to 70 percent of the population. The presence of so large a middle class, combined with the "leveling" tendencies at work in colonial society, gave the colonies a degree of equality unknown in Europe. Social distinctions did not carry the weight they did in Europe. Deference toward one's social superiors, so pervasive throughout Europe, was not a prominent feature of American life. The colonists exhibited a spirit of independent-mindedness, of defiance of authority, and a desire for economic self-betterment that would not have fit well with the static social systems and inherited class distinctions found in Europe.

The colonies also were places of considerable religious diversity. Religious intolerance was not uncommon: in Rhode Island, for example, only Trinitarian Protestants could become full citizens. Yet religious tolerance was the rule rather than the exception, and lively religious dialogues were a major staple of intellectual life.

## The political environment

By the 1770s, most of the colonial governments had been functioning for over a century. Eight of the thirteen were royal colonies, whose governors were appointed by the British king. Connecticut and Rhode Island had charters granted in the seventeenth century allowing for self-government and thus elected their own governors. Maryland, Pennsylvania, and Delaware were so-called proprietary colonies, owned by families—the Penns in Pennsylvania and Delaware, the Calverts in Maryland. All colonial governors had broad powers, including an absolute veto over acts of the legislatures and appointment power that extended to all judges and all militia officers. In most colonies, the governor also appointed the members of the upper house of the legislature.

Every colony except Pennsylvania had a legislature with an upper and a lower house. The upper houses generally exercised only advisory functions and were made up of the wealthier and more conservative citizens. In contrast, elections for the lower houses of colonial legislatures were remarkably democratic by the standards of the day. Although the franchise often was limited by property qualifications, in practice most white males were permitted to vote for legislators. It was in the lower houses that opposition to British taxation was most vociferous in the 1770s.

The colonies shared the British political tradition, based to a significant degree on the rule of law and, to some extent, on the principle of constitutionalism. Accordingly, the powers exercised by colonial governments were generally limited by written charters. Because more of them could participate more fully in local politics, the colonists may actually have enjoyed more political and civil rights than did most Englishmen.

As heirs of the liberal tradition, most colonial political leaders believed that underlying constitutions and laws were fundamental rights, violations of which entitled citizens to seek governmental redress. If the government did not respect these rights, liberal theory held, citizens could legitimately overthrow that government. Governments, in other words, could and should be held responsible for their actions and the ways in which they upheld the basic interests of citizens.

## Imperial authority and American defiance

In the early 1760s, the British Empire was growing prodigiously. Having defeated France and Spain in the **Seven Years' War** (1756–63; known in the colonies as the French and Indian War), the British had removed the threats formerly posed to their possessions in the New World by the French in Canada and the Spanish in Florida. As a result, the American colonists were feeling less dependent than ever before on the mother country. At the same time, however, the costs of empire had begun to weigh more and more heavily on the British treasury. Rather than go along with the colonists' desire for more autonomy, especially in economic matters, the British crown sought greater authority over colonial affairs—in particular, the authority to impose direct taxes to defray the costs of defending and expanding the empire.

In both financial and military terms, American participation in the Seven Years' War had fallen far short of what had been expected by the mother country, which viewed the defeat of the French and the Spanish as being of direct benefit to the colonies. Just how uncooperative the colonies generally were is reflected in the fact that only three of the thirteen contributed full quotas of troops to the war. In several ways, moreover, disobedience to the Crown and nonenforcement of British rules had become rather common in America. Various acts of Parliament imposing duties on American goods were largely circumvented or ignored by the colonists, and a thriving trade between the French West Indies and American merchants was carried on contrary to British law.

Disobedience led to defiance when the British Parliament in March 1765 passed the Stamp Act, which required "that Americans pay their own protection and defense out of revenues from the sale of stamped paper to be used on some fifty items, including newspapers, pamphlets, playing cards, wills, land deeds, marriage licenses, college diplomas, bills of sale, port clearance papers, and so on." Those who violated the act could be tried and penalized without benefit of jury. The Stamp Act had been conceived by George Grenville, First Lord of the Treasury under King George III. Grenville had argued that it was needed not merely to increase revenues, but also to assert Parliament's absolute sovereignty over the colonies. When the Americans argued that because they were not represented in Parliament, Parliament did not have the right to levy taxes on them, Grenville invoked the doctrine of virtual representation. According to this doctrine, a favorite argument of the day, each member of Parliament had a responsibility to the entire Empire, and therefore even the American colonists in some sense were represented in Parliament.

The Stamp Act was one in a series of miscalculations by British authorities. Intent upon asserting control over the colonies, they underestimated the growing colonial spirit of independence and failed to see how each further effort on their part to exercise power only aggravated the situation. Without the act, and the similar actions that followed, the British might have been able to make the most of the relative calm that had followed the Seven Years' War. Instead, many colonists came to view the Crown with increasing suspicion and to decry London's alleged exploitation of the colonies.

Colonial reaction to the Stamp Act was harsh and effective. Several months after the act was passed, the first organized resistance took place in Boston. The so-called Sons of Liberty, a radical group composed of artisans, mechanics, apprentices, day laborers, and merchant seamen, hanged effigies of Andrew Oliver, the king's designated agent for stamp distribution in Massachusetts, and Lord Bute, a close friend of the king's. The effigies were hanged from what came to be known as the Liberty Tree. To make their points, the Sons of Liberty were quite ready to employ force. One group of defiant colonists, carrying the effigies, destroyed a warehouse belonging to Oliver, and then burned the effigies in a huge bonfire on a hillside near his home. Several protes-

tors even ransacked Oliver's home, making off with his extensive wine collection. The following day Oliver resigned, and no one could be found to take his position. None of the Sons of Liberty was brought to trial.

A year after passing the Stamp Act, Parliament repealed it, only to enact the so-called Townshend duties, which taxed colonial imports of paint, tea, lead, and paper. Again the colonists protested, and eventually all the duties except that on tea were repealed. After a few years of relative calm between British authorities and American colonials, Parliament in 1773 granted the East India Company the exclusive right to sell tea to American local dealers. The mandate, under which American merchants were shut out of the tea trade, prompted the famous Boston Tea Party, in which protestors disguised as Indians dumped tea from British ships into Boston harbor. In response, the British closed the port of Boston—a drastic economic penalty for a city that depended so heavily on trading. In addition, the charter of the colony of Massachusetts was virtually withdrawn, and elections and town meetings were forbidden.

These actions provoked yet wider defiance of British authority. Groups of concerned citizens met in several colonies and sent delegates to the First Continental Congress. Convened in Philadelphia in 1774, the Congress promptly called for a boycott of British goods. Armed conflict broke out in Massachusetts the following year, when the British commander in Boston sent troops to seize weapons stored by the colonists in Concord. In 1775, the Second Continental Congress, although hesitating to make a final break with Britain, decided to raise an army and

[January, 1770]
[1773(?)]

## WILLIAM JACKSON,

an *IMPORTER*; at the

## BRAZEN HEAD,

*North Side of the* TOWN-HOUSE,

and *Oppofite the Town-Pump, in*

*Corn-hill,* BOSTON.

It is defired that the SONS and DAUGHTERS of *LIBERTY*, would not buy any one thing of him, for in fo doing they will bring Difgrace upon *themfelves*, and their *Pofterity*, for *ever* and *ever*, AMEN.

The boycott is an ancient tactic of protest. This poster was printed by angry Boston colonists opposed to importing goods from England.

Disguised as Indians, rebellious colonists toss boxes of heavily taxed tea into Boston harbor.

began making overtures to France for assistance. Shortly thereafter, the more radical American political leaders finally persuaded the moderates that independence was a necessary step, and Congress commissioned Thomas Jefferson to write a formal Declaration of Independence. A major factor in the radicals' success was Tom Paine's *Common Sense*, a pamphlet that electrified colonial America when it appeared in January 1776. In *Common Sense*, Paine placed America's struggle in a larger perspective, that of the struggle of all mankind for free government. For Paine the American cause was one of liberty versus tyranny, not simply one of colonials who had specific grievances against the British Crown.

When the Second Continental Congress reconvened in June 1776, Thomas Jefferson presented a draft of the Declaration of Independence. It was amended and approved by the Congress on July 4, 1776, two days after an official resolution of independence from Great Britain had been passed. Jefferson's declaration has been perhaps the single most influential piece of American political writing.

## The Revolutionary War

The war itself was an unexpectedly protracted and, in military terms, oddly inconclusive affair. The British had every reason to believe they could easily subdue the colonials. Their army was highly experienced and well-trained, and their navy was the world's largest. By 1778, there were almost 50,000 British troops in North America, along with 30,000

# Thomas Paine: radical democrat, pamphleteer supreme

The radical ideas and eloquent pamphlets of Thomas Paine, the son of a poor English staymaker, influenced political life in three countries during his lifetime (1737–1809). His most famous pamphlet, *Common Sense* (1776), helped to stiffen American resistance to the British monarchy. And during the Revolutionary War his series of papers *The American Crisis* did much to sustain American patriotism. It was Paine who characterized the Revolutionary War years as "the times that try men's souls."

After the war, Paine's writings also made an impact in his native England, where they stimulated considerable political reform.

Paine's power as a political pamphleteer lay in the fact that he dared to take popular ideas to their logical, if radical, conclusions. In *Common Sense*, for example, he not only attacked the particular British king then ruling, but went on to reject any form of monarchy and to call for government based exclusively on the expressed will of the people. And in *The Rights of Man* (1791–92), a defense of the French Revolution, he anticipated modern socialist ideas by portraying government as an instrument used by the rich to exploit the poor and by calling for pension systems, unemployment projects, public education, and aid to the poor—all to be paid for through progressive income and inheritance taxes.

Prosecuted for treason in Great Britain, Paine fled to revolutionary France in 1792 and there was made a member of the governing National Convention. In France he published a widely read

attack against formal religions titled *The Age of Reason* (1794–95). Upon returning to the United States in 1802, he encountered considerable resentment generated by the allegedly atheist ideas in *The Age of Reason* (an untrue charge) and by his denunciation of George Washington in

*Letter to Washington* (1796). At the time of his death, he was a social outcast in his adopted country, in whose formation he had played so significant a role.

COMMON SENSE;

ADDRESSED TO THE

INHABITANTS

OF

AMERICA,

On the following interesting

SUBJECTS.

I. Of the Origin and Design of Government in general, with concise Remarks on the English Constitution.

II. Of Monarchy and Hereditary Succession.

III. Thoughts on the present State of American Affairs.

IV. Of the present Ability of America, with some miscellaneous Reflections.

A NEW EDITION, with several Additions in the Body of the Work. To which is added an APPENDIX; together with an Address to the People called QUAKERS.

N. B. The New Addition here given increases the Work upwards of one Third.

Man knows no Master save creating HEAVEN,
Or those whom Choice and common Good ordain.
THOMSON.

Raising and supporting an army are not such simple matters, regardless of revolutionary fervor. General Washington experienced great difficulties getting both soldiers and supplies. As a result, outside help (from France, in particular) played a vital role in fighting the British to a standstill and thereby winning independence.

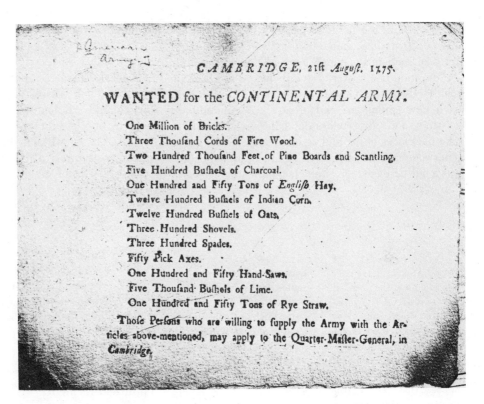

CAMBRIDGE, 21st August. 1775.

WANTED for the CONTINENTAL ARMY.

One Million of Bricks.
Three Thousand Cords of Fire Wood.
Two Hundred Thousand Feet of Pine Boards and Scantling.
Five Hundred Bushels of Charcoal.
One Hundred and Fifty Tons of *English* Hay.
Twelve Hundred Bushels of Indian Corn.
Twelve Hundred Bushels of Oats.
Three Hundred Shovels.
Three Hundred Spades.
Fifty Pick Axes.
One Hundred and Fifty Hand-Saws.
Five Thousand Bushels of Lime.
One Hundred and Fifty Tons of Rye Straw.

Those Persons who are willing to supply the Army with the Articles above-mentioned, may apply to the Quarter-Master-General, in Cambridge.

German mercenaries. The Americans, starting from scratch, eventually created a Continental Army of 5,000, supplemented by state militia units. Their officers were inexperienced, although George Washington had had some experience of actual combat in the French and Indian War.

The British, however, suffered from serious disadvantages: the war had to be waged 3,000 miles from the British Isles, the vast and mostly wild American terrain was difficult to conquer in any sense, and there was no single nerve center of revolutionary activity whose destruction would ensure a British military victory. Moreover, even if the British won the war militarily, they would have to face the daunting task of restoring imperial domination over the defiant colonials. Finally, many observers criticized the British for waging the war indecisively, vacillating between ill-thought-out attempts to gain a military victory and efforts to achieve a reconciliation with the revolutionaries.

The American war for independence also became an international contest. France supplied large amounts of munitions to the Americans, and both France and Spain eventually declared war on Great Britain. Other nations, including Sweden, Russia, and Prussia, moved to protect their shipping from British blockades of the colonies. In the end, French assistance to the colonies was critical to the success of the revolutionary effort, with elements of the French fleet and army helping to make the decisive American victory at Yorktown (1781) possible.

The revolutionaries also had to overcome formidable difficulties. Keeping an army in the field was a constant problem for the new nation. Not only was there an overall lack of manpower, but popular support was often lacking. Desertions from the Continental Army were numerous, and many farmers who did serve refused to extend their tours of duty when new planting or harvest seasons came around. Cash incentives were required to maintain more than a token force in the field. In January 1777, Congress offered 20 dollars, new clothing, and one hundred acres of land in exchange for a pledge to serve for the duration of the war. Nevertheless, there was no rush to enlist. States were given quotas to fill before each new campaign, and often slaves, indentured servants, and propertyless day laborers were paid to take the places of the middle-class farmers who would otherwise have had to serve. The revolutionary ideal was a militia based on a universal obligation to serve;

the reality was an army made up largely of the poor and others who responded principally to financial incentives.

An even greater problem for the revolutionaries was active or passive opposition to the war within the colonies. It has been estimated that up to 20 percent of the white population remained actively loyal to the Crown and that as much as 50 percent remained neutral in the struggle.[2] More and more colonials became less and less enthusiastic as the war dragged on.

In the end, however, British public opinion deserted the war faster than American public opinion. After the French-American victory at Yorktown, the British gave up their attempt to crush the rebellion, even though they still held the dominant position militarily. The Americans defeated the British not by gaining a clear-cut military victory, but simply by hanging on and refusing to lose the war.

## Independence and political ferment

In the Treaty of Paris, signed on September 3, 1783, the British government formally recognized the independence of its former colonies. Few treaties have had such profound and far-reaching political ramifications. Both in the new United States of America and in Europe, political life was irrevocably changed.

Many historians have remarked about the political folly of the British government, whose high-handedness provoked the Revolutionary War and thereby lost the American colonies. In fact, many in England opposed these policies from the start. This 1782 cartoon pictured a reconciliation between colonies (represented here as an Indian) and motherland. Prior to the birth of Uncle Sam as a national symbol, the United States was depicted as an Indian, a rattlesnake, a bucking bronco, and an eagle.

## The postrevolutionary era

In the United States new political enthusiasms emerged in the aftermath of the war. Demands for equality were everywhere, even in regard to slavery. In 1774 the Continental Congress had urged abolition of the slave trade, and in 1775 the world's first antislavery society had been formed by Quakers in Philadelphia. After the war, some Northern states gave freedom to slaves who had served in the Continental Army, and

# Comparative perspective The French Revolution

On the surface, the French and American revolutions seem to have had much in common. Both originated in rebellions against monarchical governments; and both sought constitutional rule, government by consent, and the affirmation of the basic rights of citizens. There the similarities end, however. In comparison with the course of events in France, the American revolution and its aftermath were mild and orderly indeed.

The French Revolution began in 1789 in a rebellion of a portion of the Estates-General, an assembly that had been summoned by King Louis XVI. The Estates-General was divided into three estates, or classes, based on the status system of feudal society: that of the clergy; that of the nobles; and a Third Estate consisting of everyone else, from lawyers and business people

to peasants and laborers. Once called into session, the Estates-General quickly became a forum for reformist and even revolutionary sentiment, and a struggle developed between the nobles and the Third Estate for control. As this struggle proceeded, violence broke out in many parts of the country. A mob stormed the Bastille (a state prison in Paris), murdered its governor after 98 of the insurgents had been killed, and went on to murder the mayor of Paris. In the countryside, too, peasants began to rebel against the landed aristocracy.

The Third Estate separated from the Estates-General and declared itself a National Assembly. In enacting many reform measures, it in effect abolished the feudal system that had remained a potent force in French political life. In August 1789, it issued the Declaration of the Rights of Man and Citizen. A new government, in which the king was to have only the power to suspend legislation by veto, was formed in 1791, but the king refused to participate in it and counterrevolutionary forces, both foreign and indigenous, began to threaten the revolution.

War broke out in 1792 between revolutionary France and its monarchist neighbors.

While fighting foreign foes, the revolutionary regime began a domestic reign of terror against real and suspected opponents of the government. During this period (1793–94), an estimated 40,000 people (including the king) were executed and thousands of others driven into exile.

From 1795 to 1799 France was a constitutional republic in which all literate citizens had the right to vote. But war pressures and a lack of popular support weakened the republican government. In 1799, Napoleon Bonaparte seized power and ruled France under a form of benevolent despotism until his armies were

Early days of the French Revolution. Citizens dance around the head of Princess De Lamballe as it is being carried through Paris. The French Revolution was characterized by far greater terror than ever occurred during the American Revolution.

finally defeated by foreign powers in 1815. Under Napoleon the democratic impulses of the original revolution were suppressed in the rise of what was, in effect, a new monarchy. Over the next several decades, the French government alternated between more democratic and more royalist regimes. Not until 1870 was a genuine republic established that was destined to last for a significant length of time.

# How "revolutionary" was the American Revolution?

This question may seem absurd. To many historians and political scientists, however, the American Revolution was only half a revolution. In order to see what they could mean by such a statement, we must look more closely at what the American rebels did and did not set out to accomplish.

It is certainly true that the colonists fought an anticolonial war, that they sought independence and self-rule. It can also be agreed that some of the principles on which they based their new government were genuinely innovative, including the concepts of government by consent, based on the opinions of the governed, and of basic rights and liberties enjoyed by all citizens. Certainly, they set out to create what, in their minds and in the minds of many others, was something new in political history.

But there were things they did *not* do. The American Revolution did not tear up government by the roots, in the manner of the French Revolution a decade later. In a sense, the Americans only extended and perfected political traditions that were familiar to them. The new government they created, although a genuine advance toward democratic politics, did not represent a radical break with the past political life of the colonies. Moreover, the American Revolution did not involve the overturning of a social (as opposed to a political) order. The forms of power and property that had existed in colonial life remained more or less intact after the revolution. Because America did not have an entrenched hereditary aristocratic class, there was no such class to overthrow.

The American Revolution also differed profoundly from the radical social upheavals of the twentieth century, such as the Russian and Chinese revolutions, in which private ownership of property was a principal target of the revolutionaries. In fact, a desire to defend the right to property was part of what sparked the revolution in America. Private property rights mattered very much to the colonists. There were many

---

most Northern states moved to end slavery within their borders. By 1830, the Northern black population of 125,000 included only 3000 slaves.

At the same time, a new attitude of parochialism was becoming evident in state legislatures—what James Madison described as a "spirit of locality." During and after the Revolution, legislatures increasingly became embroiled in conflicts between various narrow interests. More elections were contested, and there was an increasing turnover of legislative seats, usually in favor of individuals of humbler backgrounds. Few legislators seemed interested in looking out for the interests of the community as a whole. Critics of the actions of the Vermont legislature complained that laws were altered, real-

tered, made better, made worse—but always kept in a state of fluctuation. Many of the new laws favored particular individuals or groups. Pressure group politics was already making itself felt in U.S. political life.

Before the Revolution, many had seen the legislature as the basis for the people's sovereignty, the bulwark against executive excess. In the war's aftermath, however, fear of legislative excesses grew. As Jefferson put it, "173 despots would surely be as oppressive as one." Many people began to worry about how to ensure that fundamental law would not be tampered with, and, thus, "liberty" kept safe.

In Europe, meanwhile, the American Revolution had a profound impact. The very idea that a people

sources of friction between rich and poor in revolutionary America, but in revolting against Great Britain, Americans had no thought of instituting government ownership of the means of production, or of taking radical steps toward equalization of the life chances of the members of society.

Our revolutionary heritage is therefore of a political, rather than social, nature. The American revolutionaries sought a political framework that would free people from oppressive government and allow

them to enjoy political rights, not one that would equalize their conditions of life. But if it was not a "total revolution," the American Revolution, and the Constitution that followed it, did give the world a living example of how a large and diverse nation could achieve independence and be governed more or less by consent. For its time, this was an extraordinary achievement—truly a pioneering venture in political history.

ample in the early nineteenth century, when they fought to free themselves from Spanish domination.

Finally, the new United States was widely seen abroad as the home of the "common man," where ordinary people could enjoy political and legal rights and could participate in political life. This perception, as well as economic opportunity, made the United States attractive to immigrants from other nations. It also provided a model for those who wished to see their own societies change in an American direction.

## The Articles of Confederation

Soon after declaring independence, American political leaders turned to the task of setting up a new government. In 1781, shortly before the war ended, the last of the thirteen states ratified the nation's first written constitution—the **Articles of Confederation**. The government that the Articles created was a political failure, however. To understand the reasons for its failure is to understand why the subsequent (and present) Constitution has succeeded so well.

The principal political impulse behind the Articles was fear of a strong central authority; its authors wanted to ensure that the new national government was not endowed with the excessive power they believed lay at the disposal of the British monarch. In doing so, they created a national government that could function effectively only at the sufferance of the states. The only national political body under the Articles was a one-house Continental Congress, in which each state had one vote. There was no independent chief executive and no national court system. Congress had the power to create executive departments and to approve treaties, but it could not print money, levy taxes on the citizens of the states, or regulate interstate commerce.

Political realities soon exposed the weaknesses of this government. Controversies raged among the states that simply could not be settled without a national

could make a declaration of independence and embody in it the ideal of equal rights for all seemed to show that ideas of liberty were indeed practical—that freedom was not just an abstract concept, but something people could claim for themselves. The fact that each American state wrote its own constitution further excited European interest. These constitutions were translated into French and became items of intense curiosity. The American example certainly was one of the reasons that the French revolutionaries began by drawing up a declaration of human rights and drafting a new constitution. The Revolutionary War also demonstrated to other European-governed peoples that an anticolonial revolution could succeed. Latin American nations looked to this ex-court system and a stronger national government, and many feared that Great Britain would foment and take advantage of interstate rivalries. Further, the central government had so few powers that the focus of blame for social and political problems shifted to local governments. For instance, because only the states could print money, those who felt the squeeze of tight money in the postwar depression looked to the states for help. In Massachusetts, debt-ridden farmers who were facing foreclosure demanded that the state legislature issue more paper money. When the legislature refused, the farmers, led by Daniel Shays, took up arms in August 1786. Their first protests were directed against local courts, which they prevented from conducting business. Later, the rebels also forced the state supreme court to adjourn. Only after both state militia and federal troops were called out against Shays and his supporters was the rebellion crushed in early 1787. However, most participants, including Shays, were pardoned by the state legislature.

**Shays's Rebellion** was at least a partial success. Largely because of it, the state legislature in 1787 decided not to impose new taxes, lowered court fees, and exempted household goods, clothing, and the tools of one's trade from the debt process (preventing them from being seized to pay off debts). But the real importance of Shays's Rebellion was that it convinced many political leaders, particularly the more conservative, that a new constitution had to be created with power lodged more fully in the national government, including the power to issue currency.

national government. At the Annapolis Convention (1786), in which the states met to discuss interstate trade, he called for a national convention whose purpose would be to amend the Articles. After Shays's Rebellion, five state legislatures appointed delegates to the as-yet-hypothetical convention. The Continental Congress issued a rather tentative call for a convention as well, but carefully insisted that any revisions of the Articles would require both its approval and the approval of *all* state legislatures. When the convention finally did convene in Philadelphia in 1787, some delegates arrived with instructions to go no further than amendment of the Articles.

On May 14, 1787, the day appointed for the convention to begin, only the delegates of Virginia and Pennsylvania were present. By May 25, nine state delegations had arrived, and work on "revision" of the Articles began. State legislatures in twelve states named a total of seventy-three delegates, of whom fifty-five actually attended the convention and thirty-nine eventually signed the new Constitution. The thirteenth state, Rhode Island, decided not to participate in the process.

Of the fifty-five delegates who met at Philadelphia, thirty-three were lawyers, forty-four had been members of the Continental Congress, twenty-seven had been officers in the Revolutionary War, twenty-five had been to college, twenty-one were rich and another thirteen affluent, and nineteen were slave owners.[3] There were many relatively young delegates, including the very influential Alexander Hamilton, who was thirty-two, and James Madison, who was thirty-six. The patriarch of the group was Benjamin Franklin, at eighty-one.

## The Constitutional Convention

### A stronger national government

The movement toward what was to become known as the Constitutional Convention was anything but swift and unanimous. Alexander Hamilton, a young New York lawyer and former delegate to the Continental Congress, took the lead in efforts to strengthen the

From the start, the convention began to enlarge on its mandate to revise the Articles of Confederation. New proposals presented to the convention called for a thoroughly altered national government, one with greatly strengthened powers. The delegates readily accepted the idea of a national judiciary and that of a strengthened executive branch. There was considerable debate, however, over the nature of the new legislative structure. Benjamin Franklin, for one, favored a one-house (**unicameral**) arrangement. But most delegates supported the idea of a two-house (**bicameral**) Congress, an arrangement used by most state governments.

The earliest comprehensive proposal submitted for consideration at the convention was the **Virginia Plan**, set forth by the delegation from that state. It called for a strong national government with a bicameral legislature: a lower house, elected by the voters, and an upper house, chosen by the members of the lower house. Under the plan, either tax contributions or population would provide the basis for proportional representation in both houses. Generally, the larger states supported the Virginia Plan.

The smaller states responded with the **New Jersey Plan**, submitted by William Patterson of that state. Patterson's plan called for a national government empowered to levy taxes and to regulate interstate commerce and, significantly, a national Supreme Court with the power to review state court rulings. On the key question of legislative structure, it proposed a one-house legislature in which each state would have one vote, as had been the case under the Articles.

Debate over the relative merits of the Virginia and New Jersey plans deadlocked the convention for weeks. The problem was finally resolved through the **Connecticut Compromise**, proposed by a special committee in which the Connecticut delegation played an important role. The key element of the compromise was the concept of a two-house legislature consisting of an upper house in which the states would be represented equally and a lower house in which representation would be based on population and from which all fiscal measures must originate. Although delegates from the larger states initially reacted negatively to the compromise, they soon realized that it was the price they would have to pay for a strengthened national government. In any case, with the struggle for ratification by the states still to come, it was simply good politics to assuage the smaller states' fear that their interests would be neglected in a powerful national government based on proportional representation.

## The slavery issue

The other great compromise of the Constitutional Convention concerned slavery. The southern (slaveholding) states sought to include slaves in the population counts used to determine representation in the House of Representatives—without, of course, giving them the right to vote. The South feared that without such additional representation, a northern majority might dominate the new Union. Southern insistence on this matter led to the infamous compromise that each slave would be counted as three-fifths of a person. This was perhaps a pragmatic solution in the context of the time, since the outlawing of slavery was not yet a practical possibility. Yet the compromise revealed rather starkly the vulnerability of the new nation. This was an issue that, in the end, could not be successfully compromised.

The framers of the Constitution also had to deal with the question of the slave trade. In another compromise, the slave trade was allowed to continue until at least 1808, at which time Congress would be permitted to legislate against it. Commerce in human beings was subsequently prohibited by Congress as of January 1, 1808, although for many years thereafter a thriving smuggling business persisted.

## Fragmentation of power

Many delegates at the Convention were concerned about potential abuses of power on the part of popular majorities. Was it possible to create a government based on the will of the people but not susceptible to majority tyranny? Doubts about relying on the wisdom of "the people" were voiced by, among others, Alexander Hamilton, who argued that "The voice of the people has been said to be the voice of God; and however generally this maxim has been quoted and believed, it is not true in fact. The people are turbulent and changing; they seldom judge or determine right." Fearing mass democracy on the

*James Madison*

Some historians regard James Madison as one of this nation's most original political thinkers. His defense of the U.S. Constitution in *The Federalist Papers* ranks as some of the most significant discussion ever of power, rights, and consent in a democratic context. Madison recognized how easily power can be abused and suggested ways of counteracting such abuse.

one hand, and tyrannical monarchy or oligarchy on the other, the framers created a complex system of government designed to ensure the dispersal of power.

The electoral system they devised provided for a limited democracy. The people were given a direct voice in government through elections of the members of the lower house of Congress; members of the upper house, in contrast, were to be chosen by state legislatures. (This system remained in effect until the ratification in 1913 of the Seventeenth Amendment, which mandated direct popular election of senators.) The framers also sought to insulate the presidency from the popular vote by stipulating that the president be chosen by a group of electors (the **electoral college**) selected by the states in the gen-

eral election. This system of elections would, Hamilton averred, allow for little probability that one class of voters could dominate another. Finally, the framers left the matter of voting requirements up to the individual states, some of which had attached property qualifications to the franchise and all of which excluded women and slaves from the polls. This measure further diluted the power of the masses.

The delegates to the Convention also were concerned with concentrations of power within the government. Their deliberations on this issue reflected the ideas and influence of James Madison, whose views were set forth in 1787–88 in an impressive series of essays known collectively as *The Federalist Papers*. As a student of history and of political philosophy, Madison was aware that republican government—that based on the will of the people rather than on a hereditary ruler—was most likely to succeed in small societies whose members shared common values and in which wealth was distributed relatively equally. But the United States was a sprawling society in which different interests abounded and wealth was unevenly distributed. For republican government to succeed in a large society with many conflicting interests, Madison argued, the political system must be fragmented such that power could be used effectively but excessive concentrations of power avoided. In this way, he felt, rash or tyrannical actions on the part of powerful interests could be blocked and the necessary degree of political unity preserved.

In *The Federalist*, No. 51, Madison contended that "you must first enable the government to control the governed; and in the next place, oblige it to control itself." He went on to point out that if the responsibility for decision making could be sufficiently fragmented, both the rights of minorities could be protected and minority factions could be prevented from thwarting the properly expressed sentiments of the majority.

Madison's ideas were implemented in the constitutional system of **separation of powers and checks and balances**.

First, powers were divided between the states and the national government (a matter we will explore fully in Chapter 4). Next, governing power within

the central government was divided among the executive, legislative, and judicial branches (see Figure 3.1). Within the legislature, power was further divided between two houses. In addition to this separation of powers, the decision-making process was fragmented by a delicate system of checks and balances. For example, the president, through the veto power, was given the means to intervene in the legislative process, the Senate was granted the power to confirm or reject appointments made by the president to the Supreme Court and the cabinet, and

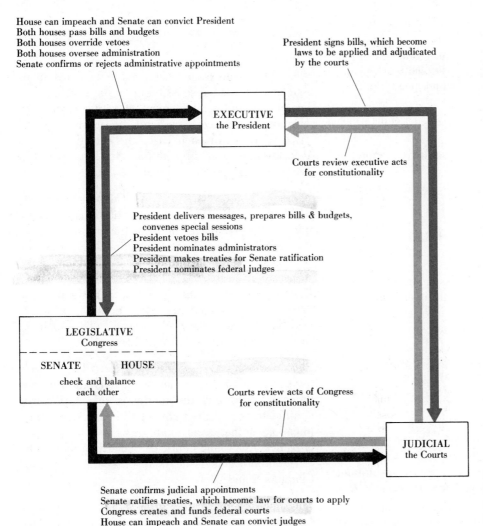

House can impeach and Senate can convict President
Both houses pass bills and budgets
Both houses override vetoes
Both houses oversee administration
Senate confirms or rejects administrative appointments

President signs bills, which become laws to be applied and adjudicated by the courts

**EXECUTIVE**
the President

Courts review executive acts for constitutionality

President delivers messages, prepares bills & budgets, convenes special sessions
President vetoes bills
President nominates administrators
President makes treaties for Senate ratification
President nominates federal judges

**LEGISLATIVE**
Congress

**SENATE**        **HOUSE**
check and balance
each other

Courts review acts of Congress for constitutionality

**JUDICIAL**
the Courts

Senate confirms judicial appointments
Senate ratifies treaties, which become law for courts to apply
Congress creates and funds federal courts
House can impeach and Senate can convict judges

FIGURE 3.1
Separation of powers in the three branches of the national government

Congress was given the power to impeach and convict the president, the vice-president, and the members of the federal judiciary.

To the original checks and balances laid out in the Constitution have been added many other refinements in a kind of unwritten constitution—traditions, laws, and procedures that have evolved through political necessity over the years. Consider, for example, the wide range of governmental and societal agencies with a voice in economic policy making today:

1. The president, whose broad economic powers include the ability to unilaterally freeze wages and prices.

2. The Federal Reserve Board, which regulates the national supply of money and credit.

3. Other bureaucratic agencies, such as the Defense Department, with its enormous budget, and the Agriculture Department, which regulates farm-support prices and quotas.

4. Congress, which regulates every sector of the national economy.

5. The courts, whose power of legislative interpretation affects economic decisions.

6. States and cities, which enjoy economic powers outside federal control.

7. Private organizations—interest groups, corporations, and labor unions—whose views help shape the economy.

Every policy area is shaped by similar power points, which interact in constantly shifting arrangements.

Madison could not possibly have anticipated the extent to which the constitutional system of checks and balances would evolve and change. Nor could he have anticipated the development of certain elements of modern politics that have skewed some constitutional checks on power. Whereas in Madison's time political parties were not a significant force, today parties link occupants of the various branches of government on many policy issues. Soon after the Constitution was written, the Supreme Court claimed the right to declare legislative acts unconstitutional (a power implied but not explicitly stated in the Constitution), and thus vastly increased the powers of the federal judiciary in the constitutional arrange-

ment. Presidents have gained the power to issue so-called executive orders in some matters, thus bypassing the need for congressional approval of all legislation. Within Congress, legislative programs must move through an elaborate thicket of decision points, subject to potential ambushes by any number of interest groups. As political scientist Robert Dahl has stated, "the making of government decisions is not a majestic march of great majorities united upon certain matters of basic policy. It is the steady appeasement of relatively small groups."[4]

## Four issues

Among the many issues discussed at the convention, four merit further discussion here: the regulation of commerce, the establishment of voting rights, the election of the president, and the guaranteeing of civil liberties. In each case, the way the framers dealt (or failed to deal) with the issue left a powerful imprint on American political life.

**The regulation of commerce:** This was one of the problems that had led to the Constitutional Convention in the first place, and the framers decided to give regulatory power to the national government. Specifically, the Constitution gives the federal government the power to regulate interstate commerce. It is a power that has served as a basis for vast expansion of national regulatory power in general, especially in the twentieth century. (This topic is discussed in Chapters 18 and 22.)

**The establishment of voting rights:** The Constitution left this issue to the states, thus allowing the framers to sidestep the thorny issues of property qualifications and the rights of non-whites. The implications of that decision are now clear: many years of battles over voting rights, particularly in the South. (The voting-rights issue is discussed in detail in Chapters 5 and 20.)

**The election of the president:** Various political compromises at the convention resulted in the electoral college as a method of choosing the president. A somewhat peculiar and complex mechanism, in which the president and vice-president are formerly elected by state electors (and each state has a number of electors equal to its number of senators and representatives). Thus the only truly national political figure is elected by a mechanism rooted in the states. As a method, the electoral college has had vast implications for political strategy—for example, in the way that candidates must win electoral, rather than popular, votes.

**The guarantee of civil liberties:** The Constitution omitted any mention of civil rights and liberties; these were added after ratification, in the first ten amendments (the Bill of Rights), and then with application specified only to the national government. Though these amendments ensured that citizens were protected against infringements by the national government, they provided no protection against state governments. The result has been a complicated and lengthy process of securing rights against the states. (This process will be discussed further in Chapter 5.)

## Ratification

The struggle over ratification of the proposed Constitution was bitter and the outcome very close. The delegates to the Constitutional Convention opted to entrust the ratification process to conventions elected by the people in each state. In this way, they circumvented the state legislatures, in which opposition to the Constitution was strong, and gained direct access to popular support for the new Constitution. The delegates also specified that once two thirds of the states had voted for ratification, the Constitution would be in force.

Supporters of the Constitution called themselves Federalists, and opponents became known as Antifederalists. Rural areas of the nation, populated by farmers and relatively poorer people who feared the growth of centralized power, tended to oppose the new Constitution. Those living in cities and coastal areas tended to support it. Many cross-currents affected the political struggle, however, and no one factor can explain the outcome.

Critics of the new Constitution immediately scored two powerful points against it. First, they noted the omission of a **Bill of Rights.** If some state constitutions included protections against government infringements on liberty, opponents argued, why shouldn't the national constitution incorporate such protections? The Federalists were forced to yield on this point, and it was agreed that a Bill of Rights would be added once the Constitution was ratified. The Antifederalists also decried what they viewed as an ill-considered rush toward ratification. New political arrangements of such import, they contended, demanded lengthy and thorough deliberation. Although aware of the merit in this argument, the Federalists knew that quick action was necessary to prevent their opponents from becoming fully organized. The Federalists also carried out a brilliant propaganda campaign centered around *The Federalist Papers,* a series of essays that appeared in New York newspapers written by Hamilton, Madison, and John Jay.

The strategy adopted by the Federalists worked well. Within a year, nine states had ratified the Constitution, making it legal. But the votes for ratification were close in several states, and two crucial states, Virginia and New York, gave their approval only after the Constitution had been adopted. Rhode Island was the thirteenth state to ratify (1790), after refusing seven times to even call a ratification convention.

## Amending the Constitution

Thomas Jefferson was one of several framers of the Constitution who worried about the tendency of governments to break down or lose touch with the people over time. Accordingly, he proposed that a new constitutional convention be called in each succeeding

Much did not run smoothly in the new republic. This print shows a brawl in Congress between Federalist Roger Griswold and Republican Matthew Lyon. Early disputes revolved around U.S. policy toward revolutionary France and laws dealing with freedom of speech. Still, the fledgling nation held together for seventy-three years before being torn apart by the Civil War.

generation, noting, "We might as well require a man to wear still the coat which fitted him as a boy, as a civilized society to remain ever under the regimen of their barbarous ancestors." Although the framers did not incorporate this idea into the Constitution, they did provide for a means of amending the Constitution as the need arose.

In order to be adopted, an **amendment** first must be proposed and then must be ratified. Each of these steps can be accomplished in either of two ways. For proposal, either two-thirds of the members of each house of Congress must approve or two-thirds of the state legislatures must petition Congress to call a national constitutional convention. Only the first of these methods has ever been employed. In the 1960s, however, opponents of the Supreme Court's rulings on reapportionment came within one state legislature of petitioning Congress to call a national constitutional convention, and as of 1985, more than half the state legislatures had petitioned for an amend-

ment requiring a balanced federal budget. If a national constitutional convention ever were to be called, unprecedented complications would have to be dealt with.[5] Who would determine if the states had presented valid petitions? Could the convention be limited to the one issue named in the petition? If the convention were to exceed its original mandate (as the Constitutional Convention did), would political and social chaos follow?

Congress can deflect the threat of petition by the states by passing its own version of the constitutional amendment involved and sending that version to the state legislatures for approval. When petitions calling for the direct election of U.S. senators began accumulating early in this century, for example, Congress recognized the thrust of public sentiment and proposed the Seventeenth Amendment. As yet unanswered is the question of whether, once two-thirds of the states have presented Congress with a call for a national convention, Congress must comply. Article V of the Constitution states that Congress *shall* call a convention—not that it *must*.

The two methods of ratifying a constitutional amendment are approval by three-fourths of the state legislatures, or approval by three-fourths of ratifying conventions called by the states. Congress determines which method is to be used in each case. Ratifying conventions have been called only once—to approve the Twenty-first Amendment, which repealed Prohibition (which had been mandated by the Eighteenth Amendment). Congress chose that method because state legislatures were expected to be less likely to vote for repeal.

The usual method of ratification has its own complications. How much time do legislatures have to ratify? Usually, Congress has stipulated that the ratification process be limited to a period of seven years. In 1978, however, the ratification period was extended for the Equal Rights Amendment, amid considerable debate over whether Congress could arbitrarily change the ground rules for ratification. Can a state withdraw approval for an amendment it previously ratified? Several state legislatures rescinded prior ratifications of the ERA, but those rescissions were never put to a legal test. The dominant legal interpretation is that states cannot rescind their approval, although they can always ratify an amendment they had previously rejected.

It is a matter of vital importance to democratic theory and practice in this country that the amending procedures be, first, sufficiently flexible and, second, sufficiently representative of majority sentiment. In two hundred years, only twenty-six amendments have been added to the Constitution, ten of which were adopted together as the Bill of Rights. Sometimes the amending process has been used in an effort to have the last word in the constitutional system—to overrule even the judgments of the Supreme Court. At other times, it has been employed in attempts to hold back social change. In yet other cases, it has represented the last resort for those seeking changes that could not be obtained other ways. Though it is difficult to judge the overall impact of amending initiatives on our governmental system, it is probably fortunate that the Constitution has

not been amended more frequently, and thus laden with prohibitions and complications that would make governing extremely difficult. Still, most people would like to be able to amend the Constitution in ways that suit them—without, of course, opening the door to all those other amendments! Democratic commitments do require that in a polity based on a written constitution, there be some method of amendment that responds to majority impulses.

## The U.S. Constitution: An enduring political legacy

The world is strewn with scraps of paper called constitutions. Many are subterfuges for coups, caudillos, and corruption. The U.S. Constitution is rare in its continuing capacity to prescribe rules of governance two centuries after its formulation.

Equally rare is the semireligious aura that envelops the U.S. Constitution. All constitutions are essentially political documents conceived in power politics and shaped by compromises made between conflicting interests. But a successful constitution eventually becomes as much symbol as document, taking on some of the qualities of Holy Writ. Written interpretations of it resemble analyses of the scriptures, it comes to prescribe civic virtue and to legitimize good behavior, and an elaborate code of laws and customs build up around it, presumably shaped by the needs of the day. Often the fact that a constitution was originally a political document is all but forgotten.

For many years the U.S. Constitution was considered an act of divine intervention in the affairs of men.[6] Those who (like the Founders) doubted that God troubled Himself so directly with the affairs of men accepted the slightly different, although equally benign, view that the Constitution represented a victory for "straight-thinking" men over "narrow-minded" men, for visionaries over parochials, for the public interest over that of the individual.[7] According to

# Comparative perspective

## Americans write another constitution

Americans have been directly responsible for the formulation of at least one constitution other than their own. In 1946 the Government Section of the Supreme Commander for the Allied Powers in Japan wrote a new constitution for the Japanese nation in six days. Adopted shortly thereafter by the Japanese parliament, that constitution has remained the governing document of Japanese politics and has never been amended.

This highly unusual procedure arose out of a singular set of circumstances. In the aftermath of World War II, Japan was occupied by the United States, which was determined to prevent the return of the political system that had led to Japan's fascist policies in the 1930s and 1940s. Allied Supreme Commander General Douglas MacArthur was charged, in effect, with the democratization of Japanese society—a task that required drastic alterations in the so-called Meiji constitution, under which Japan had been governed since 1889. It is fascinating to chart how the new, American-made constitution differed not only from the Meiji constitution, but also from the U.S. Constitution.

The most elemental difference between the old and new Japanese constitutions lay in the status of the Japanese emperor. Under the old constitution the emperor, as sovereign, was the acknowledged source of all authority. Although the emperor could act only through his cabinet

ministers, the concept that power ultimately resided in the person of the emperor represented a symbolic denial of the sovereignty of the people. The new constitution transformed the emperor from sovereign to figurehead, designating him a "symbol of the state" whose position derives "from the will of the people."

Another revolutionary feature of the new constitution was an extensive and explicit listing of inalienable, God-given rights that may not be abridged by any political authority. The rights spelled out in the 1946 constitution cover not only the familiar areas of speech, religion, and due process of law, but also such matters as employment (the right to choose an occupation); emigration; academic freedom; complete equality of the sexes in regard to property, inheritance, and all other matters; collective bargaining; and the right of each person to "minimum standards of wholesome and cultured living." In practice, many of these rights have proven difficult to realize fully. Still, it is interesting that so many social and political rights not included in the U.S. Constitution were incorporated into a modern constitution written by Americans.

The political structure created by the 1946 constitution is a parliamentary system much closer to that of Great Britain than to that of the United States. As in the U.S. Constitution, however, there is provision for an independent federal judiciary with the power to review legislation.

The most controversial element in the constitution was the famous "renunciation of war" clause, in which Japan formally eschewed the use or threat of force in international relations. In fact, the constitution seems to rule out the maintenance of *any* armed forces. There has been considerable nibbling around the edges of this clause, however, and contemporary Japan has in fact developed quite extensive "security forces."

One student of Japanese politics has summarized the 1946 constitution as follows: "The Constitution of Japan is admirably democratic. It introduces rights, institutions and practices into Japanese politics that undoubtedly go far beyond anything the Japanese themselves might realistically have been expected to establish. In fact, on the basis of the text alone, it is a considerably more democratic document than is the Constitution of the United States."*

*Robert E. Ward, *Japan's Political System*, 2nd ed. (Englewood Cliffs, N.J.: Prentice-Hall, 1978), p. 145.

this view, the framers discerned the weaknesses of the Articles of Confederation and made thoroughly rational and nonpolitical judgments as to the best ways to change our political system. For generations, this interpretation of the genesis of the Constitution was almost universally accepted.

In 1913, the historian Charles Beard, in *An Economic Interpretation of the Constitution*, made the shocking argument that the Constitution was a *political* document that had been constructed by men with political interests in mind.[8] Beard pointed out that the framers were for the most part rich and well-born, that most of them would have agreed that the preservation of property was the principal object of government, and that many of them might have agreed with John Jay that "the people who own the country ought to govern it." According to Beard, the wealthy framers, following the dictates of self-interest, developed the Constitution's checks and balances in order to prevent the unpropertied majority from making unpalatable demands on the propertied minority.

Although the historical evidence does not fully support Beard's conclusions, all serious historians acknowledge that the economic interests of the early republic were very much at issue in the framing and ratification of the Constitution. Among James Madison's fundamental assumptions, in fact, were the notions that economic factors comprised a primary motivating force in human behavior and that the seeds of political conflict were sown in the economic differences between classes of people.

However one judges the framers, it is remarkable that the institutional framework they created has endured to the present day. Although the U.S. political system has gradually evolved in a more democratic direction over the years—through the direct election of senators, the expansion of the right to vote, the emergence of mass-based political parties, and the transformation of the electoral college from a group with real power to little more than a rubber stamp—the constitutional system still reflects the framers' fears of majority tyranny and the excesses of popular control.

The Constitutional Convention, 1787. Did the men we now refer to as our Founding Fathers expect that they would be honored for their efforts two hundred years later? They knew that only some political arrangements stood the test of time—and that however necessary their efforts in Philadelphia were, they were unquestionably experimental.

## Is the Constitution outdated?

Since at least the beginning of the twentieth century, political commentators have been calling the constitutional system outdated. The main focus of criticism has been the system's built-in tensions between the various branches and levels of government. In our form of government, unlike in parliamentary democracies, one branch of government is pitted against another: instead of unity, we seek division. But division of power, however laudable as a check on excessive concentration of power, can also lead to a government of stalemate in which nothing can be accomplished except in crisis conditions and Congress and the executive are locked in a perpetual standoff that makes for irresponsible policy making, or no policy making at all.

The economic and political crises of the twentieth century have greatly strained the constitutional structure. Presidents, in particular, have been forced into many political innovations in order to keep the ship of state afloat. Many observers have argued that the vast increase in presidential power in this century has been a direct result of efforts to counteract the stalemate built into the system.

Ultimately, we cannot help but see the Constitution as impressive and enduring, but also deeply flawed. It marked a giant step forward for democratic ideas in its own time, but it also left many basic democratic questions unanswered and incorporated some blatantly undemocratic concepts. We will take up the implications of these cross-currents more fully in Chapter 5, when we discuss civil rights and civil liberties issues, and in Chapters 13–17, when we focus on governmental institutions.

## NOTES

1 James Kirby Martin, *In the Course of Human Events* (Arlington Heights, Ill.: AHM Publishing, 1979), pp. 9–11.

2 George B. Tindall, *America, A Narrative History* (New York: Norton, 1984), pp. 209–10.

3 *Ibid.*, pp. 262–63, and Charles Warren, *The Making of the Constitution* (New York: Barnes and Noble, 1967), pp. 55–60.

4 Robert Dahl, *A Preface to Democratic Theory* (Chicago: University of Chicago Press, 1956), p. 146.

5 See Daniel H. Pollitt and Frank Thompson, "Could a Convention Become a Runaway?" *Christianity and Crisis*, 16 April 1979.

6 See George Bancroft, *History of the United States*, R. B. Nye, ed. (Chicago: University of Chicago Press, 1966).

7 See John Fiske, *The Critical Period of American History, 1783–1789* (Boston: Houghton Mifflin, 1888).

8 Charles Beard, *An Economic Interpretation of the Constitution* (New York: Macmillan, 1913).

## SELECTED READINGS

### Background of the American Revolution

For various perspectives on the American Revolution, see S. M. Lipset, *The First New Nation* (New York: Basic Books, 1963); Ellen Chase, *The Beginnings of the American Revolution, Volume III* (Port Washington, N.Y.: Kennikat Press, 1970); James Kirby Martin, *In the Course of Human Events* (Arlington Heights, Ill.: AHM Publishing, 1979); and Neil R. Stout, *The Perfect Crisis—The Beginning of the Revolutionary War* (New York: NYU Press, 1976).

### The Revolutionary War

Good basic works on Tom Paine include Howard Fast, ed., *The Selected Works of Tom Paine and Citizen Tom Paine* (New York: Modern Library, 1945); Eric Foner, *Tom Paine and Revolutionary America* (New York: Oxford University Press, 1976); N. F. Adkins, ed., *Common Sense* (Indianapolis: Bobbs-Merrill, 1953); and Henry Collins, ed., *The Rights of Man* (Harmondsworth, England: Penguin, 1969).

For more-extensive discussions of the effects of the Revolutionary War on American social and political development, see Charles Royster, *A Revolutionary People at War* (Chapel Hill, N.C.: University of North Carolina Press, 1980); and J. Franklin Jameson, *The American Revolution Considered as a Social Movement* (Boston: Beacon Press, 1963).

### The Constitutional Convention

There is no shortage of commentaries on the Constitutional Convention. See particularly Vernon I. Parrington, *Main Currents in American Political Thought*, vol. 6 (New York: Harcourt, Brace and World, 1927); Garry Wills, *Inventing America* (Garden City, N.Y.: Doubleday, 1978), Chapter 27; and D. G. Smith, *The Convention and the Constitution: The Political Ideas of the Founding Fathers* (New York: St. Martin's Press, 1965).

The best discussion of the political issues involved in the writing of the Constitution is still James Madison's *Notes of the Debates in the Federal Convention of 1787*, Adrienne Koch, ed., (Athens, Ohio: Ohio University Press, 1966). The philosophical underpinnings of the Constitution can be found in Alexander Hamilton, John Jay, and James Madison, *The Federalist Papers* (Cambridge, Mass.: Belnap Press, 1966); and Paul Conklin, *Self-Evident Truths* (Bloomington, Ind.: Indiana University Press, 1974).

On Madison's particular contribution, see Saul Padover, ed., *The Complete Madison* (New York: Harper & Row, 1953); Frank Donovan, *Mr. Madison's Constitution* (New York: Dodd, Mead, 1965); and Irving Brant, *James Madison and American Nationalism* (Princeton, N.J.: Van Nostrand, 1968).

# Chapter
four

# American federalism

# Can democracy be divided fifty ways?

EVERY American holds dual citizenship of a kind: as a citizen of the United States and as a citizen of a particular state. This duality reflects what is called a **federal system,** in which power is shared by different national and regional levels of government. In a federal arrangement each level of government is an integral part of the constitutionally established political process. Each level acts directly on the people and each exercises *by right* authority that (at least theoretically) cannot be taken away from it by the other. The relationship between states and cities thus is not a federal one, for cities are chartered by the state and do not enjoy a legally independent existence.

This dual citizenship has many important consequences, most of which are so obvious that we take them entirely for granted. In many states, citizens must pay state income tax as well as federal income tax. The existence of fifty separate state jurisdictions also means that a citizen must register to vote, get a new driver's license, learn different traffic regulations, and so on, upon each move to a different state. Some states make it more difficult than others to get married or divorced. Certain crimes, such as possession of marijuana, carry rather lenient penalties in some states and severe penalties in others.

From the beginning of our political history the federal system has been a source of tension between the states and the national government. The major domestic crisis in U.S. history, the Civil War (or War Between the States, as many Southerners prefer to call it), was set off when several states attempted to secede from the Union. Moreover, the racial issues underlying the secession crisis have resurfaced recurrently in U.S. history, often in struggles pitting state against nation. In the 1960s, for example, the federal government had to intervene forcefully in Southern states to protect and extend the civil rights and voting rights of black citizens.

Other nations have suffered similar problems, and many have federal arrangements similar to ours: Canada has provincial governments; Australia, West Germany, and India have state governments. In these countries power is divided between the two levels of government in somewhat different ways. Some federal systems allow the regional governments greater responsibilities and latitude for action than do others. Whatever the exact arrangements, however, all federal systems must cope with the problem of coordinating the actions of the two levels.

The opposite political structure is a **unitary system,** in which the national government's authority is more-or-less uniformly enforced throughout the country. In such a system, obviously, no government at the regional level can hold independent power. Even so, administrative subdivisions usually are required for the efficient discharge of political activities. Although these local units are not self-governing, they often have considerable autonomy, and political power may be decentralized to a certain extent. Modern examples of unitary systems include the governments of Great Britain, France, and Sweden.

Our federal system arose out of the realities of the political situation at the time the United States was created as an independent nation. The states were a given in the political equation; no one thought seriously of trying to erase them. The real question facing the Founders was which powers should be exercised by the national government and which by the states. If the Constitution settled that question in broad outline, the meaning of that outline has been debated repeatedly ever since.

## The legal mechanisms of federalism

Before addressing the current status of our federal system, we must first examine the legal mechanisms on which that system is based.

### Division of powers

The Constitution enumerates the political powers to be exercised by the national and state levels of government, respectively (see Table 4.1). The national government possesses inherent powers, delegated powers, and concurrent powers. The states exercise concurrent and reserved powers, while certain specific activities are denied them.

**Inherent powers** are those that are integral to national sovereignty. The most significant inherent

TABLE 4.1
## The federal division of powers

*Major powers of the federal government*

To tax for federal purposes.

To borrow on the nation's credit.

To regulate foreign and interstate commerce.

To provide currency and coinage.

To conduct foreign relations and make treaties.

To provide an army and a navy.

To establish and maintain a postal service.

To protect patents and copyrights.

To regulate weights and measures.

To admit new states.

To "make all laws which shall be necessary and proper" for the execution of all powers vested in the U.S. government.

*Major powers of the states*

To tax for state purposes.

To borrow on the state's credit.

To regulate trade within the state.

To make and enforce civil and criminal law.

To maintain police forces.

To furnish public education.

To control local government.

To regulate charities.

To establish voting and election laws.

To exercise all "powers not delegated to the United States by the Constitution, nor prohibited by it to the States," except for those "reserved to . . . the people."

Source: Nicholas Henry, *Governing at the Grassroots* (Englewood Cliffs, N.J.: Prentice-Hall 1984), p. 233.

power is the power to conduct foreign policy—that is, to declare and wage war, to make treaties, and to maintain diplomatic relations. Inherent powers, obviously, cannot be possessed *both* by states and by the national government.

**Delegated powers** are those that the Constitution

specifically assigns to the jurisdiction of the national government. Among the chief delegated powers are the power to regulate interstate commerce; the power to coin money; and the power to carry out the many functions assigned to each branch of government, such as Congress's powers to legislate for the general welfare, punish violators of federal laws, and raise taxes, or the executive's power to appoint ambassadors.

These delegated powers carry certain implications. If the national government, for example, is granted the power to coin money and maintain a currency, does that not imply that the national government also has the power to create a national bank to carry out these delegated functions? In the early days of our government, Alexander Hamilton, along with others of a "nationalist" orientation, argued that such implied powers did exist, whereas Thomas Jefferson and others of a more "republican" (or state-oriented) bent supported a narrower interpretation of delegated powers. In an 1819 ruling in the case of *McCulloch v. Maryland,* the Supreme Court upheld the federal government's right to create a national bank, and thereby legitimized the concept of implied powers.[1]

This concept has played a very significant role in the gradual expansion of the powers of the federal government in the course of U.S. political history. Many activities of the federal government that now seem fundamental—such as the regulation of many aspects of economic life—are not spelled out anywhere in the Constitution. This is hardly surprising: it would have been rather extraordinary if the Founders had anticipated the complexities and problems of modern industrial life. The constitution has therefore proved to be expandable, and the doctrine of implied powers has provided a major legal means of expansion.

**Concurrent powers** are those that can be exercised by both national and state governments, including the powers to raise taxes, to charter corporations, to borrow money, and to exercise the right of eminent domain (the right to appropriate private property for public use).

The Tenth Amendment to the Constitution speaks specifically of **reserved powers:** "The powers not delegated to the United States by the Constitution, nor prohibited by it to the States, are reserved to the States respectively, or to the people." In several instances early in this century, the courts invoked the Tenth Amendment to place limits on federal power, a topic we will discuss later in the chapter.

The Constitution also forbids the states to exercise certain powers, including the powers to make war, to make treaties with foreign governments, to maintain armies and navies, and to coin money. At the same time, the national government is bound by the Constitution to keep import duties uniform throughout the nation, to respect the territorial integrity of existing states, and to see to it that each state is appropriately represented in the House and has two senators.

## Limitations on government actions

The framers of the Constitution were diligent in erecting legal barriers to arbitrary or tyrannical actions on the part of government. Thus, Article I of the Constitution sets certain limits on the actions of the states, which are forbidden to, among other things, grant titles of nobility and pass bills of attainder or ex post facto laws (see the box on page 82). Similar restrictions were applied to the national government in Amendments One through Ten, which comprise the **Bill of Rights.** Further restrictions on governmental activity were added in subsequent amendments. Under Amendments Fifteen and Nineteen, the states are forbidden to limit voting rights on the basis of race or sex, respectively. The Fourteenth Amendment requires that no state shall abridge the privileges and immunities of citizens of the United States, that states must observe "**due process of law**," and that each person is entitled to "**equal protection of the laws**." (These concepts will be discussed fully in Chapter 5.)

# Limits on government power

*Bill of Attainder* Any legislative act that singles out a specific individual or group for punishment. Perhaps the most prominent recent controversy involving the constitutional prohibition on such bills was that over the papers of former president Richard Nixon. In 1974, Nixon claimed that he was the victim of, in effect, a bill of attainder after Congress passed legislation instructing the General Services Administration to preserve and eventually make public those of his papers that had historic value. Nixon's contention that he had been singled out for special treatment, given that other presidents had been permitted to decide which of their papers would be published, was eventually rejected by the Supreme Court. The Court argued that Nixon was "a legitimate class of one," particularly because he was the only president ever to have resigned his office.* The disposition of his papers, therefore, was a special situation that Congress could reasonably act upon.

*Ex Post Facto Law* Any law that designates as criminal an act that was not a crime when it was committed, that increases penalties for a crime after it has been committed, or that retroactively alters the conditions required to prove a crime was committed. The constitutional prohibition against ex post facto laws does not extend to civil (as opposed to criminal) law and does not prohibit retroactive laws that benefit, rather than harm, the accused.

*Richard M. Nixon v. General Services Administration* (1977)

---

## Interstate obligations

Article IV requires that states grant **"full faith and credit"** to the acts of other states, return fugitives fleeing from criminal proceedings in other states, and grant all **"privileges and immunities"** to citizens of other states. Under the "full faith and credit" provision, the most far-reaching of these requirements, every state must accept as valid such legal proceedings and records of other states as mortgages, legal documents, and birth certificates. As interpreted by the Supreme Court, this provision does not include the obligation to enforce the *criminal* laws of another state: that is, a person wanted for a crime in another state must be extradited to that state for trial. State civil laws, however, usually must be enforced by all other states. Thus, whenever a person leaves one state to avoid complying with a contract made there, the state to which he fled normally must enforce that contract in a court of law.

The "full faith and credit" provision has not been uniformly followed by the states or enforced by the courts, however. In particular, the requirement that states extradite fugitives to other states has often been ignored, with the acquiescence of the Supreme Court. In several famous cases, state governors have refused to extradite fugitives on the grounds that prison conditions were unsafe or that a fair trial could not be obtained in the state seeking the return of the fugitive. Recent federal legislation has made such refusal more difficult by making it a federal crime to cross state lines in an effort to avoid prosecution.

Among the most significant "privileges and immunities" that the states are required to extend to all U.S. citizens are the right to vote and the right to travel freely. Until quite recently, many states sought to circumvent this constitutional provision by attaching lengthy residency requirements to the right to vote, even in national elections. The Supreme Court largely ended this practice by ruling that a state must demonstrate the legitimacy of lengthy residency requirements. The right to travel across state lines has generally been accepted by the states. The only significant exception to this rule occurred when thousands of migrants fleeing the Dust Bowl conditions of the Midwest in the 1930s were prevented from entering California under a state law excluding indigent immigrants. In *Edwards* v. *California* (1941), the Supreme Court struck down the California law as an unconstitutional barrier to interstate commerce.[2]

## Admission to the Union

The Constitution states that Congress may admit new states but does not establish any fixed procedures for admission. More than half of the present states were once "territories" governed by congressional appointees. One by one, these territories petitioned Congress for statehood, and each eventually was the beneficiary of a Congressional **enabling act** allowing its citizens to draft a state constitution. Next came congressional and presidential approval of the draft constitution, and after any differences had been ironed out, admission to the Union. Sometimes additional requirements had to be fulfilled: the citizens of Hawaii and Alaska, for example, were required to approve admission to statehood at special elections. Once admitted, a state stands in complete legal equality with all other states; none has unique privileges or obligations.

# The Northwest Ordinance of 1787

This 1783 map shows the geographical divisions of that time, including the American states, Florida, Canada, Quebec, and Nova Scotia. The land that would be covered by the Northwest Ordinance is situated northwest of the Ohio River.

The Northwest Ordinance of 1787 has been called the most far-reaching piece of legislation ever enacted in the United States. In mandating that new states were to be created in the area north of the Ohio River, the ordinance stipulated that the new states would enjoy the same legal status as already-existing states and that slavery would be excluded in this area. By decreeing that newly settled territories would be incorporated into the Union as full-fledged states, the ordinance defused the threat of rivalry between the older states, many of which had sought to expand into the Northwest territories. It also precluded any move toward colonial subordination of newly settled areas to established states. The system of "elastic federalism" instituted by the Northwest Ordinance, under which statehood was to be granted to those who actually settled and developed new territories, offered perhaps the most sensible method for opening the continent and expanding the Union.

## The evolution
of federalism

Abraham Lincoln once asserted that "the Union is
older than any of the states, and, in fact, it created
them as states." President Ronald Reagan has taken
precisely the opposite view, that "the federal government did not create the states; the states created
the federal government." These divergent views of
federalism have been in conflict since the founding
of the nation. In fits and starts, and through several
severe crises, the federal system has been shaped
and reshaped in U.S. history.

### Three crises
of state and nation

The crisis with the greatest impact on federalism
culminated in the Civil War. In the verbal and ideological battle preceding the war, the renowned South

Carolina politician John C. Calhoun raised basic
questions about exactly what "nationhood" meant in
the United States. "The very idea of an *American
People*, as constituting a single community, is a mere
chimera," he argued. "Such a community never for
a single moment existed—neither before nor since
the Declaration of Independence."[3] For Calhoun, as
for Ronald Reagan, the states created the nation:
each state, that is, was a sovereign community that
voluntarily entered into a compact with the other
states to form the national society. A more-or-less

Daniel Webster, 1830. One
of the greatest orators of his
day, Webster was an elo-
quent advocate of a strong
national union. Tensions
between national and state
interests are still with us
today, though we no longer
fear the integrity of the
nation itself.

The ruins of Richmond and the Union army preparing for battle at Fredericksburg. The Civil War was extraordinarily costly on all sides, taking a heavy toll in lives and leaving a wide trail of destruction. The issues that provoked it were only partially resolved and continued to haunt our national life for a hundred years, as did memories of the war itself. The war did, however, settle one basic matter: there would be only one nation on American soil. The experiment in secession was over.

logical deduction from this view was that the states, having compacted to form the union, could also dissolve it.

Calhoun's concept of federalism was vigorously opposed by Daniel Webster, the eloquent senator from Massachusetts. Webster, whom Lincoln would echo, argued that the United States was created not by a compact between the states, but "by the people of the United States in the aggregate." The Constitution, he said, was "the people's Constitution, the people's government, made for the people, made by the people, and answerable to the people." He concluded his argument with the famous line, "Liberty and union, one and inseparable, now and forever."[4]

Webster not only defended a union based directly on the people; he also pointed out that many common interests of U.S. society as a whole could not be attended to by the states. For Webster, as for Alexander Hamilton, national action was absolutely necessary to secure many worthwhile goals that the in-

dividual states were not likely to pursue. Only the national government, Webster contended, had the power and the mandate to handle the problems of land use, waterway development, and transportation that would grow increasingly important as the United States developed as an industrial society.

The North's triumph in the Civil War not only resulted in the abolition of slavery and the permanent demise of the concept of secession, but also led to a major expansion of the powers of the federal government. During and after the war, federal involvement in banking, transportation, higher education, and land management broadened considerably, as Webster and Lincoln had argued it must.

The second major crisis of federalism grew out of the vast expansion of industry throughout the nation in the last half of the nineteenth century. With the emergence of giant corporations whose interests stretched across state lines, state governments found it nearly impossible to regulate commerce and industry. Monopolistic and predatory business practices, such as price fixing, flourished despite widespread agitation by farmers, workers, and consumers for legislation restricting the power of business. Action by the federal government, principally in the administrations of Theodore Roosevelt (1901–1909) and Woodrow Wilson (1913–1921), was necessary to bring the disruptive forces of industrial power under a modest degree of social control. Congress established new regulations for the conduct of trade, encouraging competition and limiting monopolistic practices, and passed a series of statutes regulating the banking, food and drug, meat packing, and other industries. The Justice Department, with the acquiescence of the Supreme Court, vigorously enforced antitrust laws. Throughout this era (roughly, 1890–1916), then, all branches of the federal government became involved to an unprecedented degree in the regulation of business.

The third crisis of federalism developed out of the Great Depression of the 1930s, when the magnitude of the national economic collapse far exceeded the remedial powers of the states. With millions unemployed, local and state welfare efforts were stretched beyond the breaking point. In his 1933 inaugural address, President Franklin D. Roosevelt argued that since the crisis was national, the solutions also had to be national. He called for extensive planning to be carried out by the federal government. Roosevelt's New Deal inaugurated a new phase of federalism. The earliest New Deal efforts consisted of emergency steps toward national planning for economic recovery. They continued, however, initiating many programs that extended federal efforts into new areas, some of which had previously been within the province of the states—including welfare and income-maintenance programs, provision of jobs, regulation of wages and prices, and a host of other functions.

## The role
## of the courts

The federal courts, and particularly the Supreme Court, have played a crucial role in resolving the disputes between the federal government and states that have shaped the evolution of the U.S. federal system. Historically, the Supreme Court's view of federalism has undergone major shifts. In early U.S. history, the Court assisted the growth of national power. After the Civil War, it frequently championed the rights of the states—a pattern that in many ways continued until the 1930s. Since that time, expansion of the powers of the federal government has been looked upon favorably by the Court, particularly in the area of commerce.

*McCulloch* v. *Maryland*:  In the case of *McCulloch* v. *Maryland* (1819), the Supreme Court had the opportunity to choose between two different interpretations of the Constitution. The focus of contention in the case was the Bank of the United States, an institution established by Congress in 1816 to control the issuance of currency. When the state of Maryland levied a tax against the Baltimore branch of the bank, James McCulloch, a cashier, refused to pay the tax. McCulloch's lawyer, Daniel Webster, argued that a state could not tax a bank that had been established by Congress; Maryland's position was that the states had the constitutional right to levy taxes on any institutions within their boundaries.

In a historic decision, Chief Justice John Marshall agreed with the proponents of states' rights that the Constitution divided sovereignty between the states and the national government. But, he went on, "the government of the Union, though limited in its powers, is supreme within its sphere of action." Although Congress's power to charter a bank was not specifically stated in the Constitution, Marshall argued, such a power could be inferred from the "**necessary and proper**" clause of Article I, which charged Congress "to make all laws which shall be necessary and proper" for executing its powers. The Chief Justice concluded that Congress had the right to legislate with a "vast mass of incidental powers which must be involved in the Constitution, if that instrument be not a splendid bauble"—that, in other words, it could exercise a wide range of powers implied in the Constitution. It followed that no state could use its concurrent powers (the right to tax, for example) to hinder the national government's execution of its duties. "The power to tax," Marshall declared, "involves the power to destroy."

The decision in *McCulloch* represented a momentous victory for the national government. It was based on John Marshall's belief that a narrow interpretation of the Constitution (that is, recognizing only those powers explicitly named in the Constitution) would unwisely restrict the operations of the national government and thus make the problems of governing a growing nation even more difficult.

**The era of dual federalism:** After the Civil War, as the United States rapidly became a more industrialized society, the courts elaborated a complex doctrine of dual federalism, under which it charted clearly separate spheres of regulation for federal and state laws. Advocates of dual federalism argued, for example, that a distinct area of *intra*state commerce could be separated from that of *inter*state commerce, and that the former was the province of state law and the latter of federal law. In practice, such distinctions proved very difficult to maintain. A railroad might cross the boundaries of many states and yet be chartered in one particular state. Manufactured goods could be produced in one state and marketed in another.

Under the reign of dual federalism, the Supreme Court on numerous occasions invoked the reserved powers clause of the Tenth Amendment to restrict federal power. In 1871 it held that the salaries of state officials could not be taxed by the national government. In a very significant commerce case decided in 1918, the Court struck down congressional legislation that had prohibited the interstate transport of goods produced by child labor, arguing that the power to regulate child labor was reserved to the states. And in 1935, the Court again cited the Tenth Amendment in declaring unconstitutional the National Industrial Recovery Act, a crucial piece of New Deal legislation. This decision, however, proved to be one of the last of its kind. From 1937 to the present day, the Court has consistently upheld far-reaching federal ventures into social welfare, labor relations, and commerce regulation. At present, there are no clear constitutional limits on the federal power to legislate in the areas of commerce and the general

welfare. It has become increasingly difficult to invoke the Tenth Amendment or the doctrine of dual federalism to limit the scope of the national government's powers.

**Nationalizing the Bill of Rights:** The courts have also played a key role in applying the Bill of Rights (the first ten amendments) to the states. In *Barron* v. *Baltimore* (1833), the Supreme Court ruled that the restrictions on government power contained in the Bill of Rights could be applied solely to actions of the national government.[5] Only in this century did the Supreme Court gradually "nationalize" its interpretation of the protections found in the Bill of Rights, applying most of its provisions to state governments as well. This is a complex story, to which we will return in Chapter 5.

## "New federalisms"

Changes in the federal system have become commonplace in recent decades. Beginning in 1933, there have been four distinct efforts to alter the federal system. The first such "new federalism" was FDR's New Deal, under which the balance of the federal system was tilted toward Washington in an effort to deal with serious problems of national scope. Programs initiated in the New Deal period were often referred to as products of cooperative federalism, in which the national government worked directly with local as well as state governments. The key element in cooperative federalism was federal funding for programs administered by state and local governments, including Aid to Families with Dependent Children (see Chapter 19), construction projects (hospitals, highways, airports, and so on), public health programs, and unemployment compensation.

The second "new federalism" of modern times emerged in President Lyndon Johnson's Great Society program of the 1960s. Johnson termed his program one of "creative federalism"; in practice, it entailed a new and greatly heightened level of federal intervention in community affairs that had previously been handled by state and local governments. In

# The death of the Tenth Amendment?

The Tenth Amendment to the Constitution provides that those powers not granted to the federal government nor prohibited to the states are reserved "to the states or to the people." In practice, however, what exactly does such a notion of reserved powers mean?

In *National League of*
*Cities* v. *Usery* (1976) a narrow court majority of 5–4 held unconstitutional Congress's extension of the Fair Labor Standards Act to state employees, employing the Tenth Amendment's reserved powers concept as a check on Congress's right to regulate interstate commerce in a way that affected "the states as states." This was the first court decision in forty years to invalidate an action taken by Congress under the Commerce Clause of the Constitution (that is, through its power to regulate interstate commerce).

Although that case led many to expect a major shift in the federal-state power balance, such a
shift did not occur. Almost from the first, the Court failed to carry through on its *League of Cities* decision, showing reluctance to extend it to other areas.

In 1985 the Court overruled the 1976 decision in *Garcia* v. *San Antonio Metropolitan Transit Authority*. Once again it was a narrow, 5–4 majority. In *Garcia*, the Court restored the applicability of federal minimum-wage and maximum-hour standards to employees of publicly owned mass transit systems, and by implication to most other state employees. The Court ma-
jority argued in *Garcia* that the Constitution (with rare exceptions) does not limit the federal power to interfere in state affairs, calling efforts to impose such limits "both impracticable and doctrinally barren." The states were protected, it maintained, by the very structure of our political system and by their representation in Congress. The four-person minority accused the majority of creating a situation where federal officials "are the sole judges of the limits of their own power."

---

developing more than two hundred new social and economic programs, President Johnson and his supporters in Congress triggered a vast increase in federal involvement in the day-to-day affairs of U.S. citizens. These programs had a strong urban emphasis; in fact, federal funds often went directly to cities, bypassing state governments. Great Society legislation also strongly emphasized aid to the disadvantaged. Federal money flowed into such previously sacrosanct preserves of state and local authority as education and law enforcement. Between 1960 and 1970, federal aid to the states increased from $7 billion to $24 billion, and the percentage of federal funds going to urban areas increased from 55 percent to 70 percent of the total.

The Johnsonian concept of federalism was at least partially discarded during the administration of Pres-
ident Richard Nixon. The general philosophy of the Nixon administration was that financial assistance from the federal government to the states should continue, but that the policy-making and administrative functions of the federal government should be reduced. To this end, federal grants to the states were restructured in two principal ways: through the introduction of **revenue sharing** programs, under which a certain portion of federal revenues was disbursed among the states; and through the consolidation of many federal funding programs into block grants, under which states and localities were given greater flexibility in putting the funds to use. Under the State and Local Assistance Act of 1972, state and local governments were allocated $5 to $6 billion a year for five years in large noncategorical grants, to use as they saw fit. One-third of the funds was earmarked

for the states and two-thirds for local governments, apportioned according to a formula that involved population, per capita income, and other factors.

Revenue sharing became a regular part of inter-governmental relations in the 1970s, and it was enthusiastically supported by most state and local authorities. The concept also had its critics, however. It seemed to many observers that under revenue sharing, less money found its way to poorer citizens and poorer communities, and more money wound up in well-to-do suburbs. Another criticism was that because state and local record keeping was far less efficient than federal accounting had been, maladministration and corruption had increased greatly. On a more general level, revenue sharing suffered from the excessively complex system of local governments in the United States. Of the 80,000 local governments of various sorts in the United States, 21,000 do not even employ one full-time employee. Yet 11,000 of these virtually inactive local entities received revenue-sharing funds. As a consequence, money has often been distributed in futile, foolish, and wasteful ways.

For these and other reasons, federal efforts to provide direct aid to cities and localities via revenue

sharing were not as beneficial as had been expected. With more aid coming from Washington, many states simply allowed the federal government to supply what state legislatures had once furnished. As a result, local governments as well as the states themselves became increasingly dependent on federal aid. Many cities came to receive more from Washington than they raised in taxes. Many feared this increased dependence because of possible federal controls over state and local functions in areas such as education, transportation, and welfare. Government, they argued, was getting away from the people. On the other hand were critics who continued to maintain that revenue sharing involved too little federal control.

One response to these questions was President Ronald Reagan's New Federalism program, the fourth significant development in federal-state relations over the past fifty years. The Reagan strategy was based on three main elements: devolution, decremental-ism, and deregulation. *Devolution* involved an increased delegation of authority to state and local governments. Under *decrementalism*, federal aid was cut from $95 billion in 1981 (accounting for 25 percent of state and local expenditures) to $88 billion in 1982 (22 percent of such expenditures). *Deregulation* involved efforts to reduce federal regulation of business and social activities. The centerpiece of the New Federalism was to be a significant reordering of programs between state and federal levels, under which the federal government was to assume responsibility for certain state and local programs (such as Medicaid) and the states were to assume responsibility for certain predominantly federal programs (such as Aid to Families with Dependent Children). In addition, several dozen federal aid programs were to be turned back to the states.

The proposal had one major appeal to the states: it allowed for increased state control over many major programs. At the same time, however, many states and localities saw no way to finance these programs at the funding levels established by the federal government. As a result, reaction to the New Federalism proposals was mixed, and significant opposition in Congress, as well as at the state and local levels, prevented much of the New Federalism program from being enacted.

FIGURE 4.1
How federal revenue-sharing funds were spent in 1981

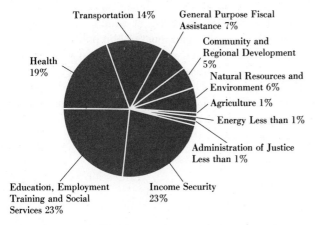

Source: Nicholas Henry, *Governing at the Grassroots* (Englewood Cliffs, N.J.: Prentice–Hall, 1984), p. 328.

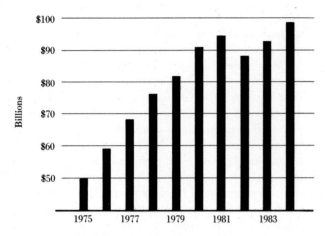

Grants-in-Aid to State and Local Governments

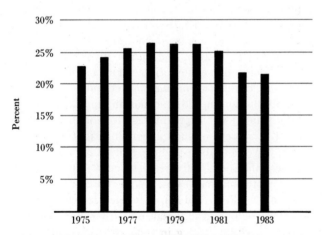

Grants as Percentage of State and Local Expenditures

FIGURE 4.2
Federal grants-in-aid to state and local governments

Nonetheless, in President Reagan's first term there was a clear shift in federal-state relationships. Most important, federal budget cuts in the early 1980s put considerable financial pressure on state and local governments. In most cases, states were able to replace the lost federal money and to maintain social programs at levels higher than had been generally anticipated. The one program that suffered most was the extension of welfare benefits to the working poor. After a Reagan administration initiative removed the

working poor from welfare rolls, most states did nothing to restore them.[6]

But, to the surprise of many, quite a few states increased their support of environmental, educational, and health programs cut back at the national level. In addition, many local governments, previously accused of discriminating against blacks and women, joined civil rights groups in defending the very quotas and affirmative action programs the Reagan administration was attacking.

In addition, revenue-sharing programs were retained only for counties and municipalities; the states themselves were dropped. And in 1985, the Reagan administration made further efforts to eliminate the revenue-sharing program altogether as an economy measure, a move sharply resisted by many local officials. Clearly, the administration had won part of its battle to reverse the patterns of federal-state relationships. But the human and social costs of these adjustments may have been high. Shifting taxes from federal to state and local levels has resulted in more economic inequality.

## Policy responsibilities of the states

Most of the nation's public business is conducted on the state and local levels, at which most political conflicts are settled and most public policy decisions are made and carried out. The areas in which state and local governments carry significant responsibilities for public policy include education, transportation, health and welfare, crime, the environment, civil rights, and taxation.

## Education

States and localities supply most of the funding for public schools, determine the content of school cur-

A pleasant-looking elementary school class, with movable desks, an integrated student group, and a rather good-spirited teacher. Education is one of the major functions of state and local governments. Without federal intervention, we should note, this integrated class might never have come about.

ricula, set teacher qualifications, and decide how education funds should be spent. Higher education also is principally a state responsibility. Federal funds account for less than 10 percent of all education expenditures.

## Transportation

Highway location, construction policies, funding for highway projects, waterways, airports, railroads, and shipping, gasoline and motor vehicle taxation, and regulation of traffic are among the many functions of state and local governments connected with the transport system. Expenditures for transportation comprise the second largest item in most state budgets. Although the federal government supplies about 30 percent of funding for transportation and is heavily involved in the construction and maintenance of the interstate highway network and of all major airports, the states and localities carry the main burden.

## Health and welfare

The states administer the largest programs in the fields of health and welfare—Aid to Families with Dependent Children (AFDC), Medicaid, food stamps, and unemployment compensation. Despite the heavy impact of federal funding in these areas, state governments generally decide how much is to be spent on, the rules of eligibility for, and the type of administration governing each program. States and localities also maintain facilities for people who cannot care for themselves, such as orphans, the aged, and those who are mentally or physically ill.

## Criminal justice

Although the federal government does have some important criminal justice responsibilities, state and local governments carry the main burden of public

Criminal justice, including the maintenance of prisons, is a state and local function—and an expensive one. In recent years the American criminal justice system has come under strong criticism; overcrowded conditions and crime *in* prisons have made many dubious about the possibilities for rehabilitation in such an environment.

safety. State and local governments employ more than 250,000 police officers, who bear the brunt of law enforcement in the United States. Criminal prosecution and the maintenance of courts are largely state and local matters. States and counties maintain extensive jail facilities; more than 90 percent of all convicts are incarcerated in nonfederal prisons.

## Other responsibilities

Protection of the *physical environment* has become an increasingly important governmental responsibility at all levels, but most environmental matters are handled by states and localities. Maintenance of streets and parks, zoning regulations, provision of basic public utilities, rubbish collection, sewage removal, water treatment and supply, the monitoring of air and water pollution—all these tasks must be

handled by state and local governments, with some help from the federal government.

States are also heavily involved in *civil rights* matters. The enforcement of both state and federal civil rights laws is largely left to states and communities, especially in the areas of employment, schools, and housing. Experience in many of these areas has shown just how complicated and frustrating it can be to try to make civil rights meaningful all over the nation when local and state governments pit themselves against federal power.

Finally, states and localities are responsible for many forms of *taxation*—sales taxes, property assessments, state income taxes. In raising hundreds of billions of dollars in taxes every year (see the box on page 93), they must decide who will bear the tax burden, how much that burden will be, and how the funds should be spent. It should be noted that the much-heralded "tax revolt" of the late 1970s began in California as a protest against state and local government tax policies.

# State and local taxes, 1980

In 1980 the fifty states collected a grand total of $136,913,324,000 in taxes and other assessments—an average of $623.91 per resident. (This figure does *not* include taxes at the local level.) The states that collected the most money were Alaska ($3,541 per capita), Hawaii ($1,091), Delaware ($886), Wyoming ($863), and California ($853). The states that collected the least were New Hampshire ($302 per capita), South Dakota ($393), Missouri and Tennessee (both $430), and Ohio ($444).

On a percentage basis, state revenues collections were derived from the following sources in 1980.

*Sales and excise taxes*

| General sales | 31.5% |
|---|---|
| Motor fuels | 7.1% |
| Tobacco | 2.7% |
| Public utilities | 2.3% |
| Insurance | 2.3% |
| Alcoholic beverages | 1.8% |
| | 47.7% |

*License fees*

| Motor vehicles | 3.6% |
|---|---|
| Corporations | 1.0% |
| Vehicle operators | 0.3% |
| Hunting and fishing | 0.3% |
| | 5.2% |

*Other taxes*

| Individual income taxes | 27.1% |
|---|---|
| Corporate income taxes | 9.7% |
| Severance taxes | 3.0% |
| Property taxes | 2.1% |
| Death and gift taxes | 1.5% |
| Other revenues | 3.7% |
| | 47.1% |

The states that derived the highest proportions of their revenues from personal income taxes in 1980 were Oregon (59.6 percent), Massachusetts (47.4 percent), Delaware (45.7 percent), New York (45.4 percent), and Wisconsin (42.5 percent). The states that derived the smallest part of their revenues from personal income taxes were Ten-nessee (1.6 percent), New Hampshire (3.9 percent), New Mexico (5.1 percent), Connecticut (5.5 percent), and Alaska (7.0 percent).

As of 1984, six states had no state income tax: Florida, Nevada, South Dakota, Texas, Washington, and Wyoming.

Source: Andrew Hacker, ed., *U/S: A Statistical Portrait of the American People* (New York: Viking Press, 1983), p. 175.

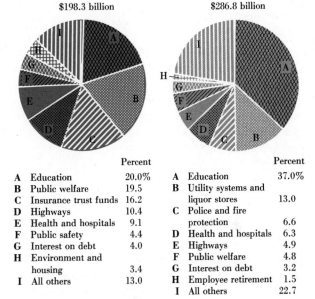

|   | State: $198.3 billion | Percent |
|---|---|---|
| A | Education | 20.0% |
| B | Public welfare | 19.5 |
| C | Insurance trust funds | 16.2 |
| D | Highways | 10.4 |
| E | Health and hospitals | 9.1 |
| F | Public safety | 4.4 |
| G | Interest on debt | 4.0 |
| H | Environment and housing | 3.4 |
| I | All others | 13.0 |

|   | Local: $286.8 billion | Percent |
|---|---|---|
| A | Education | 37.0% |
| B | Utility systems and liquor stores | 13.0 |
| C | Police and fire protection | 6.6 |
| D | Health and hospitals | 6.3 |
| E | Highways | 4.9 |
| F | Public welfare | 4.8 |
| G | Interest on debt | 3.2 |
| H | Employee retirement | 1.5 |
| I | All others | 22.7 |

Source: John J. Harrigan, *Politics and Policy in States and Communities* (Boston: Little, Brown, 1984), p. 69. Data from Bureau of the Census, *Governmental Finances in 1980–81*, GF 81, no. 5 (Washington, D.C.: U.S. Government Printing Office, October 1982), pp. 34, 65.

FIGURE 4.3
Where state and local governments spend your money

## Tensions in the contemporary federal system

Over the years the American federal system has been far from stagnant. Such factors as population movement, economic and technological evolution, investment patterns, and the aging of public works cause changes in both the politics and structure of the federal arrangement.

## Regional rivalries

Under a federal system, resources can be shifted from wealthier to poorer areas by the federal government, which can allocate to specific states more federal funds than those states contribute in tax dollars. During the Depression, the South, which was particularly impoverished, received an economic boost in the form of increased federal spending. Today, the southern states, along with the other so-called Sun Belt states in the Southwest and West, still get back more than they contribute. Meanwhile, states in the so-called Frost Belt generally pay out more to the federal government than they get back.

Frost Belt mayors and governors in recent years have complained loudly of this inequity in federal disbursements, and have called for increased federal assistance to their region. Once an area becomes dependent on government expenditure, however, it is difficult for either the president or the Congress to cut those funds. Any politician running for office

in a state faced with a significant reduction in federal funding would be hard pressed not to denounce it.

Tensions between the Sun Belt and the Frost Belt have become evident in the political arena. Since World War II, the Sun Belt's rate of population growth has considerably exceeded that of the Frost Belt. From 1950 to 1975, Frost Belt population grew by 32 percent, whereas the Sun Belt increase was 60 percent. As a result of this large population shift, the Sun Belt states gained a substantial number of seats in the House in 1982 and in the Electoral College in 1984. (See Figures 4.4 and 4.5.)

This trend carries potentially important implications for U.S. political life. Because Sun Belt states are generally more conservative in political outlook, liberal legislation and liberal presidential candidates seemingly will encounter increasing difficulties. A large question mark, however, hangs over these calculations—California, a Sun Belt state that has been growing especially fast. Despite the fact that its citizens spearheaded nationwide efforts to cut state and local taxes in the late 1970s and early 1980s, California is by no means a clearly conservative state. In fact, it has been an innovator in the environmental and energy areas, and its large and growing Chicano and Asian-American populations almost certainly will have an increasing—and possibly liberal—impact on national politics.

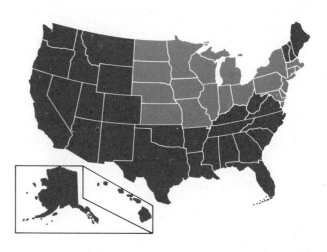

FIGURE 4.4
Shift in population in the United States, 1970–1980: The dark blue marks states where the population grew by 10 percent or more from 1970 to 1980. Source: An- drew Hacker, ed., *U/S: A Statistical Portrait of the American People* (New York: Viking, 1983), p. 16.

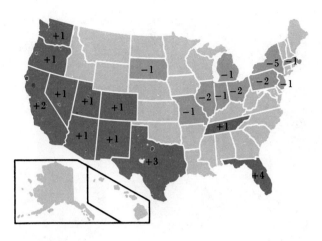

FIGURE 4.5

Changes in U.S. congressional representation, 1970–1980. Eleven states gained and ten states lost seats in the House as a result of population shifts in those years. Florida and Texas posted the largest gains, adding four and three seats respectively. New York lost five seats; Pennsylvania, Ohio, and Illinois, two each. Overall, the shift was in the direction of the Sun Belt and away from the Frost Belt. Source: Martha V. Grotton, ed., *Congressional Districts in the 1980s* (Washington, D.C.: Congressional Quarterly, Incl, 1983).

## Issues that strain federal arrangements

Another source of tension in the federal system is that individual states are ill-equipped politically to address many of the most pressing issues in American life. For example, some problems posed by water and air pollution are unique to heavily urban areas scattered throughout the country, and others, such as those concerning the Great Lakes and major river systems, have a multistate impact. Under the present federal system, how can legislation be coordinated to treat such issues effectively? The problems faced by Detroit have much more in common with those of Boston, Houston, and Atlanta than they do with issues significant in northern Michigan. How can those state governments dominated by rural, small town, and suburban votes be expected to respond vigorously to big-city problems, such as street crime, industrial unemployment, welfare, and housing deterioration? Then, too, the cities themselves often experience jurisdictional problems of their own. Most metropolitan areas contain dozens or even hundreds of separate governmental jurisdictions, and power is often fragmented among many different boards and authorities.

It is instructive to note at this point that the basic governmental structures of today are the same as those that existed at the time of the writing of the Constitution: states, counties, and municipalities. But the boundaries and political divisions we have inherited are not necessarily the ones we would find most useful at present. Perhaps a new federal arrangement—a United States divided into regions and enlarged metropolitan areas—would serve us better in the twenty-first century—or, at least, more efficiently.

## Infrastructure— whose problem?

The term *infrastructure* seemed to be on the lips of every politician in the early 1980s. The infrastructure encompasses the entire system of public works that are basic to the smooth functioning of an industrial society: bridges, highways, sewage disposal, streets, water systems, port facilities, and so on. When these public works deteriorate, the normal operation of economic and social life is constantly threatened.

In the late 1970s, U.S. Department of Transportation officials estimated that 45 percent of the nation's bridges were structurally deficient or obsolete, including 126,000 that were seriously unsafe; that more than eight thousand miles of interstate highway were crumbling, and two-thirds of other major roads were in need of repair; and that about 25 percent of bus and subway systems needed replacement. At the same time, it had become apparent that hundreds of

95

cities needed new water and sewage systems. This deterioration of the infrastructure obviously represented an urgent political priority, as evidenced by the number of politicans who invoked it. Yet the tax-cutting mood of the American public in the late 1970s and early 1980s militated against attempts to raise the funds needed for new public works. Local bond issues went down to defeat more often than not, and any proposal to raise taxes met with fierce resistance.

It has been estimated that the United States will have to invest between $2.5 and $3 trillion over the next decade to remedy past neglect of public works. Some observers have called on the federal government to make a first-ever inventory of needed public works projects. Others have argued for the establishment of a national capital budget ranging up to $100 billion per year. With state and local governments, which have funded about 75 percent of infrastructure costs, increasingly hard-pressed to raise additional revenues, it appears that only a national

approach to the problem can generate the resources necessary to deal with it. The federal system, it seems, will have to be put to use in order to work out priorities and raise the money to cope with infrastructure decay.

## Federal intervention for democratic principles

On several occasions the federal government has concluded that some or many states were failing to serve democratic principles on particular issues. In such cases the national government has intervened (however reluctantly) to set state governments on a more democratic path. We will consider two such examples of federal intervention, involving reapportionment of legislative seats and voting rights.

Infrastructure: the expensive new Miami subway system, whose construction was financed with considerable federal money, and the decaying New York City system, whose operating budget depends on federal funds. Some states and localities are far more burdened with transportation maintenance and construction costs than are others. If the federal government cuts its funding and the states and localities do not have the funds to repair old systems or initiate new ones, who will bear the responsibility for mass transit?

## Reapportionment

In 1900, three-fifths of the population of the United States lived in rural areas; by 1960 over two-thirds of the people lived in cities or suburbs. State legislatures, however, did not change to reflect this trend toward urbanization. In 1962, for example, the twenty-four inhabitants of the town of Stratton, Vermont, enjoyed the same level of representation in the state's house of representatives as did the city of Burlington, with a population of 35,531. At the same time, Los Angeles County's 6,038,771 people received the same state senate representation as did the 14,196 inhabitants of three northern California counties. Such discrepancies left urban dwellers throughout the country in a political position far weaker than that of rural constituents.

In *Reynolds* v. *Sims* (1964), the Supreme Court ruled that state legislative districts must be apportioned strictly according to population. In the words of Chief Justice Earl Warren, "Legislators represent people, not trees or acres."[7] Basic to a representative form of government, the opinion continued, was the right of the citizen to cast a vote that counts in full. Any substantial disparity in the population of legislative districts, accordingly, would have the same effect as the allotting of a different number of votes to different individuals. This principle of "one man, one vote" was later extended by the Court to cover both houses of state legislatures.

Political scientists have yet to agree on the political consequences of the widespread **reapportionment** of legislative districts that followed the Court's rulings. Some have contended that well-apportioned states are scarcely distinguishable in policy making from malapportioned ones. Perhaps reapportionment has simply shifted power from rural anticity interests to suburban anticity interests. In the late sixties, for example, the New York State legislature declined to provide significant help to the New York City subway system, which carries 2 million riders a day, but did underwrite the losses of the Long Island Railroad, which carries 100,000 suburban commuters daily. Perhaps, too, the effects of reapportionment have been more subtle and less dramatic than its proponents had expected.

## The Voting Rights Act

When, in the early 1960s, civil rights groups made an all-out effort to register black voters in the South, they ran up against a wide variety of state election laws intended to impede and restrict the registration of blacks. In 1965 the Reverend Martin Luther King, Jr., led a dramatic march on the Alabama state capitol, in Montgomery, to challenge these laws. Television captured scenes of Alabama state police attacking marchers who tried to cross one of the city's bridges. Such scenes stunned the country and provided much of the impetus needed for passage of the Voting Rights Act of 1965. Under this landmark legislation, federal officials were empowered to register voters and to suspend literacy tests in areas in which less than 50 percent of the voting age population was registered for, or had voted in, the 1964 national election. Under this formula the act applied initially to six Southern states (Alabama, Georgia, Mississippi, South Carolina, Virginia, Louisiana), Alaska,

# Comparative perspective Federalism in West Germany

West German political life was reorganized after World War II under the Basic Law, promulgated in 1949. The Basic Law, put together by representatives of the three occupying powers (the United States, France, and Great Britain) and various German leaders, was supposed to be a temporary arrangement providing a constitutional framework that would last until the two portions of Germany, divided after the war, were reunited. After the experiences of the Nazi period, the occupying authorities were suspicious of cen-

tralized power in the new German state. One of the provisions of the Basic Law, therefore, was for a federal system. The Federal Republic of Germany, or West Germany, is currently the only major European state that has such a federal system.

The Federal Republic is organized into ten constituent states (*Länder*). The spheres of authority of the states and the federal government are set out explicitly in the Basic Law. The most important powers of the *Länder* pertain to education, law enforcement, and cultural affairs. The two levels of government jointly exercise some powers, including those having to do with transportation, energy development, and criminal law. In most cases, the administration of federal legislation is left to the states; the federal government plays a supervisory role, rather than a directly administrative

one. As a result, the Federal Republic has a relatively small central bureaucracy.

A unique feature of the West German federal arrangement is the role of the states in selecting the Federal Council, the upper house of the parliament. The forty-one seats in the Federal Council are allocated to the states on the basis of population, and each state delegation in the Federal Council casts its votes as a unit based on instructions received from its state legislature. The powers of the Federal Council are considerable. All drafts of national legislation, for example, must go first to the Federal Council for approval, and about half of the bills passed by the popularly elected lower house must be approved by the Council. All executive ordinances must gain majority support in the Council. As a result, the German Federal Council is one of the most important upper cham-

bers in any democratic government, rivaling (though not equaling) the U.S. Senate in power and prestige.

The German states also participate in the selection of the president of the Federal Republic and in the selection of judges for the Federal courts. On the other hand, the states' activities are limited by certain provisions of the Basic Law. The protections of human and civil rights set out in the Basic Law also apply to each *Länder*. The death penalty, for example, is outlawed in the Basic Law and cannot be employed by any of the states.

As in the United States, there has been a gradual trend toward greater centralization of decision making at the national level. Overall, however, the *Länder* have remained a very significant force in West German political life.

---

thirty-four counties in North Carolina, and one county each in Maine, Arizona, and Idaho.

The Voting Rights Act has been, by general agreement, an extremely effective piece of legislation. It clearly demonstrated that national intervention into matters once handled by the states could quickly and thoroughly rectify serious and persistent deprivation of democratic rights. Within two years of passage of the act, black registration in the South had increased

by more than 1,280,000. The percentage of blacks in the South registered to vote jumped from 33 percent in 1964 to 59 percent in 1972. And by 1976, more than twenty-two hundred blacks held public office in the South.

The Act was renewed in 1970 and again in 1975, and its provisions were extended to bar discrimination against Hispanic-Americans, American Indians, and other minorities. In addition, certain states and counties with substantial non-English-speaking minorities were required to supply bilingual election materials.

The resounding success of the Voting Rights Act was one reason President Reagan recommended that it *not* be renewed a third time in 1982. In addition, he maintained that the act discriminated against the South and exercised a stranglehold on state and local government. In the end, however, backers of an extension of the act won the day, even gaining the support of the Reagan administration. The requirement for bilingual ballots and election materials was extended ten years, and a controversial section of the act that required the preclearance of all election law changes with the Justice Department was extended for twenty-five years.

## Conclusions

It is one of the happy accidents of the federal system that a single courageous state may . . . serve as a laboratory and try novel social and economic experiments without risk to the rest of the country.   *Associate Justice Louis Brandeis*

The states are prisoners of their own freedom.   *Barney Frank, Massachusetts state legislator, 1979*[8]

Half of all Americans now live in states other than the ones in which they were born. Twenty percent of the country's population moves every year. Problems no longer come cut to state-size shapes—if they

August 6, 1965. One hundred years after the Civil War, President Lyndon Johnson signs the bill that, once effectively enforced, would finally provide adequate protections for black voters. The consequences of the Voting Rights Act were dramatic: black registration increased tremendously. The sign shows no exaggeration: Jim Crow was finally dead.

ever did. As we have already noted, major cities often face issues of national scope, and many environmental, health, energy, and economic problems cannot be confined within convenient state boundaries. Given these facts, does it make sense to remain tied to the concept of state government.

Those who argue for the continued significance of the states can draw on traditional arguments for decentralization. States and localities still do much of the workaday business of government—schooling, policing, licensing. As Justice Brandeis noted, the states do provide many different arenas for experiment, innovation, and local adaptation. For example, elimination of the death penalty, provision for old age pensions, regulation of railroads, and decriminalization of marijuana were first accomplished at the state level. States also pioneered in developing the income tax, child labor laws, and the vote for women and eighteen-year-olds. States also serve to keep government closer to the people and give room for popular participation in policy making. State governments can occasionally respond more swiftly to popular sentiment—through processes such as the **initiative** (whereby citizens can put a proposal on the ballot) or the **referendum** (whereby citizens can vote on a piece of legislation through the ballot)—than can the federal government.

Thus, states can be experimental, can keep in touch with popular sentiment, and can help government adapt to changing conditions. But several factors work against the states. State governments are often antiquated in structure and procedures, and they frequently are even more susceptible to corruption and to the pressures of special interests—local elites or intense majorities—than is the federal government. We must also question the worth of providing fifty separate jurisdictions with fifty kinds of marriage and divorce laws, criminal courts, prison systems, alcoholic beverage controls, tax systems, educational and welfare arrangements, and so on. Is this an indication of a healthy localism or of a confusing lack of national standards?

Another growing problem in recent years has been the use of the autonomy the states possess in the economic sphere. As the states have competed with one another for industry, they commonly have granted

special tax breaks to corporations, attempted to keep union activity low, reduced corporate income taxes, and generally altered state economic policies to suit large businesses. States now take pride in the fact they have enticed industries away from other states, even when the latter desperately needed the jobs provided. States also have shown an increased reluctance to pass rules that businesses may frown upon. In 1976, for example, Massachusetts voters defeated a proposal that would have ended discount electrical rates for large industrial users. They had been persuaded that passage of such a rule would have amounted to economic suicide for the state. The one obvious remedy for this destructive state-versus-state competition is national action—a uniform federal welfare plan, national health coverage, uniform levels of workers' compensation, and a uniform policy on trade unions.

In toting up the balance sheet of democracy in relation to U.S. federalism, we must note that the federal system almost certainly helped to perpetuate the evils of racial segregation. The denial of basic rights to black citizens was probably made easier by the division of powers between the state and national governments. It can be argued, of course, that had the nation not been divided into states, a form of national segregation may have resulted. In such a case, however, a clear confrontation with the reality of racism might have come earlier, and the issues been resolved more thoroughly in a democratic direction. On balance, federalism served to shelter racism and block solutions to racial problems.

Another negative aspect of our federal system was the longstanding malapportionment of state legislative districts. In this instance, too, democracy was damaged, and that damage clearly grew out of the politics that federal arrangements made possible.

A third negative factor has been the common tendency of many states to neglect minorities, the poor, and other relatively powerless groups. Even more than the federal government, state governments are vulnerable to domination by well-organized and financially powerful groups.

The major question that we cannot answer is what U.S. political life would be like in the absence of the current federal system. What would a unitary

United States look like, or a United States divided along regional lines—say, into five or six major areas? What would we lose if we dismantled the existing states? More to the point of this book, what would democracy gain or lose? It is hard to escape the impression that democracy would lose rather little.

## NOTES

1  4 Wheaton 316.

2  314 U.S. 160 (1941).

3  Quoted in Samuel H. Beer, "The Ideas of the Nation," *New Republic*, July 1982, pp. 19–26.

4  *Ibid.*

5  7 Peters 243 (1833).

6  John Herbers, "State Finance Aid Programs Reduced by U.S., Study Finds," *New York Times*, 10 June 1984.

7  377 U.S. 533.

8  Both quotes cited in Barney Frank, "Sorry States," *New Republic*, 29 December 1979.

## SELECTED READINGS

### The legal mechanisms of federalism

Among the more provocative discussions of federalism are William Riker, *Federalism* (Boston: Little, Brown, 1964); Ivo Duchacek, *Comparative Federalism: The Territorial Dimension of Politics* (New York: Holt, 1970); and Valerie Earle, ed., *Federalism: Infinite Variety in Theory and Practice* (Itasca, Ill.: F. E. Peacock, 1968).

### The evolution of federalism

For general overviews, see Samuel H. Beer, "The Idea of the Nation," *New Republic*, July 1982, pp. 19–26; and Daniel Elazar, *The American Partnership: Inter-Governmental Cooperation in 19th Century America* (Chicago: University of Chicago Press, 1962). For further discussion of the Supreme Court's role in the evolution of federalism, see Alfred H. Kelly and Winfred A. Harbison, *The American Constitution, Its Origins and Development* (New York: W. W. Norton, 1970), Chapters 21–28.

The development of federalism is described in Daniel Elazar, "The Shaping of Intergovernmental Relations in the Twentieth Century," *Annals of the Academy of Political and Social Science*, May 1965, pp. 11–22, and Deil Wright, *Understanding Intergovernmental Relations* (North Scituate, Mass.: Duxbury Press, 1978).

For a discussion of recent federal programs, see James A. Duffy, *Domestic Affairs* (New York: Simon & Schuster, 1978), Chapter 10; Richard P. Nathan, et al., *Revenue Sharing: The Second Round* (Washington, D.C.: The Brookings Institution, 1977); John L. Palmer and Isabell V. Sawhill, eds., *The Reagan Experiment* (Washington, D.C.: Urban Institute Press, 1982).

### Policy reponsibilities of the states

For discussions of the states and state-level policy making from various points of view, see Ira Sharkansky, *The Maligned States* (New York: McGraw-Hill, 1972); Terry Sanford, *Storm over the States* (New York: McGraw-Hill, 1967); and Thomas Dye, *Politics, Economics and the Public* (Chicago: Rand McNally, 1966).

### Tensions in the contemporary federal system

On the geographic shift of political power in the United States, see Kirkpatrick Sale, *Power Shift* (New York: Vintage, 1976); Thomas R. Dye, *Politics in States and Communities*, 4th ed., (Englewood Cliffs, N.J.: Prentice-Hall, 1981), Chapter 1. On cities and infrastructure, see Roscoe C. Martin, *The Cities and the Federal System* (New York: Atherton, 1965). A wide range of issues is discussed in Jeffrey R. Henig, *Public Policy and Federalism: Issues in State and Local Politics* (New York: St. Martin's, 1985).

### Federal intervention for democratic principles

For discussions of reapportionment, see Robert B. McKay, *Reapportionment: The Law and Politics of Equal Representation* (New York: Twentieth Century Fund, 1965); and Gordon E. Baker, *The Reapportionment Revolution* (New York: Random House, 1966).

An enormous amount has been written about voting rights in the United States. For a good introduction, see the record of the voting rights hearings before Subcommittee No. 5 of the Committee on the Judiciary, House of Representatives, 89th Congress, 1st session, on H.R. 6400 (Washington, D.C.: U.S. Government Printing Office, 1965). Also see Howard Ball, *Compromised Compliance: Implementation of the 1965 Voting Rights Act* (Westport, Conn.: Greenwood Press, 1982).

# Chapter five

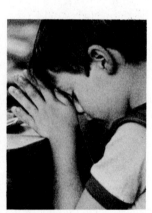

# The evolution of rights and liberties

# Democracy with a human face

IN 1968 a reform movement surged through the Communist Party of Czechoslovakia. The reformers, including several leaders of the party, wanted to "liberalize" political life in that country. They envisioned a socialist society free from official repression, in which dissent was possible, differing ideas could contend openly, individuals were protected against arbitrary arrest, and the basic civil liberties of citizens were honored by the authorities. The Czech reformers termed the goal of their movement "Socialism with a human face," to signify the shift from an oppressive to a humane form of socialist society. In August 1968, however, the liberalization movement was crushed by Soviet and other Warsaw Pact troops, with whose backing a totalitarian regime was reinstalled.

For the Czech reformers, socialism alone was far from enough: only if socialism were humanized through a respect for individual and group rights would a just society be established. The same is true of democracy. For the democratic creed to maintain its full meaning, majority rule must be accompanied by adequate provisions for individual liberties and rights. Without such protections, democracy can degenerate into yet another system of oppression and exploitation, despite the noble intentions embodied in the concept of majority rule.

The concept underlying civil liberties is that citizens must be protected against an overbearing government; that behind civil rights is that all citizens, regardless of race, sex, national origin, or religion, should receive equal treatment under the law. If these concepts sound simple enough in theory, they have not been easy to implement in practice, as U.S. history shows. In the eighteenth century, at the time the Constitution and the Bill of Rights were written, there was a particular conception of basic rights and liberties, based on the ideals of classical liberalism. This conception included freedom of speech and of religion, protection against arbitrary uses of governmental power, and protection of property rights. Other rights and liberties were not fully accepted, however. The right to vote—the most basic democratic right—was not acknowledged to apply to women or slaves. And the concept of equal treatment under the law was only in its infancy at the end of the eighteenth century.

The realities of twentieth-century life have necessarily altered our conceptions of rights and liberties. Eighteenth-century ideas of individual rights now are widely viewed as basic but insufficient. Modern societies must face not only the problem of arbitrary and unrepresentative government, as the American revolutionaries did, but also the complex

103

problems posed by industrial civilization. Accordingly, the rights and liberties of a twentieth-century citizen are generally acknowledged to include the right to form trade unions, the right to a reasonably safe and healthy environment, the right to an education, and several others. The classical liberal view of basic rights and liberties has had to be broadened considerably to cover contemporary social, political, and economic realities.

Nevertheless, this chapter opens with an examination of eighteenth-century rights and liberties, since even such long-accepted concepts have remained highly controversial in application. Throughout U.S. history, the interpretation of such basic democratic concepts as free speech and freedom of religion has been the subject of numerous and often fierce disputes. After covering those disputes, we will turn to the struggle to realize the ideal of equal protection of the law for all, and then to a consideration of rights and liberties unique to the twentieth century.

If this nation's realizations of various liberties and rights has been far from perfect, it is to our credit

104

that we have fought over them and incorporated them to a substantial degree in our political life. The Czechs would envy us at least for this.

## The Bill of Rights and constitutional protections

What we call the **Bill of Rights** was not included in the original Constitution. As noted in Chapter 3, the first ten amendments were added to mollify the Antifederalists, who agreed to back the Constitution only when promised that a specific list of liberties would be appended to the new document following ratification. This was done by the First Congress and made part of the Constitution by 1791.

The protections included in the Bill of Rights are the ones thought at the time sufficient to provide the opportunity for a decent life for each citizen, to guard against arbitrary government interference, and to

August 1968. "Socialism with a human face" comes to an end, as Warsaw Pact tanks roll into Prague. A more liberal society, with free debate and discussion, was apparently not to be tolerated by the Soviet Union.

protect dissent. The rights most central to the preservation of democratic politics are those listed in the First and Fifth amendments.

*First Amendment:* Freedom of speech, press, and assembly; the right to petition for a redress of grievances; freedom of religion, along with prohibition of an "establishment of religion."*

*Fifth Amendment:* Protection from loss of life, liberty, and property without due process of law.

Other significant protections in the Bill of Rights include:

*Fourth Amendment:* Prohibition of unreasonable searches and seizures.

*Fifth Amendment:* Protection from being tried twice for the same crime and from being forced to testify against oneself.

*Sixth Amendment:* Rights to a speedy trial, to counsel, to confront hostile witnesses, and to know the charges against oneself.

*Seventh Amendment:* Right to a jury trial.

*Eighth Amendment:* Prohibition of excessive bail and fines and of cruel and unusual punishments.

The Third Amendment deals with an issue of little importance today—the quartering of soldiers in private homes. Until very recently, the Second Amendment's guarantee of the right to bear arms for the purpose of maintaining a militia seemed equally irrelevant to modern life; gun control opponents, however, have taken to citing it as a constitutional bar to governmental regulation of gun ownership. The Ninth and Tenth amendments offer vague cautions that the enumeration of rights and powers in the Constitution does not disparage or deny other rights held by the people or the states.

U.S. legal history has been replete with controversies over the interpretation of these rights. How do they apply to particular situations? Does free speech mean citizens may criticize the government in time of war? Or advocate resistance to the draft? Does the right to assemble mean groups may gather in order to advocate violence against other groups? Does prohibition of an "establishment" of religion mean that even nonsectarian prayers in schools are unconstitutional? Does free exercise of religion mean that polygamy is permissible if one's religion sanctions it? Just when does a search become "unreasonable"? Is the death penalty a form of "cruel and unusual punishment"? Is the right to counsel applicable in *all* cases?

The issues raised by these questions have formed the constitutional backdrop for significant struggles over the meaning of civil liberties and rights in U.S. political history. Of course, many of the issues we confront today in attempting to give meaning to democratic ideals are rather different from those faced by the framers of the Constitution. The framers did not have to take into account such central elements of modern-day life as the mass media, a powerful and activist government, mass public education, and huge corporations. We can see in the Bill of Rights both issues fundamental to democratic politics at any time and place and issues that reflect more precisely the time and place in which the document originated.

## Federalism and civil liberties

*As we will see later in this chapter, the phrase "establishment of religion" has been subject to many interpretations. Some have argued that it prohibits only an official state religion; others have maintained that it excludes all favoritism toward any religion, or even toward religion in general.

For much of U.S. history the protections enumerated in the Bill of Rights were not applied to state governments. As noted in Chapter 4, the Supreme Court held in *Barron* v. *Baltimore* (1833) that the Bill of

Rights was meant to apply solely to the national government. According to the Court, the Bill of Rights placed no restrictions on the actions of state and local governments, who were free to develop their own policies on civil liberties.

This view remained largely unchallenged until the ratification, in the aftermath of the Civil War, of the Thirteenth, Fourteenth, and Fifteenth amendments, which abolished slavery and extended the rights of citizenship (including the vote) to former slaves. The Fourteenth Amendment, in particular, raised the question of state versus federal responsibility for the enforcement of civil rights and liberties. That

amendment states, in part, that "no State shall make or enforce any law which shall abridge the privileges or immunities of citizens of the United States." If the "privileges and immunities" on which the states were forbidden to encroach were interpreted to be those mentioned in the Bill of Rights, then the amendment could be viewed as providing the basis for a unitary national civil liberties policy—one applicable to every state.

The question of how the privileges and immunities clause should be interpreted came before the Supreme Court in the *Slaughterhouse Cases* of 1873.[1] At issue was a Louisiana state law creating a slaugh-

**TABLE 5.1**
## Case-by-case incorporation of Bill of Rights provisions into the Fourteenth Amendment

| Provision | Amendment | Year | Case |
|---|---|---|---|
| "Public use" and "just compensation" conditions in the taking of private property by government | V | 1896 and 1897 | *Missouri Pacific Railway Co. v. Nebraska; Chicago, Burlington & Quincy Railway Co. v. Chicago* |
| Freedom of speech | I | 1927 | *Fiske v. Kansas; Gitlow v. New York; Gilbert v. Minnesota* |
| Freedom of the press | I | 1931 | *Near v. Minnesota* |
| Fair trial and right to counsel in capital cases | VI | 1932 | *Powell v. Alabama* |
| Freedom of religion | I | 1934 | *Hamilton v. Regents of Univ. of California* |
| Freedom of assembly and, by implication, freedom to petition for redress of grievances | I | 1937 | *DeJonge v. Oregon* |
| Free exercise of religious belief | I | 1940 | *Cantwell v. Connecticut* |
| Separation of church and state; prohibition of the establishment of religion | I | 1947 | *Everson v. Board of Education* |
| Right to public trial | VI | 1948 | *In re Oliver* |
| Right against unreasonable searches and seizures | IV | 1949 | *Wolf v. Colorado* |
| Freedom of association | I | 1958 | *NAACP v. Alabama* |
| Exclusionary rule as concomitant of unreasonable searches and seizures | IV | 1961 | *Mapp v. Ohio* |
| Right against cruel and unusual punishments | VIII | 1962 | *Robinson v. California* |
| Right to counsel in all felony cases | VI | 1963 | *Gideon v. Wainwright* |
| Right against self-incrimination | V | 1964 | *Malloy v. Hogan; Murphy v. Waterfront Commission* |
| Right to confront witnesses | VI | 1965 | *Pointer v. Texas* |
| Right to privacy | Various | 1965 | *Griswold v. Connecticut* |

terhouse monopoly. Independent butchers had brought suit against the state, claiming that the establishment of such a monopoly violated their "privileges and immunities" under the Fourteenth Amendment. In rejecting that argument, the Court took an extremely restrictive view of the clause. Ruling that the clause did not extend to the states responsibility for enforcing the Bill of Rights, the Court held that national citizenship must be distinguished from state citizenship. This decision represented an enormous setback for those who wished to see the nationalization of civil liberties.

The Court maintained this stance until the turn of the century, when it began to apply national standards to state actions in the area of civil liberties under two other clauses of the Fourteenth Amendment: the due process clause, which stipulates that no state may deprive a person of life, liberty, or property without due process of law; and the equal protection clause, which mandates that no state may deny any person equal protection of the laws. In *Gitlow* v. *New York* (1925), the Supreme Court argued that "freedom of speech and of the press, which are protected by the First Amendment from abridgement by Congress, are among the fundamental personal rights and liberties protected by the due process clause of

TABLE 5.1 continued

| Provision | Amendment | Year | Case |
|---|---|---|---|
| Right to impartial jury | VI | 1966 | *Parker* v. *Gladden* |
| Right to speedy trial | VI | 1967 | *Klopfer* v. *North Carolina* |
| Right to compulsory process for obtaining witnesses | VI | 1967 | *Washington* v. *Texas* |
| Right to jury trial in cases of serious crime | VI | 1968 | *Duncan* v. *Louisiana* |
| Right against double jeopardy | V | 1969 | *Benton* v. *Maryland* |
| Right to counsel in all criminal cases entailing a jail term | VI | 1972 | *Argersinger* v. *Hamlin* |

*Other incorporated provisions*

| | | | |
|---|---|---|---|
| Right of petition | I | | Included by implication of other First Amendment incorporations |
| Right to be informed of the nature and cause of the accusation | VI | | Included by implication of other Sixth Amendment incorporations |

| | Provisions not incorporated | | |
|---|---|---|---|
| | II | | All |
| | III | | All |
| | V | | Right to indictment by grand jury |
| | VII | | All |
| | VIII | | Right against excessive bail; right against excessive fines |

Source: H. W. Chase and C. Ducat, *1980 Supplement to Constitutional Interpretation: Cases, Essays, Materials* (St. Paul: West Publishing Co., 1980), pp. 888–90.

the Fourteenth Amendment from impairment by the states."[2] Note that the Court did not automatically apply the entire Bill of Rights to the states; rather, it designated certain freedoms guaranteed in the **First Amendment** as so fundamental that they must be universally protected.

Following the *Gitlow* decision, the Supreme Court gradually expanded the number of Bill of Rights provisions that the states may not violate. Some modern-day justices—most notably Hugo Black and William O. Douglas—have argued that the entire Bill of Rights should pertain to the states—the doctrine that was rejected in the *Slaughterhouse Cases*. Although this view has never been explicitly accepted by a majority of the Court, over the years the justices have incorporated almost the entire Bill of Rights into the Fourteenth Amendment by means of the due process and equal protection clauses. As a result, proponents of a uniform, national civil liberties policy have achieved incrementally what they were unable to achieve in one blow.

This excursion into the field of constitutional law is of more than historical importance, for it reflects a significant policy choice. It can be argued that certain liberties are so basic to democratic life that they must be protected against interference in every corner of the country. Conversely, it can be contended that a large, complex nation is best served by the development of standards and policies at the local level. For example, should the interpretation of "pornography" be identical in New York City and in rural Arkansas? Or should "pornography" mean one thing in New York and something else in an area with radically different social mores? As a polity, we have moved steadily in the first of these directions over the past half-century.

## Freedom of speech

The classical liberal justification of freedom of speech (and the press) is that it is essential if mankind is to advance intellectually—that the competition of ideas is a necessary condition of progress.[3] Even if an unpopular view turns out to be entirely incorrect, in this view, it should still be tolerated, because the challenge of the false view will force the holders of truth to examine their position and to flex their intellectual muscles.

A different basis for defending free speech was provided by the political philosopher Alexander Meiklejohn. Free speech, according to Meiklejohn, becomes necessary once people have decided to govern themselves: that is, free speech is mandated by a prior commitment to self-government.[4] For the people to choose the rules under which government functions, they need free access to information so that they can make intelligent, informed choices. A logical corollary to this premise is that a distinction can be drawn between political speech (speech that is related to self-government) and nonpolitical speech, and that only the former must be protected absolutely. Thus, Meiklejohn could argue, quite consistently, that free speech for political radicals must be protected, whereas slander and libel may be outlawed.

Especially in this century, the Supreme Court has largely followed Meiklejohn's approach. Acknowledging that the basic justification for free speech is its contribution to self-government, the Court has repeatedly ruled that public policy requires greater freedom of discussion on political than on other matters.

Two sides of an argument, expressed vividly and publicly. This is one of the things free speech is all about: forming opinions, organizing them, putting them forward—and being able to do so without fear.

# The Alien and Sedition Acts of 1798

The French Revolution stirred intense debate in the new United States. Thomas Jefferson and others of similar views, known as Jeffersonian Republicans, welcomed the revolutionary developments in France. The more conservative Federalists, however, generally decried what they viewed as the increasingly destructive and radical direction the revolution seemed to be taking. Feelings grew so high that when Jefferson went to Philadelphia in March 1797 to take the oath of office as vice-president, he noted that "men who have been intimate all their lives, cross the streets to avoid meeting, and turn their heads another way, lest they should be obliged to touch their hats." This deep-seated fear of the radicalism of the French revolutionaries led to the new republic's first brush with political repression.

In 1798, the Federalist-dominated Congress passed the Naturalization Act and the Alien and Sedition Acts, which were ostensibly aimed at protecting the nation from the alleged threat from France. In reality, however, the acts were directed as much at the Republican opposition as at any supposed foreign danger. The Naturalization Act increased the period of residence required to gain U.S. citizenship from five to fourteen years, and the Alien Act and the Alien Enemies Act gave the president the power to expel foreigners by executive decree. Far more controversial was the Sedition Act, which made it a criminal offense to

---

**Setting limits on dissent:** After the Sedition Act of 1798 (see box), Congress made no attempt to regulate free speech until the passage of the Espionage Act of 1917 and the Sedition Act of 1918. Both acts were designed to curb criticism of the government during World War I. In a significant series of cases in the postwar period, the Supreme Court passed on the constitutionality of these acts in rulings that have largely shaped the legal debate on free speech matters to the present day. All three cases examined here involved extremely controversial political speech. Through these cases we can trace a gradual evolution of the Court's approach to setting limits on dissent. We should also note the profound importance in these cases of the political and social atmosphere of the times.[5]

The three cases referred to are *Schenck* v. *United States* (1919), *Abrams* v. *United States* (1919), and *Gitlow* v. *New York* (1925). All three contained similar elements.

*Schenck* v. *United States*. In 1917 Charles T. Schenck, a Socialist Party official, mailed out one hundred and fifty thousand leaflets urging eligible young men to resist the draft. The leaflets described conscription as despotism and urged citizens to defend their rights against the interests of Wall Street. Schenck was convicted under the Espionage Act.

*Abrams* v. *United States*. In 1919, Jacob Abrams and five associates, all Russian-Jewish immigrants, distributed leaflets (by throwing them out of a factory window in New York) criticizing U.S. involvement on the side of anti-Bolshevik forces in the Soviet Union. The leaflets branded President Woodrow Wilson a hypocrite and a tool of Wall Street and called on workers to join a general strike. In 1919, four of the defendants were convicted under the Sedition Act and sentenced to twenty years in prison.

*Gitlow* v. *New York*. In 1925, Benjamin Gitlow, a radical socialist, was convicted under New York State's Criminal Anarchy Act of 1902 of advocating the violent overthrow of the government. The main evidence against him was a theoretical piece he had written titled *Left Wing Manifesto*.

In none of the cases was any evidence advanced that the pamphlets, leaflets, or theoretical writings had had any noticeable effect on the conduct of those who read them. Accordingly, the issue in each case

speak or write against Congress or the president with the "intent to defame" or bring either into contempt. Such vague legislation practically invited abuse, of which examples were soon forthcoming. Not surprisingly, every person charged under the act was a Republican or Republican sympathizer, including many newspaper editors, and every judge and almost every juror in these cases was a Federalist. Of the 25 persons prosecuted under the Sedition Act, ten were convicted and punished with heavy fines or jail sentences.

Despite the intimidating presence of the act, criticism of the government continued, and the election of 1800 put Jefferson into the White House (although only after several dozen ballots in the House of Representatives were required to break a deadlock between Jefferson and Aaron Burr). All four acts were allowed to expire in 1800 and 1801.

was whether the government could limit freedom of expression because of *possible* interference with a governmental function, or because it found certain views threatening. How far, in other words, did freedom of speech extend? If some citizens opposed a war as immoral, and urged others to do the same, why would their activities not be protected under the First Amendment?

In *Schenck* the court unanimously upheld Schenck's conviction. Justice Oliver Wendell Holmes, in expressing the Court's view, attempted to define the free speech issues involved:

We admit that in many places and in ordinary times the defendants in saying all that was said in the circular would have been within their constitutional rights. But the character of every act depends upon the circumstances in which it is done. The most stringent protection of free speech would not protect a man in falsely shouting fire in a theatre and causing a panic. It does not even protect a man from an injunction against uttering words that may have all the effect of force. The question in every case is whether the words used are used in such circumstances and are of such a nature as to create a clear and present danger that they will

bring about the substantive evils that Congress has a right to prevent.[6]

Critics of this famous opinion have argued that although the government may have had the right to prevent obstruction of the draft, Schenck's pamphlet simply did not represent the "clear and present danger" alluded to by Holmes.

The convictions of Jacob Abrams and his associates were also upheld by the Court. In this case, however, Justices Holmes and Louis Brandeis dissented, arguing that

the best test of truth is the power of thought to get itself accepted in the competition of the market. . . . That at any rate is the theory of our Constitution. It is an experiment, as all life is an experiment . . . we should be eternally vigilant against attempts to check the expressions of opinions that we loathe and believe to be fraught with danger, unless they so imminently threaten immediate interference with the lawful and pressing purposes of the law that an immediate check is required to save the country.

To the Court majority, however, the convictions were justified on the grounds that the activities involved had a "dangerous or bad tendency"—that they were meant to instigate riot or revolution. These two positions set the parameters for subsequent debate over the limits of speech and opinion.

In *Gitlow*, Holmes and Brandeis again dissented from the Court's ruling. Their minority opinion sets out the implications of their views even more fully:

Every idea is an incitement. It offers itself for belief and if believed it is acted on. . . . If in the long run the beliefs expressed in proletarian dictatorship are destined to be accepted by the dominant forces of the community, the only meaning of free speech is that they should be given their chance and have their way.[7]

A majority of justices upheld Gitlow's conviction. But, as we have seen, the Court did take the important step of acknowledging that the Fourteenth Amendment applied to the freedoms of speech and press in the states.

Not until the 1930s did a majority of the Court begin to come around to the Holmes-Brandeis view. In several cases decided in that decade, the right of communists to express their views was upheld by the Court, on the grounds that the activities involved did not include plans for action, but simply the articulation of opinions.

**The Smith Act cases:** In 1940, Congress passed the Smith Act, which made it a crime to knowingly advocate or teach, or to organize or knowingly become a member of a group that advocated the violent overthrow of any governmental unit of the United States. The Smith Act, like most other sedition and criminal anarchy statutes, was more concerned with speech than with acts against the government.

In 1949, indictments were brought under the act against eleven leaders of the U.S. Communist Party. They were charged not with committing overt acts against the government, or even with the planning of such acts, but rather with teaching the duty and necessity of revolution from Marxist texts. All eleven were convicted, and the Supreme Court in 1951 upheld the convictions in *Dennis et al.* v. *United States*. Writing for the Court majority, Chief Justice Fred M. Vinson argued:

If the government is aware that a group aiming at its overthrow is attempting to indoctrinate its members and to commit them to a course whereby they will strike when the leaders feel the circumstances permit, action by the Government is required. . . . The damage which such attempts create both physically and politically to a nation makes it impossible to measure the validity in terms of the probability of success, or the immediacy of a successful attempt. . . . We must therefore reject the contention that success or probability of success is the criterion.

From this perspective, it was irrelevant whether or not there was any evidence of contemplated or planned-for future action. If people merely disseminated the idea of revolution, the government was justified in prosecuting them.

Commenting on this position in a dissenting opinion, Justice William O. Douglas wrote:

If this were a case where those who claimed protection under the First Amendment were teaching the techniques of sabotage, the assassination of the President . . . the planting of bombs, the art of street warfare . . . I would

have no doubts. . . . The case was argued as if those were the facts. That is easy and it has popular appeal, for the activities of Communists in plotting and scheming against the free world are common knowledge. But the fact is that no such evidence was introduced at the trial. . . . What petitioners did was to organize to teach and themselves teach the Marxist-Leninist doctrine contained in four books. . . . The opinion of the Court does not outlaw those texts. . . . But if the books themselves are not outlawed . . . by what reasoning does their use in a classroom become a crime? The crime then depends not on what is taught, but on who the teacher is. . . . Once we start down that road we enter territory dangerous to the liberties of every citizen.[8]

Six years later, in *Yates* v. *United States* (1957), the Court shifted its ground by returning to the "clear and present danger" test.[9] By a 6–1 vote, the Court overturned the convictions under the Smith Act of five second-rank leaders of the U.S. Communist Party and ordered that the nine other party officials involved in the case be remanded for new trials. (None was ever retried.) The Court majority in *Yates* argued that conviction under the Smith Act required proof not just that defendants had advocated a belief in revolution in the abstract, but that they had advocated action to bring revolution about. The decision in *Yates* in effect made the Smith Act relatively useless to federal prosecutors.

**Contemporary trends:** Since *Yates* the Court has not deviated noticeably from the "clear and present danger" standard in comparable cases—most notably, the so-called Pentagon Papers case in 1971. During the Vietnam War, several convictions for draft card burning, flag desecration, and similar activities were upheld by the Court, but there were no free speech convictions on the order of *Schenck* or *Abrams*.

In recent decades the Court has established three basic tests of the constitutionality of laws and regulations designed to limit free expression. Under the concept of "strict scrutiny," the government must assume the burden of proving a compelling interest in its restriction of speech. Also, under the doctrine of "overbreadth," statutes that purport to limit expression must be narrowly and specifically drawn. Finally, the Court has paid careful attention to the

Symbolic speech, 1968. Tommie Smith and Juan Carlos, medal winners at the Mexico City Olympics, raise their fists in a gesture to black power as "The Star Spangled Banner" is played. Their act stirred considerable criticism, for the summer of 1968 was a time of intense racial polarization in the United States. Only months earlier, Martin Luther King, Jr., had been assassinated.

"chilling effect" of statutes: that is, a law may be held unconstitutional if its mere existence "chills," or impairs, the exercise of First Amendment rights. In *Shelton* v. *Tucker* (1960), for example, the Court cited the "chilling effect" in invalidating an Arkansas statute that had required every schoolteacher to file an annual report of all organizations to which he or she belonged or contributed money.[10]

**Symbolic speech and "fighting words":** Not all expression of views or ideas takes the form of reasoned political speech. Often, political or social views are expressed through symbolic gestures, such as picketing, the wearing of armbands, or the carrying of signs or placards. Sometimes people express themselves in particularly heated or intense ways—cursing, screaming, haranguing. Or they may utter "fighting words," or carry on symbolic activities in sensitive places such as schools, public buildings, or other centers of public activity. Such intense and/or symbolic expressions of views have raised numerous and complicated First Amendment issues.

Over the years, the Supreme Court has applied First Amendment protections to various forms of symbolic speech and heated expression of views and denied them to others. In *Amalgamated Food Employees Local 590* v. *Logan Valley Plaza, Inc.* (1968), for example, the Court held that the "speech" aspect of picketing is fully protected under the First Amendment, but that the conduct of picketers is not. "Because of this intermingling of protected and unprotected elements," the Court decided, "picketing can be subject to controls that would not be constitutionally permissible in the case of pure speech."

Another limitation on symbolic speech came in *United States* v. *O'Brien* (1968), in which the Court held that the burning of draft cards as a symbolic protest was not a constitutionally protected form of free speech.[11] The justices could not accept the principle that an "apparently limitless variety of conduct can be labeled 'speech' whenever the person engaging in the conduct intends thereby to express an idea."[12]

In *Tinker* v. *Des Moines Community School District* (1969), however, the Court upheld the right of students to make a symbolic protest against the Vietnam War by wearing black armbands to school. Such a practice, the justices found, represented a legitimate form of free speech and so was protected under the First Amendment, except for cases in which it would cause serious disruption of school activities.[13]

As for "fighting words," the Court has shown considerable tolerance toward what might seem to be potentially disruptive forms of expression. In 1942, in *Chaplinsky* v. *New Hampshire*, the Court did uphold the right of the state to punish the utterance of "fighting words."[14] In 1972, in contrast, it refused

113

# Comparative perspective
## Political extremism in Australia and West Germany

The problem of how to define and deal with political groups regarded as extremist or politically unacceptable has troubled many democratic countries, especially in the decade following World War II. In the United States, as we have seen, groups that advocated the violent overthrow of the government were outlawed under the Smith Act. We will now examine how two other societies dealt with this issue.

In Australia, the conservative coalition government of Prime Minister Robert Menzies pushed through parliament in 1950 a bill outlawing the Australian Communist Party (ACP). The year is significant: war had just broken out in Korea, and Australian troops were involved in the fighting there. The ACP and several labor unions took the new legislation to the Australian High Court for review. The Court found that the political situation in Australia was not perilous enough to warrant such a serious infringement of civil liberties.

Another approach to the problem of dealing with political extremism in the postwar era was followed by the new Federal Republic of Germany (West Germany). The Basic Law (the equivalent of a constitution) of the Federal Republic prohibited the formation of antidemocratic political groups. This prohibition was intended principally to forestall the revival of the Nazi Party or any similar organization. In 1949, however, a right-wing political group launched the Socialist Reich Party (SRP), whose views were close to those of the Nazis. The SRP participated in elections and won several seats in state and national voting. In 1951 the West German government petitioned the Constitutional Court (equivalent, roughly, to the U.S. Supreme Court) to declare the SRP unconstitutional under the Basic Law. The Court, noting the party's similarities to Nazism, its anti-Semitism, and its recruiting of leaders who had been active Nazis, banned the SRP.

At roughly the same time, the German government also moved against the German Communist Party (KPD). With the KPD, however, the case for political extremism was less clear-cut, and the political situation more complicated. German communists had fought bitterly against the Nazis both before and during World War II, and to banish them from postwar political life seemed incongruous to many. Then, too, neighboring East Germany, with which the Federal Republic had tense relations, was committed to a communist ideology. Finally, the KPD was relatively popular, having polled a respectable 1.4 million votes in the last election. For these reasons, the Constitutional Court delayed issuing a ruling for more than four years, in the hope that the matter would be resolved in some other way. When the decision was finally handed down, in 1956, it ran to over three hundred pages. The Court found that communist doctrine was not compatible with a democratic political process, since communists were committed to the "class struggle" and were unwilling to recognize and cooperate with the results of democratic elections. Thus the KPD, like the SRP, was banned.

to permit application of a "fighting words" statute against a black man who shouted, "White son of a bitch, I'll kill you," at a white police officer (*Gooding* v. *Wilson*).[15]

More recently, the Court upheld the right of a Nazi group to hold a rally and display the Nazi emblem in a heavily Jewish Chicago suburb (*National Socialist Party* v. *Village of Skokie*, 1977), noting that "anticipation of a hostile audience could not justify . . . prior restraint." In facing this issue of the "angry audience," the Court generally has ruled that assemblies and parades that threaten physical disturbances and serious disorder can be halted by police if a risk of imminent violence has been clearly demonstrated. The justices have also made it clear, however, that the prior obligation of the police is to protect those participating in a rally or meeting, if at all possible.

## Freedom of religion

The very first issue addressed in the First Amendment is the relationship between government and religion—as sensitive an issue today as it was in the eighteenth century. In the amendment, Congress is commanded to make no law "respecting an establishment of religion" (the **establishment clause**) or "prohibiting the free exercise" of religion (the **free exercise clause**). On the most basic level, both clauses are clear: Congress may not establish a state religion or prohibit particular religions. These prohibitions were certainly relevant to the forms of religious intolerance and the official state religions found abundantly in eighteenth-century Europe and America. Throughout the nineteenth century, few controversies developed between the national government and religious groups. In the twentieth century, however, many such controversies have arisen—some of them very subtle and difficult to resolve.

**Establishment of religion:** Was it the intention of the framers of the Bill of Rights merely to prevent the establishment of a national church, such as the Church of England, or to prohibit *any* acts of government that would support certain religions, or even religion in general? Commentators who have taken the latter view have spoken of the need for a "wall of separation" between church and state, to keep government entirely out of matters associated with religion. Most recent church-state controversies have revolved around the many ways that government and religion do, or could, interact.

The best known of these debates has centered around the saying of prayers in public schools. In a series of decisions in the early 1960s, a divided Supreme Court banned even nonsectarian prayers from public schools. In the best known of these cases, *Engel* v. *Vitale* (1962), the Court majority declared unconstitutional the saying of a nondenominational prayer written by the New York State Board of Regents for use in state public schools.[16] The Court later outlawed Bible reading in public schools, even in those that permitted children to be excused if their parents objected. Because such practices aided religion in general, the Court argued, they could not be permitted under the establishment clause. As an alternative, the Court pointed out that religion could be *studied* in any academic context.

Opposition to these rulings was immediate and intense. Many school districts simply refused to comply with the Supreme Court guidelines (see Chapter 17). In addition, proponents of school prayer began working toward passage of a constitutional amendment permitting some religious practices in public schools. According to backers of the proposed amendment, the Bill of Rights was not intended to prohibit all religious exercises in schools, or *any* government involvement with religion.

In June 1985 the Supreme Court struck down by a 6–3 vote an Alabama law that permitted a one-minute period of silent meditation or prayer in public schools. In *Wallace* v. *Jaffree*, the Court affirmed its earlier rulings that "government must pursue a course of complete neutrality toward religion," but indicated at the same time that "moment of silence" laws could be held constitutional as long as they did not have as their chief intention the fostering of religious activity in the classroom. The Alabama law, the ma-

115

jority argued, had intended to characterize prayer "as a favored practice." At the time of the ruling, varying versions of the "moment of silence" law existed in twenty-five states.

Another long-running establishment clause controversy concerns public aid to private schools, most of which are church-related. Generally, the Court's position has been that the state can assist private-school students or support particular private-school programs that are not related to religion, but that it cannot provide assistance to religious instruction. Thus, whereas the Court has upheld tax aid to parents for costs of busing to private schools and the provision of nonreligious textbooks and other study aids from public funds, it has not permitted use of public funds for teachers' salaries, tuition aid, or maintenance and repair of school facilities.

One other sensitive subject has been the tax-exempt status of religious institutions. Many observers have considered the tax-exempt status of church property to be a constitutional violation. The Court ruled on this matter in *Walz* v. *Tax Commission of the City of New York* (1970).[17] Chief Justice Burger argued for the Court majority in this case that tax exemption was constitutional and represents "neither the advancement nor the inhibition of religion." He distinguished tax exemption, an indirect economic subsidy, from direct subsidies, which violate the establishment clause.

Church-related schools and colleges may not, however, keep their tax exemptions while violating federal civil rights legislation, as the Court's ruling in *Bob Jones University* v. *United States* (1983) made clear.[18]

**Free exercise of religion:** The right to the free exercise of religion has been consistently upheld by Supreme Court decisions. As Justice Samuel F. Miller wrote in an 1872 case (*Watson* v. *Jones*) involving a dispute within the Presbyterian church, "In this country the full and free right to entertain any religious doctrine which does not violate the laws of morality and property, and which does not infringe personal rights, is conceded to all."[19] Note how many possible conflicts are contained within those qualifying phrases, however. Many of the legal conflicts

associated with the free exercise clause have hinged on differing interpretations of the "laws of morality."

In *Reynolds* v. *United States* (1878) for example, the Supreme Court upheld a federal law prohibiting polygamy in United States territories.[20] The law had been challenged by the Mormon church, which encouraged its followers to practice polygamy. In upholding the statute, the Court distinguished between religious *beliefs*, which enjoy the full protection of the Constitution, and *actions* based on those beliefs, which can be regulated by government. To allow a person to engage in illegal behavior because of religious beliefs, the Court noted in *Reynolds*, "would be to make the professed doctrines of religious beliefs superior to the law of the land." But exactly *why* polygamy should be illegal, the Court did not make clear. It could be argued that this was a case of the majority deciding what "appropriate morality" should be.

Following *Reynolds*, very few free exercise questions were addressed by the Supreme Court until the early 1940s, when several cases involving the Jehovah's Witnesses reached the Court. At issue in *Minersville School District* v. *Gobitis* (1940) was the expulsion from school of two Jehovah's Witnesses children who had refused to participate in the mandatory salute to the flag and recitation of the Pledge of Allegiance, on the grounds that such an oath violated their religious beliefs and constituted idolatry.[21] The Supreme Court upheld the expulsions, rejecting the contention that the free exercise clause had been violated. Justice Felix Frankfurter, writing for the majority, noted the importance of symbols in American life and argued that "the flag is a symbol of our national unity, transcending all internal differences, however large, within the framework of the Constitution." There was only one dissenter on the Court.

Then, in a remarkable turnabout, the Court reversed itself only three years later, in *West Virginia State Board of Education* v. *Barnette* (1943).[22] Three new members had joined the Court in the intervening years, and in *Barnette* three other justices admitted that they had been wrong in *Gobitis*. In upholding the right of Jehovah's Witnesses to decline to swear an oath, Justice Robert H. Jackson, writing for the majority, stated, "If there is any fixed star in our constitutional constellation, it is that no official, high or petty, can prescribe what shall be orthodox in politics, nationalism, religion, or other matters of opinion or force citizens to confess by word or act their faith therein."

The Supreme Court has also affirmed the right to object to military service on religious grounds. In *United States* v. *Seeger* (1965), the Court extended this concept to cover "sincere and meaningful" religious beliefs that may not be related to a Supreme Being.[23] Five years later, in *Welsh* v. *United States*, the justices upheld the rights of a conscientious objector whose refusal to serve in the armed forces was based on "considerations of public policy."[24] How-

ever, the Court has consistently refused to sanction so-called selective objection to military service: that is, objection based on opposition to a particular war, as opposed to all wars.

## Due process and the rights of the accused

The rights of those accused of crime have always posed difficult issues for democratic societies. There are the inevitable tensions between the need to protect the accused, on the one hand, and to prosecute the guilty, on the other; particularly in times of social strain and tension, the balance seems to tip in the direction of increased police powers. Another complicating factor in U.S. society has been the disproportionate presence in the ranks of defendants of members of minority groups and the poor.

Under Chief Justice Earl Warren, the Supreme Court in the 1960s introduced radical changes into the process by which criminal suspects are apprehended and guilt or innocence is determined. As a rule, the Warren Court attempted to tighten the requirements for establishing legal guilt, principally by placing constraints on the kinds of evidence that could be introduced and the procedures that could be followed in criminal courts. The touchstone of the Court's approach to defining the rights of the accused was the Fifth Amendment's injunction that no person "be deprived of life, liberty or property, without due process of law." In comparison with its predecessors (and, as it turned out, successors), the Warren Court took a decidedly expansive view of the meaning of "**due process.**"

School prayer. No one can prevent students from contemplating their own thoughts, but the Supreme Court has made it clear that *organized* efforts by the government to encourage religious observance in public schools are unconstitutional.

Most fundamentally, the Court significantly broadened the accused's right to counsel, which is guaranteed in the Sixth Amendment. In a series of cases the justices ruled that the accused has the right to be represented by an attorney during interrogation by police, at line-ups, during preliminary hearings, at trial, and during the appeals process. Moreover, in the landmark case of *Gideon* v. *Wainwright* (1963), the Court held that if a defendant could not afford to hire an attorney, the state must provide one.[25] Only if representation by an attorney were guaranteed even to the most indigent defendant, the Court reasoned, would the rights of that defendant be adequately protected.

The second basic principle of the due process revolution launched by the Warren Court was that of *exclusion* of "tainted" evidence: that is, if the state's officers obtain evidence against a defendant by activities that violate the latter's constitutional rights (such as unauthorized searches or improper interrogations), that evidence must be excluded from the trial. In this way, no defendant could be convicted on the basis of illegally obtained evidence. The exclusionary rule also provided a means for regulating the conduct of police officers. If officers cannot use evidence obtained in illegal searches and seizures or interrogations, they presumably will be less likely to engage in such practices.

In a further effort to eradicate police abuses of the rights of suspects, the Court in **Miranda v. Arizona** (1963) dictated guidelines to be followed by police in the interrogation of suspects.[26] All persons arrested, the court declared, must be informed of their right to remain silent and of their right to legal representation during questioning, and must be warned that anything they say may be used against them in court.

To their proponents, the Warren Court's decisions on due process went to the very heart of civil liberties doctrine—the need to protect the dignity and humanity of citizens. The Court argued that certain police and prosecutorial procedures simply did violence to the basic human rights that citizens ought to enjoy. Another defense of the Court's approach is the argument that the best way to avoid the conviction of an innocent person is to establish strict procedural rules governing arrest, interrogation, and trial. Finally, some of the procedural protections set up by the Court, such as the principle of exclusion, were designed to prevent too much intrusion by police in the lives of citizens. Random searches, dragnet arrests, and threatening interrogations of suspects may be useful tools in catching lawbreakers, but they cannot be justified in a society of limited government.

The Warren Court's decisions on due process were and remain controversial. As we noted in Chapter 2, there is a basic ambivalence in U.S. society between the desire for efficient apprehension and punishment of those who break legal norms and the desire for restrictions on the powers of the state in its dealings with individuals.

The notion that the Warren Court had gone too far in protecting criminals at the expense of law-abiding citizens exerted an especially powerful popular appeal in the 1960s, a time of widespread social discontent and fear. The election of President Richard Nixon in 1968 ushered in a gradual retreat from the positions taken by the Warren Court. In his appointments to the Court, President Nixon selected justices who were more sympathetic to efficient law enforcement, and by the mid-1970s it had become evident that the Court's approach to due process rights had changed significantly. Under Chief Justice Warren Burger the Court has, for example, consistently narrowed the application of the "Miranda rules." The Burger Court has not explicitly overruled *Miranda*, but it has whittled away at the breadth of the Warren Court decisions in that and other due process areas.

## Civil rights

A citizen's civil rights are, in effect, guarantees that he or she will be treated *fairly and equally* by government and by those parts of society that government deems must meet those same standards. Among the most basic civil rights are the right to vote, the right to equal employment opportunities, the right to equal education, and the right to equal treatment in housing and in public accommodations. The exact limits of governmentally imposed civil rights have yet to be decided. For example, should all-male bars or clubs be permitted? Should affirmative action be employed to rectify past injustices toward blacks and others? We will discuss some of these contemporary controversies in Chapter 20. Here we will examine the most basic civil rights: the right to vote; fundamental elements of racial equality, including education equality; and equal rights for women.

## The right to vote

The right to vote, also known as the franchise, is the most fundamental of all civil rights in a democracy. Those to whom it is denied are effectively excluded from the basic element of the democratic process— the chance to register one's political views and to help shape the mandate of popular sentiment. The overwhelming importance of the right to vote can be seen most vividly in societies such as contemporary South Africa, in which more than three-fourths of the population is denied any real electoral voice. If black South Africans could express their views democratically, the current government, which supports white supremacy, would undoubtedly be quickly voted out of office.

In the case of South Africa, as in many similar cases, the exclusion of specific groups from the electoral process is part of a larger picture of deprivation of civil rights. Attainment of the right to vote may not in itself provide a total solution to the deprived circumstances of such groups, but it is a necessary step toward the righting of political wrongs.

The history of the right to vote in the United States is one of a gradual, and often bitterly contested, broadening of the franchise. At the time the Constitution was ratified, all states except Vermont still imposed property or tax-paying qualifications on the franchise. Only in Vermont was there universal *manhood* suffrage—the democratic ideal of the day. Women were not seriously considered as potential voters—and the same, of course, applied to slaves.

By the 1820s, most states had dropped property qualifications for voting, and after 1817, universal male suffrage was a prerequisite for admission to the Union. For that time in history, the United States enjoyed a far more democratic suffrage than did any other nation.

Extension of the franchise to black ex-slaves was mandated by the Fifteenth Amendment (1870) but not fully secured until the passage of the Voting Rights Act of 1965. As is described in Chapter 1, women had an even longer struggle to gain the suffrage. Not until ratification of the Nineteenth Amendment, in 1920, did *all* adult citizens of the United States attain the right to vote. Eighteen-year-olds were accorded the right to vote in federal elections in 1970, and that right was extended to state elections through the twenty-sixth Amendment, ratified in 1971.

## Blacks and equal rights

The Declaration of Independence proclaims that "all Men are created equal, that they are endowed by their Creator with certain inalienable Rights, that among these are Life, Liberty, and the Pursuit of Happiness." This revolutionary statement is constantly cited as proof of the fundamental American commitment to equal opportunity. And yet it was written by a slaveowner (Thomas Jefferson) and adopted by a Continental Congress that was unwilling to take action against the slave trade.

When Africans first arrived at Jamestown, Virginia, in the early 1600s, slavery was almost unknown in English society. Initially, blacks were treated as indentured servants who could earn their freedom. As the years passed, however, the need for cheap labor and the belief that "savages" of another race were not entitled to the protection accorded white people were reflected in court decisions that led to the legalization of perpetual servitude for blacks. Judges began to recognize sales and wills specifying complete servitude. Intermarriage between whites and blacks, which had been allowed, was now forbidden in many colonies. Step by step, the debasement and dehumanization of blacks were crystallized in law. Racial discrimination obtained legal sanction, and the law deepened and strengthened prejudice. Finally, as the institution of slavery took definite shape, it created powerful economic interests that were dependent on it. It took a bloody Civil War to alter this situation.

Abolition of slavery and full equality for ex-slaves were the primary goals of the Radical Republicans, who dominated Congress in the late 1860s. By 1876, only eleven years after the end of the Civil War, the Constitution had been permanently altered by the addition of the Thirteenth, Fourteenth, and Fifteenth amendments, which outlawed slavery, made equal protection of the laws a fundamental legal principle, and guaranteed voting rights to ex-slaves. Southern states had to ratify the amendments in order to be readmitted to the Union. During this period, the broad protections of the new constitutional provisions were supported by eleven major civil rights acts passed by Congress.

This monumental civil-rights achievement, however, did not outlast the immediate postwar period. By the 1880s, most of the post–Civil War civil-rights laws had been rendered inoperative by court interpretations and by the unwillingness of either the Congress or the executive to enforce them. It required several generations of constant struggle to alter the patterns of legal segregation established in the late nineteenth and early twentieth centuries. One of the key areas of contention in this battle was public education.

**School desegregation:** In *Plessy* v. *Ferguson* (1896), the Supreme Court sanctioned as constitutional the establishment of "separate but equal" facilities for whites and blacks. The pernicious effects of this doctrine were especially evident in the creation throughout the South of rigidly separate and decidedly unequal school systems for blacks and whites. After years of determined litigation spearheaded by lawyers of the National Association for the Advancement of Colored People (NAACP), the Supreme Court in the 1930s began to recognize that segregation in education involved a denial of basic civil rights for

blacks. A first step in this direction came in the case of *Missouri ex rel. Gaines* v. *Canada* (1938). Lloyd Gaines, a citizen of Missouri and a black graduate of Lincoln University, had applied for admission to the all-white law school of the University of Missouri. Rather than admit Gaines to the state law school, Missouri offered to pay his tuition at any other law school that would admit blacks. Gaines refused to accept this compromise and took his case to court. The Supreme Court held that Gaines was "entitled to be admitted to the law school of the state university in the absence of other and proper provision for his legal training within the state."[27]

The Court went beyond the *Gaines* decision in *Sweatt* v. *Painter* (1950), in which the justices rejected Texas's contention that its new law school for blacks provided the same educational opportunities as those at the University of Texas.[28] In this decision, the Court argued that by segregating black students from whites, the state was preventing blacks from gaining the sorts of interactions that would be essential to a successful law career. This was very close to saying that such segregated education could never in fact be "equal."

The decisions handed down in *Gaines* and *Sweatt* permitted the NAACP to challenge the whole structure of educational segregation. After the Supreme Court accepted school segregation cases for review in 1952, the U.S. Justice Departments entered the fray on the side of those arguing that segregated schools were unconstitutional. Then, in 1954, after a long delay and extremely careful consideration, the Supreme Court unanimously ruled that segregated schools were unconstitutional in **Brown** v. **Board of Education of Topeka**.[29]

The *Brown* case was a landmark in the U.S. legal system's turnaround on the issue of segregation. In the decades following *Plessy*, the Supreme Court had applied increasingly strict standards to the "separate but equal" doctrine but had not questioned the constitutionality of segregation itself. Blacks were granted relief not because they were segregated, but because they were denied equality within a segregated system. In the series of cases from which the *Brown* decision derived, however, the facts showed that in all the school districts involved, "the Negro and white schools . . . have been equalized, or are being equalized." In *Brown*, therefore, the Court chose to face squarely the issue of school segregation itself.

The substance of the Court's unanimous ruling in *Brown* was that segregated education *in itself* deprives black children of equal educational opportunities. In a famous footnote to the Brown opinion, the Court cited psychological evidence that black children suffered from a loss of self-esteem and viewed *being* black as inferior to being white. This sense of inferiority, the Court argued, interfered with the black child's motivation to learn and retarded his or her educational and mental development.

The justices therefore ordered that schools be desegregated "with all deliberate speed," under the assumption that the Southern states would accept gradual integration of the schools. Instead, decades of litigation and social strife ensued. Now, over thirty years later, it has become apparent that the struggle over the enforcement of a basic constitutional right to desegregated schools has provided a revealing test of the capacity of American institutions to resolve one of the nation's deepest social problems. Perhaps no other issue so well illustrates the extent and limits of judicial power in accomplishing social change within the U.S. federal system—as we shall see in Chapter 19, when we take a closer look at the means used to achieve school integration.

## Women and equal rights

The battle for female suffrage culminated on August 18, 1920, when Tennessee became the thirty-sixth state to ratify the Nineteenth Amendment. The magnitude of the task of winning the vote for women at that time was captured in the following statement by Carrie Chapman Catt, president of the National American Woman Suffrage Association:

[Getting] the word "male" . . . out of the Constitution cost women of the country 52 years of pauseless campaign. . . . During that time they were forced to conduct 56 campaigns to get Legislatures to submit suffrage amendments to voters; 47 campaigns to get state conventions to write woman suffrage into state constitutions; 277 campaigns to get state party conventions to include woman suffrage planks; 30 campaigns to get presidential party conventions to adopt woman suffrage planks in party platforms; and 19 campaigns with 19 successive Congresses.[30]

Following approval of the Nineteenth Amendment, women proceeded to enlarge their role in political and economic life. The League of Women Voters was formed in 1919. At the same time, women's lobbying groups were organized, as were women's branches of various professional associations, and the number of women appointed to positions of responsibility in government increased steadily. Nonetheless, women were still excluded from juries and from public office in many states. In addition, many state and federal laws discriminating against women in regard to property ownership and other matters remained in force.

During the 1940s and 1950s, organized political activity on behalf of women's political and social rights dropped to a low point, although extensive social changes, such as the growing presence of women in the work force, heralded political developments to come. The 1960s and early 1970s marked a watershed in feminist activity and legislative attempts to secure full equality for women. The Equal Pay Act of 1963 required equal pay for equal work for the first time. Title VII of the Civil Rights Act of 1964 banned discrimination in employment on the basis of sex—a provision that proved to provide significant legal protection in employment practices and stirred up considerable controversy concerning just how far equality of the sexes should go (a point discussed further in Chapter 20). Also, many states began to eliminate or alter statutes that discriminated both for and against women in matters such as divorce and family law.

For many activists, however, this step-by-step process of altering laws and customs to achieve equality for women seemed too cumbersome and slow. In the mid-1970s, the woman's movement came to focus on the proposed **Equal Rights Amendment** to the Constitution as a way of providing equality at one stroke. After a long political struggle, the amendment was finally defeated—a story we will explore more fully in Chapter 20.

## Basic social rights

Eighteenth-century liberals primarily conceived of rights and liberties as protections against the encroachments of government. It was the arbitrariness of government—its tendency to intrude into the lives of citizens, to become tyrannical—that most concerned the framers of the Constitution.

A different way of viewing the rights of citizens began to develop in the late nineteenth century, largely because of the radical social changes wrought by the Industrial Revolution. From a relatively small, largely agrarian society, the United States had been transformed into a booming industrial society powered by a modern capitalist economy and characterized by rapid urbanization and increasing mechanization of transport and industry. Out of these developments arose a series of complex social problems that involved such fundamental issues as the right to basic security in regard to health and safety. Reformers sought to have government intervene to ensure decent housing for all, to limit hours of work in factories, to protect workers against unsafe working conditions, to provide public health resources to counteract serious illnesses, to make sure that all citizens received a basic education, and so on. Unlike eighteenth-century liberals, then, the social activists of the late nineteenth century saw an activist

government—one that involved itself in the day-to-day affairs of its citizens—as necessary to the development of a just society.

In Part IV, which deals with contemporary issues of public policy, we will look at recent controversies over government intervention to protect the general welfare. In this section, the new ideas of basic social rights will be illustrated through two important examples of government action to secure such rights—in the creation of the Food and Drug Administration and in the establishment of the right to form trade unions and to bargain collectively.

## Pure food and drugs

In his novel *The Jungle*, published in 1906, Upton Sinclair provided a graphic account of the conditions then obtaining at the Chicago stockyards. Sinclair had spent seven weeks observing the situation of meat-packing workers and studying the meat inspection laws, and he wrote *The Jungle* in order to expose the abominable conditions of the factory workers. Its principal impact on the public, however, was to ignite a wave of public concern over unsanitary ingredients in food and drugs. The following passage from Sinclair's novel demonstrates why the public reacted with such outrage:

There would come all the way back from Europe old sausage that had been rejected, and that was moldy and white—and it would be dosed with borax and glycerine and dumped into hoppers, and made over again for home consumption. There would be meat that had tumbled out on the floor, in the dirt and sawdust, where the

workers had trampled and spit uncounted billions of consumption [tubercular] germs. There would be meat stored in great piles in rooms; and the water from leaky roofs would drop over it, and thousands of rats would race about on it. It was too dark in those storage places to see well, but a man could run his hand over these piles of meat and sweep off handfuls of the dried dung of rats. These rats were nuisances and the packers would put poisoned bread out for them—they would die, and then rats, bread, and meat would go into the hoppers together. . . . The meat would be shoveled into carts, and the man who did the shoveling would not trouble to lift out a rat even if he saw one—there were things that went into the sausage in comparison with which a poisoned rat was a tidbit.[31]

Sinclair's revelations, combined with the efforts of others who had revealed the widespread use of dangerous substances in food and drugs, led to the passage of the Pure Food and Drug Act and the Meat Inspection Act of 1906, under which federal authorities were empowered to ban some forms of adulteration of food and drugs and to stop the use of hazardous preservatives. Over the next two decades, additional legislation broadened the scope of government concern. A 1912 law banned false health claims for patent medicines; a 1913 law required package labels to include the quantity of various contents; a 1919 law required net-weight labels on packaged meat.

Not until 1927, however, did Congress create an agency to enforce this legislation. The Food, Drug and Insecticide Administration (which became the Food and Drug Administration in 1931) began its work with the recognition that technological changes and various court decisions had largely outdated the 1906 law under which it was to operate. Yet another scandal was required before the agency obtained adequate regulatory powers. When a new "wonder drug," elixir sulfanilamide, was marketed without prior safety testing, it caused the deaths of more than one hundred people. Under the existing law, the FDA had been powerless to prevent the drug from reaching the market—it was empowered to take action against a drug only after it had been demonstrated to cause death or illness. Public outrage over the FDA's powerlessness to stop the marketing of elixir

Coal miners, circa 1908. Child labor was an everyday fact of early industrial life, and one that required governmental action to correct. These little coal miners put in long hours and received little or no schooling. Not until the second decade of the twentieth century was child labor curtailed in the United States.

sulfanilamide led to passage of the Food, Drug and Cosmetic Act of 1938, which specified that drugs be tested prior to distribution, set tolerance levels for toxic substances, provided for factory inspection, strengthened truth-in-labeling provisions of previous laws, and extended health coverage to cosmetics.

Even this strengthening of the health and safety laws did not solve all the problems involved, but it did signal a clear recognition of the governmental responsibility to provide for the safety of food and drugs. The basic right involved—one that remains highly controversial in specific applications—is the right to safe, noninjurious products, which is really an extension of the right to life itself.

## Trade unions and collective bargaining

Although the rights of workers to organize and to bargain with management are not thought of as fundamental human rights, they are indispensable to the successful functioning of an industrial society. More important, they are closely connected with the meaning of democracy in modern times. Without the opportunity to form trade unions, workers often have little defense against exploitation by management. In the absence of an effective workers' organization,

working conditions and pay can largely be dictated by management—a situation resembling tyranny far more than democracy. The right to form a union, then, is one of the basic democratic rights required for a decent life in a modern society.

The history of the union movement in the United States has been punctuated by many episodes of almost open warfare. For many decades, government forces were brought to bear against workers who attempted to form unions. Until 1842, the courts typically held that union activity *per se* was illegal. After that date, courts were more willing to grant unions the right to exist but generally refused to recognize the right to strike or to compel employers to bargain with unions. Beginning in the 1880s, court orders against union activities were widely used to break strikes, and state militia, National Guard, and regular army forces often intervened in labor disputes on the side of employers.

The first piece of federal legislation to provide some protection for labor was the Clayton Act of 1914, which prohibited the issuance of injunctions (court orders) against strikes, boycotts, and picketing except to prevent "irreparable damage." The courts, however, remained generally hostile to unions, and Congress showed little inclination to further union interests until the onset of the Great Depression forced the recognition that fundamental changes were necessary in the economic life of the nation.

Poultry inspector, circa 1930. At the time, legal provisions to ensure safe food and drugs were still somewhat new.

# The Ludlow massacre of 1913

Attempts to unionize the coal and mineral miners of Colorado began in the 1890s. Concerted unionizing efforts early in the twentieth century led to the arrest of union organizers and the firing of union sympathizers. The mines were subsequently worked by non-union laborers, most of whom were recent immigrants from Europe or Mexico. For a time, these workers proved relatively docile, despite the wretched conditions found in the mining camps, where disease was rampant, sanitation poor, and alcoholism common. Water for drinking and washing flowed directly from the mines, without prior treatment. Miners were paid only in script, or company money, which could be only used in company-owned stores. Many conditions in the camps violated state law, but because the mining companies exerted great influence over Colorado politics, the state did not intervene to improve conditions.

Eventually the workers organized, and in September 1912 they called for a forty-hour work week, an eight-hour work day, union recognition, and various other work-related improvements. When the mining companies refused to budge on the unionization issue, the workers went on strike. Both miners and employers expected the strike to be serious and violent. The workers had stockpiled weapons, in the well-founded expectation that the companies would resort to violence to quell the strike. The companies brought in detectives and deputy sheriffs to protect their property. Finally, the governor called out the state militia. A six-month stalemate ensued, and the companies began to import strikebreakers. At this time, John D. Rockefeller, Jr., testified at a congressional hearing that his companies would rather lose all their assets than recognize the miners' union.

On April 19, 1913, in circumstances that are still disputed, a confrontation between state militia and strikers led to violence. A strikers' camp in Ludlow was burned and thirty-three people were killed, including eleven women and children. After this "Ludlow massacre," the strikers prepared for open warfare, and the governor called on President Woodrow Wilson to send federal troops. Ten days later, the U.S. Army occupied the area and calm was restored. The union failed to gain recognition.

The Ludlow massacre was one of the more spectacular examples of labor-management violence in U.S. history. Other bloody incidents marked the Great Railroad Strike of 1877, the Homestead Steel Strike of 1892, the Gastonia Strike of 1929, and the Little Steel Strike of 1937.

Two pieces of legislation, in particular, signaled governmental acceptance of unions as a permanent and legitimate force in U.S. society. The Norris-LaGuardia Act of 1932 prohibited the enforcement of "yellow dog" contracts in federal courts. Such contracts, which had been used widely to prevent unionization, required that employees sign a pledge not to join a union as a condition of employment. The Norris-LaGuardia Act also deprived the federal courts of jurisdiction to issue antilabor injunctions against strikes. In effect, then, the act neutralized the role of the federal courts in labor disputes.

The Wagner Act passed in 1935 went further. Under it, workers were guaranteed the right to form unions and to bargain with management. The Wagner Act also created the National Labor Relations Board (NLRB), which was given the power to investigate unfair labor practices by employers and to issue cease-and-desist orders enforceable through the federal courts. Not only did this act effectively end violent labor strife in the United States by firmly establishing the right to collective bargaining, but it

also helped create an atmosphere in which unions were more likely to develop. And between 1935 and 1947, union membership increased from 4 million to 15.5 million.

After World War II, federal labor legislation generally reflected a more critical view of unions. The Taft-Hartley Act of 1947, for example, regulated union activities and prohibited strikes by federal employees. Under Section 14B of the act, states were empowered to pass "right to work" laws, which require that union membership not be a *condition* of employment. Such provisions were adopted by twenty states, despite vigorous opposition by organized labor. The Landrum-Griffin Act of 1959, moreover, mandated more democratic practices *within* unions and established a union membership "bill of rights."

In the contemporary era, debates over union power and management practices have continued. Many observers have charged that unions have become too powerful and often serve to obstruct more than to facilitate labor relations. Others have pointed out that the United States is one of the least unionized

nations in the industrial democratic world and that many U.S. workers still suffer from a lack of basic protections. For our purposes, the important point to bear in mind is that political recognition and protection for basic trade union rights came only after a painful, costly battle that reflected the social class divisions in U.S. society, in which the many own little property and the few control most of it. The issue of the effects on democratic life of an extremely unequal distribution of property is one we will turn to in Chapter 6.

## Governmental repression of liberties

If a commitment to defend civil liberties and rights has been an essential part of our national history, so, unfortunately, has been the effort to undermine them. Attempts by the federal government to prosecute and harass opponents date back to the Alien and Sedition Acts of the John Adams administration, as we saw earlier in this chapter. The tempo of repression usually has quickened when some in government have perceived threats to established patterns of social and political life. As a result, throughout U.S. history groups that have called themselves radical or that merely have seemed radical have often been the targets of government repression.

In the early years of this century, for example, the Industrial Workers of the World (IWW), a militant industrial union, was the target of a concerted campaign of prosecutions that eventually resulted in the imprisonment of many of its leaders. Then, in the aftermath of World War I and the Russian Revolution, a near-hysterical fear of communism swept the country. During this "red scare," the press continually portrayed anarchists and radicals as serious threats to law and order and to the government itself. In January 1920, a wave of raids resulted in the arrest of about four thousand supposed radicals. Many were deported and many others imprisoned. Most were held without benefit of legal assistance and some were even prevented from contacting their families.

At the state level, five Socialists were deprived of their seats in the New York state legislature. Many state legislatures passed various antiradical statutes, including those requiring loyalty oaths for teachers and bills directed toward keeping the Socialist Party off the ballot. In the antired hysteria of those times, twenty-four states even passed laws making it a crime to display the red flag.

This pattern of antiradical activity combined with repression or subversion of civil rights was repeated in the 1950s. Tensions raised by the Cold War with the Soviet Union (plus the hot war in Korea) led to restrictions on free speech such as those in the Smith Act. Loyalty oaths again proliferated. Congress was also active in attempting to locate the "disloyal." The House Un-American Activities Committee, in particular, relentlessly hunted communists—past or present—and communist sympathizers in all walks of American life. Many people lost jobs, careers, friends, and self-respect in the process of being investigated. As states copied the national model, many state un-American activities committees sprang up. Civil rights and antiwar activities in the 1960s led to another outburst of repressive activities. Presidents Lyndon Johnson and Richard Nixon, believing that the antiwar movement and the New Left posed a serious threat to American society, apparently felt that drastic action was needed to stop disruptions. The federal government's intelligence gathering and investigatory agencies kept close track of many activists, such as Dr. Martin Luther King, Jr. (see box). Informers infiltrated groups considered radical, regardless of whether those groups had violated laws or been involved in violence. Illegal break-ins and wiretaps by law enforcement officials were common,

In union there is strength— but not always enough strength. The air traffic controllers who struck for better working conditions and higher wages in 1981 lost the battle and their jobs, as President Reagan fired them, and the FAA hired new controllers. Here, early in the strike, they voice their enthusiasm in a picket line, a basic liberty protected by U.S. law since the 1930s.

127

# The harassment of Martin Luther King, Jr.

For more than six years, from 1962 to 1968, the Federal Bureau of Investigation engaged in daily surveillance of civil rights activist Dr. Martin Luther King, Jr. Though not publicly revealed until after King's death in 1968, the FBI's campaign against him did much private damage to King's reputation and brought serious emotional turmoil to him and his closest relatives.

The FBI's pursuit of King began six years after he first became a national figure, during the Montgomery, Alabama, bus boycott of 1955–56. In early 1962 the FBI learned that one of King's closest political advisors was a white New York attorney, Stanley D. Levison, whom the Bureau had known of a decade earlier when he was playing a crucial role in the secret U.S. Communist Party. Wiretaps were placed on Levison's telephones and microphones covertly installed in his office, but no evidence of sinister connections or plotting was forthcoming. Nevertheless, FBI Director J. Edgar Hoover sent grim warnings about the Levison-King friendship to President John F. Kennedy and his brother Robert, the attorney-general. The Kennedy brothers finally approved Hoover's request that FBI wiretaps be placed on King's home and office phones in Atlanta.

The new electronic surveillance transformed the FBI's interest in King almost overnight. Concern about Levison quickly was replaced by an obsession that King's less-than-perfect private life was unacceptable for such a prominent minister and public leader. Agents were assigned to tail King as he traveled from city to city and hotel room to hotel room, and transcribed accounts of his most private moments were sent out to the White House and to dozens of federal agencies. Bureau operatives attempted to interest the news media in the seamy material about King, and one FBI executive mailed an anonymous threatening letter to King—enclosing an embarrassing tape and warning of imminent exposure—just days after the black leader had been awarded the 1964 Nobel Peace Prize for his pathbreaking civil rights efforts. Much to the FBI's disappointment, its efforts to smear or destroy King publicly went for naught; reporter after reporter rebuffed the Bureau's approaches on the grounds that King's private life was not news.

Frustrated but not dissuaded, the FBI kept up its close watch on King's activitites, becoming particularly agitated when he strongly denounced the Vietnam War policies of President Lyndon Johnson and advocated a massive but nonviolent "Poor People's Campaign" targeted against the nation's capitol. Thorough and painstaking congressional investigations have shown no FBI complicity in King's 1968 assassination. The full record of the Bureau's activities against King, however, reveals the expenditure of millions of dollars on one of the most appalling violations of personal privacy and civil liberties in U.S. government history.

In the early 1950s Senator Joseph McCarthy (R, Wisc.) made many rash and unsubstantiated charges of communist infiltration of the U.S. government. His accusations received wide coverage by the media and helped stir national hysteria on the subject. Loyalty oaths proliferated, and free speech was threatened. A backlash followed, however. Here he is shown at a hearing about the U.S. Army. The quiet, persistent attorney Joseph Welch (seated) was able to dramatize McCarthy's bullying tactics before national television cameras. McCarthy was later censured by the Senate, and his influence waned.

and there was considerable legal harassment of both civil rights and antiwar activists.

The states also joined in the antiradical campaign. Julian Bond, the first black elected to the Georgia state legislature in one hundred years, was denied his seat because of his association with the Student Non-Violent Coordinating Committee, which had outspokenly opposed the Vietnam War. In this case, however, the federal courts stepped in to vindicate Bond's rights.

To some observers, these outbreaks of government repression represented justifiable responses to real threats to the social order. If groups seek to violently alter society or to subvert institutions, it is often argued, repression is called for—although in this view "repression" usually is called *"maintaining order."* It is true that at times the threats have been real, and at other times it has been difficult to decide if threats were real or not. Were anarchists sending bombs through the mail in 1919? Was the U.S. Communist Party trying to subvert the government in the 1930s and 1940s? Did antiwar radicals plan to destroy property and disrupt public order during the Democratic Convention in 1968? Were black radicals of the 1960s talking revolution and violence?

There was just enough truth in these allegations to permit those in authority to persuade themselves and much of the rest of the population that drastic steps had to be taken. Yet it remains an unpalatable fact that *repression,* not just the maintenance of or-

129

der, was involved in each case. The lack of respect for civil liberties, the excessive use of force, the intimidation of people with any sympathies for the targets of repression—all these were signs that the steps taken went beyond anything needed just to maintain order, and that the active suppression of certain views and groups was contemplated.

How can such repressive activities arise in a democratic society? One theory is that U.S. government repression is usually directed against those who threaten, or seem to threaten, private property, and in doing so place themselves outside the realm of acceptable political discussion. The government, according to this view, then steps in to defend capitalism, as it would step in to defend itself. This explanation, although useful for understanding the battles between trade unions and employers, cannot account for all forms of repression.

Another more comprehensive explanation of gov-

ernmental repression emphasizes the lack of real commitment to civil liberties among U.S. political elites. Many at the top levels of our political system are concerned more with maintaining their own power than with respect for the Bill of Rights.

Of course, political elites alone cannot be blamed for repression. It also has had a popular base. As we will see in Chapter 7, tolerance for dissent has had a long struggle to become established in the United States. Even reasonable people often disagree about what should be tolerated. For example, should groups preaching racial or religious hatred be permitted to exercise First Amendment rights? Should groups that do not respect civil liberties be entitled to those liberties? The answers to such questions are not easy, but in any case, it is clear that protecting the right to dissent is a perpetual struggle and that constitutional protections play a key role in shoring up defenses against repression.

## Conclusions

Looking back over U.S. history, we can take pride in the recent progress of this country toward an increased recognition of civil rights and liberties. Thirty years ago, for example, basic civil rights were denied to many black citizens, and the civil liberties of all citizens were being threatened amid an outburst of anticommunist hysteria. In most ways, we are far better off today. But it has been a slow, costly process, and often a painful one. In our appreciation of democracy it is useful to remember this. We will return to this subject in Chapter 12, when we consider the many forms protest has taken in the search for democratic rights.

We must also acknowledge that our history contains many examples of neglect, repression, or erosion of liberties and rights. As we have seen, U.S. society has not been immune to antidemocratic impulses, which have marred our history in many ways.

Finally, it is important to understand our ideas about rights and liberties must grow and change as society changes. We must reassess rights and liberties as politics and society change. It is not appropriate for twentieth-century democrats to view civil and social rights in the manner of eighteenth-century liberals. New conceptions of rights and liberties, however, inevitably involve new controversies and disputes.

Overall, the United States of the 1980s is a freer country than it has been before—a nation more attentive to the democratic rights of its citizens. We should remember, however, at any given time some U.S. citizens are suffering deprivation of their rights—out of neglect, harassment, or the inability to put those rights and liberties to use. When this happens, the true democrat must feel that his or her own rights and liberties have lost some of their meaning.

The spectre of force— soldiers in gas masks, rifles ready. A sadly common sight in the sixties, when civil rights and antiwar activists stirred opposition to government policies. Just as some considered protesters excessive in their tactics, so others found the force used to keep order unjustified.

## NOTES

1 16 Wallace 36.

2 268 U.S. 652.

3 J. S. Mill, *On Liberty* (New York: F. S. Crofts, 1947), and John Milton, *Aeropagitica*, John Hales, ed., (London: Oxford University Press, 1961).

4 Alexander Meiklejohn, *Free Speech in Relation to Self-Government* (New York: Harper and Row, 1948) and *Political Freedom* (New York: Oxford University Press, 1965).

5 H. Pollack and A. B. Smith, *Civil Liberties and Civil Rights in the United States* (New York: West, 1978).

6 249 U.S. 47.

7 268 U.S. 652.

8 341 U.S. 494.

9 354 U.S. 298.

10 364 U.S. 479.

11 391 U.S. 308.

12 391 U.S. 367.

13 393 U.S. 503.

14 315 U.S. 568.

15 405 U.S. 518.

16 370 U.S. 421.

17 397 U.S. 664.

18 81 U.S. 3.

19 13 Wall 679.

20 98 U.S. 145.

21 310 U.S. 586 (1940).

22 319 U.S. 624 (1943).

23 380 U.S. 163.

24 398 U.S. 333 (1970).

25 372 U.S. 335.

26 384 U.S. 436.

27 305 U.S. 337.

28 339 U.S. 629.

29 347 U.S. 483.

30 As quoted in Jarol B. Manheim, *Deja Vu* (New York: St. Martin's, 1976), pp. 147–48.

31 Upton Sinclair, *The Jungle* (New York: Viking, 1946), p. 135.

## SELECTED READINGS

### The Bill of Rights and constitutional protections

The history of constitutional rights is chronicled in Martin Shapiro, *Freedom of Speech: The Supreme Court and Judicial Review* (Englewood Cliffs, N.J.: Prentice-Hall, 1966); Henry J. Abraham, *Freedom and the Court* (New York: Oxford University Press, 1977); S. E. Morison, H. S. Commager, and W. E. Leuchtenburg, *A Concise History of the American Republic* (New York: Oxford University Press, 1977); and Leonard W. Levy, *Legacy of Suppression: Freedom of Speech and Press in Early American History* (Cambridge, Mass.: Harvard University Press, 1960).

For a critical assessment of liberal ideas of freedom, consult Christian Bay, *The Structure of Freedom* (Stanford, Cal.: Stanford University Press, 1970). Discussions of these issues from various political perspectives can be found in C. B. MacPherson, *The Political Theory of Possessive Individualism: Hobbes to Locke* (London: Oxford University Press, 1962); Isaiah Berlin, *Two Concepts of Liberty* (London: Oxford University Press, 1958); Frithjof Bergmann, *On Being Free* (South Bend, Ind.: University of Notre Dame Press, 1977); and Erich Fromm, *Escape from Freedom* (New York: Free Press, 1968).

The liberal view of freedom of speech is presented in John Stuart Mill's nineteenth-century classic *On Liberty* (New York: Crofts, 1947). Meiklejohn's ideas on the subject are set forth in his *Free Speech in Relation to Self-Government* (New York: Harper & Row, 1948) and *Political Freedom* (New York: Oxford University Press, 1965).

On the Alien and Sedition Acts, see Morison *et al.*, *History of the American Republic*; and Levy, *Legacy of Suppression*.

Much of the discussion of post–World War I cases involving political speech is drawn from A. B. Smith, *Civil Liberties and Civil Rights in the United States* (St. Paul: West Publishing Co., 1978).

For discussions of the Smith Act cases, see Samuel Krislov, *The Supreme Court and Political Freedom* (New York: Free Press, 1968); Abraham, *Freedom and the Court*; and L. J. Barker and T. W. Barker, Jr., *Civil Liberties and the Constitution*, 3rd ed. (Englewood Cliffs, N.J.: Prentice-Hall, 1978), Chapter 3.

On symbolic speech and limits on expression, see Joel B. Grossman and Richard S. Wells, *Constitutional Law and Judicial Policy Making* (New York: John Wiley, 1980), Chapter 5; Thomas Emerson, *A General Theory of the First Amendment* (New York: Vintage, 1967).

On religion and the first amendment, see Leo Pfeffer, *Church, State and Freedom* (Boston: Beacon Press, 1967); Frank J. Sorauf, *The Wall of Separation: The Constitutional Politics of Church and State* (Princeton, N.J.: Princeton University Press, 1976); K. M. Dolbeare and P. E. Hammond, *The School Prayer Decisions: From Court Policy to Local Practice* (Chicago: University of Chicago Press, 1971).

For various treatments of due process rights, see Anthony Lewis, *Gideon's Trumpet* (New York: Random House, 1964); Neal A. Milner, *The Court and Local Law Enforcement: The Impact of Miranda* (Beverly Hills, Cal.: Sage Publications, 1971).

A good basic text on the contemporary legal system is Ralph Rossum and Alan Tarr, *American Constitutional Law* (New York: St. Martin's, 1982).

### Civil rights

On the right to vote, see especially K. H. Porter, *A History of Suffrage in the United States* (Chicago: University of Chicago Press, 1918); and Winthrop Jordan, *White Over Black* (Baltimore: Penguin Books, 1969). The politics of racial segregation has spawned a vast literature. For introductions to it, see R. W. Logan, *Betrayal of the Negro* (New York: Collier, 1965); Idus A. Newby, *Development of Segregationist Thought* (Homewood, Ill.: Dorsey, 1968); and C. Vann Woodward, *Reconstruction and Reaction* (Boston: Little, Brown, 1966). On school desegregation, see J. W. Peltason, *58 Lonely Men: Southern Federal Judges and School Desegregation* (Urbana, Ill.: University of Illinois Press, 1971); Clement E. Vose, *Caucasians Only: The Supreme Court, the NAACP and the Restrictive Covenant Cases* (Berkeley, Cal.: University of California Press, 1959).

### Basic social rights

For introductions to social-rights issues, see Peter Temin, *Taking Your Medicine—Drug Regulation in the United States* (Cambridge, Mass.: Harvard University Press, 1980); and John Mendeloff, *Regulatory Safety: An Economic and Political Analysis of Occupational Safety and Health Policy* (Cambridge, Mass.: MIT Press, 1979). On the FDA and its problematic relationship to the industries it regulates, see Upton Sinclair, *The Jungle* (New York: Viking Press, 1946); and M. J. Hinich and Richard Staelin, *Consumer Protection Legislation and the U.S. Food Industry* (New York: Pergamon, 1980).

For various perspectives on the genesis and evolution of the U.S. labor movement, see Stanley Aronowitz, *The*

*Shaping of American Working Class Consciousness* (New York: McGraw-Hill, 1973); Thomas R. Brooks, *Toil and Trouble: A History of American Labor* (New York: Delacorte Press, 1971). On the Ludlow massacre, see George S. McGovern and Leonard F. Guttridge, *The Great Coalfield War* (Boston: Houghton Mifflin, 1972); and James C. Dick, *Violence and Oppression* (Athens, Ga.: University of Georgia Press, 1979).

### Governmental repression of liberties
For a general survey of governmental repression of liberties, see Robert J. Goldstein, *Political Repression in Modern America: From 1870 to the Present* (New York: Schenkman, 1978); and *Political Repression and Political Development in Modern Europe* (New York: Barnes and Noble, 1983). On the "red scare," see H. M. Hyman, *To Try Men's Souls: Loyalty Oaths in American History* (Berkeley, Cal.: University of California Press, 1960). Other sources on repression of liberties include S. M. Lipset and E. Raab, "Epilogue: The 1970s," in *The Politics of Unreason: Right Wing Extremism in the United States, 1790–1977* (Chicago: University of Chicago Press, 1978); John Roche, *Courts and Rights* (New York: Random House, 1977).

# Chapter
six

# The American political economy

# Inequality and democratic politics

ECONOMIC issues have been among the most complex and divisive matters facing modern societies. In speaking of economics, we refer not only to such specific matters as the day-to-day management of inflation or the regulation of farm prices. Economics, in the larger sense, also involves such far-reaching issues as the distribution of wealth and income in society, the ownership of property, and the range of government power. All of these economic issues and questions are affected by the actions of government—and government, in turn, is shaped by the economic structure of the society of which it is a part. This is what is meant by the political economy of a society. We can learn a great deal about what a government accomplishes, and fails to accomplish, by looking at the economic organization that it shapes and is shaped by.

In this chapter, we will first take a look at the ongoing debate over how a modern economy *should* be structured, and the implications of that debate for democratic politics. We will then examine how the U.S. economy is structured. Finally, we will explore the connections between U.S. social and economic structures and the ways in which U.S. government policy is made.

## Capitalism and socialism

Unequal distribution of property and of income is inherently an unequal distribution of freedom.   *Kenneth Arrow*

What's good for General Motors is good for the country. *Charles Wilson (president of General Motors and secretary of defense in the Eisenhower administration)*

One hundred years ago, as industrial capitalism was rapidly developing everywhere in the Western world, defenders and opponents of this economic system predicted an intense struggle over its future. Capitalism and socialism were seen as the great alternatives. Socialists believed their system held out the prospect of genuine economic equality combined with democratic politics. Capitalists contended that only their system would protect individual freedom and promote economic growth and high productivity. There often seemed little way of compromising the two alternatives.[1]

By comparing the theories of socialism and capitalism, we can clarify the debate about the "just society" that has preoccupied Western political thinkers since the eighteenth century. It must be borne in mind, however, that the socialist alternative has not been a very prominent one in the United States, at least in comparison to Western Europe. In this country, the debate over the political economy has been carried on not so much between socialists and capitalists as between the more liberal reformers of capitalism and the more conservative defenders of it. Generally, U.S. liberals have sought to amend, humanize, or improve the capitalist system, rather than to substitute socialism for it.

## Capitalism

The essential elements of a **capitalist** system are private ownership of the means of production and a competitive market system, driven by the profit motive, through which wealth and resources are distributed. The major capital goods in such a society—factories, machines, land, and money—are owned by individuals or groups who have the right to use this property for private gain. What goods are produced, what they cost, and who will receive them are determined by the competitive operations of the marketplace according to the costs of supply and the demands of consumers.[2]

According to eighteenth-century exponents of capitalism, the ideal capitalist society would be made up of many small enterprises competing for a portion of the potential market. Government would play a decidedly minor role in this society: basically, it would provide various public services, such as the building and maintenance of roads; conduct foreign policy and provide for the national defense; and enforce the law. This liberal-capitalist concept of minimum government was espoused by many founders and early leaders of the United States. They, along with many other eighteenth-century liberals, saw government as the chief potential enemy of freedom. Freedom to do business as one pleased was linked in their minds, and in their actions, with other freedoms, such as

freedom of conscience and freedom of speech. For them, the ideal government was one that functioned as a "night watchman"—a guardian of the existing distribution of property.

In the early nineteenth century, it was widely believed that **laissez faire** (unregulated) capitalism would liberate society from the tyrannies of political oppression, bureaucratic control, and stifling traditions. Capitalism, many held, would create a new world of immense wealth, a far more efficient and productive economy—without any conscious direction from government. Each person could attempt to profit as much as possible, for in doing so he or she would create wealth, and this would benefit the whole society.[3] Selfishness, in other words, would serve social ends. In this ideal capitalistic world, individuals would be judged on their merits—meaning the value of their skills in the marketplace—not on such noneconomic criteria as social status, color, sex, or religion.

Capitalism's achievements were almost immediately evident. The new economic system was enormously productive. It revolutionized the production and distribution of goods, stimulated worldwide trade, and broke down ancient and often oppressive traditions and social barriers. For many, the economic freedom of capitalism and the political freedom of democracy seemed necessarily to go hand-in-hand.

Yet from the first, the capitalist system had many critics. Conservative critics viewed capitalism as inimical to communal ties and social bonds. Conservatives also were unhappy with capitalism's antigovernment stance. Government was needed, nineteenth-century conservatives argued, to protect the weak (such as children who worked fourteen-hour days in mines and factories) and to limit the ferocity of competition. There were some values, conservatives argued, more important than profit.[4]

More-radical opponents of capitalism attacked it as a system that proclaimed the value of equality but in fact created inequality. Under nineteenth-century capitalism, wealth was very unequally distributed, and it seemed likely to remain that way. Capitalism exploited the workers and was highly inefficient, radicals argued. Cycles of inflation and depression caused great suffering and wasted vast resources.

Another major criticism of capitalism was that it made real democracy very difficult to achieve. As long as wealth was so unequally distributed, the few who were rich would have excessive political power and the many who were poor would have too little power. Then, too, the fact that in a capitalist economy decisions affecting the lives of millions were made by a handful of powerful capitalists who controlled the means of production, was inherently undemocratic. For these reasons, most radicals called for some form of collective ownership of the main means of production, in order to democratize economic decision making.

## Socialism

There is less agreement on the meaning of **socialism** than on that of capitalism. Most socialists, however, would agree that private ownership of the means of production should be replaced by some form of social ownership; that the market system should be replaced by some sort of planned economy; and that the distribution of wealth should be considerably more equal than it is under capitalism.[5]

Some early socialists—including the most famous, Karl Marx and Friedrich Engels—expected that capitalism would inevitably collapse under the weight of its internal problems and that socialism would automatically take its place. Others were gradual reformers who favored a slow transition from capitalism to socialism through parliamentary processes. Almost all traditional socialists, however, expected to use the vast productive apparatus created by capitalism to achieve a more just social order. Socialism would work in a more rational, planned fashion than capitalism, avoiding the problems of economic boom and bust. Socialism would allow for a more just social order, since wealth would be more equally distributed and large concentrations of wealth abolished. The system would also create a more compassionate and community-minded society characterized by a strong concern for those who were not

economically productive. Socialism would enable individuals to pursue values more worthy than profit and would neutralize the crass commercialism of capitalism.

The critics of socialism predicted disaster.[6] How could any planner manage the complexities of a modern economy? they asked. Attempts at government planning, they argued, would only result in great inefficiency and in the concentration of power in the hands of government bureaucracy. The growth of government power under socialism would threaten democracy and freedom itself. Some critics pictured socialism as a new kind of tyranny, with government planners as the tyrants. Others feared that socialism, in attempting to bring life's uncertainties under control and provide security for all, would succeed only in producing stultification of human creativity.

## Mixed systems

The alternately apocalyptic and utopian forecasts of the early proponents of capitalism and socialism turned out to be very wide of the mark. Rather than evolve into strictly socialist or capitalist societies, the Western industrial democracies came to embody a mix of capitalist and socialist elements. The exact mix of elements differs from one society to another: the United States, for example, is more capitalist in orientation; Great Britain and Sweden, more socialist.

These mixed systems developed in fits and starts, often spurred by desperate efforts to deal with the crises of capitalism. In many countries, socialist-type reforms, backed by growing trade union movements and socialist political groups, began gathering momentum in the late nineteenth and early twentieth centuries. The first steps toward what we now call the **welfare state** were taken then, including systematic government aid to the poor and the unemployed, public housing, and government provision for old age pensions. As government became more and more involved in regulation of the economic marketplace, new governmental agencies were created to protect

# The TVA: an experiment in socialism

Although Senator George Norris of Nebraska was a Republican, he was the principal sponsor of legislation calling for the creation of a publicly owned Tennessee Valley Authority (TVA) to provide cheap electrical power to residents of the economically deprived Tennessee River valley. In the early 1930s, 98 percent of the farms in the valley had no electricity, and the few that did paid exorbitant rates to private power companies. The entire area, although rich in natural resources, was in a chronic state of poverty. Water power was being wasted, forests were being destroyed by improper cutting and management, thousands of acres of farmland were being abandoned, and much industry had left the area.

Despite these dismal facts, President Herbert Hoover in 1931 vetoed Norris's proposed TVA program. Expounding the dangers of government involvement in economic development, Hoover stated: "I hate to contemplate the future of our institutions, of our country, if the preoccupation of its officials is to be no longer the promotion of justice and equal opportunity, but is to be devoted to barter and the market. This is not liberalism, it is degeneration."* To Hoover, state involvement in the economy was "socialism," and therefore totally abhorrent.

But Norris persisted, and with the backing of President Franklin D. Roosevelt, the TVA was established by Congress in May 1933. The enterprise was gigantic in scope, involving the generation of power, the development of natural resources, and a significant amount of economic planning for an area three-fourths the size of England. It also represented the first essentially socialist project entered into by the U.S. government.

The TVA was an outstanding success by most estimates. Twenty-five dams were built, extensive flood control projects carried out, nitrate production established, thousands of miles of electric transmission lines built, and huge amounts of power sold at low rates to local communities. According to one history of the era, "Within a few years, millions of abandoned acres were returned to cultivation, forests grew in burnt-over land, industry returned to the valley, vacationers crowded its artificial lakes, and the river, navigable now over its entire length from Knoxville to the Ohio River, was one of the busiest streams in the country. The TVA itself became a model which attracted the attention and emulation of the whole world."**

The TVA is still in existence, and has even continued to grow. It has in recent years come under attack by conservatives, who have argued that government should sell off the TVA to private enterprise. It has also received sharp criticism by environmentalists, both for the monumental pollution caused by its coal-fired generating plants and for its plans to construct an enormous nuclear power plant. After the TVA installed equipment that cut pollution by 50 percent and shelved the nuclear plant, however, environmental groups began to offer praise.

Certainly, questions exist about the direction the Tennessee Valley Authority will take in years to come. As S. David Freeman, retired-chairman of its board of directors, said in 1984, "My greatest worry is that the TVA will

The TVA's Imperial Dam.

go back to sleep. That's really the natural state of a fifty-year-old bureaucracy. But our mission ought to be activist. We should be the one developing ideas for the electric car; for hammering out practical answers to acid rain. The TVA ought not to be, as President Carter once said, just another utility."***

*Quoted in S. E. Morrison, H. S. Commager, and W. E. Leuchtenburg, *Growth of the American Republic* (New York: Oxford University Press, 1977), vol. II, p. 500.
**Ibid., p. 501.
***William E. Schmidt, "The TVA Has Come to a Bend in the River," *The New York Times*, 20 May 1984, Section E, p. 5.

consumers and workers. There also were some attempts to break up large concentrations of industrial power, and a few tentative efforts to protect the environment.

The Great Depression of the 1930s represented a watershed in the evolution of mixed economies. As governments sought to deal with widespread unemployment and social dislocations, they became far more active in intervening in the market and in creating new social programs. This trend was reinforced by the experience of World War II, during which governments were forced to do extensive economic and social planning. The Western democracies emerged from the war with new capabilities for dealing with modern economic life.

In the post–World War II period, the proponents of socialism enjoyed some measure of success in Western Europe. In Great Britain and Scandinavia, socialist parties held the reins of government in the immediate postwar era, and in West Germany, France, the Netherlands, and other countries they became political forces to be reckoned with. The Labour Party of Great Britain nationalized (put under government ownership) the failing coal mining industry, as well as the steel industry, road transport, and other major industries. The British also created a socialized medical system and generally increased the reach of the welfare state.

Generally speaking, socialist parties in power proved more moderate than many had expected.[7] In Scandinavia, for example, there was very little nationalization. Instead, Scandinavian socialists concentrated on keeping employment and economic growth high and in extending the scope of government benefits. The goal was still equality, socialists argued; the exact means used didn't matter that much. In addition, the results of nationalization were often disappointing. In Britain, most workers found their lives little changed by the shift from private to government ownership.

At the same time, capitalism also prospered. The new mixed economies allowed extensive government stimulation of economic growth—and growth there was. When no serious depression occurred after World War II, many experts argued that the boom-and-bust

cycle characteristic of unregulated capitalist economies had been banished permanently, thanks largely
to government stimulation of the economy.[8]

The **mixed economies** characteristic of most
Western democracies today generally can be described as follows.

Private ownership of the means of production is predom-
inant, although the government's role in the economy is
substantial (see Figure 6.1 and Table 6.1).

Socialist ideology called for government ownership of the "commanding heights" of the economy. When they gained a popular majority in the election of 1945, the British Labour Party nationalized a consid-erable portion of the British economy, including the coal mines. Unfortunately, the mines were a failing industry at the time, and they have remained prob-lem-plagued ever since.

TABLE 6.1
## The state as boss, 1982
## Employment in the public sector*
## (% of labor force)

|  | Public enterprises | Total public sector |
|---|---|---|
| Austria | 13.7 | 33.0 |
| Belgium | 5.2 | 19.6 |
| Britain | 8.1 | 28.5 |
| Denmark | 3.4 | 18.7 |
| France | 7.3 | 21.0 |
| W. Germany | 7.2 | 20.6 |
| Holland | 3.6 | 16.6 |
| Ireland | 7.3 | 12.8 |
| Italy | 6.6 | 18.5 |
| Japan | 2.8 | 12.9 |
| Spain | 2.9 | na |
| Sweden | 8.2 | 29.6 |
| United States | 1.5 | 18.8 |

Sources: European Centre for Public Enterprises (CEEP), OECO,
national statistics.
*Countries' definitions of public sector vary.

Government regulation of the overall level of economic
life has become a normal state of affairs. Through taxation
and spending, regulation of interest rates, and other means,
the government seeks to maintain high levels of employment and economic growth and to keep inflation under
control.

The government regulates many important details of economic life, including working conditions, environmental
conditions, and matters affecting health and safety.

The government is deeply involved in promoting the welfare of the citizenry. Basic welfare state programs include
old age insurance, aid to the poor, health insurance or
socialized medicine, and other provisions for groups such
as the unemployed youth, the handicapped, and students.

Cooperation between government and business is widespread. The government provides aid to failing industries,
special tax breaks to businesses, and subsidies to various

**Who Owns How Much?**

Privately Owned: □

Publicly Owned: 25% 50% 75% All or Nearly All

| | Postal Service | Telecommunications | Electricity | Gas | Oil Output | Coal | Railroads | Airlines | Autos | Steel | Shipbuilding | Government Spending (Percent of Gross Domestic Product) 1982 | 1975 |
|---|---|---|---|---|---|---|---|---|---|---|---|---|---|
| Australia | All | All | All | All | Private | Private | All | 75% | Private | Private | † | 24.0 | 32.0 |
| Austria | All | All | All | All | All | All | All | All | All | All | † | 32.1 | 40.2 |
| Belgium | All | All | 25% | 25% | † | Private | All | All | Private | 50% | Private | 30.7 | 43.2 |
| Britain | All | All | All | All | 25% | All | All | 75% | 50% | 75% | All | 34.2 | 44.4 |
| Canada | All | 25% | All | Private | Private | Private | 75% | 75% | Private | Private | Private | 29.4 | 40.0 |
| France | All | All | All | All | † | All | All | 75% | 50% | 75% | Private | 36.3 | 40.3 |
| Italy | All | All | 75% | All | † | † | All | All | 25% | 75% | 75% | 32.4 | 41.9 |
| Japan | All | All | Private | Private | † | Private | 75% | 25% | Private | Private | Private | 19.0 | 23.4 |
| Netherlands | All | All | 75% | 75% | † | † | All | 75% | 50% | 25% | Private | 34.4 | 51.2 |
| Sweden | All | All | 50% | All | † | † | All | 50% | Private | 75% | 75% | 32.7 | 40.4 |
| United States | All | Private | 25% | Private | Private | Private | 25%* | Private | Private | Private | Private | 29.5 | 34.0 |
| West Germany | All | All | 75% | 50% | 25% | 50% | All | All | 25% | Private | 25% | 33.6 | 42.1 |

† Not applicable or negligible production *Including Conrail

Shading indicates countries in which the rate of government spending grew most rapidly

Sources: *The Economist* and the Organization for Economic Cooperation and Development.

FIGURE 6.1
The government's share of the economy

groups (such as farmers), and enters into joint private-public ventures (such as exploration for oil). The relationship between government and business is sometimes cooperative and sometimes antagonistic.

Considerable inequality in the distribution of wealth and income persists, even where socialists have held power for long periods. Generally, however, wealth is not so unequally distributed as it was fifty years ago.

Given such diverse elements, it is hard to affix an appropriate name to this type of political economy. Some observers have called it neo-capitalism—a name that emphasizes its continuity with the capitalism of the past. Others have called it conservative socialism—a name that emphasizes how much has changed, both in economic life and in the way socialists now think about economic problems.

## The U.S.
## political economy

To say that the United States is the richest nation in the world is to echo a cliché—but a cliché that contains a large amount of truth. Americans comprise only 5 percent of the world's population and yet produce 30 percent of all the goods and services produced annually in the world. The U.S. **gross national product** (the value of all goods and services produced) is more than $2 trillion a year—an amount equal to the combined GNP of all the nations of Western Europe, plus Japan and Canada. Americans also use about 40 percent of the world's output of raw materials and produce an approximately equal amount of the world's waste products and pollution.

The United States has been the dominant force in international economic life since the end of World War II. Beginning in the early 1970s, however, a noticeable erosion of that dominance set in. The Vietnam War, energy shortages and oil price increases, the effects of recession followed by huge government budget deficits, and the growing economic power of other nations have all been contributing factors in this process. Today, for the first time since the 1930s, the assumption that American affluence could only increase has come into question. As different groups of Americans are affected in dif-

INCA KOLA or COCA-COLA, which will it be? The sign says drink INCA KOLA because "it's ours," a valiant effort to outflank the pervasive influence of America and its products, but probably a failing one.

Even in nations that are officially hostile to the United States, American films, dress, songs, and sports are often immensely popular among the population at large.

TABLE 6.2
## Per capita incomes of selected nations

| Nation | Year | Income |
|---|---|---|
| Denmark | 1980 | $12,956 |
| West Germany | 1982 | 11,142 |
| United States | 1982 | 11,107 |
| France | 1980 | 8,980 |
| United Kingdom | 1979 | 7,216 |
| Italy | 1980 | 6,914 |

Source: *World Almanac* (New York: NEA, 1984).

ferent ways by these economic changes, important new political issues and conflicts will inevitably arise. No longer is the United States the world leader in **per capita income** (GNP divided by population). Latest figures show that both Denmark and West Germany have passed the U.S. (see Table 6.2).

Distribution
of income

Americans are not equal participants either in the nation's affluence or in its economic problems. Our society includes many gradations of wealth and poverty. Traditionally, sociologists have viewed societies as divided into **social classes**—fairly distinct groups, differentiated by occupation or income, that usually have different life-styles and sometimes are in conflict politically.[9] An analysis of class can be based on many different criteria. For example, some sociologists regard the distinction between white-collar and blue-collar jobs as the fundamental division in society. Others emphasize property ownership, dividing society into owners and nonowners. Yet others focus on income and life-style criteria.

## Comparative perspective Income distribution in selected nations

Income distribution is more unequal in the United States than in many other industrial democracies, as well as in some less-industrialized ones. The following table compares the share of total income received by the poorest 20 percent to that received by the wealthiest 20 percent in selected nations. In the United States, that ratio is 10 to 1.

| Ratio of Income, Top 20% to Bottom 20% of Population | |
|---|---|
| Finland | 4/1 |
| Denmark | 5/1 |
| Japan | 5/1 |
| Netherlands | 5/1 |
| Sweden | 5/1 |
| United Kingdom | 5/1 |
| Bangladesh | 6/1 |
| West Germany | 6/1 |
| Norway | 6/1 |
| Sri Lanka | 6/1 |
| Yugoslavia | 6/1 |
| India | 7/1 |
| Indonesia | 7/1 |
| Spain | 7/1 |
| South Korea | 8/1 |
| Tanzania | 8/1 |
| France | 9/1 |

| | |
|---|---|
| United States | 10/1 |
| Malaysia | 16/1 |
| Turkey | 16/1 |
| Venezuela | 18/1 |
| Mexico | 20/1 |
| Peru | 32/1 |
| Brazil | 33/1 |

Source: Lester R. Brown, "Reshaping Economic Policies," in Lester R. Brown, et al., *State of the World, 1984* (New York: W. W. Norton, 1984), p. 202. The data are for the latest year available.

The dignity of the individual worker is enhanced by the idea that he or she cannot be replaced. But the fact of modern industrial society is that virtually anyone is replaceable, particularly those who work on the assembly lines and in mass production facilities. Because of the central importance of employment, a complex set of political issues revolve around the role of government in providing and protecting the job.

Most Americans classify themselves on the basis of annual income, the amount of money brought into the household in a given year. Those with annual incomes ranging from $8,000 to $80,000 commonly think of themselves as being "middle class." But such a broad category includes people with radically different life-styles, political views, occupations, incomes, and degrees of wealth.

A truer picture of the economic classes into which U.S. society is divided can be obtained by dividing the population into fifths, according to income levels, and determining the percentage of the nation's total income each fifth of the population receives. As Table 6.3 shows, in 1980 the poorest fifth of the U.S. population received less than 5 percent of the national income, whereas the richest fifth received close to 45 percent. Moreover, the second-poorest fifth received about 10 percent of all income, whereas the next-to-the-richest fifth received just under 25 percent. Clearly, income is distributed quite unequally in our society.

Mere recitation of such dry statistics, however, tells us little about how the poorest 20 percent of the population lives or about the political consequences of unequal income distribution. Fortunately, the U.S. government has attempted to describe the economic situation of families at various income levels, including those above as well as below the so-called poverty line. Above the poverty line (in 1983, $10,178 for an urban family of four), the Bureau of Labor Statistics differentiates among low-budget, medium-budget, and high-budget levels. On the basis of these rough income categories, the U.S. population in 1978 could be divided as follows:

| | |
|---|---|
| Above the high budget | 15% |
| Between medium and high | 30% |
| Between low and medium | 25% |
| Between poverty line and low | 15% |
| Below poverty line | 15% |

TABLE 6.3
## Incomes of U.S. families before taxes, 1929–1980

| Sector of population | 1929 | 1941 | 1950 | 1960 | 1970 | 1980 |
|---|---|---|---|---|---|---|
| Lowest fifth | 3.8% | 4.1% | 4.5% | 4.8% | 5.4% | 4.1% |
| Second fifth | 8.7 | 9.5 | 12.0 | 12.2 | 12.2 | 10.2 |
| Third fifth | 13.8 | 15.3 | 17.4 | 17.6 | 17.6 | 16.8 |
| Fourth fifth | 19.3 | 22.3 | 23.4 | 24.0 | 23.8 | 24.8 |
| Highest fifth | 54.4 | 48.8 | 42.7 | 41.3 | 40.9 | 44.2 |
| Top 5% of highest fifth | — | — | 17.3 | 15.9 | 15.6 | 16.5 |

Source: *Statistical Abstract of U.S.*, 1980, and U.S. Census Bureau, *Current Population Reports*, series P-23, No. 126, August 1983.

We can see from this analysis where the common notion of the breadth of the U.S. middle class comes from. As of 1978, about half the population fell somewhere between the low and high budget limits— that is, between $11,000 and $27,000. Within this range were many types of occupations, with considerable overlap between upper-blue-collar and lower-white-collar workers. The vast majority of the high-budget group fell in the $27,000–$50,000 income range. At the very top, however, was a small subgroup of the very rich, whose incomes ranged well into the tens of millions of dollars.

Upward movement from blue-collar to white-collar occupations is common in the United States, but no more so than in other industrial countries. What is exceptional about U.S. social mobility is the degree of movement from the bottom to the top—from the working class to the ranks of owners or managers. One out of every ten sons of American fathers with manual occupations rises to an elite professional or managerial position, as opposed to only one out of 30 in Sweden, one out of 45 in Great Britain, and one out of 100 in Denmark.[10] The Horatio Alger, rags-to-riches story is more than a myth in the United States; the relative frequency with which it actually happens tends to reinforce American faith in individualism. In the structure of beliefs undergirding U.S. society, the conviction that anyone can make it to the top is a vital element.

## Distribution of wealth and ownership

**Wealth** is the monetary value of what an individual or a household owns, adjusted for indebtedness. Ordinarily, wealth is divided between durable goods (e.g., houses, cars, appliances) and financial assets (e.g., stocks, bonds, savings, life insurance).

Wealth is distributed far less equally in the United States than is income. In 1962, for example, the poorest fifth of the population had a zero share of all wealth (because of net indebtedness), the second fifth has 3 percent, the third fifth 5 percent, the fourth fifth 16 percent, and the top fifth 77 percent. Moreover, the wealthiest 5 percent of the population holds 53 percent of all wealth, and the wealthiest 1 percent holds somewhere between 20 and 33 percent.

For a more dramatic view of the uneven distribution of wealth in the United States, we can divide the total net wealth (holdings minus debts) possessed by each income group by the number of people in that group. For example, if a group of one hundred people owned a total of $10,000 in stock, each hypothetically would be worth $100. Applying this method to the income categories described above, we find that those in the bottom 20 percent are worth $0 each; those in the next 20 percent, approximately $6,000 each; those in the third 20 percent, $10,000

Much of the power exercised by the top corporate elite in America is not directly political. Corporate decision makers, however, make plans for investment, for the opening and closing of plants, for research into new areas—all of which carry significant political consequences.

## Earnings of corporate executives

It is no surprise that the chief executives of many large corporations receive phenomenally high compensation. In 1981, top executives of such corporations as Mobil Oil, International Telephone and Telegraph, Revlon, and United Technologies all received salaries of more than a million dollars a year. Such earnings are of course dozens of times higher than those of the workers they employ. The following short profile of such corporate executives is taken from an essay by Paul Blumberg, "Another Day, Another $3,000: Executive Salaries in America."

Just who are these prodigiously paid executives? In their personal background and characteristics do they reflect the diversity of the American population? Has their composition been altered by the civil rights struggles of the 1960s, the women's movement, the equality revolution in general that sought to break down barriers of exclusiveness based on race, sex, and class, and to democratize access to the desirable positions in American life?

A recent study of the social background of 450 top executives from 250 of America's largest corporations answers all these questions in the negative. The executive suite today is full of the same old faces. They are all men, all white, nearly all from upper- or upper-middle-class families, are overwhelmingly Protestant (85 percent) and mainly Episcopal and Presbyterian, nearly all college-educated, with Harvard, Yale, MIT, and Columbia the most frequently attended schools, and almost all Republicans. In short, top management has been virtually untouched by any of the movements toward equality of the last decade and a half, and the executive suite remains one of the most highly segregated sanctuaries in the land.*

*Paul Blumberg, "Another Day, Another $3,000: Executive Salaries in America," *Dissent*, Spring 1978, pp. 157–168.

each; those in the fourth 20 percent, $32,000 each; those in the top 5 percent, $200,000 each; and those in the top 1 percent, $800,000 each.

Such facts of economic life not only imply radical differences in life-style among Americans—they also have direct and profound political and social consequences. Economics can translate into political power through contributions, advertising, and various sources of influence and assistance. Higher social status itself usually permits a greater voice in political life. Great concentrations of wealth also place in the hands of a few decision-making power in economic matters that affect the lives of the multitude—factories can be closed or opened, investments shifted, new products marketed or not developed. The partial democracy of the political arena, then, faces what is primarily an oligarchy in the economic sphere.

It is important to recognize that the U.S. economy is largely a *corporate* economy. Although there are still vast numbers of small businesses, most manufacturing is done by a fairly small number of large corporations. The eighteenth-century capitalist image of a marketplace populated by many small enterprises has little meaning and less relevance in an economy in which a few major firms dominate the market in most industries.

A major economic trend in recent decades has been toward ever-increasing concentration of industrial power. In 1955 the five hundred largest corporations controlled 65 percent of all manufacturing and mining assets in the country. By 1965, that figure had increased to 73 percent. By 1977, it had hit 80 percent. This development raises serious questions about the nature of the U.S. economy: How much real free enterprise remains? How much competition can there be when it is almost impossible to challenge the leading companies in an industry? As fewer and fewer companies dominate the market, don't collusion and price fixing become more and more likely? Has the well-being of huge corporations become tied up with our national well-being? Can we allow major companies to fail economically, when that will mean hundreds of thousands out of work?

Of course, the U.S. economy is by no means entirely "corporatized," and corporations are not the only groups that wield political clout. As politics has penetrated every area of economic life, individuals with common economic interests have formed pressure groups in an effort to achieve political influence. Doctors, teachers, blue-collar workers, sellers of insurance—all are politically organized. This is inevitable in an economy in which political and economic

The New York Stock Exchange, a frenzy of activity during the peak trading hours. A symbol around the world of U.S. capitalism, the stock market has become a highly sensitive barometer of shifting national and international political and economic trends.

factors are interwoven so thoroughly. If an industry, a corporation, or some sector of the economy fails to become organized in a politically effective way, it may well find itself vulnerable to political forces outside its control.

## Poverty

Any assessment of the distribution of wealth in the United States must deal with the question of poverty. How many suffer severe deprivation from the inequalities in U.S. society? And perhaps more importantly, what progress is being made toward reducing their number? The issue is not a simple one. Most of us do not interact with the poor, who pop-

TABLE 6.4
## Poverty level in America, 1960–1982

| | Persons below poverty level | | | Median income of all families |
|---|---|---|---|---|
| | Number (millions) | Percent of total population | Average poverty line for nonfarm family of four* | |
| 1960 | 39.9 | 22.2% | $3,022 | $ 5,620 |
| 1966 | 28.5 | 14.7 | 3,317 | 7,532 |
| 1972 | 24.5 | 11.9 | 4,275 | 11,116 |
| 1976 | 25.0 | 11.8 | 5,815 | 14,958 |
| 1982 | 34.4 | 15.0 | 9,862 | 21,023 |

*Dollar equivalent of minimal nutrition intake is tied to the consumer price index, and thus increases with inflation.
Source: Adapted from U.S. Statistical Abstract, 1982–83.

American capitalist ideology usually focuses on small, self-started businesses as its ideal. Many Americans dream of being their own bosses, but maintaining a small business is a tough venture, and large numbers go under. Millions of small businesses exist, but the American economy is dominated by corporate giants.

shansky for the Social Security Administration in the early 1960s.[11] At the core of her computations was an estimate of the dollar equivalent of the minimum amount of nutrition needed for a person to survive. She then multiplied this economy food budget by three, to reflect the findings of a series of studies in 1955 that low-income families spent two-thirds of

ulate the margins of our society—the ghettos, barrios, migrant farm worker camps, and Indian reservations. Also, who exactly "the poor" are, and how prevalent poverty is, are matters of some dispute.

**Definitions:** The federal government's definition of poverty is based on calculations made by Mollie Or-

Poverty has remained an intractable problem in the United States. But, as many observers have pointed out, our current poverty is often hidden from view. It was for this reason that Michael Harrington coined the term "the other America" to refer to this hidden poverty in urban ghettoes, isolated rural areas, and, as in the photo below, on Indian reservations.

TABLE 6.5
## People likely to be poor, 1980

| Characteristics | Percent below the poverty line |
|---|---|
| Unrelated individuals | 22.9% |
| Persons in families with a female head | 32.7 |
| Blacks | 32.5 |
| Black persons in families with a female head | 49.4 |
| Persons of Spanish origin | 25.7 |
| Spanish-origin persons in families with a female head | 51.3 |
| Unrelated individuals over age sixty-five | 30.6 |
| Children under fifteen | 19.1 |
| Persons living in families with a head under age twenty-five | 21.0 |
| Persons living in families whose head had less than eight years school | 24.9 |
| Persons in families with no wage earner | 27.2 |
| Persons in families with seven children or more | 51.6 |

Source: Bureau of the Census, *Current Population Reports: Characteristics of the Population Below the Poverty Level: 1980*, series P-60, no. 133 (Washington, D.C.: U.S. Government Printing Office, July 1981), Tables A, 1, 11, 17, 24, 31.

their budgets on nonfood essentials such as clothing, shelter, and fuel. The figure then arrived at became the basis for establishing poverty lines for various groups of people—those in urban or rural areas, families of four or single individuals, and so on. A person whose income fell below the poverty line of his or her group was counted as "poor."

As Table 6.4 demonstrates, progress toward the eradication of poverty, as that term is officially defined, has been disappointing over the last two decades: much headway was made between 1960 and 1972, no improvement was noticeable in 1972–76, and a dramatic *rise* in poverty was recorded in 1976–82. And if one takes issue with the government's statistical definition of poverty, the picture becomes even less encouraging. By the government's own admission, the nutrition provided by the economy food budget is only *minimally* adequate—and only certainly so for "emergency or temporary" periods.

150

**Distribution:** Poverty is not randomly distributed in U.S. society. Although more than 60 percent of all poor people are white, a disproportionate 30 percent are black (blacks make up 11 percent of the population). Also, female-headed households make up 44 percent of the poor. As we will see, social attitudes and policies sharply affect who will become and remain poor. Poverty is largely a product of generations of discrimination, sexism, exploitation, and neglect. Being born into a poor family places heavy burdens on even the most enterprising of people— the fight for a good education, a decent job, and other opportunities is steeply uphill.

Government policies have had a marked effect on the distribution of poverty. Over the past 20 years, the percentage of elderly people who are poor has declined sharply, largely because of higher Social Security payments. In comparison with the late 1960s, the poor today are more likely to be young, black, and female (see Table 6.5).

Victims of the Great
Depression—the mother
and children of a migrant
family living in a patchwork
trailer in an open field. In
the 1930s large numbers of
homeless Americans roamed
the land in search of work,
shelter, and help. The 1980s
saw another epidemic of
homelessness, much of
it concentrated in urban
areas.

## Public policy and the political economy

## Government spending, taxation, and regulation

The U.S. government has always been involved in our economic life. Yet until relatively recently, its spending, taxation, and regulatory policies were only marginally significant in terms of the overall economy. In 1929, federal spending represented only 9.8 percent of the U.S. gross national product. Outlays to combat the Depression of the 1930s pushed government spending to 19 percent of the GNP. During World War II government expenditures rose dramatically—to finance military production, the government spent 41 percent of the GNP in both 1943 and 1944. When peace came, government outlays temporarily dropped back to prewar levels, only to rise again in the Cold War era, to 23 percent of the GNP. Today, the federal government normally accounts for between 20 and 25 percent of the U.S.

gross national product. The two largest budget items are usually defense and Social Security.

When the government disposes of a quarter of a nation's GNP, it is obvious that the priorities of government spending will have great social and political ramifications for the society. The basic issues involving the federal budget are: How large should the overall budget be? Is the national debt a problem? Who should carry the tax burden? What priorities should government expenditures follow?

On the first two issues, modern-day liberals and conservatives generally split. Liberals tend to see many uses for an involved and active government, and they frequently argue that government spending is too low. Conservatives, in contrast, tend to regard government spending as a major social issue in itself and to campaign vigorously for budget cuts. Conservatives also often call for a balanced budget— that is, one in which the outflow of funds is roughly matched by government revenues from taxes and other sources. Liberals tend to argue that deficit spending can help stimulate economic growth. These positions are not written in stone, of course: liberals as well as conservatives have opposed too-large budget deficits, and it was the conservative administration of President Ronald Reagan that amassed the largest government debt in U.S. history.

The question of who should carry the tax burden is an even more controversial one. Should individuals pay most of it, or should corporations? Is there a proper balance to be struck between the two? The majority of the tax burden currently falls on individuals—a subject we will return to in Chapter 19.

Whatever the spending level decided upon, and whoever ultimately foots the tax bill, there will be differences of opinion about spending priorities. Here, too, the broad political patterns are fairly easy to discern. Conservatives have long emphasized military preparedness as a top priority, whereas liberals have usually called for increased spending on social programs. (Of course, the full political picture is not so devoid of shadings—many liberals, for example, have been, and continue to be, strong proponents of defense spending.)

The battles fought over the size and composition of the federal budget each year reflect these differences in political beliefs and commitments. They also reflect the views of the social groups from which lawmakers draw support. The president, who has the major hand in shaping the budget, also determines the terrain on which the budget battles will be fought. President Lyndon Johnson's Great Society programs helped shape the federal budget of the mid-1960s, as his commitment to the Vietnam War shaped those of the late 1960s. More recently, President Reagan's emphasis on military preparedness had a tremendous impact on the budget deficits run up by the federal government in the early 1980s.

Since the 1950s, defense spending as a percentage of GNP has alternately risen and fallen. Government expenditures on defense declined from 9.5 percent of GNP in 1968 to 5.1 percent in fiscal 1979, only to rise again under the Reagan administration. Generally, U.S. outlays on defense exceed those of other Western democracies, because of the heavier defense burden the United States carries.

Federal government spending on social programs has increased significantly since 1965. Currently, expenditures for social programs comprise about 50 percent of all federal expenditures; they also account for more than 70 percent of recent growth in the national budget.[12] Many of these programs are exempt from budgetary limits, and so it is difficult to control their growth. Higher Social Security payments, for example, have been responsible for much of the rise in social spending. In 1981, for example, the elderly, a group making up about 11 percent of the U.S. population, received about 25 percent of all federal government spending, in the form of Social Security payments, Medicare and Medicaid payments, and such other programs as food stamps and housing.

Despite these recent increases in social welfare spending, the U.S. government still spends significantly less than its European counterparts on public welfare. Our income tax levels are also significantly lower, and they have increased less over the past twenty-five years (see Table 6.6). It is no wonder, then, that the more elaborate European welfare states have gone further than the United States, to eliminate poverty, deprivation, and neglect. In Norway, for example, government policy has virtually ended poverty, despite the fact that the pretax distribution of income in Norway is very similar to the pretax distribution in this country. The Norwegians allot more of their total GNP for use by the government, and a greater percentage of government expenditures is directed into **transfer payments** (money paid to individuals through social programs). The Norwegian tax structure is also a highly progressive one (that is, the higher one's income, the higher the rate of taxation).

The example of Norway illustrates that even in a predominantly capitalist society (as Norway is), the government can go to great lengths to deal with deprivation. It also reflects profound differences in Norwegian and American attitudes toward what government should do, and for whom. It has often been pointed out that Americans tend to focus the blame for economic failure on the individual, not on the society as a whole. Many Americans who are not successful, accordingly, blame themselves for their

TABLE 6.6
## Tax revenue as a percentage of gross domestic product, 1955–80

| | 1955 | 1965 | 1980 | 1982 | 1955–82 percentage increase |
|---|---|---|---|---|---|
| Britain | 29.8% | 30.8% | 35.9% | 39.6% | 9.8% |
| France | 32.9 | 35.0 | 41.2 | 43.7 | 10.8 |
| Netherlands | 26.3 | 35.5 | 46.2 | 45.5 | 19.2 |
| Sweden | 25.5 | 35.6 | 49.9 | 50.3 | 24.8 |
| United States | 24.6 | 26.5 | 30.7 | 30.5 | 5.9 |
| West Germany | 30.8 | 31.6 | 37.2 | 37.3 | 6.5 |

Sources: *Revenue Statistics of OECD Countries 1965–1980* (Paris: OECD, 1984). *Long-Term Trends in Tax Revenues of OECD Member Countries, 1955–1980* (Paris: OECD, 1981).

situation, and often their faith in the "American dream" of individual success[13] remains unshaken.

But if the U.S. government has often not accorded the highest possible priority to the alleviation of deprivation, it does perform many essential social welfare functions, as well as other functions that are deeply embedded in the nation's socioeconomic life. As already noted in our discussion of the mixed economy, the government regulates the trade cycle (though often unsuccessfully, at least in detail); provides social welfare benefits to individuals, without which many more people would fall below the official poverty line; and oversees a wide system of economic regulation designed, in many respects, to protect individuals.

## Government and inequality

Should government actively promote economic equality? Some argue that government has no business interfering with the distribution of income and wealth in society. Others maintain that the redistribution of income is a legitimate governmental activity—to increase equality and assist those in greatest financial need.[14]

In fact, governments seem inevitably to become deeply enmeshed in economic activity, and their rules and programs do provide benefits and protections to various groups. The question is, How much should government do, and for whom? American conservatives say that since the New Deal governmental programs have had the effect of distorting the workings of the marketplace and even resulted in a deadening of incentive. Government has tried to produce too much equality, they claim, and has done so rather badly. Liberal and socialist critics, on the other hand, point out that those reforms undertaken in the direction of greater equality have usually been necessitated by the obvious failings of capitalism, and have not fundamentally changed U.S. economic patterns.

Both sides can cite evidence for their views. Since the 1930s, government-administered social programs clearly have led to a certain amount of redistribution of income (not wealth). Also, government regulatory activities in the areas of health and safety have helped to protect workers and consumers from serious hazards, and civil-rights legislation has helped to improve the economic lot of women and minorities.

# Selected U.S. government subsidies

The U.S. government provides a variety of subsidies for various groups. These include special tax advantages, direct cash payments, and loans with favorable conditions as well as regulations designed to encourage particular activities. Following is a selected list of beneficiaries of such subsidies and the value of the subsidy in the early 1980s.

### Cash payments
The maritime industry, $600 million

Business aviation, $660 million

### Tax breaks
Savings and loan institutions, $3.3 billion

Trucking companies, $60 million

Multinational corporations, $500 million

High-technology firms, $600 million

Timber companies, $470 million

Oil and gas companies, $1.9 billion

### Favorable regulations
Trucking (limits on competition)

AM broadcasters (limits on competition)

Nuclear power industry (limits on liability in case of accident)

### Interest and loan subsidies
Farmers (price supports)

Exporting companies (loans to promote the export of U.S. goods)

Source: *Common Cause*, August 1981, pp. 24–29.

---

Still, much government activity has undeniably been designed to bolster big business interests and keep capitalism running as smoothly as possible. Efforts at aiding social change, critics have argued, usually have left the majority of the disadvantaged unaffected.

Recent studies have shown that the federal income tax, contrary to many popular notions, does not redistribute all that much income. Although the income tax does take proportionately more from wealthier taxpayers, its overall effect is very limited. According to the Congressional Joint Committee on Taxation, in 1977 the wealthiest 25 percent of taxpayers took home 55.5 percent of all income and after taxes still held onto 53.2 percent of it. At the same time, the poorest 25 percent of taxpayers received just 4.6 percent of income, and after taxes their share rose to only 5.2 percent.

Those redistributive effects that are achieved through government take place as a result of transfer payments. The income of the poorest sector of the U.S. population is significantly increased by these payments, as well as by such noncash assistance as food stamps and public housing. Government action does make a real difference to these individuals, though, as we have seen, it falls far short of eliminating poverty and severe deprivation.

The growth of the welfare state and the various sorts of benefits and burdens it has to distribute has also led to new social conflicts, many of which revolve around the legal rights and entitlements the welfare state can grant or withhold. Should disadvantaged groups be given preference in hiring policies? Which programs should have priority in the federal budget—those dealing with the elderly, unemployed youth, cities, or environmental matters? In many ways, economic competition, once more-orless confined to the marketplace, has now been partly redirected into the political arena.

Another troubling aspect of the current U.S. political economy is that it is difficult to judge how just our current arrangements are. As many critics have pointed out, our system facilitates each interest group's attempts to bring pressure on the political process to get special benefits or to protect its position (a matter we will take up in detail in Chapter 11). And even if every organized group enjoys some degree of access, the best organized and the most persistent usually win the greatest benefits.[15]

Overall, then, we see a mixed picture in regard to the role that government plays in promoting equality or inequality. Our national governments have done both, with emphases varying from one administration to another. The social programs of Lyndon Johnson's "War on Poverty" significantly improved the lot of the poor, while, on the other hand, the policies of the Reagan administration appear to have resulted in an increase in poverty and inequality.

## Conclusions

The successes of mixed economies have left many important issues unresolved.[16] From the capitalist standpoint, Western societies have moved too far to the left. From the socialist standpoint, many of the old problems of capitalism remain, if less intense in form. The issues confronting U.S. social and economic life today are skirmishes in a long-running battle over what sort of economy and society is a healthy and just one. In the United States, as we have noted, the struggle is not so much between capitalists and socialists as between liberals and conservatives. American liberals are considerably more moderate than are European democratic socialists, while American conservatives are usually somewhat to the right of European conservatives.

From the perspective of democratic theory, the key issues here are two: How much economic equality is necessary to make democracy workable and reasonably just? And what are the implications for the quality of democratic life? Does a government-owned economy spell trouble for political freedoms, as some conservatives argue, or can it produce a more equitable social system than we now have? These are not easy questions, yet they may well be among the most intricate and important issues that democrats face today.

Orthodox apologists for capitalism often have argued that democracy is incompatible with government ownership of large segments of the economy.[17] Only private ownership, they have contended, confers the economic freedom that makes political freedom meaningful. Critics of this position have replied that pure, unregulated capitalism in itself threatens democracy, since it creates so much inequality and so many serious economic problems.

There is general agreement, however, that the industrial democracies face two new sets of problems. For one, the successful methods of economic management that Western democratic governments pioneered in the 1930s and expanded in the 1950s no longer seem able to cope fully with the complex economic problems of today. For another, energy/environment issues—problems of declining energy sources, depletion of land and forest, population pressures, unprecedented international debt difficulties, environmental pollution that affects air and oceans—have added new dimensions to the economic equation, especially in a changing international economic system. Neither conservatives nor liberals (nor, in Europe, democratic socialists) have turned out to have very persuasive solutions to these difficulties. As we will see in Chapters 19 and 23, the solutions we find to our new economic dilemmas also have important democratic dimensions.

## NOTES

1 For a provocative discussion of this period and the ideological alternatives, see Karl Polanyi, *The Great Transformation* (Boston, Mass.: Beacon Press, 1957); Adam Smith, *The Wealth of Nations* (New York: Modern Library, 1937); and George Lichtheim, *A Short History of Socialism* (New York: Praeger, 1971).

2 Joseph Schumpeter, *Capitalism, Socialism and Democracy*, 3rd ed. (New York: Harper and Row, 1950); David Ricardo, *Principles of Political Economy and Taxation* (New York: Dutton, 1962); John Maynard Keynes, *The*

*General Theory of Employment, Interest, and Money* (New York: HBJ, 1965).

3 An early expression of this novel concept can be found in Bernard Mandeville, *The Fable of the Bees*, published in 1714.

4 These views can be found in the works of the poet Samuel Taylor Coleridge as well as in the writings of Thomas B. Macaulay and the British Prime Minister Benjamin Disraeli.

5 For two thoughtful discussions, see George Lichtheim, "What Socialism Is and Is Not," *New York Review of Books*, April 9, 1970; and Robert Heilbroner, "Socialism and the Future," *Commentary*, December 1961, pp. 35–45.

6 See, for example, the apocalyptic fears of one conservative in Friedrich Hayek, *The Road to Serfdom* (Chicago, Ill.: University of Chicago Press, 1944).

7 For an example of this moderation, see C. A. R. Crosland, *The Future of Socialism* (New York: Macmillan, 1957).

8 A good discussion can be found in Andrew Schonfield, *Modern Capitalism* (New York: Oxford University Press, 1965).

9 For some interesting examples, see Peter Blau and Otis Dudley Duncan, *The American Occupational Structure* (New York: Wiley, 1967); and Stephen J. Rose, *Social Stratification in the United States* (Baltimore: Social Graphics, 1979).

10 Blau and Duncan, *ibid*.

11 Mollie Orshansky, "Counting the Poor," *Social Security Bulletin*, 25 (1963), pp. 2–21.

12 Reported by Robert D. Reischauer, deputy director of the Congressional Budget Office in a talk at Duke University, 1979.

13 Kay Scholzman and Sidney Verba, *Injury to Insult: Unemployment, Class, and Political Response* (Cambridge, Mass.: Harvard University Press, 1979).

14 See the discussion in Irving Kristol, *Two Cheers for Capitalism* (New York: Basic Books, 1978); and Michael Harrington, *Decade of Decision* (New York: Simon & Schuster, 1980).

15 Grant McConnell, *Private Power and American Democracy* (New York: Random House, 1970).

16 A useful, iconoclastic discussion of these issues can be found in Paul Goodman, *People or Personnel: Decentralizing and the Mixed System* (New York: Random House, 1965).

17 Milton Friedman, *Capitalism and Freedom* (Chicago: University of Chicago Press, 1964).

## SELECTED READINGS

### Capitalism and socialism

On capitalism see John Kenneth Galbraith, *American Capitalism* (Boston, Mass.: Houghton-Mifflin, 1956); Edward S. Mason, ed., *The Corporation in Modern Society* (Cambridge, Mass.: Harvard University Press, 1960); Thomas S. Ashton, *The Industrial Revolution, 1760–1830*, Revised ed. (New York: Oxford University Press, 1964); Beth Mintz and Michael Schwartz, *The Power Structure of American Business* (Chicago, Ill.: University of Chicago Press, 1984).

Among the more readable and provocative presentations of socialist ideas are Michael Harrington, *Socialism* (New York: Bantam Books, 1973); George Lichtheim, *A Short History of Socialism* (New York: Praeger, 1971); and Ross Terrill, *R. H. Tawney and His Times* (Cambridge, Mass.: Harvard University Press, 1973).

For accounts of the new "mixed system" from various points of view, see Daniel Bell, *The End of Ideology* (New York: The Free Press, 1965) and *The Coming of Post Industrial Society* (New York: Basic Books, 1976); Andrew Shonfield, *Modern Capitalism;* Robert Heilbroner, *Between Capitalism and Socialism;* Herbert Marcuse, *One Dimensional Man* (Boston: Beacon Press, 1964); and M. D. Hancock and G. Sjoberg, eds., *Politics in the Post Welfare State* (New York: Columbia University Press, 1972).

### The U.S. political economy

For a general discussion of the field of political economy, see Charles E. Lindblom, *Politics and Markets: The World's Political-Economic Systems* (New York: Basic Books, 1977); and Ralph Miliband, *The State in Capitalist Society* (New York: Basic Books, 1969).

On poverty, see Bradley R. Schiller, *The Economics of Poverty and Discrimination* (Englewood Cliffs, N.J.: Prentice-Hall, 1976); Harrell Rodgers, *Poverty and Plenty* (Reading, Mass.: Addison-Wesley, 1979); and Nick Kotz, *Let Them Eat Promises: The Politics of Hunger in America* (Englewood Cliffs, N.J.: Prentice-Hall, 1969).

## Public policy and the political economy

For discussions of various ways politics and economics are interrelated, see Robert Heilbroner, *Between Capitalism and Socialism* (New York: Vintage, 1970); A. J. Heidenheimer, H. Heclo, and C. T. Adams, *Comparative Public Policy* (New York: St. Martin's Press, 1983); and H. L. Wilensky, *The Welfare State and Equality* (Berkeley, Cal.: University of California Press, 1975).

## The problems of a mixed economy

For analyses of the problems of the mixed economy, see Seymour Melman, *The Permanent War Economy* (New York: Simon and Schuster, 1974); Leo Srole, *Mental Life in the Metropolis* (New York: McGraw-Hill, 1975); and Anne Ehrlich, Paul Ehrlich, and William Holdren, *Ecoscience* (San Francisco: W. H. Freeman, 1977). Irving Howe, ed., *Beyond the Welfare State* (New York: Schocken, 1982).

# Part
two

# Politics

# Chapter
seven

# Political socialization and public opinion

## Informed awareness or complacent ignorance?

WHERE do our political attitudes come from? How do we learn to "believe in" democratic politics (to the extent that we do)? How do we become Democrats or Republicans, or choose to shun party affiliation? Where do we acquire political information, and how adequate is the information acquired? In this chapter, these and similar questions will be explored and related to the state of democratic politics in the United States today.

The two major areas we will discuss are political socialization and public opinion. Examination of the process of socialization will reveal how political attitudes are shaped in this country; examination of trends in public opinion will reveal what those attitudes actually are. In the process of exploring these areas, we will come across several significant issues related to the major themes of this book. At the broadest level, for example, we will be asking whether the American public can generally be characterized as an informed, thoughtful, and democratic group. Do most Americans understand the ideals and the realities of democratic politics? Do we tend to be articulate and aware in a political sense, or apathetic and ignorant? What is the acceptable level of public information in a democracy?

We will also want to know if American political values are truly democratic. Do we endorse freedom of speech and press? Are we committed to equality? Do we support a reasonable level of tolerance for unpopular views?

We will consider, finally, the implications for U.S. political life of alienation from politics in general. Does the fact that many citizens have become cynical and disillusioned imperil democratic life? Do Americans as a group exhibit trust in their government and faith in the efficacy of political activity?

A logical starting point for any exploration of these issues is the complex of factors that shapes us as political and social beings—principally, the family and the school system. Through these agencies, we are socialized: that is, inculcated with distinctly American social and political values and attitudes. Because much of the imprint of early socialization is retained throughout life, an interest in the workings of democracy naturally leads us back to the shaping of the values of the child.

## Political socialization

The words have a heavy ring, but their meaning is not all that difficult to comprehend. **Political so-**

**cialization** refers to the processes through which an individual acquires the political attitudes and behavior common to a particular culture. Every culture must socialize its members—that is, indoctrinate them into its language, customs, mores, and institutions. By the time a child is just a few years of age, he or she has been stamped by the formative forces of society.

If every society inculcates some values into children, the key questions to be asked are, Which values? and Whose interests do the values serve? To recall that American blacks and women were long socialized to believe in their own inferiority is to understand that socialization can serve exploitative purposes. It is easier for most Americans to acknowledge that this phenomenon takes place in other societies—such as the Soviet Union or Cuba—than to admit that it occurs in the United States as well. It would serve us well to remember, however, that socialization is a two-edged sword in all societies, including our own.

Most Americans take substantial pride in their country and regard its capitalistic economic system favorably. These attitudes, which are inculcated very early in an individual's development, usually form a deeply rooted base of diffuse support[1] for the political and economic structures of U.S. society. A base of *diffuse support* is a set of favorable attitudes toward political and social objects that is independent of day-to-day events. For most citizens, that is, temporary discontent with the government of the day or with the government's approach to specific problems leaves untouched a reservoir of good will and tolerance toward governmental institutions. Such fundamental support provides government with a stable foundation even in times of great crisis. Because of this foundation, the United States has been able to weather the many crises of the last twenty-five years with relatively little change in its fundamental political structures and practices.

Diffuse support can be distinguished from *specific support*, which is tied much more closely to approval of particular policies and practices and is therefore more subject to change. From the standpoint of democratic politics, the issue to be explored is not so much whether most of us have acquired a generally

## Comparative perspective
## National pride and willingness to fight for one's country

The two questions here were asked in 1982 by Eurobarometre, a European opinion poll. The survey includes samples from the United States and Japan as well as various Western European nations. Notice that it also includes a composite score for Continental Europeans as a group (excluding Great Britain and Ireland).

Americans, according to this survey, express considerably more national pride than do Europeans. A substantial majority of Europeans do express positive attitudes toward their nations, but not such positive ones as Americans voice. This finding may reflect several things: greater American self-love, a European tendency toward self-criticism or a sense of disillusion, since two world wars have been fought on European soil in this century.

Americans are also far more willing at least to

positive feeling about the main institutions of U.S. society—that seems to be the case in all reasonably stable societies. Rather, the key issue is how diffuse support and specific support are balanced at any given time. If diffuse support is carried too far, or prevents citizens from appreciating current realities, it will hinder critical inquiry and cripple political debate. There must be a balance between appreciation of the virtues a system exhibits and willingness to see its flaws and deficiencies. Otherwise, socialization becomes a tool for exploitation and domination, rather than a means of instilling knowledge.

How proud are you to be a (citizen of a particular country)?*

|  | U.S. | Great Britain | Ireland | Japan | Europe | West Germany | France | Italy | Spain |
|---|---|---|---|---|---|---|---|---|---|
| 1. Very proud | 80% | 55% | 66% | 30% | 38% | 21% | 33% | 41% | 49% |
| 2. Quite proud | 16 | 31 | 25 | 32 | 38 | 38 | 43 | 39 | 34 |
| 3. Not very proud | 2 | 8 | 5 | 28 | 12 | 18 | 8 | 11 | 8 |
| 4. Not at all proud | 1 | 3 | 1 | 3 | 7 | 11 | 9 | 6 | 4 |
| 5. Don't know | 2 | 3 | 3 | 7 | 6 | 12 | 7 | 2 | 5 |

Of course, we all hope that there will not be another war, but if it were to come to that, would you be willing to fight for your country?*

|  | U.S. | Great Britain | Ireland | Japan | Europe | West Germany | France | Italy | Spain |
|---|---|---|---|---|---|---|---|---|---|
| 1. Yes | 71% | 62% | 49% | 22% | 43% | 35% | 42% | 28% | 53% |
| 2. No | 20 | 27 | 31 | 40 | 40 | 41 | 46 | 57 | 27 |
| 3. Don't know | 9 | 11 | 20 | 38 | 17 | 24 | 12 | 15 | 20 |

say that they would fight for their country. Only the British come close to the American score of 71 percent; the overall European average is only 43 percent "yes" answers. In some nations— most notably Japan, West Germany, and Italy—the balance is heavily tilted in the "no" direction.

*Source: Stichting European Value Systems Study Group, Tilburg, Netherlands.

## Childhood

Although much remains to be discovered about how children acquire their views of society and politics, we do know that both family and school are critical mediators of socialization and that socialization is both a direct and an indirect process. Direct socialization involves the deliberate teaching of specific political views, values, and behaviors. Indirect socialization involves attitudes and behavior patterns that are not deliberately taught, but acquired through emulation. For example, children may acquire through direct socialization the idea that all Americans have equal rights guaranteed by the Constitution. Through indirect socialization, however, they may gain a sense that some are "more equal than others," as they pick up cues subtly conveyed by adults.

For a typical child the first object of political awareness is not politics itself, but the political community—the nation and the symbols associated with it, such as the flag. By the age of six or seven, most children have come to realize that they are "Americans," to associate themselves with the American

163

It is usually not hard to perceive the importance of parental influence on child development. Children model themselves on parents and, until adolescence, usually adopt attitudes and styles similar to those they find at home.

flag, and to believe that theirs is a "free" country. For children, feelings about politics are acquired before knowledge about politics. A sense of national loyalty develops before children are aware of the specific ways in which U.S. politics works.

Young children see the national government as consisting mainly of the president and his "helpers." Similarly, they identify local government principally with the mayor or other local executive and, perhaps, the neighborhood police officer. To children, then, authority is highly personalized and idealized. "Government" appears to consist of a series of individuals performing executive functions; legislatures and courts are not significant elements in a child's political consciousness.

According to studies conducted in the late 1950s and early 1960s, American children tend to view the president as a "benevolent leader," or a "superfriend"—well-intentioned, helpful, hard-working, honest, and invariably correct in his decisions and

actions. Why such a benign and favorable image of the president? For one thing, children tend to transfer feelings from parents (especially fathers) to others in authority; thus, presidents and other authority figures are viewed as children wish to view their parents. Also, the "benevolent leader" image often is deliberately advanced by parents, teachers, and other adults. Even adults who are critical of the president when with other adults may screen out negative references and introduce children to politics in a positive manner.[2]

When these findings about socialization were first published about twenty-five years ago, they were thought to apply to all American children. Later investigators, however, discovered that they applied principally to middle-class white children. Studies of poor white children in Appalachia and of Mexican-American children in the Southwest uncovered almost opposite feelings (see Table 7.1). These children were far less likely to see the president as more honest, harder-working, or more knowledgeable than most people—or even as a good person.

These findings highlighted a phenomenon that students of politics had noted in other areas: namely, that social class and ethnicity make a significant difference in attitudes and behavior. Generally, middle-class children are more aware of partisan differences, show a greater sense of political efficacy (i.e., that political action will be worthwhile), and are more likely to want to participate in politics than are lower-class children.

During the Watergate scandal of the early 1970s, researchers set out to contrast the responses of grade school students to the questions that had been put to such students in 1962.[3] The results of their survey

TABLE 7.1
## Views of the president among three groups of U.S. children

| Question | Response | Mexican-American children | Appalachian children | Suburban Chicago children |
|---|---|---|---|---|
| 1. How hard does the president work compared with most men? | Harder | 49% | 35% | 77% |
| | As hard | 27 | 24 | 21 |
| | Less hard | 24 | 41 | 3 |
| 2. How honest is the president compared with most men? | More honest | * | 23% | 57% |
| | As honest | * | 50 | 42 |
| | Less honest | * | 27 | 1 |
| 3. How knowledgeable is the president compared to most men? | Knows more | 41% | 45% | 82% |
| | Knows about the same | 42 | 33 | 16 |
| | Knows less | 17 | 22 | 2 |
| 4. What kind of person is the president? | Best in the world | 11% | 6% | 11% |
| | A good person | 63 | 68 | 82 |
| | Not a good person | 26 | 26 | 8 |

*Data not reported.
Source: Appalachian and Chicago data reported in Dean Jaros, Herbert Hirsch, and Frederic J. Fleron, Jr., "The Malevolent Leader: Political Socialization in an American Sub-Culture," *American Political Science Review* 62 (1968):568. The Mexican-American data are reported in Herbert Hirsch and Armand Gutiarrez, "The Socialization of Political Aggression and Political Affect: A Subcultural Analysis," an unpublished paper.

were revealing. Whereas 58 percent of fourth-graders surveyed in 1962 rated the president as "my favorite" or "almost my favorite" person, only 7 percent of those surveyed in 1973 did so. The fourth-graders of 1973 also were able to distinguish between negative feelings toward the current occupant of the office, Richard Nixon, and the office of the presidency itself—a distinction that had been considered beyond the grasp of such young children. Despite the Watergate scandal, the children generally retained positive feelings about the presidency, while showing an openness to negative evaluations of the current president.

Political partisanship is also transmitted to children rather early. One study found that by age nine, 60 percent of children were expressing partisan loyalties.[4] Often, political loyalties, like religious affiliations, are basically inculcated through the child's unconscious identification with parental preferences. Loyalties acquired early in life are subject to later reexamination, however—socialization does not end at adolescence. Moreover, there is some evidence that children often—perhaps as much as half the time—do not follow the political leads of their parents. Many children declare themselves to be "Independents," thus moving some distance away from the

TABLE 7.2
## Party identification
## of parents and children

| | Parents | | |
| Children | Democrat | Independent | Republican |
|---|---|---|---|
| Democrat | 66% | 29% | 13% |
| Independent | 27 | 53 | 36 |
| Republican | 7 | 17 | 51 |
| | 100% | 99% | 100% |

Source: Bruce A. Campbell, *The American Electorate* (New York: Holt, Rinehart and Winston, 1979), p. 112.

political party preference of their parents (see Table 7.2). When the parents do not agree on party affiliation, it is even more likely that the children will strike out on their own.

Children acquire through the family not only specific political attitudes or behaviors, but also general emotional orientations that may shape later political responses, such as tolerance, generosity, fear of being different, or confidence in oneself. Psychological studies have shown that children who grow up in authoritarian households are more likely to take on authoritarian attitudes and to display prejudice and hostility toward those who challenge authority.[5] Likewise, liberal attitudes and behavior are usually acquired in the family. Of course, many "authoritarian" or conservative families produce liberal children, and vice versa. The mysteries of human character development sometimes remain just that.

## The role
## of the
## school

Although socialization begins in the family, the school also plays a large role in the process. Studies conducted in many different nations have led social sci-

entists to conclude that schools play a central role in the socialization process. Certainly, American schools have helped along the "melting pot" process. Through education in public schools, various economic, ethnic, and religious groups have come to share a common socialization experience. In this sense, schools potentially can teach tolerance and respect for differences—values essential to democratic life. It is not known, however, how successfully schools have performed this function.

Schools also represent a major source for the inculcation of certain basic cultural values. The textbooks used in elementary schools, for example, usually represent preferred cultural norms. The *McGuffey Readers*, the nineteenth-century American reading texts, expounded the values of self-reliance, hard work, thrift, free enterprise, and individualism, overlaid with nationalism and religiosity. Through such materials, U.S. public schools indoctrinated and reinforced predominantly middle-class values. Given the powerful role textbooks play in the socialization of children, it is not surprising that many controversies have arisen over their contents. In recent decades, blacks, native Americans, women, and others have protested alleged biases in school texts. Textbooks also have been the focus of debates over the teaching of evolution, as opposed to biblical views of creation, sex education, and a long list of other topics. Recent years have seen extensive efforts at book censorship, in both classrooms and school libraries and parents' groups have organized to gain the right to exercise veto power over school materials. In 1985, a Maryland parents coalition listed 32 topics they wished to have subject to parental permission, including nuclear war, religion, abortion, and euthanasia.

Another way in which schools instill cultural values is through emphasis on nationalistic rituals, including salutes to the flag, recitation of the Pledge of Allegiance, and the singing of patriotic songs. Children also are taught early on to respect leading figures in U.S. history, particularly the Founders and various presidents. Many children even seem to view the Pledge of Allegiance as a prayer; in the United States, nationalism and religion often are mutually reinforcing.

Finally, socialization in schools proceeds indirectly, by example. Children learn in school to compete on an individual basis with other students. They learn much about the need to comply with authority (and, frequently, the need to suppress dissent) and about how and why majorities rule on some matters. Like parents, teachers also serve as role models. Are teachers willing to discuss controversial issues? Do they emphasize the virtues of U.S. political life while deemphasizing its problems? How teachers approach such matters can help shape the child's growing awareness of how to deal with politics.

There have been systematic critiques of the way U.S. public schools have taught students about politics. A committee of the American Political Science Association has suggested that U.S. schools typically fail to convey a realistic picture of our political life, to transmit knowledge of behavior and processes instead of just formal institutional arrangements, and to develop critical and judgmental abilities in students. Generally speaking, the panel charged, the schools fail to give students a sense of what civil liberties are about, or of what role dissent plays in a democratic society.[6]

One of the problems inherent in judging the impact of schools on political socialization is that it is difficult to disentangle the effects of education from those of normal physical, cognitive, and emotional maturation. As children grow older, their sense of how society works grows more subtle, no matter what or how they are taught. For example, younger children commonly take a fairly simplistic view of justice, which they tend to see as a matter of an eye for an eye. Teenagers, in contrast, are more likely to argue the same questions from a point of view that includes criticism of society's norms and operations.[7] Older children also display greater ease in dealing with political abstractions, such as "democracy," and in grasping the inter-relations among the various parts of the government.

Adolescence has frequently been characterized as the time of identity-seeking and experimentation. Sometimes these explorations take a political form, sometimes not. As one noted expert has pointed out, many adolescents begin to acquire not just political views (often highly related to the views of their peers) but also *ideologies*—more-comprehensive political viewpoints that may put them in conflict with the adults in their world.[8] Politically based adolescent rebellion has been a rarity in the United States, al-

"I pledge allegiance to the flag. . . ." How many times have we each repeated the lines of the Pledge? Do such patriotic rituals of loyalty have any effect on impressionable minds? The evidence seems to be that they do. Democracy demands loyalty to majority decisions, but it also demands that there be a limit to loyalty. Can that also be taught?

though in the 1960s the radicalism of college students had a marked effect on U.S. politics. This brings us to the final element in our discussion of school and socialization—the effects of higher education.

| College
| and politics

Until 1964, Republican presidential candidates were usually favored on U.S. college campuses. More than anything else, this political choice reflected the social backgrounds of most college students. Adolescents from poorer families, who were less likely to be Republicans, were also less likely to find themselves on college campuses. Even if, as seems to have been the case, a college education tended to exert a liberalizing effect on students of all political persuasions, U.S. college campuses historically were not scenes of intense political involvement. All that changed in the 1960s.

In February 1960, four black undergraduates at North Carolina Agricultural and Technical State University in Greensboro, N.C., staged the first "sit-in" protest, refusing to leave the whites-only section of a store lunch counter. Four years later, students at the University of California sat-in at an administration building to protest college policies limiting student political activities. From this point on, political protests involving the Vietnam War, civil rights, and other cultural and social issues pervaded college campuses. In the decade of protest activities that followed, various radical student groups appeared, made their mark, and then disappeared again. The most notable of these groups was the Students for a Democratic Society (SDS), which finally splintered into several small political sects by the end of the 1960s.

Student activism was the subject of bitter debate in the 1960s and early 1970s. Some observers saw activist students as basically humane, conscientious, and committed individuals who had the courage to act on widely shared ideals. Others saw them as irrational rebels acting out their own troubled emo-

tional lives in the arenas of campus and national politics. To critics of the protest movement, college campuses seemed to be serving as breeding grounds for political radicalism. By the end of the 1960s, there was widespread speculation that some universities might be torn apart by sustained protest.

But in the 1970s, student activism diminished as worsened economic times set in and the Vietnam War wound down. By the mid-1970s a general disillusionment with politics had become evident. Student values also changed, in the direction of conservatism and pragmatism. In the 1984 election, a majority of college students voted for Republican candidate Ronald Reagan (see Chapter 8 for a fuller discussion). Figure 7.1 shows the way college freshmen from 1970 to 1984 characterize their political views.

Did the 1960s, then, represent only an aberrant period, one not likely to recur? Has the socializing impact of higher education reverted to its pre-1960s form—namely, a slight liberalizing influence, especially in the areas of tolerance, equality, and respect

The quintessential 1960s moment: Bob Dylan and his guitar, blacks and whites, the activist young. For a time, activism seemed to pervade college campuses, only to fade drastically in the 1970s. By the 1980s, collegiate activism had revived somewhat, as students on many campuses called for divestment by their schools in corporations doing business in South Africa.

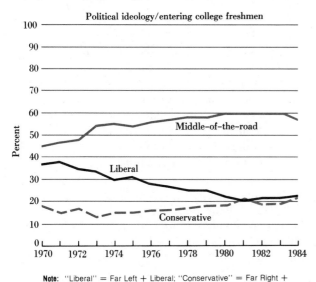

Political ideology/entering college freshmen

**Note:** "Liberal" = Far Left + Liberal; "Conservative" = Far Right + Conservative.

FIGURE 7.1
How college freshmen characterize their political views, 1970–1984
Source: *Public Opinion*, April/May 1985, p. 39.

for freedom of speech? Such questions are difficult to answer with any degree of certainty, but it does seem probable that the unique constellation of developments that contributed to the student activism of the 1960s will not be seen again soon.

## Public opinion

Having examined the various factors that mold our political opinions, we must now explore the dimensions of those opinions and their effects on U.S. political life. In this section we focus on that much-discussed but often elusive phenomenon, **public opinion**—what it is and how it is gauged, how informed the American public really is, how supportive American public opinion is of democratic norms. Public opinion is one of the basic ingredients in the complex recipe for democracy. For a truly comprehensive understanding of U.S. political life, we need to know not only the extent to which Americans are politically informed and democratically inclined, but

169

how political opinions interact with policy-making and what those interactions imply for democratic life.

## Gauging public opinion

Polls of public opinion have become a fixture of national political life. As of 1980, close to 150 separate polling organizations were operating in the United States. What is involved in trying to gauge public opinion? How is it done? What are its values, limits, and problems?

In a democratic polity, the study of public opinion is a particularly significant art, since political life is supposedly based on a government that is responsive to public sentiment. Only since the end of World War II, however, have systematic efforts been made to gauge that sentiment. Contemporary studies of public opinion use *surveys,* in which responses to set questions are elicited from a sample of the population. Survey research is based on two assumptions: that a fairly small sample of people can accurately represent the views of a much larger population, and that the answers people give to survey questions are at least reasonably meaningful.

The first problem faced by the survey researcher is to define an appropriate *sample* of opinion. The larger the sample selected, the more likely it is to reflect the opinions of the population as a whole. Beyond a certain point, however, the law of diminishing returns takes over, and financial considerations enter the picture. In surveying the U.S. population, a sample of 1,000–1,500 individuals will provide a result with a maximum error of only 3 percent, which is acceptable for most purposes. For example, if the results of a poll indicate that one candidate will receive 52 percent of the votes cast in an election, the likelihood is 95 percent that the candidate will actually receive between 49 percent and 55 percent of the ballots. To reduce the maximum error to only 1 percent, one would have to increase the sample size to five thousand—not a practical alternative financially, and not necessary most of the time.

The second criterion governing sample selection is *randomness*. Ideally, every individual in the population should have an equal chance of being selected. In practical terms, this is difficult to accomplish, since there is no master list of each individual in the United States—and even if there were, the cost of following up on each person randomly selected would be prohibitive. Instead, survey researchers use *cluster sampling*, which involves the selection of a number of geographic units (clusters) within which individuals are sampled. Selection of a national sample might proceed as follows.

1. Divide the United States into four regions.

2. Select, randomly, a certain number of counties within each region (in proportion to population).

3. Select several census tracts within each county.

4. Select blocks (in urban areas) within census tracts.

5. Select households within blocks by some arbitrary rule—say, every third house.

6. Interview one person of voting age within each household.

Use of such a method reduces survey costs considerably while keeping the selection random. Departures from cluster sampling can lead a surveyor astray. Interviewing people at subway stations or on street corners, for example, can lead to highly selective samples and unrepresentative results, as can attempting to judge public sentiment on the basis of letters to the editor or on the number of people who come out to work for a candidate at precinct meetings.

An equally important facet of survey research is the nature of the questions asked. Questions must be understandable, unbiased, and include reasonable categories of answers. Most commonly, survey questions are "close-ended"—that is, the interviewee is asked to choose among specific responses, such as "yes" and "no" or "agree" and "disagree." But because such pat alternatives fail to tap the intensity of people's feelings, surveyors have attempted to provide a more varied set of responses in some cases. The Survey Research Center at the University of Michigan, for example, once offered respondents a "feeling thermometer" on which they could evaluate twelve major political figures, rating each on a scale from zero to one hundred. Sometimes interviewers ask people not only if they agree or disagree with the question posed, but also how strongly they feel in either direction. Such open-ended questions often yield greater riches in terms of the complexity of answers obtained, but they are time-consuming to administer and difficult to analyze quickly and reliably.

How accurate is public opinion polling? Since the 1950s, the major polls have generally provided accurate predictions of who will win presidential elections, even in the very close elections of 1960, 1968, and 1976. During the 1980 presidential primaries, in contrast, the polls frequently erred in predicting the victor, because many voters remained undecided until the last minute and because many states allowed crossover voting (i.e., permitted registrants of one party to vote in the other party's primary).

The accuracy of a poll is also a function of how the results are interpreted. Much of what a poll "means" is a product of the alternatives the interviewees are offered. For example, an interviewer who asks only if people approve or disapprove of the pres-

ident's performance will get one set of results, one who asks respondents to rate the president on a "feeling thermometer" will get another, and one who attempts to determine how people feel about a specific set of presidential actions will get yet another. All of these results may or may not match up.

There are other problems with polls. For one thing, they can "create," rather than reflect, public opinion, usually by fostering the mistaken impression that the public knows or cares more than it really does about public issues. Moreover, poll findings don't usually measure to any meaningful extent the depth or sensitivity of public opinion. Polls can also turn people off. Asking people their views has become such a commonplace matter that many people don't believe that surveyors care very much how they *really* feel. More-probing, open-ended discussion might show that many of the respondents who routinely answer "don't know" or "no opinion" care very much about political issues but cannot easily articulate their views.

Then, too, most sample surveys tend to include only very small numbers of various minorities, such as Jews, blacks, or Hispanics. As a result, polls

In the 1970s and 1980s exit polling became a common practice on election day, as shown here in New York City in November 1984. Such polls allowed networks to broadcast early predictions, a practice that became highly competitive. But these early predictions came under attack as diminishing the significance of voting, especially for those who would vote later in the day because of time-zone differences.

171

often tell us very little about the differences of opinion *within* such groups. It is common to see black and white opinion compared, but much rarer to see comparison of blacks with other blacks. There simply aren't enough blacks in a typical sample to allow for any dependable generalizations. This condition leads to a neglect of the nuances and conflicts within such groups. Finally, polls can intimidate policy-makers, who can become more concerned with not contravening public opinion than with taking realistic action when faced with difficult social problems. Poll results also can affect the outcomes of elections. On the one hand, supporters may not bother to go out and vote for a candidate who is far behind in the polls; on the other, supporters of a candidate who looks like a sure winner may not bother going to the polls, since the outcome seems so certain.

Whatever their inherent problems, however, polls do help us estimate public feeling more accurately than was possible before. In the material that follows, we will refer often to survey results.

## Public opinion and democracy

Because public opinion plays so crucial a role in democratic politics, a viable democracy requires a politically informed public.

**Political knowledge:** Those who have studied the political attitudes and knowledge of Americans have characterized the public as roughly divided into four groups: chronic know-nothings, the general public, the attentive public, and the opinion- and policy-makers.[9] Estimates of the sizes of these groups vary. For example, one analyst estimated the chronic know-nothings at 20 percent of the public, whereas another put the size of this group at only 4 percent. The size of the general public is also hard to gauge; it seems to vary according to the issue involved. Unlike the know-nothings, who never become informed or involved, the general public has some information and can sometimes be stirred to political action. At the

next highest level of political involvement is the attentive public, sometimes estimated as 15–20 percent of the population. The attentive public seeks information, develops opinions, and can have a significant effect on policy making. Clearly, the size of the attentive public grows as a particular issue develops and becomes dramatized. Most Americans were only vaguely aware of Watergate or Vietnam when they first came to public attention. As time went on, however, more and more citizens became attentive to those matters—and that attention had an effect on policy-makers. Beyond the attentive public are those who most shape opinions and policies. This group includes leaders in politics and the media.

Exactly how much does the general public know about politics? To explore this question is to receive some sobering information. Most people know a few fundamentals but not much else. According to one survey taken in 1978, for example, a large majority can name the current vice-president, but only a bare majority know how many senators represent each state (see Table 7.3).

One can draw either optimistic or pessimistic conclusions from the data given in Table 7.3. It is com-

TABLE 7.3
## Political knowledge of the U.S. public, 1978

| Question | Percent correct answers |
|---|---|
| Name the current vice-president. | 79 |
| How many senators represent each state? | 52 |
| How many years in a U.S. representative's term? | 30 |
| Name the current secretary of state. | 34 |
| Which party has the most members in the House? | 69 |
| Name one senator from your state. | 59 |
| Is the government of China communist? | 63 |

Source: National Opinion Research Center (Chicago: 1978).

President John F. Kennedy on television in the early 1960s. Electronic media allowed politics to find its way daily into the homes of virtually all Americans. Although large numbers of citizens remained ignorant of the basics of political life, the influence of media in shaping attitudes in recent decades is undisputed.

forting to know that most Americans could name one of their senators, knew how many senators represent each state, knew that China has a communist government, and so on. On the other hand, it is troubling to note that even in the 1970s more than a third of Americans didn't know that China was communist. Equally troubling is the fact that 70 percent of the U.S. public didn't know the length of a representative's term, and that 66 percent couldn't name the secretary of state. In general, the public's knowledge of foreign policy is even sketchier than its grasp of domestic affairs. Other polls have revealed that as much as 20 percent of the American public believes that the Supreme Court is a part of Congress and that as few as 1 percent know what congressional committees their representatives serve on or what their representatives' areas of expertise are.[10]

This level of political ignorance apparently is not affected by instruction in civics. One poll of four-teen- and seventeen-year-olds, taken in the early 1970s, found that one out of every two respondents in both groups believed that the president appoints members of Congress; that one of every eight 17-year-olds thought that the president did not have to obey the laws; and that half of the fourteen-year-olds believed that starting a new political party was illegal.[11]

A widely held truism of political science is that the older—and further away from school—one gets, the more knowledgeable one becomes about politics. The assumption underlying this observation is that with age, one is more motivated to participate in politics and thus to know about it. Yet adults generally do not fare much better than teenagers in surveys of political knowledge, even though today much more information is available than ever before.

Perhaps even worse, much of the public remains uninformed about pressing public issues of the day.

More people seem to have a better idea of what they think the government ought to be doing than of what it is doing. This is not a totally dismal state of affairs from a democratic point of view; after all, it is encouraging that people are willing to say what they want from government. But it is unsettling to find that so many base their opinions on little other than personal preferences, with very few facts to go on. What this portends in terms of the democratic process is that catchwords, slogans, and simplistic formulas may become the common coin of public discourse, that a largely ignorant public may respond only to the very broad contours of policy alternatives, and that leaders may try to work over public sentiment based on prejudice, shallow emotional rhetoric, and the like. The more such demagogic practices prevail, the worse for democracy.

The reality is that most of us, most of the time, focus far more on personal than on social and political concerns. Most people, that is, express far more concern about personal health, family matters, and the like than the issues of public life. This is, perhaps, as it should be—but too much privatism obviously can lead to neglect of the public sphere. Generally speaking, Americans tend not to make a direct connection between their personal situations and the situation of the country as a whole. In the usual American view, the fate of an individual is determined largely by that individual, rather than by society or government. As a result, Americans commonly express the belief that they, as individuals, will fare well in the future, but that the nation as a whole may not.

Thus, the level of public information, a basic element in the democratic equation, is in many ways not what it should be in U.S. society—a factor that degrades the integrity of the democratic process.

**Democratic norms:** A second fundamental element of democracy is the range of popular tolerance and support for democratic norms. This element has two facets: the level of acceptance of democratic politics, and the level of tolerance for dissenting views.

Americans emphatically support the basic rules of democratic politics. According to most surveys, more than 90 percent of the public would agree with the following statements.

Democracy is the best form of government.

Public officials should be chosen by majority vote.

Minorities should be free to criticize majority decisions.

Every citizen should have an equal chance to influence government policy.

Note, however, that these are very abstract statements. As more-specific elements are introduced into survey questions, the democratic consensus begins to crack. On questions pertaining to areas such as demonstrations and protest, undemocratic responses often outnumber democratic responses. It is also notable that so many people are not sure what they think on such issues. Whenever any hint of political extremism appears in a question—such as demonstrations or protests—support for democratic values declines considerably.

Given these findings, it is difficult to escape the conclusion that the typical American attitude toward free speech combines an acceptance of the general principle with an unwillingness to extend that principle to concrete situations involving political dissenters or other nonconformists. This is a worrisome situation for democratic values, and one that bears further examination.

How do people react to political situations involving controversial groups? How much tolerance is there for unpopular ideas? In 1954, during a period when civil liberties were greatly threatened, Samuel Stouffer conducted a study of the state of political tolerance in the United States. Many of his findings came as an unpleasant surprise. He discovered, for example, that the level of support for the political rights of those with controversial views was low indeed. Stouffer constructed his survey questions around three types of people: an admitted communist, a person who opposes churches and religion, and a person who favors government ownership of railroads and big industries. (In the second and third cases, the words "atheist" and "socialist" were *not* used.) The subjects of the survey were asked if they would allow any such person to make a speech or teach at a university, and if they would oppose removing from the public library books written by such persons. The "tolerant" response totals on these issues were quite low, as Table 7.4 shows. Only 6 percent said they would allow a communist to teach, only 37 percent indicated that they would allow an atheist to make a speech, and a bare majority opposed removing socialist books from the library. In view of such findings, it is hardly surprising that civil liberties seemed in great jeopardy at that time.

It is encouraging to note that public attitudes on these same questions have grown considerably more

TABLE 7.4
## Percentages supporting freedom of expression in specific situations

|  | Percent tolerant | | |
|---|---|---|---|
|  | *1954* | *1977* | *1982* |
| **Allow speech by:** | | | |
| *Atheist* | 37 | 62 | 65 |
| *Socialist* | 59 | — | — |
| *Communist* | 27 | 56 | 58 |
| *Racist* | — | 59 | 61 |
| *Militarist* | — | 51 | 61 |
| *Homosexual* | — | 62 | 68 |
| **Oppose removing from library books written by:** | | | |
| *Atheist* | 35 | 59 | 63 |
| *Socialist* | 53 | — | — |
| *Communist* | 27 | 55 | 59 |
| *Racist* | — | 61 | 63 |
| *Militarist* | — | 55 | — |
| *Homosexual* | — | 55 | 58 |
| **Allow to teach in college:** | | | |
| *Atheist* | 12 | 39 | 47 |
| *Socialist* | 33 | — | — |
| *Communist* | 6 | 39 | 46 |
| *Racist* | — | 41 | 44 |
| *Militarist* | — | 34 | — |
| *Homosexual* | — | 49 | 57 |

Source: Michael Corbett, *Political Tolerance in America* (New York: Longman's, 1982), p. 36.

tolerant in the period since Stouffer's study. A 1977 study found that in every category tolerance had increased, often by a great deal. According to one estimate, there was a 25 percent increase in tolerance in the United States from the mid-1950s to the mid-1970s. Part of this increase in tolerance has been attributed to an increase in the overall educational level of the population, and part to changing socialization patterns in family and school.

Of course, these issues are not really so straightforward. When dealing with particular groups and particular circumstances, people of reasonably good will frequently disagree about how far tolerance should extend. Should American Nazis be permitted to march in a Jewish neighborhood? Should the Ku Klux Klan be allowed to picket a black church? The answers to such questions are certainly not simple. The level of tolerance in the American public may have increased significantly over the past thirty years, but a considerable amount of intolerance remains, especially for groups that are, for whatever reason, highly controversial or disliked.

Attitudes toward minorities also have undergone very significant changes over the past fifty years. In the early 1940s, for example, antiblack feeling was dominant among the white population of the United States. Over 80 percent of whites favored confining blacks to separate sections of towns, almost 70 percent favored separate restaurants, a similar percentage supported segregated schools, and approximately half favored segregation in public transportation and in the armed forces. Since that time, racial attitudes have undergone an enormous change. By the mid-1970s, only 9 percent of Americans supported segregation, whereas 39 percent favored desegregation and 49 percent favored something "in-between."[12]

Similarly, whereas in 1936–37 only 31 percent of Americans said they would vote for a woman candidate for president, in 1983 80 percent indicated a willingness to support a woman presidential candidate. Over the same time span, willingness to vote for a Jewish presidential candidate rose from 46 to 88 percent. And between 1958 and 1983, the percentage of Americans willing to vote for a black for president rose from 38 percent to 77 percent.[13]

Other survey results have not been so encouraging. When asked, for example, if various minority groups are actually discriminated against, most Americans in 1977 said that they did not believe so. Apparently, what were once openly racist attitudes have been partly displaced into other, less clear-cut issues, such as the pace of black progress, or support for federal intervention to integrate schools.[14] Overall, Americans have indicated only lukewarm support for laws and activities through which racial integration can be achieved. According to many observers, there has been a substantial change in American attitudes toward minorities, but a substantial amount of prejudice remains.

## Efficacy and alienation

Americans are often cited as a people with a strong sense of **political efficacy**. This means that they not only are willing to participate in politics, but also believe that such participation can be effective—that something will happen as a result of their actions. Surveys comparing political attitudes in various democratic countries have shown that Americans, to a much greater extent than citizens of other democracies, believe that ordinary people should be active in the community, that ordinary people can do something about unjust national regulations, and that citizens can successfully challenge harmful local regulations. Such survey results give the impression that the United States is a nation of avid political participants who have a strong sense of their ability to set the political process right, to shape it and make it respond.

Unfortunately, political reality is far more complicated. To begin with, **alienation** from government has grown sharply in recent decades. The social upheavals of the 1960s and early 1970s, involving civil rights, the Vietnam War, the growth of government, and the Watergate scandals, contributed to a widespread loss of faith in government. People of very different political views became disillusioned by the war and the government's failure to carry through on

176

## Comparative perspective
## Attitudes on freedom versus equality

The results reproduced here are based on a 1980 Gallup survey in six European nations and the United States.

Both Americans and British choose "freedom" rather heavily over "equality"—Americans by a ratio of about 3½ to 1. In West Germany, Italy, and Spain, more people chose "equality," although in each case by a very narrow margin. The overall European average shows a slight edge for "freedom," 49 percent to 35 percent.

[1]Data for "Europe" refers only to Continental Europe; Great Britain and Ireland are not included. *Source: Stichting European Value Systems Study Group.

social programs. Many on the political right were equally unhappy with the government efforts to enforce school integration and to aid the poor.

Alienation from political life has three major components: feelings of distrust, of meaninglessness, and of powerlessness. *Distrust* can take the form of lack of faith that the government will or can govern effectively; alternatively, it can show itself in the attitude that government is run by and for a few big interests, rather than for the benefit of all people. *Meaninglessness* springs out of a sense that the existing political choices are irrelevant, that it makes no difference who is in power, and that personal goals are unrelated to party politics. *Powerlessness* involves feelings of political impotence—that one is ignored, or that the group one identifies with is not taken into account.

All three dimensions of alienation increased sharply during the 1960s and 1970s, according to most surveys. Interestingly, in the early 1980s people began to express slightly more trust in government. This trend was evident among both Republicans and Democrats, as well as among both men and women.

Which of these two statements comes closest to your own opinion?*

A. I find that both freedom and equality are important. But if I were to make up my mind for one or the other, I would consider personal freedom more important, that is, everyone can live in freedom and develop without hindrance.

B. Certainly both freedom and equality are important. But if I were to make up my mind for one of the two, I would consider equality more important, that is, that nobody is underprivileged and that social class differences are not so strong.

| | U.S. | Great Britain | Ireland | Europe[1] | West Germany | France | Italy | Spain |
|---|---|---|---|---|---|---|---|---|
| 1. Agree with "freedom" | 72 | 69 | 46 | 49 | 37 | 54 | 43 | 36 |
| 2. Agree with "equality" | 20 | 23 | 38 | 35 | 39 | 32 | 45 | 39 |
| 3. Neither (volunteered information) | 3 | 4 | 5 | 9 | 19 | 8 | 5 | 13 |
| 4. Don't know | 5 | 4 | 11 | 7 | 5 | 7 | 7 | 12 |

Whites in general showed an increased trust in government, and although distrust remained high among blacks, it did not rise noticeably from earlier levels. One possible explanation for this decrease in feelings of alienation is that many who wanted to see the government doing less in general were gratified by the policies of the Reagan administration. Another factor probably was the improved economic picture in those years. In any case, the dropoff in alienation was slight in comparison with the increase in such feelings over the previous two decades.

How significant a factor has alienation been in political life? It probably fueled the growth in antigovernment sentiment of recent years. It may also have played a role in generating political apathy, which remains a deep-seated problem in U.S. politics. Alienation has also led to violence and antisocial behavior, triggered when political frustration reaches an extreme point and there is little faith that grievances will receive attention. At the same time, however, most Americans have retained a high estimate of the nation, and have continued to say that they are highly satisfied with life as a whole.

## Opinion and policy

The relationships between public opinion and governmental policy-making are complex, but it is possible to discern several patterns. When public opinion clearly supports programs already in existence, such as Social Security, politicians find it very difficult to make changes in them. Such programs usually have very wide impact, touching almost everyone to some degree. Another recognizable pattern is that of popular rebellion, which occurs when public opinion becomes stirred to the point of demanding action (or taking action itself, as through a referendum). In recent years, popular rebellions have broken out over taxation, environmental issues, and the Vietnam War. Policy-makers who ignore broad-based discontent often do so at peril to their careers.

A more complex situation arises when a particular matter becomes a central and intense issue to an influential or well-organized minority. Abortion, for example, has stirred such intense feelings in some

177

# Comparative perspective

## Confidence in institutions

Both Americans and Europeans place their highest confidence in the police and the military, but Europeans put the police first, whereas Americans favor the armed forces. Europeans, like Americans, display the lowest level of confidence in labor unions, major companies, and the press. Overall, Europeans show less confidence in major institutions than Americans display. Americans, as is noted in Chapter 1, also tend to express more confidence in religion than do Europeans as a whole.

[1]Data for "Europe" refers only to Continental Europe; Great Britain and Ireland are not included.
*Source: Stichting European Value Systems Study Group, Tilburg, Netherlands.

### Percentage of respondents claiming confidence in different institutions*

| | U.S. | Great Britain | Ireland | Japan | Europe[1] | West Germany | France | Italy | Spain |
|---|---|---|---|---|---|---|---|---|---|
| The police | 76 | 86 | 86 | 67 | 71 | 71 | 64 | 68 | 63 |
| The armed forces | 81 | 81 | 75 | 37 | 60 | 54 | 53 | 58 | 61 |
| The legal system | 51 | 66 | 57 | 68 | 57 | 67 | 55 | 43 | 48 |
| The educational system | 65 | 60 | 67 | 51 | 55 | 43 | 55 | 56 | 50 |
| The church | 75 | 48 | 78 | 16 | 52 | 48 | 54 | 60 | 50 |
| Parliament/Congress | 53 | 40 | 51 | 30 | 43 | 53 | 48 | 31 | 48 |
| The civil service | 55 | 48 | 54 | 31 | 40 | 35 | 50 | 28 | 38 |
| Major companies | 50 | 48 | 49 | 25 | 39 | 34 | 42 | 33 | 37 |
| The press | 49 | 29 | 44 | 52 | 32 | 33 | 31 | 46 | 31 |
| Labor unions | 33 | 26 | 36 | 29 | 32 | 36 | 36 | 28 | 31 |

people that no other issue matters to them. There have been abundant examples of well-organized minorities and poorly organized majorities in U.S. politics. Usually this occurs because the well-organized have more clearly defined and intensely felt interests at stake. For instance, although the majority of the population supports gun control legislation, those who oppose it are so committed to their cause that they have effectively blocked such legislation for years. The medical profession has successfully postponed action on national health insurance time and again. In the same way, small numbers who will benefit greatly from particular tax loopholes press their case on tax reform with great insistence.

A somewhat different pattern emerges when public sentiment and legal edicts conflict. The busing issue provides a clear example of the courts ordering the implementation of policies that most of the public and much of the political elite oppose. Efforts to overturn these policies through legislation or constitutional amendment largely have failed, but the lack of public and elite support for such policies has had a significant impact on their implementation. Enforcement agencies have been deprived of adequate funding. Protesting parents have kept children out of school, or moved from city areas where integration has been required. And at every level of government, from local school boards to the federal administrative

A woman wears a yellow star with *Jude* ("Jew") inscribed on it—a symbol of the horrors of the Nazi era. She was demonstrating on the day in 1985 President Ronald Reagan visited the Bitburg cemetery in West Germany, which contained the graves of German soldiers who fought in World War II. Although Reagan saw this gesture as a symbol of German-American reconciliation, his short visit stirred deep resentment among many who regarded it as insensitive. In response to the negative reaction, the White House altered Reagan's itinerary and added a visit to the site of the Bergen-Belsen concentration camp, shown in the photo at the left.

apparatus, attempts to slow down implementation of busing have been made. Generally, then, public opposition usually makes itself felt somewhere in the process of turning policies into realities.

In many areas, public opinion is neither well-formed nor well-organized, even though it may exist. When this is the case—as it often is in matters of foreign policy, for instance—politicians have considerable leeway in policy-making.

A study of the connections between public opinion and policy shifts in the United States between 1935 and 1979 demonstrated that policy is definitely affected when public opinion shifts are sufficiently large.[15] The researchers studied hundreds of national opinion polls and 357 federal, state, and local issues on which public opinion showed a "significant" shift—defined as a change of at least 6 percent. In 153 such cases (43 percent of the total), governmental action fairly quickly followed major shifts of opinion. For example, the Civil Rights Act of 1964 was passed after a 12 percent shift of public opinion

in the direction of greater support for equal rights for black Americans. Not surprisingly, the larger the shift in opinion, the greater the likelihood that policy will shift in the same direction. When the opinion shift was 20 percent or greater, the researchers found, policy shifted 90 percent of the time.

This study helps us see that public opinion *is* connected with policy. It does not tell us, however, what factors are involved in causing those shifts in public opinion. A whole range of factors can come into play here, including mass movements, organized protests, the quality of leadership, media attention, and the general readiness of the public to respond to a particular issue. As we will see in chapters to come, the factors that affect *both* opinion and policy are often complex.

## Conclusions

To all democrats, there is much that is troubling in the American socialization process and in the patterns of American public opinion on issues that reflect democratic values. It seems reasonable to observe that the socialization process does not stress sufficiently the significance and application of democratic practices. In particular, too many Americans have grown up intolerant of others and lacking in a commitment to protect the rights of dissenters and to treat others equally. On these counts, it is true, Americans have progressed in a democratic direction over the past thirty years; but there is still a considerable distance to cover.

Americans also tend to be lamentably ill-informed on many important political matters. In addition, many citizens—perhaps a majority—have become alienated from government—a fact that is both easy to understand and difficult to interpret. At a minimum, we can say that it is an aspect of U.S. political life that should stir unease.

Public opinion counts only so much in democratic politics. It does not always shape public policy. Many majorities are ignored because their members lack intensity of feeling or the will to organize politically,

or because better-organized and more-intense minorities are more effective politically. These realities of contemporary politics in the United States show us some of the current limits of democracy in practice.

Finally, we should remember that public opinion does not come ready-made. True, political socialization does much to shape people's opinions. Yet the socializing agencies themselves—families, media, schools, and so on—must derive *their* values from somewhere. In examining these questions, we should attempt to define the essence of what a sensible political education and of a truly informed and democratic public opinion would be, and to decide how we can best realize those ideals. The chapters that follow will take up, in turn, voting and elections, the political parties, the media, interest groups, and mass movements. In each case, we will be dealing with processes that form and reflect public sentiment. How satisfied we should be with that formative process and that reflection is a question to which we will return.

## NOTES

1 This term is taken from David Easton, *A Systems Analysis of Political Life* (New York: Wiley, 1965), Chapter 17.

2 Fred I. Greenstein, "The Benevolent Leader: Children's Image of Political Authority," *American Political Science Review* 54 (1960):943–45.

3 F. C. Arterton, "The Impact of Watergate on Children's Attitudes Toward Political Authority," *Political Science Quarterly* 89 (1974):269–88.

4 Fred I. Greenstein, *Children and Politics* (New Haven, Conn.: Yale University Press, 1965).

5 T. W. Adorno, et al., *The Authoritarian Personality* (New York: Harper, 1950).

6 Bernard Hennessey, *Public Opinion* (Belmont, Cal.: Wadsworth, 1970), Chapters 13 and 14.

7 See Joseph Adelson, "The Political Imagination of the Young Adolescent," *Daedalus* 100 (1971):1013–50; and Alan C. Elms, *Personality in Politics* (New York: Harcourt, Brace, Jovanovich, 1976), Chapter 1.

8 Erik Erikson, *Childhood and Society* (New York: W. W. Norton, 1963).

9 Much of the material in this section was derived from Alan D. Monroe, *Public Opinion in America* (New York: Harper & Row, 1975).

10 R. S. Erikson and N. R. Lattbeg, *American Public Opinion: Its Origins, Content, and Impact* (New York: Wiley, 1973), Chapter 2.

11 Ibid.

12 Andrew M. Greeley and Paul R. Sheatsley, "Attitudes toward Racial Integration," in Lee Rainwater (ed.), *Social Problems and Public Policy: Inequality and Justice* (Chicago, Ill.: Aldine, 1974), p. 242.

13 Michael Corbett, *Political Tolerance in America* (New York: Longman's, 1982), p. 50.

14 Ibid., p. 80.

15 Benjamin I. Page and R. Y. Shapiro, "Effects of Public Opinion on Policy," *American Political Science Review* 77 (1983):175–90.

## SELECTED READINGS

Among the classic introductions to the issues involved in political socialization are R. D. Hess and J. V. Torney, *The Development of Political Attitudes in Children* (Chicago: Aldine, 1967); Bruno Bettelheim, *Children of the Dream* (London: Macmillan, 1969); Fred I. Greenstein, *Children and Politics* (New Haven, Conn.: Yale University Press, 1965); and Erik H. Erikson, *Childhood and Society* (New York: W. W. Norton, 1963).

For stimulating discussions of political attitudes, see Kenneth Keniston, *Young Radicals* (New York: Harcourt, Brace and World, 1968); Samuel Stouffer, *Communism, Conformity and Civil Liberties* (New York: Doubleday, 1955); Michael Corbett, *Political Tolerance in America* (New York: Longman's, 1982); and John Mueller, *War, Presidents and Public Opinion* (New York: Wiley, 1973).

For more-specialized studies of particular aspects of political psychology and public opinion and their interaction with political action, see Murray Edelman, *Politics as Symbolic Action: Mass Arousal and Quiescence* (New York: Academic Press, 1971); Irving Janis, *Groupthink* (Boston: Houghton Mifflin, 1982); Sara Evans, *Personal Politics* (New York: Knopf, 1979); Stanley Milgram, *Obedience to Authority* (New York: Harper & Row, 1974); Erich Fromm, *Escape from Freedom* (New York: Avon, 1965); and Nevitt Sanford and Craig Comstock, *Sanctions for Evil* (Boston: Beacon Press, 1971).

### Public opinion

Attitudes toward democratic norms are treated in James W. Prothro and C. W. Grigg, "Fundamental Principles of Democracy: Bases of Agreement and Disagreement," *Journal of Politics* 22 (Spring 1960): 276–94; and Herbert McCloskey, "Consensus and Ideology in American Politics," *American Political Science Review* 58 (June 1964): 361–83. See also R. S. Erikson, N. Luttbeg, and K. L. Tedin, *American Public Opinion* (New York: Wiley, 1980); Corbett, *Political Tolerance in America*; J. L. Sullivan, J. Pierson, and G. E. Marcus, *Political Tolerance and American Democracy* (Chicago: University of Chicago Press, 1982); David Lawrence, "Procedural Norms and Tolerance: A Reassessment," *American Political Science Review* 70 (1976): 80–100; and Stouffer, *Communism, Conformity and Civil Liberties*.

On alienation, see Robert S. Gilmour and Robert B. Lamb, *Political Alienation in Contemporary America* (New York: St. Martin's Press, 1975). There is an extensive literature on alienation as an idea and a phenomenon. See, for example, Daniel Bell, "Two Roads from Marx," in his *The End of Ideology* (New York: The Free Press, 1962); Joel D. Aberbach, "Alienation and Political Behavior," *American Political Science Review* 63 (1969): 86–99; William Gamson, *Power and Discontent* (Homewood, Ill.: Dorsey Press, 1968); James S. House and William M. Mason, "Political Alienation in America, 1952–1968," *American Sociological Review* 40 (1975): 123–47; Murray Levin, *The Alienated Voter* (New York: Holt, Rinehart and Winston, 1960); and Lewis Lipsitz, "The Grievances of the Poor," in P. Green and S. Levinson, eds., *Power and Community* (New York: Pantheon, 1970).

# Chapter eight

# Public sentiment and electoral trends

# Is there a meaningful majority?

THE underlying premise of democratic political life is that elections actually matter—that the hoopla of campaigns, the political competition, the media blitz, the primaries, the vote, and the different political parties fundamentally influence the course of society. But do they?

In one sense, it is obvious that they do. Throughout modern history, struggles to obtain the right to vote and to create real political competition have helped citizens of many countries to gain control of government. It is equally apparent that in many countries without elections (or without honest elections), citizens are deprived of any dependable method of retaining or removing those in office. Governments can be changed by other means—revolutions, coups d'etat, politically directed strikes, and so on. But such methods are costly and uncertain. Elections furnish a regular, and safe, means of choosing who will occupy political offices.

The question is more complicated than that, however. In many countries, elections change very little. The same individuals or types of individuals are reelected over and over, and they maintain the same political situation. In many Latin American countries, for example, one group of oligarchs succeeds another, and the well-being of the mass of citizens is ignored. As a slogan written on a wall in Ecuador once stated: "One hundred years of elections—one hundred years of misery."

Elections, then, are not magic. They make meaningful change possible, but they do not guarantee it. What factors make for meaningful elections? An informed and involved citizenry is one vital factor. Another is that competing political parties offer programs that differ from each other, that will be carried out to a significant degree, and that actually address major social issues. Also, the process of political campaigning must help raise public knowledge and clarify issues, rather than disguise or cloud them. Such, in any case, is the democratic ideal.

In the next three chapters, we will examine the factors that, taken together, make up the major portion of the electoral process. In this chapter we will look at the structure of public sentiment and the pattern of electoral competition. In Chapter 9, we will examine the workings of our political parties. Finally, in Chapter 10, we will consider the role of campaigning and media in U.S. political life. The key questions we will ask are, Are American elections meaningful? and How close do we come to satisfying the democratic ideal?

We will start by trying to assess the meaning of **majority sentiment** in the United States. Do we actually have electoral majorities? How do they express themselves? How is public sentiment structured, and how does that affect the electoral process? Do people vote the way they think, or do short-term factors, such as a candidate's personality, intervene? Finally, why do some people (in some elections, a majority) not vote at all?

## Understanding
## public sentiment

How structured is the political thinking of most Americans? It seems safe to say that the average American does not espouse an **ideology**: that is, a highly structured system of ideas applied to political and social issues in a coherent manner. The intense political combat of highly ideological parties, a staple of certain European polities, has largely been absent in the United States. We have something closer to a politics of the center—a politics of pragmatism and moderation, or of incoherence and irresponsibility, depending on how one views it.

## Liberalism and
## conservatism

**Liberal** and **conservative** have been the most common labels in U.S. politics since at least the 1930s. It is often hard to define exactly what these terms mean, mainly because each has several dimensions. For example, there are economic conservatives (who might favor a balanced federal budget), foreign policy conservatives (who might favor taking a hard line toward the Soviet Union), law-and-order conservatives (who might strongly support the death penalty), and cultural conservatives (who might oppose changes in the traditional roles of men and women). Similar categories could also be applied to liberals. Is it likely that an individual will be consistently conservative or liberal across so many dimensions? Some investigators have argued that a common core of attitudes differentiates liberals from conservatives. One often-proposed distinction is that conservatives generally resist change, whereas liberals generally accept or support change. Still, the applicability of this dichotomy often depends on exactly what is being changed.

In examining U.S. politics, we will first of all find out where people place themselves, overall, along the liberal/conservative spectrum, and then trace national changes along that spectrum as the public mood has shifted. We will also look at more-specific dimensions of liberalism/conservatism, such as economic issues, foreign policy matters, and such social issues as abortion.

## Contemporary trends
## in U.S. politics

A casual survey of U.S. politics over the past twenty years might well register two rather drastic shifts in popular sentiment: a shift in the direction of liberalism during the 1960s and one in the direction of conservatism in the late 1970s and early 1980s. Upon closer examination, however, the evidence for shifts in popular views is far more elusive than might be expected. Over the period 1964–83, in fact, there was surprisingly little change in the percentages of the Americans who viewed themselves as conservative or liberal (see Table 8.1). Self-professed liberals comprised 18 percent of the population in 1983, as opposed to 23 percent in 1964; for conservatives, the figures were 39 percent and 36 percent, respec-

TABLE 8.1
## Self-professed political perspectives
## of Americans, 1964–83

|  | 1964 | 1968 | 1972 | 1978 | 1981 | 1983 |
|---|---|---|---|---|---|---|
| Conservative | 39% | 37% | 32% | 32% | 33% | 36% |
| Middle-of-road | 38 | 31 | 35 | 41 | 45 | 40 |
| Liberal | 23 | 17 | 22 | 18 | 17 | 18 |
| Radical | — | 2 | 2 | 1 | — | — |
| Not sure | — | 13 | 9 | 8 | 5 | 6 |

Source: Louis Harris surveys of June 26, 1967, February 20, 1978, and June 6, 1983.

tively. Such figures do not reflect very startling shifts in political philosophy. More noteworthy, in view of the relatively nonideological nature of U.S. politics, is the fact that even during these two decades of intense social conflict and rapid change, a significant percentage of Americans did not see themselves as either liberal or conservative. Since 1972, middle-of-the-roaders have outnumbered adherents of either liberalism or conservatism.

One question raised by these data is just how meaningful self-identification by the public actually is. Often, people who identify themselves as, say, conservative, are unable to explain what that term means. We might also ask whether being a liberal or a conservative in 1964 meant the same thing as being a liberal or a conservative in 1983. The content of these terms may have changed considerably in the intervening period.

Less problematic then self-identification surveys are those in which Americans are asked to identify those issues they believe distinguish a liberal from a conservative. About two-thirds of the country, for example, consistently has characterized "beefing up national defense," "abolishing welfare," "cutting federal income taxes," and "giving corporations a better tax break" as conservative views. Just as consistently, most people have identified "supporting the ERA (Equal Rights Amendment)," "increasing spending to prevent air and water pollution," and "helping blacks move faster toward equality" as liberal positions.

## Liberal and conservative views on specific issues

By taking a closer look at specific issues, we can discern more clearly the pattern of liberal and conservative views among the public.

**Social issues:** Many of the most significant social issues of the last two decades involve aspects of sexuality—abortion, the ERA, gay rights, and sexual morality itself. The public has generally leaned to-ward liberalism in the areas of women's rights and abortion. In 1974, when the ERA first surfaced as a significant issue, 78 percent of the population supported it. After considerable controversy about the issue raised by conservatives, the level of support declined to 64 percent in 1978 and to 61 percent in 1982. On the abortion issue, a solid majority has opposed the passage of a constitutional amendment banning all abortions, as well as a legislative ban on federal abortion funding.[1] (It should be noted, however, that responses to questions on abortions often vary considerably depending on how the question is phrased.) As for gay rights, the public has remained almost evenly divided between those opposing the legalization of homosexual relations between consenting adults and those supporting legalization.

The evidence on matters of law and order is mixed. Public support for capital punishment rose to 72 percent in 1984, from 38 percent in 1965; and 81 percent of the public felt that the courts were too easy on criminals in 1984, as compared with 49 percent in 1967.[2] But in 1982, almost two-thirds of the nation supported a law requiring the registration of handguns, and 45 percent backed a ban on handguns altogether.[3]

Of all social issues, the one on which the public has rallied most firmly behind a conservative position is school prayer. In 1982, 73 percent of those polled favored a constitutional amendment to permit prayer in public schools. Support was strongest among those over age fifty and those living in the South and Midwest, but in no region or age group did support fall below 60 percent.[4]

**Economic issues:** New Deal–style economic programs have remained popular with most Americans, a majority of whom has continued to support efforts to aid the poor, to help improve housing in urban areas, and to provide assistance to people in their old age. For approximately thirty years, most of the population has favored national provision for health protection. And since the Great Depression, most people have believed that the government ought to guarantee jobs for those unemployed. Generally, then, public opinion has remained solidly committed to the **welfare state** programs that originated in the 1930s.[5]

Public attitudes toward business have been re-markably ambivalent. On the liberal side, a large majority has expressed a lack of confidence in those running major companies and supported the idea of consumer representatives on the boards of corpora-tions. Yet Americans have consistently and over-whelmingly expressed faith in the capitalist system.

In analyzing public sentiments toward business, many experts have concluded that the main factor involved is antagonism to bigness *per se*, and the concentration of power that goes with it. Interest-ingly, support for business is notably weak not only among blue-collar workers—where one might expect this view to prevail—but also among high-status, well-educated professional people to whom business val-ues are unappealing.

Doubts about big business do not necessarily translate into support for organized labor. A 1984 survey showed that the public had far more favorable views toward both environmental and women's polit-ical action groups than toward such groups operating on the behalf of either business or labor.[6] Ameri-cans, it seems, take a skeptical attitude toward both big business and organized labor, but strongly sup-port the capitalist system as a whole.

**Foreign policy:** Until recently the liberal/conserv-ative dimension was more difficult to define in the foreign policy arena than in others. Most major for-eign policy initiatives were supported by both polit-ical parties, and the range of debate about alterna-tives was rather limited. Beginning with the Vietnam War years, however, that picture changed drasti-cally, as intense debate over foreign policy matters became a well-established feature of the national po-litical scene.

On the whole, conservatives have favored a build-up of U.S. armed forces, whereas liberals have sup-ported arms agreements and other negotiations with the Soviet Union. Conservatives have also tended to be more **interventionist**, especially in military terms, whereas liberals generally have argued for other means of engagement—or, sometimes, for nonintervention. Such differences could be seen very vividly in the mid-1980s debate over the Reagan administration's Central American policies.

William Adams has suggested that in the area of foreign policy, the public is far more likely to agree with the **human-rights** position of liberals than with the interventionist arguments of conservatives.[7] He has argued that most Americans, at least in the ab-stract, support a foreign policy that emphasizes hu-man rights and looks to negotiated settlements. At the same time, he has noted that the public is quite capable of shifting in an interventionist direction in certain circumstances. Americans, Adams has con-tended, want a strong defense and do not want to be threatened or intimidated.

Some of these same tensions have been reflected in public attitudes toward defense spending and re-lations with the Soviet Union. From the late 1960s to 1976, the public was generally critical of heavy defense spending and favored cuts. Then the trend reversed, as the public became convinced that our international status was weak and that the Soviet Union was engaging in a military buildup. As a re-sult, most of the public supported the U.S. defense buildup of the early 1980s. By 1984, the trend had reversed again. A Harris poll published in 1984, for example, found that a large majority of the public preferred cuts in defense spending to cuts in Social Security, Medicare, aid to education, veterans' bene-fits, or federal health programs.[8]

In the area of nuclear weapons, American atti-tudes have remained relatively fixed since the first atomic bomb was dropped in 1945.[9] Most Americans have from the start favored curtailing the arms race, even while fearing that the Soviets could not be trusted. A 1983 study showed that a vast majority (79 per-cent) supported the idea of a **nuclear freeze**, in which both the United States and the Soviet Union would cease producing new nuclear weapons, though eighty percent believed the Soviets would probably cheat on such an agreement. At the same time, more than half (55 percent in 1981) believe the United States should have military superiority over the So-viet Union (and very few, a scant 4 percent, believe we don't need to be as strong).[10]

It is interesting to note that between 1978 and 1984, attitudes about dealing with the Soviet Union also shifted dramatically. In 1978, 53 percent of the public favored a tougher stand toward the Soviets, and only 30 percent favored reducing tensions. By 1984, however, 55 percent favored reducing tensions and 26 percent said that we should be tougher.[11]

**The overall picture:** One of the most difficult aspects of public opinion analysis is judging how long a trend will last. Was the conservatism of the 1970s—such as it was—a temporary trend, or will it grow and deepen through the 1980s? Can the antiabortion or anti-ERA movements succeed, or are they last-ditch, rearguard actions doomed to failure? Pollsters have often been wrong in their predictions about such developments. If the mildly conservative trend of the late 1970s and early 1980s continues, however, there will probably be a shift of national attention to areas conservatives consider important.

Overall, there seems to be a durable element of schizophrenia in the views of the American public. Some studies have shown that between one-half and two-thirds of Americans generally think conservative but often are willing to vote liberal and tend to agree with many specific liberal policies. Also, the ethic of individualism has retained a strong hold on American ideas, even as the welfare state and big government have enjoyed considerable popular support. In U.S. politics, conservative individualism, populist appeals to the common man, and a distrust of "bigness" often coexist in a confusing melange. It is no wonder that most students of U.S. public opinion have asserted that few Americans have clear-cut ideological stances. In fact, the very odd mix that we have found *is* the common ideological stance in this nation.

## Some key influences on public sentiment

Students of public opinion have long relied on comparisons among different segments of the population. Key factors are such variables as education, age, sex, religion, and region. Some of the resulting conclusions are very elementary, for example, that poor people tend to support the political party that prom-

ises the most assistance. Yet even this simple generalization can be qualified. Sometimes race or religion might matter more than poverty in choosing a political party, for example. Other questions are harder to peg: Are women more liberal than men about divorce? Are younger people more likely than elderly people to support the death penalty?

We will now look at a few of the many interesting factors that seem to affect people's attitudes. Specifically we will consider class, education, and gender. Examination of such factors allows us to recognize and understand some of the forces that affect public opinion.

**Class:** One of the most enduring divisions in modern politics springs from inequalities in the distribution of wealth and status. Most European political conflict has revolved around such class politics—with workers aligned against the middle class, and labor and socialist parties against the bourgeois parties. We can see such patterns clearly in England, West Germany, France, Italy, and Scandinavia. Even though Americans are much less class conscious than Western Europeans, these divisions still play a significant role in U.S. politics. People's occupations are clearly related to views on many economic questions, and are in turn related to political party preference.

Comparing lower-status and higher-status people (in terms of income, education, and occupation) over a range of issues, the general conclusion we reach is that lower-status people are more liberal on economic questions, while higher-status people are more liberal on civil rights and liberties. On foreign policy, the situation is a little complicated. Higher-status people are more likely to be internationalist, whereas lower-status people are usually more isolationist.

How do such realities affect U.S. politics? We can draw one clear conclusion: that the economic liberalism of the poorer sectors of the population generally means support for the Democrats, and for trade unions. But qualifications remain. For example, the greater conservatism of less-educated people on civil rights and liberties, as well as on some foreign policy questions, can lead to the sorts of events we saw in the 1960s and early 1970s, when construction workers attacked students protesting the Vietnam War and the AFL-CIO president refused to endorse Democratic presidential candidate George McGovern. To consider a more current example, we can point to Ronald Reagan's successful political strategy of appealing to the blue-collar, white ethnic voters' patriotism and moral values.

**Education:** One fascinating development in recent years has been the widening ideological split between the better-educated and the less-well-educated Americans. As Figure 8.1 indicates, education seems to make a difference on many sorts of questions, including personal values as well as views on social issues and foreign policy.

Some now argue that the fundamental source of division in U.S. society is education, which, they say, is the new basis for defining one's social class.[12] We have blue-collar conservatives on the one side and the new professionals on the other. The new professionals tend to be more liberal on a host of social issues, more permissive personally, and more critical of the political leadership, especially on foreign and defense policies. The working class, on the other hand, has acquired a real stake in the system and now defends it staunchly, taking a somewhat conservative stance socially while maintaining its traditional economic liberalism.

It is hard to say, from the perspective of the mid-1980s, whether education will continue to have so much political significance. The mid-eighties saw the

FIGURE 8.1
American views on foreign
and defense policy, by
educational attainment.

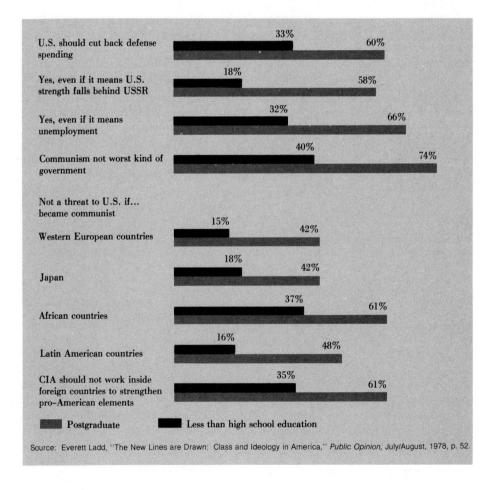

Source: Everett Ladd, "The New Lines are Drawn: Class and Ideology in America," *Public Opinion*, July/August, 1978, p. 52.

emergence of a somewhat new phenomenon: **yuppies**. First seen as a political force during the 1984 presidential campaign, these young, urban professionals (ranging in age from twenty-five to forty) are educated, affluent, and, often, tuned in to political matters. As a group, they are hard to categorize politically. Disillusioned by Vietnam and Watergate, they are liberal on such issues as rights for women and minorities, environmental regulation, and abortion. They are in some respects conservative, however, tending to oppose government intervention in the marketplace, for instance. They have been characterized as selfish and career-oriented. Yuppies are also considered to be antiparty, for they seem to identify neither with labor and the New Deal nor with Republican business interests or the Moral Majority.

**Gender:** On the whole, American women tend to be both more "puritanical" and more "tender-minded" than men on most issues. On social measures women take a somewhat more conservative position than men. Men are more likely to favor easier divorces, legalized abortion, legalization of marijuana, and premarital sexual relations.[13]

As for "tender-minded" questions, women tend to be more in favor of gun control and less supportive of capital punishment. In recent years, women have shown less faith in the economic system than men have.

By the early 1980s, talk of a "gender gap" became common political parlance as certain differences grew more marked. Ronald Reagan's presidency seemed to underline these differences. For example, women have tended to see Reagan's economic policies as "unfair" and his foreign policies as "risky," whereas men have been more likely to characterize the president as "forceful."[14] This gender gap proved significant in the 1984 presidential election, when the Democrats, to their chagrin, discovered a powerful new minority group: white males. Of this group, two-thirds voted for President Reagan, while the women's vote was far more evenly divided.[15] There was also a marked decline in the percentage of men who identified themselves as Democrats from 1980 to 1984, with no decline among women. It is of course important to remember that in generalizing about sex

differences, we may be, and probably are, overlooking important differences *within* the women's group, such as among various age groups, or levels of education, or occupational status.

## Electoral trends

Having looked at the structure of political sentiment among Americans, we now turn to the question of how political attitudes are or are not reflected in the electoral process. The question of why people vote the way they do has spawned a vast and complex literature among students of politics. There has been so much to say about voting because over the past thirty years, our understanding of the factors that shape voting behavior has changed considerably. As the political and social realities have changed, so have our ways of voting—and, in turn, our understanding of what voting is all about. This may sound a bit vague and slippery, so we will go through the problem step by step, adding complexity at each stage.

### Social bases of voting patterns

The basic features of contemporary U.S. politics were established in the 1930s, when a significant realignment of the electorate took place. A **realignment** is a major, long-term change in political party allegiance among the electorate, reflecting a shift in the coalitions that support each party. During the Great Depression, there was a massive repudiation of the Republican Party, whose policies were widely blamed for the economic crisis. The beneficiary of this realignment was the Democratic Party of President Franklin D. Roosevelt, who forged a majority coalition primarily made up of Northern blue-collar workers (many with ethnic and immigrant backgrounds) and Southern voters of all classes (a holdover from the South's affiliation with the Democrats since the Civil War). Generally speaking, any un-

Why are these nuns smiling? Could it be because they have found a candidate who particularly suits them? Indeed! They are cheering for the Catholic Robert Kennedy during his 1966 Senate campaign in New York.

derstanding of the workings of U.S. politics in the period from the 1930s to the present must be based on this fundamental realignment—even though, as we will see, a crucial question today is whether Roosevelt's New Deal coalition has begun to come apart.

In a study of the presidential election of 1940, Paul Lazarsfeld and colleagues analyzed voting patterns through the use of an "index of political predisposition."[16] This index, based on key elements of the New Deal coalition, was made up of three factors: socioeconomic status, religion, and place of residence (urban or rural). The authors found that a high socioeconomic status, affiliation with Protestantism, and a rural residence tended to lead to a Republican vote. Democrats tended to be poorer, more urban, and Catholic.

Let us examine how these and other demographic characteristics have been related to voting behavior in the United States.

*Religion.* Both Catholics and Jews have been much more likely to vote Democratic. This preference can be traced to the patterns of emigration to the United States. Most

190

Catholic and Jewish immigrants—Irish, Russians, Italians, Poles, and others—settled in cities already dominated by Democratic Party political machines. During the waves of immigration of the nineteenth and early twentieth centuries, the Republican Party contained a strong nativist, antiforeign element, which also helped drive the newcomers toward the Democrats. Catholics, and Jews as well, frequently saw themselves as economic and social underdogs in this country, and in the New Deal period, both groups strongly identified with Roosevelt's policies. For Jews, this identification was solidified during World War II. Protestants (outside the South), in contrast, have been the most strongly Republican of the three major religious groups, partially because of the heavier representation of Protestants in the business classes in small-town America and (until recent decades) among the wealthier, and hence, the better educated.

*Social class.* Struggles between haves and have-nots have always been a factor in U.S. politics. At least as far back as Andrew Jackson and the election of 1828, the Democratic Party has proclaimed itself to be the party of the "common man." On the whole, the effects of class struggle on U.S. politics have been muted. They were evident, however, in the 1930s, when the Republicans, thanks to Herbert Hoover and the Depression, became solidly established as the party of big business and the middle classes. The working class voted for the Democrats by at least 10 percent more than the middle class in every national election between 1952 and 1972. In the presidential elections of 1972, 1980, and 1984, however, the Republicans were able to cut into the Democrats' percentage of the working-class vote.

*Race.* Until the New Deal, most blacks voted Republican—in those places where they were able to vote. This preference was rooted in an attachment to the party of Lincoln and in opposition to the role of Democrats in the South in disenfranchising blacks around the turn of the century. Black loyalty to the GOP began failing in the New Deal period, as many blacks came to support New

A notable feature of the 1984 Democratic party primaries was the presence of Jesse Jackson, who waged an active, nationwide campaign. His effort focused on getting black voters registered as well as on showing that a black candidate could appeal to nonblack citizens.

Deal economic programs. Blacks moved closer to the Democrats in the 1940s, when the party began to take some steps on the civil rights front. Since the election of 1952, at least 60 percent of black voters have cast their ballots for the Democratic presidential candidate. The election of 1964 represented another turning point for the black vote, as over 80 percent of the black electorate chose Democrat Lyndon Johnson over Republican Barry Goldwater. The black vote has remained over 80 percent Democratic since then, reaching 87 percent in 1984. In the early 1980s, blacks began to exert an increasing influence in U.S. politics, principally through heavy voter registration drives. Between 1980 and 1983, over 1 million new black voters were added to the registration lists.

We could consider other demographic factors—age, region, and level of education, for example—but the general picture should be clear. At least since the political realignment of the 1930s, particular groups have remained more-or-less attached to each party. This picture only gives us the broad outlines of modern U.S. political life, however. A large number of people don't fit neatly into the traditional categories

used to analyze voter preferences. For example, what sort of voting pattern could be expected from a middle-class Catholic, or from a working-class Protestant living in an urban area? When various demographic factors are mixed, prediction and understanding of voting behavior becomes more difficult. Then, too, as the issues, and even the social bases of political life, change over time, voting patterns can be transformed. This happened, for example, as a college education, once reserved almost exclusively for the upper middle class, became available to a wider spectrum of Americans, as hundreds of thousands of Southern blacks moved north, and as the New Deal and the Depression faded in the minds of many voters. Finally, there is the question of whether voters

understand their political preferences in terms of ideology. In other words, do people have a coherent view of political issues and can they make sense of the political spectrum in terms of liberal or conservative ideals?

## The demise of ideology in the 1950s

In the 1950s, political scientists, dissatisfied with the incompleteness of earlier answers to the question of why people vote as they do, began to seek more-refined answers.[17] What they found was startling and discouraging. When investigators tried to tap the

The Irish have played an important role in the U.S. for over 100 years. Here New York's Mayor Ed Koch shows his enthusiasm during the St. Patrick's Day parade in 1984. Such ethnic celebrations tend to bring out politicians, who are usually loathe to offend any significant ethnic or other group.

A new voting group—the elderly—began to make themselves felt in U.S. politics in the 1970s and 1980s. Working sometimes through the ballot and sometimes through interest group activity and protest, symbolized here by Maggie Kuhn, leader of the Gray Panthers (*top left*), older Americans promised to become a significant and permanent factor on the political landscape.

ideological dimension of people's thinking—to see if voters viewed elections in terms of liberalism versus conservatism—they discovered that very few Americans exhibited a consistent political outlook. In studying the 1956 national elections, for example, researchers at the Michigan Survey Research Center classified only 3 percent of the voters as "clear ideologues" and only 13 percent as "near ideologues." The researchers did find that the underlying social bases of U.S. politics had remained intact, in that a large percentage of the electorate seemed to vote on the basis of group benefits promised by different candidates—such as, "Candidate X will help the working people."

These findings about liberalism/conservatism were important because they appeared to show that most Americans did not—or perhaps could not—think about politics in a complex and consistent manner. Citizens also lacked the basic information (such as what the positions of the two parties were) necessary to make considered political choices. And there often seemed to be little connection between the stand people would take on one issue and the stand they would take on another. People who had a liberal outlook on economic matters, for instance, might take a conservative stance on others. It almost appeared as if many voters chose political positions at random.

In the 1950s, voters usually decided whom to vote for on the basis of party affiliation, the personality characteristics of the candidates, or specific issues. Issue voters would weigh which party would do better in dealing with unemployment, the Korean War, or some other issue. Personality-oriented voters would stress the honesty, leadership abilities, or experience of a particular candidate. Party loyalists would pick the party that seemed likely to prove more helpful to themselves and to the country. During this period, party identification was still very high in the United States—about 75 percent of the public claimed party affiliation. It turned out, in fact, that party affiliation was one of the best predictors of how people would vote in the 1950s. During that decade, over 90 percent of the voters stuck with their party of choice in congressional elections. Of course, millions of Democrats also voted for Republican presidential candidate Dwight Eisenhower, although chiefly on the basis of his personality and his standing as a war hero.

The overall political picture in the 1950s was a confusing, discouraging, but strangely simple one. Basically, most people voted according to party affiliation, which was, in most cases, inherited from and linked to those structural and historical features of U.S. political life discussed above. In this period, too, the Democratic Party enjoyed a significant built-in edge in every national election, as between 40 and 50 percent of the electorate professed allegiance to that party. Nevertheless, the Republicans, with whom only about 30 percent of the public identified, were able to capture the presidency both in 1952 and 1956, and to win control of both houses of Congress in 1952. How could this happen? The GOP won because of short-term factors that worked in the party's favor—candidate personality (Dwight Eisenhower) and performance failures by the Democrats (as in Korea). Such short-term factors did not lead people to repudiate the Democratic Party, but they

did lead to a temporary Republican dominance of the federal government. The issues of the Depression era, which had loomed so large in U.S. politics for two decades, were fading. Although party identification remained strong, personality and other factors often proved decisive in the 1950s.

### The reemergence of ideology

The U.S. political scene underwent a radical change in the 1960s. Two students of voting behavior summed up this transformation as follows.

The year 1956 was the middle of the Eisenhower Era; the Korean War and the McCarthy hearings were in the past, and in a very real sense, not much was happening politically. . . . Politics was indeed, as Robert Dahl

Ike pledged to go to Korea if elected and go he did. He is pictured here eating with U.S. troops in December, 1952. Ike's image as a victorious World War II commander helped him win the 1952 presidential election, a triumph at least in part of personality over party allegiance.

described it at the time, merely a sideshow in the circus of life.

The first big change in this picture occurred in 1960 with the advent of a deliberately activist administration, a new focus on the problems of race and poverty and, perhaps most important, a Kennedy-inspired conviction, on the part of many citizens, that involvement in politics could actually bring about desired changes. . . .

The tremendous media focus on Kennedy's assassination brought politics even more to the forefront of national life. . . . The 1964 election, and the impetus it provided to citizens to structure their political beliefs into a coherent liberal/conservative ideology, was not merely a transient phenomenon. Americans were bombarded with one social and political crisis after another in the middle and late 1960s . . . by the late 1960s the positive involvement of the early and mid-60s had turned decidedly sour. The war lingered on, the Great Society programs appeared to have failed, and it seemed as if the government was incapable of dealing with new problems such as crime, pollution and inflation. The cynicism which arose from government's failure to deal with the society's problems by no means decreased the salience of politics—the feeling that what happens in Washington affects one's life—but, we believe, did cause many people to withdraw from politics in frustration.

The important point is that the pattern of attitudes found among Americans in the 1950s was a transient phenomenon and not an inevitable characteristic of mass politics.[18]

Between 1964 and 1972, ideology, which seemed to have disappeared as a significant political factor in the 1950s, came back with a vengeance. As issue-oriented politics reemerged in the United States, the tendency of the 1950s electorate to embrace unstructured jumbles of beliefs gave way to a trend toward ideological political thinking. People who held liberal views on one issue, such as Vietnam, were more likely to be liberal on other issues—and the same was true with conservatives. The political spectrum grew more polarized and clearer, partly because many Americans came increasingly to feel that politics affected them, had an influence on their personal lives.

Candidate personality remained an important political factor through the 1960s, but the salience of issues increased sharply. At the same time, party affiliation became much less significant. In 1972, only 21 percent of those surveyed mentioned party as an important element in evaluating the presidential candidates.[19] Again and again, party proved to be of secondary importance in presidential politics. In 1964, millions of Republicans defected to Johnson; in 1972, millions of Democrats defected to Nixon.

As the number of people who identified with either major political party declined, the percentage of independent voters grew rapidly. By the late 1970s, an estimated 35–40 percent of Americans were characterizing themselves as political independents. Younger voters were particularly inclined to reject party affiliation, and the lowering of the voting age to eighteen, starting in 1972, increased the ranks of independents dramatically. The youth vote, however, was not the only source of new independents. Many former party members rejected old affiliation, often out of disillusion with the events of the 1960s and early 1970s. Partisanship in general weakened, except among those who considered themselves "strong Republicans." Solid evidence for this trend was provided by the rising popularity of split ticket voting. From the 1950s to the late 1970s, the percentage of voters who voted a straight party line in both presidential and congressional elections dropped drastically.

We should note that the 1976 election marked a return to more traditional voting patterns. Jimmy Carter was able to recreate some of the New Deal coalition involving the South, the blue-collar vote, and, very importantly, blacks. (Carter actually lost the election among whites alone.) In 1976, Carter was able to attract 80 percent of Democrats, whereas Gerald Ford won the support of over 90 percent of all Republicans.

The Democratic defeat in the 1980 election showed just how fragile Carter's revived New Deal coalition turned out to be. With Reagan's victory came renewed assertions that a Republican majority was taking shape and that a major political realignment was underway. Some observers traced the origins of this realignment back to the 1950s, pointing to the two Eisenhower victories as signs of developments to come. And yet the shape of U.S. partisan politics was any-

thing but clearcut, a situation that was to persist even after the election of 1984.

## The election of 1984

If, as almost all observers agree, the fundamentals of U.S. electoral politics have been changing for thirty years, the import and ramifications of that process of change is a topic that has summoned up considerable disagreement. Eisenhower's two easy presidential victories in 1952 and 1956 led to predictions that the era of Democratic dominance of national politics was coming to an end. But Lyndon Johnson's landslide triumph in 1964 induced some experts to argue that the Republicans were about to expire as a political entity. Then, during the height of political unrest in the 1960s, other observers forecast the emergence of a new political party of the left in the United States, or at least a sharp leftward turn for the Democrats. The political events of the 1970s only added to the confusion. Was Richard Nixon's 1972 landslide victory a freak event? Could Jimmy Cart-

er's narrow win in 1976 be interpreted as a resurrection of the New Deal coalition after 1976? And was Ronald Reagan's victory in 1980 more a rejection of Carter than a positive vote for Republican conservatism? The election of 1984 did not provide definitive answers to these questions, but it did give some indications of the directions in which U.S. politics was likely to go.

In 1984, Reagan won a victory of substantial proportions. How was the victory accomplished? There were many plausible explanations: the economic recovery, popular support for Reagan as a leader, brilliant use of the media by the Republicans during the campaign (see Chapter 10 for details), the failures of the Democrats to mount a telling attack on the administration, the growing conservative trend among American voters. All these elements deserve a place in any comprehensive explanation of the outcome.

Economic factors had perhaps the greatest bearing on the election. In the 1982 off-year elections, the Democrats made substantial gains that many observers attributed to the recession then in progress. In 1984, however, 60 percent of voters stated that they were "better off" than they had been in 1980, and Reagan captured the votes of this group by a 6–1

One objective of political campaigning is to appear before a large variety of groups, seeking their support and creating an image for the candidate. Here, candidate Jimmy Carter speaks to a group of handicapped people during his 1980 campaign for the presidency.

margin.[20] Among those who said they were "worse off" in 1984, the margin was 4–1 for Democratic candidate Walter Mondale. With the exception of Jewish voters, all the groups among which Mondale did best were those facing economic hardship—the poor, blacks, union members, and families that had been hit by unemployment. This observation alone could explain the outcome of the elections.

Apart from economic factors, Reagan's victory could be attributed to his strong appeal to white males, who made up 42 percent of the electorate—an electoral bloc second only to white females in size.[21] Reagan captured 66 percent of the white male vote, carrying a majority of white males even among the poorest sectors of the population. The president also outpolled Mondale among women, but by a considerably narrower margin.

The male vote for Reagan was linked to positive perceptions of him as a leader. Among white males, he was widely viewed as a "man's man," a leader who would "stick to his guns," and who was "tough enough" to deal with international problems.[22] Mondale, in contrast, was viewed as cautious. The only leadership dimensions on which the Democratic challenger scored more favorably than Reagan were "caring about people" and physical ability to deal with the job. But Mondale was unable to capitalize on these assets during the campaign.

Overall, the Mondale strategy of discussing issues rather than attacking a popular president failed to ignite the voters. When Mondale emphasized the need

to be honest about raising taxes to deal with huge federal budget deficits, the public disagreed with him by a margin of 2–1. Many voters did agree with him on specific issues such as the need for arms control agreements or opposition to an amendment to end abortions, yet they preferred to vote for Reagan anyway.[23]

What did the 1984 election indicate about contemporary U.S. politics? It represented the fourth Republican presidential victory in the past five elections, and the sixth in the past nine. Yet, as usual, Republicans failed to capture the House of Representatives, and Democrats continued to dominate governorships, dropping only one of the thirty-five they held. Although the Republicans once again won the presidency, Democrats were the majority party

Despite vigorous efforts by the Democrats, the Republicans were able to register more new voters in 1984, and perhaps most strikingly, many of them were young voters. Ronald Reagan's popularity was one of the factors involved.

197

# Classifying presidential elections

Political scientists have devised a classification system for elections based on two major dimensions of voting results: how well the majority party does, and the degree of change (if any) in the voter coalition that has supported the majority. In a *maintaining election*, the majority party retains its strength and enjoys the same pattern of support as in the previous election. In a *converting election*, the majority remains a majority but its supporting coalition shows serious

signs of change. In a *deviating election*, the basic majority coalition remains intact but short-term factors lead to a victory for the minority party; in such a case, the deviation is not considered likely to last. In a *realigning election*, not only does the former minority party win, but basic changes also take place in the voter affiliations and a new majority is created.

Throughout U.S. political history, maintaining elections have been by far the most common. In recent years, however, examples of all four election types have cropped up. The great realigning election of the New Deal occurred in 1932. In the elections of 1936 through 1948, the New Deal coalition maintained its majority. The Republican victories of 1952 and 1956 are considered deviating elections; although the Republican candidate won,

the basic pattern of electoral loyalties apparently did not change. Both the 1960 and the 1964 elections were of the converting type. The Democrats, still a majority, won both, but new patterns of voter attachment seemed to be in evidence. Some experts have argued that 1964 should be considered a realigning election, in that basically new coalitions were established in the form of conservative Republicans and liberal Democrats. In retrospect, however, the new coalition that seemed within reach of the Democrats after 1964 never crystallized, and since then, party loyalties have grown less, rather than more, intense. The Nixon victories of 1968 and 1972 are considered deviating, as is Ronald Reagan's 1980 triumph. Carter's 1976 win represented the only maintain-

ing election among the last nine.

Beginning with the 1952 election, then, the patterns of party loyalty established definitively in 1952 have been changing. But in what direction? This question has been stumping political analysts for more than a decade. The hard-to-interpret results of the 1984 election have led to speculation that there may no longer be a pattern to deviate from. Perhaps the 1984 election should be characterized as "pre-aligning," in that the old Democratic majority disappeared, but no new, durable voting pattern emerged. Or perhaps it represented a "dealigning" election— one that reflected merely the continued breakdown of old political loyalties.

---

in terms of the number of national electoral offices held.

This seeming contradiction in voting patterns requires some explanation. In fact, a majority of Americans seemed to *prefer* a divided government. Fifty-four percent of voters said the country would be better off if Republicans did *not* control the Congress during a Reagan presidency.[24] It seems that many voters disagreed with the president on a wide range of issues, including cuts in social programs, Central

American policy, abortion, and defense spending, and perceived that Democratic control of one house of Congress would serve as a check on the president and his programs.

Looking at the pattern of U.S. elections from 1948 to 1984, can we see signs of a political realignment? Opinions vary. Some changes are clear. Most prominently, the New Deal coalition has lost one of its major elements and may be about to lose another. The once-solid Democratic South has steadily been turning Republican, and in 1984, a majority of southerners identified with the GOP for the first time. In the North, big-city Catholics have been defecting from the Democrats as well. Whether this latter shift is a permanent one is not so clear. Nonetheless, the GOP has managed to appeal to core elements of the New Deal coalition, at least in terms of presidential voting.

On the other hand, the social bases of U.S. voting patterns have not really shifted since the 1930s. Higher income and higher occupational status still correlate with voting Republican. Trade-union members, blacks, Jews, Hispanics, and Catholics are still more likely to vote Democratic than whites, Protestants, and non-union members.

An interesting question arises about the politics of younger voters. Some commentators see these voters as having caused a basic realignment in U.S. voting patterns.[25] Republicans did in fact do very well at registering younger voters for the 1984 election, and polls showed a majority of voters under thirty identifying with the GOP. But it remains to be seen whether this pattern will prove to be a temporary one, in response to one particular election. As one student of the subject said, "Younger voters have no real commitment to the GOP. They seem fond of Reagan, but it is a soft sentiment, not a strong devotion. . . . Younger voters are decisively *not* ideological conservatives. They voted for Reagan on pragmatic grounds. . . . Shaped by change and uncertainty, younger Americans are inclined to be self-protective and fearful of deep commitment. . . ."[26]

Other observers interpret the 1984 election as evidence of dealignment rather than a realignment. Pointing out that Americans now often switch parties to match their preference in presidential candidates, these commentators argue that party identification no longer means very much to U.S. voters. In this view, the American electorate has continued to become more volatile, but has yet to settle decisively into a new voting pattern.[27]

Yet another view holds that the apparent loosening of party ties is in fact part of a new realignment. In this interpretation, the Republicans may be on their way to becoming the new majority party, but public perception of their performance as a governing party will be crucial to their future. Ronald Reagan's first term, according to this view, provided a considerable boost to the GOP cause since most of the public were positive about his leadership and gave him credit for the economic recovery.[28]

## Nonparticipation: the Achilles' heel of U.S. politics

That nonparticipation in the political process is the most serious problem facing U.S. democracy is reflected in the following figures.

From 1970 to 1980, more than 15 million Americans who were eligible to vote, including many regular voters, stopped voting altogether.

Between 1960 and 1980, the percentage of eligible voters who actually cast ballots in presidential elections decreased sharply, from 64 percent to 52.6 percent; and in 1984, there was only a marginal increase in turnout, to 53 percent. A similar trend has been evident in local, state, and congressional elections—and at a substantially lower level of participation than in presidential elections.

Nearly 75 million eligible Americans failed to cast ballots in the 1980 presidential election; nearly 100 million did not vote in the congressional elections in 1974.

Fewer than 27 percent of Ronald Reagan's fellow citizens voted for him for president in 1980. Governor Brendan Byrne of New Jersey received a "mandate" of less than 15 percent of the eligible vote in his successful 1977 reelection bid. Mayor Ed Koch was the choice of less than 12 percent of New York City's eligible voters in 1981. Senator Henry Jackson won the 1976 New York presidential primary by garnering less than 6 percent of the potential vote.

One bright spot in this disturbing picture of nonparticipation in recent elections was the slight increase in turnout for the 1982 congressional elections, in which voter participation increased by 3.6 percent over that in the off-year elections of 1978. Another is that the ideological thrust of the Reagan administration's policies galvanized many groups to conduct voter registration campaigns in the early 1980s. Black organizations, the National Organization for Women, and both political parties were among the

TABLE 8.2
## Ranking of countries by turnout in their most recent national election*

*Vote as a percentage of voting-age population*

| | |
|---|---|
| Italy | 94.0% |
| Austria | 89.3 |
| Belgium | 88.7 |
| Sweden | 86.8 |
| Portugal | 85.9 |
| Greece | 84.9 |
| Netherlands | 84.7 |
| Australia | 83.1 |
| Denmark | 82.1 |
| Norway | 81.8 |
| West Germany | 81.1 |
| New Zealand | 78.5 |
| France | 78.0 |
| United Kingdom | 76.0 |
| Japan | 74.4 |
| Spain | 73.0 |
| Canada | 67.4 |
| Finland | 63.0 |
| Ireland | 62.3 |
| United States | 52.6 |

*Most recent as of 1981.
Source: D. Glass, P. Squire and R. Wolfinger, "Voter Turnout: An International Comparison," *Public Opinion*, December/January, 1984. The figures for the United States are from the *Statistical Abstract of the United States* 1982–83. The data for all other countries for the number of voters and the number of persons registered are from *The International Almanac of Electoral History*, 2d ed. by Thomas T. Mackie and Richard Rose. The voting-age population was derived from the countries' year books. It was occasionally necessary to extrapolate the present age breakdown on the basis of the last census.

most successful such groups. Figures indicate that the Republicans were able to outregister Democrats in most parts of the country.[29] Since people tend to vote once they are registered, these campaigns almost certainly will bear fruit in later elections.

American voting levels are the lowest of all democratic nations, as is shown in Table 8.2. Obviously, democracies can continue to function with large numbers of nonparticipants, but such largescale nonparticipation is in itself worrisome. American voting has been declining since 1960, and even then had reached just the 60 percent level (see Table 8.3).

From a democratic perspective, there is reason for concern when so many citizens are so uninvolved with their society's political life.

TABLE 8.3
## Turnout in presidential and congressional elections, 1920–1984

| | Office | |
|---|---|---|
| Year | Presidential | U.S. House |
| 1920 | 43.5% | 40.8% |
| 1922 | — | 32.1 |
| 1924 | 43.9 | 40.6 |
| 1926 | — | 29.8 |
| 1928 | 51.9 | 47.8 |
| 1930 | — | 33.7 |
| 1932 | 52.4 | 49.7 |
| 1934 | — | 41.4 |
| 1936 | 56.9 | 53.5 |
| 1938 | — | 44.0 |
| 1940 | 58.9 | 55.4 |
| 1942 | — | 32.5 |
| 1944 | 56.0 | 52.7 |
| 1946 | — | 37.1 |
| 1948 | 51.1 | 48.1 |
| 1950 | — | 41.1 |
| 1952 | 61.6 | 57.6 |
| 1954 | — | 41.7 |
| 1956 | 59.3 | 55.9 |
| 1958 | — | 43.0 |
| 1960 | 62.8 | 58.5 |
| 1962 | — | 45.4 |
| 1964 | 61.9 | 57.8 |
| 1966 | — | 45.4 |
| 1968 | 60.9 | 55.1 |
| 1970 | — | 43.5 |
| 1972 | 55.5 | 51.1 |
| 1974 | — | 36.3 |
| 1976 | 54.3 | 49.6 |
| 1978 | — | 37.9 |
| 1980 | 52.6 | 47.4 |
| 1982 | — | 48.5 |
| 1984 | 52.9 | — |

Sources: Data for 1920–80 from U.S. Bureau of the Census, *Statistical Abstract of the United States, 1982–1983* (Washington, D.C.: U.S. Government Printing Office, 1983). Data for 1982 from U.S. Bureau of the Census, "Voting and Registration in the Election of November, 1982," *Current Population Reports*, series P-20, No. 383 (Washington, D.C.: U.S. Government Printing Office, 1983).

## Barriers to voting

The consistently low voter turnouts in U.S. elections can be at least partially attributed to features of the law and of the election system that make it difficult, or even impossible, for some people to vote. For example, residency requirements have sometimes served to restrict voting. Until a decade or so ago, most states made eligibility to vote contingent upon residence in the state for at least a year and in a specific county and precinct for several months. Because Americans move so often, as many as 5 million voters may have been barred from recent presidential elections on these grounds. Supreme Court decisions in 1970 and 1972 reduced residency requirements for national, state, and local elections.

The registration process itself has often been a barrier to voting. In a number of European countries, a voter can register merely by showing up at the polling place on election day. The registration process in many parts of the United States, in contrast, is closed down well before election day. Some states even require voters to reregister if they have failed to vote for two successive years.

Registration requirements were cited by 31 percent of nonvoters in one poll taken in 1984.[30] Obviously, then, other factors are at work here. One major deterrent to voting can be an overwhelming superiority on the part of one political party. In such **one-party districts** or states, supporters of the excluded party tend to feel that voting is useless, and supporters of the dominant party tend to feel that voting is unnecessary.

## Who votes?

Not all groups or classes of Americans are equally likely to vote (see Table 8.4). In general, the socially disadvantaged are more likely not to vote, and the socially advantaged more likely to show up at the polls regularly. The following factors influence voting habits.

1. *Income*. The more money a person makes, the more likely he or she is to vote.

2. *Education*. The higher a person's level of education, the more likely he or she is to vote.

3. *Age*. People between the ages of thirty-five and fifty-five are considerably more likely to vote than are younger or older persons. People do not seem to develop regular voting habits until they have established themselves in life. The falloff in voting among the elderly seems attributable to physical infirmity.

4. *Gender*. Men are more likely than women to vote. In recent elections, however, the voting gap between men and women has disappeared.

5. *Race*. Whites are more likely than nonwhites to vote. In the past, large differences in turnout between the races stemmed from discrimination against black voters. The difference that remains can be ascribed primarily to education and income differences between whites and non-

TABLE 8.4
## Voting turnout by population characteristics, 1968–80

|  | 1968 | 1972 | 1976 | 1980 |
|---|---|---|---|---|
| **Male** | 69.8% | 64.1% | 59.6% | 59.1% |
| **Female** | 66.0 | 62.0 | 58.8 | 59.4 |
| **Age** |  |  |  |  |
| *18–20* | — | 48.3 | 38.0 | 35.7 |
| *21–24* | 51.0 | 50.7 | 45.6 | 43.1 |
| *25–34* | 62.5 | 59.7 | 55.4 | 54.6 |
| *35–44* | 70.8 | 66.3 | 63.3 | 64.4 |
| *45–64* | 74.9 | 70.8 | 68.7 | 69.3 |
| *65 and over* | 65.8 | 63.5 | 62.2 | 65.1 |
| **Education** |  |  |  |  |
| *8 years or less* | 54.5 | 47.4 | 44.1 | 42.6 |
| *9–11* | 61.3 | 52.0 | 47.2 | 45.6 |
| *12* | 72.5 | 65.4 | 59.4 | 58.9 |
| *More than 12* | 81.2 | 78.8 | 73.5 | 73.2 |
| **Race** |  |  |  |  |
| *White* | 69.1 | 64.5 | 60.9 | 60.9 |
| *Black* | 57.6 | 52.1 | 48.7 | 50.9 |
| *Hispanic* | N.A. | 37.4 | 31.8 | 29.9 |

Source: U.S. Department of Commerce, Bureau of the Census, *Statistical Abstract of the United States, 1982–1983* (Washington, D.C.: U.S. Government Printing Office, 1983), p. 493.

# Comparative perspective
## Fewer voters, but more voting

While the United States lags far behind other Western nations in the proportion of its citizens voting at national elections, it is far ahead of any other Western nation in the *number of votes* cast by the average citizen in a given four-year period.

The first reason for this is federalism. Americans typically vote in at least four jurisdictions—federal, state, county, and town elections. This four-layer system of government is not usually found in Europe.

The second reason is the separation of powers. Americans are unique in being able to vote for both legislative representatives and executive leaders at all levels from city council members and mayors to congressmen and president. In a parliamentary system, individuals vote only for legislative representatives; those elected choose the prime minister and cabinet.

A third reason is the long ballot. When Americans vote, they vote for many executive offices from dog-catcher or coroner to governor and president. By comparison, parliamentary regimes do not allow citizens to vote for any incumbent of an executive office. France is unique in Western Europe in having a powerful directly elected president. Countries with figurehead presidents often still choose the president indirectly (e.g., Italy) or without a contest (e.g., Ireland), and only a few by popular election (e.g., Finland and Austria). America is also distinctive in that some of its judges, and in some cases, police commissioners or sheriffs, are subject to direct election.

Fourth, there are many special purpose jurisdictions—school boards, sewer districts, etc.—which are directly elected. In Europe, such bodies almost invariably are appointed by the government of the day, or do not exist at all. For example, education is often a branch of central government; its officials are no more subject to direct election than would be military commanders.

Fifth, many Americans are able to enact or repudiate legislation through referenda on legislation and some taxes affecting current or capital expenditure. The principle of the referendum is not unique to America, and at the national level, it is most important in Switzerland. But state and local governments do use the autonomy of federalism to hold more such ballots collectively in a given year than does the whole of Europe put together. The recall of elected officeholders is another distinctive American institution, but rarely used and hardly needed if terms of office can be as brief as two years.

Sixth, primary elections in which all registered electors have the right to cast a ballot and choose among a party's potential candidates are unique to America. In continental Europe, the mechanics of proportional representation "slate-making" normally compel centralized decision making by party committees determining the party's candidates for safe and hopeless seats. Voters have a limited opportunity to alter party endorsements. Primaries at multiple levels of government can double many of the opportunities to vote described above. In southern states where a run-off election is prescribed when no candidate secures half the vote in the first primary contest, it can treble an individual's opportunity to vote.

Such a contrast might first lead an American to ask: Why do Europeans have so few opportunities to vote? The answers are several: the heritage of aristocratic rather than populist decision making; the belief in the efficacy and impartiality of civil servants as executive agents of government; and reliance upon parties to organize and direct government through parliamentary institutions. A European who enquired about the advantages and disadvantages of the American system of multiple voting would first of all be met with answers emphasizing the principle of direct determination of issues by citizens (e.g., bond issues or school tax referenda) and the superiority of decision making by elected representatives. A European might wonder whether something was not lost by reducing the standing of experts and civil servants, and by the disintegration of parties.

Extracted from Richard Rose, "Citizen Participation in the Presidential Process," *Society*, November/December, 1978, pp. 43–48.

whites. Minority voter turnout rises greatly when a member of a minority is a candidate for office.

6. *Party*. Because Republican voters are more likely to be college-educated and to earn high incomes, Republicans are more likely to vote than are Democrats.

7. *Partisanship*. Persons who identify themselves either as Republicans or Democrats are more likely to vote than are persons who call themselves independents.

Angus Campbell and his associates have attributed these differences in voting habits to the individual's sense of **political efficacy**—the degree to which a person believes that "the affairs of government can be understood and influenced by individual citizens."[31] Campbell's findings showed that a person with a firm belief in his or her own political efficacy virtually always votes.

It is hardly surprising that those groups most likely to vote—the educated, the well-to-do, the middle-aged, whites, and Republicans—are much more likely to believe in their ability to influence government. One reason for such confidence is that by producing much higher voter turnouts, these groups do indeed have an impact on elections far out of proportion to their actual numbers. A rich man's vote does not count for any more than a poor man's—except if the rich man votes and the poor man does not.

It is important to note, nevertheless, that recent studies have identified a growing number of nonvoters who defy the normal generalizations. In a study of the 1976 elections, Arthur Hadley found that 35 percent of nonvoters were what he termed "positive apathetics." Such individuals, according to Hadley, "refrain from voting because their lives are going so well that voting seems irrelevant. They are apathetic not out of misery but out of contentment."[32] Positive apathetics have a much higher sense of personal—if not political—efficacy than do other nonvoters; they also have more education and money. What distinguishes positive apathetics from others of the same income and education is a failure to connect politics to personal life. Whether this type of dissociation was a transitory product of the mid-1970s or a more enduring perception of the postindustrial affluent remains to be seen.

Another, and hotly disputed, question is whether voters and nonvoters differ very much in their political preferences. Some students of politics have argued that even if American turnout were 100 percent, the results of elections would usually be about the same. Others have maintained, however, that increased turnout would either aid the Democrats or threaten the system itself, because of the influx of poorly informed and easily manipulated new voters.

## Other forms of political participation

As we have seen, nearly 50 percent of Americans of voting age do not vote in presidential elections. Moreover, between 20 and 25 percent do not vote in any elections, or participate in politics in any way.[33] Voting is not the only normal form of political participation (unusual forms are discussed in Chapter 12). One can join in political life by taking part in campaign activities, discussing politics, contributing money, going to meetings, writing to public officials, and so on. Some people participate at the local level and ignore national politics; others operate in the reverse fashion. What is the normal level of political involvement in U.S. society, and how does it compare with that in other societies?

About 15 percent of Americans engage in campaign activity, and about 20 percent give money to candidates. Another 20 percent don't participate in campaigns but do get involved in political issues, usually by contacting officials or joining groups. Perhaps 10 percent of Americans are politically active in all of the usual forms of political activity.

The extent of political involvement varies from group to group. Better-educated and higher-status people are more likely to involve themselves in all forms of activity than are less-educated and lower-status citizens. Urban dwellers, Catholics, and blacks are more likely to participate in campaigns, whereas Protestants and small-town residents are more likely to join in community activities. Compared with citizens of

TABLE 8.5
## Percentages of citizens active in politics in seven countries

| | Austria | India | Japan | Netherlands | Nigeria | United States | Yugoslavia |
|---|---|---|---|---|---|---|---|
| **Voting** | | | | | | | |
| *Regular voters* | 85% | 48% | 93% | 77% | 56% | 63% | 82% |
| **Campaign activity** | | | | | | | |
| *Members of a party or political organization* | 28 | 5 | 4 | 13 | — | 8 | 15 |
| *Worked for a party* | 10 | 6 | 25 | 10 | — | 25 | 45 |
| *Attended a political rally* | 27 | 14 | 50 | 9 | — | 19 | 45 |
| **Communal activity** | | | | | | | |
| *Active members in a community action organization* | 9 | 7 | 11 | 15 | 34 | 32 | 39 |
| *Worked with a local group on a community problem* | 3 | 18 | 15 | 16 | 35 | 30 | 22 |
| *Helped form a local group on a community problem* | 6 | 5 | 5 | — | 26 | 14 | — |
| *Contacted an official in the community on some social problem* | 5 | 4 | 11 | 6 | 2 | 13 | 11 |
| *Contacted an official outside the community on a social problem* | 3 | 2 | 5 | 7 | 3 | 11 | — |

Source: Sidney Verba and Norman H. Nie, "Political Participation," in Fred I. Greenstein and Nelson W. Polsby, eds., *Handbook of Political Science* (Reading, Mass.: Addison-Wesley, 1975), 4:24–25.

other countries, Americans are less likely to be members of a political party or to vote, but more likely to be involved in communal activities, such as neighborhood organizations or groups established to deal with local problems (see Table 8.5).

There is some evidence that more Americans have become more politically active in ways other than voting since 1960. More of us are writing to Congress and/or engaging in such unconventional forms of politics as demonstrations and protests. As the educational level of the population as a whole increases and people become more knowledgeable about politics, it stands to reason that political participation will rise. But even if that is the case, widespread apathy toward electoral politics remains a serious problem for American democracy.

## Conclusions

Majority rule is the chief pillar of democratic politics. Millions of people have fought, and sometimes died, for the right to vote and the right to influence the direction of government. Yet in the contemporary U.S. polity, far too many citizens do not even make the simplest and easiest of political gestures—that of entering the polling booth and pulling down the lever.

Some observers of the U.S. political scene have found this situation undisturbing. They have noted that U.S. politics has remained remarkably stable, that our constitutional system has endured many tests. In recent times, they have pointed out, one president was assassinated, another refused to stand for re-election, and yet another resigned from office—and none of these seeming catastrophes shook the foundations of U.S. political life. This is quite remarkable evidence for the basic stability of our political system.

Yet there is another side to the picture. In the 1960s, black Americans felt it necessary to take to the streets in an effort to make themselves heard politically. Many black protesters, especially in the South, were trying to break *into* the democratic process. But those who participated in riots that broke out in large cities across the country had another message—they were angry at social injustice and alienated from the political process. At a basic level, they felt that they had been left out of the political system. Others who do not participate in politics may also become alienated and angry—and, sooner or later, their voices, too, will be heard.

Nonparticipation also entails the loss of the chance to experience democratic politics at work. And the fact that nonparticipation is particularly characteristic of the poor and the less educated means that the latter are doubly deprived. Overall, anyone who values active, participatory democratic politics cannot help but be worried by the recent growth of non-participation in U.S. society.

Whether or not majorities participate, how meaningful is majority sentiment in U.S. politics? On this question, we have to take a cautious view. As we have seen, public sentiment in the United States is not structured along ideological lines. Nevertheless, there are majority sentiments, some of which have been enacted into law and some of which have not. But the majority sentiment tends to shift on many issues, and trends are sometimes difficult to discern. We can safely say that in general, the major shifts in U.S. electoral politics are clearly related to shifts in public sentiment. The New Deal enjoyed strong majority support, much of which remains in place today. Other shifts in law and political practice, such as those involving women's rights, tolerance, and racial equality, also reflect—and, in turn, influence—the views of emerging majorities. Other majority sentiments have not become law: stricter gun control has not been enacted, national health insur-ance has not been created, the federal budget has not been balanced.

You may have noticed a missing link in our discussion. One can discuss the meaningfulness of majority sentiment, or the importance of participation, only so long before noting the crucial significance of political parties—the institutions that connect mass sentiment to public policy. In the following chapter, we will address that dimension of the electoral process.

## NOTES

1 *Gallup Report*, no. 206, November 1982.

2 Harris polls of May 24, 1982, and February 10, 1983. It is interesting to note that two-thirds of the respondents did not think that the death penalty was fairly applied. *The Washington Post*, national weekly ed., February 11, 1985, p. 38.

3 *Gallup Report*, no. 206, November 1982.

4 *Ibid*.

5 *Ibid*.

6 Harris survey, May 31, 1984.

7 See William C. Adams, "Why the Right Gets It Wrong in Foreign Policy," *Public Opinion*, August/September 1983, pp. 12–15.

8 Harris survey, January 26, 1984.

9 Everett Carll Ladd, "The Freeze Framework," *Public Opinion*, August/September 1982.

10 *Public Opinion*, August/September 1983, p. 30.

11 Harris survey, April 1, 1984.

12 Everett Carll Ladd, "The New Lines Are Drawn: Class and Ideology in America," *Public Opinion*, July/August 1978.

13 R. S. Erikson, N. Luttbeg, and K. L. Tedin, *American Public Opinion* (New York: Wiley, 1980), p. 187.

14 *The New York Times*, September 30, 1984, p. 14 and October 21, 1984, p. 15.

15 Dan Bolz, "Democrats Discover a Power Bloc: White Males," *The Washington Post*, national weekly ed., December 24, 1984, p. 15.

16 Paul Lazarsfeld, et al., *The People's Choice* (New York: Columbia University Press, 1948).

17 See Philip Converse, "The Nature of Belief Systems

in Mass Publics," in David Apter, ed., *Ideology and Discontent* (New York: The Free Press, 1964), pp. 238–45; and Angus Campbell, et al., *The American Voter* (New York: Wiley, 1960).

18 N. H. Nie and K. Anderson, "Mass Belief Systems Revisited: Political Change and Attitude Structure," in N. G. Niemi and H. F. Wiesberg, eds., *Controversies in American Voting Behavior* (San Francisco: W. H. Freeman, 1976), pp. 94–137.

19 Paul Allen Beck, "The Dealignment Era in America," in R. J. Dalton, S. C. Flanagan and P. A. Beck, *Electoral Changes in Advanced Industrial Democracies: Realignment or Dealignment?* (Princeton, N.J.: Princeton University Press, 1984), pp. 242–46.

20 Hedrick Smith, "The Economy: Still the Key for Reagan," *The New York Times*, November 7, 1984.

21 Dan Bolz, "Democrats Discover a Power Bloc: White Males," *The Washington Post*, national weekly ed., December 24, 1984, p. 15.

22 *Ibid.*, pp. 1 and 14.

23 David E. Rosenbaum, "Polls Show Many Choose Reagan Even If They Disagree with Him," *The New York Times*, September 19, 1984, p. 1.

24 Seymour Martin Lipset, "The Elections, the Economy and Public Opinion: 1984," *Political Science*, Winter 1985, p. 34.

25 Gerald W. Pomper, "The Presidential Election," in Gerald Pomper, et al., *The Election of 1984: Reports and Interpretations* (Chatham, N.J.: Chatham House, 1985), p. 85.

26 Wilson Carey McWilliams, "The Meaning of the Election," in Pomper et al., *op. cit.*, p. 178.

27 Lipset, *op. cit.*, pp. 34–38.

28 Everett Carll Ladd, "As the Realignment Turns: A Drama in Many Acts," *Public Opinion*, December/January 1985, pp. 6–7.

29 Thomas B. Edsall, "The GOP's Registration Coup," *The Washington Post*, national weekly ed., October 1, 1984, p. 6.

30 Gallup poll, December 9, 1984.

31 Campbell, et al., *The American Voter*.

32 Arthur Hadley, *The Empty Polling Booth* (Englewood Cliffs, N.J.: Prentice-Hall, 1978), p. 40.

33 Sidney Verba and Norman H. Nie, *Participation in America: Political Science and Social Equality* (New York: Harper & Row, 1972), Chapter 4.

## SELECTED READINGS

For general discussions of public opinion in the United States, see Richard Hamilton, *Class and Politics in the United States* (New York: Wiley, 1972); S. M. Lipset, *Political Man* (Garden City, N.Y.: Doubleday, 1960); Robert E. Lane, *Political Ideology: Why the American Common Man Believes What He Does* (New York: The Free Press, 1962); and Studs Terkel, *Working* (New York: Avon, 1974).

On the meaningfulness of elections, consult Herbert Asher, *Presidential Elections and American Politics* (Homewood, Ill.: Dorsey Press, 1976); R. G. Neimi and H. F. Weisberg, *Controversies in American Voting Behavior* (San Francisco: W. H. Freeman, 1976); Paul N. Abramson, et al., *Change and Continuity in the 1980 Elections* (Washington, D.C.: Congressional Quarterly Press, 1982); and Bernard Berelson, et. al., *Voting* (Chicago: Rand McNally, 1965).

On political participation, see Everett C. Ladd, Jr., *Where Have All the Voters Gone?* (New York: Norton, 1978); L. W. Milbrath and M. L. Goel, *Political Participation* (Chicago: Rand McNally, 1977); Kristi Amundsen, *A New Look at the Silenced Majority* (Englewood Cliffs, N.J.: Prentice-Hall, 1977); and Carole Pateman, *Participation and Democratic Theory* (New York: Cambridge University Press, 1970).

### Understanding public sentiment

On the general topic of ideology, see David Apter, ed., *Ideology and Discontent* (London: Free Press of Glencoe, 1964); William F. Stone, *The Psychology of Politics* (New York: The Free Press, 1974), discusses liberalism and conservatism from a psychological perspective. For the substance of American political attitudes, see the discussion in Robert Shogun, "The Upright Stuff: Our Values and Our Politics," *Public Opinion*, December/January, 1984.

### Electoral trends

The classic studies of voting in the United States are Berelson, et al., *Voting*; Paul Lazarsfeld, et al., *The People's Choice* (New York: Columbia University Press, 1948); Angus Campbell, et al., *The American Voter* (New York: Wiley, 1960); and A. Campbell, et al., *The Voter Decides* (New York: Harper & Row, 1954). For a discussion of recent trends, see Theodore H. White, "New Powers, New Politics," *The New York Times Magazine*, February 5, 1984.

For other discussions of the "responsible voter" controversy, see Asher, *Presidential Elections and American Politics*, especially Chapter 4; and Bruce A. Campbell, *The American Electorate: Attitudes and Action* (New York: Holt, Rinehart and Winston, 1979). See also Philip E. Converse, "The Nature of Belief Systems in Mass Publics," in Apter, ed., *Ideology and Discontent*.

### Nonparticipation: the Achilles' heel of U.S. politics

For overviews of this subject, see Sidney Verba and Norman Nie, *Participation in America* (New York: Harper & Row, 1972); Verba and Nie, "Political Participation," in F. I. Greenstein and N. W. Polsby, eds., *Handbook of Political Science* (Reading, Mass.: Addison-Wesley, 1975); and Milbrath and Goel, *Political Participation*.

For two different views on the subject of participation, see George F. Will, "In Defense of Nonvoting," *Newsweek*, October 10, 1983; and Pateman, *Participation and Democratic Theory*. On the question of the meaningfulness of elections, see: Stanley Kelley, Jr., *Interpreting Elections* (Princeton, N.J.: Princeton University Press, 1983).

# Political parties

## Do they offer a choice?

POLITICAL parties generally are given short shrift in the classic works on democratic theory, which concentrate on rights, equalities, liberties, and elections. And to many of the Founders of the United States, parties represented a potential threat to decent politics. Viewing partisan organizations as essentially selfish groups that would seek to exploit government to serve their own interests, they believed that parties would constitute a constant irritant in political life, a source of conflict and contention and of corruption and deception. James Madison warned of the dangers of "factions" that would use public power to further their own goals. George Washington shuddered at the thought of one faction alternately dominating another—a prospect he characterized as "a frightful despotism."

Even so, U.S. political parties began to develop very early. The beginnings of party disputes were apparent in the controversy over ratification of the Constitution. After George Washington left office, political disputes broke out during the administration of the second president, John Adams. These disputes laid the basis for the new republic's first political parties, the Federalists and the Democratic-Republicans.

Why was it that political parties seemed to develop so quickly and so naturally even among men who distrusted the very idea of party? With two hundred years of hindsight, we can see that political parties are necessary components of the democratic process. In fact, our perception of democratic politics has shifted 180 degrees from that of the Founders: they could not bear the thought of a political life that included parties, whereas we cannot imagine it without them.

Why are parties vital to the democratic process? And how effectively do contemporary U.S. parties fulfill the roles they are assigned in democratic politics? These questions will serve as focal points for this chapter.

## The role of parties in democracies

There have been attempts to define exactly what a political party is. Edmund Burke, the great English statesman of the late eighteenth century, declared that a **political party** was "a body of men united, for promoting by their joint endeavors the national

209

interest upon some particular principle in which they are all agreed." Burke thus focused on the *ideological* basis of a political organization—on what a party stood for. In his time, Burke saw various groups coalescing within the British governing structure. He realized that to combat groups that he and like-minded people opposed, it was necessary to attract and organize followers and allies who were willing to fight for certain principles.

Another way to look at political parties was offered by political scientist Leon Epstein. He defined a political party as "any group, however loosely organized, seeking to elect government office-holders under a given label."[1] The focus in this definition is on the major activity of political parties—the contesting of elections. In this view, a common label and the nomination of candidates for office suffice to establish the existence of a party.

Yet a third way to view political parties is to focus on organization. According to French social scientist Maurice Duverger, parties can best be characterized as structured groups. "A party," he wrote, "is a community with a particular structure."[2] As political parties have evolved in modern times, Duverger pointed out, they have developed particular structural characteristics, and methods of organization become a crucial element in the concept of party. Some parties are very loosely organized, whereas others have tightly disciplined arrangements. Every party, however, organizes itself in order to engage in political competition.

All three of these factors—ideology, activity, and organization—must figure significantly in any discussion of parties, and we will touch on all three in this chapter. Before leaving the matter of definition, however, we should take note of a summary description of a political party developed by political scientist Hugh Leblanc: "An organized effort to win elective office in order to gain political power and control the policies of government."[3]

### Three facets of political parties

A political party usually has three distinct aspects: it is a formal organization, with distinctive internal

politics; it is a part of the electorate, in that it organizes electoral support; and it is a part of the government, in that it is composed of officeholders on every level.

As a formal organization, a party conducts business outside of government. The formal party structure includes the national organization and its leadership, various local organizations, and numerous professionals and activists who are heavily involved in party life. Many European political parties have millions of formally enrolled members, whereas U.S. parties usually depend on cadres of full-time staffers.

As a part of the electorate, a party relies on the long-term allegiance of voters to its views. Identification of citizens with the party serves as the solid base of political support at election time. As we will see, party loyalties in the United States have grown distinctly weaker in recent times, and candidates have often established personal organizations that function outside the party structure.

The party-in-the-government is made up of the many officeholders at all levels who run under the party label, and of the more numerous officeholders who are appointed by elected officials. Collectively, these elected officials and appointees are responsible for policy-making.

The three aspects of party overlap, of course. Some party professionals may hold office, and strong party-identifiers may work for the party organization. There is no simple way to ascertain the strength of parties, since they function in so many different ways. Generally, however, U.S. parties are considered to be among the weakest political parties in modern democracies—meaning that they are very loosely organized and relatively undisciplined.

### Political parties and democracy

It is possible to conceive of a small, democratically organized community that functions without political parties. Neighbors would gather for weekly meetings to discuss the community's business. Since the meetings would be small and the issues familiar and fairly easy to understand, there usually would be no need for factions or parties within the community. In fact,

210

the appearance of anything like a political party would probably have a disruptive influence on the community. Such is the ideal. Yet even in such a small group, factions and organized interests sometimes would form when there were disagreements on important issues, when some began to fear they were being neglected, or when others acquired a taste for power. And in any democratic society in which face-to-face discussion is not possible, numerous issues must be dealt with, and governing is a highly complex operation, political parties perform extremely significant functions.

Parties provide key links between citizens and government. First of all, they serve as vehicles for the selection of candidates for office and mobilization of the electorate. By channeling votes toward their candidates, parties limit and focus the choices of citizens. As parties come to stand for certain policies, voters link themselves to those policies. Other voters simply identify strongly with a party label. In this way, the political parties simplify the seemingly complex choices that face voters.

Parties also organize the government: that is, they are responsible for the functioning of the legislative and executive branches. In the United States, the party with a majority in either house of Congress organizes that House along partisan lines, selecting a majority leader and structuring the committee assignments in its favor. Likewise, the newly elected president generally makes appointments along party lines. Sometimes, of course, presidents deliberately make appointments across party lines in order to widen their base of support, or to demonstrate fair-mindedness.

Finally, parties provide for "responsibility" in government. In modern democratic societies, the governing political party generally is held responsible for the conduct of government. Its candidates run on the party record, and voters can pass judgment on the way government was conducted by deciding whether to reelect those in office or to turn them out.

This description of the functions of political parties in a democracy leaves many questions unanswered. What if parties do not behave responsibly? What if they fail to organize the government in an effective fashion? What if the opposition is itself divided and confused? What if party labels have lost their meaning and voters no longer pay much attention to them? What if control of government is so split among various parties that no clear lines of

Political party competition vanished from Spain for 30 years during the dictatorship of Francisco Franco. Here, Socialist voters celebrate the victory of their party and candidate, Felipe González, in the 1982 elections. Spain's new democracy remained on a fragile footing in the early 1980s, however, with the threat of a military coup an ever-present possibility.

responsibility emerge? What if political conflict grows so intense that governing parties threaten to outlaw other parties? And what if there are too many political parties—or too few? We cannot deal adequately with all such questions here, but as the chapter proceeds, we will address those with the greatest bearing on our own party system.

## Two-party and multiparty systems

"The best system is to have one party govern and the other party watch," asserted Thomas Reed, Speaker of the House, in 1880. The United States, with its two-party system, fits into this category. Most European democracies, however, have multiparty systems: West Germany, for example, has two major parties and two minor ones, whereas Denmark and Italy have ten or more parties apiece.

The U.S. political system has become almost exclusively a two-party system. In recent decades, third parties have had a very difficult time electing any legislators to Congress or to state legislatures. In other democracies with predominantly two-party systems, such as West Germany, Great Britain, and Canada, third or even fourth parties are often able to elect some members of the national legislature and may play significant political roles. In West Germany, for example, the small Free Democratic Party for years played a decisive role in coalition governments, since neither major party, the Social Democrats and the Christian Democrats, was able to win a majority in the national parliament. Even in Great Britain, where the Conservative and Labour parties have alternated in office since the 1930s, the small Liberal Party has been able to retain its identity and compete for office. And very recently, the Social Democrats, a new party formed by breakaway members of the Labour Party, has met with modest electoral success.

At several points in U.S. history, third parties have helped to shape the course of national politics—a subject we will return to. Overall, however, the United States has tended strongly in a two-party

212

direction. A principal reason for this tendency is our reliance on the **single-member district**: that is, whoever gets the most votes in a legislative district represents that district. In such a system, obviously, votes for a minor party are usually wasted. Countries with multiparty systems, in contrast, commonly use a method of election known as **proportional representation**, in which each party is awarded seats in the legislature in more-or-less direct proportion to its percentage of the popular vote. Since votes are not wasted in a proportional system, minor parties have an incentive to compete.

Another factor in the evolution of our two-party system has been the strong ties of party identification established between the voters and the two major parties. People have come to think of elections in strictly two-party terms. Moreover, electoral laws provide the two major parties with distinct advantages—for example, new parties must petition to get on the ballot in most states. And since the two major parties are composed of many factions and interests, new groups usually have been able to make their presence felt *within* an established party, rather than in a new political group. In the United States, political coalitions most often are worked out *within* the parties; in multiparty systems, governing coalitions are worked out *between* parties when no one party wins a clear electoral majority.

A unique feature of U.S. political life that lends further support to the two-party arrangement is the way the chief political leader, the president, is selected. In many other democratic nations, the executive leader is chosen by the party (or parties, in a coalition government) that controls the parliament, whereas we hold an entirely separate election for president. The national attention focused on this office makes presidential elections far and away the most dramatic political events in the United States. The two established parties, with their party loyalists, organizations, and patterns of identification, have a nearly insurmountable advantage in the presidential race.

Finally, it may be that the overall moderate nature of American public opinion has pushed us in the direction of two middle-of-the-road political parties. As noted in Chapter 2, the heritage of U.S. political

TABLE 9.1
# The political spectrum
# in several democratic nations

| Country | Radical Left | Communism | Democratic Socialism | Liberalism | Christian Democracy | Conservatism | Reactionary Right |
|---------|-------------|-----------|---------------------|------------|--------------------|-------------|-------------------|
| Britain | | | Labour Party | Liberal Party | | Conservative Party | |
| | | | Social Democratic Party | | | | |
| France | Unified Socialist Party (PSU) | French Communist Party (PCF) | Socialist Party | Radical Party | Democratic Center | Independent Republicans (RI), Gaullists (UDR) | |
| West Germany | | German Communist Party (DKP) | Social Democratic Party (SPD) | Free Democratic Party (FDP) | Christian Democratic Union (CDU) | Christian Social Union (CSU) | National Democratic Party (NPD) |
| | | | Greens | | | | |
| Italy | Proletarian Democracy (DP) | Italian Communist Party (PCI) | Italian Socialist Party (PSI) | Republican Party (PRI) | Christian Democratic Party (DC) | Liberal Party (PLI) | Italian Social Movement (MSI) |
| | | | Social Democratic Party (PSDI) | | | | |
| United States* | | | | Democratic Party | | Republican Party | |

*Note that the United States is one of the few democratic countries with only two political parties, although there are some nations (Britain and West Germany, for example) where two parties predominate.
Source: Adapted from David M. Wood, *Power and Policy in Western European Democracies*, 2nd ed. (New York: Wiley, 1982), p. 78.

culture is generally liberal. Both the extreme left and the extreme right have been notably weak in U.S. political life, and there has been little room for political success outside of the mainstream. Patterns of opinion and party identification in other nations are quite different (see Table 9.1).

## The U.S. party system

Over the years the U.S. party system has undergone several basic shifts. Let us now look at how it has evolved and how its evolution has affected the function of democratic politics in the United States.

## Origins of contemporary parties

In his farewell address, delivered in 1797, President George Washington called on the nation to be wary of the "baneful effects of the spirit of party." This warning resulted from events during his administration that, much to his dismay, clearly signaled the emergence of political party divisions in the new nation.

Two main factions had been developing during Washington's eight years in office. Members of one faction, calling themselves the **Federalists,** were led by Secretary of the Treasury Alexander Hamilton (and by George Washington himself, despite his disdain for parties in principle). The Federalists were generally men of wealth and high social position. Members of the second group, the so-called **Democratic-Republicans**, were led by Thomas Jefferson and James Madison. Jefferson's party, a coalition of small farmers, small property owners, and local political leaders in the Southern and Mid-Atlantic states, soon came to dominate U.S. politics. By the mid-1820s, the Federalists had ceased to exist as a political force.

With the election of Andrew Jackson to the presidency in 1828, the party of Jefferson and Madison, renamed the **Democratic Party**, was transformed into a mass membership organization and became the dominant force in U.S. political life. Presidents Jackson and Martin Van Buren reorganized their party to accommodate the new states admitted to the Union and to gain support among those who became eligible to vote as economic qualifications limiting the suffrage were eased.

Between 1828 and 1856, the Jacksonian Democrats faced opposition mainly from the **Whig Party**. Generally speaking, the Democrats found their political base along the frontier, among farmers in the western states, whereas the Whigs appealed more to New England and especially to those with business interests. Although the Democrats won the presidency and a majority in the House of Representatives in most of those elections, the Whigs were able to attract a substantial following, electing both Zachary Taylor and William Henry Harrison to the presidency. The Whig-Democratic rivalry extended beyond the national level to state and local politics.

Both parties were deeply divided by the slavery issue. The Democrats became dominated at that time by their southern wing, which controlled Congress. In the 1850s, the Whigs disappeared altogether, many of them merging into the newly formed **Republican Party**. In 1860 its presidential candidate, Abraham Lincoln, won election, as the Democratic Party broke into Northern and Southern factions that fielded separate presidential candidates. The Republicans, originally a small, radical party formed chiefly to oppose the further extension of slavery, quickly put together a coalition of northern industrialists, merchants, workers, farmers, and freed slaves.

Although the Democratic Party survived the Civil War, the Republican coalition won every presidential election for the next five decades except for those of 1884 and 1892. During this time, the Republican base of support slowly shifted to businessmen and middle-class white Protestants, while the Democrats began to attract the urban, Catholic immigrants and to erode Republican support among workers.

The system
of '96

Events of the 1890s shaped U.S. politics for generations to come. At that time, socialist parties were becoming a political force in Europe, and the United States seemed ripe for such a development. The **Populist Party**, which had arisen in the South and West in the 1880s, demanded many socialist-sounding measures, and a growing trade union movement was also making its presence felt on the U.S. political scene. Workers and Populists together might have formed the nucleus for a new party of the left, or precipitated a decisive shift to the left in the Democratic Party. But the Democratic candidate in 1896, William Jennings Bryan, though a populist in rhetoric, steered clear of the labor movement and big-city ethnic populations, and thus failed to put together an electoral coalition that might have realigned the U.S. party system along left/right political lines. William McKinley's victory in the presidential election of 1896 reinstated Republican dominance, which was reinforced by certain political reforms instituted in 1896.

Prior to 1896, Americans took an intensely partisan view of politics. Electoral contests were waged as full-scale battles, in which each party drummed up partisan enthusiasm through torchlight parades, elaborate campaigns, wide-reaching party organization, and extensive patronage. Elections turned on party preference more than on individual candidates. Partisan competition was keen and voter turnout high.

The reforms of 1896 changed political life dramatically. Supporters of the "system of '96," as these reforms came to be known, succeeded in passing new registration laws, in reforming the civil service, and

William Jennings Bryan,
one of the great orators of
his time, delivers a campaign
speech. Despite his elo-
quence, Bryan was unable
to rally the forces to defeat

William McKinley in the
1896 presidential election,
and his loss began a decline
of the Democrats that lasted
almost 40 years.

Burnham felt that the system of '96 left a permanent
hole in the American political universe, one that in
Europe was filled by Labor and Social Democratic
parties. The large-scale politicization of the poor and
the working class that might have taken place in the
United States in the 1890s, in other words, simply
did not occur.

## The New Deal coalition

HECKLER: I'm a Democrat.

THEODORE ROOSEVELT: May I ask the gentleman why
he is a Democrat?

HECKLER: My grandfather was a Democrat, my father
was a Democrat, and I am a Democrat.

ROOSEVELT: My friend, suppose your grandfather was a
jackass and your father was a jackass, what would you
be?

HECKLER: A Republican.

Between 1896 and 1932, only the victories of Woodrow Wilson in 1912 and 1916 interrupted the Republican lock on the presidential office. And Wilson's election in 1912 was made possible by a split
among the Republicans that led to Theodore Roosevelt's candidacy on a third-party ticket.

The Republican Party's support in this period came
principally from a coalition of middle-class Protestant and native-stock Americans (those whose ancestors came here before the twentieth century, mostly
from Britain and Germany). Democratic strength was
centered in the so-called solid South. The border
states also leaned toward the Democrats, and there
were pockets of Democratic strength in the larger
cities of the Northeast among immigrant voters and

in creating direct primaries (whereby voters, rather
than party leaders, could choose nominees), in establishing split-ticket balloting. One result of civil
service reforms was that parties were denied the patronage that helped build loyal followings. By these
means, reformers hoped to introduce a calmer, less
intensely partisan political life. But ballots without
party labels confused many voters, and registration
complexities contributed to keeping many from voting in the first place—a particularly significant factor
in view of the growing number of foreign-born potential voters. Turnout declined, the parties lost much
of their vitality, and the era of modern, candidate-
centered politics began. Walter Dean Burnham estimated that after 1896, fully 50 percent of potential
U.S. voters remained outside the political process,
alienated from parties and politics, and that only
about one-third remained firmly attached to the usual
electoral systems. The functional result of the system
of '96, Burnham stated, "was the conversion of a
fairly democratic regime into a rather broadly based
oligarchy."[4]

Many experts have disagreed with this highly critical judgment of the contraction of the active electorate at the turn of the century, but there is no doubt
that a major depoliticization took place at that time.

215

the industrial working class. Overall, the distribution of voter support was decisively in favor of the Republicans.

The collapse of the economy in 1929 gave the Democrats an opening. It is interesting in retrospect that during the Depression, no third party mounted a serious challenge to the dominance of the two major parties. In any case, Franklin Roosevelt won an overwhelming majority in the 1932 election. As we saw in the last chapter, Roosevelt's landslide victory ushered in a new era in U.S. politics, and one that has continued in many ways to the present day.

The coalition that brought the Democrats to power in 1932 and reelected Roosevelt three times was not entirely new. Some elements of the pre-1932 Democratic strength were still present—the solid South and working-class, Catholic voters. But new groups of voters were largely responsible for the strength of the New Deal coalition. The black population, long affiliated with the Republicans, now began to switch to the Democrats in large numbers, attracted by the Roosevelt administration's tentative attack on discriminatory practices and by federal programs for the hungry and the jobless. Jews, heavily concentrated in major cities, also joined the coalition. FDR's sup-

port for the poor and downtrodden and his early opposition to the Nazi regime in Germany were key elements in this development.

Perhaps most important, the experience of the Depression and the economic appeal of New Deal programs redirected U.S. politics along lines of social class. For the first time since 1896, class factors exerted a decisive influence on election outcomes. The Democrats were able to attract heavy working-class support and to repoliticize many voters who had lost interest in politics, thus overcoming some of the heritage of the system of '96. Still, even in the Depression years, class voting in America was not so clearly defined as it was in other democratic nations.

## Since the New Deal

Since the 1930s, the U.S. political party system has evolved greatly, as both parties have undergone considerable change without fully altering their basic identities. The Democrats, for example, have gradually lost their once-solid hold on the South. This process began abruptly in 1948, when the so-called Dixiecrats (southern Democrats who opposed integration) broke from the party after a civil rights plank was passed at the Democrats' national convention. Since that point, Southern disaffiliation from the Democratic Party has run a more gradual course. It took until 1960 for the Republicans to win more than seven congressional seats in the deep South. Finally, in both 1976 and 1980, Democrat Jimmy Carter, himself a Southerner, failed to win the support of a majority of voters in the Southern states. Clearly, a portion of the New Deal coalition had shaken loose.

At an ideological level, the shift of portions of the South away from the Democrats showed the liberal direction the party had taken. More-conservative Southerners moved toward the Republicans—a step in line with their true ideological position. Some Southern politicians, such as South Carolina Senator Strom Thurmond, actually shifted their partisan identities, proclaiming themselves Republicans and running successfully on the Republican ticket. On the other hand, Southern blacks remained firmly committed to the Democrats.

Another factor that helped to undermine and reshape the New Deal coalition was the prominence of a set of social issues that, at times, eclipsed economic questions. In the presidential election of 1952, the issues were communism, corruption, and Korea. In the 1960s, attention focused on violence in the streets, corruption in high office, and the loss of values among youth. In 1968 and 1972, Richard Nixon campaigned on a "law-and-order" platform, focusing on dissenters, crime, and riots in the cities. In 1984, such issues as abortion and school prayer held center stage. Of course, many other factors were involved in Democratic defeats in 1968, 1972, 1980, and 1984. But overall, it seems safe to say that such social issues have made an important contribution to the gradual decay of the New Deal coalition. Because of these issues, many white, ethnic, working-class groups once strongly affiliated with the Democrats have shifted, on occasion, to Republican candidates, especially in presidential contests.

Both parties have also undergone internal conflicts. Among the Republicans, the long-term struggle for control between the more liberal Northeastern and Western party members and the more conservative Sunbelt group seemed to be decided in 1980 in favor of the latter, but conflicts on specific issues continued. As for the Democrats, very sharp splits began to appear over Vietnam in the 1960s and continued throughout the 1970s and into the 1980s between the more liberal, affluent, and better-educated McGovern-Kennedy wing of the party and various more conservative factions.

Between the end of World War II and the mid-1980s, then, the U.S. party system has been in a process of gradual transition. But transition to what?

On this matter, the experts are far from sure. As we will see later in the chapter, many scenarios have been proposed for the future shape of our party system—including the prediction that the party system is in deep trouble and is likely to decompose in the years ahead.

## Dilemmas and contributions of third parties

Third parties have an unenviable position in the United States, partly because of the many legal and financial barriers they face. Whereas the two major parties are guaranteed columns on the ballot in all states, third parties must go through elaborate, time-consuming, expensive processes to obtain official recognition. California, for example, requires a petition signed by 713,000 registered voters to be delivered before January 20 of the election year. In New Hampshire, each such signature must be a separate petition duly certified by the town clerk. Estimates are that about 2.2 million signatures are required to get on the ballot in all 50 states—and the same process must be repeated each election year.[5]

As for financing, the major parties receive millions of dollars through the federal election law—a total of $105 million in 1980. Third-party candidates, however, receive no public funds unless they obtain at least 5 percent of the popular vote. In 1980, for example, John Anderson barely made this threshold and thereby saved himself from years of struggle to pay off campaign debts.

In U.S. history, only once has a third party (the Republicans) replaced one of the major parties (the Whigs)—and that was 130 years ago, during the crisis that led to the Civil War. But as hard as third parties have had to struggle to play a significant role in the political process, several have made valuable contributions to U.S. political life.

**A history of third parties:** Egalitarian issues dominated third-party movements in early U.S. history. The Anti-Masons, the nation's first significant third

party, emerged in the 1820s. They saw themselves as challengers of privilege, of which the Masonic order was a symbol. In 1840, the Liberty Party was launched as the country's first explicitly antislavery political party. The American (or Know-Nothing) Party attracted wide support in the 1850s. Its main aim was to limit immigration, particularly of Irish-Catholics.

After the Civil War, a new set of third parties developed in response to issues related to industrial growth, capitalism, and class conflict. After the economic depression of the early 1870s, the Greenback Party organized to urge the issuance of paper money and the rejection of the gold standard. Then, in the late nineteenth century, the People's Party, better known as the Populist Party, arose in the farm areas

of the Midwest, South, and Far West. The Populists favored the coinage of silver (rather than gold), government ownership of railroads, a graduated income tax, and direct election of U.S. senators (who at the time were still elected by state legislatures). Among the other parties of economic protest that appeared around the turn of the century, the most prominent was the **Socialist Party** led by Eugene Debs, who ran for president five times. The Socialists reached the peak of their electoral power in 1912, when 667 party members held state or local offices and Debs received about 900,000 votes for president.

Two particularly prominent Republican figures also led third-party efforts early in this century. In 1912, ex-president Theodore Roosevelt ran on the Bull Moose ticket after failing to gain the nomination of the Re-

Left: One of our first third parties, the Know-Nothings, is satirized in this 1856 cartoon. Anti-foreign sentiment was the party's dominant policy, an issue that was to arise again and again later in the country's history.

Middle: Theodore Roosevelt campaigning in 1912 on the Bull Moose ticket after he broke with the Republicans. A vigorous campaigner and a reformer, Roosevelt's candidacy permitted Woodrow Wilson to win the election.

Right: The greatest third party vote-getter in U.S. history, George Wallace. Here, his supporters demonstrate their enthusiasm. Despite his plan to hold the balance of power in the 1968 election and perhaps prevent any candidate from receiving a majority of electoral votes, Wallace was unable to achieve this objective.

publican Party; he received over 4 million popular votes and eighty-eight votes in the electoral college. Like Roosevelt, Robert LaFollette came from the liberal wing of the Republican Party and ran on a reformist platform as the candidate of the Progressive Party in the 1924 election.

Third-party efforts continued after World War II. In 1948, Henry Wallace ran on the left-leaning Progressive Party ticket and Strom Thurmond was standardbearer of the Dixiecrats. George Wallace, the conservative Democratic governor of Alabama, launched a presidential bid on the American Independent Party ticket in 1968. Wallace, who made the often-quoted statement that there "isn't a dime's worth of difference between the Republicans and Democrats," was able to attract almost 10 million popular votes (the most ever for a third-party candidate) and forty-six electoral votes. The most significant third party effort since 1968 was mounted by the National Unity Party, under whose banner John Anderson ran for president in 1980.

**The role of third parties:** Although no third party has successfully challenged a major party since the 1850s, third-party and independent candidacies have served useful functions in U.S. political history. With the major parties usually seeking to stick to the middle ground and avoid controversy, third parties have often provided an outlet for protest politics centered on controversial issues. Third parties helped to bring the issue of slavery onto center stage in U.S. political life and were moderately successful in raising im-

219

# Comparative perspective
# A new party in West Germany

When an electorate becomes extremely frustrated with the dominant political parties and their policy positions—or lack of positions—one solution is to form a new party. Perhaps the most dramatic (and to some, disquieting) new party to be formed in recent years is the Green Party in West Germany.

The Greens defy the usual left-right categories. Their policies stress new issues such as environmental degradation and the need for alternative lifestyles. They call for sharp reductions in nuclear armaments and want West Germany to leave NATO. They draw supporters from all groups and age levels in German society, but their core activists are younger, unconventional people who look back to the 1960s, when grassroots action had startling effects on political life. Not all Greens, however, agree on a common agenda.

Begun in 1980, the party's membership by 1983 was estimated at 1.5 to 2 million people. Though they captured only 1.5 percent of the vote in the 1980 national elections, far short of the 5 percent necessary to gain representation in the national parliament, the Greens won 5.3 percent of the vote in a state election later that year and entered the state parliament. That victory was followed by showings of 5 percent or better in four other state elections, with the Greens in some cases replacing the Free Democrats as the third parliamentary party. In the March 1983 national election, the Greens captured 5.6 percent of the vote and entered the 498-member lower house of the national parliament with 27 seats.

Whether they can develop the flexibility and expertise needed to generate policies and programs that will compete in the political marketplace and still retain the loyalty and support of millions of voters is a question just beginning to be answered. The Greens may reject the system in some respects, but the fact that they are a political party, participating in the day-to-day legislative business of the country, is a vote of confidence in that same system. One key question they may well face in the near future is whether they will be willing to forge coalitions with the Social Democrats, or whether they will choose to remain in opposition.

---

portant questions about industrial capitalism in the late nineteenth and early twentieth centuries. Third parties have also pointed the way toward procedural reforms. A third party held the first national nominating convention. Third parties were the first to advocate women's suffrage and to call for a wide range of electoral reforms.

## Party organization

When Will Rogers quipped, "I belong to no organized political party—I am a Democrat," he was poking fun at his own party, but what he said could be applied to either of the major U.S. parties. They are organized in only the loosest sense on the national level, where one might expect them to be most coherent. State party organizations range from the quite active to the virtually moribund. Local party organizations tend to be the most tightly structured. At all three levels, U.S. political parties have undergone significant changes in recent decades.

**Local parties:** The most notorious—and frequently, most successful—form of political organization in the United States has been the local **political machine**, a coterie of party professionals who get out the vote and provide constituent services. The most successful of these machines, based on "boss" rule and strong standards of loyalty, reached from the mayor's office through the precincts down to the

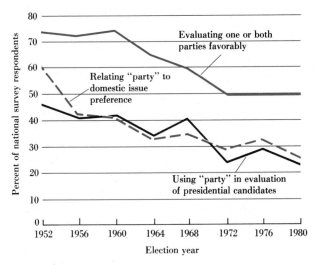

FIGURE 9.1
Party as a Point of Reference for Voters, 1952–80.
Source: David Price, *Bringing Back the Parties* (Washington, D.C.: Congressional Quarterly Press, 1984), p. 18.

ward and block levels. Most arose in Eastern and Midwestern cities after the Civil War, and a few retained power through the 1960s.

The machines were successful partly because they served important political and social functions. They provided the means through which newly arrived immigrant groups were integrated into U.S. politics. And in return for votes, rank-and-file members of the machines provided aid to needy families, supplied city jobs, and generally gave ignored groups recognition they could not find elsewhere. As one summary of the classic machine politics put it: "An effective political party needs five things: offices, jobs, money, workers, and votes. Offices beget jobs and money, jobs and money beget workers, workers beget votes, and votes beget offices."[6] This is a neat little circle—and one that invites corruption, nepotism, favoritism, inefficiency, and dictatorial trends.

Machines were long the object of reform efforts at both federal and state levels. The introduction of civil service was intended to limit boss rule by cutting back on the number of patronage appointments. Sometimes, nonpartisan elections were used to limit the influence of machine-controlled voting. The introduction of the direct primary was inspired at least in part by a perceived need to wrest the control of nominations from the machine bosses.

The overall decline of the urban political machine was a slow process. As social conditions changed, the machines no longer met the needs they had earlier. Immigrants found a more secure place in the nation's economy. Federal programs such as Social Security, unemployment insurance, workmen's compensation, and welfare took over many of the functions once performed by the machines.

Even before their demise, however, machines represented only one facet of local politics. Local political life in the United States has always been a highly varied affair, ranging from minimally organized and contested elections to highly partisan and sharply fought campaigns for city councils, county governing bodies, even school boards. One of the unique features of U.S. politics is the number of different local officials who are elected, rather than appointed.

Local politics has often served as the initial point of entry for people who want to become politically involved. Many recent studies have focused on the increasing number of "amateurs" or "purists" who become involved in local politics and then make their way onto the national political scene. Such "purists," as they are often called, see politics as a realm of ideas and principles, whereas the old machine-oriented professionals were far more interested in maintaining party organization and winning elections.[7]

**State parties:** At the top of the state party organization is the state committee, consisting of anywhere from a few dozen to several hundred members. Typically, the county is the basic unit of representation. Members of the state committees are selected in a variety of ways, including primaries, caucuses, and selection by state convention delegates.

Whatever their theoretical powers, few state committees play active roles in state party matters. Usually, the committee meets a few times a year and leaves day-to-day business to the party chairperson, normally the key figure in party matters. Most often the state party chairperson is closely associated with the governor or other high-ranking state officials. As state politics has grown more competitive in recent decades, the chairpersons, and the state parties in general, have widened the scope of their functions. They employ opinion poll data and work to develop issues for future campaigns. Chairpersons now engage in more fund-raising activities, as the costs of statewide campaigns have risen sharply. One area in which state party organizations have come to exert less influence than in the past is candidate selection. As candidate personality and use of the media have become more central to campaigns, some of the traditional roles of state parties have been lost. As a result, the state parties now emphasize fund-raising and professional services to candidates.

**National parties:** Originally, the sole function of the national party was to nominate a presidential candidate, who was selected by party leaders in Congress. By the 1830s, however, national conventions had become the accepted means of selecting the party's presidential hopeful. Each state was allowed to decide how to choose its delegates to the convention. The adoption of the national convention system, in turn, made it necessary to create an ongoing organization that would make arrangements for the convention and coordinate the campaign. This function was performed by the **national committee**, created by the Democrats in 1848 and adopted by the Republicans eight years later. In both parties, each state elected a single member to the national committee until the 1920s, when a committee*woman* was added for each state.

For over a century the national committees served only as links from one convention to the next. They did not effectively centralize party control, as power still resided mainly in the hands of the state chairpersons. Only a few national chairpersons had a strong

222

enough influence over party affairs to exercise some control over the nominating process. The decentralized nature of party politics was made evident whenever a president tried to influence party politics at the state or local level. In 1938, for example, Franklin Roosevelt unsuccessfully attempted to purge thirteen Democratic congressmen who had opposed his New Deal programs. The hard feelings raised by Roosevelt's purge effort were voiced by national committee chairman James Farley, who accused the president of having violated a "cardinal political creed" by intervening in state politics.

Not until after the tumultuous 1948 convention did strong pressures develop within the Democratic Party to diminish the overwhelming influence of state parties in the national convention process. At the 1948 convention, several state delegations were allowed to participate despite the fact that they were pledged to support the so-called Dixiecrat ticket rather than the Democratic ticket. This capitulation by the national party to Dixiecrat delegations set off a struggle to nationalize party rules. Finally, in 1956 the convention resolved that state parties selecting national convention delegates had to "assure" that the official Democratic Party nominee would appear under the party label on the state ballot. (In the 1948 election, Dixiecrat candidate Strom Thurmond, not Democratic candidate Harry Truman, had been listed as the "Democratic" candidate in four states.) In the 1960s, the Democrats took several additional steps in the direction of greater national control of state delegations, most notably by stipulating that state delegations be selected on a nondiscriminatory basis. After the strife-ridden 1968 Chicago convention, extensive new rules governing delegate selection were instituted (see the following section).

Despite these moves toward nationalization of party rules, the Democratic Party, like the Republican Party, has remained a highly decentralized organization. There has been no effort to formalize party membership through requirements that members pay dues and carry party cards. Nor has there been any significant effort to require candidates to adhere to a clearly drawn set of party principles.

The Republican Party has pursued nationalization in its own way. Under a series of dynamic national

## Comparative perspective Disciplined parties of Great Britain

In Great Britain, members of parliament (MPs) used to be able to keep their seats so long as they remained personally popular with their constituents. Political reforms instituted in the late nineteenth century, however, served to make personal appeal less practical (and corrupt campaigns less feasible) by extending the franchise, limiting campaign spending, and introducing the secret ballot. Under the new political rules, party organization in the constituencies became crucial to an MP's reelection chances. Thus, party leaders, who controlled the organization, were largely able to decide an individual MP's fate. This disciplined party system, in turn, gave the government (the Prime Minister and the Cabinet, collec-

tively) close control over party members in Parliament.

The ramifications of this political system are apparent today. Within Parliament, party discipline is enforced by the structure of roles and by informal norms and sanctions. Members are expected to attend party meetings in the House and, if possible, to join party committees concerned with various policy areas. MPs are also expected to attend important debates and support the party's position; lack of attention to party chores may mean the closing of paths to advancement for the offending member.

Responsibility for enforcing discipline rests with the Whips. Each party leader in the House of Commons chooses his or her own Chief Whip, who then appoints assistant, or junior, Whips. The Whips' authority is real, even though their methods, for the most part, are informal. They use persuasion, if they must, to enforce party discipline. One of the best arguments a majority Whip can use is that a vote against the government could help to bring the latter down. Whips seldom have to resort to appeals, however. By dispensing favors and

British Prime Minister Margaret Thatcher talks to citizens on the streets of Birmingham in 1979. A British party leader usually holds considerably greater centralized power over party affairs than does any American politician.

accommodating individual MPs, the Whips seek to instill reflexive party loyalty in MPs.

An MP who consistently opposes party policy may, theoretically, be expelled from the party, making a future political career far more difficult. A prominent case in point was Alfred Edwards, elected as a Labour member in 1935 and expelled from the Party in 1948 for opposing the government deci-

sions on nationalization of industry. Expulsion is an extreme measure, however; it is reserved for those who have abandoned basic party principles not only in Parliament but also in public speeches and activities.

Party loyalty and discipline are mirrored in parliamentary voting. In practice, this means that if the party in power has a solid majority, the opposition has virtually no chance of influencing government policy. It must wait until the next election to try to gain the advantage.

Sources: A. H. Birch, *The British System of Government*, 2nd ed. (London: George Allen and Unwin, 1968); Vernon Bogdanor, *Multi-Party Politics and the Constitution* (Cambridge, England: Cambridge University Press, 1983); Robert J. Jackson, *Rebels and Whips* (London: Macmillan, 1968); Richard Rose, *Politics in England* (Boston: Little, Brown, 1980); Donald Searing and Chris Game, "Horses for Courses: The Recruitment of Whips in the British House of Commons," *British Journal of Political Science* 7 (July 1977):361–85.

chairpersons, the GOP ("Grand Old Party") has expanded the operations of its national office over the past two decades. Beginning in the mid-1960s, the GOP national organization mounted extensive fund-raising efforts using direct mail. Enough money was raised for the GOP to build its own national headquarters in 1971—the first ever owned by either party. Through the 1970s, the GOP also established a highly complex network of services and activities, including the recruitment and training of candidates for state and local races on an unprecedented scale; opinion polling, research, media production, and data processing; financial assistance to candidates, totaling almost $11 million in 1980 (including the presidential race); national advertising campaigns focused on alleged Democratic failures and Republican "new ideas"; the development of issues on a long-term basis through the use of advisory councils; and publication of a party monthly, numerous brochures, and a semiacademic journal.

Both national parties, then, are alive and well. Neither, however, serves as an overall coordinator of party policy. Instead, both have followed a course of partial nationalization along lines of party reform, provision of services, and campaign strategy. The basically decentralized quality of U.S. politics has remained intact.

## Party reforms after 1968

**Democratic reforms:** Political events in 1968 stimulated efforts to reform the Democratic Party's nominating process. Prior to the 1968 convention, President Lyndon Johnson elected not to seek renomination. Robert Kennedy (before his assassination) and Eugene McCarthy then waged a highly visible and intense battle for the presidential nomination in states that had primaries. Meanwhile, Vice-President Hubert Humphrey, fearful of widespread opposition to the Vietnam War among rank-and-file Democrats, chose to avoid most presidential primaries. Humphrey based his strategy on the strength of

224

his support among party regulars in those states that did not hold primaries. At that time, 60 percent of the delegates to the Democratic national convention were selected by state conventions or state committees. And even in states that held primaries, the delegates selected by popular vote often were not bound to a particular candidate. Humphrey's strategy enabled him to quietly garner enough party support to gain the nomination. Many Democrats were outraged by this result, largely because they suspected that Humphrey could not have won nomination in the primary battles.

The 1968 Democratic Convention in Chicago represented one of the political low points of the 1960s. At the convention itself control of the proceedings was very tight, and some delegates accused the party bosses of police-style tactics. In the streets of Chicago, protesters of many sorts roamed or paraded through the city, sometimes taunting police, sometimes set upon and beaten by police without provocation. The protesters sought the passage of an anti–Vietnam War plank and a more open convention, as did many inside the convention hall. When some convention delegates accused Chicago Mayor Richard J. Daley, the convention's host and leading Democratic power broker, of condoning "Gestapo tactics" against demonstrators, Daley shouted profane epithets at his critics in front of a national television audience. At the deepest level, the legitimacy of the entire U.S. political process was being called into question. More specifically, many Democrats became convinced that reform of the nominating process was absolutely necessary.

After the 1968 election, national party chairman Fred Harris appointed a reform commission headed by Senator George McGovern of South Dakota and later chaired by Representative Donald Fraser of California. The McGovern-Fraser Commission introduced several ambitious reforms, the most significant of which were the following.

A requirement that each state delegation take steps to assure that blacks, women, and those under thirty would be represented in "reasonable" relationship to the state's population.

The development of written rules governing each state's method of choosing delegates.

Abolition of the *unit rule*, under which state delegations had been allowed to vote as a unit for one candidate. Henceforth, each delegate's vote would be recorded.

Prohibition of proxy voting in delegate selection (to prevent control by a few power brokers).

Reform of the apportionment of delegate slots given to each state.

A limit on the number of delegates (10 percent) selected by party committees.

These reforms significantly reduced the capacity of Democratic Party leaders to control or even influence the process of delegate selection. Here was the backlash of the insurgent Democrats against the "boss-controlled" convention of 1968. That such reforms should even be suggested came as a shock to many political observers; that they were actually carried out was even more surprising.

The nomination of George McGovern as the party's 1972 candidate for president was a triumph for the reformers. McGovernites were highly active in primaries and, with the aid of the rule changes, were able to wrest control of the convention from party professionals. The nomination was achieved at a heavy price to the party, however. Many regular Democrats, most notably labor union leaders, failed to support the party's nominee. After McGovern's decisive defeat in the general election, accordingly, it appeared that a thorough reform of the reforms might take place. Instead, over the course of the next decade, a series of gradual changes were made in the delegate selection processes. The McGovern-Fraser reforms were rolled back, but only to a degree.

**Republican reforms:** The GOP never experienced the intense pressures for reform that buffeted the Democratic Party. There was no Republican analogue to the traumatic 1968 Democratic convention, and the GOP was not under the pressure of strong minority groups demanding change or a liberal ideology that seemed to require it. Moreover, the Republican Party had dropped the unit rule in the mid–nineteenth century. After 1968, GOP party leaders warned against "McGovernizing" the party; nonetheless, they instituted a more open delegate selection process at the local level. There also was

some discussion of positive action to end discrimination, but plans to require action were pointedly dropped, and the 1976 convention refused to endorse any procedures designed to assure compliance. A party committee in 1981 did recommend that

political parties should (themselves) determine how their nominees are chosen; state party organizations should have the authority to adjust the delegate selection process to fit their local political traditions; national, time zone or regional primaries should not be imposed; and changes in party rules which require state legislative action should be drafted in a manner which would permit rather than require a party to adopt the change.[8]

Such recommendations were unlikely to disturb any sectors of the party, a deliberate contrast with the conflicts among Democrats.

**Effects of the reforms:** The reforms of the nominating process in both parties led to a sharp increase in the number of presidential primaries. Opening up the caucus meetings of the party led to an influx of new people at the local level. Both of these shifts meant that the power of party professionals to control the nominating process was greatly reduced. It was no longer so important for candidates to line up the support of party leaders and officeholders. There was clearly a gain here for democratic principles, in the sense that the reforms encouraged more widespread popular participation and closed the door to the kind of "backroom" control that had characterized past conventions. The reforms also led to broader representation of women, blacks, and younger party members at national conventions (see Table 9.2).

In both 1972 and 1976, the Democrats nominated candidates who would have stood little chance under the prereform system. The successes of George McGovern and Jimmy Carter demonstrated, among other things, that committed political amateurs could capture the nominating process, that good showings in the early primaries could earn even an unknown candidate a great deal of momentum, and that the new system placed a premium on the shrewd use of mass media and on the personality and ideas of particular candidates. In both races, the Democratic

Police stand guard at the scene of the 1972 Democratic convention. Despite the fears of violence, there was no repetition of the deep and extensive clashes that marked the 1968 Democratic Convention in Chicago.

candidate was picked by the voters, rather than by party professionals.

Who are better equipped to judge a person's presidential caliber—the voters or the party professionals? That is a difficult question to answer. In primary

contests, the turnouts are generally far lower than those in general elections, and the better-educated, wealthier, and more issue-oriented voters turn out.[9] Party professionals can no longer ignore new issues and new blood, but they also face increased difficulty in welding together a united party. In 1984, twenty-five states held Democratic party primaries (a slightly lower number than in 1976 and 1980). Some experts have contended the staging of so many primaries, strung out over a period of several months, made it difficult to put together an effective campaign to challenge GOP incumbent Ronald Reagan.

Many supporters of the enlarged primary process and more open conventions are willing to admit that the new system is flawed and that further reforms are necessary. Most maintain, however, that there is no going back to the days of the politician-controlled nominating convention. As one student of the subject put it: "We wouldn't have primaries if the old system had worked. The party machines collapsed in the late 1950s and early 1960s when the electorate changed totally."[10]

Overall, it seems clear that the reforms have created a more competitive and open nominating process. Whether they will consistently produce candidates competent to govern the nation is another question.

TABLE 9.2
**Percentage of black, women, and young delegates to national conventions, 1964–84**

|  | Democratic delegates | | | Republican delegates | | |
|---|---|---|---|---|---|---|
|  | Black | Women | Under 30 | Black | Women | Under 30 |
| 1964 | 2 | 13 | * | 1 | 18 | * |
| 1968 | 6 | 13 | 4 | 2 | 17 | 1 |
| 1972 | 15 | 40 | 22 | 3 | 32 | 7 |
| 1976 | 11 | 33 | 15 | 3 | 31 | 7 |
| 1980 | 15 | 49 | 11 | 3 | 29 | 5 |
| 1984 | 18 | 50 | 8 | 4 | 44 | 4 |

*Figures not available. Note the substantial increases in blacks, women, and younger delegates between 1968 and 1972 at the Democratic conventions. While blacks have held their own, and the percentage of women has increased, delegates under 30 have declined sharply in the last decade. As for the Republicans, only women have experienced a marked increase since 1964.
Source: David Price, *Bringing Back the Parties* (Washington, D.C.: Congressional Quarterly Press, 1984), p. 192.

| Do the
| political parties
| differ?

To some observers, the Republicans and the Democrats are like two sides of the same well-worn coin: they may differ, but only at the surface. If the decorative markings are different, they are basically made of the same materials. Others have argued that Republicans and Democrats offer the electorate clear choices on many issues. Who is right?

One way to investigate this question is to look at the promises made by each party in election years

and to ascertain how much these promises have differed. Fortunately, considerable research has been carried out on this subject. Studies of platform pledges over the past forty years have shown that Democrats and Republicans have held different images of themselves and have made different promises to the citizens.[11] The Republicans typically have placed greater emphasis on national defense and on issues relating to how the government is run, whereas the Democrats have given greater weight to labor and welfare matters. However, the parties have tended to overlap in many areas, particularly foreign policy.

Party differences have carried over into Congress, as one would expect. Typically, the parties have divided on many of the questions reflected in their

TABLE 9.3
## 1984 delegates and ordinary party members

|  | Democratic delegates | All Democrats | Republican delegates | All Republicans |
|---|---|---|---|---|
| Liberal | 50% | 25% | 1% | 12% |
| Moderate | 42 | 45 | 36 | 44 |
| Conservative | 5 | 24 | 60 | 40 |
| Family income |  |  |  |  |
| Less than $12,500 | 3 | 22 | 2 | 11 |
| $12,500–$24,999 | 12 | 36 | 6 | 34 |
| $25,000–$34,999 | 18 | 24 | 12 | 25 |
| $35,000–$50,000 | 25 | 14 | 21 | 18 |
| More than $50,000 | 42 | 6 | 57 | 11 |
| High school or less | 11 | 72 | 12 | 60 |
| Some college | 18 | 16 | 25 | 19 |
| College graduate | 20 | 12 | 28 | 21* |
| More than college | 51 |  | 35 |  |
| Protestant | 53 | 60 | 71 | 70 |
| Catholic | 32 | 35 | 22 | 24 |
| Jewish | 9 | 3 | 2 | 1 |

*Figures include both college graduates and those with graduate study or degrees. Convention delegates in 1984 were in many ways unlike rank and file party members. They were far richer for one thing, and also much better educated. Overall, Democratic delegates were somewhat better educated than Republicans, but the Republicans were richer. Note also that Republicans were far more likely to be Protestants, both at the rank-and-file and delegate levels. Perhaps most interesting, Democratic delegates were much more liberal than rank-and-file Democrats, while GOP delegates were far more conservative.
Sources: *New York Times* polls, CBS News polls, and *New York Times*/CBS News polls

platforms. In the first two years of the Carter presidency, for example, there were sharp partisan disagreements on about 40 percent of all votes in the Congress.

President Reagan took office in 1981 determined to carry out his party's promises. He immediately froze federal payrolls, decontrolled oil prices, and proposed to cut social welfare programs. Here too we can see the influence of partisan commitments on performance.

Can we safely say, then, that Democrats and Republicans differ enough to offer voters a meaningful choice? Unfortunately, that question cannot easily be answered from what we have seen so far. We know that the parties do differ in some respects, but that they also overlap considerably. Statistics do not reflect the fact that on some important issues both parties have failed to present any real alternatives. For example, neither the Democrats nor Republicans have presented clear alternatives on energy issues, and many other party positions are confused and even contradictory.

It has been argued that both U.S. parties lean toward the center, and tend to fudge their disagreements, because that is where the voters are. Party leaders must moderate their views if they do not want to leave the voters behind. The crushing defeats suffered by Goldwater and McGovern in 1964 and 1972, respectively, have often been explained in these terms: the leaders went further either to the right or to the left than most of the electorate was ready to follow.

To sum up, research has shown what common sense indicates: that the major parties do differ on many issues and that their pledges do make a difference, but at the same time, that parties ignore some important issues, fudge others, and fail to convince the public that the choices they offer are truly meaningful. Part of the reason for this confusing picture of U.S. political life lies in the internal disarray and lack of overall cohesion of both major parties. Were U.S. parties more closely disciplined, it would be far easier to see and to judge the relationships among party pledges, party differences, and the outcomes of government action.

## Current issues

In this final section we will consider the current state of the U.S. party system. We will examine, in particular, two somewhat related topics: the disaffiliation of voters from the major parties, and the prospects for significant shifts in the party system.

### Decline of the U.S. party system

Most political scientists would agree that the major U.S. political parties are in a decline. Some of the signs of decline are obvious. For example, fewer people identified themselves as Democrats in 1984 (39 percent) than did so in 1937 (50 percent). Those identifying themselves as Republicans declined from a high of 39 percent in 1944 to a low of 24 percent in 1980, before increasing to 35 percent in 1984. Meanwhile, those who identify themselves as independents increased from 16 percent in 1937 to 26 percent in 1984. Among younger voters, the trend toward independent status has been marked. Of all voters under thirty in 1984, 45 percent called themselves independents, and only 16 percent considered themselves "strong" partisans. It also seems clear that younger voters who have identified themselves as independent do not tend to shift toward one of the parties in later years. [12]

Another sign of party erosion can be seen in the many defections from traditional party patterns in voting behavior. Over the past thirty years, large numbers of Democrats, for example, have voted for Republican candidates. The same is true for Republican-identifiers. The trend toward ticket-splitting and general defection from party labels is as widespread among older as among younger voters.

If we add the fact that the voters' perception of the parties has grown increasingly negative, we can make a strong case for the long-term decay of party allegiance in the United States. Between 45 and 55

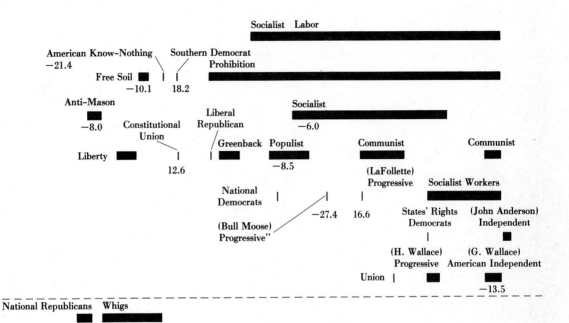

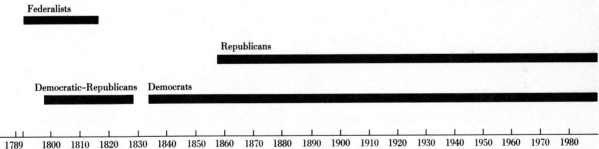

FIGURE 9.2

Source: Frank Smallwood, *The Other Candidate, Third Parties in Presidential Elections* (Washington, D. C.: Brookings, 1974) p. 4. The dates give the years parties either ran presidential candidates or held national conventions. The lifespan for many political parties can only be approximated because parties existed at the state or local level before they ran candidates in presidential elections; and parties continued to exist at local levels long after they ceased running presidential candidates.

percent of the nation persists in stating that there are no important differences between the parties and to see parties as more and more irrelevant to the nation's and the individual voter's main concerns.[13] Voters have come to focus increasingly on candidates and issues regardless of party. There has been a notable decline in the use of party labels to evaluate domestic-issue preferences as well as presidential candidates. Other signs of party decline include the rise of single-issue groups (such as Right-to-Lifers),

FIGURE 9.2
American Political Parties since 1789: There have been a considerable number of third parties in American history, but few of them have had any significant effect on electoral outcomes. The highest percentage of votes gained in an election are given for some of the more popular parties.

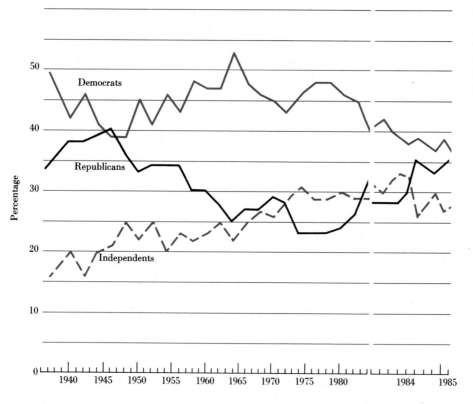

FIGURE 9.3
Political Party identification, 1937–85.
Source: *Gallup Report*, nos.
228, 229 (August, 1984),
p. 33.

the loss of party cohesion in voting in Congress, and the decreasing need for candidates to use party labels in election and reelection efforts.

The decline of the parties is, of course, linked to the growth of political alienation and mistrust, as well as to the decline in voter participation noted in Chapter 8. Taken together, these elements indicate a growing crisis in the U.S. polity that might lead to a basic realignment of the parties and of voter preferences.

### Realignment: who's got the majority?

Ronald Reagan's first presidential victory in 1980 and his landslide reelection in 1984 led many to

speculate that a political realignment of major proportions had finally occurred. The breakdown of the New Deal majority had been predicted for decades, and evidence had been pouring in since the 1950s that FDR's unique coalition of "urban ethnics, Southern Protestants, dirt farmers, Jewish intellectuals, illiterate coalminers, poor blacks and virulent racists"[14] had come apart at the seams.

Democrats were told that their party had lost its vision, that its old constituencies had moved on, that it had become identified as the party of special interests, and that it had run out of ideas—particularly, ideas about how to get the U.S. economy on track once again. Congressman Tim Wirth of Colorado, one of a group of younger Democrats who became loosely known as "neoliberals," offered this troubled assessment: "Our problem is that we do not have a single bumper-sticker solution. We're working through some pretty complicated notions."[15] Others had a simpler explanation for the 1984 presidential debacle: "A winning party has to have a vision and a message . . . Mondale's message is Hubert Humphrey."[16] This reference to the heyday of Democratic liberalism implied that Mondale's campaign appeal was largely outdated.

Could New Deal liberalism be updated to suit the closing years of the twentieth century? Would Democrats turn away from their party's ties to blue-collar workers, blacks, and ethnic minorities? The future of the New Deal party was certainly not clear.

Meanwhile, it was equally unclear how much of a realignment was taking place in the Republican Party. Four Republican presidential victories in five outings between 1968 and 1984 added up to an impressive showing, but Republicans also failed in three strong tries—1980, 1982, and 1984—to come close to gaining a working majority in the House of Representatives. And Democrats held their own in many state races. Noting these facts, some commentators attributed the size of the 1984 Republican landslide to astute management of the use of television. Others saw the GOP successes in 1980 and 1984 as merely personal triumphs for Ronald Reagan. Some Republican conservatives were critical of the president precisely because of his failure to campaign effectively for the rest of the party's ticket. Reagan was even accused of double-crossing his own party's lower-level candidates by refusing to stump the country on their behalf. Finally, there were doubts that a Republican Party dominated by its conservative wing could ever constitute an effective national majority. As political observer Kevin Phillips put it: "The Republicans' economic sobriety and commitment to national defense must somehow be . . . broadened and infused with a sense of the common man."[17]

One analyst summed up the situation in the following way:

"The election [of 1984] tells us [little] about Reagan's impact upon the thinking of the U.S. public. The President has thus far succeeded in changing the images of the two parties. The Republicans are no longer seen primarily as the party of businessmen, and the Democrats (to their distress) are no longer the party of prosperity. But has he changed Americans' view of what approach (to government) is best?"[18]

As we look toward 1988, it does not yet seem possible to predict the directions each of the major parties will take. Will the Democrats remain close to the New Deal tradition, or will they reshape themselves and nominate a neoliberal such as Gary Hart or Bill Bradley? Will George Bush, a fairly conventional Republican, inherit Reagan's mantle, or will the Republicans turn toward a more conservative candidate? It is a testimony to the continuing volatility of U.S. politics that these questions will likely prove impossible to answer until the actual campaigning begins again.

## Conclusions

Do the two major parties really perform the way "responsible" parties should in a democratic society? Many students of the subject have thought the answer to be no. In 1950, a committee of the American Political Science Association published a document titled "Toward a More Responsible Two-Party System," in which the authors outlined how U.S. parties could become more disciplined and programmatic.[19] In criticizing the existing parties of that period (and such criticisms would probably apply equally well today), the authors found U.S. parties to be deficient in several basic ways: they did not offer citizens fundamentally distinct policy choices; they were too weak organizationally to carry through their programs; they were not united on any basic principles; they failed to reflect the opinions of the electorate sufficiently. The committee looked for a reorganized party system along British lines, whereby each party would be highly disciplined, with strong leadership and a large mass membership.

The report did not meet with instant approval. Many political scientists maintained that a weakly organized, somewhat irresponsible pattern of governing had, overall, been a good thing for the United States. Precisely because U.S. parties had not been radically different, or based around ideological principles, this argument ran, they had helped to keep the political temperature low and to create an atmosphere of compromise and conciliation, rather than one of distrust and fierce ideological battling. Because the major parties are not entirely different, elections are not highly disruptive in the United States. There is considerable continuity as well as a certain measure of change. The electorate is not faced with having to decide between extreme positions.

Although it seems commonsensical to acknowledge some of the points made by advocates of "nonresponsible" parties, we should also note that democratic theory requires parties that *approach* the "responsible party" model. No one wishes to see parties divide on every issue and fight every battle to the finish. That is a recipe for civil war, not democratic politics. But if party lines are heavily blurred, if lines of responsibility are not clear, the electorate will find it impossible to figure out what parties stand for—if anything. Each of the major U.S. parties has been such a hodgepodge of differing and often conflicting interests that no coherent policy-making could reasonably be expected.

Perhaps the key to the problems in responsible policy-making unique to U.S. politics lies in the complexity of our governmental systems. Unlike other democratic systems, ours sets the federal legislative and executive branches against each other, and splits regional policy-making into fifty separate jurisdictions. Our parties must try to reach across these jurisdictional differences to create policy that reflects at least a minimal coherence. Unfortunately, they frequently fail at this Herculean task. When they do, citizens are often left bewildered, and policy-making itself becomes incomplete and even contradictory. Despite the increasing talk about party realignment, it appears that in the near future, our party system will remain largely a "nonresponsible" one.

We should note, however, that the first Reagan administration did provide a taste of what "responsible" politics might look like. The firmly conservative approach of the Reagan program represented a marked change from past policies in many areas. Moreover, although Reagan did not carry through on all his major campaign promises, he did follow through on enough to achieve what many considered a mini-

232

revolution in U.S. politics. What would have happened if the presidential landslides of 1980 and 1984 had been accompanied by similar victories in the House and Senate? Had that taken place, we would have seen the fuller development of the Reagan program, and that administration would have had the full responsibility for its actions and their consequences.

## NOTES

1 Leon Epstein, *Political Parties in Western Democracies* (New York: Praeger, 1967), p. 9.

2 Maurice Duverger, *Political Parties* (New York: Wiley, 1954), pp. xiii–xv.

3 Hugh L. Leblanc, *American Political Parties* (New York: St. Martin's Press, 1982), p. 3.

4 W. D. Burnham, "The Changing Shape of the American Political Universe," *American Political Science Review* (1965):27.

5 Frank Smallwood, *The Other Candidates: Third Parties in Presidential Elections* (Hanover, N.H.: University Press of New England, 1983).

6 Quoted in David E. Price, *Bringing Back the Parties* (Washington, D.C.: Congressional Quarterly, Inc., 1984), p. 22.

7 See James Q. Wilson, *The Amateur Democrat: Club Politics in Three Cities* (Chicago: University of Chicago Press, 1962); and Aaron Wildavsky, "The Goldwater Phenomenon: Purists, Politicians and the Two-Party System," in his *Revolt Against the Masses* (New York: Basic Books, 1971).

8 Quoted in Price, *Bringing Back the Parties*, p. 159.

9 See Leblanc, *American Political Parties*, Chapter 7.

10 Richard Wade, quoted in *The New York Times*, April 12, 1984, p. 15.

11 See Leblanc, *American Political Parties*, Chapter 10; Gerald R. Pomper, *Elections in America: Control and Influence in Democratic Politics* (New York: Dodd, Mead, 1968); and Anthony King, "What Do Polls Decide?" in D. Butter, H. R. Penniman, and A. Ranney, eds., *Democracy at the Polls* (Washington, D.C.: AEI, 1981), pp. 293–324.

12 Price, *Bringing Back the Parties*, p. 51.

13 *Ibid.*, p. 17.

14 *Newsweek*, July 16, 1984, p. 15.

15 *Ibid.*, p. 16.

16 *Ibid*.

17 *The New York Times*, April 19, 1984, p. 25.

18 Scott Keeter, "Public Opinion in 1984," in G. Pomper, et al., *The Election of 1984* (Chatham, N.J.: Chatham House, 1985), p. 109.

19 Committee on Political Parties, "Toward a More Responsible Two-Party System," *American Political Science Review*, Sept. 1950, supplement.

## SELECTED READINGS

For perspectives on political parties, look at Maurice Duverger, *Political Parties* (New York: Wiley, 1954); Richard Hofstadter, *The Idea of a Party System* (Berkeley, Cal.: University of California Press, 1969); W. E. Binkley, *American Political Parties* (New York: Knopf, 1965); and Frank Smallwood, *The Other Candidates* (Hanover, N.H.: University Press of New England, 1983).

On party reform and our changing party system, consult David E. Price, *Bringing Back the Parties* (Washington, D.C.: Congressional Quarterly Press, 1984); Gerald R. Pomper, *Elections in America* (New York: Dodd, Mead, 1968); W. N. Chambers and W. D. Burnham, eds., *The American Party System* (New York: Oxford University Press, 1975); and James L. Sundquist, *Dynamics of the American Party System* (Washington, D.C.: Brookings, 1973).

### The role of parties in democracies

The antiparty sentiments of the Founders are explored in Richard Hofstadter, *The Idea of a Party System* (Berkeley, Cal.: University of California Press, 1972). The role of parties in democratic societies is discussed in Maurice Duverger, *Political Parties;* E. E. Schattschneider, *The Struggle for Party Government* (College Park, Md.: University of Maryland Press, 1948); and Leon D. Epstein, *Political Parties in Western Democracies* (New York: Praeger, 1967).

Chapter
ten

# Campaigns, money, and media

## Packaging politics

IN the contest for the 1984 Democratic presidential nomination, Walter Mondale launched a devastating attack on Gary Hart, his chief opponent, by deriding the alleged lack of substance in Hart's campaign. Borrowing a slogan from a contemporary television commercial, Mondale kept asking Hart, "Where's the beef?" By the "beef," he meant the content, or substance, of Hart's ideas—a critical element in the conduct of democratic politics. In one way or another, we all want to know "Where's the beef?" in politics. We want to find out what is really behind what we see and hear in political campaigns—behind the promises, styles, phrases, and the general whirl of events and proposals.

In this chapter, we will try to discover where the "beef" is in the process of political campaigning and in the role of the media in politics. These are complicated subjects. Our focal point will be how campaigning and media contribute to or detract from democratic hopes. Do campaigns enlighten? Do they bring forward capable leadership? Or do they wind up packaging candidates and selling them like commercial products? Do the media give voters the information needed to make informed choices? Do voters learn about meaningful alternatives? Do they have the chance to hear critical and constructive commentary? Or do the media distort and play up the superficial as opposed to the substantial? Just how much of the "beef" comes through to us as citizens?

## Political campaigns

In a democracy, the electorate is asked to make choices—that is what elections are all about. How do the "choices," as represented by opposing candidates, get onto the ballot? In the United States, it is through an often long and tedious process that involves getting recognition, receiving the endorsement of a party, obtaining funds from supporters, and seeking approval by the voters. Together, these activities comprise a political campaign.

A campaign can serve democracy well in several ways: by providing a forum for new political leadership; by disseminating information to potential voters; by mobilizing the electorate, and thus ensuring that the electoral process reflects popular consent. Sometimes, of course, campaigns do not fulfill all, or any, of these functions. The political leaders presented to the electorate may not be qualified to deal with problems of the day. Issues may not be clarified; worse, they may be obscured. Finally, when a campaign does not reach many potential voters, the legitimacy of the electoral process may be undermined.

It is difficult to generalize about political campaigns in the United States, because U.S. elections are so varied. Different campaign strategies are appropriate for primaries or general elections; for congressional, senatorial, or presidential races; for incumbents or challengers. It is possible, however, to identify four distinct stages in the typical campaign.

First comes the *decision to run*. Some potential candidates actively seek party approval; others are recruited by party leaders or by interest groups.

The second—and often the hardest—stage is *nomination* by a party. To be nominated for office by a major party, a person must first gain the support of local and state party officials and then, in many cases, run in a **primary**. In a primary election, potential candidates vie for nomination as the party's designated candidate in the general election. Primaries may be wide-open affairs or virtual walkovers, depending on the circumstances. If a particularly popular incumbent is seeking renomination, he or she may go unchallenged in the primary. In fact, incumbents are challenged less than half the time in congressional races. In those states in which one party is dominant, the primary election may be more important than the general election that follows.

Primary elections can follow one of three formats:

*Closed primary*. Voters registered as belonging to a particular party can vote only in that party's primary (forty-one states).

*Open primary*. Voters can choose either party's primary (Michigan, Minnesota, Wisconsin, North Dakota, Montana, Utah, and Vermont).

*Blanket primary*. Voters can choose either party's primary for different offices—for example, the Democratic primary for senator and the Republican primary for governor (Alaska and Washington).

The third stage of the campaign process is the *contest for electoral victory*. The candidate's main tasks at this stage are to raise funds, to make use of the media, to meet the voters, to gain support from prominent groups and individuals, to activate the party faithful, and to mobilize campaign workers. In the larger campaigns, armies of professionals work behind the scenes on campaign strategy. Such professionals, including pollsters, computer experts, and media strategists, have become almost indispensable to campaigns for major offices. Most other campaigns, however, are run on a shoestring basis. Modest expenditures and small, or even nonexistent, campaign staffs are still common in congressional campaigns—particularly those in which an incumbent has no substantial opposition. In 1976, for example, only 25 percent of all congressional campaigns were run by salaried campaign managers. However, about 10 percent of the congressional campaigns that year accounted for 50 percent of all the money spent by congressional candidates. In 1984, expenditures on congressional campaigns rose above the $300 million mark. Spending on Senate races increased 150 percent over 1978 and on House contests 126 percent in the same period. In one California race, a candidate spent a record $1.8 million on his campaign in 1984. Even House races can become very expensive.

The final stage of the campaign process (or the first, depending on how one views it) encompasses what takes place *between* elections—what we might call the *interelection stage*. Once elected, a representative or senator must continue to attend to the political situation in his or her district or state. Ties with important groups, individuals, and the party itself must be maintained. Congressional representatives usually must try hard to serve constituents, in order to build up a reservoir of good will for future use. They generally make every effort to bring as much federal money as possible into their districts. In this connection, conservatives usually do not differ much from liberals. The chance to benefit his or her constituents, along with the higher name-recognition that comes with incumbency, can be of great help to a candidate seeking reelection. Incumbency can also have disadvantages, however. An incum-

236

In one of the classic photos of U.S. electoral politics, the Republican candidate Wendell Willkie parades through the streets of Elwood, Indiana, before accepting the party's nomination in 1940. Willkie ran a surprisingly strong contest against Franklin D. Roosevelt.

bent may offend some constituents by particular votes or actions, or may suffer from association with an unpopular administration.

## Presidential campaigns

Although all political races have certain elements in common—stumping for votes, getting media exposure, fund-raising, taking the pulse of the electorate—the intensity and importance of these activities varies from race to race. In presidential campaigns, *everything* counts. These are the most intense, most expensive, most drawn-out political campaigns in any modern democracy. Let us now examine some of the major events in a presidential race.

**Preconvention activity:**  Given the significance of the presidency in U.S. politics, it is not surprising that some politicians have been willing to spend years generating the level of support needed to gain the nomination of a major party. George McGovern, Jimmy Carter, and Walter Mondale started their presidential efforts at least two years in advance. Ronald Reagan campaigned for at least four years before his 1980 success. And as soon as the 1984 presidential election was over, several potential candidates from both parties launched undeclared bids for the 1988 nominations. For those seeking the office of president, years of public appearances, lectures, and wooing of state and local party leaders usually precede the formal opening of the contest.

We saw in Chapter 9 that until relatively recently, presidential nominees generally were selected by powerful party leaders at or before party conventions. Because of reforms instituted by both parties in recent decades, however, primaries now play a crucial role in the selection process. As primaries have become more numerous and more important, presidential campaigns have become lengthier and lengthier affairs. In 1984, thirty-six Republican and twenty-nine Democratic presidential primaries were staged over a period stretching from February to June. Of course, many candidates focus their efforts on particular contests—either those they believe are crucial to them or those they regard as critical to an opponent. In 1960, for example, John Kennedy mounted a major effort in the West Virginia primary in order to demonstrate that a Catholic candidate could do well in a largely Protestant state.

The primary process can produce quite unpredictable results. For example, Jimmy Carter's victory over a dozen other Democratic presidential hopefuls in 1976 came as a considerable shock to most analysts and party professionals. The former governor of Georgia started out as one of the least-known candidates in a field that included several prominent Democratic figures. But unexpected and decisive victories in a few primaries were sufficient to establish Carter as a force to be reckoned with. Conversely, a string of early primary defeats can doom the candidacy of even the best-known politician.

Not all delegates to the party conventions are selected through the primary process. In some states, delegates are chosen at party conventions following **caucuses** in local electoral precincts and counties. Those candidates who put years of effort into building political relationships with local leaders usually are rewarded at caucus time.

Because the primary process has been a crucial factor in presidential nominations for such a short period of time (since 1972), politicians and the electorate alike are still learning its ins and outs. The Democratic Party's nominating process in 1984 contained several interesting developments. Most notably, a black candidate, Jesse Jackson, was able to garner enough votes to be taken seriously as a contender. Jackson received 18.6 percent of all the primary votes cast, including 77 percent of the black votes.[1] One seasoned political observer contended that after the Jackson candidacy, "American politics will never be the same."[2]

Another significant development was the role played by televised debates among the eight Democratic contenders in shaping the way the primaries evolved. Overall, the debates tended to help such lesser-known candidates as Gary Hart and Jesse Jackson, who were able to gain extensive media exposure. The debates

hurt the well-known John Glenn, who was not able to impress viewers, and did little for leading contender Walter Mondale, who was the target of attacks from all the others. Thus, the debates proved to be a great equalizer in some senses, even though Mondale was able to gain the nomination on the first convention ballot.

**National conventions:** The national political conventions have retained some of the flavor of the past. Mass demonstrations, marches, music, and behind-the-scenes negotiations take place now as always, complete with exhausted delegates and smoke-filled rooms. For both major political parties, national conventions remain significant undertakings. But today the identity of the nominee is generally known in advance.

At every national convention held between 1956 and 1984, one ballot sufficed to select the nominee. In 1924, by contrast, the Democrats took a record 103 ballots to nominate John W. Davis. Yet some drama has continued to linger around convention maneuvering. Even though the delegate count is now much better defined, because of primary voting, it is still unclear at times whether a candidate has all the votes needed for nomination. Reagan and Pres-

The old national convention featured a good bit of back-room deal-making and strategy, all of which was symbolized by the term, "smoke-filled room." There is no smoke or backroom in this photo, but the strategy effort seems clear. It is 1956 and Senator John F. Kennedy of Massachusetts is consulting. Kennedy made a surprise effort to gain the vice-presidential nomination at the Democratic convention that year.

Political conventions are certainly not all serious business. To make sure they are not, you can hire the Kilgore Texas Rangerettes, who here arrive at the 1984 Republican National Convention.

ident Gerald Ford were almost tied going into the 1976 Republican convention, and both made every effort to woo the small number of uncommitted delegates. Also, the dominant candidate often has had to struggle to keep his forces unified. Democratic delegates to the 1984 convention were not "bound" to candidates (i.e., their votes did not automatically go to the candidates they represented), so Mondale had to make sure his delegates did not defect to his opponents. Dominant forces, finally, must try to retain control of critical convention committees—in particular, the one charged with drafting the party's platform. It is more than awkward for a presidential candidate to run on a platform that is strikingly at odds with his own views.

The chief remaining source of drama at convention time is the selection of the vice-presidential nominee. This process occasionally involves some of the anxiety, bargaining, and high drama of old-style convention politics. The Republican convention of 1980, for example, was enlivened by ultimately fruitless backroom negotiations over the second spot on the ticket between Reagan and former President Ford.

Generally speaking, vice-presidents have been selected to balance the ticket geographically or ethnically and/or to pacify another wing of the party. In 1960, Democratic presidential nominee John Kennedy chose Senator Lyndon Johnson of Texas, his chief opponent for the nomination, in order to attract Southern votes in the election. Reagan's choice of George Bush in 1980 was made partly as a gesture toward more moderate Republicans and partly because Bush's foreign policy experience filled a gap in Reagan's background. In 1984, Mondale selected Geraldine Ferraro, the first female vice-presidential candidate of a major party in U.S. history, partly in order to appeal to women's rights proponents.

**The run for general election:** In the eight weeks between Labor Day (the first Monday in September) and Election Day (the first Tuesday in November), the candidates and their staffs work ceaselessly to woo voters. During this period, candidates must not only seek to convince voters to vote for them, but also broaden their appeal to diverse parts of the electorate and touch base with a variety of special interests.

The candidates work hand-in-hand with paid political consultants to devise an overall campaign strategy and create a desirable image. Public opinion samples tell consultants what areas of the country the candidate should concentrate on and which issues he or she should emphasize in specific regions. The consultants schedule public appearances, stage "news events" (such as walking tours, rallies, and hospital visits), and make certain that advance work is done properly before a candidate arrives at a destination. Most important, they coordinate a political advertising campaign that culminates in a media blitz the last two weeks of the campaign. (Image-making through the media will be discussed at length later

239

in the chapter.) The candidate, meanwhile, follows a grueling schedule that involves flying from one part of the country to the other for daily rounds of speech making, interviewing, and crowd working.

In view of the exhausting and drawn-out campaign process, many critics have wondered if the present system offers the most sensible way of selecting a president. The most fundamental question raised in regard to this system is, Does it attract the best people to political life? Many observers have contended that the most statesmanlike public figures, the potential Jeffersons and Lincolns, are precisely those who are driven away from political life by the intensity and cost of the campaign process. Why should anyone be asked to spend two or three years running and preparing to run for office? To do so may well imply an uncommon measure of devotion to public service, or it may reflect merely an all-consuming ambition. The fear is that we have turned campaigns into huge circuses that necessarily favor the sorts of candidates who are good at performing, but not necessarily at governing.

If this is true, what remedies are available? The primary process could be shortened, to reduce the cost and strain of campaigning. The political parties could be restored to substantial health, which would help to attract better people into politics by making politics seem a reasonable long-term career. Most importantly, perhaps, the role of financing in political campaigns could be diminished—a subject we will now address.

## Campaign financing

The cost of winning and holding office has skyrocketed in recent years (see Table 10.1). In 1956, candidates for public office spent a total of $155 million trying to get elected. By 1980 the cost of presidential campaigns alone had increased to $250 million, and congressional election costs topped $300 million. Much of this rise in spending came from the increased use of television and radio advertising (see Table 10.2), public opinion polling, and computers,

as well as from the need for ever-larger campaign organizations.

In 1984, the average one-minute commercial in prime-time cost $50,000 on network television and $1,500 on a typical local station.[3] Multiplication of these figures by the number of commercials one sees during large federal or state campaigns gives some idea of the expense involved—but only some. Media campaigns must be thought up and produced by consultants who usually charge $500 and up per day, plus between $100–$200 daily for each staff member assigned to the job. Presidential aspirants can spend as much as $200,000 on consulting fees alone; Senate hopefuls, $50,000; and candidates for the House of Representatives, $20,000. Polling can also be costly, particularly when it involves face-to-face interviews.

Financial outlays cannot guarantee victory in an election. No amount of campaign spending could get a Republican elected in some heavily Democratic districts or a Democrat elected in traditional Republican strongholds. Nor could the most lavish expenditures get an outspoken opponent of farm subsidies elected in a rural Iowa district, or a committed segregationist elected in a black ghetto. Moreover, some campaign resources cannot be bought. Scholars, artists, entertainment figures, and the like usually do not hire themselves out to campaigns; if they are sufficiently attracted to a particular candidate, however, they may volunteer their time and efforts. Sometimes a candidate can come up with a stratagem that garners free media attention. In 1970, for example, Lawton Chiles of Florida successfully campaigned for a U.S. Senate seat against a better-financed opponent by taking a long walking tour of the state. As a result of the tour, Chiles received so much coverage in the mass media that he had little need to buy media advertising to get his name and his platform known to the voters.

But if large-scale campaign expenditures cannot guarantee victory in an election, they can greatly increase the probability of electoral success. In the 1978 senatorial elections, for example, the winners raised more than twice as much as the losers; and in thirty-two of the thirty-four Senate races, the biggest spenders won. Facts such as these are well known

TABLE 10.1
## Costs of presidential general election campaigns, 1860–1980

| | Republicans | | Democrats | |
|---|---|---|---|---|
| 1860 | $100,000 | Lincoln* | $50,000 | Douglas |
| 1864 | 125,000 | Lincoln* | 50,000 | McClellan |
| 1868 | 150,000 | Grant* | 75,000 | Seymour |
| 1872 | 250,000 | Grant* | 50,000 | Greeley |
| 1876 | 950,000 | Hayes* | 900,000 | Tilden |
| 1880 | 1,100,000 | Garfield* | 335,000 | Hancock |
| 1884 | 1,300,000 | Blaine | 1,400,000 | Cleveland* |
| 1888 | 1,350,000 | Harrison* | 855,000 | Cleveland |
| 1892 | 1,700,000 | Harrison | 2,350,000 | Cleveland* |
| 1896 | 3,350,000 | McKinley* | 675,000 | Bryan |
| 1900 | 3,000,000 | McKinley* | 425,000 | Bryan |
| 1904 | 2,096,000 | T. Roosevelt* | 700,000 | Parker |
| 1908 | 1,655,518 | Taft* | 629,341 | Bryan |
| 1912 | 1,071,549 | Taft | 1,134,848 | Wilson* |
| 1916 | 2,441,565 | Hughes | 2,284,590 | Wilson* |
| 1920 | 5,417,501 | Harding* | 1,470,371 | Cox |
| 1924 | 4,020,478 | Coolidge* | 1,108,836 | Davis |
| 1928 | 6,256,111 | Hoover* | 5,342,350 | Smith |
| 1932 | 2,900,052 | Hoover | 2,245,975 | F. Roosevelt* |
| 1936 | 8,892,972 | Landon | 5,194,741 | F. Roosevelt* |
| 1940 | 3,451,310 | Willkie | 2,783,654 | F. Roosevelt* |
| 1944 | 2,828,652 | Dewey | 2,169,077 | F. Roosevelt* |
| 1948 | 2,127,296 | Dewey | 2,736,334 | Truman* |
| 1952 | 6,608,623 | Eisenhower* | 5,032,926 | Stevenson |
| 1956 | 7,778,702 | Eisenhower* | 5,106,651 | Stevenson |
| 1960 | 10,128,000 | Nixon | 9,797,000 | Kennedy* |
| 1964 | 16,026,000 | Goldwater | 8,757,000 | Johnson* |
| 1968 | 25,402,000 | Nixon* | 11,594,000 | Humphrey |
| 1972 | 61,400,000 | Nixon* | 30,000,000 | McGovern |
| 1976† | 21,786,641 | Ford | 21,800,000 | Carter* |
| 1980‡ | 29,188,188 | Reagan* | 29,352,767 | Carter |

*Winner.

†The first year public funding was used for presidential elections. The Republican National Committee spent an additional $1.4 million on Ford's campaign. The Democratic National Committee spent an additional $2.8 million on Carter's campaign.

‡In 1980 the Republican National Committee spent an additional $4.5 million on Reagan's campaign. The Democratic National Committee spent an additional $4 million on Carter's campaign.

Source: Herbert E. Alexander, *Financing Politics*, 3rd ed. (Washington, D.C.: Congressional Quarterly Press, 1984), p. 7.

to political consultants, one of whom once said, "Money—get it early, get as much as you can."[4]

Who spends the most money? Republicans are usually far better financed than Democrats. It is not unusual for the Democratic candidate to be deeply in debt after a presidential election year, whereas Republican campaigns frequently generate a surplus. In 1980, for example, the Republican National Committee received funds from more than 1 million contributors and spent $47 million on Republican candidates, whereas the Democratic National Committee raised most of its money from organized in-

TABLE 10.2
## Expenditures for radio and television time in presidential general election campaigns, 1952–80

|      | Republicans  | Democrats   |
|------|--------------|-------------|
| 1952 | $2,046,000   | $1,530,000  |
| 1956 | 2,886,000    | 1,763,000   |
| 1960 | 1,865,000    | 1,142,000   |
| 1964 | 6,370,000    | 4,674,000   |
| 1968 | 12,598,000   | 6,143,000   |
| 1972 | 4,300,000    | 6,200,000   |
| 1976 | 7,875,000    | 9,081,321   |
| 1980 | 12,324,000*  | 18,400,000  |

*Does not include about $245,000 in coordinated expenditures by the Republican National Committee on behalf of Reagan-Bush or approximately $4.2 million spent by the RNC during the general election period on a media campaign supporting all Republican candidates.
Source: Herbert E. Alexander, *Financing Politics*, 3rd ed. (Washington, D.C.: Congressional Quarterly Press, 1984), p. 13.

terest groups and spent only $12 million. Similarly, the Republican House and Senate campaign committees outspent their Democratic counterparts by 5–1 and 10–1, respectively. On the other hand, individual Democratic candidates outraised Republicans in three of the four House and Senate elections between 1976 and 1982. So the picture is mixed.

Much of the money raised by the parties and candidates comes from various interest groups. Business and conservative groups, which generally support Republican candidates, tend to outspend labor and liberal groups, who traditionally support Democrats. Lately, the contributions of such groups have been limited by campaign finance reform laws, as we will see in the following section.

## Reform efforts

The financing of political campaigns—particularly presidential campaigns—has long been a sore point in U.S. politics. In 1962, President John F. Ken-
nedy's Commission on Campaign Costs concluded that there was a need to remove the taint of "shoddiness" from campaign political finance and that the requirements of the Federal Corrupt Practices Act of 1925 were outdated and useless. It was not until 1971, however, that any substantial action was forthcoming from the Congress. The Federal Election Campaign Act (FECA) passed that year limited media spending by candidates in federal elections, required detailed reporting of contributions, and provided for a voluntary $1 checkoff on individual income tax forms to help pay for presidential elections. To avert a threatened veto by President Nixon, Congress stipulated that the act would apply only after the 1972 elections.

Ironically, it was financing irregularities in the 1972 presidential election, culminating in the Watergate scandal that forced Nixon to resign from office, that finally triggered large-scale efforts to reform campaign financing. Why did Watergate trigger a serious reform effort? The U.S. system of privately financed politics always invited secret and unreported funding, but in the Nixon reelection effort of 1972, such abuses reached new heights. Public anger was also ignited by the revelation that Nixon received very heavy contributions from a very small group of wealthy individuals. These were practices that reformers in Congress intended to stop.

The 1974 off-year congressional elections swept into office a new wave of representatives and senators bent on changing the way campaigns were conducted. This "Watergate class" was instrumental in passing the far-reaching Federal Election Campaign Act of 1974, which set sharp spending and contribution limits on federal campaigns, beefed up requirements for financial disclosure, and established a scheme for public financing of presidential primaries and of presidential general elections. The Federal Election Commission was created to enforce these new rules.

To undercut the influence of rich contributors who had played such an important role in the financing of previous campaigns, the new law placed strict limits on the amount of money an individual could contribute: $1,000 to any candidate in a primary, $1,000 to any candidate in a general election, and

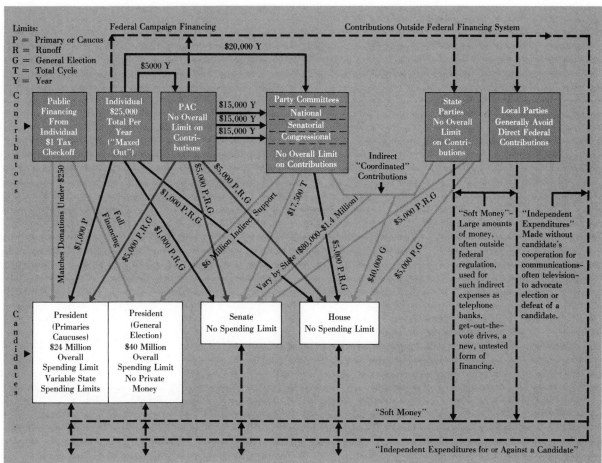

Limits:
P = Primary or Caucus
R = Runoff
G = General Election
T = Total Cycle
Y = Year

Federal Campaign Financing

Contributions Outside Federal Financing System

Source: Thomas B. Edsall, "The Ins and Outs of the American Money Machine," *Washington Post*, national weekly edition, December 12, 1983, p. 7.

FIGURE 10.1
This rather mind-boggling chart shows the immense complexity of the rules governing the spending of money in federal elections. Individuals, for example, can contribute to a candidate directly, to a PAC, or to a political party, or they can make "independent" contributions. In each of these cases, the rules governing the contributions are different. Likewise, there are different rules for each type of committee—candidate, political party, or ideological. In addition, some funding is exempt from all restrictions and other categories of funding fall into a gray area where restrictions are unclear. Overall, this does not appear to be a useful way to control the role of money in campaigns, although many would argue it is better than no control at all.

$20,000 to a party's national committee. The law also allowed individuals to give up to $5,000 to a **political action committee** (PAC), an organization formed for the purpose of channeling funds to selected candidates and working for certain political goals. In any election year, an individual may not contribute more than $25,000 in total. Considering that two individuals had given Richard Nixon at least $1 million in 1972, and that nineteen others had each contributed over $200,000 to his campaign that year, these new contribution limits seemed austere.

In 1976 the Supreme Court upheld Congress's power to set limits on individual and group contributions made directly to campaigns, but it declared unconstitutional the $1,000 limit on contributions of individuals not clearly connected with candidates. The Court also voided limits on candidates' expenditures of their own money and on the overall spending in a campaign, unless a candidate voluntarily accepted public funding.[5]

The FECA was amended in 1976 and 1979. It provided for limits on contributions by individuals ($1,000 per election to a federal candidate) and by political action committees ($5,000 per election to a federal candidate). It also set restrictions on expenditures. Presidential candidates who accept public financing were limited to $10 million for the campaign for nomination and $20 million for the general election (to be adjusted for inflation). Expenditures by national parties for presidential nominees were restricted, as were those by both state and national parties for Senate and House candidates. Finally, the act provided for public financing of presidential campaigns for all candidates who can raise at least $5,000 in each of twenty states. Notably, millions of Americans have been willing to contribute to the public financing of presidential elections through the income tax checkoff. Over a quarter of all taxpayers used the checkoff in 1980, for example, when the amount raised was $41 million.

Early in 1985, the Supreme Court further curtailed the impact of campaign spending limits. In *Federal Election Commission* v. *NCPAC* (National Conservative Political Action Committee), the Court declared unconstitutional the limits on spending by political action committees on behalf of presidential candidates in general elections. Writing for the seven-person majority, Justice William Rehnquist argued that limiting such expenditures is "much like allowing a speaker in a public hall to express his views while denying him the use of an amplifying system."[6]

The case involved NCPAC, a group that had spent $5.5 million on behalf of Ronald Reagan in 1984. One other group, the Fund for a Conservative Majority, gave $2.5 million, and total independent spending for Reagan was $15.3 million. Independent contributions to Walter Mondale's campaign that year amounted to $621,000.

In dissent, Justice Byron White argued that the Court had "transformed a coherent regulatory scheme into a nonsensical loophole-ridden patchwork."[7] Though many agree with Justice White, there is still no clear consensus on how campaign laws should now be revised.

## The consequences of reform

The presidential campaigns of 1976, 1980, and 1984 conformed, in many ways, to congressional intentions. In 1976, for example, 60 percent of campaign expenditures were publicly financed, and private funding declined to 50 percent of its previous level. Overall, all three campaigns appear to have been relatively free of financial trickery. But the reforms have also had other, unintended consequences. Perhaps most significant has been a dramatic increase in the number and activities of political action committees. In 1974, there were 608 PACs; by 1984, there were 4,000. A large part of that increase was accounted for by business and corporate PACs (see Table 10.3).

Under the new campaign finance laws, restrictions were placed on the amount of money PACs could contribute to an individual's campaign, but not on money spent independently. In other words, PACs were allowed to make unlimited expenditures on a candidate's behalf or in support of certain policy views, provided that those expenditures were not directly coordinated with the candidate's campaign. In prac-

TABLE 10.3
## The ten largest money raisers and contributors among PACs, 1981–82

**Top Ten Money Raisers**

| | |
|---|---|
| 1. *National Conservative Political Action Committee* | $9,990,931 |
| 2. *National Congressional Club* | 9,742,494 |
| 3. *Realtors Political Action Committee* | 2,991,732 |
| 4. *Fund for a Conservative Majority* | 2,945,874 |
| 5. *American Medical Association Political Action Committee* | 2,466,425 |
| 6. *National Committee for an Effective Congress* | 2,430,886 |
| 7. *Citizens for the Republic* | 2,415,720 |
| 8. *Committee for the Survival of a Free Congress* | 2,359,477 |
| 9. *Fund for a Democratic Majority* | 2,307,605 |
| 10. *Committee for the Future of America, Inc.* | 2,190,264 |

**Top Ten Contributors to Federal Candidates**

| | |
|---|---|
| 1. *Realtors Political Action Committee* | $2,115,135 |
| 2. *American Medical Association Political Action Committee* | 1,737,090 |
| 3. *UAW-V-CAP (United Auto Workers)* | 1,623,947 |
| 4. *Machinists Non-Partisan Political League* | 1,444,959 |
| 5. *National Education Association PAC* | 1,183,215 |
| 6. *Political Action Committee of the National Association of Home Builders* | 1,005,628 |
| 7. *Committee for Thorough Agricultural Political Education of Associated Milk Producers* | 962,450 |
| 8. *American Bankers Association BANKPAC* | 947,460 |
| 9. *Automobile and Truck Dealers Election Action Committee* | 917,295 |
| 10. *AFL-CIO COPE Political Contributions Committee* | 906,425 |

Source: Federal Election Commission.

tice, such a fine line between direct and indirect financing has often been difficult to draw.

Despite these restrictions, PAC contributions to individual candidates have remained substantial. According to one source, more than one hundred members of the House got 50 percent or more of their campaign funds from PACs in 1982.[8] In 1984 Senate races, moreover, PACs supplied almost 30 percent of candidate funding on average. PAC contributions to Senate races rose by more than 200 percent between 1976 and 1984, discounting the effects of inflation. PAC contributions to House races in 1984 reached $104 million, a 25 percent increase over 1982. It should be noted that the role of PAC money varied greatly in different campaigns. For example, one senator raised almost 75 percent of his campaign funds from PACs, whereas others received less than 10 percent from that source.[9]

Top PAC contributors to 1984 congressional races included the National Association of Realtors ($2.6 million), the American Medical Association ($2 million), the National Education Association ($1.9 million); the Seafarers Union ($1.4 million) and the National Automobile Dealers Association ($1 million). Interestingly, 73 percent of all these contributions went to incumbents, and often to incumbents with little or no opposition. The goal is clearly to maximize access and influence with key members of Congress. There are more PACs connected with corporations than any other type, but the largest growth rate is among those labeled "nonconnected" by the Federal Election Commission—these including such ideologically oriented groups as NCPAC.

Many representatives and senators have found PACs to be particularly handy when large campaign debts must be paid off. One long-time senator noted that the problem of financing congressional campaigns "virtually forces members of Congress to go around hat in hand, begging for money from Washington-based special interests, political action committees whose sole purpose for existing is to seek a *quid pro quo*."[10] Other observers have argued that PACs do not exert excessive influence, if only because there are so many in existence that their efforts tend to cancel out. Even if this is true, however, the increasing political role of PACs raises legitimate concerns.

One such concern is heavy spending by PACs on efforts to defeat specific representatives and senators. In recent elections, conservative PACs, such as NCPAC, have targeted various liberal candidates for attack, spending large sums to aid in attempts to defeat them. Senator Jesse Helms (R., N.C.), a favorite of conservative PACs, was the recipient of over

TABLE 10.4
# Number of registered political action committees, 1974–1984

| Type of committee | 1974 | 1976 | 1978 | 1980 | 1982 | 1984 |
|---|---|---|---|---|---|---|
| Corporate | 89 | 433 | 784 | 1,204 | 1,467 | 1,682 |
| Labor | 201 | 224 | 217 | 297 | 380 | 394 |
| Trade, membership, health[a] | 318 | 489 | 451 | 574 | 628 | 698 |
| Nonconnected | . . . | . . . | 165 | 378 | 746 | 1,053 |
| Cooperative | . . . | . . . | 12 | 42 | 47 | 52 |
| Corporation without stock | . . . | . . . | 24 | 56 | 103 | 130 |
| Total | 608 | 1,146 | 1,653 | 2,551 | 3,371 | 4,009 |

Source: Gary C. Jacobson, "The Republican Advantage in Campaign Finance," in John E. Chubb & Paul E. Peterson, eds., THE NEW DIRECTION IN AMERICAN POLITICS (Washington: Brookings, 1985), p. 147.

$4 million in PAC funds for his 1978 Senate campaign. Ideological targeting of this kind has contributed to the decline of political parties, by supplanting the parties' fund-raising and support functions. (For further discussion of PACs, see Chapters 11 and 14.)

## Proposed reform measures

In the eyes of many observers, the reforms of the 1970s were too limited in scope. With the weakening of the major parties, the proliferation of PACs, and the increasing importance of the mass media in political campaigns, sentiment for more-radical reforms has grown. Several far-reaching reform measures have been proposed:

Limitations on the costs of political advertising on television, or the granting of free TV time to candidates.

Curbs on the independent spending of PACs, especially that used to discredit candidates. (There is some question whether such restrictions might not violate the First Amendment protections—a position taken by the Supreme Court in 1976.)

Checks on the unrestricted use of personal wealth by individual candidates.

Provision for public financing of congressional as well as presidential election campaigns.

The last recommendation has been proposed in Congress several times but has not been passed by both houses. Some critics have argued that public financing would assist incumbents, who already enjoy many advantages. Others have taken the opposite view—that it would unfairly aid challengers.

## The role of the media

That the mass media (television, radio, newspapers) play a significant role in U.S. political campaigns is obvious. To pursue the issue further, we must ask what functions the media serve and whether they help educate citizens about the issues and sensitize them to matters of importance in democratic politics. In this section, we will look at four aspects of the media's role in elections: the growing political importance of the mass media, the use of the media for candidate image-making, the potential educative role of political debates, and overall news coverage of elections. We will then try to assess the relationship between the media and politics in terms of democratic theory.

246

The pre-media campaign often featured the candidate touring by train, stopping to address crowds along the route. The last major whistle-stop presidential campaign effort was Harry Truman's in 1948. In the picture above, the candidate is William Howard Taft, and the year, 1912.

## Impact on elections

Democratic elections have always involved efforts by candidates and parties to communicate with potential voters. Since at least the 1950s, however, the manner in which politicians communicate with the electorate has undergone a fundamental change. The mass media, and especially television, now play such a significant role in that communication process that the process itself has been and continues to be transformed. The new-found potency of the mass media to rearrange the political landscape was first apparent in the tremendous impact on public opinion of the first of the Kennedy-Nixon televised debates in 1960. Many analysts have credited that single event with being the decisive factor in Kennedy's victory. More recently, the remarkable emergence of the previously unknown Jimmy Carter as a serious contender for the 1976 Democratic Party presidential nomination owed much to extensive media coverage of his successes in early primaries. One study of the role of the media during the early primaries in 1984, in fact, found that shifts in media attention were invariably followed by shifts in public sentiment. Before the primaries began, leading contenders Walter Mondale and John Glenn were helped by media attention; then, the media focus turned to Gary Hart's surprising showing in early primaries, and Hart's standing among the voters rose accordingly. The other potential nominees, meanwhile, were hurt by lack of attention from the media.[11]

These examples serve to highlight the fact that the media can sometimes make or break a candidate—can enhance a campaign, or undermine it. The media undeniably have become a singularly powerful element in virtually all major U.S. elections.

How did this situation come about? Some of the reasons are obvious. Public attention to mass media is pervasive in the United States: Americans spend almost half their leisure time watching TV, listening to the radio, or reading newspapers and magazines. This adds up to seven hours per day of media exposure, 75 percent of which is accounted for by television.[12] Also, television is a powerful medium of communication. The chance to reach millions in one exposure is one no candidate can afford to ignore. Through the media, candidates can create images that can decisively influence elections.

Other reasons for the growth in importance of media are not so obvious. As more and more U.S. voters have disaffiliated from the two major parties, for example, candidates have increasingly sought to target specific audiences with media messages. Then, too, the enhanced importance of primaries has made the nominating process more visible—and thus more newsworthy. Media organizations, on their part, have

247

# Public information, media power, and bias

People tend to believe much of what the media tell them, and they believe the media more than they believe politicians. But social scientists have mixed opinions on how influential the media are, and whether they mold or reflect mass opinion. It is probably accurate to say that the media focus attention and thereby help establish the agenda of politics. A spectacular demonstration of this attention-focusing capacity was the daily TV coverage between 1979 and 1981 of the Iranian hostage crisis. An earlier example was the media focus on the Vietnam War, called by some the "livingroom war."

There is no doubt that such coverage of the war influenced public attitudes and policy decisions. Some observers believe that the amount of media attention contributed directly to public exhaustion with the war. The lesson is clear: Any major issue highlighted by the media can become one that is very difficult for political leaders to ignore.

Obviously, from the standpoint of democratic politics, the accuracy and general worth of the media are a critical component in maintaining meaningful public discussion. If the media fail—either in terms of accuracy, depth of coverage, or the airing of diverse views—public discussion suffers. One problem for the media is obtaining the information to be conveyed or interpreted as "news." Surprisingly, a great deal of data comes directly from government sources. A study of the *New York Times* and the *Washington Post*, reputed to be the most critical and independent national newspapers, found that the vast majority of information used as the bases of stories was originally obtained through official channels. Less than 20 percent of stories came from nongovernmental sources, while only 1 percent were the result of a reporter's own analysis. In such a situation, the media can all too easily become the captive of their sources.

Nonetheless, in recent years there have been many charges of a liberal, antigovernment bias in the media. The Nixon administration com-

also been changing. The three major broadcasting networks—CBS, NBC, and ABC—now cover campaigns in great detail, and even commission their own public opinion polls. Finally, media involvement in political campaigns has been aided by several Supreme Court decisions. In 1957 the Court ruled that broadcasters could not be held responsible for the content of political spot ads, and thereby opened the airwaves to such ads. Two years later, the justices relaxed "equal time" requirements for news coverage of candidates. Before that ruling, a network that covered a news event involving one candidate was obligated to provide equal time for coverage of opposing candidates. Then, in 1976, the Court also relaxed the equal time requirements for political debates, freeing broadcasters from the necessity of including minor party candidates in a debate.[13]

The growth of the media's importance in political life has led, perhaps inevitably, to heightened tensions between candidates and the media. Candidates and their organizations (which usually include sophisticated media specialists) seek to use the media to advance their own perspectives. On the other side, journalists have to decide which candidates to cover, what activities are newsworthy, and how to treat the "themes" of a campaign. In covering the candidates, the media almost invariably create images that can have important consequences. In 1976, for example, Democratic candidate Henry Jackson was portrayed as humorless, somber, and dull and President Gerald Ford was seen as a bumbler and fumbler. The tensions between media and candidate have been summed up as follows.

[T]he needs of the media and the objectives of candidates differ. The candidates strive to flood television and the press with selective information conducive to their election. Reporters and editors want news—defined as conflict, controversy, duplicity, scandal. They probe for candidates' weaknesses, deceptions, closeted skeletons. Candidates and their aides try to impose their definitions of what is important in an election on the media. They assert the primacy of the issues which favor them. . . .

plained that a liberal elite decided what the nation would learn about world events. Conservative critics have pointed out that studies show that journalists are considerably more liberal than the average American. Liberals respond to these critics for pointing out publishers and those who own the media are frequently politically conservative. In the 1980s new attacks by conservatives were mounted on the media. Senator Jesse Helms (Republican, N.C.) launched a bid to take over CBS and eventually replace its news staff.

Some studies of bias have not found the sort of liberal-left propaganda conservatives claim is there. For one thing, most newspapers endorse Republican candidates. A study of the content and themes of network evening news and weekly news magazines found that they frequently pictured the United States as the best nation in the world, and that criticisms of our politics were usually focused on personal dishonesty and bureaucratic inefficiency and not on any basic matters of principle.

Of late, conservatives have been able to make their voices heard quite effectively in the media. Religious broadcasts featuring fundamentalist social and political views have become the fastest growing portion of the TV industry, and conservative columnists are widely disseminated.

It is probably inevitable that tension should exist between the media and politicians. Although each needs the other, their purposes are quite distinct and often opposed.

As in the case of campaigns, what the media often fail to do well is to convey the facts accurately, and to offer sufficient interpretation in depth. The media are also prone to pander to the public's wishes for sensationalist news. The media face a dilemma: to gain mass attention, stories must be told simply and dramatically, but this style leads to oversimplification. We also find, especially with TV news, that fragmentation is the rule, making issues difficult to follow and understand. As we have already discussed (see Chapter 7) much of the public remains uninformed on many issues of vital significance. The media are part of that problem.

Who observes the observers? The ubiquity of the media is itself a major social and political fact. These photographers are on the floor of the 1976 Democratic National Convention in New York City.

# Marketing a candidate

The following excerpts are taken from a strategy report produced by advisers to President Gerald Ford in his 1976 campaign against Jimmy Carter.

*Strategy specifics (actions aimed at specific objectives)*
Establish leadership qualities:

Avoid self-deprecating remarks (Ford not a Lincoln) and acts (being photographed with a cowboy hat).

Carefully plan, prepare and execute *all* on-camera appearances. The President should be seen on television as in control, decisive, open, and candid. Prep time (15–30 minutes) should be built into the President's schedule . . . immedi- ately preceding on-camera events. . . .

Use ads and advocates to compare the President's personal characteristics and experience with Carter's.

The President must not go on the attack personally (not only because it results in a negative voter reaction) because the country does not want strident, divisive tactics. The country is coming together . . . and part of this healing process is a rejection of politicians who are perceived to be aggressive attackers.

*Attack and Carter's reaction*
Carter's popularity is based primarily on his perceived credibility, but it is very soft. The voter's perception of Carter can be substantially changed. Our basic objective should be to change the perception of Carter:

Move him to the left on social issues and away from traditional American values.

Identify him as a partisan Democrat.

Show that he is devious and arrogant, driven by personal ambition in ruthless pursuit of power.

*General Goals*
1. Cause the swing voter to reevaluate the President. This will take an "attention getter" (such as a good acceptance speech) so that people will reevaluate their assumptions about the President's personal characteristics and once again begin to listen to what he has to say.
2. Develop a major and highly disciplined attack on the perception of Carter. We must close the gap between Carter's perception and his actual weaknesses. He must be seen as:

An unknown. A man whose thirst for power dominates. Who doesn't know why he wants the Presidency or what he will do with it.

Inexperienced.

Arrogant (deceitful).

Devious and highly partisan (a function of uncontrolled ambition).

As one who uses religion for political purposes; an evangelic.

As liberal, well to the left of center . . . the old-line Democratic majority.

Carter's campaign must be linked (in the public's mind) to Nixon's '68 and '72 campaigns—very slick, media-oriented. A candidate that takes positions based on polls— not principles.

Source: Excerpted from Martin Schram, *Running for President 1976: The Carter Campaign* (New York: Stein and Day, 1977), in Richard Joslyn, *Mass Media*, pp. 23, 26, 27.

---

The media varyingly accept, ignore, or reject these attempts while seeking stories of their own devising.[14]

But how do the media affect the public? Are citizens better informed by the way campaigns are portrayed in the media? Are their political perceptions altered? Is their belief in the electoral process reinforced, legitimizing the way the system works, or are elections a disillusioning experience?

## Image-making

Public opinion pollsters and professional political consultants have become key figures in modern campaigns, often usurping the advisory roles previously filled by party officials. What they bring to a campaign is the expertise needed to understand and use

the media and other tools of modern campaigning. Among the services they provide are

advertising campaigns for radio, television and newspapers, including layout, timing and the actual placing of advertisements; public relations and press services, including the organization of public meetings, preparation and distribution of press releases and statements and detailed travel arrangements for the candidate; research and presentation of issues, including preparation of position papers, speech-writing and arranging for consultations between candidates and outside experts in appropriate areas of public policy; fund-raising solicitations, both by mail and through testimonial dinners and other public events; public opinion sampling to test voter awareness of the candidate, voter response to the campaign and voter attitudes on major issues; technical assistance on radio and television production, including the hiring of cameramen and recording studios for political films and broadcasts; campaign budgeting assistance designed to put campaign funds to the best possible use; use of data processing techniques to plan campaign strategy based on computer evaluations of thousands of bits of information; mobilization of support

through traditional precinct-level organizations, door-to-door campaigns and telephone solicitation of votes.[15]

Consultants devise strategies on how best to present a candidate to the media, based on public perceptions of the candidate's strengths and weaknesses (see box). In 1980, professional pollster and strategist Patrick Caddell shaped President Jimmy Carter's reelection bid on the basis of information gathered from opinion polls. Caddell later described his advice to Carter as follows.

[T]here was no way we could survive either a primary or general election contest on the first three years of the Carter administration. . . . [In the primaries] we had to make the choice *not* President Carter's record, but Senator Kennedy's issue stands and ideology. . . . [In the general election] we had to keep the focus on the candidates and we had to try to keep it on the future as opposed to the past. If the election were based on the past, we would lose flat out . . . there was a lot of doubt about what would happen with Reagan as president. We tried to put him on the defensive on exactly what his programs would mean. . . . Our job was to make people make a choice between two candidates—two personalities—and, to the extent that we could, between two parties.[16]

The tactics formulated by Caddell and by President Ford's advisers add up to a form of political persuasion that verges on manipulation of public opinion. Fundamentally, modern campaign strategists seek to alter or strengthen images of their candidate. In order to do so, they contrive contrary images of the opposing candidates and attempt to persuade the public of the value of such images. Such efforts can have educational and informative aspects, but at their core is image-making—a process closer to the marketing of products than to public debate and education.

It is important to add, however, that this kind of political image-making is nothing new, that it is not unique to the age of mass media. In 1840, the Whigs won a presidential campaign by successfully portraying William Henry Harrison as a man of the people and a successful general. In a campaign legendary for its hoopla and lack of content, the Whigs promised "Tippecanoe and Tyler Too," referring to the Battle of Tippecanoe, an insignificant skirmish with Indians in 1811, and vice-presidential candidate John Tyler. Other candidates have also cultivated specific images, from Teddy Roosevelt the "rough-rider" to Abe Lincoln the honest "rail-splitter." The issue in each of these cases, as with modern media campaigns, is the degree to which pure image-making takes over from a more reasoned and thoughtful assessment of a candidate's character and his stands on the issues.

**Political advertising:**  The first presidential candidate to hire an advertising agency was Dwight D. Eisenhower in 1952. His Democratic opponent, Adlai Stevenson, considered advertising beneath the dignity of the political process. Since that time, few politicians competing for major electoral offices have done without media advertising strategies.

In television advertising, the most money is spent on so-called spot ads, which usually run thirty seconds or less. The vast majority of spots are candidate-oriented: that is, they ask the electorate to judge the candidate as a person, not as the representative of a party or the champion of a political philosophy. When spots do bring up political issues, they generally do so in a very vague way, only loosely connecting the candidate to a particular position. In 75 percent of all spot ads there is no mention of a political party. Only 20 percent contain enough specific information about a candidate's position on an issue to allow the audience to draw inferences about the candidate's future behavior (see Table 10.5). As for the format and effectiveness of such political spots, the following guidelines are generally accepted by experts in the field.[17]

Commercials can help to make a candidate known—to enhance name-recognition.

Commercials can polish a candidate's image considerably, shifting voter perceptions even of a highly visible incumbent.

It is best to pretest ads before selected audiences, in order to weed out those that do not produce the intended effect.

The riskiest sort of ad is a negative one that voters and the press might label as unfair.

Ads cannot entirely blot out reality: they cannot make defeat look like victory, or entirely alter the perception of a candidate's character.

What effect, overall, do political ads have on citizen awareness? They apparently have a modest effect on the audience's perception of issue positions

TABLE 10.5
## Content of 156 televised political ads

| | |
|---|---|
| **Partisanship** | |
| *Overt* | *9.6%* |
| *Marginal* | *15.4* |
| *Nonpartisan* | *71.2* |
| *Bipartisan, cross-partisan* | *3.8* |
| | *100.0* |
| **Issue position** | |
| *Specific* | *19.9%* |
| *Vague* | *37.8* |
| *Salience only* | *19.2* |
| *None* | *42.3* |
| | *119.2** |
| **Candidate qualities** | |
| *Yes* | *47.4%* |
| *No* | *52.6* |
| | *100.0* |
| **Groups** | |
| *Yes* | *39.7%* |
| *No* | *60.3* |
| | *100.0* |

*This category sums to more than 100 percent because more than one type of policy appeal may appear in each ad.
Source: Adapted from Richard A. Joslyn, "The Content of Political Spot Ads," *Journalism Quarterly* 57 (Spring 1980):95. Reprinted by permission. Ads were chosen from a variety of campaign situations over a number of years. The sample is not representative, but the data are suggestive.

The theme of Ronald Reagan's presidential re-election bid was a renewed and stronger America. Here the man is somewhat dwarfed by the giant U.S. flag displayed in the atrium of a Dallas hotel. In politics, as in dreams, symbols count.

and of the personal characteristics of the candidates, and they can sharpen perceived differences between candidates on the issues. Recent research has indicated that political ads may contain more issue content than TV news coverage. This may not be saying much, however, since TV news, as we will see, is typically unattentive to issues. Moreover, issues are always presented with a partisan flavor in political ads. A thirty-second spot accusing one's opponent of favoring "baby murder" (a euphemism for abortion) ostensibly deals with an issue, but it does not do much to increase our political understanding. The real danger of political advertising, then, is that it may more often befuddle or misinform than enlighten the electorate.

**The 1984 campaign:** Television ads had clear-cut effects on the ways in which voters perceived the two candidates in the 1984 presidential campaigns. The ad campaign mounted by President Ronald Reagan's organization was unique in that the spots were designed primarily to make people feel good about the country and then to link that good feeling with the president. Reagan's ad team, which included some of the biggest names in the advertising business, apparently succeeded in associating the incumbent with feelings of patriotism and optimism. The ads were very low on specific issue content.

On the Democratic side, Walter Mondale proved a reluctant TV performer. His spot ads, which focused on issues, never caught on. But Mondale clearly understood the potential of television. "Modern politics requires television," he said. "I don't believe it's possible anymore to run for President without the capacity to build confidence and communications every night. It's got to be done that way."[18]

# The Lincoln-Douglas debates

Perhaps the most impressive political debates in American history were held during the 1858 Illinois senatorial campaign. The debates pitted one of the nation's most prominent politicians, Stephen A. Douglas, against a rising Illinois Republican who had served two years in the House of Representatives and had two years earlier unsuccessfully sought the Republican vice-presidential nomination, Abraham Lincoln.

By general agreement, conditions at the start of the campaign favored Douglas, by far the better known candidate. Douglas's plan was to solidify his support in Illinois as his base for a run at the presidency in 1860. In an effort to offset Douglas's well-established reputation, Lincoln challenged him to a series of debates. Douglas reluctantly accepted. Seven three-hour debates were held. In each, the first speaker opened with a one-hour presentation, the other was allowed ninety minutes to reply, and the first had the final thirty minutes.

The debates attracted considerable attention. Large audiences assembled, coming by train and wagon. Newspapers across the country covered the debates, sometimes publishing entire speeches. The contrast between the two candidates was striking: Douglas, less than five feet tall, a shrewd and ingenious debater; Lincoln, tall and awkward, master of the clear moral statement.

The core question of the debates was slavery, a matter that had almost reached the boiling point in the United States.

Douglas had established a reputation as a pragmatist on this matter, maintaining that the question should be resolved by popular sovereignty, with each state deciding whether to be slave or free. He seemed to accept unquestioningly the conviction of most whites that blacks were inherently inferior and accused Lincoln of being a radical and of advocating racial equality. In response, Lincoln admitted there was "A physical differences between the white and black races. . . ." but nonetheless favored the containment of slavery within its

## Televised presidential debates

Presidential debates are not required by law. In fact, they have been the exception, rather than the rule, since 1960, when Vice-President Richard Nixon surprised observers by giving his challenger, John Kennedy, the chance to appear on national television on an equal footing. Kennedy took advantage of the opportunity by demonstrating a mental quickness and command of facts that Nixon could not match, especially in the first of their debates. And because TV lighting made Kennedy look fresh and Nixon haggard, millions of television viewers came away with a more favorable impression of the young challenger. It is generally agreed that the debates gave Kennedy a perhaps crucial boost toward victory in the election.

Thereafter, frontrunners in presidential campaigns were understandably reluctant to give their opponents a chance to shine on national television. The next series of TV debates did not take place until 1976, when challenger Jimmy Carter faced President Gerald Ford. Ford was not the usual incumbent, having been appointed to the office of president rather than winning it on his own. By general agreement, Carter, the challenger again came away with the prize, although by only a slim margin. Through the debates, Carter was able to establish himself as a legitimate leader, on an equal footing with the president.

In 1980 the presidential debates were complicated by the presence of a third-party candidate, John Anderson. Carter, the incumbent, refused to debate with both Anderson and Republican candidate Ronald Reagan, on the grounds that he would be facing two Republicans (both had run in the Republican pri-

existing borders and looked toward its gradual extinction. He accused Douglas of being indifferent to the moral content of slavery. "That is the issue which will continue in this country when these poor tongues of Judge Douglas and myself shall be silent. It is the eternal struggle between these two principles—right and wrong—throughout the world."

Douglas spent $80,000 on the campaign, Lincoln $1,000. In the popular vote to elect the state legislature Lincoln's forces won, 126,084 to 121,940. But because Douglas's backers controlled more seats, Lincoln failed to be elected to the Senate. The larger moral and political victory belonged to Lincoln, however, who had established himself as a future national leader able to influence the terms in which slavery would be discussed during the coming crisis.

Sources: A. L. Boulton, ed., *The Lincoln and Douglas Debates* (New York: Henry Holt, 1905); Don E. Fehrenbacher, *Prelude to Greatness* (Palo Alto, Cal.: Stanford University Press, 1962); Harry V. Jaffa, *Crisis of the House Divided* (Garden City, N.Y.: Doubleday, 1959).

---

maries). This refusal may have been based on genuine conviction, but it seems more likely that Carter calculated that such a three-cornered debate could only enhance the status of the challengers, as previous debates had done. Reagan, however, did agree to debate Anderson, and that debate probably helped Reagan.

As election day neared, a one-shot debate between Reagan and Carter was finally arranged. Neither camp was truly anxious to hold the debate, yet both were ensnared by previous statements they had made about being willing to debate. Reagan's advisers thought a debate could only hurt their candidate, who was 5–6 percentage points ahead in the polls. Carter's advisers, on their part, doubted that the president could score a "knockout" against Reagan in the debate. In the event, Carter was judged to be the loser by a decisive margin.

In 1984, President Reagan, despite holding a wide lead in the polls, agreed to confront challenger Walter Mondale in two debates. The first debate was a near-disaster for the president, who was off his usual form and gave the impression of being confused and slow-thinking. As a result, many viewers felt that Reagan's age was starting to show. Reagan improved considerably in the second debate, seeming more confident, optimistic, and relaxed. When Mondale was unable to score another clear victory in the second debate, there was a sense that the election, then two weeks away, had been decided.

Have such debates been worthwhile? On the positive side, they have attracted huge audiences, stimulated interest in the election, and given voters a chance to see the candidates side-by-side. Presidential debates also have helped citizens learn more about the policy positions of the candidates, especially since many of the most *un*informed citizens are attracted to the debates. As two political observers noted in reference to the 1976 debates, "Watching the debates increased the level of manifest information that all citizens had . . . those individuals who watched the debaters exhibited a heightened political awareness at exactly the time when political information is crucial."[19]

On the negative side, debates have tended to emphasize the superficial; rarely has there been in-depth discussion of issues. One political scientist has characterized the debates as "the political version of the Indianapolis Speedway. What we're all there for . . . is to see somebody crack up in flames."[20] All too often, gaffes, hesitations, sweat on the upper lip, trivial errors, and the like have overshadowed the actual discussion of issues and positions. The media have usually focused on the "winner" in each debate, rather than on what was said or not said.

As currently organized, then, TV debates leave much to be desired. Improvements that have been suggested include having the candidates question each other, increasing the number of debates, or combining these and other alternatives in some sequence. Debates *can* be meaningful and informative. The more loosely organized debates among the Democratic Party primary candidates in 1984, for example, proved to be less tense, more exploratory, and far more interesting than the presidential ones have been.

# Comparative perspective
## The election game in Great Britain

Among the many startling differences between the U.S. and British political systems, one in particular stands out: the relative number and types of elections to national office. In contrast to the different elections Americans hold for president, senator, and representative, Britain has only one type of national election—that of the individual member of Parliament. All MPs are elected at the same time, and the government is then formed by the party with the most seats in the House of Commons. Parliamentary elections are thus all-important. The campaigns for these elections are very short—just a matter of weeks from the time a prime minister calls an election (which he or she must do within five years of taking office).

British campaigns are of two distinct types. An *official* (and therefore legally regulated) local campaign takes place in each of the nation's legislative districts. An *unofficial* (and almost completely unregulated) national campaign is directed by national party leaders and conducted mainly through the mass media. Laws regulating campaign finance apply only to the local campaigns; there are no legal limits on contributions to or expenditures by national campaigns. Still, party expenditures in the national campaign seem small by American standards: in 1979, for instance, the total reported spending was under $7 million. The main reason for the relatively low level of campaign spending is that parties may not spend money on television and radio advertising. Instead, the free airtime is provided for all parties, each of which controls the format and content of its broadcasts. The number of broadcasts allowed is based roughly on the relative electoral strength of the parties. Each party-controlled broadcast runs ten minutes and usually focuses on the party rather than on individual candidates.

But party-controlled broadcasts tell only part of the story. Elections are, after all, news. Covering the campaign as news, broadcasters produce interview programs, "man-in-the-street" surveys, and so on, and provide extensive coverage of individual party leaders. In addition, the centralized nature of British politics is reflected in the relatively large number of national newspapers—including the *Guardian* and the London *Times*—that take partisan positions.

---

## Media coverage of the "horse races"

Jimmy Carter made a telling remark in his 1976 campaign for president: "The only presidents I know who emphasized the issues were Presidents Dewey, Goldwater, and McGovern." Of course, none of these men won election, perhaps because they *were* more concerned with issues than image. The very nature of the mass media works against issue-oriented candidates. It takes much time (in broadcasting) or space (in print media) to explore issues, and time and space are at a premium in the media. Hence the disproportionate emphasis in the media on a candidate's personality, campaign strategy, and relative standing against rivals. These are features of the political "horse race"—an inherently more colorful and exciting media subject than is discussion of the issues. In a study conducted in 1975 and 1976, Thomas Patterson found that network news programs devoted 24 percent of their presidential campaign coverage to issue-related matters and 62 percent to the "horse race."[21] Studies of the 1980 and 1984 nominating process have produced similar findings. Newspaper and television coverage of campaigns do not differ

Is it love, admiration, respect? Whatever the emotion, it seems to be something intense as Robert Kennedy touches the hands of well-wishers during his 1968 presidential campaign.

significantly in this respect. In the 1976 presidential contest, 51 percent of newspaper coverage focused on the "horse race."

Then, too, the candidates themselves often deemphasize issues. In part, this may be due to the centrist thrust of U.S. politics, which encourages the blurring of differences. Some candidates, calculating that an emphasis on issues will cost them votes, turn to personality factors and campaign hoopla in an effort to divert the public's attention. Others become personality candidates reluctantly, realizing that issues are not dealt with well by the media and that personality and television seem made for each other. Of course, issues are not entirely neglected, but in the extraordinarily lengthy U.S. presidential campaigns, they are usually eclipsed by other matters. In 1984, Democratic contender Gary Hart was able to attract attention by his emphasis on "new ideas"— a phrase that vaguely suggested an issue-focus combined with a personality dimension.

What is the overall effect of media coverage of elections on public awareness? Most citizens get most of their information from the media, which they generally view as credible, trustworthy, and unbiased. We have seen—at least by way of example—that the media *can* have a powerful shaping effect on public perception of candidates. The media also play a role in setting the agenda of a campaign—that is, in influencing which issues, persons, events, and themes are perceived as important.

The public's perception of the candidates' posi-

Politics often stirs passion, but, at times, a good bit of the mundane is present. Here, Walter Mondale encounters a group of women who emerged from a beauty parlor to meet him on a Michigan street in 1976.

tions on the issues apparently corresponds to how much emphasis the candidates themselves place on issues during the campaign process.[22] Significantly, those exposed to network news do not learn any more about positions on issues than do those who do not watch the news. Citizens who read newspapers, however, are somewhat better informed on issues than are nonreaders. Daily television, accordingly, seems to do little to inform the electorate about the positions of candidates.[23]

On occasion, television can make a very powerful contribution to general public awareness through coverage of important events such as the nominating conventions. Those who watched the Democratic convention in Chicago in 1968 and saw, live on TV, the intensity and turmoil on the convention floor and the protests in the streets of Chicago could not help but be affected by what they had seen. These images had different effects on different people, but the fact that they were seen was important in itself.

It is difficult to generalize about the media's contribution to how the public evaluates candidates. One expert has noted that "there is evidence that citizens *use* . . . news reports to expand, refine and fill in existing belief systems in a process that is complex and varied. The effect of the news on such . . . evaluations . . . is seldom direct, simple or overwhelming; it is more often indirect, complex, marginal and subtle."[24] This picture may not be definitive, but it seems the best available at the present time.

## Conclusions

In many ways, U.S. politics is an exciting spectator sport. Candidates appear and disappear; contests drag on for months, even years; great amounts of cash are raised and spent; television keeps an eye on the progress of the "horse race." But what do citizens gain from the extraordinary spectacle of political campaigning and from the media coverage of political life? Not as much as they could, it seems.

From a democratic perspective, political campaigning in the United States has several shortcom-

ings. As we have seen, money plays far too substantial a role in the electoral process—and will continue to do so in the absence of fundamental reforms. Also, much of the campaign process has the effect of draining meaning out of elections rather than instilling in the electorate a clear sense of the issues involved. Compared with most other democratic nations, the American way of selecting and electing candidates is very open, very long, and very complicated.

As for the media, what is required is more depth, more emphasis on issues than on aspects of the "horse race," and a willingness to educate rather than merely entertain.

As one observer of the media has pointed out, the great strength of journalism is its ability to focus on *facts*, not theory. The media can be of vital assistance to the public in exploring reality in all its detail. What is happening in Nicaragua? Why are people unemployed? Does a missile gap actually exist? Focusing on "the facts" during a presidential campaign, for example, could help journalists rise above their "losing preoccupation with the nuances of hypothetical opinion, symbolic epistemology, electoral bookie work, and the tired search for someone to quote."[25] If the media did a thorough job of fact-gathering and presented stories dramatically enough, presidential candidates would be pressed a good deal harder to know, and explain, what they are talking about. And at a deeper level, the public itself must *want* to learn more about political life, must come to understand issues more clearly, and then, in turn, demand more of both media and the campaign process.

Richard Joslyn, in an effort to judge the democratic worth of U.S. campaigns and elections, set out four alternative models of how popular consent works:[26] the "prospective policy choice" approach, the "retrospective policy satisfaction" approach, the "selection of a benevolent leader" approach, and the "election-as-ritual" approach. In the first of these models, citizens choose candidates on the basis of what they anticipate *future* policies will be. In the second, electoral choices are based on satisfaction with *past* policies. In the third, voters select a reassuring personality as leader. In the fourth, elections serve principally to reinforce deeply held cultural myths.

The model that fits an election conforms to the

educative value of the campaign. Joslyn concluded that U.S. elections do not, in general, measure up to the "prospective policy choice" model, although issue-oriented elections have occurred and some voters are informed enough to make prospective policy choices. Much of what candidates and the media discuss during campaigns, Joslyn noted, has little to do with the issues and typically is vague and ambiguous. Given these styles of candidate rhetoric and campaign news coverage, it seems improbable that our elections have the sort of educative effect that would allow citizens to make an informed judgment on future policy directions.

The model that better fits contemporary U.S. elections is the "retrospective policy satisfaction" approach. It is far easier for the average citizen to assess with some knowledge what has been going on in the world than what directions policy will take. Basically, each presidential election provides an answer to the question, Do you want four more years of this? Although administrations are certainly capable of covering up past policy failures, their ability to do so is limited. Events frequently confound the pleasing pictures administrations try to cultivate of their policy successes. Studies have found that voters do, in fact, "punish" administrations when economic conditions take a turn for the worse or foreign policy problems get out of hand.[27]

Joslyn also found evidence for the applicability of the third approach: the selection of a "benevolent leader." Candidates themselves often cultivate such an approach by stressing their personality qualities. Image-making that projects reassuring notions of a powerful leader who can take care of the nation has become a commonplace aspect of contemporary elections.

As for the fourth idea of elections, the "elections-as-ritual" approach, Joslyn presented some evidence in support of this view as well. Usually, all candidates refer to the great myths of U.S. culture—patriotism, economic success, individual worth, Christian values, and American destiny. Campaign propaganda utilizing these concepts often is directed at people's emotions, tugging at their values and prejudices.

What do these observations contribute to our evaluation of public opinion, elections, and campaigns—the subjects of the last four chapters? On the one hand, we can take comfort in the fact that most citizens have a sufficiently good idea of what has happened in political life to make retrospective judgments on an administration and its policies. On the other hand, there is a great deal of public ignorance, much of it cultivated by candidates and not remedied by the media. In the words of political scientist James David Barber, "Normatively speaking, consent from ignorance can never be genuine, no more so than conversion by the sword . . . an ignorant citizenry is dangerously unready when the time comes for choice."[28] Our overall situation, then, is ambiguous. Our democratic electoral processes are less than satisfactory, but not disastrously flawed.

## NOTES

1 Adam Clymer, "The 1984 National Primary," *Public Opinion*, August-September 1984, p. 53.

2 Theodore White, as quoted in *The New York Times*, April 5, 1984, p. 27.

3 David E. Price, *Bringing Back the Parties* (Washington, D.C.: Congressional Quarterly Press, 1984), Chapter 8.

4 Quoted in Ruth K. Scott and Ronald Hrebenar, *Parties in Crisis* (New York: Wiley, 1979), p. 9.

5 On the constitutional dimensions of campaign financing reforms, see Albert Cover, "The Constitutionality of Campaign Expenditure Ceilings," *Public Studies Journal* 2 (Summer 1974): 267–73.

6 *The New York Times*, March 19, 1985, p. 1.

7 *Ibid*.

8 Fred Wertheimer, chairman of Common Cause, as quoted in *The New York Times*, February 3, 1983.

9 *The New York Times*, January 6, 1985, p. 13.

10 Senator Thomas Eagleton, as quoted in *The New York Times*, February 3, 1983.

11 William C. Adams, "Media Coverage of Campaign '84: A Preliminary Report," *Public Opinion*, April-May 1984, pp. 9–13.

12 Doris A. Graber, *Mass Media and American Politics* (Washington, D.C.: Congressional Quarterly Press, 1984),

Chapter 1; and Richard Joslyn, *Mass Media and Elections* (Reading, Mass.: Addison-Wesley, 1984), Chapter 1.

13 Richard Joslyn, *Mass Media*, Introduction.

14 David L. Paletz and Robert M. Entman, *Media, Power, Politics* (New York: The Free Press, 1981), pp. 32–3.

15 *Congressional Quarterly Weekly Report*, April 5, 1968, as quoted in Richard Joslyn, *Mass Media*, p. 33. Reprinted by permission of Congressional Quarterly, Inc.

16 As quoted in Richard Joslyn, *Mass Media*, p. 30.

17 Edwin Diamond and Stephen Bates, "The Political Pitch," *Psychology Today*, November 1984, pp. 22–32.

18 *The New York Times*, November 9, 1984, p. 13.

19 Arthur H. Miller and Michael MacKuen, "Learning About the Candidates: The 1976 Presidential Debates," *Public Opinion Quarterly* 43 (Fall 1979): 344.

20 Nelson Polsby, as quoted in *Time*, October 29, 1984, p. 31.

21 As reported in the *Washington Post*, December 5, 1976.

22 Richard Joslyn, *Mass Media*, Chapter 6.

23 *Ibid.*, pp. 178–83.

24 *Ibid.*, p. 191.

25 James David Barber, *The Pulse of Politics: Electing Presidents in the Media Age* (New York: Norton, 1980), p. 315.

26 Joslyn, pp. 273–96.

27 See, for example, Benjamin I. Page, *Choices and Echoes in Presidential Elections* (Chicago: University of Chicago Press, 1978), pp. 223–27.

28 James David Barber, "Character in the Campaign," in J. D. Barber, ed., *Race for the Presidency: The Media and the Nominating Process* (Englewood Cliffs, N.J.: Prentice-Hall, 1978).

## SELECTED READINGS

For insight into political campaigns, consult T. Ferguson and J. Rogers, *The Hidden Election* (New York: Pantheon, 1981); L. Chester, et al., *An American Melodrama* (New York: Viking, 1969); or any of the books of Theodore H. White covering the presidential elections since 1960.

On money and politics, see Herbert E. Alexander, *Financing Politics: Money, Elections and Political Reform* (Washington, D.C.: Congressional Quarterly Press, 1984);

and Elizabeth Drew, *Politics and Money: The New Road to Corruption* (New York: Macmillan, 1983).

On the media and politics, see Joe McGinness, *The Selling of the President, 1968* (New York: Trident, 1969); Doris A. Graber, *Mass Media and American Politics* (Washington, D.C.: Congressional Quarterly Press, 1980); and David Paletz and Robert Entman, *Media, Power, Politics* (New York: The Free Press, 1981).

### Political campaigns
For an interesting discussion of campaign styles and strategies, see E. N. Goldenberg and M. W. Traugott, *Campaigning for Congress* (Washington, D.C.: Congressional Quarterly Press, 1984). Two stimulating treatments of U.S. presidential campaigns are Thomas Ferguson and Joel Rogers, *The Hidden Election: Politics and Economics in the 1980 Presidential Election* (New York: Pantheon, 1981); and Lewis Chester, *et al.*, *An American Melodrama: The Presidential Campaign of 1968* (New York: Viking, 1969).

Two perspectives on national party conventions are offered in Judith H. Parris, *The Convention Problem: Issues in Reform of Presidential Nominating Procedures* (Washington, D.C.: The Brookings Institution, 1972); and Jeane J. Kirkpatrick, *The New Presidential Elite: Men and Women in National Politics* (New York: Russell Sage Foundation, 1976).

### Campaign financing
For current information on campaign costs, consult Herbert E. Alexander, *Financing Politics: Money, Elections and Political Reform*, 3rd ed. (Washington, D.C.: Congressional Quarterly Press, 1984). See also George Thayer, *Who Shakes the Money Tree?* (New York: Simon and Schuster, 1973); and Robert Agranoff, "The New Style of Campaigning: The Decline of Party and the Rise of Candidate Centered Technology," in Robert Agranoff, ed., *The New Style in Election Campaigns* (Boston: Holbrook, 1972), pp. 31–3.

### The role of the media
A critical account of the development of political advertising can be found in Malcolm MacDougall, "The Barkers of Snake Oil Politics," *Politics Today*, January-February 1980, p. 35. See also Joe McGinness, *The Selling of the President*. More-general treatments are Robert Agranoff's *The Management of Election Campaigns* (Boston: Holbrook, 1976); and Doris A. Graber, *Mass Media and American Politics* (Washington, D.C.: Congressional

Quarterly Press, 1980). The mindset of consultants is explored in David Lee Rosenbloom, *The Election Mess: Professional Campaign Managers and American Democracy* (New York: Quadrangle, 1973).

Discussions of debates can be found in Arthur H. Miller and Michael MacKuen, "Informing the Electorate: A National Study," in Sidney Kraus, ed., *The Great Debates* (Bloomington, Ind.: Indiana University Press, 1979), pp. 209–270; and Austin Ranney, ed., *The Past and Future of Presidential Debates* (Washington, D.C.: American Enterprise Institute, 1979).

For general treatments of the influence of media see: David Paletz and Robert Entman, *Media, Power, Politics;* Todd Gitlin, *The Whole World Is Watching: Mass Media in the Making and Unmaking of the New Left* (Berkeley, Cal.: University of California Press, 1980); David Halberstam, *The Powers That Be* (New York: Knopf, 1979); Edward Epstein, *News from Nowhere* (New York: Random House, 1973); Doris A. Graber, *Mass Media;* Herbert Gans, *Deciding What's News: A Study of CBS Evening News, NBC Nightly News, Newsweek and Time* (New York: Pantheon, 1979); W. Lance Bennet, *Public Opinion in American Politics* (New York: Harcourt, Brace, Jovanovich, 1980), pp. 304–307; and M. B. MacKuen and S. L. Coombs, *More Than News: Media Power in Public Affairs* (Beverly Hills, Cal.: Sage, 1981).

# Chapter
eleven

# Interest-group politics

# Democracy to the highest bidder?

IN early 1980, headlines were made by yet another in a long series of "influence-buying" incidents involving members of Congress. The influence-buyers in this case were actually FBI agents who, posing as representatives of wealthy Arabs, sought favors from the legislators in return for substantial bribes. Although the FBI's methods were widely criticized, the Abscam operation, as it was known, reinforced a common image of how U.S. politics works. To many Americans, political life is riddled with corruption.

Consider another case. In 1974, the Senate voted, 53–42, in favor of no-fault auto insurance legislation, but the House failed to act on the measure. Opposition to the bill, which would have severely limited automobile accident suits, had been led by the American Trial Lawyers Association (ATLA), whose members earn substantial sums from such suits. In 1975, ATLA organized a campaign fund for congressional candidates in an effort to help prevent passage of a similar bill.[1] Overall, ATLA contributed $250,000 to candidates in the 1976 Senate races. Seven senators who had voted for no-fault in 1974 switched their positions and subsequently received $5,000 campaign contributions from ATLA, which also gave $10,000 to primary opponents of the senator who had been the floor-manager of the no-fault bill. In addition, eleven of the seventeen newcomers

to the Senate in 1976 received ATLA contributions either before or after the elections. There was nothing illegal about these campaign contributions. ATLA had simply done what hundreds of other groups do—use its resources to influence the outcome of the political process.

Influence-seeking is not confined to the legislative arena. Over decades of legal struggle, lawyers for the National Association for the Advancement of Colored People argued for equal treatment under the law for black Americans. The NAACP maintained that the segregated conditions imposed on blacks in many states denied them the equal protection of the laws. Finally, in the famous *Brown* v. *Board of Education* school desegregation case of 1954, NAACP lawyers achieved what they had sought—a clear reversal of the 1896 Supreme Court ruling that separate facilities could be equal. For American blacks as a group, the federal court system had offered the main avenue through which influence could be sought. As slowly as litigation proceeded, it had been their most powerful tool, and gradually the system of segregation crumbled under the legal pressure brought to bear.

Let us consider one more case. Recently, local landlords in a small American city, seeing an opportunity to make a substantial profit, sought permission from the town board to transform their apartment complexes into condominiums—a transformation process that had become very common in major cities. In this case, tenants in the apartment complexes organized and protested to the board that they needed the apartments, that they could not afford to buy condominiums, and that the owners were interested only in a quick profit, not in the long-term good of the community. The landlords argued that the property was theirs and that condominiums were an entirely proper use for these apartments. Keeping up the pressure, the tenants organized neighborhood protests, continually appeared at board meetings, and met informally with board members. Eventually, the board rejected the owners' request.

What do these four cases tell us? First, influence-seeking is an everyday part of our political process. Second, interest groups come in all shapes and sizes,

and their interests are as varied as their make-up. Third, influence can be exercised at many political access points in many different ways, ranging from lawsuits and campaign contributions to personal conversations. Fourth, there are winners and losers in these battles, although the vast majority of the public may know little of how the battles are either fought or resolved. Fifth, the system of influence-seeking is open to corruption.

These fairly straightforward perceptions lead to a series of more difficult questions. In this process of group pressure, whose interests are represented most effectively? Are all of us, and our many interests, part of the process of group representation and pressure? Which groups get the lion's share of the benefits that the political process has to offer, and why? What types of groups are there, and how do they make themselves felt in the political process? Ex-

One of the victims of Abscam, Senator Harrison Williams of New Jersey. Accused of taking bribes, Williams fought his case through the courts and lost.

actly how does this complicated group-process system operate? Is it democratic? Fair? Reasonable? These are the questions we will take up in this chapter.

## Interest-group dynamics

Democratic politics lends itself naturally to group activity. People in all democratic societies tend to coalesce around shared interests and ideas. Most Americans have many such interests. Concerns about wage scales or job security might lead a person to join a union or other work-related association. The same person might also contribute to an environmental group, because of worries about nuclear power plants being built nearby. He or she might also take an interest in better town recreational facilities, and hence attend town meetings or sign petitions. Finally, our hypothetical American might join a synagogue or church, and thereby affirm his or her religious identity—representing a *potential* interest that might be activated under certain circumstances. In U.S. society, many such interests are givens, a product of the country's economic, religious, regional, ethnic, and racial diversity.

Traditionally, the United States has been characterized as a nation of joiners. Foreigners have often marveled at this aspect of American life. In the early 1800s, Alexis de Tocqueville remarked:

The Americans make associations to give entertainments, to found seminaries, to build inns, to construct churches, to diffuse books, to send missionaries to the antipodes; in this manner they found hospitals, prisons and schools. If it is proposed to inculcate some truth or to foster some feeling by the encouragement of a great example, they form a society. Wherever at the head of some new undertaking you see the government in France, or a man of rank in England, in the United States you will be sure to find an association.[2]

This observation remains pertinent today. According to public opinion polls, about 40 percent of Americans are active in at least one organization, and 40 percent of those who are active have more than one membership. Group membership is closely related to social class and education, however. Better-educated, middle-class people are much more likely to be joiners, which means that their views usually are better represented in the process of group expression.[3]

Organizations that commonly direct their efforts toward political influence are called **interest groups**. This term is slightly less laden with negative connotations than the term *pressure group*, which was popular in the past. Nonetheless, interest groups have also demonstrated that they can effectively pressure legislators, bureaucrats, and public officials. And,

265

Why do people join organizations? The reasons are extremely varied, including the desire to protect economic and other interests, the wish to meet others, to have fun, to establish an identity. Although many Americans belong to no organization, as a society we are famous as joiners. Here, a group of Masons in festive garb.

as we shall see, there are good reasons for being concerned about the ways such groups go about their business.

## Various functions

Interest groups may have any of several different objectives. Some groups serve mainly *symbolic* functions: ethnic, religious, or racial associations, for example, generally seek to bolster their members' sense of group identity. Such groups may also seek to affirm the symbolic significance of their members' identity in relation to the rest of society. In lobbying to make the Reverend Martin Luther King, Jr.'s, birthday a national holiday, black groups were making such a symbolic statement.

Groups may also pursue *instrumental* functions seeking more concrete returns. *Economic* functions naturally loom large in the aims of many interest groups. Often, interest groups promote the economic well-being of whole classes of people or sets of institutions, such as doctors or hospitals. Trade unions and business associations are formed almost entirely for economic purposes.

Groups may also pursue a whole range of non-

economic policy goals. Such goals range from amnesty for Vietnam war resisters or aid for Cambodian refugees to the preservation of historic sites. Some groups focus on more *ideological* concerns. In this category are, among others, Americans for Democratic Action (liberal causes), Americans for Constitutional Action (conservative causes), and Common Cause (the cause of honest, open government). Ideological and instrumental groups often overlap, since particular issues and overall ideologies tend to blend together.

Finally, groups may serve *informational* functions: that is, may disseminate information on matters of interest to members. The environmental group Friends of the Earth, for example, publishes a magazine that keeps members up-to-date on environmental issues and related public policy questions.

## Inherent problems

Although interest groups clearly play useful political and social roles, the proliferation of such groups clearly has created serious problems in democratic life. As far back as the Constitutional Convention, James Madison warned of the deleterious effects of "factions" on the political process; in his eyes, factions represented potentially dangerous social elements that by nature would oppose the public interest. The only way to counteract the dangers of faction, Madison believed, would be to ensure that factions counteracted another, so that no majority faction could tyrannize society. This image of counterbalancing factions accords with a commonly held view of the U.S. political process: that no one interest group possesses enough power to enforce its views on a wide range of issues, since each group will be counteracted by other groups.

It would be comforting to think that the system of interest groups is balanced such that in the end, the "public interest" (however that is defined) is ultimately served. Unfortunately, there are good reasons for thinking that this is not the case. Perhaps the primary flaw in this theory is that the system is heavily biased in the direction of those who have the resources that matter most: money, organizational clout, and political and social legitimacy. The effectiveness of interest groups, in other words, is not decided by the size of their memberships or the intellectual or social worth of their goals.

Another problem with the interest-group system is that many potential interests have not always been effectively represented. At the time of the drafting of the U.S. Constitution, for example, women, blacks, and those with little property were shut out of the political process. At any given time, some groups are not considered "legitimate," however representative they may be. As a result they must battle—often violently and at considerable cost—to break into the system of group politics. The barriers facing such groups can be daunting. Invariably, they must overcome the psychological barrier of being ignored or scorned by the rest of society. Often, they must also overcome legal hurdles, such as those that confronted blacks and women in their decades-long battles for equal rights. Other barriers are organizational in nature—for example, new groups often lack the resources of more-experienced and better-financed groups.

Frequently, those interests that are almost universal—such as interests in clean air and safe consumer goods—are most difficult to organize. Some observers have argued that broadly shared interests do not usually possess the elements essential to organizational success. For potential members of groups dedicated to such causes, clear personal benefits may seem lacking, and it may be hard to see how joining will make much of a difference. As Mancur Olson has pointed out, the payoffs to any one individual for joining a large interest group dealing with diffuse public issues usually are exceeded by the costs of joining and acquiring information.

Narrowly focused interest groups, in contrast, are often quite cohesive, because those who are seriously affected by a specific public policy have a very strong incentive to organize. Suppose, for example, that regulations allowing competition in the sale of eyeglasses were proposed. Consumers might benefit from such regulations, but most of them would have only a vague idea of what those benefits might be. Opticians, however, surely would organize to lobby *against* regulations that would, in effect, force them to lower prices. Here we see a chronic problem of interest-group politics: widely shared interests that affect many people slightly are less likely to lead to organized representation than are narrowly shared interests that affect a few people more deeply.

A related problem is that the process of influence-seeking is often hidden from public scrutiny. Interest-group lobbying more often resembles subtle osmosis than it does pressurized arm-twisting. This coziness has been decried by many critics as destructive of the open, public debate of alternatives that democracy requires.

## Major
interest groups

That interest groups exist, that they exert much influence, that they raise serious problems for democracy—each of these points has been established. Now we must take a closer look at how the interest-group system is organized and how influence is actually exerted.

## Business

The interests of people in business are highly diverse. An executive of a large corporation who comes to Washington to lobby for restrictions on Japanese imports and a local florist who needs a small business loan have little in common. Accordingly, the business community does not always speak with one voice, and splits within that community often lead to political conflict. Small businesses seek protection against larger rivals. Businesses in depressed areas seek government aid, whereas those that prosper generally oppose such assistance. Import policies are often the focus of business rivalry. Finally, several major pieces of business legislation, such as the Interstate Commerce Act and the Sherman Antitrust Act, originated in the efforts of smaller companies to protect themselves against larger competitors.

Nevertheless, there is a certain degree of unity within the business community. Generally, business interests oppose tax increases, support restrictions on the power of organized labor, favor protection against foreign competition, and encourage government to create a favorable climate in which business and investment can grow. A reduction in governmental regulation of business is usually viewed as the key feature of such a climate.

Major business organizations include the Chamber of Commerce, with a membership of two hundred thousand businesses and individuals and four thousand associations and a budget of $63 million in 1985; the National Association of Manufacturers (NAM), commonly viewed as representing the interests of "big business"; and the Business Roundtable, which represents 190 large companies through the lobbying efforts of high-level business executives.

Specific industries are represented by a host of other groups, such as the Associated Milk Producers, the National Cotton Council, and the American Meat Institute.

Business interests, which are affected by so many government programs, engage in many forms of influence-seeking. They attempt to shape the general climate of public opinion through advertising. They lobby extensively in Washington, D.C., and the various state capitals. They litigate to delay and to defeat the purposes of regulatory legislation. They seek the appointments of those favorable to business to top administration positions. They fund campaigns and candidates. Several of these strategies will be examined in detail later in this chapter.

## Labor

Most American workers are not trade union members. At their peak, in the 1950s, unions claimed almost 25 percent of the work force. That figure has now declined to below 20 percent. American unions certainly are not insignificant, but they are weaker than those in any other advanced industrial democratic nation.

For most of U.S. history, only a very small sector of the economy was organized in unions. Until the Great Depression and the prolabor New Deal of the 1930s, only the skilled crafts, such as carpentry and other building trades, and railroad workers were organized to any significant extent. The rapid expansion of unionization in the 1930s was spearheaded by the growth of the Congress of Industrial Organizations, which organized industrial workers in auto, steel, and other major industries. After a period of intense rivalry, the CIO and the much older American Federation of Labor merged in 1955 to form the AFL-CIO. Despite the importance of several large individual unions, the AFL-CIO remains labor's paramount organization and the source of most of its politically directed activity.

The AFL-CIO attempts to influence national politics on a whole array of domestic issues—social welfare, employment, job training, minimum wages, child labor, occupational health and safety, consumer protection, the tax code. Individual unions often lobby separately for their own agendas. Sometimes labor and business find themselves on the same side of an issue, as when both try to get government help to improve the competitive position of an industry.

Since the end of World War II, labor has also

been heavily involved in U.S. foreign policy. The AFL-CIO has frequently given aid to anticommunist organizations in other societies, sometimes with help from the Central Intelligence Agency. Many unions took a pro–Vietnam War position, and in the 1972 presidential election found themselves at odds on this issue with the hierarchy of the Democratic Party, with which labor had long been affiliated.

Labor's overall political strategy has been to work within the Democratic Party. Few unions overtly support Republican candidates, although both Richard Nixon and Ronald Reagan were endorsed by some segments of organized labor. The AFL-CIO's Committee on Political Education was, in effect, one of the nation's most significant political action committees long before such organizations began to proliferate in the 1970s. COPE has provided indirect funds and services for Democratic candidates, by mailing campaign literature, making phone calls, getting out the vote, and so on.

As for lobbying, the AFL-CIO carries the most clout among labor interest groups. Its 106 affiliated unions, representing everyone from teachers and plumbers to meat cutters and garment workers, enlist some 14 million dues-paying members; counting the families involved, the organization actually represents close to 50 million Americans. The AFL-CIO also supports three hundred lobbyists who work on behalf of fifty member unions, along with hundreds of local pressure groups in all states and congressional districts. On issues that are generally considered crucial to all of labor, such as minimum wage legislation, the entire organization will be mobilized. On many other issues, only various affiliates take an interest. Sometimes portions of the organization conflict; at other times, the leadership and the rank-and-file are at odds.

Other active union lobbies include those of the United Mine Workers, the United Auto Workers, and the Teamsters. Overall, though, labor's record in the post–World War II period has not been impressive on issues closely related to its immediate interests. For the most part, organized labor has been fighting a defensive battle since 1950.

Trade unions were once one of the most important sources of protest in all industrialized nations. In recent decades, unions generally have become institutionalized and considerably less radical than in the past. Here we see a small part of the democratic process at work at a union meeting of striking West Virginia coal miners.

# Comparative perspective
## British trade unions

Organized labor plays a far more important political role in Great Britain than in the United States. In a sense, the British Labour Party is a creature of organized labor—the political voice of a long-active and still powerful social and economic institution. In 1983, trade unions represented about 10.5 million Brit-

ons, or nearly 50 percent of the working population—more than double the percentage of union membership found in the United States. The Labour Party outside Parliament is organized as a federation of trade unions and individual dues-paying members. The party is almost wholly dependent on trade unions for its routine income.

Trade union involvement with the Labour Party goes far beyond interest-group lobbying and American-style endorsements and campaign activity. Through the National Executive Committee of the Labour Party, trade unions are able to shape party policy. At the annual NEC conference, each union commands a voting

strength equal to its total number of members, who contribute part of their union dues to the party. In the 1970s, two unions, the Transport and General Workers Union and the Amalgamated Union of Engineering Workers, exercised enough combined voting power (about 30 percent of NEC votes) to determine the composition of the NEC and the outcome of almost any controversial issue. In 1973, for instance, Jack Jones of the Transport Workers initiated an incomes policy proposal that became official government policy in 1975.

Most British trade unions are members of the Trades Union Congress, which represents the interests of member unions. During the tenure of the 1974–79 Labour government, leading members of the TUC and

the government kept in close contact through monthly meetings and regular private meetings at the Prime Minister's residence.

Until early 1979, the Labour Party's ability to get along with trade unions was its chief electoral advantage over the Conservatives. But in 1979, Labour lost that edge, at least temporarily, when it failed to prevent or mitigate the effects of a wave of industrial strikes. As a result, the Labour government fell. The party's relationship with organized labor appeals to voters when it is perceived as "party control"; support fades when it is perceived as "party captivity."

---

## The defense lobby

Defense is very big business. The Pentagon is the biggest single purchaser of goods and services in the nation. Defense spending creates as many as thirty-five thousand jobs for every $1 billion spent—and the defense budget exceeded $200 billion in 1985. The peaks and valleys of defense spending have extraordinary effects on particular sectors of the economy. This is particularly true in highly defense-dependent areas such as Southern California, Texas, and Connecticut. In California, one job in ten is defense-related.

Nationwide, more than 30 percent of mathematicians, 25 percent of physicists, 47 percent of aeronautical engineers, and 11 percent of computer programmers work in the military-industrial complex. Many defense contractors are single-customer industries entirely dependent on defense spending for survival. The number of top defense contractors, however, is rather small. In 1982, ten companies received more than 30 percent of all large defense contracts and almost 50 percent of all research and development contracts given out by the Defense Department.

Defense contractors often use high-powered advertising and public relations techniques to lobby within the government for new contracts. Under the current system, as Senator William Proxmire (D., Wisc.) put it, "contractors get generous allotments from the government to produce weapons systems. But rather than using all of it for production of these weapons systems, they siphon some of it off to lobby for even more money. . . . There is enough favoritism and behind-the-scenes influence on large defense contracts without the added insult of having the taxpayer pay for the bill."[4] The Rockwell Corporation, for example, produced and made one hundred prints of the film *The Threat—What Can One Do?* which dealt with the need to build the B-1 bomber. The film was then shown to the public and members of Congress. Rockwell maintained that this project represented merely a public relations effort, and therefore was a deductible business expense. Government tax auditors saw the film as part of an extensive lobbying effort to get the government to build the B-1 and to make sure that Rockwell got the contract.

Often, weapons systems are kept alive not because of their military value, but because they contribute to the financial health of the area of the country in which they are located. Senator Carl Levin (D., Mich.) described the situation this way: "I think the pressures on Congress from the [military-industrial] complex are great and often successful when they shouldn't be. . . . Part of the problem is that we have a democratic government and every member of Congress is going to try and get as much for his district or state as he can. That's the price we pay for democratic government."[5]

The defense lobby has strong allies, then, both among members of Congress, who want defense contracts in their districts, and Department of Defense bureaucrats, who want to strengthen weapons systems. This kind of alliance is known as an *iron triangle*. Typically, it involves a set of interest groups, a portion of the federal bureaucracy, and a congressional committee or some members of a committee. The three sides of this triangle reinforce one another in a strong, protective framework of mutual influence. Another element in the picture is that people

flow from one part of the triangle to another. Frequently, people who have worked for the Defense Department acquire jobs within the defense industry. Sometimes the traffic flow goes the other way as well—from industry into government employment. According to political scientist Gordon Adams, "Once molded, the triangle sets with the rigidity of iron. The three participants exert strenuous efforts to keep isolated and protected from outside points of view." In the iron triangle, Adams went on, those outside the government (the defense contractors) are "so close to government that they not only carry out military policy, but often create it."[6]

## Public interest groups

The rise of public interest lobbies has been one of the most significant developments in recent U.S. political history. One student of the subject has defined **public interest group** as "one that seeks a collective good, the achievement of which will not selectively and materially benefit the membership or activists of the organization."[7]

Common Cause and the Ralph Nader organizations are the most prominent of the general-purpose public interest lobbies. **Common Cause**, founded in 1970 by former Health, Education, and Welfare Secretary John Gardner, attracted one hundred thousand members in its first six months of existence. As of 1983, its membership stood at about two hundred and forty thousand, down from three hundred thousand during the Watergate days of 1974. Common Cause has both a paid staff and a volunteer force working out of its Washington office. It has frequently focused on procedural issues, such as open-hearings requirements in Congress, because it believes that better procedures will yield more honest policy-making. Common Cause has also supported public campaign financing and reform of the lobbying disclosure laws.

**Ralph Nader**'s career as a consumer activist and the large number of public interest organizations he has helped create constitute an extraordinary story

in recent U.S. political life. Nader started his career as champion of the ordinary citizen by taking on some of the biggest targets in U.S. industry—beginning in the mid-1960s with General Motors, whose Corvair he attacked as "unsafe at any speed." Nader's battle with GM ended in a clear-cut victory for the activist, as reflected in the passage of the Motor Vehicle Safety Act of 1966. That was just the beginning. Nader's efforts have spawned at least fifteen public interest groups, focused on consumer issues, environmental concerns, health, science, regulatory reform, energy, and other matters.

In the 1960s alone, fourteen major pieces of consumer legislation passed Congress with the help of public interest group lobbying. These bills dealt with auto safety, credit bureaus, drugs, flammable fabrics, interstate land sales, natural gas pipeline safety, postal fraud, poultry inspection, product safety, toy safety, truth in lending, truth in packaging, and meat wholesaling.

Not all consumer group efforts, however, have been so successful. The Food and Drug Administration,

for example, has been widely criticized for its allegedly cozy relationship with the industries it was established to regulate. Efforts to reform the FDA have had only limited success, and battles over issues such as adequate testing of food additives have continued. The Consumer Product Safety Commission, created in 1972, has also met with many failures and difficulties. On another level, consumer advocates have not succeeded in attempts to persuade Congress to create a cabinet-level consumer agency.

Despite these setbacks, public interest groups have had a noticeable impact in U.S. political life. Their success can be attributed partly to their ability to tap the resilient capacity for middle-class activism and youthful idealism in the country. They also have been able to pinpoint weaknesses and problems in politics and social life—particularly, problems created by entrenched powers in the economy, Congress, and the governmental bureaucracy. The public interest organizations have made many more people aware of what has actually happened, or, often, not happened. The informational function of such groups is vital. Had Ralph Nader not researched the Corvair and published a book warning of its design flaws, very few Americans would have known anything about that automobile's unsafe design. Public interest organizations have repeatedly revealed, and therefore shaken up, long-standing relationships among industry interest groups, regulatory agencies, and Congress.

The struggle waged by public interest groups has been of the David-and-Goliath variety. Few such groups have the finances, the organizational clout, or, on the whole, the long-established legitimacy of the major interests they attack. In addition, since they are often critical of the political process itself, they tend to provoke antagonism from many of the political actors whose support they need in the long run. Yet, they carry a few large rocks in their slingshot: they can evoke an enduring streak of public idealism, they can tap the widespread discontent many alienated Americans feel with the political process, and they, unlike most other interest groups, are not looking out for number one.

In recent years, some participants in the public interest movement have become part of the political establishment. Cities, states, and the federal government have set up consumer protection agencies, for example, and many former activists are now responsible for making and enforcing policy. Moreover, tactics have sometimes changed. As Carol Tucker Foreman, former president of the Consumer Federation of America, stated: "You score your points now by negotiation, by data, not by marching around the White House."[8] It should also be noted that some in business have also become more attentive to the rights of the consumer. And the nature of the issues has changed as well. As Stuart M. Statlee of the U.S. Consumer Product Safety Committee said, "the problems that remain are much more esoteric, much more complicated . . . and in some ways much more costly."[9]

## Single-issue groups

A **single-issue group** is a well-organized and intensely active organization that focuses exclusively on one issue or set of issues. Among the best known of these groups are the pro- and anti-abortion organizations, the **Moral Majority** (interested in moral/religious issues), environmental and consumer groups, and the gun lobby. For many of these groups, their particular areas of interest override all other considerations, dictating whether a legislator will be supported or opposed. Almost all such groups have enjoyed at least a measure of success in state and national politics. They have proliferated to such an extent that some observers worry about the fragmentation of U.S. politics, such that interests are so intense, narrow,

and well-organized that compromise becomes virtually impossible.

Moral intensity and a single-issue orientation are not new elements. The current single-issue groups, however, represent a break with the main patterns of the recent past, as represented by the New Deal and the post–World War II political consensus. During this period, single-issue economic groups were somewhat neutralized, as each won a "piece of the pie" through subsidies, tax breaks, favorable legislation, and the like. Moral issues seemed to be disappearing from political life as Americans apparently grew more tolerant and as older moral concerns, such as Prohibition, faded away. A bipartisan consensus on foreign policy also muted discontent.

The breakdown of these patterns began in the 1960s, with the emergence of new and intensely felt moral and social issues. In that decade, many people learned that they could make a political impact. Marching, picketing, signing petitions, and participating in campaigns seemed to make a difference. The single-issue groups of the 1970s put these lessons to work. Let us look more closely at some of these groups.

**The antiabortion lobby:** Antiabortion groups have often been viewed as among the most successful of all single-issue interest groups. They first came to prominence after the Supreme Court, in *Roe* v. *Wade* (1973), struck down many state laws that had restricted abortion. Since that time, they have played substantial roles in several senatorial and congressional races. Many observers have credited them with the defeat of several liberal legislators, although there has been considerable debate over just how decisive their political role actually has been.

Antiabortion activists have been highly emotional and occasionally violent. At the National Right to Life Convention in 1979, speakers compared abortion to genocidal Nazi extermination of the Jews, and U.S. drug companies supplying abortion services were compared with German industrialists who used slave labor. In 1984, several abortion clinics were firebombed, allegedly by antiabortionists. Such intense emotion and extreme tactics have made rational discussion of this issue very difficult.

The National Right to Life group claimed 12 million members in two thousand chapters in 1984. Besides contributing to the defeat of proabortion legislators, antiabortion groups were influential in the passage of legislation prohibiting the use of federal Medicaid funds for abortions except in a few limited circumstances. Finally, antiabortion activists have led the campaign for passage of a constitutional amendment banning abortions. Such an amendment has passed several state legislatures and been introduced in the House and Senate sixty-five separate times.

**The gun lobby:** An overwhelming majority of Americans favor more restrictive regulation of handguns. The political clout and financial resources of the gun lobby, however, have thwarted all gun control efforts at the national level. The chief element

in that lobby is the National Rifle Association. At present, the NRA is a loose union of hunters, indoor shooting sportsmen, firearms and ammunition manufacturers, conservationists, and sporting goods businessmen. With the aid of refined computer and direct-mail techniques, the NRA has been able to mobilize its membership around gun-control issues. In addition to lobbying Congress directly, the NRA has effectively campaigned for or against selected senators and representatives. In the 1978 election, for example, the NRA and its allies spent $500,000 on behalf of twenty-one Senate and 142 House candidates.

NRA backers are committed, well-organized, persistent, and well-financed. Their opponents, although comprising a numerical majority, are not well-organized and lack the money and intensity of the progun forces. Still, there are signs that the once seemingly invincible power of the NRA may be waning. Support for gun control legislation remains high in the country as a whole, and particularly among younger Americans. A wide range of gun control proposals have been placed on the ballot in various states and localities, and some municipalities, such as San Francisco, have banned the possession of handguns altogether.

**Environmental groups:** The presence in U.S. politics of groups concerned with protecting the environment is not new. Environmental issues such as land use, national parks, and wildlife protection originated in the nineteenth century. Early in this century, President Theodore Roosevelt brought such issues to the forefront of national politics. In many ways, however, environmental activism ebbed for more than half a century thereafter. Amidst the rising affluence of U.S. society after World War II, few

Demonstrating in front of the Supreme Court building, anti-abortion protesters state their views. Reversing policy made by the Supreme Court may be the toughest battle any interest group can confront.

# Comparative perspective
# Guns
# and
# public policy

Alone among the Western democracies, the United States allows a vast number of guns to circulate in society. According to one estimate, Americans currently possess 200 *million* guns of all descriptions, of which 60 million are handguns. Every fifty minutes an American is killed with a pistol. From 1963 through 1980, more than 388,000 Americans were killed by gunfire: 170,000 were murdered, a

roughly equal number committed suicide, and 48,000 were victims of accidental shootings.[*]

In contrast, Western European nations impose tough standards for gun ownership. To obtain a gun in West Germany, individuals must undergo physical and mental tests and prove they have a need to protect themselves. Permission to own a handgun is seldom granted in Great Britain, and rifle ownership is very carefully regulated. The penalty for carrying a gun illegally is six months in jail, and that for using a gun in a crime is fourteen years imprisonment. Most British police officers do not carry guns, although they

[*]M. Stone, *U.S. News and World Report*, September 28, 1981, p. 82.
[†]Statistics supplied by Handgun Control, Inc., Washington, D.C.

There was little doubt about Ronald Reagan's feelings toward the NRA. Despite his brush with violent death, Reagan, like the NRA, opposed most gun control legislation.

can be specially authorized to use them in certain circumstances. In 1980, handguns killed seventy-seven people in Japan, eight in Great Britain,

eighteen in Sweden, four in Australia, and 11,522 in the United States.[†]

There is no organization comparable to the NRA in any European nation. What nurtured the NRA's development in the United States? American defenders of the gun base their arguments on the Second Amendment to the Constitution, which refers to the right of the people to bear arms (although in the view of most experts, this provision was intended to apply not to individuals, but to state militias). The individualistic American tradition has also been an important factor. The right to own a gun has become associated, for some, with personal autonomy and freedom.

---

Americans attended to the hidden and not-so-hidden costs of creating a complex, industrial society.

Only over the past two decades have environmental issues moved to the front burner of national politics. Often these issues are complicated and deeply felt. They can take many forms, from local air and water pollution questions to toxic waste disposal, the preservation of wildlife and wilderness, and worker health and safety matters. As a result, environmental interest groups of all sorts have emerged. More-traditional groups such as the Sierra Club have expanded the range of their concerns, and many new

environmentally concerned organizations have sprung up, including the Friends of the Earth, Environmental Action, Greenpeace, the Environmental Defense Fund, and a host of antinuclear groups.

Like other interest groups, some environmental organizations have singled out legislators for political attack. A particular target of environmental activists in the early 1980s was James Watt, Ronald Reagan's first secretary of the interior. Watt earned the ire of environmentalists through his support of commercial development of nationally owned lands. Environmental groups also have campaigned strongly on a

Affirming their identity and political preferences, supporters of the state of Israel stage a parade. For the smaller marchers, this socialization experience may have importance much later.

cess of pro-Israel electoral efforts was the 1982 defeat of Representative Paul Findley, the ranking Republican on the House Foreign Affairs subcommittee that authorizes aid to Israel. Findley had grown increasingly critical of Israel. Both he and his successful opponent noted that pro-Israel money could well have made the difference in their close congressional contest.

## How lobbying works

variety of local and state issues: nuclear power, bottle return laws, shipment of radioactive wastes, pollution standards, and others. They have employed the courts, civil disobedience, and referenda, as well as more conventional lobbying activities.

**The Israel lobby:** In focusing on the single foreign policy issue of aid to Israel, pro-Israel groups have been strikingly effective. One member of a House Foreign Affairs subcommittee has noted that whenever he has complained in committee hearings about aid for Israel, he usually has received a visit from a representative of one of the pro-Israel PACs. He described it this way: "Not once, I told them, have I ever strayed from the cause. And they said, 'Well, you abstained once.' That's how good they are."[10]

Thirty-one pro-Israel groups spent $1.67 million in the 1981–82 congressional season, helping to elect certain legislators and defeat others. A variety of Jewish political organizations belong to a national umbrella group, called simply the National PAC, which carries on the work of various regional groups in a more systematic fashion. One impressive suc-

The major resources available to interest groups are money, the clout that comes with membership size, organizational skills, leadership skills, expertise, knowledge of the political process, motivational commitment, and the intangible but very significant factor of prestige, or legitimacy. How are these resources used by groups that seek to influence policymaking?

Money can buy a great deal. It translates into a vast array of potential weapons in the influence-gaining process—campaign contributions, media exposure, the ability to procure the talents of able people. Wealthy organizations can afford to employ large lobbying staffs and offer substantial lecture fees to legislators as a means of winning influence.

Size can also translate fairly readily into power. The AFL-CIO, for example, has organizations in every congressional district. Farm groups wield considerable political clout in certain districts. Even business has become aware of the potential of grass-roots activism. One Chamber of Commerce lobbyist noted that "lately we've grown aware of the potential impact of the grass-roots membership we have. The Chamber has business proprietors and executives in every congressional district, and we can use them to open a lot of doors for us that were closed before."[11]

Membership unity also matters. Unless a group's members are united around and deeply concerned about an issue, lobbying efforts may fail to make much of an impression. One House member, speaking of agricultural interest groups, put it this way: "If they can't get their own members together, they aren't going to start lobbying."[12]

Political reputation and prestige can also translate into influence. The most influential lobbyists often are those who obtain the trust of legislators. Lobbyists in general put great store in a reputation for honesty and expertise. Such a reputation is especially important, of course, for those lobbyists with little else to offer by way of political power. A group's overall prestige can also matter. Because the Business Roundtable is made up of the chief executive

directors of the country's largest corporations, its status among business groups is very high.

One lobbyist summarized the whole matter of group resources and efforts to obtain influence as follows.

Different kinds of assets can be effective, but the individual has to, to some extent, decide what are his assets and then use them to the maximum. That is, if you have a special asset that you can develop arguments, you can do research and develop tight information that is useful and reliable to senators and congressmen. Then you use that to the maximum. If your asset is sitting around the Congressional Hotel, in the Democratic Club, drinking cocktails and just hitting issues lightly but maximizing your contacts with senators and congressmen, then you use that to the maximum. . . . On the other hand, . . . being a source of reliable information to congressmen . . . tends to work better and be a more effective tactic if you are a small group or if you're working for a group that doesn't put large amounts of money into campaigns, one that has good contacts with a minimum number of senators and congressmen. . . . The tactics have to vary with the kind of organization.[13]

## Overall strategies

There are many different influence-gaining strategies. Some groups concentrate their efforts on the legislative process, others on grass-roots organizing, others on the executive branch and such regulatory agencies as the Federal Trade Commission or the Securities and Exchange Commission. Still other groups focus on the courts. Overall, however, most lobbyists seek to influence Congress, either directly (by lobbying for or against legislation) or indirectly (by campaigning for or against congressional candidates).

It is hard to ignore the point being expressed by this demonstrator at the San Francisco Civic Center. Whether the point will become accepted as policy, however, depends on many factors, the clout of the demonstrator's group being one.

# A theorem on special interests

A theorem developed by Representative [Fortney H.] Stark was proved true by a line of tax-bill lobbyists that stretched from the door of the Ways and Means Committee room thirty-six meters, twenty-one centimeters down the hall. This was precisely the length predicted by the Stark Theorem. Two working days later, a line of lobbyists waiting to observe the Medicare mark-up [bill consideration] stretched (as Stark had predicted) only fifteen meters, thirty-seven centimeters.

Stark's theorem is as follows:

$$L = \frac{P}{I} \, (AF^2 \times DF)$$
$$- \; 93 \; (AFDC + SSI + \text{food stamps})$$

Basically, Stark postulated that the Length of a Line of Lobbyists ($L$) equals the Population of the nation ($P$) divided by the number of Individuals impacted ($I$), multiplied by the Arcaneness Factor squared ($AF^2$), times the Dullness Factor ($DF$), minus 93 times the number of references to poor people.

In other words, the fewer the number of taxpayers affected, and the duller and more arcane the subject, the longer the line of lobbyists.

This was borne out by the small group of lobbyists covering the Medicare hearing (which affects 26,758,000 people) compared with the standing-room-only group listening to the debates on coal royalties, nuclear power plant decommissioning, and certain corporate taxes.

Said Stark, "The Arcaneness Factor was the hardest to postulate. The figure I've developed is obtained by counting the number of 'subparagraphs' in the law being amended after excluding the first ninety lines; adding two lines for each 'except that'; adding 4.2 lines for each 'provided that'; and adding sixteen lines for each Greek alphabet symbol used."

The Dullness Factor is simply the number of crossword puzzles being worked on in the hearing room in any sixty-minute period.

A final element in the Stark Theorem factors in the lack of interest among lobbyists in poor-people issues. Every mention of AFDC, SSI, or food stamps is multiplied by 93 and then subtracted from the total.

Source: A press release issued by California Representative Fortney H. (Pete) Stark, reprinted in *Harper's* magazine, December 1984, p. 15.

---

Lobbying groups employ two general strategies. To start with, they keep track of important political action. Since so many parts of the government can have an effect on issues of concern to an interest group, simply keeping track of government activity is a major task in itself. As a representative of one business group once put it:

It's impossible to follow everything. . . . Just the *Congressional Record* and the *Federal Register* take all day to read. We have one person who follows the *Record*, the *Register*, *CQ* [*Congressional Quarterly*] and things like that, and I'll spend a lot of time on the Hill, talking to members and staff about what's going on. I learn more from gossip and idle chatter about what might happen than from anything else.[14]

The next step is to initiate or oppose government action. Consumer groups, for example, have supported bills to establish a Consumer Protection Agency, whereas most (though not all) business groups have opposed such legislation. To have some effect on the political process, a group must know what it wants and have *points of access*. According to one lobbyist, "You have to have lines into the right committee and the right subcommittee. I always make sure I have a friend on the subcommittee, someone who will look after my interests, who will introduce and push bills or amendments for me. If you don't have a friend on the inside, then you're really on the outside looking in."[15]

**Lobbying in Congress:** How do lobbyists attempt to influence legislators? They can provide information that bears on important policy decisions, and they can help plan political strategies. Lobbyists also can supply innovative ideas and approaches, especially when the organizations involved have special expertise in important political areas such as health or welfare policy. Perhaps most obviously, groups can offer campaign support or threaten opposition.

Lobbying groups can also try to influence the internal structure of Congress itself. During the 1950s and 1960s, for example, oil lobbyists succeeded in barring from membership on the House Ways and Means Committee representatives who did not favor the large oil depletion allowance enjoyed by the industry. Having sympathetic members of vital committees is crucial to the long-term success of lobbyists.

Finally, we should note that lobbyists and legislators are often personally close. Much interaction between them is informal—parties, vacations, lunches, country club sports, and so on. Such friendships are not surprising, given the shared attitudes and backgrounds of many lobbyists and legislators. Former legislators often become lobbyists and maintain ties with ex-colleagues.

**Lobbying in the executive branch:** Lobbying is not confined to Congress. Executive branch lobbyists also play a significant political role in trying to influence the shape of proposals before they are sent to Congress. Efforts of this kind generally are focused on the White House. Labor groups, business leaders, consumer representatives—all seek meetings with the president. Executive branch lobbying also involves foreign policy questions, as when Jewish leaders seek to influence policy toward Israel, or black leaders policy toward South Africa. Frequently, interest groups and the White House work together; for example, both consumer groups and President Jimmy Carter's consumer representative sought creation of the Consumer Protection Agency in 1977.

Just as members of Congress often have close relationships with lobbyists, many executive branch agencies maintain close ties with those they serve. The Department of Commerce has links with the business community, the Agriculture Department looks toward the interests of farmers, the Veterans' Administration looks toward those of veterans, and so on.

Relations between executive agencies and interest groups are frequently very cordial. The groups usually seek to perpetuate their friendships by influencing the choice of political appointees to the top positions in these executive hierarchies.

The independent regulatory commissions are also prime targets of lobbyists. Since many of the day-to-day operations of major industries are deeply affected by the rules made by bodies such as the Federal Communications Commission and the Interstate Commerce Commission, interest groups often go to great lengths to set forth their views before these agencies. Here, too, relationships between the regulator and the regulated are often rather cozy.

**Intragovernmental lobbying:** Lobbying also goes on within the executive branch itself, as well as between the White House and Congress—a phenomenon known as intragovernmental lobbying. The first administration to establish a congressional liaison office in the White House in order to lobby Congress was that of President Dwight Eisenhower. Today, many executive branch agencies maintain special congressional liaison staffs. Each cabinet department has such an office, as do most regulatory agencies and many federal bureaus. Typically, agency lobbyists coordinate their activities with White House lobbying efforts.

## Influence-seeking through the courts

Yet another facet of interest-group activities is the pursuit of specific goals through the courts. Often, an interest group will mount a legal challenge to a new regulation, as various industries have commonly done in regard to regulations promulgated by the Environmental Protection Agency or the Occupational Safety and Health Administration. Less commonly, legal efforts will represent the most vital element in an interest group's strategy. As we have already seen, the NAACP's long struggle to win equal protection under the law for blacks was focused principally on the courts; to this end, the NAACP established a special Legal Defense and Educational Fund in 1939. Ralph Nader created the Public Citizen

Litigation Group to represent consumer interests in the courts, and those groups opposed to the death penalty have concentrated on the legal arena.

Groups sometimes attempt to exercise influence by joining in a lawsuit brought by others. Groups also sponsor research that might affect court decisions and attempt to shape the selection and confirmation of judges. The shift in decision-making patterns from the more liberal Supreme Court under Chief Justice Earl Warren to the more conservative Court under Chief Justice Warren Burger shows how vital court appointments can be in shaping the life chances of individuals and groups in the United States.

## Insider and outsider strategies

Some students of the lobbying process have described strategies as "insider" or "outsider." Insider methods revolve around direct connections between interest groups and the main political actors involved —legislators, bureaucrats, or other members of the executive branch. Outsider strategies build on connections between legislators and their home districts.

**Insider strategies:** The keys to insider strategies are social relationships, friendships, and the political needs of legislators; often, these elements are brought into play while the intricate mechanisms of the political process slowly grind toward a decision. Interest groups that use insider strategies often try to lighten a legislator's work load by supplying information, writing speeches, or answering criticisms offered by opponents. According to one student of the subject, "The corporate representative is often effective because he is a specialist, trading in information about an industry that may be crucial to the wording and effect of a given piece of legislation. 'Every industry has its little quirks,' explained one liberal Democrat. . . . Even if you are against them . . . you need their lobbyist to help you get your head on straight.' "[16] The powerful role of expertise, of specialized knowledge, could not be put more clearly. As legislation has become increasingly intricate and regulation more extensive, the insider's

knowledge has become increasingly vital to lawmaking. Hence, interest groups that are believed to have the special knowledge required often have considerable political leverage at their disposal.

Insider lobbyists also try to exert influence by pointing out to a legislator what effects a particular piece of legislation will have on the lawmaker's home district—that it will hurt a certain local hospital, mean three thousand more jobs, lead to federal funds being taken away from that area, and so forth. Groups sometimes supply speech-making materials to overworked legislators and their staffs. As a Senate aide once noted: "My boss demands a speech and a statement for the *Congressional Record* for every bill we introduce or co-sponsor. . . . I can't do it all myself. The better lobbyists, when they have a proposal they are pushing, bring it to me along with a couple of speeches, a *Record* insert, and a fact sheet. They know their clout is tripled that way."[17]

The most subtle insider tactic involves the gradual development of social relationships with legislators. In this way, business involvements and friendships between lawmakers and lobbyists take hold. Social gatherings have often been cited as exercising an important influence on political life. Speaking of such gatherings, one Senate aide declared:

They're damned important, especially with the new congressmen. The new man arrives in town with his wife. They're both a little awed. And what happens? All of a sudden, they are invited to a little dinner party given by the Washington vice president for a billion-dollar corporation. They're impressed, but there's more to it than that.

Let's say the congressman is a liberal. He's suspicious of big business. What does he find? The big shot is a darned nice guy. He doesn't have horns and a tail. He charms the wife and he's deferential to the congressman. They go away feeling a little differently. Maybe it doesn't affect the way he votes, at least not right away. But it's a softening process.[18]

**Outsider strategies:** Outsider methods of lobbying depend on the effective use of grass-roots sentiments to influence legislators. Such strategies may be chosen for a variety of reasons. In some cases, they represent the most effective way to influence policymaking. In others, they offer the only alternatives left after insider strategies have failed. Finally, they may comprise one element in a long-term effort to influence the direction of public opinion. In that case, the outsider strategy may not be linked to a particular piece of legislation, or to any specific outcome.

There have been some prominent grass-roots outsider efforts in recent years. The Chamber of Commerce has successfully generated opposition among businessmen to labor legislation. In 1983 the American Bankers Association led a highly successful lobbying blitz in which banks encouraged their customers to send letters and postcards to legislators urging the repeal of a withholding tax on interest payments. Thirteen million pieces of mail arrived, and the measure was repealed. A less successful outsider strategy was that developed by Common Cause, the AFL-CIO, and the Ralph Nader network to bolster the fading effort to create a federal consumer protection agency. In their joint "nickel" campaign, citizens were to send nickels to members of Congress—the five cents representing the cost of the new agency to each American. This outsider strategy failed, just as the insider one had, in the face of determined business opposition.

Grass-roots lobbying has grown enormously in recent years, as single-issue campaigns and organizations have focused on arousing intense public support or opposition to particular proposals, such as gun control, abortion, or antitax measures. Moreover, many corporations, taking a longer-range view of political influence, have begun to use so-called advocacy advertising to gain public support for their interests. It has been estimated that as much as one-third of all corporate advertising is now devoted to advocacy ads. Mobil Oil, for example, uses ads in the media to offer its views on energy and regulatory issues related to business.

Other outsider strategies are directed mainly toward influencing the general tone of public discussion. A number of corporations contribute to conservative think tanks, which in turn produce scholarly and popular materials that make their way into public discussion on many issues. The role of intellectual leadership in shaping the issue-agenda of politics is very significant. Those who have a hand in shaping the agenda of politics condition the atmosphere in which interest group activity takes place.

## The new lobbying

Since the early 1970s, there has been a quantitative and qualitative change in the business of political lobbying. The absolute volume of interest-group endeavors has increased dramatically. The number of lobbyists registered in Washington, D.C., has almost doubled, to fifteen thousand, in recent years (and that figure does not include thousands of unregistered lobbyists). Lobbies now spend an estimated two billion dollars to influence public policy; about half of that amount is spent on government lobbying, and the other half in attempts to influence public opinion.

Five hundred corporations now operate their own lobbies, as opposed to only 100 in the mid 1970s. Why this substantial increase? The increase in the size and complexity of the federal government has been the main factor. The government now regulates a great many matters of interest to a wide array of groups. Many seemingly trivial rules or requirements have important ramifications on the well-being of towns or companies. The stakes are often very high for the contending interests.

A second, related factor is the growing sophistication and expertise of lobbyists, who have become more aware of how government does or could affect their interests. Most lobbyists now are able to give guidance and advice to those in government who create the new rules and make the expenditures, as well as to provide information on the possible impact of their work.

Finally, fundamental changes in the power structure in Congress in recent years have given outside influences greater access to legislators. Many members of Congress, especially Democrats, have won election without the benefit of close party ties. Such legislators are less likely to be brought into line by party pressures or to be influenced by party leaders in Congress. As party organizations have declined in power, the nonideological politics of specific issues has replaced party politics to a large extent. For example, business-oriented political action committees have supported many of the new Democratic congressmen, who in turn are opposed to many of the party leadership's prolabor policies.

## Regulation, representation, and the public interest

Concern about the excesses of lobbying date back to the 1830s, when the term *lobbyist* was first coined. Scandals or alleged scandals were common in the pre–Civil War period. In the 1850s, Washington was a wide-open city "filled with a variety of gambling houses whose proprietors worked closely with the lobbyists. When a representative or a senator was unlucky enough to fall into debt, as he frequently did, the managers of the gambling halls had him where he would do them the most good."[19] Lobbying scandals continued through the late nineteenth and early twentieth centuries. Not until 1946, however, was legislation regulating lobbying activities actually passed.

### Regulatory efforts

The Federal Regulation of Lobbying Act, part of the Legislative Reorganization Act of 1946, required that persons paid to influence Congress be registered, that they disclose the source and use of all compensation over $500, and that they state their general legislative objectives in a report to Congress. The bill, then, did not actually restrict lobbying at all: it simply required disclosure, on the theory that publicly available knowledge would create a healthier political climate.

Since its passage, the law has been criticized on legal and constitutional grounds, and deemed both ineffective and ambiguous. Contentions that it violates the First Amendment protections of free speech and right to petition were rejected by the Supreme Court in 1954, but the justices interpreted the act very narrowly. Basically, the act reflected Congress's ambivalence toward interest group activity. Relations between legislators and lobbyists have often been mutually beneficial, as we have pointed out. Congress has been uneasy about taking action that would require closer policing of its members.

The 1946 act suffers from obvious weaknesses, even if one accepts disclosure (as opposed to control) as a reasonable objective. The disclosure rules apply only to lobbying aimed directly at Congress—executive branch, grass-roots, and other forms of lobbying are not addressed. Interest groups are given considerable latitude in interpreting how much of their money is spent on lobbying, and only those groups that declare their "principal purpose" to be direct contact with legislators are covered. Then, too, the act does not make clear exactly what constitutes a lobbying effort. Finally, another weakness is that no clear enforcement agency is designated in the law, as a result of which the law has been rarely enforced.

Perhaps the best way to demonstrate the gross inadequacies of federal regulation in this area is to look at a specific lobbying case. The lobbying effort devoted to the defeat of President Jimmy Carter's 1977 energy package was nothing short of fierce. American Gas Association Vice-President Nick Laird called it one of the most all-out efforts he had ever witnessed. Of the millions of dollars spent on this campaign, very little was reported under the federal lobbying act. Total oil industry expenditures in the first nine months of 1977 were only reported as $639,329, and the gas industry reported only $507,047. One registered lobbyist for an oil company, Standard Oil of Indiana, reported spending $2.94 from July to September—a period of intense lobbying efforts. Other groups also claimed extremely small expenditures.

Efforts to develop new and tougher regulations for lobbying have blossomed in almost every recent session of Congress, only to fail for lack of a consensus. Some of the questions involved in regulatory efforts are: Who should have to register? What sorts of lobbying should be covered? Should contributions to lobbies be made public? Should the overall expenditures of lobbies be limited? and How much regulation is constitutional? Some states, most notably California, have passed tough regulatory legislation. On the federal level, however, interest-group lobbying has remained intense, well-organized, well-funded, and largely beyond the reach of governmental regulation or control.

Government and inter-
est groups: cooperation
and corruption

We have already noted that the interests of lobbies frequently coincide with those of both executive agencies and members of Congress. Thus, for example, tobacco growers and manufacturers may find steady allies on the agriculture committees in both houses and in the Department of Agriculture. Such close relationships, like those between regulated industries and regulatory commissions, have led critics to ask who is looking out for the public interest in such situations. Too often, the answer is "no one." It often seems as if our political system were built around the premise that good policy is that which is acceptable to the major interests involved, regardless of what would benefit the majority of Americans.

This policy-making process has been fiercely attacked by public interest lobbies, who have called for greater independence on the part of government agencies and a more open and publicly reported lobbying process. Although the task of defining the "public interest" has yet to be resolved in an entirely satisfactory way, it is easy to see what clearly is *not* in the public interest: policy-making that ignores important affected interests; policy-making carried on out of public view by small, well-organized groups seeking benefits for themselves; policy-making that loses sight of the more permanent and deeper commitments we supposedly share as a society, such as those to honesty, equality, and fairness.

Further, is it in the public interest for an expert on the payroll of a private industry to serve the government without compensation for an extended period of time and then return to his private post? He may well have knowledge that is otherwise unavailable to the government, and he may be completely honest—yet he knows that his public service is temporary and that his future lies with the company he will return to. What of the situation in which a high government official finds herself in charge of regulating matters that affect a major corporation? She knows that, as a government official, she is likely to be replaced when a new administration is voted into office, yet she will have acquired valuable knowledge in the course of government service that she will be understandably reluctant to see go to waste. The thought of a subsequent career with the corporation under jurisdiction may well affect her decisions in office. Although it would be difficult to impugn the integrity of the particular individuals in either of these instances, it must be recognized that a serious problem of persistent and insidious bias exists. There may be no conspiracy—or even corruption, in the common sense of that term—but the public interest may well suffer.

An admiral in charge of procuring great quantities of steel retires and joins a steel company; a general leaves the armed services to head a corporation with important military contracts; a civil aviation administrator resigns to become head of a major airline—such moves have become commonplace. Of the top twenty-nine officials of the Ford administration who left office in 1976, twenty went to work for industries in jobs that required them to interact regularly with their old agencies over governmental policy.

In an attempt to curb this disturbing trend, Congress passed an ethics law under which former government officials are permanently prohibited from representing those interests they regulated as civil servants. But "representing interests" is a vague term, and the law permits "business contacts" between former civil servants and their agencies after one year. In addition, the ethics law does not deal with the past connections of regulators. One expert, writing in 1982, underlined the consequences of this omission with the following list.

1. More than 100 government officials who decide what drugs can be sold and what chemicals can be added to food once worked for drug or chemical companies.

2. More than 300 top-level regulatory officials are now making the rules for sale of stocks and bonds to the public by their former employers—including brokerage firms and stock exchanges.

3. Common Cause has found that 429 or 65% of top level officials of the Nuclear Regulatory Commission have come from private enterprises, all holding licenses, permits, or contracts from NRC.[20]

Such overlaps between regulators and those they regulate are almost certain to produce a subtle yet important bias in the policy-making process.

## Conclusions

Since the 1960s, interest groups in general, and the increasingly numerous single-issue groups in particular, have grown more skillful and influential. This trend has taken place at a time when Congress has become more vulnerable to interest-group strategies. As the power and effectiveness of political parties has ebbed, interest groups have begun to step into the political vacuum created. For a time it appeared that these developments would improve the chances of the new public interest variety of interest group. By the mid-1980s, however, narrowly focused interest-group politics seemed more prevalent than ever before. As the number of interest groups has increased and their goals have narrowed, U.S. political life has been subject to an ever greater degree of fragmentation.

It is true that single-issue groups may coalesce under ideologically based umbrella organizations, such as the New Right. They may also play constructive political roles by spotlighting grievances and dramatizing neglected public issues or by counteracting the influence of more powerful but often less visible interest groups. Overall, however, the fragmentation of politics makes compromise difficult and the "public interest" a neglected notion.

Another problem in U.S. interest group activity is the pervasiveness of business influence, which has become even more prominent in recent years with the spectacular growth of corporate political action organizations. The political action committees representing the oil-and-gas lobby alone outspent the entire Democratic Party in 1980. As we have seen, heavy corporate PAC contributions have often had telling effects on the political process. Business lobbyists also direct their attention to the federal agencies whose regulations affect business life. Corporations mount extensive grass-roots efforts, organized by well-financed computer-based operations.

Organized labor at one time could match the lobbying efforts of business groups, but those days are long over. And the public interest lobbyists spent less than one-thousandth of the amount spent by business interests. Especially in recent years, big business has effectively been able to veto any legislation it deems sufficiently threatening. Business lobbyists do not always get precisely the legislation they wish, but they can generally stop legislation that they think will hurt them.

Business influence is actually part of the larger problem of unequal distribution of power and influence in our pluralistic system. It would be comforting to think that all works out for the best in the clash of interest group politics, but that is often not the case. Although many groups exert influence on policy-making, money, persistence, organizational capacities, intensity, and legitimacy determine the degree of influence various groups exercise. Theoretically the system is open to all interest groups. On a practical level, however, only some groups have substantial input. The direction of decisionmaking is heavily biased toward those who can wield political clout—and that is not what democracy is supposed to be about.

Imagine trying to tell migrant farm workers or young, unemployed black people that the interest group system was open to their efforts at influence. The idea of an open system, in which each group can make its voice heard effectively, does not accord with the day-to-day realities faced by these and many other Americans. The weakness of pluralism is that it both reflects and helps to sustain the undemocratic distribution of power and influence in U.S. political, social, and economic life. This situation is exacerbated when the major political parties do not make issues sufficiently visible to the public and when a large portion of the population, disproportionately poor and poorly informed, is not really a part of the political process.

Besides the problem of excluded or relatively powerless groups, what about the public interest? In the clash of battles for group influence, the long-term public interest is sometimes lost sight of. Are agricultural policies that help to destroy the family farm really far-sighted? Were oil subsidies that contributed to domestic shortages of the 1970s really in the national interest? If welfare policy undermines the point of finding work, if the gun lobby keeps millions of new pistols circulating—are those policies really desirable in the long run?

Some observers have regarded the rough-and-tumble politics of the interest group network as a price that must be paid for open, democratic politics. Robert Samuelson, for example, argued that

> the prejudice against special interests strikes at the heart of the democratic process. One person's special interest is another's crusade. The function of politics is not only to govern in the general interest and to reconcile differences among specific interests; it is also to provide outlets for political and social tensions. . . . No one, of course, should pretend the resulting system is problem-free. . . . The growth of government authority and political activism has led to severe tensions. . . . This is the ongoing drama of government, but it should not be mislabeled. The system is struggling, but it is not corrupt.[21]

Samuelson also recognized serious difficulties with interest group activities: "On the one hand, government faces paralysis: a collision of competing interests so severe that nothing happens. . . . On the other hand, there looms the sort of pervasive contradictions that compels government to act in ways that are ultimately self-defeating." These are sobering reflections on the state of the U.S. polity.

## NOTES

1 Common Cause, *In Common*, March-April 1983, pp. 5–11.

2 Alexis de Tocqueville, *Democracy in America* (Garden City, N.Y.: Doubleday, 1969), p. 485.

3 S. Verba and N. H. Nie, *Participation in America* (New York: Harper & Row, 1972).

4 Quoted in *In Common*, August 1981, p. 27.

5 Quoted in Rorie Tempest, "U.S. Defense Establishment Wields a Pervasive Power," *Los Angeles Times*, July 10, 1983, p. 3.

6 Quoted in *In Common*, August 1981, p. 7.

7 Jeffrey Berry, *Lobbying for the People* (Princeton, N.J.: Princeton University Press, 1977), p. 7.

8 *The New York Times*, April 13, 1985, p. 18.

9 *Ibid.*

10 J. J. Fialka, "Pro-Israel Politics," *Wall Street Journal*, August 3, 1983, p. 1.

11 Norman J. Orenstein and Shirley Elder, *Interest Groups, Lobbying and Policymaking* (Washington, D.C.: Congressional Quarterly Press, 1978), p. 73.

12 *Ibid.*, p. 75.

13 *Ibid.*, p. 79.

14 *Ibid.*, p. 56.

15 *Ibid.*, pp. 57–58.

16 *Ibid.*, p. 84.

17 *Ibid.*, p. 85.

18 *Ibid.*, p. 86.

19 *Ibid.*, p. 97.

20 Charles Dunn, *American Democracy Debated*, 2nd ed. (Glenview, Ill.: Scott Foresman, 1982).

21 R. J. Samuelson, "The Campaign Reform Failure," *New Republic*, September 5, 1983, pp. 35–36.

## SELECTED READINGS

For basic coverage of what interest groups are and how they function, consult Norman J. Ornstein and Shirley Elder, *Interest Groups, Lobbying and Policymaking* (Washington, D.C.: Congressional Quarterly Press, 1978); and Allan J. Cigler and Burdett A. Loomis, eds., *Interest Group Politics* (Washington, D.C.: Congressional Quarterly Press, 1983).

For critical assessments of interest group politics, see Theodore Lowi, *The End of Liberalism* (New York: Norton, 1969); Michael Parenti, *Democracy for the Few* (New York: St. Martin's Press, 1983); and B. M. Russett, *What Price Vigilance* (New Haven, Conn.: Yale University Press, 1970).

On public interest lobbies and the general issue of the public interest, see Jeffrey M. Berry, *Lobbying for the People* (Princeton, N.J.: Princeton University Press, 1977); Robert P. Holsworth, *Public Interest Liberalism and the Crisis of Affluence* (Cambridge, Mass.: Schenkman, 1980); C. J. Friedrich, ed., *The Public Interest* (New York: Atherton, 1962); and Richard Flathman, *The Public Interest* (New York: Wiley, 1966).

Andrew S. McFarland, *Common Cause: Lobbying in the Public Interest* (Chatham, N.J.: Chatham House, 1984).

# Chapter twelve

# Mass politics
# and protest

# A threat?
# or a necessity?

On February 1, 1960, four black students from the North Carolina Agricultural & Technical University entered Woolworth's in downtown Greensboro, North Carolina. Violating the norms of the segregated society of that day, the four seated themselves at the lunch counter and asked for cups of coffee. The waitress, adhering to the Southern tradition of race relations, refused them service. But the four did not leave. They remained on their stools until the day ended. It was the first sit-in of the 1960s.[1]

The Greensboro sit-in proved contagious. The next day, twenty students joined the original four. By the end of the week, thousands of A&T students and other blacks had violated segregation norms in downtown Greensboro. Some of these protestors were attacked by Ku Klux Klan members and other indignant whites. A few demonstrators were arrested, but all remained nonviolent. With tensions increasing, Woolworth's closed its doors at the end of the week. But the sit-in movement spread, and within a month sit-ins had taken place in more than fifty cities in nine states.

It was a tactic and an objective whose time had come. Yet no one had planned the sit-ins. The four students who initiated the sit-in at Woolworth's had decided on that method of protest quite casually.

Their action ultimately represented only a small part of a far larger movement involving race relations in the South and, in many ways, the rest of the nation as well. The walls of segregation were about to come tumbling down, but not without the efforts and commitment of tens of thousands and the sympathetic support of millions.

In April 1963 a series of demonstrations and sit-ins took place in Birmingham, Alabama, led by the Reverend Martin Luther King, Jr. While black demonstrators remained largely nonviolent, city police used police dogs, firehoses, and clubs to control them. A national television audience was treated to the sight of dogs, fangs bared, leaping at black people and other blacks being pinned against storefronts by powerful streams of water. President John Kennedy was said to have been sickened by the picture of the police dog attack.[2] Later that year, King led the March on Washington for Jobs and Freedom, at which he made his famous "I Have a Dream" speech. The momentum for racial change had been created, and the following year, Congress enacted legislation prohibiting segregation in public places.

These events—sit-ins, marches, nonviolent protest campaigns—were not the stuff of ordinary politics. They were extraordinary, unsettling, challenging. They involved dimensions of personal

287

commitment, of mass organization and arousal, and of conflict that lay outside the day-to-day agenda of political life.

In this chapter we take up some of the issues raised by **extraordinary politics**—that is, the politics of protest and mass involvement. This form of politics can involve conscience, but it also can involve violence and intimidation. It can be a politics of progress toward social justice, but also a politics of repression. There are many kinds of protest and many kinds of mass involvement. What is the place of such politics in a democracy? Do mass politics and protest enlarge democratic options, help fulfill the promise of democracy? Or do they threaten the civil order and respect for law required in a democracy?

## Extraordinary politics

The distinguishing features of extraordinary politics are strategies or actions that heat up the political atmosphere beyond its usual level—that seriously intensify the stakes in political struggles. Of course, what is ordinary in one political system can be extraordinary in another. A protestor carrying a sign reading "Down with the Government" would be a

288

fairly ordinary sight in Lafayette Park, across the street from the White House, but a quite extraordinary one in Red Square in Moscow, where the police would surely orchestrate his rapid disappearance. Still, even in a society in which such activity is protected, public protest represents a step toward extraordinary political action.

Extraordinary politics can be violent or nonviolent in nature. It can involve the actions of millions of individuals or the solitary protest of one dedicated person. The most extreme form of extraordinary politics is violent revolution. Even democracies have justified the resort to violence (as in the case of the American Revolution) by arguing that nothing less would have altered an intolerable political situation. Any comprehensive survey of world politics over the last two hundred years would reveal that instances of extraordinary politics have been extremely common in virtually all nations.[3]

Protestors and protest movements have many tactics at their disposal. We saw in Chapter 3 how varied were the tactics employed by the American colonists in protests against the British government. They refused to pay certain taxes; they held demonstrations; they intimidated governmental officials and vandalized property; they banded together in secret and semisecret organizations; they armed themselves; and in the end, they made war. New protest tactics are forever being invented.

The simplicity of the sit-in tactic made it easy to practice in many situations, although sit-ins often brought real danger to the participants, who were sometimes beaten, harassed, and arrested. These blacks sit at a lunch counter in Charlotte, N.C. in the early 1960s, shortly after the initial sit-ins in Greensboro.

One of the purposes of a democratic political process is to allow the preferences of citizens to be expressed through nonviolent political means and through established political channels on a regular basis. Yet, as we have already noted on several occasions, democratic practices are never perfect—and even if they were, issues that could not be addressed within the context of ordinary politics might arise. Often, the avenues of change seem to be blocked, or issues are particularly pressing and significant for moral or other reasons. Under such conditions, people are likely, sooner or later, to resort to extraordinary politics. In doing so, they raise the political ante and take the risks that such tactics involve—both for themselves and for the polity as a whole. Reviewing U.S. history, we can easily isolate the issues that led to such significant protest movements as the antislavery movement, the movement for women's suffrage, the Ku Klux Klan, the Prohibition movement, the antiwar movements of World War I and the Vietnam War, the civil rights movement, the environmental movement, the nuclear freeze movement, the anti-abortion movement.[4]

Some readers may be startled to find the civil rights movement and the Ku Klux Klan placed in the same category. Of course, it *does* make a difference from the viewpoint of democratic theory whether a movement is violent or nonviolent, and whether it is prodemocratic or antidemocratic in aim. We will examine such questions as the chapter develops. But it must be understood that extraordinary politics can be used by forces of any political or social persuasion; can be employed to help prevent change as well as to make change possible; and can be used by the powerful as well as by the weak, although we usually associate it with the latter. As we will see, government itself sometimes resorts to extraordinary politics in dealing with politically difficult and explosive situations.

Move and countermove in Warsaw, Poland, August, 1981. When police blockaded the route of a planned demonstration, bus and trolley drivers retaliated by creating a massive traffic jam. In the struggle for power and democracy in Poland in the early 1980s, a military government took the extreme step of declaring martial law (1981), arresting Solidarity union leaders, and declaring the movement illegal. But Solidarity, though stunned, went underground and by the mid-1980s had shown its capacity to survive. Polish protesters proved particularly creative in finding new ways to express their grievances, even under conditions of extensive police control.

# The invisible empire

The Ku Klux Klan was born in December 1865 as an organization dedicated to the use of violence and terror to ensure the social and political subordination of blacks in the South. It flourished in the late 1860s, then ceased to exist as an organized group. The Klan lay dormant for close to fifty years, during which time two developments set the stage for a resurgence of Klan activity.

First of all, between 1878 and 1914 about 23 million people emigrated to the United States.

These immigrants were not always welcomed by the sons and daughters of earlier immigrants. Second, World War I left many Americans leery of change and modernity. To them, modernity meant only the waning of church influence, a breakdown of parental control over children, and the decline of customs and traditions. Distrustful of aliens and threatened by economic dislocation and rapid social change, some Americans responded by developing a siege mentality, which manifested itself in the rebirth of the Klan.

In 1915 the Klan was reconstituted as the Invisible Empire of the Ku Klux Klan, whose stated purpose was to defend the country against "aliens, idlers, strike leaders and immoral women." By June 1920, membership stood at a few thousand. That year, however, its founders reorganized the Invisible Empire. The new pitch was "pro-American," and anyone perceived as a threat to "American" interests was considered anti-American. The Klan of 1920 has been described as chameleonic: anti-Japanese on the West Coast, anti-Mexican in the Southwest, anti-Catholic in the Midwest, anti-black in the South, anti–foreign-born in the big cities, and anti-Jewish on the East Coast. By appealing to people's fears of economic and social change, it found an increasingly large audience. By 1921, as the list of Klan enemies grew to include "bootleggers, dope, graft, nightclubs,

Above, members of the Ku Klux Klan urge resistance to integration. The Klan also supported, and sometimes ran, candidates for public office. But such legal, public activity was not typical. The Klan gained its legendary reputation for violence with cross-burning ceremonies, shootings, and lynchings (right).

---

| | The whys |
| | of protest |

Some of the reasons why protests develop in democratic states have already been alluded to. At times, vital issues are at stake and many people feel that they must take extraordinary action (as in the case of freeze advocates or contemporary antiabortion demonstrators). At other times, protestors view governments as unresponsive to moral issues or involved in immoral actions (as did those who opposed slavery or the Vietnam War). Protest can also be directed toward arousing the conscience of one's fellow citizens (as was the case with the civil rights movement), or it can simply represent a moral statement (as in the case of conscientious objectors). Finally, protest activities can be directed against the private, rather than the public, sector. Civil rights demonstrators sat-in at a Woolworth's in Greensboro, not at a city office. Auto workers staged dramatic sit-ins at General Motors plants during the 1930s, protesting the refusal of the company to recognize their union. In all these examples of extraordinary political activity, people have been moved to protest because they believed it necessary either to resist a perceived evil or to dramatize a commitment.

Protest may take the form of a chaotic riot rather

violations of the Sabbath, sex and scandalous behavior," membership swelled to about one hundred thousand.

In 1922 the Klan helped elect governors in Georgia, Alabama, California, and Oregon. Texas sent a Klansman to the Senate, and Klan campaigns helped unseat two Jewish congressmen. By 1924 nationwide membership was estimated at 2 to 3 million. In August 1925, forty thousand Klan members marched down Pennsylvania Avenue and on to the Washington Monument.

After peaking at 4 to 5 million in the mid-1920s, Klan membership declined precipitously. Klan violence finally backfired, and scandals involving Klan leadership hastened the organization's deterioration. A march in 1926 attracted only half the previous number of participants. Klan-controlled candidates were routed at the polls that fall, and in 1928 the Democratic Party nominated Al Smith, a Catholic, as its presidential candidate. By 1930, membership had fallen to a few hundred thousand. It was not until the civil rights struggles of the 1950s and 1960s that a much-reduced Klan revived yet again.

than a concerted political movement. In the "long, hot summers" of the 1960s, for example, rioting, arson, and looting erupted in the black ghettos of many U.S. cities. This nation has a long history of race riots, most of which have begun with attacks by whites on blacks. The political content of such outbursts has often been hard to determine, because they characteristically have lacked concrete political goals. We must recognize, however, that riots often do have important political consequences and that they almost invariably represent a form of social assertion, even if a self-destructive one.[5] As Emerson once said, "Sometimes a scream is better than a thesis." In these situations, mass preferences and hatreds are articulated in visceral ways. In many cases, the social system and its values have prepared the way for such activities. Mob violence against and the lynching of blacks, for example, was made possible by a sociopolitical value system in which blacks were viewed as inferiors—as less than fully human. And the black riots of the 1960s were facilitated by widespread cynicism and hopelessness within the ghetto, where crime was common and police authority often despised.

This point brings us to another aspect of protest. One of the most widely argued theories of protest and rebellion (not confined to democratic political contexts) is that most political protest grows out of a

291

sense of *relative deprivation:* that is, the feeling that one's group is being deprived of the life chances enjoyed by other groups in the society.[6] The exact form that deprivation-caused protest takes depends on how intensely people feel about their deprivation, how they feel about resorting to protest, how much force is likely to be used against them, how many allies they have, and numerous other factors. Nonetheless, we can use the concept of relative deprivation as a starting point for exploring the origins of certain forms of protest. Interestingly, people often do not feel deprived until after they have entertained *increased* expectations of a better life in the future. Many revolutions have broken out after people who had experienced some improvement in their situation subsequently lapsed into worsened circumstances.

Value differences between groups can trigger a move toward extraordinary politics, especially if one group fears that it is losing power or influence. Threatened groups sometimes reach far beyond the usual range of political action to embrace genuinely violent measures. After the Civil War, for example, Southern whites who felt threatened by the new social order founded the Ku Klux Klan and attempted, through violence and intimidation, to prevent blacks and their white sympathizers from gaining or maintaining political control in the South (see box).

Between the normal political activities—voting, giving money, lobbying, debating, organizing campaigns—and the extreme politics of revolution, violence, and intimidation, is an extensive repertoire of extraordinary political actions and tactics, including marches, sit-ins, and various acts of civil disobedience. As this chapter will make clear, however, many of these protest tactics are difficult to use successfully.

| Extraordinary politics and government action

Protestors do not have a monopoly on extraordinary political activities. Governments, too, often resort to force, intimidation, coercion, and other unconven-

tional techniques in efforts to control or keep track of citizens.

The United States has a long and controversial history of the use of governmental force in social conflicts. The Civil War represents the prime such case. For many years governmental force was employed to protect the property rights of businesses in labor disputes. In more recent years we have the example of the National Guard shootings at Kent State in 1970 that killed four students and injured others. Though some people maintain that the troops needed to protect themselves from students protesting the Vietnam War, others argue the shootings were not necessary.[7]

The government has also resorted to other forms of extraordinary political activity. In 1919, government agents conducted a nationwide mass arrest of political and labor agitators and deported hundreds of aliens. Similarly, at the outbreak of World War II, thousands of Japanese-Americans were rounded up and interned (see Chapter 5). Perhaps the most subtle of all extraordinary methods the government employs are those used by investigative agencies such as the FBI and the CIA. In recent times, both agencies have engaged in such illegal or questionable practices as the infiltration of political groups, wiretapping, bugging, and harassment of individuals or groups.

There is another side to unconventional government actions, however. If governmental force has been used to control or repress legitimate dissent, it has also been employed for more-positive goals. In the 1950s and 1960s, for example, federal or state forces protected black students in the process of integrating schools and protest marchers in dangerous situations.

In the ideal democratic society, all government officials would understand the need for dissent and thus respect the rights of dissenters. They would have a sensible perspective on the meaning of conflict in a democratic society, and they would be able to tolerate criticism of their own policies—even serious, sustained criticism—without feeling the need to repress dissent. In the real world, unfortunately, even democratic leaders have been willing to resort to rather extreme measures to curb dissent. An almost paranoid attitude toward dissenters on the part of the Nixon administration was clearly revealed on the tapes of Oval Office conversations that were made public during the Watergate scandal of the early 1970s. An unpleasant tactic of the Establishment-under-attack is to try to link protest with treason. President Lyndon Johnson, for example, believed that the protest movement against the Vietnam War was aided by North Vietnam. More recently, President Ronald Reagan charged that the Soviet secret police were somehow involved in the peace movement in the United States and Western Europe. Such attitudes betray a failure to understand what the right of dissent is all about in a democracy.

In dealing with dissent or with alleged threats to national security, the government must carefully judge the amount of force to be used in particular situations. Governmental authorities may simply lose patience and unleash far more force than is necessary. Or they may display a lack of respect for the rights and dignity of those against whom force is applied.

Of course, dissenters, too, may interfere with the rights and well-being of other segments of society. During the Vietnam War era, supporters of the war

often were not permitted even to state their views on college campuses. In 1983 United Nations Ambassador Jeane Kirkpatrick was prevented from giving a speech at the University of California at Berkeley by protesting students who shouted her down. Actions of this nature raise basic questions about the limits of protest and the meaning of the rights guaranteed by the **First Amendment**.[8]

## Protest
## and disobedience
## in a democracy

That people living under a dictatorial regime might express political protests through mass demonstrations, sporadic violence, and even organized warfare does not seem surprising. When the normal channels of political expression are closed, citizens with intense grievances must find other ways to express their discontent. To the Nicaraguan citizens who, through popular protest and armed insurrection, overthrew the dictatorship of Antonio Somoza in 1979, such

National Guard troops at Kent State University, May, 1970. A fusillade of bullets, and in a few seconds four were dead and many wounded—people who had happened to be in the area when the Guard opened fire. This instance of government violence was variously condemned as an atrocity and applauded as a necessary use of force to maintain order.

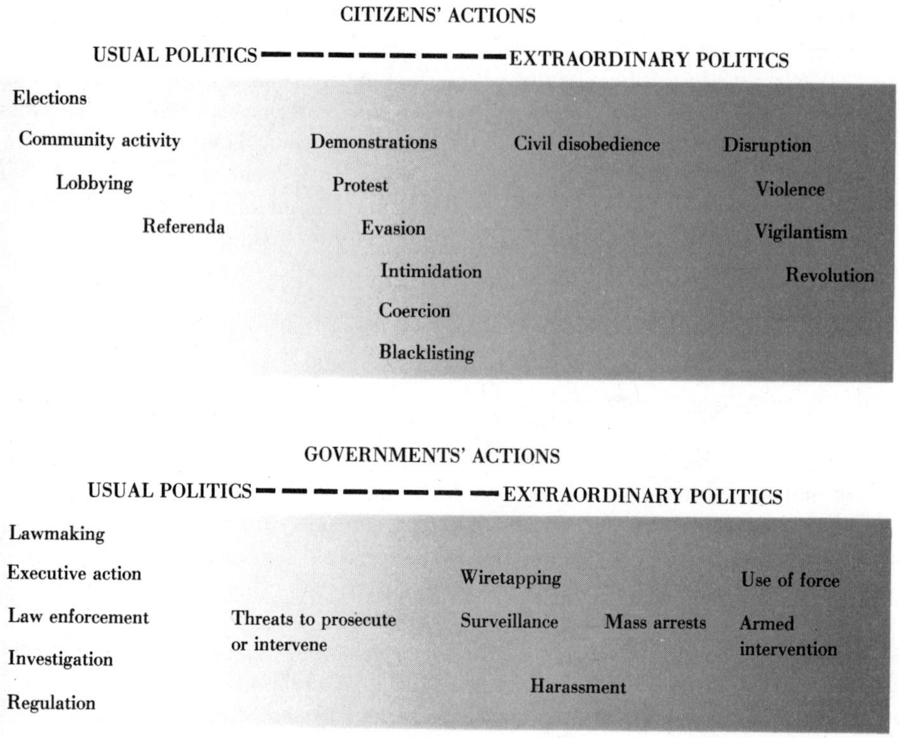

CITIZENS' ACTIONS

USUAL POLITICS — — — — — — — EXTRAORDINARY POLITICS

| | | | |
|---|---|---|---|
| Elections | | | |
| Community activity | Demonstrations | Civil disobedience | Disruption |
| Lobbying | Protest | | Violence |
| Referenda | Evasion | | Vigilantism |
| | Intimidation | | Revolution |
| | Coercion | | |
| | Blacklisting | | |

GOVERNMENTS' ACTIONS

USUAL POLITICS — — — — — — — EXTRAORDINARY POLITICS

| | | | | |
|---|---|---|---|---|
| Lawmaking | | | | |
| Executive action | | Wiretapping | | Use of force |
| Law enforcement | Threats to prosecute or intervene | Surveillance | Mass arrests | Armed intervention |
| Investigation | | | | |
| Regulation | | Harassment | | |

FIGURE 12.1

Types of political actions by citizens and governments.

extraordinary political activities offered the only realistic means of toppling a tyrant.[9] Similarly, the strikes that paralyzed Poland in the summer and fall of 1980, leading to the departure of the Polish leader Edward Gierek, represented the understandable response to dictatorship of a citizenry that was forbidden to organize an opposition political party or to engage in open political activity against the government.[10]

Extraordinary politics is easier to understand when democratic forms are lacking. What else can people do, it seems reasonable to ask, when they cannot express themselves freely, when there is no First Amendment, when there are no competing political parties or genuine elections? Yet many forms of extraordinary politics also take place under more-or-less democratic regimes. Here we will explore the complicated questions of why citizens of democracies sometimes feel compelled to engage in extraordinary political activities, and when and how such activities can be justified.

294

## Law and disobedience

The idea that disobedience to existing law may sometimes be necessary has a long lineage. The ancient Greeks recognized a higher law that prevailed over manmade law. Christian theologians have long argued over the meaning of Jesus's statement that one should "render unto Caesar that which is Caesar's, and render unto God that which is God's." What if the demands of conscience ("render unto God") conflict with the demands of the government ("render unto Caesar")?[11] What if moral justice conflicts with societal laws? In the view of some theologians, a higher law, as expressed in Christian teachings, can *compel* disobedience to manmade laws in some circumstances. Thus, many pacifists have argued that their consciences forbade them to kill, even if the state required military service.[12]

Perhaps the most eloquent and influential advo-

# Comparative
# perspective
# Gandhi
# and *satyagraha*

Mohandas K. Gandhi (1869–1948), widely regarded as one of the premier political innovators of the twentieth century, pioneered the use of nonviolent direct-action campaigns for political and social justice. After being educated as a lawyer in England, Gandhi returned briefly to his native India and then moved to Africa, where he led the Indian population in efforts to combat racial discrimination. After returning to India in 1915, he led nonviolent campaigns designed to gain independence from British rule and to correct injustices in Indian society.

Gandhi coined the term *satyagraha*, or "truth-

force," to describe the essence of a nonviolent mass campaign. Those who follow *satyagraha*, Gandhi wrote, believe that it is better to suffer than inflict suffering on others; that one's opponents are also human and therefore can be persuaded; that nonviolence is a truth-seeking instrument through which a political situation can be opened up; and that deep-rooted injustice must be confronted, and in many cases organized nonviolence offers the only real alternative to violence. In Gandhi's view, a *satyagrahi* (fol-

lower of *satyagraha*) must be more than simply a passive sufferer—he or she must confront evil with an intense, disciplined conviction. Yet, Gandhi also believed that even a sincere *satyagrahi* could be mistaken, which made nonviolence toward others all the more important.[*]

Gandhi felt that a well-thought-out nonviolent campaign should involve two stages.[†] In preparing for mass action, the campaigners should launch an educational effort to acquaint people with the issues involved. After such preparations should come the action

phase of the campaign, in which *satyagrahis* commit carefully considered acts of civil disobedience. Communication with opponents should be maintained during this phase, for the campaigners must be ready to negotiate at all times, so long as basic principles are not sacrificed. Gandhi's own mass campaigns ranged in duration from seven weeks to sixteen months.

Not all of Gandhi's campaigns were entirely successful or entirely nonviolent. But they had a tremendous cumulative effect in demonstrating the possibility of employing organized nonviolence as a method of social struggle. There is no doubt that not only were they crucial in India's evolution toward independence, but that they had a profound impact on the civil rights movement in the United States.

[*]Mohandas K. Gandhi, *An Autobiography* (Boston: Beacon Press, 1971).
[†]Joan V. Bondurant, *Conquest of Violence* (Berkeley, Cal.: University of California Press, 1969).

cate of disobedience in American history was Henry David Thoreau (1817–62). In the 1840s, as a protest against both the Mexican-American War and the continued existence of slavery, Thoreau refused to pay a portion of his local taxes. For this action, he was arrested and jailed. He defended his position in a brief essay titled "On the Duty of Civil Disobedience," in which he referred to "a government in which the majority rule in all cases cannot be based on justice." He went on: "I think that we should be men first, and subjects afterward. It is not desirable to cultivate a respect for the law, so much as for the right." And finally: "There will never be a really free and enlightened State, until the State comes to recognize the individual as a higher and independent power."[13]

Was Thoreau a fanatic—the apostle of views that, if widely accepted, would make any viable politics impossible? Or was he a man of justice who sought to awaken a democracy to its own cruelties? Indisputably, his writings had an enormous impact on modern political and social history. Particularly influenced by Thoreau's defense of civil disobedience were Mohandas Gandhi, India's famous advocate of nonviolent disobedience to unjust law (see box), and U.S. civil rights activist the Reverend Martin Luther King, Jr.

**Letter from the Birmingham jail:** In 1963, Dr. King led a major civil rights campaign in Birmingham, Alabama. The campaign involved protest marches and deliberate, nonviolent confrontations with city authorities in an effort to break the hold of segregation. Large numbers of protestors were jailed, including King himself. Eight Alabama clergymen published a letter raising questions about King's decision to confront the law rather than negotiate. In a letter written from the Birmingham city jail, King attempted to answer these questions.[14] Although this letter does not provide complete answers to all the issues involved in civil disobedience, it does offer some compelling arguments for deliberate disobedience of unjust laws.

In the letter, King argues that one can judge whether

a law is unjust, and thus may be disobeyed, by means of four criteria: it degrades human personality, it binds one group but not another, it is enacted by an unrepresentative authority, or it is unjustly applied. In King's view, the first three of these criteria applied to Birmingham's segregation ordinances and the fourth applied to otherwise valid laws, such as the need for proper parade permits, that were being unfairly applied to civil rights protestors.

How valid are these criteria? Although they are not crystal clear, they do furnish reasonable guidelines. The clearest and most easily applicable is the second—that a law should not bind one group and not another. When majorities make rules that discriminate against minorities, as was the case with segregation statutes, democratic norms clearly are violated. Of course, there are also sensible laws that bind one group and not others, such as those that deny children access to pornography or alcohol. Such laws, however, are based on *reasonable* criteria. They are not arbitrary.

Similarly, with regard to the third criterion (un-representative authority), it is often clear when democratic norms have been violated—particularly when the political process has been deliberately and systematically skewed against one group. A much more problematic criterion is that of degradation of human personality. Clearly, different people would apply such a general principle in different ways. Yet it is also clear that segregation degraded blacks through systematic inequality.

Dr. King concluded his letter with a warning about the consequences of disobeying a law:

One who breaks an unjust law must do so openly, lovingly, and with a willingness to accept the penalty. I submit that an individual who breaks a law that conscience tells him is unjust, and who willingly accepts the penalty of imprisonment in order to arouse the conscience of the community over its injustice, is in reality expressing the highest respect for law.

The case for direct action against laws perpetuating segregation was, in a way, an easy one to make—although we should remember that it was highly controversial at the time and that King was charged with

Marches were a major dramatic element in the civil rights movement of the 1960s. In these two photos, Martin Luther King, Jr., leads protesters against segregation. The march served as a symbolic affirmation of unity and a courageous public declaration of a people's grievances.

A multitude of flags, most of them American, but some representing the Viet Cong and North Vietnam, fly at the huge Moratorium Rally in Washington in 1969 protesting the Vietnam War. The antiwar movement grew from its early roots in universities to embrace a wide spectrum of the population by the late 1960s.

As in many large and diverse movements, tensions arose among different factions over basic philosophies, goals, and strategies. Protest politics, like all politics, calls on symbolic forms of expression to embody the feelings of the group and communicate to others.

fomenting anarchy and worse. If we turn to the issues posed by the Vietnam War, however, matters grow more complicated.

**Vietnam and illegitimate authority:** There has been domestic opposition to most American wars. Abraham Lincoln, as a young congressman, had opposed the Mexican War in 1848. Many voices were raised against U.S. involvement in World War I and, as we saw in Chapter 5, important civil liberties cases developed out of that dissent. And although World War II was a highly popular war, many conscientious objectors refused to serve in the armed forces. The Vietnam War, however, aroused greater and more sustained domestic opposition than had any previous war. During the 1960s and early 1970s, antiwar activities raised many serious questions about the value and limits of dissent in a democracy.

Opponents of U.S. involvement in Vietnam tried many tactics in attempting to end the war and to

alter foreign policy decisions. Many individuals refused to serve in the armed forces, and some publicly burned their draft cards. Others committed acts of civil disobedience such as blocking the entrances to military facilities with their bodies and sitting-in against military recruiters on campuses. In most of these cases the protestors were practicing classic forms of civil disobedience.[15] As the war went on and disenchantment grew more intense, however, some segments of the antiwar movement advocated an escalation in acts of protest. A more aggressive form of resistance or coercion, they argued, was needed to bring about meaningful change. These radicals visualized thousands of protestors blocking all the buildings of the federal government, sitting-in day after day at the White House, perhaps even bringing to a halt the machinery of government. Some argued that such large-scale protests should be recognized as a legal right.

There was an obvious problem with such proposals: What if those who did not favor antiwar policies reacted by doing their own "coercing"? Activities of this nature actually did take place, most notably when construction workers attacked student antiwar demonstrators in New York City in 1971. Once the Pandora's box of coercion is opened, one cannot know exactly how far developments may go. Yet, it is also easy to understand the frustration of those who felt that because the war was immoral, even extreme protest measures were justified, whatever the risks involved. How should we judge protest activities, then? By the motives of those who commit them? On the basis of how much harm they inflict on society? Or by the goals they embody?

## Civil disobedience:
## a compromise

It is clear even in a perfect democracy, all the problems of making just, sensible, humane public policy would not disappear. And present-day democracies are far from perfect. Political representatives in democracies can and do act cruelly, unjustly, foolishly. Democratic processes do furnish citizens relatively good means by which to change or affect public policies. But these means are limited: elections occur only occasionally; public opinion may be easily swayed; leaders may deceive, or lack judgment or political courage. As a result, citizens may be confronted with difficult moral choices. What then?

The classic stance of the democratic protestor has been to embrace a form of civil disobedience that straddles the line between law and justice. Classic **civil disobedience** (that espoused by Thoreau, Gandhi, and King) involves a public act committed to arouse the conscience of the society by a person who is fully willing to accept the punishment prescribed by law. Such persons must be morally serious. They must not act secretly, or use violence to intimidate or harm. In expressing protest or violating laws, they stay within a context of respect for others and for law itself. This strategy seems to offer a sensible compromise—one that democracy can live with, and that enriches our sense of what democracy means and of how individual conscience and social norms interact.[16] According to one student of the subject,

What society needs is a struggle sufficiently equal to compel a process of public reasoning, which is its best protection against error. To prohibit freedom of speech, to forbid strikes and boycotts, and to punish civil disobedience by death would enable governments to overwhelm protest without having to reason. At the other extreme, not only to permit free speech, strikes and boycotts but also to legalize civil disobedience and disruption . . . would enable the dissenting minority to dictate to the majority. . . . A more equal and fruitful balance might be obtained by permitting boycotts but forbidding disruption, and penalizing civil disobedience, but only moderately.[17]

We should recognize, however, that no matter what balance is struck between order and protest, some citizens will feel that it is sometimes morally imperative to protest policies or disobey laws they view as unjust. At the same time, some public officials will always regard civil disobedience as just another sort of crime, ignoring its morally significant content.

## How
## protest
## works

Effective protest involves more than simply the voicing of objections to policies or conditions. Many complex concepts are associated with protest activity.

## Consciousness-
## raising

The first step in the development of protest is the shaping of the consciousness of the protestor. The core of protest is, always, the protestor—the person who is willing to make the commitment, to take the step of publicly declaring a grievance. Many students of rebellion have acknowledged that radicalization of the victims of an unjust social system is the most difficult step that a protest movement must take. This is why leadership is so important in protest movements. Leaders must demonstrate that a new consciousness and a new courage are possible, and that inner change must precede public action.

## Activating
## others

Once a new mass consciousness begins to develop, the protest group usually must seek to forge alliances with other groups in a society. The civil rights movement in the United States, for example, needed significant nonblack support to topple the pillars of segregation. To that end, civil rights leaders sought to activate third parties, to find help both within and outside the governmental structures. The activation of such help can be difficult. It is usually accomplished by appeals, by threats, or by a combination of the two tactics.

In making appeals, protestors try to call attention to the injustice, suffering, or deprivation they face in such a way that outside groups or individuals will be moved to help them. The extent to which appeals will generate public concern, which in turn will activate government officials, depends on many factors: the actual degree of suffering, the extent to which the public acknowledges this suffering and regards it as unjust, the extent to which the protesting group is regarded as worthy of social concern, and the extent to which the public perceives that the system has the resources necessary to remedy these concerns.

If appeals fail, threats can be employed. One of the principal weapons of protestors is the threat of disruption—of making it more difficult for society to carry on its business. Gandhi astutely combined appeals and threats in his nonviolent campaigns. He knew that when the streets are filled with demonstrators, the jails filled with protestors, and the court dockets jammed with cases, governments find it difficult to maintain business as usual, and thus are more willing to listen to protestors.

# Getting into the system: the migrant farmworkers

Protest groups usually are successful only if (1) they are motivated, (2) they are capable of mobilizing political resources, and (3) they can outlast the efforts to oppose them. For decades, migrant farmworkers did not meet either of the first two conditions, and their employers, in collusion with local, state, and federal authorities, were able to crush the few efforts at organization that looked as if they might succeed.

This was the situation in the 1960s, when Cesar Chavez began his efforts to organize migrant workers. Chavez had experience both as a migrant farmworker and as a labor organizer in Los Angeles. Chavez was the energizer, the galvanizer: he spoke of sacrifice and the need for Chicanos (Mexican-Americans) to overcome white cultural dominance. He led protest marches and strikes, and he fasted for several weeks when violence threatened to take over his peaceful movement. He proclaimed the farmworkers' group *La Causa*, "the movement," and set as its goals cooperative farming, worker control, and fundamental social change.

Along with being an inspirational leader, Chavez was a shrewd organizer. Knowing that the farmworkers needed immediate small victories if the movement was to enlist the energies of the poor, he organized in an area where farmworkers were not transient and crops grew all year. It was also a less poor area, where union dues, although not exorbitant, were initially sufficient for the seed money to print materials and hire lawyers.

Perhaps Chavez's cleverest strategy was the secondary boycott, aimed at the large markets on which fruit and vegetable producers depended. Chavez and the United Farmworkers Union (UFW) enlisted the help of volunteers, churches, and even some grocery chains across the United

Cesar Chavez, organizer of migrant farm workers, in a moment of repose during one of his hunger strikes. Following the example of Gandhi, Chavez used the fast to dramatize the movement's grievances. Such tactics, however, take their toll on the leader, who must confront his own uncertainties and the possibility of failure.

States to call attention to farmworker problems and to help mount a boycott of agribusiness produce in general, and of grapes in particular. By 1970, 85 percent of the table-grape growers in California had been forced to sign contracts with unions. Strawberry and lettuce growers soon followed suit. The election of a sympathetic Edmund G. Brown, Jr.,

Threats can also take more sinister forms: for example, protesting groups can threaten or carry out acts of violence. Such tactics, however, often backfire, toughening the resolve of opponents and creating emotional antagonism.

| Contexts for
| effective protest

Protest is most effective when it takes place in a favorable context. Protestors have a better chance of success when other, more powerful groups in the society can be mobilized on behalf of protest objectives or when protest tactics coincide with the objectives of influential politicians or public officials. The actions of the civil rights movement in the early 1960s, for example, coincided with the election of a liberal Democratic administration.

Protest tactics can sometimes force a government to recognize that the protestors have a valid claim to be heard in the political process. But once they gain such a hearing, protestors must rely once again on influence of a more routine kind. So although it may place issues on the public agenda, help provide a protest group with higher standing in public controversies, or enhance the group's organizational development, protest by itself is not enough to accom-

as governor of California helped the cause considerably. At Brown's urging, the state legislature granted farmworkers the right to choose which union would represent them—something that had been denied previously. By 1978 the UFW had signed one hundred contracts with growers.

The farmworkers' movement thus resulted in a victory for group politics. But the price was very high: years of extreme economic deprivation, jailings, beatings, intimidation. That was what it had taken for a socially weak, marginal group to join the system of group politics and make its voice heard in the political process.*

*For an overview of the farmworkers' situation, see Peter Matthiessen, *Sal Si Puedes* (New York: Dell, 1969).

plish policy objectives. In fact, it is a somewhat precarious tool on which to rely, as we will see.

### Limitations of protest tactics

Effective protest usually lies uneasily on the borderline between legitimacy and illegitimacy. Because of this delicate balancing act, protest demonstrations often run the risk of alienating potentially sympathetic groups and of arousing opposing groups to action. It is a matter of strategy (rarely an easy calculation) to anticipate whether the costs of a given protest tactic will outweigh its benefits. Decisions regarding protest strategy are particularly delicate when a protest group has begun to gain success, for the wrong choice may lead to the loss of alliances that have been forged with other groups.

An understandable reluctance to alienate supporters and sympathizers may account in part for the tendencies of protest groups to become more cautious and restrained as they grow in power and status. The decision to try protest tactics and to risk the possible alienation of newly developed allies is easier to make for protest groups with relatively little power, because they have relatively little to lose. Such groups, however, may not have the resources to organize protest campaigns. The lack of such resources may even place an effective protest campaign beyond their reach. Protest success also depends on gaining media coverage, which aids greatly in activating outside groups. Without publicity, protest tactics may be meaningless. The most successful protest leaders in recent years have been those who have raised the ability to gain publicity to an art form.

As we saw in Chapter 10, the news media not only report the news—they also can shape it in significant ways. Protest leaders design tactics in response to their understanding of what editors will consider newsworthy. Tactics often escalate in severity or militance for the simple reason that what is news on one day will be old hat the following week. The drama and symbolism of protest are often integral parts of its forceful communication. The Boston Tea Party

springs to mind in this regard, as does the Reverend Martin Luther King's March on Washington for Jobs and Freedom in August 1963.

Sometimes those who are the targets of protest command significant resources to limit or undermine protest strategies. Such resources include

*Delaying tactics*—e.g., appointing a commission or relegating a problem to study.

*Tokenism*—conceding a tiny fraction of what is desired while giving the impression that a significant concession has been made.

*Discreditation*—attempting to damage a group's credibility or legitimacy in the public arena.

*Suppression*—utilizing police actions of various kinds.

Thus, although protest is one of the few resources available to relatively powerless groups, its potential is often highly limited.

### Protest through the ballot: initiatives and referenda

One form of mass participation that has become increasingly prominent in U.S. state politics in recent years stands between protest and normal electoral politics. This is a form of **direct legislation**, specifically, the initiative and the referendum.[18] An **initiative** allows citizens to present a measure directly to voters, thus bypassing the legislature. A **referendum** is a direct popular vote that allows the electorate to approve or reject a law or policy. Referenda and initiatives are not necessarily forms of protest; often they deal with decidedly uncontroversial issues—a 1978 referendum in Oregon passed a measure allowing lab technicians to fit false teeth, for instance. Sometimes, however, they serve as vehicles

One of the more famous initiatives in recent U.S. history, Proposition 13, to cut property taxes in California, takes a resounding lead on election night.

for deeply felt, urgent issues—nuclear power plants, the death penalty, property taxes, gun control, the manufacture of nuclear weapons.

Referenda in this nation date back to the American Revolution, when several states submitted their new constitutions to citizens for approval. The use of the initiative did not develop until the end of the nineteenth century. The form of referendum most widely used today is the constitutional referendum; every state but Delaware requires that proposed constitutional amendments be submitted to voters in this way. Many states also submit certain local measures to voters as referenda. These local referenda number from ten to fifteen thousand a year and typically include such items as local bonds, tax rate changes, and school financing, as well as such controversial issues as fluoridation of local water supplies.

The United States is one of the few democratic countries that does not have a national referendum or other form of direct national legislation. A proposal submitted in the Senate in 1977 that would have created a national initiative failed to pass.

There is some debate about whether this kind of direct legislation generally leads to liberal or to conservative outcomes. A number of states have used initiatives and referenda to pass laws regarding political honesty, consumer protection, nuclear waste disposal, and nonreturnable cans and bottles, all liberal measures that may well not have passed state legislatures because of powerful interest-group lobbying. A recent study of initiatives and referenda between 1945 and 1984 that involved liberal/conservative choices concluded that the split was close to fifty/fifty.[19]

# Comparative perspective the Swedish nuclear referendum

One of the weaknesses of representative democracy is that political parties, parliaments, and congresses are often slow to address crucially important problems and issues. One way for constituents to supplement—or supplant—legislative representation is with a referendum.

In March, 1980, some 4.7 million Swedes, about 95 percent of the electorate, participated in a national referendum on nuclear energy policy. It was one of the first plebiscites ever held on the nuclear energy issue and the culmination of several years of debate within Swedish politics. The Swedish Establishment—

the Social Democratic Party, the trade unions congress, big business, and most major newspapers—had long opposed a referendum on the issue. At stake was the most extensive nuclear energy program in Europe: six reactors already in operation, four ready for start-up, and two under construction. Dismantling the existing reactors would be enormously expensive, both in terms of lost jobs and wasted expenditures. There was also the problem of finding alternative energy sources. Sweden has no oil and little coal. However, it happens to sit on a huge uranium deposit, one of the key materials for generating nuclear energy.

The turning point on the issue came after the 1979 accident at Three Mile Island. Within days, Prime Minister Olof Palme, speaking for the Social Democrats, reversed his opposition to a referendum, and the government quickly agreed. Voters were presented with three alternatives on the referendum ballot. Alternatives I and II were virtually identical, calling for the completion of the partly-

finished program but with a phase-out of nuclear power in twenty-five years (coincidentally the average lifespan of a nuclear reactor). Alternative II, supported by the Social Democrats and liberals, differed from the conservative-backed Alternative I by using language that favored government ownership, energy conservation, and the development of alternative energy sources (chiefly hydroelectric power). Both alternatives were a plea to maintain the status quo for the time being. Alternative III, led by the People's Campaign against Nuclear Power and the Center Party, called for the program to be dismantled and mandated the phase-out of nuclear power in ten years.

The outcome, after a heated campaign on both sides, might best be described as yes/no: 58 percent voted for one of the first two Alternatives; 39 percent chose Alternative III. The referendum was not constitutionally binding, but it did oblige the government to go ahead with the national program for twenty-five years. This go-ahead includes some qualifications, however. Swedish

voters decidedly did *not* embrace nuclear energy as a long-term solution to energy problems, and twenty-five years is not a very long time in which to devise alternative energy policies.

Although the 1980 referendum did not, in itself, change Swedish energy policy, it did provide a framework within which Swedes could discuss and debate policies. Out of that debate emerged a changed orientation to the issue of nuclear power, which in turn resulted in a new energy policy. A major energy bill passed in 1981 called for reduced dependency on oil imports, total abandonment of nuclear power after 2010, development of sustainable and renewable energy sources, and a largescale effort to reduce energy demand.

Direct legislation has been widely used in California. In recent years especially, initiative and referendum campaigns have become highly organized and often very expensive. Media campaigns have come to be used extensively, complete with carefully engineered images, slogans, and brief TV spots. Citizens in California sometimes use initiatives as a means of public education. For example, a proposal to decriminalize marijuana use has no chance of obtaining the needed majority, but has appeared on the ballot several times.

What are the pros and cons of direct legislation? On the pro side we can look to the Progressives in the early days of this century, who argued that "the cure for the ills of democracy is more democracy." They maintained that the initiative and referendum would bring government closer to the people, would allow issues to be raised and discussed rather than being suppressed by politicians, would provide an accurate gauge of public sentiment, and would revive interest in political life. Overall, the increased involvement of the citizens through referenda and initiatives, the Progressives argued, would serve the public interest rather than that of political parties, officeholders, and other politicians. Direct democracy would help to clarify public purposes and create a more informed and mature public opinion.

What are the arguments on the other side? For one, many have doubted the ability of ordinary citizens to understand, let alone decide, complex questions of public policy. Moreover, there is the threat that temporary or passionate majorities may arise which will enact laws that may in fact be ill-considered or discriminatory. The delays and compromises required to pass bills in a legislature often serve to protect minority rights. Another danger is that more-direct democracy may weaken governmental institutions and the process of representation in general. Citizens may come to respect legislatures and politicians less than they do now, and potential candidates may be less inclined to seek office if they know that their powers may be easily undermined by direct legislation. Whereas some commentators insist that direct legislation will be used only if politicians fail to respond to popular needs, others argue that it will

always be difficult to prevent well-organized (and diverse) interests from using them, regardless of how elected officials conduct themselves.

## Conclusions

If we could devise a system so perfect that it would never turn out wrong decisions, then we could forget about protest tactics and stick to politics as usual. It hardly needs to be said that such a political process is nowhere in sight. In the nature of real democratic politics, some needs are ignored, others deliberately neglected. Not all interests are heard in the interest-group process. As society changes, some groups and individuals find their values threatened, their status undermined, their expectations dashed.

"A little rebellion now and then is a good thing, and as necessary in the political world as storms are in the physical," declared Thomas Jefferson, in a particularly revolutionary mood. Protest is useful to a democratic society. For those whose consciences are offended, it provides a way of expressing discontent or voicing disagreement. Protest is also a signal that some of our fellow citizens are aroused. It can educate us about the problems others face. It can arouse the typically lethargic conscience of the majority. Protest, when successful, helps to focus our attention on matters that otherwise might be ignored.

On the other hand, protest and extraordinary politics can be a nuisance—or worse, a serious danger to life, liberty, and democratic processes. Protest can be animated by a spirit that is alien to democracy, or carried out in such a way that basic democratic values are put in jeopardy. When the Ku Klux Klan sought to stop blacks from exercising basic political rights—when vigilantism was rampant and intimidation a common fact of life—extraordinary politics posed a deeply serious threat to democratic progress.

It is often not easy to decide whether protest is justified. One thing we can say, however, is that when protest is a tool of the weak, when it is carried out in a spirit of moral seriousness, and when its goals are compatible with democratic values (as in the case of the civil rights movement of the 1950s and 1960s), then it surely will enrich our political life.

## NOTES

1 For a careful description, see Milton Viorst, *Fire in the Streets* (New York: Simon and Schuster, 1979), Chapter 3.

2 Frederich F. Siegel, *Troubled Journey: From Pearl Harbor to Reagan* (New York: Hill & Wang, 1984), pp. 148–49.

3 There is a detailed analysis of civil strife and protest in many nations in Ted R. Gurr, "A Comparative Study of Civil Strife," pp. 572–626, and Raymond Tanter, "International War and Domestic Turmoil: Some Contemporary Evidence," pp. 550–69, both in Ted R. Gurr and Hugh D. Graham, eds., *The History of Violence in America* (New York: Praeger, 1969).

4 See Alec Barbrook and Christine Bolt, *Power and Protest in American Life* (New York: St Martin's, 1980), Chapter 9 for a discussion of what issues generate protest and how group power is exercised in U.S. politics.

5 David O. Sears and John B. McConahay, *The Politics of Violence: The New Urban Politics and the Watts Riots* (Boston: Houghton Mifflin, 1973).

6 Ted Robert Gurr, *Why Men Rebel* (Princeton: Princeton University Press, 1970), Chapters 2 and 10.

7 James Michener, *Kent State: What Happened and Why* (New York: Random House, 1971).

8 See John Bunzel, *Anti-politics in America* (Westport, Conn.: Greenwood Press, 1979); Robert Paul Wolff, Barrington Moore, Jr., and Herbert Marcuse, *A Critique of Pure Tolerance* (Boston: Beacon Press, 1965).

9 Eduardo Crawley, *Dictators Never Die: Nicaragua and the Somoza Dynasty* (New York: St. Martin's, 1979).

10 Neal Ascherson, *The Polish August* (New York: Penguin, 1982).

11 One fascinating discussion can be found in Oscar Jaszi and John D. Lewis, *Against the Tyrant* (Glencoe, Ill.: Free Press, 1957).

12 See A. J. Muste, "Of Holy Disobedience," in Hugh Adam Bedau, *Civil Disobedience: Theory and Practice* (New York: Pegasus, 1969), pp. 127–34.

13 Henry David Thoreau, *Walden and Civil Disobedience* (New York: Signet, 1961), p. 223.

14 The letter can be found in M. L. King, Jr., *Why We Can't Wait* (New York: Signet, 1964). For a useful commentary on it, see Curtis Crawford, ed., *Civil Disobedience: A Casebook* (New York: Crowell, 1973), pp. 226–29.

15 David Dellinger, *More Power Than We Knew* (Garden City, N.Y.: Anchor Press, 1975).

16 See Elliot Zashin, *Civil Disobedience and Democracy* (New York: Free Press, 1972), Chapters V–IX.

17 C. Crawford, *Civil Disobedience: A Casebook*, p. 241.

18 Much of the information in this section is derived from David Butler and Austin Ranney, ed., *Referendums: A Comparative Study of Practice and Theory* (Washington, D.C.: American Enterprise Institute, 1978).

19 Austin Ranney, "Referendums and Initiatives, 1984," *Public Opinion*, December/January 1985, pp. 15–17.

## SELECTED READINGS

For mass politics and protest, see David J. Garrow, *Protest at Selma* (New Haven, Conn.: Yale University Press, 1978); Arnold Rice, *The Ku Klux Klan in American Politics* (New York: Haskell House, 1972); Robert Jay Lifton, *Revolutionary Immortality: Mao Tse-tung and the Chinese Cultural Revolution* (New York: Norton, 1976); Irwin Unger, *The Movement: A History of the American New Left, 1959–1972* (New York: Dodd, Mead, 1975); Lawrence Weschler, *Solidarity: Poland in the Season of its Passion* (New York: Simon and Schuster, 1982).

For more personal accounts of involvement in protest politics, see Robert Coles, *Children of Crisis: A Study of Courage and Fear* (New York: Dell, 1967); Sara Evans, *Personal Politics* (New York: Knopf, 1979); Kenneth Keniston, *Young Radicals* (New York: HBJ, 1968); William H. Grier and Price M. Cobbs, *Black Rage* (New York: Bantam, 1969); Alice Wexler, *Emma Goldman* (New York: Pantheon, 1984). On the moral issues involved in disobedience and protest, see Michael Walzer, *Obligations* (Cambridge, Mass.: Harvard University Press, 1970); John Rawls, *A Theory of Justice* (Cambridge, Mass.: Harvard University Press, 1972), pp. 363–91; Walter Stein, ed., *Nuclear Weapons and Christian Conscience* (London: Merlin Press, 1965); J. Roland Pennock and John W. Chapman, eds., *Nomos XII: Political and Legal Obligation* (New York: Atherton Press, 1970).

# Part three

# Institutions

# Chapter
# thirteen

# The workings of Congress

## Specialization or fragmentation?

THE act of legislating has long been regarded as the heart of the democratic political process. Early democratic theorists enshrined "the people" as the ultimate arbiters, the makers of law, who would both limit and extend their own freedom through the legislative acts of their representatives. Lawmaking would be a dignified and solemn process in which representatives of the people would gather to debate the issues of the day, develop policy for the entire society, compromise differences, and resolve disputes. Democratic politics would remain viable so long as the people were effectively and honestly represented and their representatives were intelligent and committed enough to create workable and democratic laws.

The descent from the lofty realm of democratic theory to the real world of democratic political practice, however, is a steep one. A pungent old saying bears on this topic: "There are two things one should never watch being made: sausage and legislation." The reasoning behind this observation is obvious. A close look at the democratic process may disillusion us, or worse. We will have to acknowledge how tawdry, imperfect, deceptive, confused, and occasionally corrupt this process can be.

This contrast between real and ideal will be the principal theme of Chapters 13 and 14. We will take an honest look at our own national legislature, the Congress, in order to arrive at plausible conclusions about how our particular legislature measures up to democratic requirements. Is Congress organized to do its job effectively, honestly, democratically? Are the many varied interests in our society, including the public interest, effectively represented? Are our legislators generally honest and competent?

Unlike most national legislatures, the U.S. Congress is an independent legislative body that does not merely pass laws, but also initiates and creates them. Congress decides how revenues are to be raised and spent, regulates commerce among the states and with other nations, and has the power to declare war. More generally, the Constitution gives Congress the power "to make Laws which shall be necessary and proper for carrying into execution the foregoing powers, and all other powers vested by this constitution in the government . . . or in any department or officer thereof."[1] This innocuous-sounding statement, which has come to be known as the "elastic clause," has provided the basis for a vast expansion of congressional power. To do what is "necessary and proper" gives Congress a great deal of latitude in deciding when and how to legislate.

These tasks add up to a heavy legislative burden, and one that has grown more onerous as the world

The U.S. Capitol. The formal dignity of the building itself is striking for Washington visitors. In the hurly-burly of everyday politics, it is easy to overlook the ultimate significance of the institutions we have created and sustained. But Americans are often of two minds about political life—revering the institutions, while disliking the politicians who people them.

has grown increasingly complex and societal interests more diverse and polarized. Does Congress consistently play a creative, constructive role in democratic life? Or does it more often fail to fashion workable policy, to resolve differences sensibly— even to stand for democratic principles?

Before we can answer these questions, we must examine the workings of Congress—its functions, its structure, its mode of operation. As a first step, we must establish what is meant by the term *representation*. As many a member of Congress has discovered, that is by no means an easy task.

## The nature of representation

There are two classic views of how legislators should represent their constituents. One group of political theorists has argued that *representation* should be taken literally: that is, that legislators should vote the way the majority of those who elected them would vote. This position is known as the *delegate theory*. Adherents of the opposing view, which is called the *trustee theory*, have maintained that representatives have a responsibility to vote their own convictions and to educate and lead their constituents. Constituents who don't like the results can vote the representative out at the next election. In practice, most members of Congress operate at various times under both of these theories, along with a third one—that of the *politico*, whose actions are conditioned to some degree by the need to compromise and make deals in the legislature itself.

An added complication in the representative function is that none of the members of Congress represents the whole of the country. Each of the 535 national legislators represents a specific segment of the society, and the interests of that segment often conflict with the interests of society as a whole. This fundamental problem in the way Congress functions is reflected vividly in the matter of defense spending. Were defense spending to be cut, many states and districts would lose local defense installations that may employ thousands of local inhabitants and pump millions of dollars into local economies. Although the national interest might best be served by cutting back on defense, that interest is likely to be pale in the face of local or regional economic needs. Of course, legislators often do look toward the larger interest, but in general they tend to be sharply constrained by constituency questions.

## Functions of Congress

Congress is more than a machine designed to crank out laws in a mechanical fashion year after year. Among other valuable functions, it provides the set-

ting for the airing of public policy issues and the deliberative crafting and shaping of legislative proposals, it helps to develop and oversee a national budget, and it oversees the administration of the laws it enacts and initiates investigations when called for. The Senate has the added function of accepting or rejecting numerous executive and judicial appointments made by the president. Each of these functions deserves close examination.

How do policy issues get aired in Congress? One might expect this to take place in debate on the House or Senate floor, but that is generally not the case. Most policy issues are thrashed out in committee and subcommittee hearings, in which legislators go over, often in considerable detail, the particulars of public policy.[2] A good example of the degree of public attention that can be focused on congressional hearings occurred in connection with U.S. policy toward El Salvador in 1981. At that time, the administration of President Ronald Reagan had requested more military aid for the Salvadoran government to counteract what it saw as a communist-backed insurgency. Robert White, the ambassador to El Salvador under former president Jimmy Carter, was able to voice his criticisms of this new policy

In the chamber of the House of Representatives, the president (Ronald Reagan, Jan. 22, 1983) delivers the annual State of the Union address before the assembled members of Congress, justices of the Supreme Court, members of the Cabinet, the Joint Chiefs of Staff, and foreign ambassadors. The momentary formal appearance of governmental unity present on such occasions quickly gives way to the push and shove of political battling that is characteristic of our system of separation of powers.

before television cameras at the congressional hearings. Thus, a point of view at odds with administration policy gained significant public attention through the hearings of a congressional committee. Given the usual preponderance of media attention accorded to administration spokesmen, this chance for critics to air their views plays an important role in keeping debate both public and lively.

The airing of policy matters may also take place in a larger forum, as when legislators use the media or the lecture circuit to address contemporary issues. Senators, in particular, often can locate a national audience to whom they can speak. Communication travels the other way, too: interest groups come to

Washington to make their voices heard in the corridors of Congress.

Congress's contribution to the shaping of laws is many-sided. Sometimes Congress initiates legislation, rather than waiting for direction from the president. At other times a president picks up ideas originally voiced by members of Congress. Another crucial element of law-shaping is the detailed consideration of proposed legislation. This process usually takes place in the committee and subcommittee hearings and in committee meetings, where legislation is "marked up"—that is, prepared for final consideration. In these discussions, lawmakers delve into the implications of legislative proposals, resolve conflicts, and fine-tune the wording of proposed legislation.

Congress also is responsible for legislating a budget. For many years, the budget process was an extremely chaotic one, characterized by the lack of a central-ized overview of what was being allocated and spent. In the 1970s, however, the budgetary process was reformed and the House and Senate budget committees established.[3] (The work of these committees will be discussed more fully later in the next chapter.)

Congress's *oversight* function involves following up on the implementation of programs that have already been approved. Until relatively recently, Congress usually performed this task in a somewhat haphazard way. Then, public concern over excessive taxes and governmental waste endowed the oversight function with enhanced political appeal. Methods of oversight range from routine audits and reporting requirements for agencies to more assertive legislative investigations, congressional vetoes, and even impeachment proceedings (by which Congress can remove certain officials from office). In recent years, Congress has moved toward a balanced, serious, and consistent evaluation of federal agencies and programs, prin-

---

# National versus local interests— an example

In May 1984, Dennis E. Eckart, a second-term Democrat from Ohio, cast the decisive vote to kill proposed legislation dealing with power plant emissions that allegedly were causing acid rain. What was most surprising about Eckart's vote was that he had been considered to be among the most environmentally-oriented legislators in the House. The League of Conservation Voters had given him a very favorable rating on environmental issues, and as a legislator in Ohio, he had made a strong reputation as an environmentalist. Eckart was also acutely aware of the environmental problems posed by acid rain, and he believed that power plant emissions were a major source of the pollutants that caused it. He had been under tremendous pressure from environmentalists to vote in favor of the proposals.

Explaining his "no" vote, Eckart argued that local effects of the new rules were of primary concern to him. "This is not just an environmental issue. . . . It is an economic and consumer and geopolitical issue as well." Eckart cited the effects of the new rules in terms of plant closings and higher electric rates in his district. One county in his district, Eckart said, already suffered from 16 percent unemployment, and many marginally profitable factories there would be forced to close by regulations requiring them to install expensive antipollution equipment.

"This is how Representatives get whipsawed . . . I vote one way and people say, 'Aren't you supposed to represent the national interest?' I vote the other way and people say, 'We sent you there to represent us.' . . . It is not an easy issue. I'd just as soon not be in this position. But that's what we get paid for."*

*Quoted in Philip Shabecoff, "A Lesson From Whipsawing 101," *The New York Times*, May 4, 1984.

cipally through studies focused on efficiency and effectiveness in reaching program goals and through investigations. Congressional investigations—not just of federal programs, but of various controversial aspects of political life as well—can be wide-ranging and highly publicized affairs. Over the past few decades, for example, committees have looked into the assassinations of John F. Kennedy and Martin Luther King, Jr., corporate influences on American foreign policy, organized crime, corruption in the labor movement, and many other matters of consequence.

The duty of providing *advice and consent* on presidential appointments is solely a Senate function. Some delegates to the Constitutional Convention of 1787 favored a system whereby the Senate would make all cabinet appointments; others maintained such appointments should be the prerogative of the president. Under the compromise position incorporated into the Constitution, "The President shall nominate, and by and with the Advice and Consent of the Senate shall appoint Ambassadors, others public Ministers and Consuls, Judges of the Supreme Court, and all other Officers of the United States." Although only eight cabinet nominees have been rejected by the Senate since 1789 (the latest in 1959), hundreds of appointees to cabinet and other offices have been withdrawn when it became clear that they would not get approval. Many other appointees have had to face tough questioning in Senate committee rooms. Confirmation hearings provide opportunities for the party out of power to retaliate against the "ins," by bringing up potentially damaging issues for the governing administration. They also give legislators a chance to elicit from appointees specific policy statements.

Although most confirmation hearings are mundane affairs, some have been marked by dramatic confrontations. One of President Franklin Roosevelt's nominees to the Supreme Court, Hugo Black, was grilled in committee hearings about his youthful membership in the Ku Klux Klan in Alabama; his appointment was confirmed anyway, and he turned out to be one of the more liberal members of the Court. President Richard Nixon ran into difficulty with two of his Supreme Court nominees: Clement Haynesworth, whose ethics were questioned, and G.

Harrold Carswell, who had made a campaign speech pledging himself to uphold white supremacy. Their names were withdrawn. Conservative senators forced President Jimmy Carter to withdraw the nomination of Theodore Sorensen as head of the Central Intelligence Agency. Several of President Ronald Reagan's cabinet nominees met with stiff questioning. For example, William Clark, a nominee as deputy secretary of state, was forced to admit he could not name the prime ministers of South Africa or Zimbabwe; he was confirmed anyway.[4]

## The structure of Congress

Democratic legislatures can be either **unicameral** (consisting of a single house) or, like the U.S. Congress, **bicameral** (consisting of two houses). In bicameral legislatures, all laws must run the legislative gauntlet twice—in the case of the U.S. Congress, through the larger House of Representatives and the smaller Senate. The political complexities arising from this situation constitute one facet of the **"checks and balances"** system created by the framers of the Constitution. It was intended that one house of Congress "check" the actions of the other. The framers also stipulated that one house be elected on the basis of population and that the other be made up of two members from each state. At the time the Constitution was written, it was thought that the House, directly elected every two years by the people, would serve as a populist forum. Senators, on the other hand, were to be selected by state legislatures, and only one-third of the Senate body would be chosen every two years. Senators were to be at least thirty years old (House members could be twenty-five) and to have been citizens for at least nine years (as opposed to seven years for House members). Thus, it was thought, senators would serve as the elder statesmen, shielded from popular pressures, who would check the more populist impulses of the House.[5]

In 1913 the lofty political status of senators was altered by the Seventeenth Amendment, which required that they be popularly elected. Today, senators are subject to many of the same political pressures faced by House members. The way the Senate is structured still confers political advantages, however. The one hundred Senators serve six-year terms—a lengthy time in office that, potentially at least, allows them to execise more independence from the immediate concerns of their constituents. Prominent senators can capture wide public attention, thus counterbalancing to some degree the attention focused on the president. This is a position rarely available to the 435 members of the House, who serve two-year terms and usually represent smaller constituencies. As we will see in the next chapter, a House member must always keep one eye cocked to constituents' needs and reelection concerns. (Table 13.1 summarizes some of the major differences between the two houses.)

Congress has developed certain structural or organizational traits in response to the demands imposed by its size, workload, and political environment. In the rest of this chapter, we will look at the most important of these traits: *hierarchy* of leadership, *specialization* of function, and *routinization* of procedure.

## The hierarchy of Congress

Party leaders orchestrate the efforts of various congressional work groups to produce coherent legislative results.[6] In attempting to influence the legislative course of events, party leaders have several resources at their disposal. In many cases, they can use parliamentary rules for partisan ends. One tactic that is frequently used, especially by the majority party, is to delay the scheduling of a controversial bill until the leaders gather enough votes for passage. Another leadership resource is control or influence over many of the tangible rewards available to individual members, such as choice committee assignments. Party leaders also control many psychological rewards; they are often able to influence the attitude of House colleagues toward a member, with isolation the possible fate of the maverick. Finally, by dominating the legislature's internal communications process, party leaders monopolize vital information: knowledge of the upcoming schedule, the substance of bills, and the intentions of other congressmen or

TABLE 13.1
## Major differences between the House and Senate

| House | Senate |
|---|---|
| Larger (435 members) | Smaller (100 members) |
| Shorter term of office (two years) | Longer term of office (six years) |
| Less-flexible rules | More-flexible rules |
| Narrower constituency | Broader, more varied constituencies |
| Policy specialists | Policy generalists |
| Less press and media coverage | More press and media coverage |
| Power less evenly distributed | Power more evenly distributed |
| Less prestige | More prestige |
| More expeditious in floor debate | Less expeditious in floor debate |
| Less reliance on staffs | More reliance on staffs |
| Initiates all money bills | Confirms Supreme Court justices, ambassadors, and heads of executive departments |
| | Confirms treaties |

Source: Walter J. Oleszek, *Congressional Procedures and the Policy Process* (Washington, D.C.: Congressional Quarterly Press), 1978, p. 24.

The Speaker's job is not an easy one, especially these days. So Speaker Thomas (Tip) O'Neill's meditative expression seems to be telling us as he ponders the president's State of the Union address. O'Neill presided over a reformed House of Representatives in which party leadership played a diminished role.

of the president. As we will see, the powers wielded by party leaders tend to be greater in the House than in the Senate.

## Leadership in the House

**The Speaker of the House,** its presiding officer, is the most influential person on Capitol Hill. Although he (there has never been a female Speaker) is chosen by the members of his own party, his authority extends over the entire House. By managing the business of the House, he controls an array of formal powers that permit him to regulate the flow of legislation. The Speaker has the power to recognize members on the floor (that is, grant them the right to speak), to break tie votes, and to refer bills to committees. The Speaker's unwritten powers depend on his personalilty and skills. He may influence the assignment of members to committees, influence the activities of the various committee chairmen, or take

the lead in scheduling legislation for floor consideration.

Despite the potential for power vested in the position of Speaker, the House of Representatives has had only a sporadic history of strong leadership. The few powerful Speakers of the nineteenth and early twentieth centuries included Henry Clay, Thomas ("Czar") Reed, and Joseph ("Uncle Joe") Cannon. When Cannon pushed the Speaker's powers beyond limits acceptable to the membership, the House voted in 1910 to strip the office of some of its formal powers. Today the Speaker's resources are more personal and informal. In this century, only one Speaker has converted these informal resources into real power—Sam Rayburn, a Texas Democrat, who wielded the Speaker's gavel for all but two years in the period 1940–61.

The Speaker is aided by the **majority leader,** the chief floor spokesman for his party and the person charged with mobilizing party voting strength. The majority leader, in turn, is assisted by the majority **whip,** who notifies members of pending business, polls them on their voting intentions, and endeavors to bring them to the floor at the right moment to vote on key issues. The **minority leader** (who is the opposition party's candidate for Speaker) and minority **whip** perform similar tasks, although they have fewer rewards to dispense among their colleagues.

## Leadership in the Senate

In the Senate, strong leadership has been much more the exception than the rule. Not until the end of the nineteenth century did coherent leadership patterns appear, and even then Senate leaders were no match for the powerful Speakers presiding on the other side of the Capitol building.

The presiding officer of the Senate has almost no formal power. The vice-president, the constitutionally mandated presiding officer, rarely attends sessions. The **president pro tem** of the Senate is merely an honorific title bestowed on the senior majority-party senator; usually, the Senate is presided over day-to-day by freshman senators who take turns. The most important Senate leader is the **majority leader**, who helps to steer his party's legislative program through the upper house. The majority leader schedules legislation and influences many of the rewards available to senators, such as committee assignments, travel allowances, and office space.

In this century, majority leaders have varied widely in effectiveness. Lyndon Johnson's success as Democratic majority leader (1955–60) was largely a result of his unique persuasive skills, which he used to foster an atmosphere of consensus between senior,

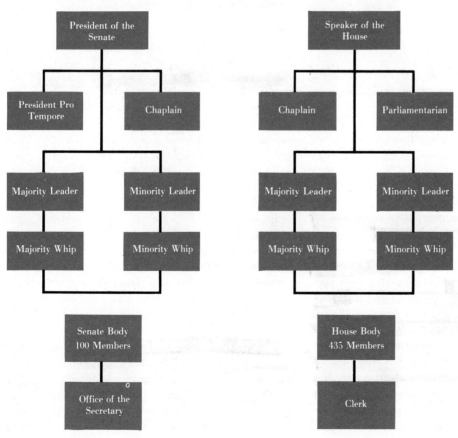

FIGURE 13.1
Leadership of Congress:
Source: John Clements,
*Taylor's Encyclopedia of Government Officials*, vol. 9 (Dallas: Political Research, Inc., 1983), p. 26.

more-conservative members of the party and more-liberal newcomers. Johnson assured each new Democratic senator at least one major committee assignment, thus bringing about a broader distribution of desirable committee seats.[7]

The opposition party elects the **minority leader,** who looks after the interests of his (or her) party members and those of the president, if the latter belongs to the same party. Both floor leaders are assisted by **whips,** who operate much as House whips do, although with noticeably looser reins on the troops.

## Legislative specialization: the committees

A frequently expressed sentiment on Capitol Hill is, "You can't write a bill on the floor." Complex measures simply can't be worked out by a large body of legislations. Only through dependence on specialized work groups, or committees, can Congress simultaneously consider a variety of matters, and individual legislators concentrate on a manageable range of problems.

Committees are the key policy-making bodies in Congress. Of the thousands of bills introduced into Congress each year, only a few are seriously considered by the committees—and only those few have a chance to be enacted into law. As President Woodrow Wilson once observed, "Congress in session is Congress on display, but Congress in committee is Congress at work."

Legislative specialization in Congress has increased as the congressional workload has grown more burdensome and diverse. New work groups have been formed as new public problems have been identified or new governmental responsibilities assumed. The Legislative Reorganization Act of 1946 consolidated and reduced the number of standing (permanent) committees (see Table 13.2 for a complete list) but did nothing to halt the proliferation of subcommittees and such other work groups as single-purpose, temporary, and joint committees (those composed of members from both houses).

TABLE 13.2
### Standing committees of the House and Senate (1985–86)

| Committee | Number of members | Number of subcommittees |
|---|---|---|
| **House** | | |
| Agriculture | 41 | 8 |
| Appropriations | 57 | 13 |
| Armed Services | 44 | 7 |
| Banking | 46 | 8 |
| Budget | 31 | 9 |
| District of Columbia | 11 | 3 |
| Education and Labor | 31 | 8 |
| Energy and Commerce | 42 | 6 |
| Foreign Affairs | 37 | 8 |
| Government Operations | 39 | 7 |
| House Administration | 19 | 5 |
| Interior | 39 | 6 |
| Judiciary | 31 | 7 |
| Merchant Marine | 39 | 5 |
| Post Office | 24 | 7 |
| Public Works | 48 | 6 |
| Rules | 13 | 2 |
| Science and Technology | 41 | 7 |
| Small Business | 41 | 6 |
| Standards of Official Conduct | 12 | none |
| Veterans' Affairs | 33 | 5 |
| Ways and Means | 35 | 6 |
| | | |
| **Senate** | | |
| Agriculture | 18 | 7 |
| Appropriations | 29 | 13 |
| Armed Services | 18 | 6 |
| Banking | 18 | 9 |
| Budget | 22 | none |
| Commerce | 17 | 8 |
| Energy and Natural Resources | 20 | 6 |
| Environment and Public Works | 16 | 6 |
| Finance | 20 | 9 |
| Foreign Relations | 17 | 7 |
| Governmental Affairs | 18 | 7 |
| Judiciary | 18 | 9 |
| Labor and Human Resources | 18 | 7 |
| Rules and Administration | 12 | none |
| Small Business | 19 | 9 |
| Veterans' Affairs | 12 | none |

Source: *Congressional Quarterly Weekly,* January 26, 1985, p. 142.

## TABLE 13.3
## Jurisdiction of House Committee on Education and Labor

1. Measures relating to education and labor generally
2. Child labor
3. Institutions in the District of Columbia: Columbia Institution for the Deaf, Dumb, and Blind; Howard University; Freedmen's Hospital
4. Convict labor and the entry of goods made by convicts into interstate commerce
5. Labor standards
6. Labor statistics
7. Mediation and arbitration of labor disputes
8. Regulation or prevention of importation of foreign laborers under contract
9. Food programs for children in schools
10. United States Employees' Compensation Commission
11. Vocational rehabilitation
12. Wages and hours of labor
13. Welfare of miners
14. Work incentive programs

Source: Walter Oleszek, *Congressional Procedure and the Policy Process* (Washington, D.C.: Congressional Quarterly Press, 1978), p. 54.

Outside the congressional hierarchy, the effective influence of members of Congress is based primarily on committee assignments and positions. In committee work, members can afford to give detailed consideration to bills, can cultivate close relationships with interest groups and executive agencies affected by legislation, and can develop expertise in particular areas. Such expertise is often deferred to by other members, who may not feel they have the specialized knowledge necessary to challenge committee judgments.[8] (For an example of the range of issues considered by a typical congressional committee, see Table 13.3.)

## Committee assignments

Committee assignments are made by the political parties in each house. For the Democrats, the Steering Committee nominates committee members; for

The two sides of the Congressional committee hearing. Right, Representative Henry Waxman (D, California), chairing the House Subcommittee on Health and Environment, addresses a witness. Left, Alexander Trowbridge, President of the National Association of Manufacturers, testifies before the Senate Foreign Relations Committee.

the Republicans, the Committee on Committees does the same. Each party caucus (made up of all members of the party in each house) then ratifies the selections. Assignments hinge on the prestige of the committee involved, the goals of particular legislators, the seniority of legislators, and whether the committee has in the past maintained a particular state or regional representation pattern. Although party leaders exercise some influence on all assignments, they generally concentrate on the most prestigious committees—Rules, Appropriations, and Ways and Means in the House; Appropriations, Finance, and Foreign Relations in the Senate. To be appointed to such committees, members must usually demonstrate "responsibility"—the ability to cooperate and accommodate different viewpoints. The most important factors in committee assignments, however, are a member's own desires and whether the assignment will help his or her reelection. As a result, like-minded legislators usually end up on the same committees, as do members who come from constituencies with similar interests, such as urban areas or farm states.[9]

Freshman members, along with those who incur the hostility of their colleagues or of party leaders or who are considered unreliable, may not be happy with their initial committee assignments. For instance, two new representatives from New York City once were assigned to the House Agriculture Committee, despite the fact that, as one of them phrased it, "there isn't any crop in my district except marijuana." Obviously, congressmen want to serve on committees that deal with areas of personal or political interest. The problem with this arrangement is that a committee made up of such members may pay more attention to the special interests of each local representative than to the overall public interest.

Once assigned to a committee, legislators generally have a right to stay there for as long as they

serve in Congress. The majority-party member who has served on the committee the longest usually is named chairman. This practice, known as **seniority rule**, once was invariably followed. Today, however, party caucuses can and do pass over the senior member and install a more junior member as chairman.

Committees such as Budget and Appropriations have been particularly popular in recent years, partly because federal spending has been such a central issue. Assignments on the House Commerce Committee have also been much sought after by those freshman members who campaigned against excessive federal regulation. Some committees are perennially unpopular: House and Senate ethics panels, the District of Columbia Committee, and, lately, the House Judiciary Committee. In the absence of applicants, party leaders must twist some arms to fill vacancies on such committees.

## Subcommittees

Over the past fifty years there has been a definite trend toward what has been called "subcommittee government." Subcommittees of the standing com-

mittees have increasingly taken over the basic responsibility for detailed legislative work, including hearings, debates, and the writing of bills.[10] The sheer number of subcommittees has increased also, from eighty-three in the Eighty-fourth Congress to 139 in the Ninety-eighth. Each standing committee has at least two subcommittees, and the major committees as many as thirteen (the Senate Appropriations Committee). The growth of subcommittee government has enhanced the effectiveness of lobbying and single-issue groups. By targeting the relatively few legislators sitting on a subcommittee, lobbies can effectively focus their concerns, often at the expense of the interests of other groups.

Numerous attempts have been made to restructure the Congressional committee system, particularly to streamline it and to abolish certain committees. All such efforts have failed in the House. Whenever the specter of abolishing a committee or subcommittee is raised, many interested members of Congress and interest groups organize to oppose it. There has been some movement toward reform in the Senate. Senators are now permitted to hold no more than eleven committee and subcommittee assignments, instead of the previous limit of eighteen. Conscientious fulfillment of eleven assignments, however, means spreading oneself rather thin.

319

# The House Un-American Activities Committee

In 1938 the House created the Special Committee on Un-American Activities under the chairmanship of Representative Martin Dies (D, Texas), a bitter critic of President Franklin Roosevelt's New Deal programs. Dies complained that the Roosevelt administration was filled with left-wingers and radicals "who do not believe in our free enterprise system." Further, in November 1938, he published a list of "purveyors of class hatred," among whom were not only the Russian dictator Josef Stalin, but also the secretaries of labor and the interior in the Roosevelt administration. Dies was the first in a series of powerful legislators who achieved notoriety by claiming that the federal government was riddled with subversives. These claims of subversion reached a climax in the career of Senator Joseph McCarthy (R, Wisconsin) in the early 1950s.

After World War II, with the Cold War looming on the horizon, the House Un-American Activities Committee was established as a standing investigatory committee—the only such body in the House. The committee was authorized to investigate the extent, character, objects, and diffusion of un-American propaganda in the United States. HUAC's official purpose was a legislative one: to help formulate new laws to deal with the problems it uncovered. But in fact, HUAC functioned for most of its history as an agency of intimidation and public exposure. Its members attacked not just problems of "subversion," but any views they considered "un-American"—a term that, of course, is rather difficult to define.

HUAC became infamous for its rigidity and excesses and for its general refusal to respect basic democratic rights, such as the right to dissent. The committee made it a common practice to harass witnesses and their lawyers and to spread publicity about "suspected" people, who often lost their jobs as a result. HUAC had two sets of files; an investigative file, based on confidential reports; and a public file, which consisted of all sorts of information, including unverified rumors. Although HUAC issued reports and information from these files, it refused to vouch for their accuracy. In 1947–48, the HUAC staff reported over twenty-five thousand requests for security checks on individuals and organizations by members of Congress.

The committee last functioned in 1968. During its two and a half decades of existence, however, HUAC helped to undermine respect for democratic rights, create a hysterical atmosphere surrounding alleged subversion in the United States, and to leave in tatters the reputations of many innocent Americans.*

*For thought-provoking commentary on the HUAC, see Victor Navasky, *Naming Names* (New York: Penguin, 1981) and Walter Goodman, *The Committee* (New York: Farrar, Straus and Giroux, 1968).

## How a bill becomes a law

The routinization of procedures in Congress is nowhere more evident than in the way a bill becomes a law. As Figure 13.2 shows, passage of a bill is the final step in a laborious process that involves several prescribed stages in both the House and the Senate.

Nothing is assured once a bill enters the labyrinth of committee perusal and floor debate. At any stage along the way a proposal can be killed or simply left to die a natural death. In fact, the vast majority of proposals never make it out of committee. Those that do are often so loaded with controversial amendments (or **riders**) that legislators refuse to pass them or the president to sign them. Let us now look at each step of the process of passing a bill, to see where these pitfalls lie.

FIGURE 13.2
How a Bill Becomes Law:
Source: *Guide to Congress*,
November 1976 (Washington,
D.C.: Congressional Quar-
terly, Inc.), p. 345.

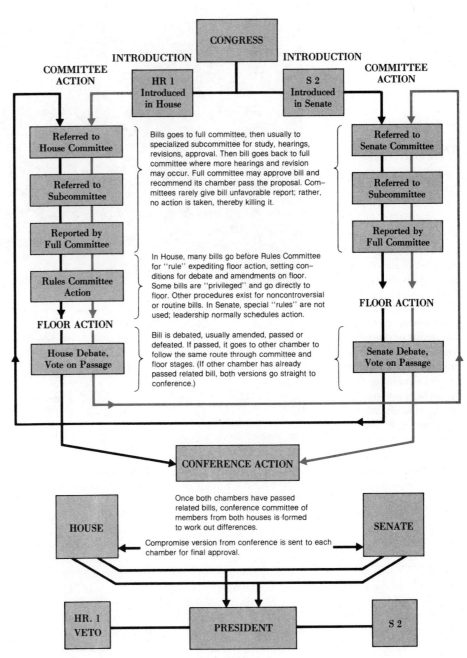

# Comparative perspective the British Parliament

The British Parliament, often referred to as "the mother of parliaments" because of its long tradition and wide influence, is made up of the House of Commons and the House of Lords. The functions of the latter are largely ceremonial or advisory; for most purposes, the House of Commons is the equivalent of the U.S. Congress.

In some ways, the House of Commons seems to be a very weak legislative body. The Cabinet (made up of members of Parliament chosen by the governing party or coalition) initiates virtually all legislation. Party control is very tight, so the majority party rarely fails to win a vote when the chips are down. Members of Parliament (MPs) gener-

ally follow party instructions, for failure to support the government in a crucial vote could end an MP's political career. The committee system in Commons is also quite weak. There are few standing committees, none of which have anything like the powers and resources enjoyed by congressional committees.

Debate in Commons is informal. Members speak from their own places,

The British Parliament is notable for the intimacy of its setting and the many rituals that attend its functioning. Here government and opposition face each other across the aisle of the House of Commons. In

this photo we see the ceremony preceding the opening of Parliament. The Gentleman Usher of the Black Rod (standing, center) has come to summon the Speaker (full wig, seated in background) and the members of the

rather than from a podium, and are not permitted to read their speeches. Filibustering is impossible, since all debate must be "germane" to the bill under consideration. Budgets are submitted by the Cabinet, and MPs are permitted only to propose decreases, which then serve as the basis of debate. In general, the opposition parties in Commons have no effective way to obstruct Cabinet policy. During the recent war in the

House of Commons to come to the State opening of Parliament in the chamber of the House of Lords. At that opening, the Monarch reads a speech written by the governing party on public policy matters.

Falkland Islands, for example, the opposition Labour Party criticized Prime Minister Margaret Thatcher's policies but could not change them. The U.S. Congress can have a very important influence in such situations, especially through use of its powers of appropriation.

A unique and significant tradition in Commons is the Question Period, during which Cabinet ministers must answer, on the floor of the Commons, written questions previously submitted to them by MPs. If an MP is not satisfied with the response, he or she can raise further questions orally. Such questioning sometimes develops into a full-fledged debate on important aspects of policy. The Prime Minister also must submit to such questioning. The U.S. president, in contrast, cannot be questioned directly by Congress, and such questioning of cabinet members as does occur takes place in committee hearings.

One of the most interesting contrasts between the British and U.S. political systems is the official recognition of the opposition's role in the British parliamentary system. The opposition in Britain is an organized countergovernment within Parliament that stands ready to take power at the next election, or should the present government lose its majority. The recognized leader of the opposition even receives a government salary and has a salaried assistant. Thus, most political leaders come up through Parliament and have had considerable experience in national politics.

The British House of Lords is an odd, anach-ronistic institution that one might have expected would have been abolished some time ago. Early in the eighteenth century, the Lords was the dominant house of Parliament, made up of the hereditary aristocracy. Commons stripped if of various powers until today it has very little role in legislating. The current House of Lords consists of 809 hereditary peerages, 300 life peerages, 26 bishops, nine law lords, and a few archbishops. Reforms in 1958 admitted women to the body for the first time and established the life (as opposed to hereditary) peerages, both of which breathed some new life into a very unrepresentative aristocratic body. Theoretically, the House of Lords has the power to hold bills up for a year, but this power is almost never employed. In general, it does some amending of legislation and conducts unhurried and sometimes useful debate.

**Origination:**  Legislation can originate in any of several ways. Some proposals arise from obvious national problems, as the New Deal legislation of the 1930s did from the Great Depression. Others originate in local problems or constituency demands, such as flood control or the building of a harbor. Still other proposals represent efforts to amend or renew existing legislation. On another level, bills can originate within either Congress or the administration. In the latter case, proposals are prepared, or drafted, either by particular government agencies or by administration officials; in the former, bills are usually drafted by congressional staff members or by experts placed at the disposal of members of Congress. About one-third of all bills that are passed are private bills, which deal with the grievances or needs of particular citizens. The other two-thirds are public bills—those that treat matters that affect the general public.

**Introduction:**  A proposal is introduced into each house by a member who supports its contents. In the House, the member simply hands the bill over to the clerk; in the Senate, a member must announce the proposal formally on the Senate floor. Although most bills are introduced simultaneously, or nearly so, in the two houses, a bill may undergo consecutive consideration—first passing through one house, then being considered in the other.

**Committee consideration:**  After the proposal is given an official number, the Speaker (for the House) and the president pro tem (in the Senate) refer it to the appropriate standing committees. Because most of the substantive work on legislation is done in committee, this stage often is the crucial one in the process of lawmaking. Once assigned to a standing committee, most bills are then referred to a specialized subcommittee for detailed discussion. The subcommittees hold hearings, at which interested individuals or groups can voice their views on the proposed legislation. The bill is also referred to committee staff members, who seek expert opinion on its likely effects and costs.

Next, in what is known as the "mark up," the subcommittee goes over the bill in detail—often rewriting it on the basis of what the hearings have

# The filibuster— the Senate's sacred cow

The English word *filibuster* is ultimately derived from the Dutch *Vrjibuiter* ("freebooter"—a term once commonly used to describe pirates), by way of the Spanish *filibustero*. In legislative parlance a *filibuster* is an attempt to talk a bill to death. If unlimited debate is permitted on a bill, a few legislators can theoretically thwart the majority and stop the legislative process by talking nonstop until the bill's proponents agree to kill it. The actual practice of filibustering began in the House but was quickly put to an end there through passage of a variety of measures designed to curtail debate. In the Senate, however, filibustering became a revered right. Senator Strom Thurmond of South Carolina holds the record for the longest speech—24 hours and 18 minutes of nonstop talk in an effort to stop the Civil Rights Act of 1957.

In 1917 the Senate adopted a cloture rule, which stipulated that debate on any specific measure could be curtailed provided that two-thirds of the senators present and voting agreed to do so. This rule was revised in 1975 to require a three-fifths vote of the whole Senate, or sixty votes. Under the current rule, one hundred hours of debate is allowed after cloture is invoked. Generally, filibusters are most effective at the close of a congressional session, when members are in a hurry to wind up pressing legislative business. A bill that is effectively killed by a filibuster has to be put through the entire legislative process again in the next session of Congress.

Is the filibuster a useful institution? In some cases a modest filibuster can provide public information or allow for a worthwhile delay while more senators inform themselves on an important question. But filibustering for days on end (often by reading out of the Washington, D.C., telephone directory) in order to prevent action on important legislative matters seems a self-indulgent way of conducting government in the twentieth century.*

*Lawrence C. Dodd, "Congress, The Constitution and the Crisis of Legitimation," in Lawrence C. Dodd and Bruce I. Oppenheimer, eds., *Congress Reconsidered*, 2nd edition (Washington, D.C.: Congressional Quarterly Press, 1981), pp. 156–85.

---

revealed and what the subcommittee members believe will be acceptable to members of the larger committee. Finally, the marked-up bill is reported back to the larger committee with a favorable or unfavorable recommendation. If the committee votes to approve the bill, it goes to the full chamber for consideration. Bills that are not approved in committee are killed.

**Floor debate:** Scheduling a bill for consideration by the full chamber is a fairly simple process in the Senate, in which the majority leader is in charge. A majority of the Senate can vote whether to consider a bill on the floor, or the majority party's Policy Committee can schedule floor action after consultation with the minority leader. In the House, the bill must be listed on a particular "calendar" (according to what type of bill it is—private or public, revenue or nonrevenue, controversial or noncontroversial), which determines when the bill will reach the floor. Most bills must also pass through the House Rules Committee, which decides how the bill will be debated—for example, whether or not it can be amended. Once the rules of debate are established, floor consideration is set by the Speaker.

**Floor action:** Every bill must be considered and voted on by each house. In the House of Representatives, each member is allowed one hour of debate (unless the Rules Committee has decided otherwise). In debates over amendments to a bill, members are allowed only five minutes of speaking time apiece. In the Senate, debate is not limited or subject to specified rules. The smaller size of the Senate permits the luxury of prolonged debate, although in a **filibuster** (see box) this privilege can be taken to extremes.

After the debate, a vote is taken on the bill. Ordinarily, each house passes its own version of a bill. Those versions may differ in, for example, the amounts of money allocated to a particular program, certain specifics of the legislation, or the riders that have been tacked on. When the bills differ, House and Senate leaders appoint a conference committee to work out a version acceptable to both houses. The

five to ten members of the conference committee generally include several members of the relevant standing committees, plus other interested members. The version hammered out in conference must then be voted on by each house exactly as it is written; no further amendments are permitted.

**Presidential consideration:**   A bill approved by both houses is sent to the president, who may consider it for up to ten days. If the president signs the bill, it becomes law. If he vetoes (rejects) the bill,

---

# The rider: a key part of the legislative process

Legislators often seek to gain attention for pet proposals by attaching them as riders (nongermane amendments) to important pieces of legislation.* Once a rider has been attached to a bill, it is often hard to break them apart, and the rider may gain approval as part of a larger package. This process

*Theoretically, only the Senate can add nongermane amendments to a bill; but by twisting the rules, House members can also vote on riders.

occurs most frequently with appropriations bills.

In February 1984, for example, President Reagan made a noncontroversial proposal to provide $90 million in emergency food aid to drought-stricken nations in Africa. The House appropriations subcommittee on agriculture approved the request. Then the full committee upped the sum to $150 million, added to the bill a proposal for $200 million in energy assistance to low-income Americans, and sent the package to the House floor. The full House approved the measure. In the Senate, the African aid measure was diverted by the chairman of the appropriations subcommittee on foreign relations, who wanted to attach a rider appropriating $93 million in military aid for El Salvador. The full Senate

committee then added to the measure the $200 million in energy assistance contained in the House bill and tacked on a further $21 million for insurgents fighting the government of Nicaragua.

At this point, the main sponsors of the original African aid bill, fearing it would go down to defeat amid battles over Central America policy, shrewdly proposed creating a separate bill that would include $80 million in African aid plus the $200 million in low-income energy assistance. It passed both House and Senate and was signed by the president. Meanwhile, the original bill became even more laden with riders, including money for nutrition programs, summer youth employment, drug interceptor aircraft, various dams, and construction of the proposed Cumberland Gap tunnel, among other things. House

leaders reacted angrily: "We sent the Senate a $90 million piece of legislation to feed the poor in Africa and it ends up as $1.3 billion."†

This case was extreme, but it illustrates the strange intricacies possible in the U.S. legislative process. In many cases, proposals have been killed or derailed by being loaded with so many additions that they ultimately became unacceptable to their sponsors. It is easy to see why many observers have criticized the rider system as an unreasonable obstruction to the legislative process.

†Martin Tolchin, "Hitching a Ride on Capitol Hill," *The New York Times*, May 2, 1984.

it is returned to each house with a message explaining the reasons for the veto. To override a veto, each house must repass the bill by a two-thirds majority; otherwise; the bill is killed for that session of Congress. If Congress adjourns within the ten-day period allotted for presidential consideration of a bill, the president can exercise what is known as a **pocket veto**: that is, he kills the bill by refusing to sign it by "pocketing" it). If the president does not sign the bill within the ten days *and* Congress is in session, the bill automatically becomes law.

**Implementation:** Once a bill has become law, it must be put into effect. This may mean, for example, the issuance of new rules in accordance with the bill, or the establishment of a new governmental agency or independent commission. Implementation may also require the allocation of funds to a particular project, or the go-ahead for a study. In other words, legislation does not implement itself; rather, the executive branch must carry out the wishes of the legislative branch. In implementing a bill, the executive branch may have to interpret the intentions of Congress, and if Congress does not agree with the interpretation, it may pass further laws to clarify what was meant.

**Reaction:** Responses to legislation can range from widespread approval to intense disagreement. Supporters may anxiously await implementation and hope that Congress's purposes will be effectively carried through. Opponents, realizing that they have lost one major battle, may seek to stop implementation through legal challenges of the new law, which will at least delay implementation. If implementation does not proceed smoothly, Congress may take new initiatives to clarify or amend the bill. At this point, the legislative cycle begins again.

## Conclusions

As we have seen, Congress has a highly decentralized and fragmented decision-making structure cen-

tered on specialized committees and subcommittees that carry most of the legislative burden. From a democratic point of view, this structure has both positive and negative consequences. On the positive side, the process of specialization helps members focus their energies and talents on particular areas of policy, and thereby develop the expertise that many consider the finest benefit of a legislative career. Decentralization and specialization also help Congress to process the overwhelming volume of information and legislative business that it must deal with.

But specialization also has many defects. Because policy-making in Congress is highly fragmented, there is often little coherence in the way the legislature conducts its affairs. Also, since committees usually operate in a highly independent fashion, each committee tends to develop a protectionist attitude toward its own area of jurisdiction. Frequently, legislators of a certain ideological persuasion, or those from a certain geographic area or a certain kind of constituency, will predominate on a particular committee—those from farm states on agriculture committees, for example. And like-minded members often wind up with a highly partisan view, supporting those policies that will aid their particular interests. In addition, they develop close relationships with those interest groups and those agencies in the executive branch that work along similar lines. Congress thus tends to serve many small constituencies, rather than to look toward the larger view—the good of the whole society, or the public interest. Finally, it is often the practice in Congress for one committee to defer to another—a tendency that results in a kind of mutual admiration society in which each special area is able to get something of what it wants. Although this process may be useful in building congressional majorities, it often serves only the many special interests involved.

Former Texas Representative Bob Eckhardt called the committee structure of Congress the chief source of both strength and weakness in the congressional system. One political scientist viewed the matter more somberly: "Congress has proven increasingly incapable of creating an internal structure that could produce decisive, innovative, independent, and authoritative policy decision on major policy issues."[11] Yet, it would not be fair to blame structural idiosyncracies alone for Congress's difficulties in forming and implementing coherent policy. The constitutional system of separation of powers and checks and balances, along with the fragmentation of U.S. political parties, contributed to the evolution of these problems in Congress.

## NOTES

1 Detailed descriptions of these functions can be found in Malcolm E. Jewell and Samuel C. Patterson, *The Legislative Process in the United States*, 3rd edition (New York: Random House, 1977); and Randall B. Ripley, *Congress: Process and Policy*, 3rd edition (New York: Norton, 1983).

2 For detailed discussion, see Jewell and Patterson, *op. cit.*; Gary Orfield, *Congressional Power: Congress and Social Change* (New York: HBJ, 1975); and, particularly, Richard Fenno, *Congressmen in Committees* (Boston, Mass.: Little, Brown, 1973).

3 Joel Havemann, *Congress and the Budget* (Bloomington, Ind.: University of Indiana Press, 1978).

4 James Conaway, "Advise and Consent Revisited in the Senate," *Washington Post National Weekly Edition*, April 2, 1984.

5 For a detailed treatment of congressional structures and procedures, see Lewis A. Froman, Jr., *The Congressional Process: Strategies, Rules and Procedures* (Boston, Mass.: Little, Brown, 1967).

6 For a debate about the effectiveness of party leadership, see Ripley, *op. cit.*, Chapter 6.

7 See John G. Stewart, "Two Strategies of Leadership: Johnson and Mansfield," in Nelson W. Polsby, ed., *Congressional Behavior* (New York: Random House, 1971), pp. 61–92.

8 On specialization, see David E. Price, "Congressional Committees in the Policy Process," in Lawrence C. Dodd and Bruce I. Oppenheimer, eds., *Congress Reconsidered*, 2nd edition (Washington, D.C.: Congressional Quarterly Press, 1981), pp. 156–85.

9 Ripley, *op. cit.*, pp. 168–74.

10 See Ripley, *op. cit.*, Chapter 5; and L. C. Dodd and B. I. Oppenheimer, "The House in Transition: Change and Consolidation," in Dodd and Oppenheimer, *op. cit.*, pp. 31–61.

11 Lawrence C. Dodd, "Congress, the Constitution and the Crisis of Legitimation," in Dodd and Oppenheimer, *op cit.*, p. 414.

## SELECTED READINGS

Selected readings about Congress appear at the end of Chapter 14.

# Chapter
fourteen

# Congress at work

## Representing some of the people some of the time?

*They're corrupt. They're bought. It's the big interests, the people with money and political clout. That's who the Congress listens to.*

*Congress is controlled by a small group of powerful men. They've gotten themselves into strategic positions and they're the ones who allocate the goodies. There's no getting around it.*

*The job is tremendously wearing. The pressures are just enormous. . . . What it takes to get the job done is eighty hours a week. That's just not compatible with how much time I'd like to spend with my family. I just wanted to get to know my kids before it was too late.*

*Yes, government is getting bigger, but what's eating this place alive is the growth of one-issue groups. . . . Neither side listens to the other. Consensus can't be achieved. . . . Moses couldn't lead the country today.*

*The most disappointing part of being in Congress is the financial pressure. . . . I'm not as good in my job as I could be because I'm always worried about money. Every minute I waste on campaign fund-raising is a minute I should be using for the taxpayers.*

THE fact that each of the images of Congress presented above contains some measure of truth should stir anxiety about the state of Congress today. Such anxiety would be justified, for the 535 men and women who represent us in Congress have heavy responsibilities and, some would say, an almost impossible task—enacting and overseeing the basic rules by which Americans live and the programs that help to sustain U.S. society.

Would-be legislators face a tough struggle to gain expertise, to master the arts of legislating, and to learn how and when to compromise, to reconcile various interests, to withstand pressure. Undoubtedly, most members of Congress wish to be honest and to do a good job—but can they? Do they have enough time to acquaint themselves with (much less master) the components of complex legislation? Is it possible to hold to one's convictions and still get reelected? Does Congress work in a creative and constructive fashion, or does it merely rubber-stamp the wishes of powerful interests? In short, do our representatives in fact represent only some of the people some of the time?

## Members of Congress

Before addressing more-complex questions, we must first examine the types of people who represent us in Congress and the kinds of functions they perform.

## Personal characteristics

The typical member of Congress is a well-educated, affluent, fifty-year-old white male, Protestant in religion and a businessman or lawyer by profession. Of course, many representatives lack some of these characteristics, and a few have almost none, yet the average carries considerable weight. The Ninety-ninth Congress (1985–86) contained only nineteen blacks, ten Hispanics, and twenty-four women (including two in the Senate)—about 4 percent, 2 percent, and 4 percent, respectively, of the total membership. These percentages do not approach those of blacks, Hispanics, and women in the U.S. population. Even more severely underrepresented are blue-collar workers, union members, teachers, housewives, and the like.

In recent years, several demographic trends have become evident in Congress. The percentage of lawyers has declined in both houses. Also, members are younger, on the average, than they used to be: the average U.S. representative was forty-five in 1983, as opposed to fifty-two in 1968. One factor in this trend has been that as the job has become more demanding, the number of members retiring has increased, and the average age of retirees has dropped. More than forty House members retired before each of the elections of 1972, 1974, 1976, and 1978—a considerably higher number of retirees than there were from 1946 to 1972. Senate retirements in this period also increased. Whether this was a passing phenomenon of the 1970s due to age and the other factors already mentioned is not clear. Retirements dropped somewhat at the beginning of the 1980s, but overall, there has not been a sharp increase in

Rep. Lindy Boggs (D, Louisiana), one of a small number of women in the U.S. Congress. In her case, a political career became possible through bad luck. Her husband, Hale Boggs, was killed in a plane crash, and she was elected to his former seat.

the number of newly elected members. In 1981, 17 percent of the House was freshmen, a figure that was average for the period since the end of World War II.[1] But the cumulative effect of recent turnover in both House and Senate has, however, resulted in a somewhat less experienced legislature than we had twenty years earlier.

One of the more outspoken members of the House, conservative Republican Newt Gingrich of Georgia, takes up the case of school prayer before a crowd on the Capitol steps. Gingrich was able to gain national prominence through his activism both in and out of the House.

## TABLE 14.1
## Profile of the Ninety-ninth Congress (1985–86)

| | House | Senate |
|---|---|---|
| **Party** | | |
| Democrats | 253 | 53 |
| Republicans | 183* | 47 |
| **Average Age** | | |
| 98th Congress | 48.6 | 53.6 |
| 99th Congress | 49.4 | 54.2 |
| **Sex** | | |
| Men | 413 | 98 |
| Women | 22 | 2 |
| **Religion** | | |
| Protestants | 263 | 69 |
| Roman Catholics | 122 | 19 |
| Jews | 30 | 8 |
| Others | 20 | 4 |
| **Profession** | | |
| Lawyers | 159 | 53 |
| Business persons | 109 | 24 |
| Public officials | 78 | 8 |
| Educators | 30 | 3 |
| Farmers, ranchers | 15 | 4 |
| Journalists | 12 | 1 |
| Congressional aides | 10 | - |
| Professional athletes | 1 | 1 |
| Clergy | 2 | - |
| Judges | 2 | 1 |
| Dentists | 1 | - |
| Admirals | - | 1 |
| Airline pilots, astronauts | - | 2 |
| Economists | - | 1 |
| Veterinarians | - | 1 |
| Others | 16 | - |
| **Race** | | |
| Whites | 403 | 98 |
| Blacks | 19 | 2 |
| Hispanics | 10 | - |
| Orientals | 2 | - |
| Polynesians | 1 | - |

Source: *U.S. News & World Report*, January 14, 1985.
(*Election of 1 House Republican was being contested in 1985.)

In financial terms, our representatives are considerably better off than the average citizen. A code of ethics passed in 1977 requires members to file financial disclosure reports. Frequently these reports turn out to be vague and inadequate—and in a few cases, deliberately deceptive—but they do tell us more about Congress than we knew before. Although most legislators live largely off their $72,600 annual salary, most receive additional income from investments, legal fees, lecture fees, real estate, partnerships, or businesses. There are about twenty-five millionaires in Congress. Also, many members obtain committee assignments that create substantial opportunities for conflicts of interest. When members retain financial interests in areas they deal with as legislators, descision-making is, at the least, not disinterested.

Professional
concerns

The individual legislator has two principal tasks: to legislate and to provide constituent service. Simply keeping up with these tasks taxes the average member's resources of time, energy, and intellect. But another time-consuming task goes with the job—running for reelection. Campaigning and fund-raising are particularly onerous burdens for House members, who must run every two years; senators, with six-year terms, don't have to put the same amount of time and energy into reelection efforts.

**Legislating:** Most legislators devote a considerable amount of time to the complicated work of lawmaking. As we saw in the last chapter, the forging of a

bill into a law requires that legislators attend numerous committee and subcommittee meetings and that they be present when important debates take place on the floor of Congress. Proper consideration of a bill also requires a great deal of study, much of which cannot be done while other business is being conducted. Representatives must make time to read, think, consult with others, and sometimes search out important issues. Familiarity with a particular issue or set of issues is a significant asset, and many legislators try to develop expertise in specific areas.

**Serving constituents:** Another large block of time in a representative's day is devoted to constituency service: answering mail, helping to solve constituents' problems, writing and delivering speeches aimed at constituents, disseminating information by newsletter or press release, meeting with constituents.

Senate Majority Leader Robert Dole (R, Kansas) holds the peace pipe, symbolic of efforts to reach an agreement on the pending budget. Acrimony can often flare, even within one party, in the process of working out serious disputes. Like most legislatures, the U.S. Congress employs various methods to keep political temperatures within bounds, one of those being symbolic gestures of peacemaking.

## TABLE 14.2
## A Representative's average day

| | Minutes | Hours |
|---|---|---|
| In the House chamber | | 2.53 |
| In committee/subcommittee work | | 1.24 |
| *Hearings* | 26 | |
| *Business* | 9 | |
| *Markups* | 42 | |
| *Other* | 5 | |
| In office | | 3.19 |
| *With constituents* | 17 | |
| *With organized groups* | 9 | |
| *With others* | 20 | |
| *With staff aides* | 53 | |
| *With other representatives* | 5 | |
| *Answering mail* | 46 | |
| *Preparing legislation, speeches* | 12 | |
| *Reading* | 11 | |
| *On telephone* | 26 | |
| In other Washington locations | | 2.02 |
| *With constituents at Capitol* | 9 | |
| *At events* | 33 | |
| *With leadership* | 3 | |
| *With other representatives* | 11 | |
| *With informal groups* | 8 | |
| *In party meetings* | 5 | |
| *Personal time* | 28 | |
| *Other* | 25 | |
| Other | | 1.40 |
| Total | | 11.18 |

Source: Roger Davidson and Walter Oleszek, *Congress and Its Members* (Washington, D.C.: Congressional Quarterly Press, 1981), p. 111.

Much of this work involves so-called casework tasks, which arise when individual citizens ask for help in coping with government bureaucracy (see Table 14.4). For example, the representative's staff might investigate alleged errors in Social Security or veterans' payments to constituents.

Legislators also provide services to interest groups. For instance, they may be called upon to supply pertinent economic and technical data to a group of computer manufacturers, to introduce a bill on behalf of an environmental group, or to work against a bill opposed by the building industry. In some cases, finally, a legislator may seek to benefit his or her whole state or district—by getting federal highway money for highway construction, for example, or steering a defense contract to a home district firm.

## TABLE 14.3
## A Senator's average day

| | Hours* |
|---|---|
| In Senate chamber | 1.35 |
| In committee or subcommittee | 2.25 |
| Talking with constituents, interest groups | 1.40 |
| Working with staff, reading staff papers | 2.35 |
| Mail and public information | 2.10 |
| Events outside the office (speeches, meetings) | 2.10 |

*Due to overlap among activities, the total time exceeds the eleven-hour average day of senators. Time figures are based upon accountings for entire days in Washington.
Source: Roger Davidson and Walter Oleszek, *Congress and Its Members*, p. 111.

## TABLE 14.4
## Breakdown of constituency casework activities

| | Percent* |
|---|---|
| Inquiries about legislation | 16 |
| Requests for a government job | 8 |
| Help with Social Security | 8 |
| Hardship discharges from the military | 7 |
| Requests for government publications | 7 |
| Requests for appointments to military academies | 4 |
| Help with unemployment assistance benefits | 4 |
| Tax problems | 2 |
| Legal problems | 1 |
| Miscellaneous problems | 49 |

*Figures total more than 100 percent because some respondents are included in more than one category.
Source: U.S. House of Representatives, Commission on Administrative Review, *Final Report* (95th Congress, 1st session, 1977, H. Doc. 95-272): II, p. 830.

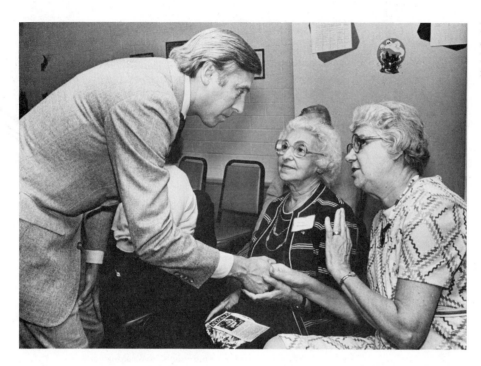

Keeping in touch with
constituents. Rep. Steny
Hoyer visits a nursing home
in his district.

**Reelection concerns:** Constituency service is not altogether altruistic; much of it is motivated by the desire to get reelected. For members of the House, in particular, reelection is a constant preoccupation. A study in the late seventies found that, on average, House members return to their home districts thirty-five times a year. Most trips are made by newer members looking to consolidate a political base. A member who acquires the reputation of being out of touch with constituents is much more likely to be challenged successfully. When the population of a district changes, or redistricting occurs, a member must work particularly hard to reestablish strong local ties.

Senators enjoy a more relaxed reelection schedule (every six years), but Senate races tend to be more competitive than House races. From 1960 to 1984, well over 90 percent of all House members up for reelection have retained their seats. In the Senate, on the other hand, the reelection success of incumbents over the same period fluctuated between 55 and 95 percent (see Table 14.5).[2]

House districts, then, have become less and less "marginal"—that is, less closely contested—over the

years.[3] This is due to several factors. Since party-oriented voting has declined for congressional seats, incumbency has become more significant. Incumbents become known at least by name to a significant number of voters. Anyone challenging an incumbent must therefore overcome the invisibility factor, which is far more serious in House than in Senate races. Ironically, it is often easier for a challenger to raise funds for the more expensive Senate races, which usually feature extensive TV coverage. Senators must face more competition, principally because their constituencies are larger and more diverse and because it is usually harder to please a state than a district. Moreover, senatorial concerns tend to be more national in scope than are those of House members, and senators more visible in the stands they take on controversial issues. Finally, the greater prestige of a Senate seat brings out better-financed and more-organized opposition.

Of course, incumbency usually confers several advantages. Both House and Senate members, for example, are given substantial financial allowances: for the average House member, about $450,000 a year for staff and office expenses; for senators, anywhere from $700,000 to $1.5 million, depending on the population of the state represented. Also, incumbents can use government facilities for making tapes and films, and they have free mailing privileges for publications distributed to constituents. Finally, congressional computer services aid incumbents in directing their mail to specialized groups. According to one estimate, every House incumbent has a $500,000 advantage over any challenger, based on the various perquisites of office. Not surprisingly, legislators tend to use these privileges very heavily in election years.

Despite the advantages of incumbency, House members have been retiring younger. Increased workloads, closer public scrutiny, mounting constituency demands, and the increasing need to raise one's own campaign funds have led some older representatives to call it quits earlier than they might have under the old congressional lifestyle.

This trend toward early retirement, coupled with the electoral vulnerability of senators in general, has created substantial changes in the composition of Congress since 1974. One clear effect of these changes has been fragmentation. Those elected owe little to their party. Members, thinking about reelection, must be heavily oriented toward their particular constituencies. Party leaders in Congress exert less influence on members, since they have had little to do with the members' electoral success. This has always been the case in the Senate, but in recent years it has become increasingly true for the House as well.

## Influences on voting patterns

What influences a legislator's vote in Congress? If Congress were like practically any other democratic legislature, the answer would be easy: party discipline. But as we have already seen, U.S. political parties are relatively undisciplined organizations. Party identification still exerts a significant influence on the way a legislator votes, but so do ideological commitments (especially along liberal/conservative lines),

TABLE 14.5
# The advantages of incumbency in reelection

| | Total number of incumbents, general elections | | | Percentage of incumbents winning |
|---|---|---|---|---|
| | Running | Winning | Losing | |
| **1960** | | | | |
| House | 400 | 374 | 26 | 93.5 |
| Senate | 29 | 28 | 1 | 96.6 |
| **1962** | | | | |
| House | 396 | 381 | 15 | 94.3 |
| Senate | 34 | 29 | 5 | 85.3 |
| **1964** | | | | |
| House | 389 | 344 | 45 | 88.4 |
| Senate | 32 | 28 | 4 | 87.5 |
| **1966** | | | | |
| House | 402 | 362 | 40 | 90.1 |
| Senate | 29 | 28 | 1 | 96.6 |
| **1968** | | | | |
| House | 401 | 396 | 5 | 98.8 |
| Senate | 24 | 20 | 4 | 83.3 |
| **1970** | | | | |
| House | 391 | 379 | 12 | 96.9 |
| Senate | 29 | 23 | 6 | 79.3 |
| **1972** | | | | |
| House | 380 | 367 | 13 | 95.6 |
| Senate | 25 | 20 | 5 | 80.0 |
| **1974** | | | | |
| House | 383 | 343 | 40 | 89.6 |
| Senate | 25 | 23 | 2 | 92.0 |
| **1976** | | | | |
| House | 381 | 368 | 13 | 96.6 |
| Senate | 25 | 16 | 9 | 64.0 |
| **1978** | | | | |
| House | 378 | 359 | 19 | 95.0 |
| Senate | 22 | 15 | 7 | 68.1 |
| **1980** | | | | |
| House | 398 | 361 | 31 | 90.7 |
| Senate | 29 | 16 | 9 | 55.2 |
| **1982** | | | | |
| House | 393 | 354 | 29 | 90.0 |
| Senate | 30 | 28 | 2 | 93.3 |
| **1984** | | | | |
| House | 408 | 396 | 16 | 96.1 |
| Senate | 29 | 26 | 3 | 89.7 |

Source: *Congressional Quarterly Weekly*, November 10, 1984, pp. 2897, 2901.

# Base-building
—one way
to stay
in office

Consider the case of
Representative Bruce
Morrison, first elected to
the House in 1982 from
Connecticut's Third
District. A narrow victor
over his Republican
opponent, Morrison
knew he had to stay
closely in touch with the
needs and demands of
various individuals and
groups back home. When
Congress recessed in the
summer of 1983, Morri-
son headed home to
engage in base-building—
making sure he was
firmly in touch with what
people were saying back
in the district.

On a typical day back in
the district, Morrison
did the following:

Attended a meeting with
the Wallingford Chamber
of Commerce, which was
seeking federal funds
for sewers.

Met with a group that
delivers free food in the
New Haven area.
Through the congress-
man's efforts they had

Part of the base-building
process involves gaining as
much support as possible
among others with political
power and visibility in one's
home area. Here Rep. Bruce

Morrison meets with Gov.
William O'Neill before
announcing his intention to
run for a second term from
Connecticut's third district.

been able to obtain a
small portion of a $4.6
billion federal allocation
for areas hard hit by
recession. They were
worried about getting
more money after the
allocation ran out.

Attended a dedication
ceremony marking the
rehabilitation of a group
of Victorian townhouses,
a task partly financed
by federal funds.
Through his presence,
Morrison staked a claim
to some of the credit.

Toured an abandoned
church that local doctors
were converting into
medical offices. Since the

building was a historic
landmark, the conversion
required the permission
of the U.S. Department
of the Interior. Morrison
decided he would try to
help the doctors get the
permits they needed.

Went to a local nursing
home that was seeking
better bus service in its
neighborhood. Bureau-
cratic complications had
thus far prevented the
Department of Transpor-
tation from helping with
federal funds.
Received at his local
office a group, including

two men in wheelchairs,
who advised him on
problems of the handi-
capped.

Attended a cocktail party
to raise money for a local
landmark, the Schubert
Theatre.

Thirteen of Morrison's
twenty-one staff members
are based in New Haven
and charged with staying
in touch with the constituency. They, like he,
know that his reelection
prospects could hinge on
many small efforts in
the district. Like many
legislators, Morrison has
financial problems. His
campaign debts in 1984,
in which he was narrowly
reelected, ran between
$80,000 and $90,000.
Fund-raising issues
therefore occupy much of
the staff's time, and can
sometimes take priority.
As one staff member
said, no matter how busy
the congressman is,
"check-presentation
ceremonies always get
scheduled immediately."

Source: Steven B. Roberts,
"A Freshman Tends to the
Task of 'Base-Building,' "
*The New York Times*,
August 18, 1983. The author
also acknowledges the help
of Representative Morri-
son's office staff, and par-
ticularly Ms. Barbara
Geller.

informal groups in Congress, constituent desires, and interest-group pressures.

## Party

Over the years, party identification has been one of the more clearcut factors in congressional voting. As we might expect in a legislature containing only two parties, many issues are fought out along party lines. But we also know that American parties are anything but unified. Party allegiance, therefore, can only partially explain why legislators vote as they do. For example, in 1984, the average Democrat voted with a majority of the party 74 percent of the time, the average Republican 72 percent. This was a slightly higher degree of party voting than in the recent past: the average in 1978 was 64 percent for Democrats and 67 percent for Republicans. Within each party, certain groups tend to vote with the party majority less than this. Not surprisingly, Southern Democrats, many of whom are closer ideologically to the Republicans than to the Democrats, have been less likely to vote with the party majority: in 1983 and 1984 Southern Democrats backed the party 55 percent of the time in the Senate; 61 percent in the House. Southern Republicans, on the other hand, supported their party 87 percent of the time.[4]

Another measure of the influence of party on congressional voting is the number of times each party majority votes against the other party majority, indicating a clear division of opinion. This "party-unity" voting has fluctuated considerably over time. In 1984, for example, only 44 percent of all votes in both houses saw party majorities in opposition, indicating that strong party differences accounted for less than half of all voting. In the years from 1970 to 1985, party-unity voting has only once exceeded 50 percent, ranging from 32 percent in 1970 to 51 percent in 1983.[5] The exact meaning of party-unity voting, however, varies: at times majorities of both parties vote the same way, and at other times no clear party lines exist.

As might be expected, party voting has been strongest on organizational issues, such as those voted on at the opening of a session. Party members almost invariably vote for their party's candidates for the chairmanships of committees and for the leadership positions. Members also tend to follow the party line if a policy issue is heavily emphasized by the president and/or by party leaders. For the most part, however, members of Congress understand that having pleased one's constituents, rather than one's party, is most important at election time. Thus, party loyalty often is subordinated to loyalty to the legislator's district or state.

## Ideology

Another significant determinant of voting patterns is ideology. Certain members of Congress may vote together because they agree on a range of issues, regardless of party affiliation. Beginning in the late 1930s, a coalition of conservative Democrats (mainly Southerners) and Republicans banded together to defeat many liberal initiatives. This coalition was most effective in 1971, when it accounted for 30 percent of all votes cast in the House and Senate and enjoyed a success rate of 83 percent. Since then the condition has waned in influence; in 1984, it accounted for only 16 percent of all votes cast in Congress.[6]

You will not find the conservative coalition listed as one of the formal caucuses in the House; it has no staff, no designated leaders, no special inducements for membership. This lack of formal organization reflects the fact that it depends on the "natural" inclinations of conservative members. Moreover, until recently it has principally been a veto group—one seeking not so much to initiate its own legislation as to block liberal efforts in the areas of civil rights, social welfare, civil liberties, and foreign policy. In recent years, however, the coalition has started taking the legislative initiative in matters such as school prayer, abortion, and a balanced budget.

Particularly in his first term, President Ronald

Reagan received crucial legislative support from this coalition. Although the Democrats held a large nominal majority in the House of Representatives in 1981, the Reagan administration won enough votes from conservative Democrats to pass its two most critical and controversial measures that year: a budget that incorporated substantial shifts in governmental priorities and a tax cut.

## Informal congressional groups

Congress is home to almost forty informal groups organized around various interests and identities. One of the first such groups, or caucuses, was the Democratic Study Group, which was organized by liberal Democrats after the party made major gains in the House in 1958. During the 1960s, GOP moderates organized the Wednesday Group, and antiwar legislators formed the Peace through Law group. In the 1970s, many more caucuses appeared, although unlike earlier groups, they tended to be bipartisan and to focus on specific issue areas. At the present time, there are caucuses on tourism, on exports, on coal, on the Northeast, on gasohol, on metropolitan Washington, on rural America, and so forth (see Table 14.6). One representative noted: "There's a caucus for just about everything around here and I guess it doesn't hurt. You know, they teach kids in school that this is the United States. But in reality, it is a group of regions and caucuses. It's not the UNITED States."[7]

The extent of the caucuses' influence is hard to gauge. About half of them have paid staff. Some seem to operate more on a symbolic than a practical level, whereas others try to educate and supply information. A few, such as the steel caucus, have occasionally demonstrated political clout on issues that concern them most. Overall, the rapid growth of caucuses in the 1970s demonstrated how Congress has become the generator of single-interest groups, reinforcing the particularism that always strongly characterized it.

## Other influences

Constituency interests and outside interest groups are not simply "other" influences on members of Congress—their impact on voting patterns often is crucial. Constituency preferences figure prominently among legislators interested in reelection. Interest groups also carry clout because of the potency of their political action committees at election time. These subjects, however, have been discussed in detail elsewhere in this chapter and also in Chapter 11.

## An institutional portrait

Until fairly recently, Congress was the most criticized of our national institutions. Many people maintained that given its structure, Congress was inherently incapable of responding sensibly to new developments and problems in U.S. society. It was considered antiquated, conservative in both attitudes and operations, and dominated by behind-the-scenes deal-making orchestrated by a few powerful legislators. With some justification, moreover, many citizens viewed the politicians representing them as not particularly ethical either in their private or their public lives.

Newcomers to Congress, sensitive to these criticisms and frustrated by the seemingly undemocratic way Congress went about its business, made determined efforts in the 1960s and 1970s to reform congressional procedures. In the sections that follow we will take a brief look at the "old" Congress before we consider the reforms that have opened up Congress and made its operations more democratic in nature. We will also touch on the question of congressional ethics and the attempts made to improve ethical standards.

TABLE 14.6
# Informal congressional groups, 1981

| House | Senate |
|---|---|

**Democratic**
- Conservative Democratic Forum
- Democratic Research Organization
- Democratic Study Group
- New Members' Caucuses
- United Democrats of Congress

**Republican**
- "Gypsy Moths" (Northern liberals)
- Republican Study Committee
- Republican Clubs
- Wednesday Group

**Bipartisan**
- Ad Hoc Congressional Committee for Irish Affairs
- Alcohol Fuels Caucus
- Auto Task Force
- Congressional Ad Hoc Monitoring Group on South Africa
- Congressional Arts Caucus
- Congressional Black Caucus
- Congressional Coal Caucus
- Congressional Port Caucus
- Congressional Shipbuilding Coalition
- Congresswomen's Caucus
- Domestic Energy Supply Coalition
- Export Task Force
- Fair Employment Practices Committee
- Federal Government Service Task Force
- Great Lakes Conference
- Hispanic Caucus
- Industrial Innovation Task Force
- Metropolitan Area Caucus
- Missing in Action Task Force
- Mushroom Caucus
- New England Congressional Caucus
- Northeast-Midwest Economic Advancement Coalition
- Rural Caucus
- Steel Caucus
- Suburban Caucus
- Sun Belt Caucus
- Textile Caucus

**Senate**

**Democratic**
- Midwest Conference of Democratic Senators
- Moderate/Conservative Democrats

**Republican**
- Republican Steering Committee
- Wednesday Club

**Bipartisan**
- Coal Caucus
- Concerned Senators for the Arts
- Copper Caucus
- Export Caucus
- Freshman Senators
- Northeast-Midwest Coalition
- Rail Caucus
- Steel Caucus
- Western State Coalition

*Bicameral, Bipartisan*

- Children's Lobby
- Coalition for Peace through Strength
- Congressional Clearinghouse on the Future
- Environmental and Energy Study Conference
- Friends of Ireland
- High Altitude Coalition
- Jewelry Manufacturing Coalition
- Members of Congress for Peace through Law
- North American Trade Caucus
- [Pentagon] Reform Caucus
- Pro-life Caucus
- Solar Coalition
- Tourism Caucus
- Vietnam Era Veterans in Congress

Source: Roger Davidson and Walter Oleszek, *Congress and Its Members* (Washington, D.C.: Congressional Quarterly Press, 1981), p. 354.

### The "old" Congress

Perhaps the most common image of the "old" Congress is that of an aging Southern senator, who had served for many years as a powerful committee chairman.[8] This powerful senator would vote conservative on most matters; on some others, perhaps, he would vote the party line. Above all, he would take a conservative view of the operations of Congress itself—its rules, procedures, traditions, and unspoken understandings.

The Congress typified by such a figure was the object of liberal ire for many years. Many liberals argued that support for significant social change was all but impossible in such a Congress. Much of the power was centered in the committees, whose chairmen usually were able to determine unilaterally how committee business would be conducted. Many of the chairmen of the most important committees in both houses were Southern Democrats who came from relatively noncompetitive districts and states, and thus attained seniority by being reelected term after term. From a liberal standpoint, this was a recipe for political disaster—or, more precisely, for political stalemate.

The old Congress had two features that added to this stalemate: the filibuster in the Senate and the role of the Rules Committee in the House. For many years the filibuster was a favorite tool of conservative senators seeking to delay or kill liberal legislation. The House Rules Committee performed a somewhat similar role in blocking legislation. The Rules Committee supplies a "rule" for a bill, stating when it will be discussed on the floor and under what conditions. For many years chairmen of that committee were not above using their power arbitrarily to prevent particular bills from reaching the House floor.

Another force for conservatism in the old Congress was the strong tradition of deference toward senior colleagues. New members were expected to wait a considerable time before they first rose to speak on the Senate floor. In the House, the norm was succinctly articulated by Speaker Sam Rayburn (D,

Texas), who once advised new members that "to get along, you have to go along."

In the old Congress, finally, much of the serious legislative work was not subject to public scrutiny. Committee and floor votes often were not recorded, so legislators couldn't be held accountable for their votes on particular issues. Committee hearings frequently were closed to the public. Commonly, deals would be worked out between powerful committee chairmen and powerful interest groups behind closed doors. Who protected the *public* interest in these transactions? Usually, that question did not arise.

What a curious spectacle the old Congress presented: a supposedly democratic legislature ruled by officeholders who often were not elected in a truly democratic fashion and who usually shaped and passed legislation not by open, responsible policy debate, but by unwritten rules and behind-the-scenes dealing. This portrait is no doubt one-sided, in that it does not fairly represent the full spectrum of Congress's operations. Yet the problems and practices it depicts were real, and they troubled all who cared about democratic politics in the United States, including many members of Congress.

### Reform in the 1960s and 1970s

The situation described above persisted for several decades, until new forces gradually produced changes in Congress. The election of President John Kennedy in 1960, the emergence of the civil rights movement in the South in the early 1960s, and President Lyndon Johnson's landslide victory in 1964 all contributed to the erosion of the old ways of doing things in Congress. Beginning in the mid-1960s, liberal Democrats, working through the Democratic Study Group, began to seek changes in House rules. Over the following decade, reform elements in the House

Succeeded in getting the Democratic Caucus to adopt rule changes allowing the caucus to vote separately for each committee chairman (previously, all had been voted on together) and limiting the chairmen's powers (1971).

Amended procedures on the floor of the House and in committees, allowing recorded votes on amendments on the floor (1970).

Got the caucus to approve a "subcommittee bill of rights" further limiting the chairmen's powers and democratizing committee and subcommittee procedures (1973).

Won passage of a rule stipulating that a committee meeting could be closed to the public only if the committee so voted (previously, a vote had been required in order to conduct an *open* meeting); as a result of their rule, closed meetings dropped to 16 percent of all committee meetings in 1973, from 40 percent in 1965.

Prodded the caucus to remove three committee chairmen and two subcommittee chairmen, on the grounds of their arbitrary actions and unresponsiveness to members of their committees; reform the powerful Ways and Means Committee (which handles all tax legislation) and drastically curtail its influence; and authorize the Speaker to appoint and remove members of the Rules Committee (1975).

These reforms had many significant ramifications. In particular, House subcommittees, endowed with greater freedom of action, began delving into new and more controversial areas, such as the political activities of the Internal Revenue Service, CIA invasions of privacy, and malfeasance in the food stamp program. In general, there was a significant increase in legislative activity, especially by the freshman class of 1974—the so-called Watergate class, which was strongly reformist in sentiment.

In the Senate, change was also on the agenda in the 1960s and 1970s. After years of effort, the filibuster was curtailed somewhat by a rule change allowing debate to be shut off by a vote of three-fifths of the Senate (previously, it had taken a vote of two-thirds of the senators present). Another important change in the Senate was the virtual disappearance of the tradition that new senators should not fully participate in Senate work or take positions of leadership. In the 1960s and 1970s, Majority Leader Mike Mansfield (D, Montana) made a point of bringing newer senators into decision-making positions more rapidly by encouraging them to speak on the floor and by giving them subcommittee chairman-

ships. By the 1980s, the Senate had become a far more egalitarian body in which junior members played significant roles.

## Congress today

Even after more than two decades of reform, many traditions of the old Congress have survived in some form. Seniority is still the rule. In the Senate, deference to the traditions of the institution and to its older members is still expected, and the filibuster remains a potent obstructionist tactic. Most observers would agree, however, that liberal-sponsored reforms have made the operations of Congress more democratic. With a sharp reduction in the power of committee chairmen, power has become highly decentralized in some respects. The fact that a greater number of participants can now affect the outcome of legislative battles is vividly illustrated by the emergence of junior senators in influential roles. In recent years, for example, freshmen senators have played key roles in battles over the Panama Canal treaties, labor law reform, and the writing of tax legislation. In the House, too, junior members have assumed more influential positions.

The greater decentralization of power in Congress has certainly meant greater fragmentation in policymaking. But has it also resulted in *better* policymaking? Although presidential legislative initiatives now receive more scrutiny and are less likely to be rubber-stamped, it has become more difficult for House members to take common initiatives, and easier for interest groups to influence the course of events. From the hands of party hierarchies and committee chairmen, much of the real power in Congress has now passed into the hands of those who can exert the most pressure, through direct or indirect lobbying in the legislative process.

Events of the first two years of President Ronald Reagan's first term in office seemed to contradict such generalizations. By mustering a disciplined Republican vote in Congress and inducing a level of bipartisan cooperation that seemed little short of a political miracle, Reagan was able to get through Congress several wide-ranging and highly controversial programs. Such legislative discipline, however, did not survive the 1982 off-year elections, as centrifugal forces within Congress and within the parties once again reasserted themselves.

## Congressional ethics

Congress has never enjoyed a reputation for scrupulous ethical behavior. Perhaps the low point in congressional morals was reached in the 1880s and 1890s, when railroads and other big corporations paid cash to advance their interests in Congress.[9] In this century, after several decades of what seemed a clean slate, several members of the 94th and 95th congresses (1975–78) were convicted and imprisoned on charges ranging from accepting bribes to taking kickbacks from employees, conspiring to extort money, committing perjury, and violating assorted morals statutes. Thirteen representatives and two senators were caught in the years 1976–78 alone. In early 1980 came the spectacular Abscam scandal in which FBI agents posing as Arab businessmen caught several representatives and one senator taking bribes in exchange for legislative favors.

Perhaps the most disturbing aspect of this problem is that Congress has been very reluctant to take action against members who have lied, taken bribes, or been involved in other questionable or illegal activities. Some observers have argued that punishment should be left to the voters, whereas others have maintained that Congress has been unwilling to apply to itself the strict standards it has set for judges and members of the executive branch.

An even more subtle and probably more important issue involving congressional ethics today is that of conflicts of interest. Should a senator accept a lecture fee from a prominent lobby group? Should a legislator accept campaign contributions from corporations and then push legislation that will aid them? Members of committees often have financial involvements in the very areas dealt with by their commit-

tees, such as real estate and banking. Should they divest themselves of these involvements before taking part in votes that would affect them?

Both House and Senate have rules governing conflicts of interest, but in general it is up to members to decide for themselves when a conflict exists. In 1977 the Senate killed, by an overwhelming vote, a proposal to prohibit senators from aiding in the passage of legislation that would serve to help their own financial interests.

In the same year, Congress did pass new disclosure laws that applied both to members of Congress and to other public officials. These new regulations require more complete disclosure of income, gifts, assets, and debts, although some loopholes remain open. Ethics codes passed that year also control expenditures from office accounts, restrict gifts from lobbyists, prohibit travel by lame-duck members (those on the way out of office), and limit outside income. (Five years later, however, the Senate dropped restrictions on outside income from speaking fees.)

## Congress and the president

Perhaps the most striking difference between the U.S. Congress and other democratic legislatures is the adversary relationship between the U.S. legislative and executive branches. The two branches both supplement and check each other, as part of the system of **checks and balances** and **separation of powers** deliberately built into the Constitution. As we have seen, this system was designed to prevent too much power from accumulating in any one place, or in the hands of any one group. Because the president and the Congress are elected separately and have different constituencies, the president may or may not belong to the party that commands a majority in either house of Congress. As a result, presidents frequently have had to deal with a hostile majority in at least one house.

Contrast this situation with the simplified system of a **parliamentary democracy**, in which executive and legislature are one and the same. Elections are held for the parliament, and whichever party succeeds in obtaining a majority organizes the government. Rather than a separation of powers between the different branches, a fusion of power exists. And because party discipline within parliaments usually is strong, the majority party normally is able to pass its basic program.

Of course, parliamentary systems also can be plagued by complications, such as the absence of a clear majority in a multiparty system. And it is true that presidents and congresses have often worked together harmoniously despite party differences. Nevertheless, the U.S. system of government practically invites muddled lines of legislative responsibility. When legislation is passed or defeated, it can be difficult to sort out which party and which branch is responsible for what results. One observer described the situation as follows.

A president . . . may have a coherent program to present to Congress. But each House can add to each of his bills, or take things out of them, or reject them outright, and what emerges from the tussle may bear little or no resemblance to what the president wanted. So when an election comes, the president, the senator, the representative, reproached with not having carried out his promises, can always say, "Don't blame me!" . . . It ends up that nobody . . . can be held responsible for anything done or not done. Everybody concerned can legitimately and honestly say it was not his fault.[10]

The separation of powers built into the U.S. system of government leads to other anomalies. For example, what would happen if Congress were to allocate money and the executive refuse to spend it? Or if Congress were to create a vague piece of legislation and then ask the executive to carry it out—reserving the right, however, to disapprove of any specific action the executive might take under the vague mandate? Or, if Congress were to seek to curtail the president's power to wage war, by prohibiting the president from sending troops into action or keeping them in action? After all, although the Constitution gives Congress the exclusive right to declare war, the president is designated Commander-in-Chief. As these and other complex interactions between Congress and the executive branch have been worked out, powers of Congress have experienced periods of eclipse and revival.

## Congress in eclipse

Despite its status as one of the democratic world's most independent and powerful legislatures, Congress for much of this century found its powers gradually diminished in relation to those of the executive branch. The fundamental cause of this trend was the paramount importance in twentieth-century politics of crisis management and of organizational sophistication. Both factors—the need to deal effectively with crisis and the need for higher levels of organizational development—have contributed to the growth of power of the more centralized and flexible executive branch. Thus, the presidency became the focus for national action and the overall guidance of national policy. Increasingly, Congress became an institution that reacted, while initiative rested with the president.

Ideological factors also supported the growth of presidential power. Liberals, in particular, championed the presidency, seeing in it the only possible focus for effective and progressive national leadership. We will discuss the growth of presidential power in the next chapter. What we must note here is that after decades of relative quiescence, particularly in the area of foreign policy, Congress began to reassert itself in the late 1960s and early 1970s, largely as a result of the Vietnam War and the Watergate scandal.

## Congress and foreign policy

As the Vietnam War wore on, many in Congress realized that they had allowed the president too much freedom in shaping foreign policy. Presidents Johnson and Nixon both had hidden important developments from Congress. Whereas Johnson usually tried to finesse (or, in some cases, deceive) Congress, Nixon

# Congress manipulated: the Gulf of Tonkin Resolution

In the summer of 1964, President Lyndon Johnson and his advisers were planning to increase U.S. involvement in the fighting in Vietnam. In early August, North Vietnamese ships fired on a U.S. destroyer in the Gulf of Tonkin, in what the administration characterized as an unprovoked incident that had taken place in international waters. The next day another incident took place, this one involving two American destroyers; it has never been made clear what (if anything) happened in this incident. President Johnson and his advisers saw these incidents as an opportunity to get Congress to authorize any action necessary to deal with the situation in Vietnam. That way they would not have to go through the lengthy and potentially difficult process of obtaining a formal declaration of war.

The president told congressional leaders that he intended to retaliate against North Vietnamese targets and that he wanted a Congressional resolution to back him up. Although he emphasized that he wanted only a "limited resolution," the one that reached the floor of Congress authorized him to "take all necessary measures" to repel "any armed attack" on American troops and to prevent "further aggression" in Vietnam. Johnson asked Senator William Fulbright (D, Arkansas), the chairman of the Senate Foreign Relations Committee, to guide the Gulf of Tonkin Resolution through the Senate.

Although Fulbright had recently been critical of the war, he and Johnson had cordial relations, so he rushed the Resolution through his committee. His main opposition in the Committee was Senator Wayne Morse of Oregon. Morse warned Fulbright that the resolution would give the president all the authority he needed for carrying on an expanded Vietnam war. Congress, Morse warned, would never be consulted about the war again.

Part of the reason Morse was fearful about the resolution was that he had been alerted to certain falsehoods and distortions in the administration's version of what had actually taken place in the Gulf of Tonkin.

---

confronted Congress with direct challenges to its power. He refused to allow administration representatives to testify before congressional committees, and he refused to heed Congress's call to halt the bombings in Indochina.

Congress responded with the **War Powers Resolution** in 1973, which it passed over Nixon's veto. This act requires the president to consult with Congress before sending U.S. troops into combat.[11] In 1975 and 1976, Congress formally terminated four states of emergency declared by various presidents. It then passed measures providing for automatic congressional oversight and review of such emergencies. In another assertion of its prerogatives in foreign policy matters, Congress set limits on the way loans to developing countries could be spent.

During the presidency of Jimmy Carter (1977–81), Congress made it clear that it would not be taken for granted in foriegn affairs. The Panama Canal treaty (providing for return of the canal to Panama in 1990) barely passed, despite intense lobbying by the administration. The ratification of SALT II (arms control) treaty was in serious trouble even before the Soviet invasion of Afghanistan shelved it indefinitely. Similarly, the Reagan administration encountered intense congressional opposition to its policies in Central America. Congress insisted on tying funding for El Salvador's armed forces to administration certification of human rights progress in that nation. Support for rebel forces opposing the leftist government of Nicaragua also faced significant congressional criticism.

(Later, Congressional investigations discovered that the destroyers had been engaged in harassing North Vietnamese radar (with electronic interference). Morse pleaded with Fulbright to hold open hearings on the resolution. What was the emergency? he inquired. Why the need to rush the resolution through? But Fulbright and Johnson had their way: the resolution passed the Senate with two dissenting votes, and the House without a dissent.

Thus, the president was given what amounted to a blank check for conducting the war in Vietnam. But Lyndon Johnson eventually paid a price for his manipulation of the Congress. Fulbright, after learning that he had been lied to and that the administration had manipulated the evidence about the Tonkin Gulf incidents, became a determined enemy of the Vietnam War and used his power as Foreign Relations Committee chairman to direct a steady stream of serious criticism at the war. The Gulf of Tonkin Resolution triggered the beginning of a widespread distrust of the credibility of the administration. This distrust culminated in the passage of the War Powers Resolution of 1973, which limited presidential warmaking powers.

**Effects of the War Powers Resolution:** The War Powers Resolution has been law for over a decade now. The resolution states, in part: "The President in every possible instance shall consult with Congress before introducing United States armed forces into hostilities or into situations where imminent involvement in hostilities is clearly indicated by the circumstances." In addition, it requires that in the absence of a declaration of war, the president must report to Congress within forty-eight hours after troops are sent (in cases where it is not possible to "consult" beforehand). If Congress does not approve the involvement within sixty days, troops must be withdrawn.

President Ford "reported" to Congress on four occasions, the most prominent of which was the 1975 rescue operation of the U.S. seamen from the *Mayaguez*, which had been seized off the Cambodian coast. Many remarked at the time of the Mayaguez rescue (in which many more died than were saved) that the president should have "consulted" with Congress beforehand rather than "reporting" afterward.

In April 1980 President Carter's attempted rescue operation of American hostages in Iran presented a similar situation. The attempt was aborted when some helicopters broke down and collided, but Carter also had failed to consult Congress in advance. Did he violate the spirit or letter of the War Powers Resolution?

In 1982 Ronald Reagan sent U.S. forces into Lebanon in a peacekeeping effort after Israel had invaded that country. Reagan thereafter obtained permission from Congress to keep the troops there for eighteen months. They were withdrawn considerably earlier, however, after the peacekeeping efforts failed and several hundred Americans were killed in the process. Nonetheless, in consulting with congressional leaders in order to obtain support for the mission Reagan had acknowledged the significance of the War Powers Resolution. It was the first real success of the resolution, actually placing limits on the size and scope of a U.S. mission.

In 1983 the Supreme Court declared a portion of the resolution unconstitutional when it argued Congress did not have the authority to order withdrawal of forces before sixty days. The main force of the resolution remained in place, however. Overall, the War Powers Resolution has yet to be truly tested, either in terms of its constitutionality or of Congress's willingness to terminate U.S. involvement in combat in the face of presidential opposition. Its mere existence, however, is a sign that executive-legislative relations have changed in the arena of foreign policy.

This newfound assertiveness in foreign policy has been applauded by many in Congress. A deeper and more sustained interest in foreign affairs by Congress, they have argued, is healthy for U.S. politics. Whether increased consultation between Congress and the executive will lead to more coherent and consistent policy-making in this area, however, remains to be seen.

One problem is that Congress is not easy to consult

Members of the Joint Budget Committee come to an agreement on the proposed 1986 Federal budget. Leaning across the table are Senate Budget Committee Chairman Pete Domenici of New Mexico (*right*) and House Budget Committee Chairman William Gray of Pennsylvania (*left*). Hammering out a budget agreement proves extremely difficult because of disagreements with the White House on the deficit and other matters.

with. Individual members have strong interests, as do various committees and subcommittees. Constant jurisdictional squabbles develop. And as a by-product of the changeover from the "old" to the "new" Congress, few individuals now can speak for the whole Congress on foreign policy matters.

Then, too, Congress's role in foreign policy seemingly suffers from inescapable weaknesses. According to some critics, Congress always approaches policy-making in a piecemeal fashion, never looking at the whole picture. Others have found Congress's main problem to be an unwillingness to *act*. One adherent of the latter view was Senator Fulbright, who felt Congress had the means but lacked the will to end the war in Indochina. Yet the same Senator Fulbright argued some years later that "those of us who prodded what seemed to be a hopelessly immobile herd of cattle [i.e., Congress] a decade ago, now stand back in awe in the face of a stampede."[12]

The skirmishes between the president and Congress over foreign policy often cause considerable confusion for foreign governments. They do not understand what the constitutional separation of powers involves, or that presidential power in foreign affairs is not unlimited. Whom exactly are they to negotiate with, Congress or the president? Congress halted the SALT II treaty, for example, after the Carter administration had successfully negotiated that pact with the Soviet Union. In the view of some observers, Congress approaches foreign policy as if it were another aspect of lawmaking, and thus tends "to place a straitjacket of legislation around the manifold complexity of our relations with other nations."[13]

Despite the accuracy of some of these criticisms, Congress has actually accomplished a great deal through its newly aggressive stance on foreign policy.

Admirers of the new Congress have pointed out that it has helped to make future Vietnams less likely, reversed the trend toward unchecked presidential power in foreign affairs, shifted the pattern of American commitments abroad in constructive ways, and broadened the base of foreign policy-making.[14]

## Congress and the budget

Traditionally, the budget process in Congress involved what has been described as a "war between the parts and the whole." The president's budget was divided up among a large number of committees, each of which dealt with one facet of it. Because little attention was paid to how the various parts would affect the whole, Congress, unlike the president, had no overview of the budget. Much of the time congressional committees simply deferred to executive judgment on authorizations and appropriations of funds for programs. Moreover, presidents sometimes made their own decisions on how much to spend, unilaterally impounding the funds authorized for programs they disapproved of.

In the early 1970s a push to reform the budget process in Congress was launched, for several reasons. Some members of Congress feared a steady rise in government spending that might bring larger and larger deficits, and the lack of control over much of the budget bothered many others. That part of the budget subject to congressional consideration usually amounted to less than half of total federal expenditures, the remainder not being subject to annual authorizations. As a result, the executive had a relatively free hand. Moreover, reform of the budget process could provide Congress with firmer control over its priorities. For without some means of weighing programs against each other, how would difficult choices in spending priorities be decided? Finally, many legislators felt it was time to reassert Congress's authority as an institution. A reformed budget process would provide Congress with much more information, and would help it to confront presidential tactics such as impoundment of federal funds. In particular, President Nixon's campaign to cut expenditures through impoundment in the early 1970s was viewed as a serious constitutional challenge to Congress's authority.

As enacted, reform of the budget process was embodied in the Congressional Budget and Impoundment Control Act of 1974, which was designed to provide Congress with a way of dealing with the total level of spending and taxation every fiscal year. To this end, the act established a budget committee in each house and a Congressional Budget Office to provide information and technical assistance. The plan was for the committees to set out two budget resolutions annually for Congress's approval: one to set overall spending and tax goals early in the budget planning process, and another to set binding figures before the fiscal year began (July 1). Then, in a step known as reconciliation, the House and Senate would agree on a set of matching proposals for each portion of the federal budget.[15] The act also prohibited presidential impoundment of funds appropriated by Congress.

The reformed budget system has been received with a mixture of dissatisfaction and pride. Conservatives wanted to use the system to place a ceiling on expenditures, but have not been able to get that ceiling down as low as they wished. Liberals, who wanted to use the process in order to set new priorities,

sought open debate about the overall emphasis in each new budget. Some such debates have taken place, but liberals have not been entirely happy with the results.

According to less-ideological members of Congress, the main effect of the budget reforms has been a clearer way of thinking about the budget. Improvements cited include earlier planning, better coordination among various committees, more careful scrutiny of certain spending programs previously left out of budget discussions, and wider dissemination of information to legislators about the consequences of their decisions.

Another gain, in the view of reform proponents, was the creation of the **Congressional Budget Office**, whose professional staff of two hundred aids Congress in dealing with budget issues. The CBO was to serve as a counterweight to the expertise of the executive branch's Office of Management and Budget. The CBO reports to Congress on economic consequences of both proposed and enacted legislation. It develops a yearly report on alternative budget options and also provides expert advice for the congressional committees considering specific fiscal issues. In fact, the CBO is widely thought to be both more accurate in its assessments and more politically neutral than the increasingly politicized OMB.

On the negative side, constant budget problems in recent years have forced Congress to spend an inordinate amount of time debating money issues, sometimes to the detriment of other aspects of policymaking. This was particularly true beginning in 1983, when record deficits developed.

## The legislative veto

In 1932, in a deal with President Herbert Hoover, Congress passed a law that allowed the president to reorganize the executive branch but reserved to itself the right to override what he did if it disapproved. This arrangement set an important, if largely unnoticed, precedent by establishing what has come to be called the **legislative veto**—a technique by which Congress delegates authority to the president and at the same time retains enough authority to interfere with the way the presidential power is used. This procedure reflected the increasing intricacies of modern government and the inability of Congress to deal with many such complexities directly.[16]

As the government entered areas that had previously been left to the states or handled in the private sector, Congress often wrote vague, general legislation, leaving the details to be worked out by the executive branch and its bureaucracy. But by writing in a legislative veto, Congress was able to keep its finger in the pie of policy-making and implementation. Congressional subcommittees could and often did dictate to executive branch agencies exactly how they wanted particular rules to be applied. According to some observers, this procedure enhanced the powers of special interests, operating through Congress, to undermine regulatory legislation.

Nonetheless, there was little serious debate about the legislative veto until the Nixon presidency. In various pieces of legislation, Congress reserved the right to remove troops from hostilities, to veto arms sales to certain nations, to restrict export of U.S. technology, to force the president to spend money on specific projects, to overturn the rulings of regulatory commissions, and to disapprove of federal land sales. This far more extensive use of the legislative veto device was justified by many members as a legitimate response to abuses of presidential power in domestic and foreign policy.

After the Nixon years, the practice continued, but more arguments arose about its constitutionality. Proponents maintained that it was a perfectly reasonable practice—in fact, one that modern governments require—whereas detractors warned that its constitutional standing was shaky. The latter turned out to be correct. In 1983, the Supreme Court ruled that the legislative veto violated the separation of powers—that it was, in effect, an effort by Congress to make law without taking the trouble of actually legislating. The Court's decision encompassed all forms of the legislative veto; how many of the 2,000-odd laws including veto provisions will be ruled *entirely* unconstitutional remains to be seen.

## Conclusions

How should we evaluate the Congress from a democratic standpoint? The first fact to remember is that the U.S. national legislature is unique because the U.S. political process is unique. Unlike parliamentary systems, in which the executive and legislative branches are fused, our system sets these branches at odds. On the one hand, this situation creates unique opportunities for legislative action and power; on the other, it leads to severe and probably insoluble problems involving legislative coordination and responsible policy-making. In its role as critic, gadfly, and check on the initiatives of the executive, Congress has shown vast improvement in recent decades. That is a definite plus. Regardless of what one thinks of particular presidential policies, it is heartening to see informed and searching debate on those policies on the legislative side. It is also a plus that Congress has reformed some of the procedures that centralized power too greatly in the hands of an unrepresentative few. The new Congress may seem at times like a Tower of Babel, but that seems better than an institution devoted to whispering in the corridors.

On the negative side, it seems unlikely that under current conditions, Congress will ever be able to engage in coherent policy-making. This is the fault not so much of Congress as of our party system, which does not provide the discipline necessary to keep members attuned to national needs as well as to local constituency interests.

There are remedies available for some of Congress's current problems. Most notably, public financing of congressional elections might diminish the power of well-oiled interests in using money to purchase legislative access. Also, a strict rule that legislators not serve on committees that could enhance their own financial or personal interests would lessen the likelihood of conflict-of-interest situations arising. Congress has been strangely lax in not moving in this direction.

Overall, Congress is interesting, exasperating, occasionally a commanding presence in U.S. politics—frequently an embarrassment, the legacy of a simpler time when chaos looked appealing. Only major constitutional changes, however, could fundamentally alter its place in the American scheme of things.

## NOTES

1 Randall B. Ripley, *Congress: Process and Policy*, 3rd ed. (New York: Norton, 1983), pp. 105–09.

2 See Albert D. Cover, "One Good Term Deserves Another: The Advantage of Incumbency in Congressional Elections," *American Journal of Political Science*, August 1977, vol. 21, no. 3, pp. 523–41.

3 Morris Fiorina, "The Incumbency Factor," *Public Opinion*, September/October 1978.

4 *Congressional Quarterly Weekly Report*, October 27, 1984, pp. 2809–11.

5 *Ibid.*

6 *Congressional Quarterly Weekly Report*, October 27, 1984, p. 2821.

7 Quoted in Roger M. Davidson and Walter J. Oleszek, *Congress and Its Members* (Washington, D.C.: Congressional Quarterly Press, 1981).

8 Much of the material in this section was drawn from Norman J. Ornstein, "The Democrats Reform Power in the House of Representatives, 1969–75," in Allan P. Sindler, ed., *America in the Seventies* (Boston: Little, Brown, 1977); and Thomas B. Edsall, "Political Reform—Social Retreat," *Dissent*, Summer 1979, vol. 26, pp. 261–65.

9 For a discussion of this era, see Norman J. Ornstein and Shirley Elder, *Interest Groups, Lobbying and Policy-Making* (Washington, D.C.: Congressional Quarterly Press, 1978), Chapter 4.

10 Quoted in "TRB," in *The New Republic*, May 3, 1980, p. 3.

11 For a good discussion of the War Powers Resolution, see Cecil V. Crabb, Jr., and Pat M. Holt, *Invitation to Struggle: Congress, the President, and Foreign Policy* (Washington, D.C.: Congressional Quarterly Press, 1980), especially Chapter 5.

12 Quoted in C. V. Crabb and P. M. Holt, *Invitation to Struggle*, p. 204.

13 *Ibid.*, p. 205.

14 *Ibid.*

15 The budget committees have received considerable attention. See James H. Duffy, *Domestic Affairs* (New York: Simon and Schuster, 1978); Randall B. Ripley, *op cit.*; Joel Havemann, *Congress and the Budget* (Bloomington, Ind.: University of Indiana Press, 1978).

16 Steven R. Weisman, "Impact of the Decision," *The New York Times*, June 24, 1983; and John Herbers, "Government Poised for Grand Realignment," *The New York Times*, June 26, 1983.

## SELECTED READINGS

For general overviews of Congress, see Richard Bolling, *House out of Order* (New York: Dutton, 1965); Morris P. Fiorina, *Congress: Keystone of the Washington Establishment* (New Haven, Conn.: Yale University Press, 1977); Donald R. Matthews, *U.S. Senators and Their World* (New York: Vintage, 1960); David R. Mayhew, *Congress: The Electoral Connection* (New Haven, Conn.: Yale University Press, 1974); Walter J. Oleszek, *Congressional Procedures and the Policy Process* (Washington, D.C.: Congressional Quarterly Press, 1978).

On more-specific aspects of Congress, consult L. C. Dodd and B. I. Oppenheimer, *Congress Reconsidered* (Washington, D.C.: Congressional Quarterly Press, 1981); Richard F. Fenno, Jr., *Home Style* (Boston: Little, Brown, 1978); John A. Ferejohn, *Pork Barrel Politics* (Stanford Cal.: Stanford University Press, 1974); C. V. Crabb, Jr., and P. M. Holt, *Invitation to Struggle: Congress, the President, and Foreign Policy* (Washington, D.C.: Congressional Quarterly Press, 1980); William R. Shaffer, *Party and Ideology in the United States Congress* (Lanham, Md.: American University Press, 1980).

# Chapter
fifteen

# The
# American
# president

# Unique,
# necessary,
# and dangerous

THE framers of the Constitution were faced with a dilemma when it came to setting up the executive branch. The political situation under the Articles of Confederation, which had essentially done away with a central executive authority, had clearly been disastrous. Yet few Americans desired to return to the days of monarchy. Some delegates to the Constitutional Convention suggested a Council of States—a plural executive that would administer the departments. At the other extreme was the suggestion for a disguised monarchy, in which the president would have monarchial prerogatives but would not be a hereditary ruler. Another option, which the delegates finally settled on, was to establish an effective executive branch whose powers would be limited by checks and balances.

It was clear that a majority of delegates favored a strengthened executive. The question was, How strong? What powers would he have?* And what checks would there be on those powers?

The delegates enumerated certain powers—such as the powers to direct all military operations, to grant reprieves and pardons, to see that laws are

*The use of "he/him/his" is not intended to imply that the presidency is necessarily a male preserve (although it has been so since 1787). A woman can be—and perhaps not too long hence, will be—president.

faithfully executed, to appoint federal officers—but they were also careful to balance executive power with powers granted to the other branches. The ultimate check on the president devised by the delegates was impeachment, a procedure by which Congress could remove the chief executive from office. In this two-step process, the House first must vote on whether or not to impeach (to bring charges against) a president, and then the Senate must try the case.

On many matters relating to the executive the Constitution remained silent. Out of those silences came some epic battles between presidents and other elements in our political system. For the most part, presidents have been able to expand the power of the office through interpretation of the Constitution. For example, they have sought to combine powers—as when Presidents Woodrow Wilson and Franklin Roosevelt combined "executive power" with those of "commander in chief" to control mobilization of the domestic economy during wartime. Some presidents have claimed **inherent powers**, which provide latitude for actions in international affairs not specifically mentioned in the Constitution, such as diplomatic recognition of foreign governments. President William Howard Taft spoke of **delegated powers**, by which he meant powers that were implied in the specific grants of powers made in the Constitution.

The end result of what the Founders concocted—and what chief executives over the years have refined and elaborated—is an office that is at once *unique* among democratic nations, *necessary* in terms of the role of leadership in our political processes, and *dangerous* in regard to the potential threat of a powerful executive to democratic politics. These three characteristics will serve as the focal points for this chapter.

## The unique president

In most democratic countries, executive leadership is divided between a symbolic president or monarch and the political leader who actually runs the government—usually the prime minister or premier. In Great Britain, for example, the monarch functions as a symbolic head of state and the prime minister as the actual head of state. The prime minister is the leader of the party (or coalition of parties) that holds a majority in Parliament. Typically, the prime minister will have been involved in political life and in party affairs for many years. Few prime ministers have been newcomers to party politics or to the national political scene.

The U.S. president, in contrast, serves as both actual political leader *and* symbol of the nation. The

president also runs for office separately: he does not become national leader by being selected as head of the majority party or coalition, but must win on his own in our only genuinely national election. On occasion, presidents have emerged from outside the major parties altogether, as war hero Dwight D. Eisenhower did in 1952, or from the periphery of the national political scene, as Jimmy Carter did in 1976. With the increasing importance of primaries in the presidential nominating process, the presidential race has been opened to contenders who enjoy little national recognition at the start. Accordingly, a president may come to office with little, if any, national political experience and few or no connections with other major political figures, even within his own party.

The unique political position of the U.S. president also stems from the peculiar strengths and weaknesses of the office. Because the U.S. governmental process is based on a **separation of powers**, the president commonly has a partly antagonistic relationship with both Congress and the federal judiciary. And because of the relatively undisciplined nature of U.S. political parties, the president, unlike most European prime ministers, can rarely expect complete support even from his own party members.

Compensating for these structural weaknesses, however, are the unusual strengths of the office. The president towers over all other figures in U.S. politics. Because he is a symbolic head of state as well

The President triumphant, or seemingly so. Woodrow Wilson, who played a central role in peace negotiations, is welcomed in Europe after WWI. Jimmy Carter joins hands with Israel's Begin and Egypt's Sadat in 1978, after hammering out the Camp David Accords, which were to provide a framework for a Mid-East peace settlement. The president has often gained his greatest power and visibility through foreign policy initiatives. But Wilson's League of Nations was never approved by the U.S. Senate and the Camp David Accords, though important, proved inadequate to end the conflict between Israel and its neighbors.

as a political leader, he can position himself above the struggles of party. In addition, the average citizen's psychological investment in the president is very high.[1] Presidents can rally the nation and command support as no other political figure can.

This ambiguity in the nature and range of presidential powers and responsibilities has often led presidents to seek to expand the powers of the office. Such attempts most often have come in crisis situations, as we shall see.

## Expansion of powers

One student of presidential power has argued that presidents who have pushed their powers to the limit have exemplified "prerogative government," which bears many resemblances to monarchy.[2] Typically in such cases, presidential decisions are made without congressional collaboration, and often in secret. Events are managed by the White House rather than by the appropriate executive departments. The president justifies decisions on constitutional grounds—either on enumerated powers or on those claimed or created

## Comparative perspective The head of state in West Germany

Only one other democracy has a presidential system somewhat similar to ours—France under the Fifth Republic, which dates from 1958. In other democracies, there is a prime minister or premier and a separate head of state. The latter may be either a monarch or a civilian, usually known as the president. (Switzerland, the exception, has neither a monarchy nor a civilian head of state—showing, as one writer put it, that "a country can survive without any head of state."*

The civilian head of state in the Federal Republic of Germany (West Germany) is the president, who is elected by a special assembly of the federal parliament and deputies from the state parliaments. Since the office was established in 1949, all of its occupants have been leading politicians who had lost all chance of becoming the actual head of the government (called the chancellor). The president serves for a five-year term and may be re-elected once. He must sign all legislation, decrees, and letters of appointment and dismissal—and does not have a choice in doing so.†

The West German president has more power than a symbolic monarch, but this power stems largely from personal prestige and respect. He can exercise a certain amount of influence on basic political questions, but very little on day-to-day politics. Thus, he can exercise some degree of political leadership, but must avoid becoming excessively political. As one student of the subject put it: "He must earn his prestige through his public statements, which should be neither trivial, abstract nor too concretely political."‡

It is not entirely clear exactly how far a West German president might be able to push his powers to intervene in affairs of state or to influence public opinion. Thus far, the rule has been that a chancellor backed by a solid majority in parliament need not pay much attention to a president's views.

*Jurg Steiner, *European Democracies* (New York: Longman's, 1986), p. 161.
†Lewis J. Edinger, *Politics in West Europe* (Boston: Little, Brown, 1977), p. 19.
‡Jurg Steiner, *European Democracies*, p. 164.

by his interpretation of the Constitution. When his expansive interpretation is challenged, he appeals to the public for support by defining his actions in terms of "national security" or the "national interest." Prerogative presidents usually refuse to tailor their actions to party requirements or to majority sentiment in Congress.

The prerogative style has not always been a successful one. One expert in the field cataloged three possible outcomes of the exercise of **prerogative powers** by the president: *frontlash, backlash,* and *overshoot-and-collapse*.[3] In the case of frontlash, the president wins: the courts and Congress acquiesce in his exercise of power, and he capitalizes on this acquiescence to extend the range of his influence. In the backlash effect, the president keeps the crisis under control but his interpretation of his powers is challenged by the other branches; this may result in the erosion of his and his successors' powers. When overshoot-and-collapse occurs, a constitutional crisis develops over the president's use of power, and he is censured or impeached.

**Frontlash:** Two historical cases—one of recent vintage and one from the beginnings of the Republic—illustrate the frontlash effect. In the early 1790s, George Washington decided that the country should remain neutral in the war between Great Britain and France, despite the fact that the United States and France were allied by treaty. He issued a proclamation of neutrality and refused to engage the British in naval warfare, as the French had requested. His actions led to a major constitutional debate over the question of whether the president had the authority to declare the nation neutral. His defenders claimed such powers were inherent in the Constitution, and those who disagreed did not have the votes to defeat Washington in Congress. Shortly thereafter, Congress actually passed neutrality legislation, and Washington went on to assert other new powers—recognition of foreign governments, the breaking off of relations with other nations, and the negotiation of foreign agreements by the executive alone.

In the second frontlash case, the president and Congress switched roles. After World War II began in Europe, President Franklin Roosevelt wanted to help Great Britain in the latter's desperate struggle against Germany, whereas Congress seemed determined to preserve a strict neutrality. Roosevelt thereupon engineered a highly controversial military aid deal with Great Britain by using an **executive agreement,** an arrangement between a president and a foreign nation not subject to Senate approval. Under this agreement, known as Lend-Lease, the United States "loaned" Britain fifty old destroyers in return for the lease of several bases in the Caribbean. Roosevelt's critics claimed that transfer violated the 1940 Neutrality Act, but Roosevelt argued it was an inherent power of the chief executive to dispose of military material. Congress, which had been fully informed about the deal, acquiesced. The frontlash effect then took over, and Roosevelt quickly signed a series of war-related executive agreements with other countries. Congress's reluctance to act in the period before Pearl Harbor set a pattern of executive initiative that was to persist at least until the 1970s.

**Backlash:** One modern case illustrates the pattern of the backlash effect. In 1950, during the Korean War, President Harry Truman ordered the Army to take over the nation's steel mills, which had been idled during a strike. When the steel companies took the matter to court, Truman argued that a combination of constitutional and statutory powers gave him the authority to intervene in such a situation, in order to preserve the national welfare. There were, in fact, many precedents for Truman's actions, and the Supreme Court had not ruled against a president's use of prerogative powers since 1866. But Truman had misjudged both the temper of the country (public opinion opposed him, 43 percent to 35 percent) and the disposition of the Supreme Court. A majority of the Court held that Congress had already mandated what should be done in strike situations in the Taft-Hartley Act, which Truman had chosen not to employ in this case. The majority opinion argued that Truman had taken the power of Commander in Chief and had "turned inward, not because of rebellion, but because of a lawful economic struggle between industry and labor."[4] Truman's defeat limited the ways in which future presidents could deal with labor disputes. After this episode, presidential seizure of factories was no longer credible unless backed up by special legislation from Congress.

**Overshoot-and-collapse:** There are two famous instances of overshoot-and-collapse: President Richard Nixon and Watergate, and President Andrew Johnson and Reconstruction. Since the Watergate affair will be examined later in this chapter, we will focus on the Andrew Johnson case here. In this situation, as in Watergate, a president attempted to subvert the law and the usual rules of the political game, with results that destroyed his administration.

Soon after inheriting the presidency upon the assassination of Abraham Lincoln, Johnson became embroiled in a fierce struggle with Congress over Reconstruction—the political restructuring of the recently defeated South. Johnson was more conciliatory toward the South than was the majority in Congress, which consistently overrode presidential vetoes of Reconstruction legislation. Matters came to a head with passage of the Tenure of Office Act, a measure designed to keep Secretary of War Edwin Stanton, a Johnson opponent, in office. Johnson challenged the constitutionality of the act and fired Stanton. The House then voted to impeach Johnson. Although the focus was on the Stanton issue, Johnson's impeachment could have been brought on many other grounds, including encouraging violations of law and obstructing Reconstruction.

Johnson survived the Senate trial by a single vote, and Stanton was removed from office. But in the process, the presidency was dealt a heavy blow. Congress acquired close control of executive departments, and for the rest of the nineteenth century, the presidency was greatly weakened. During this period, there was widespread sentiment for a move toward parliamentary government, with the president remaining as a ceremonial figure. This sharp decline of the presidency only began to change around the turn of the century, when presidents used foreign policy issues to regain center stage.

Since Richard Nixon resigned rather than face impeachment proceedings, the only U.S. president actually to have faced impeachment was Andrew Johnson, in 1868. Here we see the managers of Johnson's impeachment in the House of Representatives.

## Paradoxes of the office

Part of the unique nature of the U.S. presidency are the ambiguities and even contradictions built into the electorate's expectations concerning the office.[5] Americans generally want a "good person" in the White House—someone honest and trustworthy. Yet they also tend to like tough, forceful, perhaps even ruthless presidents. They admire statesmen who can lift the White House above the grubby day-to-day infighting of political life—leaders who can lead *all* the people. Yet the job of president requires preeminently political skills—coalition-building, manipulation, partisan dealings. Most Americans want a president who can pull us together, yet one who can also put forward a forceful national agenda, create a sense of priorities. Finally, we seem to want a chief executive who will both act as a referee, presiding over the conflict of group interest, and take a part in that process of conflict, using his powers to serve the public interest.

Winning the office of president—making it through the primaries, the conventions, and the general election—requires ambition, flexibility, and great skill at image-making and public relations. But excessive emphasis on these same skills can be disastrous once in office. It has been argued that winning a presidential election requires an electoral coalition—the assembling of a majority of voters, strategically located across the country—whereas actually running the government requires a governing coalition, which is something quite different. As one student of the subject put it: "What counts then is to mobilize support from the leaders of the key institutions in society and government. . . . This coalition must include key people in Congress, the executive branch, and the private sector 'establishment.' "[6]

In a sense, no president will be able fully to satisfy popular expectations. Nonetheless, high expectations of presidents lead chief executives to develop programs and "go to the people" to validate their proposals. Thus, in recent decades, the "necessary president" has made an appearance—the priority-setter and manager of government.

The optimistic, activist president: Theodore Roosevelt, Franklin Roosevelt, and Reagan all had a large agenda and exuded a positive attitude about achieving their goals, which, of course, were wildly different.

## The necessary president

The presidency is obviously "necessary" in that the office is required by the Constitution. But to many students of U.S. politics, the president also can be characterized as necessary in another sense: as a strong, well-organized leader who can define the main dimensions of national policy. The president, in this view, is a creator of priorities, an articulator of national needs, a figure who can rally the national energies. Given the general fragmentation of power in our political processes, the lack of discipline in U.S. political parties, and the profound issues the nation faces, the president commonly is seen as the only political figure who can draw together the threads of national policy and provide a minimum of political coherence.

At least since Franklin Roosevelt's New Deal programs of the 1930s, Americans have expected presidents to "organize" a government—to stand for something, to present some sort of program. Truman offered a Fair Deal; Eisenhower, Peace and Prosperity; Kennedy, a New Frontier; Johnson, a Great Society; Carter, New Foundations; and Reagan, a New American Revolution. Each of those slogans represent efforts to convince the public that a would-be president has actually had some ideas in mind—some changes and improvements in the conduct of government.

The necessary president indisputably has grown more important in U.S. national life. Of course, presidents, too, are often captives of the times in which they come to power—victims of the pressures of the moment.[7] Many presidents have not taken the organizing initiatives available to them. Still, when the system works, it is the president who must organize power, gather ideas and put them to use, and cope with crisis. In this section we will examine how presidents try to fulfill those functions, and how they can be aided or opposed by Congress and bureaucracy.

Presidential campaigns are full of promises. Once in the White House, however, the president must attempt to transform his promises into workable policies or programs. To accomplish this task, the president needs help from an institutionalized presidency. His most basic needs are for advice and for action.

The president needs two types of advice: political advice (Is there enough support in Congress to pass a revenue-sharing bill? Will Congress and the public accept a tax increase?) and technical advice (How can the administration reduce inflation? What will the Soviet Union do if the United States accelerates its defense build-up?). Both types of advice call for the uncertain art of prediction, and there are frequently no clear answers. To confound matters even

357

# Ronald Reagan, revolutionary president?

In his acceptance speech at the 1980 Republican national convention, Ronald Reagan shocked some of the delegates by concluding with a lengthy quotation from the man many conservatives consider their archenemy, Franklin Delano Roosevelt. Not surprisingly, Reagan quoted one of the conservative-sounding statements FDR made during the 1932 campaign, promising to cut government and balance budgets. Reagan, who remained a somewhat schizophrenic FDR enthusiast even after he himself had turned conservative, knew quite well that Roosevelt violated such statements as soon as he took office.

In Reagan's first term, however, many observers drew a comparison with FDR. Reagan, it was said, was accomplishing the most massive shift of government priorities since the New Deal. He was reconstructing the American political agenda, by deemphasizing the role of government and reemphasizing the private sector; pulling the nation out of economic troubles; and establishing an enduring new majority coalition for the years to come. Also, like FDR, Reagan seemed to have a certain magic, a capacity to communicate that reached the common person.

How true were these comparisons? Was Ronald Reagan a new FDR, fifty years later? In some respects, obviously, the comparison did *not* hold. Roosevelt took office in 1933 in the midst of the gravest economic crisis in American history. Desperation and confusion stalked the land. When Roosevelt told the country that it "had nothing to fear but fear itself," a line that Reagan likes to quote, he was speaking about a fear that far

fewer Americans nowadays are likely to experience. No doubt, there were also economic problems inherited by the new President in 1981, but they were of quite a different order; economic stagnation, recession, high inflation—intricate and troubling issues, but not life-threatening.

On the other hand, like FDR, Reagan was able, from the start, to wrest control of the political agenda from his opponents. Following through on conservative promises, Reagan marshalled an impressive legislative program, especially in his first two years in the White House. Extensive tax cuts were passed. Defense spending was rapidly increased. Heavy cuts were made in various social programs and in discretionary spending. On the other hand, the national debt increased vastly.

Some saw in this a Rooseveltian stance: "Folks laughed in 1980 when Reagan invoked FDR's name," wrote George

Will, "but in 1981 he began doing for the welfare state what FDR did for capitalism: saving it by tempering its excesses." Other found such comparisons slightly amusing. The historian Robert McElvaine put it this way: "FDR's supporters rode in freight cars, Mr. Reagan's travel in Lear jets; FDR's people stood in soup lines; Mr. Reagan's stand at cocktail parties. . . ."

Overall, the growth of government was not halted, but it was slowed, and, in nondefense areas, cut back. Some regarded this achievement as a turnaround as impressive as Roosevelt's vast expansion of government through the New Deal. Whether that would turn out to be true depends largely on how enduring the Reagan reemphases become. If taxes are not raised, if spending on programs like highways, energy research, job training, education, health and the arts, are not significantly expanded in coming decades, then the conservative Reagan "revolution" will have left its permanent mark on our policy. But we cannot yet say if the Reagan era will be remembered as a temporary interlude whose main legacy is a greatly increased national debt.

Apart from the matter of programmatic substance, there is also a question of style. Reagan became known as "the great communicator," and "the Teflon president." His success in gaining a positive public reaction was likened to FDR's shrewd use of the media, as in his famous fireside chats. No doubt, Reagan did seem to lead a charmed life. Like Roosevelt, he also narrowly escaped a would-be assassin's bullet. Reagan, to a degree, modeled his style on FDR's—confident, cheerful, theatrical, larger than life.

Reagan's popularity seemed to extend beyond agreement with his programs. Many who did not see eye-to-eye with the president nonetheless said they liked him and trusted him. He seemed to have touched a sympathetic nerve in America.

His frequent mistakes, insensitivities, and exaggerations did not seem to much affect popular perception of him. The exact nature of his unusual popular appeal proved hard to pin down, however. Some said it was his simple and optimistic approach to things. Others said it was his ultrapatriotism and hardline macho manner. Still others argued that Reagan's popularity was quite brittle and that any significant policy failure, especially domestic economic setbacks, would reduce his appeal.

Overall, in regard to the impact of presidential leadership on American politics, it should be remembered that Roosevelt served more than three terms as president and presided not only over the depression struggle but also led the nation through World War II. It would be surprising if Reagan's tenure, impressive as it is in some respects, could occasion the intensity of feeling that developed in regard to FDR. But then, are we the same people in 1985 we were fifty years earlier?

more, the two modes are rarely independent. Often technical advice—for example, to raise taxes—has unpleasant political fallout. The president's need for action has two basic components. On one level, there are operational needs: speeches must be written, trips planned, strategy outlined with congressional allies, and so on. On the policy-making level, the president's needs are more subtle and complex. A president must plant the stamp of his administration on the operations of the federal government, because the various executive agencies and departments— that is, the federal bureaucracy—do not automatically respond to presidential dictates and desires. Once an order has been given, someone must follow up on presidential instructions. For example, in 1962 President Kennedy was astonished to discover that the United States still had missile bases in Turkey, even though he had ordered the Defense Department to arrange their removal more than a year before. Presidential instructions must be enforced by a coterie of assistants whose primary loyalty is to the president.

On entering office, a new president must make a series of vitally important appointments. Without Senate consent, he appoints sixty or so potentially very powerful aides; with Senate consent, he fills about eight hundred "executive level" positions. The two main sources of advice and action the president can turn to are the Executive Office and the cabinet. To all intents and purposes, these groups comprise "the administration."

## The Executive Office

The needs for action and advice became particularly acute during the administration of Franklin Roosevelt. To deal with the Depression, Roosevelt had to expand the scope of governmental activity drastically; and in doing so, he established the preeminence of the president as the national policy-maker. In 1937, Roosevelt appointed a committee to come up with recommendations on administrative management. The committee's recommendations were tersely

Serious business, it appears, is on the agenda. A somber-looking President Kennedy meets with a group of his advisors.

summed up in one sentence: "The President needs help." In response, Congress established the **Executive Office of the President,** which represented an important departure from the time when presidents discharged their duties with the aid of a personal secretary and a handful of clerks. The president has direct control over the various components of the Executive Office (see Figure 15.1), the five most important of which are examined here.

Closest to the president is the White House Office, which consists of the president's top personal aides. The titles and corresponding duties change from president to president, but whatever their titles, these assistants are a president's most trusted associates. They are responsible only to the president, who can hire and fire them at will.

The White House Office both advises and acts for the president in the areas of national security, the economy, urban affairs, and other domestic policy matters. Some assistants provide liaison with Congress and lobby for the president's legislative program. Others write speeches, handle press relations, plan trips, work with state and local political leaders, and take care of the ceremonial and social aspects of the office. The key aide in the White House Office is the president's chief of staff, who schedules the president's appointments and filters the papers that

reach the Oval Office. In general, the chief of staff has instant access to the chief executive and works closely with him.

The largest of the Executive Office components is the **Office of Management and Budget** (OMB), formerly known as the Bureau of Budget. This little-known office with the somber title is a vitally important component in government operations—and one that has greatly increased the powers of the presidency.

The OMB has two main functions: to prepare the federal budget and to clear all legislation submitted to Congress by agencies of the executive branch. It also provides the president with summaries and analyses of the budgetary implications of legislation enacted by Congress.

When the Executive Office was reorganized by President Nixon in 1970, OMB was given additional responsibilities. Among other things, it was charged with the coordination of governmental programs among various agencies, and it became increasingly active in evaluating the efficiency and effectiveness of executive branch programs. President Carter included OMB in some aspects of policy formulation. President Reagan gave OMB Director David Stockman a major policy-making role.

The **Council of Economic Advisers** (CEA) interprets economic developments for the president and advises him on economic policy. The three members of the council are chosen by the president but must be approved by the Senate. Although council members are usually chosen on the basis of professional reputation, they have at times been accused of tempering their public economic pronouncements with political expediency.[8]

The **National Security Council** (NSC) was created by the National Security Act of 1947 in response to the need to coordinate domestic, diplomatic, and military policies in matters of national security. Invariably, the president, the vice-president, the secretary of state, the secretary of defense, and the director of the CIA sit on the council. The president may also include other officials whose knowledge he considers relevant to defense planning or in whom he has particular confidence. Thus, President Kennedy included his brother Robert, then the attorney-general, in NSC meetings, although the Justice Department is not normally involved in defense planning.

The NSC is served by its own staff, which prepares detailed analyses and policy options. Once small, this staff grew to over two hundred under President

Nixon's special assistant for national security, Henry Kissinger, and has remained at that level. Kissinger, a particularly strong national security advisor, drew national security policy-making firmly into the White House, thereby circumventing normal bureaucratic channels of decision making in the State Department and Defense Department. Under President Carter the State Department reasserted itself in the foreign policy-making process, but the NSC remained a strong participant. Under President Reagan, the NSC, the State Department, and the Department of Defense seemed to be in considerable conflict.

The newest addition to the Executive Office is the Domestic Council, or Policy Staff. Created by President Nixon in 1970, the council was set up to formulate and coordinate the president's domestic policy recommendations. The council was originally envisioned as the domestic policy equivalent of the National Security Council, but it has yet to achieve that stature.

Carter effectively dismantled the Domestic Council Nixon had created. Its successor was the Policy Staff, which shared domestic policy-making with the OMB. President Reagan created the Office of Policy Development to coordinate all domestic policy rec-

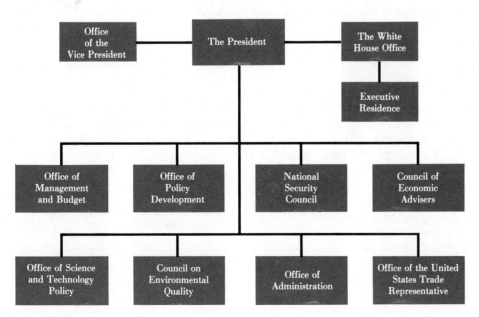

FIGURE 15.1
Executive Office of the President Source: *United States Government Manual, 1983/1984* (Washington, D.C.: Government Printing Office, 1983), page 815.

ommendations. In practice, the office did not do much coordinating, and domestic policy ideas continued to flow from a number of sources, each competing for attention.

## The cabinet

There is no mention of the cabinet in the Constitution. Since George Washington first gathered his principal government officers together in council, presidents have varied greatly in their use of the "cabinet." Andrew Jackson did not even convene his cabinet for two years, while James Polk held 350 cabinet meetings.

Today the **cabinet** consists of the thirteen heads of the major administrative departments—Justice, State, Treasury, Defense, Interior, Agriculture, Commerce, Labor, Health and Human Services, Education, Housing and Urban Development, Energy, and Transportation—plus the U.S. representative to the United Nations. Each member is subject to Senate approval.

The typical cabinet is full of political tensions. Often, cabinet secretaries are appointed for political reasons—to appease particular portions of the party or to disarm rivals or critics—yet presidents also demand loyalty and competence from the appointees. Another problem is that the president invariably wants his appointees to be responsive first of all to directives from him, yet, just as inevitably, cabinet members must also be responsive to the needs and interests of their departmental constituencies if they are to become effective department managers. Presidents then complain that cabinet members have become too independent and are being run *by* the bureaucracy, rather than the other way around. Finally, clashes between presidents and cabinet members are frequent, particularly as national and international crises take up more and more of the president's time and his personal contacts with most cabinet members diminish. He loses touch, and they do as well. If a cabinet member is not part of the president's inner circle, tensions are bound to arise.

Some Washington observers have noted that cabinet secretaries rely heavily on the many assistants who serve under them. While the secretaries deal with the headline issues, the real management of programs often is handled by the so-called subcabinet—undersecretaries, assistant secretaries, general counsels, and their staffs. These little-known officials generally exert a profound influence on key policy decisions, and finding trustworthy and competent people for these positions can be crucial to the success or failure of large programs.

## The rest of the bureaucracy

Most presidents experience more frustration than success in efforts to turn the federal bureaucracy toward their own ends. A president has only a few years to impress his views on the departments, but the federal bureaucracy is an ongoing set of institutions, with its own routines, priorities, practices. Segments of the bureaucracy have well-established connections with Congress and interest groups, and have no interest in seeing their programs gutted, curtailed, or changed by an incoming administration. According to a former cabinet secretary,

The longer one examines the awesome burdens and limited resources of those who help the president from within his immediate circle, the more skeptical one becomes of a strategy for overseeing government by "running" it from 1600 Pennsylvania Avenue. The semiheroic, semihopeless posture has been captured many times in several administrations: dedicated men, of great intelligence and energy, working selflessly through weekends and holidays to master an endlessly increasing array of detail on complex subjects beyond their understanding on which decisions must be made "here" because a resolution elsewhere is not to be trusted. . . . Yet, in the end, the effort to help the president in making government work has not succeeded.[9]

Many members of White House staffs have defined conflict within the executive branch as the single most significant problem in contemporary government. Some have reported more intense and serious conflict between president and bureaucracy than between president and Congress. Although a few staffers have seen bureaucratic noncooperation as a product of conspiracies and malevolent designs against the president, the more thoughtful have recognized that to some extent, the conflicts are inevitable. Bureaucrats have many constituents, whereas White House staffers have only one person to please. On their part, many career bureaucrats have found White House staffers to be arrogant and bossy—interfering in matters they know very little about and politicizing issues needlessly.

## Relations with Congress

In Chapter 14 we saw that Congress and the president frequently have an adversarial relationship. Although Congress has powerful constitutional tools on its side—control of the purse strings, approval of presidential appointments and treaties, and veto override—the president can use a wide array of tactics in dealing with Congress. These stratagems can be divided roughly into six categories: wooing, lobbying, exchange of favors, hardball tactics, going to the people, and the veto. Before examining them more closely, we should note that today, presidents have less trouble with entrenched committee chairmen, and more with independent-minded legislators. Instead of having to make deals with a few very powerful members of Congress, then, contemporary presidents must persuade and compromise with numerous less-powerful ones.

**Wooing:** If a president does not enjoy firm support within his party (e.g., John Kennedy), or if that party does not have majorities in Congress (e.g., Richard Nixon and Gerald Ford), the president often must woo members of the opposition. Republican presidents Nixon, Ford, and Reagan, faced with Democratic majorities in one or both houses of Congress, used wooing tactics to build on the conservative coalition that already existed in Congress (see Chapter 14).

**Lobbying:** Getting the president's point of view across to Congress is the work of the legislative liaison branch of the White House staff. Liaison staffers work closely with relevant congressional committees, consult and negotiate with legislators on critical points, and above all, try to convey a firm sense of the president's personal commitment. If they do not succeed in convincing Congress that the president is committed to a certain program, White House lobbying for that program will be useless.

Support for the president's policies also can be cultivated through contacts with interest groups, state and local party officials, and public officials, as well as by the wining and dining of important members of Congress. These efforts may not directly change votes, but they can help to keep relations cordial between the administration and Congress.

**Exchange of favors:** In exchanging favors with members of Congress, patronage is the president's main resource. Up to five hundred federal district judges, U.S. attorneys, and federal marshals, as well as numerous executive branch officials, are presidential appointees. Presidents have often used these positions as beginning chips in negotiations with opposition-party legislators. President Truman, for example, promised congressional Republicans that they could name the staff of the Marshall Plan (the U.S. program to assist Europe after World War II) if they would support the program in the first place. A president may also seek to placate a wing of his own party through an exchange of favors, as President Kennedy did when he refrained from issuing an executive order ending racial discrimination in federally assisted housing and made other gestures designed to placate Southern Democrats.

Such exchanges can backfire if members of Congress feel they are being pressured to literally trade votes for favors. As a result, exchanges must often be quite subtle. President Johnson, for example, declared unequivocally that he could not trade patronage for votes in any direct exchange. If word had spread that he was trading, everyone would have wanted to trade and other efforts at persuasion would automatically have failed. But a stubborn unwillingness to trade can also mean trouble, as President

Carter discovered when, early in his term, he cut nineteen water projects from the budget and said another 320 would be reviewed. Protests burst from Congress, which was not used to facing such blatant presidential interference in its pork-barrel traditions. Eventually, Carter decided not to review 307 projects and to restore funding to three of those he had originally dropped from the budget.

**Hardball tactics:** When all else fails, a president can resort to outright threats—usually, that federal projects will be eliminated or reduced in the state or district represented by an uncooperative legislator. President Johnson took such actions against Vietnam War opponents, and President Nixon threatened to do so against legislators he thought likely to oppose his Supreme Court nominees. Nixon also threatened to order IRS audits of particular senators' taxes. In 1985, President Reagan indicated he would have "more time" to campaign for the reelection of those Republican senators who voted for his MX missile program. When this strong-arm attempt appeared to be backfiring, Reagan quickly backed away publicly from that position. But he got the votes he needed.

**Going to the people:** Perhaps the president's main advantage in dealing with a recalcitrant Congress is that he can focus national attention on selected issues. The president's audience is always larger than that of an individual legislator, or even a group of legislators. It is also larger than that which can be commanded by the opposition party. For example, Republican President Gerald Ford's State of the Union Address was seen on TV by 75 million viewers, whereas the televised reply by Democratic congressional leaders drew only 47 million. However, too many presidential appearances can lead to diminishing audiences, so this tactic must be used with care.

Presidents can also offer off-the-record press briefings and interviews to get their views across. Televised press conferences offer presidents another forum from which they can appeal to the public, although the risk of committing a blooper is great in the relatively uncontrolled give-and-take of such conferences. Ultimately, if the president can create a sense of national crisis, his own popularity is likely to increase.

**The veto:** The veto power gives the president considerable leverage with Congress. Knowing a veto is likely, Congress may modify a bill to meet presidential objections; after a veto, it may pass legislation altered to meet presidential demands. Presidential vetoes are rarely overridden—only 4 percent suffer such a fate. Yet a few vetoes of extremely important matters have been overridden—for example, President Nixon's veto of the **War Powers Resolution** and President Truman's veto of the **Taft-Hartley Act.**

Presidents cannot veto everything Congress passes. They cannot veto constitutional amendments, or measures related to the internal organization of either house. Also, battles within the executive branch over whether vetoes should be employed in particular situations are common. Typically, conflict erupts between cabinet members and White House staffers or OMB people.

## The dangerous president

In the mid-1970s, in the wake of the Watergate scandals, great concern was voiced about the "imperial presidency," which some observers characterized as threatening to undermine the checks and balances that limit presidential power. This problem is not a new one, however. Throughout U.S. history, presidents have used the wide latitude available to them in foreign policy-making and their position as symbolic leader to create crises, go to war, or harass opponents. In the early days of the Republic, Presidents John Adams, Thomas Jefferson, and Andrew Jackson were accused of abusing the powers of the office. Then, during the Civil War, President Lincoln stretched the powers of the office considerably. In this century, Franklin Roosevelt, John Kennedy, Lyndon Johnson, and Richard Nixon have been charged with abuses of power.

Not every such accusation has been justified, of course. Partisanship has often played a role here. For many years, beginning in the 1930s, conservative Republicans attacked the growing power of the presidency, largely out of dislike for particular policies or particular incumbents. Those who attacked the power of the president, who saw it as a threat to the constitutional system, often seemed to be the same people who did not want an activist government—who preferred to see society remain as it was. During this period, liberals usually championed the strong presidency, seeing in that office an opportunity for implementing change and meeting national needs.

In the 1960s, this pattern of debate changed, as liberals began to voice concern about excessive presidential power and many conservatives found themselves backing the president in power. The Vietnam War, more than any other single factor, accounted for this shift. As many liberals came to oppose the war, they also grew alarmed at the dangerous growth of presidential power associated with it. Conservatives, on the other hand, generally supported the war and threw their weight behind the tactics of Presidents Johnson and Nixon.

Partisanship aside, there is real cause for concern that the president's constitutional powers and the additional functions of the modern presidency could easily threaten democratic politics. Presidential abuses of power generally fall into three categories: betrayals of public trust, in which the president and/or his aides deliberately mislead the public or whip up public emotion in a manipulative way; efforts to undermine the separation of powers by usurping functions that properly belong to Congress or the courts; and manipulation of the political and legal processes.

A clear example of the first type of abuse was Lyndon Johnson's portrayal of himself as the "peace candidate" in the 1964 election. It was later learned that Johnson's election tactics represented a deliberate attempt to mislead the public. Efforts to undermine the separation of powers have taken several forms: for example, the withholding of information from Congress, the circumvention of normal constitutional processes, and various forms of deception. Attempts to manipulate the political and legal processes were best exemplified in the Watergate affair. In the next two sections, we will explore more fully the second and third forms of presidential abuse of power.

## The imperial presidency

According to the historian Arthur Schlesinger, we had a taste of the imperial presidency under Presidents Lyndon Johnson and Richard Nixon.[10] From 1963 to 1974, Schlesinger suggested, presidential power was expanded and abused, and the nation was threatened with a presidential style that ignored reasonable limits on the office.

Schlesinger focused on two aspects of the expansion and use of presidential powers: war powers and the manipulation of secrecy. In an era of nearly constant crisis, the president's war powers gradually expanded until they came to include prerogatives once associated with monarchs, not elected officials. Both presidents deliberately misled Congress and the public about matters of war and peace. Nixon conducted a secret air war in Cambodia in 1969–70. Johnson shrewdly arranged for Congress to pass the Gulf of Tonkin Resolution of 1964, which gave him virtually a free hand in Vietnam. The information the president supplied to Congress on this occasion turned out to be at the least misleading and probably deliberately deceptive (see Chapter 14).

Both Johnson and Nixon also made it a practice to circumvent the need for congressional approval of treaties by the use of the executive agreement. The Supreme Court has upheld the executive's right to negotiate such agreements, which date from the presidency of George Washington. What was distinctive about the 1960s and 1970s, however, was that presidents asked for Senate approval of fairly trivial matters, while reserving truly significant negotiations for private diplomacy about which Congress often was not even informed.

Emergency powers had also accumulated in the president's hands. From the 1930s to the 1960s, Congress passed approximately five hundred laws granting the president such powers, including the powers to seize property, control production, institute martial law, and restrict travel. These laws were used by President Franklin Roosevelt to justify the internment of Japanese-Americans in 1942, and by President Nixon to justify his cover-up of the bombing of Cambodia.

Two other Nixon tactics drew special fire from those who attacked the imperial presidency: his claims of "executive privilege" and his impoundment of funds allocated by Congress. Many presidents have invoked **executive privilege** to withhold information from Congress, on the grounds that disclosure would damage the national interest or interfere with the exercise of executive responsibilities. During the Watergate inquiries, however, the administration's habit of invoking executive privilege at every conceivable juncture became a major focus of debate. As for impoundment, Nixon again made what had been a fairly rare use of power into a regular instrument of policy. As we saw in Chapter 14, **impoundment** involves the executive's refusal to spend funds Congress has allocated. Whereas other presidents had limited impoundments to small sums, Nixon impounded $18 billion—including funds for such popular programs as water treatment, urban assistance, and loans to farmers. In this case, impoundment amounted to the exercise of an **item veto**—the selective rejection of parts of a law—and the president is given no such power in the Constitution.

A final point in the inventory of imperial powers was the power to pardon. When Ford pardoned Nixon after taking office in 1974, many argued he had violated the pledge made during his confirmation hearings that he would not do precisely that. Pardon power is absolute. There is no check. Although it was intended as a corrective to errors in the judicial process, it could be put to rather broad use.

In response to these and other perceived abuses of presidential power, Congress passed the War Powers Resolution of 1973 and the Budget and Impoundment Act of 1974, curtailed the president's emergency powers, and imposed some restrictions on future executive agreements (see Chapter 14 for details).

| The Watergate
| affair

On the night of June 17, 1972, five burglars were apprehended in the headquarters of the Democratic National Committee, located in the Watergate com-

plex in Washington, D.C. Seized along with the intruders were devices for listening in on conversations. The discovery of this break-in attempt marked the beginning of a trail that led, over two years later, to the resignation of President Richard Nixon.

At first, administration spokesmen dismissed the break-in as a "third-rate burglary." But two reporters for the *Washington Post*, Carl Bernstein and Bob Woodward, traced a connection between the break-in and Nixon's reelection campaign committee (the Committee to Re-Elect the President, or CREEP), along with several White House aides in contact with CREEP. A plan to cover up these connections was put to work. Incriminating documents were destroyed, and there were efforts to buy off the Watergate burglars by providing money for their defense and their families. Despite some efforts by the Democrats to focus attention on Watergate, the cover-up efforts were generally effective prior to the elections of November 1972, in which Nixon was returned to office in a landslide.

In January 1973, however, the Watergate burglars were convicted and sentenced to jail terms, and one of the burglars told Judge John Sirica that they had been pressured into pleading guilty. Sirica reopened the case and grand jury hearings were held. A Senate Select Committee on Watergate began an investiga-

Some of the significant people and moments in the Watergate story: (*left, top*) an intense-looking Sam Ervin (D, NC), chairman of the Senate Committee that investigated Watergate and uncovered much of the damning evidence, including the existence of the White House tapes. (*left, bottom*) John Dean testifies before the Committee. A White House staff member, Dean's revelations of intrigues in the White House and in CREEP resulted in a searching examination of Nixon's staff. (*right, bottom*) President Nixon consults with top aide Bob Haldeman. Despite efforts to shield them, the inquiry reached the President and his chief aides. Haldeman, among others, was forced to resign and was tried and convicted. (*right, top*) A unique moment in U.S. political history: the resignation of a president. Richard Nixon announces that he will step down August 9, 1974, less than two years after his landslide victory. His wife, Pat, watches.

tion in May 1973. Under pressure from Congress and the press, Nixon appointed a special prosecutor to look into the matter, although he and his aides continued to maintain their innocence.

The media started to pay more attention to the case. Despite the initial findings of Woodward and Bernstein, the press had done little to investigate the affair before the election. Then someone within the administration—a someone still unknown—began providing tips to Woodward and Bernstein. As the Watergate cover-up began to unravel, the media covered the story thoroughly.

The Senate hearings soon brought increasingly unpleasant facts to light. Nixon's one-time White House counsel, John Dean, testified extensively about a concerted cover-up of the Watergate affair and other illegal activities directed from the White House. Slowly, it became clear that the Nixon administration had violated most of the usual rules of U.S. political life. White House personnel and Republican Party members illegally wiretapped political opponents, stole documents, lied to grand juries, and engaged in large-scale falsifications about illegal campaign contributions. As the evidence grew closer to the Oval Office, some of Nixon's aides resigned. (Several were later convicted for their roles in the affair, including top presidential aides John Ehrlichman and H. R. Haldeman and former attorney general John Mitchell.)

Yet Nixon himself might have been able to weather the Watergate storm had it not been for the discovery that he had installed a taping system that secretly recorded every conversation in the Oval Office. It was immediately evident to the Senate investigative committee that such tapes could provide invaluable evidence for or against the president and his top aides. Claiming executive privilege, Nixon refused to release the tapes until the Supreme Court unanimously ordered him to supply copies of the tapes to the court hearing the Watergate burglary case.

The tapes doomed Nixon. On them, Nixon and his aides emerged as vindictive schemers interested in evening scores with their enemies and increasing their power to the extent they could get away with it. With impeachment proceedings apparently imminent, Nixon resigned in August 1974.

Were Nixon's activities so different from those of other presidents? Yes and no. Many of the complaints against Nixon involved activities that other presidents had engaged in or condoned. Other chief executives had received illegal campaign contributions, used "dirty tricks" in political campaigns, provided direct or indirect payoffs to those who had helped in election efforts, used government agencies to harass enemies, tried to manage the news, and attempted to keep some activities secret from public and Congress. On the specific matters for which articles of impeachment were contemplated, however, Nixon stood alone. His personal involvement in the cover-up of crimes and the obstruction of justice distinguished him from other presidents. In the final analysis, the combination of so many violations of law and norms, of so many questionable activities designed to enhance the powers and prerogatives of a president and his cohorts, was unique to the Nixon administration.

Why did the Watergate scandals occur at all? The answer is not simple. Part of the blame can be placed on the political and moral views of Nixon and his closest advisers. Inside the Nixon administration, there was a strong sense of moral righteousness. Some in the White House saw politics as a battleground between the forces of "law and order," as represented by the administration, and rebellious students, blacks, and others who were seen as undermining the American way of life. It may seem ironic that the Nixon people could cast themselves in a law-and-order role—but to a large degree, they did. No doubt the previous growth in the power of the presidency, especially in connection with foreign policy matters, also set the stage for Watergate. Here was a president and a group of advisers who not only tried to get around the law, but who actually believed that the president (at least *their* president) was above the law.

With Nixon's resignation, many breathed a sigh of relief. We must recognize, however, that the problem of the imperial presidency has not yet been solved. Although the immediate issues raised by the Johnson and Nixon presidencies have been dealt with, still unanswered is the larger question of the president's dominant role in U.S. political life. Most Americans would prefer not to weaken the presidency in any constitutional manner. And most remain attracted to the idea of an activist president who vigorously leads the nation. So long as those views are dominant, the risk of presidential abuse of power will remain.

## Transition of power

Transitions at the top levels of a political system are frequently very difficult to manage. In many polities, such changeovers touch off intense struggles for power among individuals and groups seeking to gain political control. When Josef Stalin died in 1953 after ruling the Soviet Union for twenty-five years, the succession crisis lasted several years. Similarly, Mao Zedong's death in 1976 touched off epic political struggle in China.

One of the strengths of democratic nations is that in them, struggles for leadership can usually be settled by legal, constitutional means. As a result, democratic political leaders normally do not attempt to employ illegal means to remain in office following

electoral defeat. Yet many intricacies can develop in the process of transition at the top. What happens when a president is disabled or dies, or is removed from office?

## Modes of succession

Under normal conditions, presidents leave office because they choose not to run again or are defeated in an election. Only about one-third of U.S. presidents—thirteen in all—have won a second term in office, and only Franklin Roosevelt served more than two terms. (His election to four terms is no longer possible: under the Twenty-second Amendment, ratified in 1951, presidents are limited to a maximum of two terms in office, and a person who has gained the presidency through succession as vice-president is limited to only a single election if he serves more than two years of the unexpired term of the previous president. This means that no one may serve more than ten years as president today.)

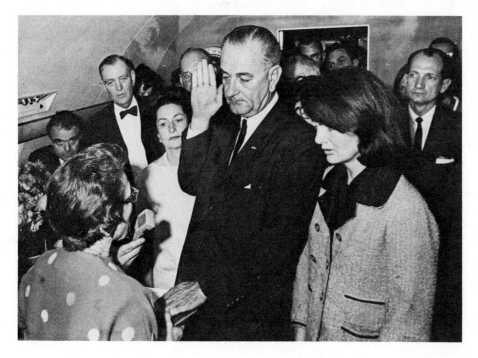

As the shock of John F. Kennedy's assassination in Dallas on November 22, 1963, spreads through the nation, Lyndon Baines Johnson takes the oath of office on Air Force One, with Jacqueline Kennedy looking on.

Slightly over 20 percent of U.S. presidents have died in office, including four who were assassinated: Abraham Lincoln (1865), James Garfield (1881), William McKinley (1901), and John Kennedy (1963). Since 1945, moreover, four out of eight presidents have been attacked by assassins—certainly a record among contemporary Western democracies. So far, no president has been removed from office via the impeachment process, although Andrew Johnson came close and Richard Nixon resigned before impeachment could be brought.

The mechanics of presidential succession are not spelled out in the Constitution. When President William Henry Harrison died one month after taking office in 1841, John Tyler, the vice-president, assumed the presidency. It was the first time that a president had died in office, and something of a controversy ensued. Should Tyler simply become president, or should he take office temporarily until a new election could be held? Tyler preferred the first alternative, and Congress went along.

The Succession Act of 1886 mandated specific procedures for presidential succession. Among other things the act made the secretary of state second in line behind the vice-president, followed by the other members of the cabinet in order of seniority. Such a system seems odd, since it places a whole series of unelected officials in line for the presidency. It also allows a vice-president who inherits the presidency to pick his own successor by choosing the secretary of state.

This pattern of succession was altered in 1947, when the Speaker of the House and the president pro tem of the Senate were placed next in line after the vice-president. The problem with this system was that it placed in the line of succession officials who might not be of the president's party. Finally, the Twenty-fifth Amendment, ratified in 1967, took up the twin issues of succession and presidential disability. Twice in U.S. history, presidents had become seriously disabled—James Garfield after being shot in 1881, and Woodrow Wilson after a stroke in 1919. Others, such as Dwight Eisenhower, had been temporarily incapacitated by illness. The Twenty-fifth Amendment provided that if the president were unable to carry out his duties, the vice-president

would serve as acting president. If the president were to decline to step down, he could be removed by a two-thirds vote of each house of Congress. In dealing with succession, the amendment specifies that on assuming the presidency, the vice-president must nominate a new vice-president, who must then be confirmed by a majority of both houses. If no new vice-president has been selected and the new president must be replaced, the 1947 arrangements prevail.

Not long after the Twenty-fifth Amendment was ratified, its provisions were put to use. Nixon's vice-president, Spiro Agnew, resigned from office after pleading no contest to bribery charges. Nixon then nominated Gerald Ford to the vice-presidency. Not long thereafter, Nixon resigned the presidency, and Ford became president. He in turn nominated Nelson Rockefeller as vice-president, and Rockefeller was confirmed by both houses. When he was sworn in as vice-president on December 19, 1974, it marked the first time in U.S. history that two men occupying the highest offices of the nation were both unelected. The procedure worked smoothly, despite the turmoil of Watergate and the novelty of the succession process. The procedures were also put into effect in 1985, when Ronald Reagan was briefly unable to serve as president during an operation for colon cancer. George Bush became acting president for that short period.

## The vice-presidency

Scorn for the vice-presidency has been common in U.S. history. According to John Nance Garner, who gave up his position as Speaker of the House to become Franklin Roosevelt's running mate in 1936, the vice-presidency was "not worth a pitcher of warm spit." And when Daniel Webster rejected a nomination for the vice-presidency in 1848, he declared, "I do not choose to be buried until I am really dead."

The vice-president's duties are minimal. The only official function is to preside over the Senate and to break tie votes in the Senate—quite a rare event. Vice-presidents have sometimes been allocated cer-

# Comparative
# perspective
# Political crisis
# and transition
# in France,
# 1958

During World War II, General Charles de Gaulle served as the acknowledged leader of the Free French. After the liberation of France, he presided over a provisional government while an assembly wrote a new constitution establishing the Fourth Republic. Disgusted with the weak government he felt had been created, de Gaulle repaired to the political sidelines in 1946.

By May 1958, the Fourth Republic had gone through twenty-four governments, and the country was being torn apart over the problem of

Sources: Don Cook, *Charles de Gaulle* (New York: Putnam, 1983); and Bernard Ledwidge, *De Gaulle* (New York: St. Martin's, 1982).

Algeria—whether to acknowledge the grievances of Algerian rebels opposing French rule or to repress all symptoms of colonial unrest. The Algerian question proved too much for the successively weaker governments. In 1956, the French Army had stood by while French settlers in Algiers attacked their own premier, socialist Guy Mollet, whom they felt had been too weak in dealing with the rebels. The disaffected military coalesced into a powerful and potentially antidemocratic threat to French political stability.

The twenty-third government of the Fourth Republic fell on April 15,

1958, when the hardline Algerian lobby withdrew its support. Four tense weeks passed before a new government could be formed. Meanwhile, de Gaulle was poised to reclaim political power. As anti-Gaullist politicians scrambled to scrape together enough support to keep him out of power, several prominent military officers planned a coup d'etat against the Republic, to be carried out on the orders of the senior military command in Algiers.

What came next has been termed the de Gaulle revolution. Through a process of secret negotiations with members of the government and public pronouncements warning

the military to "maintain exemplary behavior," de Gaulle was able to position himself for an official call to establish a new government. Legality was preserved as de Gaulle, like his predecessors, was voted into office by the National Assembly. But his terms for taking the reins of government were stiff: emergency powers and governance by decree, the temporary (six-month) dissolution of the Assembly, and the mandate to draw up a new constitution. France had preserved the form, if not the substance, of institutionalized succession.

tain functions by the president, such as chairing government commissions or undertaking foreign assignments of various sorts. For the most part, however, vice-presidents are hemmed in by the constraints of the position. They cannot openly break with the administration they serve without inhibiting the development of their own political careers.

Some observers have argued that given its general uselessness, the vice-presidency should be done away with and presidential succession handled through the holding of a second national election. Others have contended that to make the office more meaningful, presidential candidates should select their running mates early and run for nomination as a team. Neither proposal seems likely to find political acceptance in the near future.

## Conclusions

There is a tendency to reach for extremes in dealing with the presidency. To one generation, presidential leadership is the key to political soundness, progress, and effective policy-making. To another, the president is chief ogre and the presidency a source of unrestrained hubris. Today, when the president has his finger on the nuclear trigger, all the issues that had seemed important before have become enormously magnified. What sort of person should sit in the White House? What sort of latitude should we permit the occupant of the Oval Office? Is the president the fulcrum of the constitutional system or the chief source of danger to democracy? Although these questions may seem easy to answer at times, particularly when there is a heated reaction to a certain president, they are usually not amenable to simple reactions. As times and political challenges change, our image of the president changes, too.

What about the democratic component? Clearly, presidents can prove of great value in championing democratic causes. Why Lyndon Johnson asserted that "we shall overcome," and introduced the Voting Rights Act of 1965, it marked a turning point in

U.S. history. Lending the weight of the presidency to democratic causes can make the difference between progress and stagnation. But presidents can also work against democratic politics, as Richard Nixon did in so many ways, and as Lyndon Johnson did in not being truthful about his Vietnam policy. Presidents have most latitude, can do the most damage, and are most likely to play on popular fears in the area of foreign policy. Therefore, it is in this area that the most immediate problems for democratic values are encountered. Only an informed and vigorous Congress and an attentive public can make sure that presidents do not overreach in this critical aspect of policy.

We expect presidents to lead. But is it possible for presidents to lead without deception and without offering simplistic solutions? Does the public long for a leader who breathes confidence and optimism, such as Ronald Reagan or Franklin Roosevelt, whatever the logic of his proposals? This seems another of the dangers to democracy inherent in the U.S. presidency. The post may be, as Theodore Roosevelt termed it, a "bully pulpit" from which to rouse the nation—but that also means it can be used to exploit public fears, to play on popular stereotypes, to offer facile solutions to tough problems.

In the end, we have to face the fact that presidents, regardless how politically talented, are not supermen. All presidents are confronted with many "givens," problems and events that the president can neither change nor wish away. Yet, it is clear that *the person* can make a difference. How would Reagan have reacted to the Bay of Pigs crisis? How would Eisenhower have handled Vietnam? Would Ford have launched a human rights policy as Carter did? Had he been elected to a second term, would Carter have proposed a Reaganite tax policy?

It is troubling for us to have to admit that so much which matters in our democratic polity depends on one person and those who surround that person. And it is perplexing for us to recognize that someone can become president without the benefit of experience in any similar office. It is therefore on the president, most of all, that democrats must keep their eyes.

## NOTES

1 Richard Pious provides an interesting discussion of American attitudes toward the presidency in *The American Presidency* (New York: Basic Books, 1979), Introduction and Part 1. Fred Greenstein, who studied reactions to the Kennedy assassination, reported that 43 percent of adults suffered loss of appetite; 48 percent, insomnia; 25 percent, headaches; 68 percent, nervousness and tension; 26 percent, rapid heartbeat; and 17 percent, perspiration. See his "Popular Images of the President," *American Journal of Psychiatry*, 122 (1965). Also on this subject consult B. S. Greenberg and E. B. Parker, *The Kennedy Assassination and the American Public* (Stanford, Calif.: Stanford University Press, 1965).

2 See Richard Pious, *The American Presidency*, Chapter 2.

3 These examples are derived from Richard Pious, *The American Presidency*, Part II, Sections 2, 3, and 4.

4 *Sawyer, Petitioner*, v. *Youngstown Sheet and Tube Co. et al.* (1952).

5 The following discussion is derived from Thomas E. Cronin, *The State of the Presidency*, 2nd ed. (Boston: Little, Brown, 1980), Chapter 1.

6 *Ibid.*, pp. 19–22.

7 For a good discussion of the point, see Bruce Miroff, *Pragmatic Illusions: The Presidential Politics of John F. Kennedy* (New York: McKay, 1976), especially Chapters 2 and 7.

8 See James Tobin, *The New Economics* (Princeton, N.J.: Princeton University Press, 1974), for an interesting treatment of the Council of Economic Advisers.

9 Cronin, *op. cit.*, pp. 228–29.

10 See A. M. Schlesinger, Jr., *The Imperial Presidency* (Boston: Houghton Mifflin, 1973).

## SELECTED READINGS

For various overviews concerning the presidency, see Richard Neustadt, *Presidential Power* (New York: Wiley, 1960); Richard Pious, *The American Presidency* (New York: Basic Books, 1979); Thomas Cronin, *The State of the Presidency* (Boston: Little, Brown, 1980); and Arthur M. Schlesinger, Jr., *The Imperial Presidency* (Boston: Houghton Mifflin, 1973).

On more specific aspects of the presidency and the executive branch, see Michael Nelson, ed., *The Presidency and the Political System* (Washington, D.C.: Congressional Quarterly Press, 1984); Robert Shogun, *None of the Above* (New York: NAL, 1982); Theodore C. Sorensen, *Watchmen in the Night* (Cambridge, Mass.: MIT Press, 1975); James David Barber, *Presidential Character* (Englewood Cliffs, N.J.: Prentice-Hall, 1985); James M. Burns, *Roosevelt: The Lion and the Fox* (New York: Harcourt, 1956); John W. Dean, *Blind Ambition* (New York: Simon & Schuster, 1976); and David Halberstam, *The Best and the Brightest* (New York: Bantam, 1972).

# Chapter
sixteen

# Bureaucracy

# Servant or master?

CERTAIN terms carry connotations that are hard to escape. *Bureaucracy* is such a term: inevitably, it evokes thoughts of endless red tape, inefficiency, and unresponsiveness. To most people, the bureaucracy is that faceless entity responsible for forcing them to fill out tax forms or stand in line at post offices or wait for Medicare refunds. But the workings of bureaucrats touch people's lives in many other ways. The food we eat, the prescription drugs we take, the planes we fly on, the cars we drive, the sports equipment we play with, even the inflammable Dr. Dentons we wore as children—all of these disparate things fall under regulations established by the federal bureaucracy.

As used here, the term **bureaucracy** will be loosely applied to the millions of full-time career employees who do the day-to-day work of government. The bureaucracy's impact on government policy is immense. Whatever laws are enacted by Congress or directives issued by the president, in an important sense government policy is no more and no less than what the bureaucrats do. Often, bureaucrats must interpret the meaning of vague and sometimes contradictory directives from Congress or the president. Despite the superficial image of the bureaucracy as nonpolitical, bureaucrats often must make controversial decisions that are the subjects of intense political struggle, as this chapter will illustrate. If a bureaucracy can facilitate the carrying out of policies (at least when those policies are clear), it can also thwart, redirect, and even work in direct opposition to either Congress or the president.

It is important to keep in mind that the government bureaucracy is not a monolith—rather, it is a huge complex of bureaus, agencies, boards, and commissions with many different functions and different mandates, created at different times. Frequently, one portion of the federal bureaucracy will be at odds with another, as when a jurisdictional dispute erupts between two agencies, or when policies and clienteles differ. For example, whereas the Department of Health and Human Services tries to discourage smoking, the Department of Agriculture helps farmers grow tobacco more efficiently. Similarly, plans by the Army Corps of Engineers to build a dam may be opposed by the Environmental Protection Agency, on the grounds that the dam will adversely affect wildlife. The government has grown so large and complex that agencies often must go to considerable lengths just to coordinate their efforts. Simply keeping abreast of what other agencies are doing is not an easy task.

Is the concept of bureaucracy in accord with democratic ideals? Those who attack bureaucracy claim that through it, big government too often harasses individuals and groups, places too many restrictions on people's actions, and engages in costly and in- efficient practices. In this view, bureaucrats have become a power unto themselves, dictating from Washington the way people throughout the country ought to live their lives. In rejoinder, the defenders of bureaucracy argue that in a modern society, bu- reaucratic procedures are required. After all, they say, someone must send out the Social Security checks and make the appropriate rules for eligibility, some- one must police mine safety and check on air pol- lution, and so on. In addition, they maintain that at times government bureaucracy is the only defender of individual citizens who would otherwise be pow- erless against discrimination and other violations of rights and threats to health and safety. What is needed, they conclude, is not the abolition of bureaucracy, but a better, more responsive, more efficient bu- reaucracy. Even if we accept this view, however, we must still answer two fundamental questions: How much bureaucracy is enough? and How well do our current bureaucratic arrangements function?

In this chapter, we will examine three basic issues relating to the federal bureaucracy. First, just what *is* the bureaucracy? What are its components and its

tasks? Second, how do bureaucrats relate to the po- litical process? Are they servants of that process, or are they routinely unresponsive to the popular will? Third, what are the current proposals for reform of the bureaucracy? Specifically, we will look at the debate over federal regulation.

## The national bureaucracy

The Constitution's only reference to the structure and role of the federal bureaucracy is a recognition of the president's right to demand periodic reports from the head officials in the executive departments. The Founders almost certainly recognized that the ad- ministrative apparatus of government would need to remain flexible, to change with the times. But it is likely that they also failed to anticipate how much the government would grow. To them, executive de- partments were small operations aiding the presi- dent—hardly a major matter in 1792, when the en- tire federal government had only 780 employees.

One of the most significant, but least known, of govern- ment agencies, the Army Corps of Engineers, rein- forces a sagging roadbed along the shore of Lake Michigan. The Corps builds dams, creates lakes and recreation areas, dredges harbors, and carries on a vast array of construction activities.

Are we all just numbers in a file drawer? You get that feeling sometimes. Here, a government employee examines a strip of film against a backdrop of seemingly endless file cabinets.

Today the federal government has approximately 2.8 million employees (excluding the armed forces). The bureaucracy grew most spectacularly during and after the New Deal, when government took on many more social programs. Since 1950 the overall growth of federal government employment has been minimal. But federal expenditures and regulations have risen dramatically over the past three decades, particularly during the 1970s.

## Extent of federal service

Perhaps the best way to indicate the size, reach, and nature of the federal bureaucracy is to look at a number of isolated facts.

1. Only 10 percent of government civilian employees work in the Washington, D.C., area; the rest work in regional or local offices spread throughout the country.

2. In addition to its uniformed personnel the Department of Defense employs more than 1.3 million *civilian* workers, who comprise approximately 40 percent of the total government work force. The DOD is not only the biggest government employer—it is also the largest single employer in the United States. (The largest private employer, General Motors, has about 800,000 employees.)

3. Despite the great size of the federal bureaucracy, it is relatively small in comparison with the total number of state and local government employees. Only 22 percent of all government employees work for the federal government.

4. About eight-five percent of every one hundred workers are career civil service employees, whose salaries are set by Congress. In 1984 the lowest civil service salary was $9,023, and the highest, $69,600.

5. Only about a half-million government employees have characteristically bureaucratic positions, such as those of clerk or general administrator. The government also employs 147,000 engineers and architects, 84,000 scientists, and 2,400 veterinarians.

6. Most government employees are white males. In the lower levels of government service, however, blacks are overrepresented. Similarly, although nearly one-third of all federal employees are women, the vast majority of female federal employees occupy such lower-level positions as secretary and typist. In the upper salary ranges, the proportion of women dwindles rapidly.

7. Much of the work of government at all levels is done by so-called *contract bureaucracies*—private firms hired by the government. The Department of Defense, for example, hires firms such as Boeing and Lockheed to design and to build military hardware, the Army Corps of Engineers hires private firms to design and construct dams and hydroelectric projects, and most of the personnel involved in the space program are contract bureaucrats. In this way, a great many Americans work for the government indirectly—they are not on the federal payroll and their jobs are not protected by civil service regulations.

We do not always remember that the Department of Defense is a major portion of the federal bureaucracy. The vast Pentagon building itself seems to represent the huge numbers, power, and complexity involved.

## Components of the bureaucracy

Bureaucracies tend to be structured according to areas of specialization—one agency handles only law enforcement, another only medical care, and so on. Such specialized competence is the basis of bureaucracy. The principle of organization by specialization can be seen in the structure of the federal executive branch, as outlined in Figure 16.1.

Before we consider the problems engendered by bureaucratic specialization, we must examine the primary components of the bureaucracy—the cabinet departments, the independent executive agencies and government corporations, and the regulatory commissions.

**Cabinet departments:** In 1789, there were only three **cabinet departments**—State, War, and Treasury. As new needs arose, new departments were created. In 1849 the Department of the Interior was

set up to deal with the government's vast land holdings and with the Native American population. The Department of Agriculture was established in 1862, the Justice Department in 1870, and the departments of Commerce and of Labor in 1913. The War and the Navy departments were merged into the Defense Department in 1947. Health, Education and Welfare, created in 1953, was redesignated Health and Human Services in 1979. Housing and Urban Development appeared in 1965, Transportation in 1966, Energy in 1977, and Education in 1979.

The thirteen cabinet departments comprise the bulk of the federal bureaucracy, employing a majority of federal workers (although the Veterans' Administration, an independent agency, is larger than many cabinet departments). As we saw in Chapter 15, the head of a department is appointed by the president and is the department's representative in the president's cabinet. The other top officials in cabinet departments are also appointed by the president. Many of them have no prior experience in the department, and they rarely remain in office for more than a few years. Just below them, however, are career civil servants who have risen through the ranks and whose experience and skill are vital to the efficient functioning of the departments. These senior civil servants have powers that must be reckoned with when policies are being formulated. Running a department is something akin to running a small government.

**Independent executive agencies:** Like cabinet secretaries, the heads of the independent agencies serve at the pleasure of the president. With several exceptions, **independent agencies** are smaller than cabinet departments and tend to have considerably more focused missions. Most came into being to serve specific functions and, for various reasons, were not

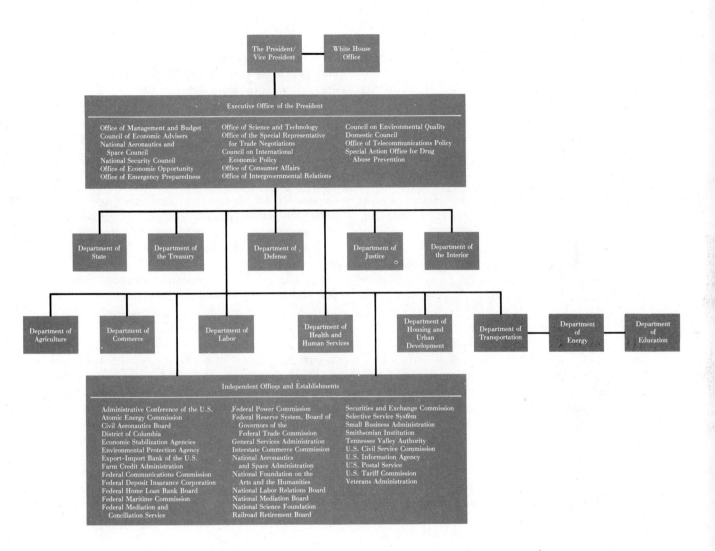

FIGURE 16.1
The Executive Branch of the U.S. Government: This organizational chart does not do justice to the complexities and tremendous size of the agencies involved, but it does provide a generalized map of the major groupings of the executive bureaucracy. The Executive Office is of direct aid to the president with relation to special issues and areas of operation that cross over departmental jurisdictions. The thirteen executive departments (the cabinet) are slightly more removed from direct presidential control. The independent offices and establishments are even more independent of presidential control, although the president maintains a degree of influence by virtue of his power to appoint their governing officials. Source: National Archives and Records Services, General Services Administration.

placed under a cabinet department. An example of such an agency was the Selective Service System. Created hastily prior to World War II, it was kept independent of the War Department (now the Department of Defense) to reassure citizens that the draft was a civilian operation and was expected to be in existence for only a limited time. The Central Intelligence Agency is another independent organization. Established through the fusion of many competing governmental intelligence agencies, the CIA was not placed under a cabinet department because its creation was intended to resolve interdepartmental power struggles.

Also included among the independent agencies are government corporations—the Post Office, the Tennessee Valley Authority (TVA), and the Federal Deposit Insurance Corporation.

**Regulatory commissions:** Another type of independent agency is the **regulatory commission.** The purpose of these agencies is to regulate certain kinds of activities, particularly in the economic sphere. They perform a quasijudicial function, in that they can bring charges, hold hearings, and impose penalties for violations of rules. The Federal Communications Commission, for example, may revoke the licenses of television and radio stations for a number of reasons, including a station's failure to provide sufficient community-service broadcasting. Regulatory commissions are also quasilegislative bodies, in that they can make, as well as interpret, rules. For example, the Federal Trade Commission imposes a wide variety of regulations on manufacturing and on advertising in order to protect consumers from unsafe or misrepresented merchandise.

The independent regulatory agencies were set up outside the normal executive branch chain of command in an effort to keep them "free" from politics. Commission members are appointed by the president to relatively long terms, subject to Senate confirmation. Once in office they are not required to report to the president and may not be removed until the end of their terms, except through impeachment. Unlike cabinet officers and heads of other executive agencies, then, they do not resign when a new president is elected. A new president can only name

members to commissions as terms expire or as vacancies occur because of death or retirement. By law, moreover, members of these agencies must be drawn from both major political parties.

In spite of these precautions, the regulatory commissions have been deeply immersed in behind-the-scenes politics. Their activities are of intense concern to interest groups, which, over time, often develop close and sometimes cozy relationships with the agencies. Critics have pointed out that some commission members seem more interested in protecting the interests of drug companies, trucking firms, brokerage houses, and other concerns that they are supposed to regulate than in protecting the interests of the public.

The history of the Interstate Commerce Commission illustrates this tendency. Originally set up in 1887 to protect consumers against the predatory practices of railroad monopolies, the ICC by 1920 was almost solely responsive to the railroad interests. In case after case, ICC rulings benefited the railroads. More recently, the ICC has struck a balance between the interests of railroads and those of trucking companies, with consumers running a poor third.

An additional barrier to effective regulation stems from the fact that federal commissions typically don't have enough staff members to fulfill their regulatory functions. Hearings to develop new regulations for an industry often pit a handful of civil service accountants and lawyers against battalions of highly paid industry lawyers and accountants.[1]

## Civil service system

The first federal job appointments were made by George Washington, who declared that his choices were based entirely on "fitness of character." It soon became apparent, however, that most of those found fit were associated with the emerging Federalist Party, which Washington and Alexander Hamilton headed. When Thomas Jefferson became president in 1801, he set a precedent by dismissing hundreds of Fed-

## Comparative perspective

# The British and French bureaucracies

One of the best-known aspects of the British bureaucracy is the "administrative class," made up of approximately seventy-five hundred senior personnel selected through a civil service system. These top civil servants are closely involved in the formulation of public policy. It is their job to screen important information for the ministers of each department, to provide political advice, and to comment on the wisdom and practicality of various policy proposals. What they do *not* do is "administer" the various departments of the bureaucracy; that task is left to others. British civil servants usually view their jobs as lifetime commitments, not as steppingstones to positions in industry or politics. Most regard themselves as the long-term protectors of the public interest and the upholders of high civil standards. They are sometimes criticized for being too cautious and unimaginative.

France was one of the first European nations to create a modern-style bureaucracy, and the existence of a top administrative class similar to the one in Great Britain has been a distinguishing feature of French bureaucratic organization. At the top of the French administrative hierarchy are several thousand bureaucrats, three to five hundred of whom are highly active in the political decision-making process.

What is most striking about the top French administrators is that they have come to comprise almost a hereditary group. The entrance exams for the two schools that train French administrators tend to favor people from upper-class backgrounds. Over the last thirty years, there has only been a very gradual increase in the number of middle-class students admitted, despite various government efforts to open the schools to all talented individuals. Candidates from working class and farming backgrounds are almost never accepted. Of the top seven thousand French civil servants in the most prestigious sectors of the bureaucracy, about 75 percent come from the highest levels of Parisian society.

These administrators have long considered themselves not mere civil servants, but managers for society as a whole and agents of change in the modernization of France. Many top bureaucrats have resented French political parties and the French legislature for interfering with plans hatched among the administrative class. A large number of top bureaucrats will move into industry if their ambitions are not fulfilled within the bureaucracy. Over 40 percent of the major French business concerns are headed by former bureaucrats.*

When the Socialist government of François Mitterand came to power in 1981, it implemented proposals to decentralize the French bureaucracy. Mitterand's goal was to loosen central bureaucratic control and provide more decision-making to local governments in France. It was the first such move in the direction of decentralization in a bureaucratic system that had been highly centralized for centuries.

*Henry W. Ehrmann, *Politics in France* (Boston: Little, Brown, 1983), pp. 161–74.

---

eralists from government jobs and installing his supporters in their places.

Thereafter, under what became known as the **spoils system,** elected officials routinely rewarded friends and supporters with government jobs. The spoils system reached its peak under President Andrew Jackson. After his election in 1828, Jackson dismissed more than one-third of the six hundred upper-level officeholders and from 10 to 20 percent of the ten thousand government officials who occupied lower-level positions.

To some extent, the spoils system made sense. The political parties needed some form of patronage (the power of appointment to government jobs) in order to reward party workers. During the nineteenth century, the government had little need for trained specialists, so a high turnover in personnel usually did not endanger operating efficiency. Furthermore, any president is entitled to fill key positions with people who share his political philosophy.*

Nevertheless, by the 1870s, obvious abuses of the spoils system had produced a clamor for reform. These demands led to action after President James A. Garfield was assassinated by a disappointed office seeker in 1881. With the support of Garfield's successor, Chester A. Arthur, Congress passed a bill establishing a bipartisan Civil Service Commission to administer competitive examinations and make appointments to office based on merit. Under the **civil service system** now in place, the commission sets up formal descriptions of job requirements and classifies civil servants according to job description. Once the various civil service positions have been described and classified, examinations are given to determine those candidates best suited for the available positions. After taking examinations, the candidates are placed on lists, from which agencies select employees.

The federal civil service system is so well developed that it is commonplace to find most bureaus filled with college graduates. It is also common to find very high levels of educational specialization in the federal bureaucracy. Chemists employed by the Department of Agriculture, biologists employed by the National Institutes of Health, safety engineers employed by the Federal Aviation Agency—all of these professionals typify the high degree of specialization and education found in modern public service.

Yet this emphasis on expertise, to the exclusion of political factors, has its costs. Most civil servants cannot be removed from their jobs except for gross misconduct, and many promotions are based on seniority rather than on merit. The laudable purpose of these procedures is to insulate the bureaucracy from unwarranted political interference—but they also

protect bureaucrats from demands for high performance. As Peter Drucker has pointed out, "Mediocrity in the civil service [may be] a lesser evil than politics [but] a good many people today have come to believe that we need some way of rewarding performance and of penalizing nonperformance, even within the civil service."[2]

These and other concerns have led to attempts to make the system more responsive to considerations of merit. President Jimmy Carter instituted a number of civil service reforms designed to enhance the role of merit in promotions, salary increases, and firings. Under Carter, top managers were given the option of trading job security for higher pay and rewards for superior performance. Of the first four thousand eligible bureaucrats, all but ten opted for the chance to make potentially higher salaries, even at the risk of losing their positions.

Another of the Carter reforms called for pay raises based on performance, not just longevity, for thousands of middle-level managers and supervisors. The civil service system was given greater flexibility in firing and demotion, but safeguards for the employee

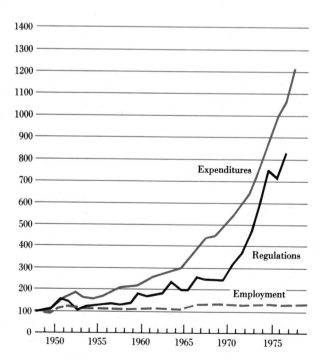

*There is a difference, it should be noted, between a patronage system that rewards political loyalists regardless of competence and a system of partisan appointments that rewards competent loyalists with key policy-making positions. In practice, however, this distinction is sometimes hard to discern.

were provided by an appeals process and union arbitration proceedings. In addition, the Civil Service Commission was split into two bodies: the Office of Personnel Management, charged with managing the federal work force; and the Merit System Protections Board, charged with protecting the rights of employees.

The basic reasoning behind the Carter reforms was not only that merit should be rewarded, but also that top civil servants should not become too deeply entrenched in their positions and unresponsive to changes in policy. In its first few years of operation, however, the new system seemingly has had little overall impact. Of the six thousand senior civil servants who gave up tenured positions in the late 1970s and early 1980s, only one was dropped for poor performance, and very few were shifted from one part of the bureaucracy to another.[3]

## Bureaucracy and the political process

Bureaucracies are embedded firmly within the political process. Consider the example of automobile safety. In 1966, alarmed by rising highway fatalities and alerted to auto design hazards by Ralph Nader's book *Unsafe at Any Speed,* Congress passed highway safety legislation creating the National Highway Traffic Safety Administration. Under this legislation, federal standards were issued affecting steering columns, brakes, door locks, windshields, and other features. One exciting new safety device developed in Detroit about that time was the so-called air bag. The bag, normally stored beneath the windshield, inflates instantaneously on collision impact to cushion occupants in a front seat. In 1971, President Richard Nixon's transportation secretary, John Volpe, issued Safety Standard 208, which required the installation of air bags or safety belts in all new cars. The Nixon White House, however, postponed implementation

FIGURE 16.2
Federal Government Growth: Money, Rules, and People (1949 = 100)

of the standard in 1972, apparently responding to pressure from the automobile industry. Four years later, in 1976, President Gerald Ford's secretary of transportation rescinded 208.

In 1977, with the Carter administration friendlier to consumer safety, the attempt to get an air bag ruling began again. A revised version of 208 providing automakers with greater time for installation, was promulgated. Either automatic seat belts or air bags would be mandatory on new cars in 1984. But in 1981 the Reagan administration took office with a philosophy determined to deregulate. Shortly thereafter, 208 was completely revoked. In reaction, a coalition of consumer groups filed suit in federal court. Their litigation was upheld in 1982. The administration and the auto companies appealed the ruling to the Supreme Court, which, in 1983, found unanimously against them, saying: "For nearly a decade the automobile industry waged the regulatory equivalent of war against the air bag and lost—the inflatable restraint was proven sufficiently effective." (Motor Vehicle Manufacturers Assoc. v. State Farm Mutual Automobile Insurance Co. [1983] 103SC2856.) In late 1983, reacting to the decision, Secretary of Transportation Elizabeth Dole postponed compliance until 1987 and, at the same time, proposed several other alternatives to air bags. As of mid-1985, only one automobile (Mercedes-Benz) sold in the United States offered air bags as an option. If statistics are correct, in the 10 years from 1976 to 1985, ninety thousand Americans lost their lives and six hundred fifty thousand were injured in cars that might have been equipped with air bags. While political struggles overwhelmed the processes of bureaucratic decision-making, thousands lost their lives.* Congress? The courts? Or should bureaucrats look first to their own conception of the public good or the public interest? Or to their professional norms and codes of ethics?

This issue is further complicated by the need for accountability in government. It can be argued that a president should be able to put a stamp on an administration. As Charles Peters, a seasoned bureaucrat, has observed, "The key to democratic pol-

*Joan Claybrook, et al., *Retreat from Safety* (New York: Pantheon, 1984), pp. 166–85.

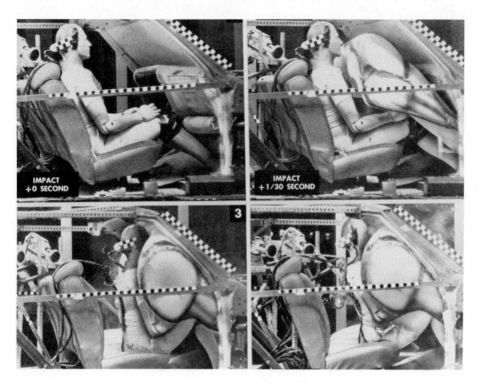

In these 1977 photos from General Motors, an air bag is shown cushioning the impact of a crash.

itics is accountability. If you don't deliver the goods, the voters can throw you out."[4] Peters went on to argue in favor of filling administrative positions with qualified politicians and making administrative decisions on a partisan basis, with reelection the compelling motive.

The problem with this attitude, as other political observers have pointed out, is that political considerations can lead to short-term planning and the implementation of splashy programs that actually serve the public worse in the long run. In trying to make government *appear* to be running well, partisan bureaucrats might ignore long-range planners.[5]

Apparently, then, a balance must be worked out between the need for unfettered administrative expertise and the need for responsible political control. To understand the complications of this issue, we must analyze how and to what extent the bureaucracy is involved in the political process. As we will see, the bureaucratic apparatus has evolved into a collection of highly specialized subdivisions, sometimes highly insulated (from the public), sometimes essentially self-governing; often backed by subdivisions of Congress and by powerful interest groups.[6] Bureaucratic discretion, expertise, and support systems serve to strengthen the bureaucracy's political position, whereas the extensive use of contract bureaucrats weakens it somewhat.

384

## Bureaucratic discretion

Legislation is never so specific as to deny bureaucracies considerable latitude in applying it to particular cases. This administrative discretion is the basis for bureaucratic political participation. For example, according to the Food and Drug Amendments of 1962, new drugs must be effective, as well as safe, in order to receive approval from the Food and Drug Administration. But Congress left it up to the FDA to determine specific standards of drug efficacy. Similarly, the Justice Department has the power to decide whether or not to prosecute an antitrust case—a decision that may have vital consequences for national economic policy. In these and thousands of other cases, government bureaucrats make policy through the application of the broad powers given them by Congress and the president.

Several aspects of the legislative decision-making process contribute to bureaucratic discretion. Most fundamentally, it would be impossible for the legislature to establish clear rules covering all contingencies—an exercise for which it has neither the time nor the expertise. Then, too, vague rules or guidelines often reflect legislative conflicts that could not be resolved in Congress and so are handed over to the bureaucracy. In this sense, bureaucratic administration represents an extension of the legislative process, as affected parties seek to advance their interests by lobbying in the offices of the bureaucracy. Indeed, administrative lobbying is as important as legislative lobbying in Washington.[7]

In policy-making matters, bureaucracies are not entirely neutral players. They have interests of their own, and they push those interests in the political process. Like most participants in the political system, bureaucrats usually claim that the programs they administer are in the public interest and that expansion of those programs would benefit the nation. Some such claims are cynical, but most are entirely sincere. Believing in the value and efficacy of their programs, bureaucrats seek to expand, or at least to protect, those programs by pushing for favorable legislation and appropriations.[8]

### Bureaucratic expertise

Expertise is another source of bureaucratic power. A basic function of a bureaucracy is to apply specialized competence to an area of policy. Bureaucrats frequently have a near-monopoly on expertise in certain political areas. Who, for example, knows more about sending a person to the moon than do the experts at the National Aeronautics and Space Administration? When other policymakers accept such claims of expertise, the bureaucracy gains an important political resource.

Economist John Kenneth Galbraith has pointed out that technology has become so complex that it would take a formidable genius to command all of the knowledge and skill required to deal with even a few of the ordinary decisions confronting business or government organizations.[9] Responsibility for decision making has therefore passed to groups composed of various specialists. As Galbraith put it, one could do worse than to think of modern organizations as composed of a "hierarchy of committees." Decisions tend to flow upward from these committees, and the person at the top ordinarily lacks the special knowledge and skills to challenge those decisions.

Galbraith saw that under present conditions of technical and organizational complexity, power in business concerns and governmental agencies inevitably passes into the hands of a great many subordinate specialists. He labeled this powerful set of specialists "the technostructure." The alternatives that they favor are ultimately reflected in public policy, because other political participants presume that these specialists must know what the best alternatives are.

Expertise can be used as a political resource in two principal ways: through important advisory roles, particularly in relation to the president; or through the presentation to Congress of complex matters about which most legislators know little. Simply because bureaucrats are more knowledgeable does not mean that they always get their way, of course. Under the present system, though, they are far better off than would be the case if Congress always had an equally knowledgeable alternative source of information.

### Mobilization of support

Another political resource of the bureaucracy is its ability to mobilize support among the general public, Congress, and its clientele groups. Government agencies like to demonstrate that they provide useful and beneficial services to the public. These public-relations efforts can take the form of public-service television messages, such as the FDA's TV spots on the proper use and storage of hazardous household products, or of free pamphlets, such as the Agriculture Department's extensive series of booklets on cooking, canning, and gardening, and other topics. In fact, such efforts are part of one of the most significant bureaucratic functions: supplying the public with needed information, although they also serve to advertise the agency and enhance its public reputation. Sometimes, however, efforts to mobilize public support may cross the line from information dissemination to sheer "public relations." The advertising efforts of the Department of Defense, for example, were thought to do so, as Senator William Proxmire insisted when he coined the term "Pentagon Propaganda Machine." In order to promote a favorable image of the military, the services aided in the production of "war" movies, gave tours of military installations to prominent citizens, provided speakers for civic groups, and produced an extensive set of advertisements for military life.

Bureaucratic agencies also try to maintain good relationships with those interest groups that are directly affected by their activities. Such groups are commonly referred to as *clientele groups*. The railroads and trucking companies are clientele groups of the Interstate Commerce Commission, labor unions are the clientele groups of the Labor Department, and so on. As long as these groups benefit from agency programs, they will lobby on the agency's behalf in Congress and the Oval Office. For example, when President Lyndon B. Johnson attempted to merge the Labor and Commerce departments in 1967, both labor and business groups, unwilling to give up what

each perceived as "its" department, protested vigorously. Johnson abandoned the idea.

An important source of the strength of clientele groups is their ability to influence Congress. Indeed, as we saw earlier, it is common for a bureaucratic agency, a clientele group, and a congressional subcommittee to be linked in a three-way alliance. For example, the Pentagon is very closely linked with large defense contractors, who in turn have a great deal of influence in Congress.

## Third-party government

Although bureaucrats are often political participants, they are sometimes denied the means necessary to effectively control the programs for which they are

## Making public tasks private

One ideological goal of the administration of President Ronald Reagan was to reduce government's role in society and enhance the role of private enterprise. As a step in this direction, the administration made an effort to transfer a wide range of public assets and programs to the private sector. The administration's argu-

ment was that private industry would do a better, cheaper job than government bureaucracies in providing many services.

In keeping with this philosophy, the administration placed both Conrail, the government-run freight rail system of the Northeast, and Landsat, the government's land-mapping satellite, on the market. It also housed aliens in detention centers that were privately operated; contracted with private firms to run many airport control towers; and used private consumer credit companies to screen applicants for government loans. Finally, the administration identified eleven thousand commer-

cial activities conducted by government that could be carried on by private contractors, including fire protection, landscaping, protective services, laundry and food services, movie-making, medical laboratory work, transportation data processing, and geological surveys.

These actions triggered an ideological debate that reflected basic philosophical differences about the nature and purposes of government. Was it government's appropriate role to deliver services itself, or was the job of government simply to guarantee that those services would be deliv-

ered? Some critics in Congress charged that the administration's real purpose was to get the government out of social policy matters altogether. Others feared that privatization would rob Congress of effective control over many programs, or that the quality of services would suffer when private firms took over. Finally, some argued that privatization simply could not get the job done in many areas.

responsible. In the case of **third-party government**, federal programs are farmed out to states, localities, special districts, nonprofit corporations, hospitals, manufacturers, banks, and other groups outside the bureaucracy. Many federal programs, in other words, are no longer run by federal bureaucrats.

The federal government's much-criticized social welfare apparatus, for example, is in reality fifty different programs run separately by the fifty states—or, more precisely, about three thousand programs run by the nation's counties. State and local officials have the power to decide the eligibility rules for and the duration and exact amounts of assistance given out under these programs. Likewise, the U.S. Labor Department distributes billions of dollars for employment and training assistance, but the money is actually spent by four hundred fifty "prime sponsors" organized by local politicians and community groups.

In addition, grants-in-aid, loan guarantees, new forms of contracting and procurement, credit insurance, and a host of other programs are handled through nonfederal organizations. Such programs pose thorny management problems and difficulties in coordination. The main problem is that those who operate the programs are not responsible to Congress, which authorizes the programs. The "bureaucrats in Washington" have far less actual control in many areas than the American public believes.

Third-party government programs do have some advantages. They allow the federal government to use the talents and resources of those outside the government, and they give the government greater flexibility in adapting programs to local needs and circumstances. Partly because of such arrangements, the size of the federal work force has not increased nearly so rapidly as have the rate of federal spending and the number of federal programs.

## Bureaucracy evaluated

In recent years, U.S. political life has been regularly punctuated by a variety of attacks against the bureaucracy. Both Jimmy Carter and Ronald Reagan ran for president at least partly on antibureaucracy platforms. In pledging radical cuts in government waste and a thorough reorganization of the bureaucracy, they were aligning themselves with what appeared to be strong public sentiment against bureaucracy.

In fact, however, most Americans have mixed attitudes toward bureaucratic institutions. When people have been asked by pollsters about actual relationships they have had with various agencies, the report card is generally quite good. But when surveyors inquire about bureaucracy in the abstract, very negative opinions surface. One study found that whereas 71 percent of respondents reported that their own problems had been handled well, only 30 percent thought that government agencies do well in general in handling problems.[10]

What are the specific charges against bureaucracy? What are the facts, and the theories about the facts? After addressing these questions, we shall take a close look at a particularly controversial bureaucratic function—regulation.

## Charges against bureaucracy

The principal charges made by critics of the bureaucracy can be summarized as follows.

1. *There are too many rules and rulemakers*. Specifically, there are over five thousand different government forms, and billions of dollars are spent each year filling them out. It has been estimated that colleges and universities alone spend several billion dollars dealing with government forms and trying to adhere to government regulations.

2. *The bureaucracy has too great a capacity for arbitrariness*. Bureaucracies are small empires that, as they grow, incorporate more and more functions. They employ an esoteric language—"bureaucratese"—that few outsiders can completely understand. They "dehumanize" citizens, turning them into mere numbers.

3. *Bureaucracy is too costly, full of unnecessary frills and programs that are self-perpetuating*. Once programs are

Knowledge is power, and power sometimes breeds fear in those who lack it. Whose fingerprint appears on the FBI screen? Will bureaucracy be run fairly and openly, or will agencies pursue their own political or personal vendettas?

started, they are almost impossible to end; they continue growing and developing support in Congress and among certain portions of the public. What starts out as a good program too often ends up as an agency more interested in protecting itself and its clients than the public interest.

4. *Bureaucracy is a breeding ground for timidity and conservatism.* The term *bureaucrat* conjures up an image of cautiousness and inactivity. According to the stereotype, bureaucrats at all costs will avoid the adventurous, the experimental, the progressive. Because of this tendency toward bureaucratic conservatism, the zeal that attends the establishment of many agencies soon disappears— particularly as the agencies develop close relationships with the very interests they are charged with regulating.

5. *Bureaucracy is authoritarian—insensitive to civil liberties.* The FBI's long-time chief, J. Edgar Hoover, used his agency to compile dossiers on many political figures. The CIA has been misused for domestic spying purposes. The general charge is that bureaucratic agencies easily lend themselves to the abuse of citizens' rights.

All of these charges are true to at least some degree. Yet, they present only one side of the picture. Of the millions of persons who work for federal, state, and local agencies, the vast majority are honest and

388

hard-working. And if some agencies are overstaffed and wasteful, others are short of staff, underbudgeted, and faced with overwhelming tasks. The Workman's Compensation Bureau has only five hundred employees to process all applications for benefits; as a result, a Labor Department task force found that it took an average of 630 days to process a claim for black lung benefits. Other overworked and understaffed agencies are the Immigration and Naturalization Service, which must patrol thousands of miles of border with a comparative handful of personnel, and the Food and Drug Administration, whose staff is far too small to check on all the ways we may be poisoning ourselves.

Then, too, the well-publicized mistakes made by some agencies should be put into perspective. For example, the oft-criticized Social Security Administration makes about 340,000 errors in its monthly mailings of checks—but those errors represent only 1 percent of the 34 million checks sent out each month.[11] We also should remember that many bureaucratic agencies are charged with enforcing complex laws and with making decisions on who does or does not qualify for benefits on the basis of only slight differences among applicants. These are not easy tasks.

Bureaucracies are inevitable in large, complex societies. Thus, the question to be asked here is not whether we want a bureaucracy—it is, rather, What kind of bureaucracy do we want? What sort of agencies, run in what fashion, and with what mandates from Congress and the people? Will the bureaucracy be run humanely and openly, and will it be run in the larger interests of the public, rather than in the interests of the strategically placed few?

## Regulation: perspectives, problems, and remedies

Apart from the general charges just discussed, many criticisms of bureaucracy are actually attacks on specific programs and agencies. And few parts of the

bureaucracy have sparked as much debate as have regulatory agencies.

Federal regulatory agencies affect the health and safety of most individuals, the rules under which most business is carried on, and many other vital matters. Critics of these agencies have argued that far too much regulating goes on, and that the regulators are not very efficient. It has been asserted that government regulation costs the country $100 billion per year[12]—although it is rarely estimated how much is saved thereby. Particular regulations and regulatory agencies are often singled out as the most burdensome, such as the health and safety rules for the workplace created and enforced by the Occupational Safety and Health Administration. Of course, the regulatory picture is not so black-and-white. As has already been pointed out, the bureaucracy is not of a piece, and criticisms applicable to one agency may be entirely inapplicable to another. We must also understand that frequently, those who participate in the regulatory debate are not disinterested observers.

In the discussion that follows we will look at the

The Immigration and Naturalization Service border patrol seizes a group of suspected "illegals" near the Mexican border. The man being searched was shipped back to Mexico the next day.

## Slowing the bureaucratic process

Why should the Environmental Protection Agency require years to issue regulations needed to carry out antipollution laws and then many more years before the rules are put into effect? The answer: The bureaucratic rulemaking process has been arranged so that all affected parties may continuously challenge regulations at every stage of the approval process. A classic example was the EPA's inability to formulate and then to carry out rules affecting wood preservatives. In 1976, the agency began to investigate the effects on the environment and on health of three chemicals used to preserve wood: creosote, pentachlorophenol, and inorganic arsenic compounds. In 1984, after three extensive studies and hearings about the new rules, EPA promulgated its guidelines limiting use of the preservatives. A year later, however, the guidelines still had not been put into effect, and the products remained on the market. Further challenges to the rules could require years to adjudicate.

Under the law, EPA rules can be challenged by makers or users of the products involved. Challengers are entitled to a first hearing before an administrative judge, after which they may take their case into the courts. Sixty companies challenged the proposed wood-preservative rules.

Some EPA administrators point to this case as an example of how, in the name of fairness, rules can be abused. A representative of a coalition of consumer groups argued that this was a "prime example of how administrative procedures . . . provide an advantage to manufacturers that want to keep their products on the market despite health and safety information that shows a clear danger to the public."

Some call for changes in the law in order to shorten the administrative process. Others maintain that such rules are necessary in order to protect the companies whose business is at stake.

Philip Shabecoff, "This Sisyphus Rolls a Wooden Stone," *New York Times*, June 29, 1985, p. 8.

---

nature of regulation and then at several proposed reforms of the regulatory process. Two points to keep clear are, first, that regulation usually costs someone and benefits someone else, and that these costs and benefits must be weighed; and second, that pro-regulation and antiregulation trends seem to occur in cycles, and that what is topical at the moment is not necessarily what makes sense.

**Types of regulation:** Both critics and proponents of government regulation—particularly the former—commonly make the mistake of lumping together two different types of regulation.[13] One group of regulatory agencies regulates prices, competition, and entry into various industries. Examples of such agencies are the Interstate Commerce Commission and the Federal Communications Commission. Both were created at the request of the regulated industries, whose principal motive was to prevent competition from invading the marketplace. Generally, regulatory agencies of this type have helped the regulated industries maintain artificially high prices and avoid the rigors of competition.

A newer variety of regulatory agency enforces standards of health, safety, and fairness. Agencies of this type include the Environmental Protection Agency, the Occupational Safety and Health Administration, the Consumer Product Safety Commission, and the Equal Employment Opportunity Commission (see Table 16.1). These regulators are usually attacked for limiting the freedom of business to do as it wishes and for adding to the costs of doing business, despite estimates that this second group of regulatory agencies has been responsible for considerably less than half the costs of all regulation.[14]

The problems attacked by the newer agencies have been significant ones—"Urban air had become unhealthy as well as unpleasant to breathe. Rivers were

TABLE 16.1
## Regulating health, safety, and the quality of the environment

| Organization | Regulatory function | Year established |
|---|---|---|
| The Packers and Stockyards Administration, Department of Agriculture | Determines plant conditions and business practices in livestock and processed-meat production so as to provide healthful meat products. | 1916 |
| The Food and Drug Administration, Department of Health, Education and Welfare | Controls the labeling and content of foods and drugs. | 1931 |
| The Agricultural Marketing Service, Department of Agriculture | Determines healthful standards for most farm commodities and also sets minimum prices for milk in some areas. | 1937 |
| The Federal Aviation Administration, Department of Transportation | Operates air-traffic-control systems and sets safety standards for aircraft and airports to reduce accidents. | 1948 |
| The Animal and Plant Health Inspection Service, Department of Agriculture | Sets standards for plant safety and inspects and enforces laws relating to meat and poultry quality. | 1953 |
| The Federal Highway Administration, Department of Transportation | Sets safety regulations for interstate trucking services. | 1966 |
| The Federal Railroad Administration, Department of Transportation | Sets safety standards for interstate railroad transportation. | 1970 |
| The National Highway Traffic Safety Administration, Department of Transportation | Sets safety standards for automobiles so as to reduce highway accident fatalities. | 1970 |
| The Environmental Protection Agency | Develops environmental quality standards and approves abatement plans operated by state agencies to curtail individual industry pollution emissions. | 1970 |
| The Consumer Product Safety Commission | Sets product safety standards. | 1972 |
| The Mining Enforcement and Safety Administration, Department of the Interior | Sets mine safety standards. | 1973 |
| The Drug Enforcement Administration, Department of Justice | Controls trade in narcotics and drugs. | 1973 |
| The Occupational Safety and Health Administration, Department of Labor | Sets and enforces workers' safety and health regulations to reduce work-related accident and disease. | 1973 |
| The Nuclear Regulatory Commission | Licenses the construction and operation of civilian nuclear power plants and other uses of nuclear energy. | 1975 |

Source: *The Challenge of Regulatory Reform: A Report to the President from the Domestic Council Review Group on Regulatory Reform* (Washington, D.C.: U.S. Government Printing Office, 1977), pp. 50–54.

This photo was staged to dramatize the argument that government regulatory efforts had gone too far. The boxes represent the additional paperwork federal rules forced on one major corporation in one year. The people in the line represent the extra employees hired to process the paperwork.

reduced, as have pesticide levels in rivers. Racial and sexual discrimination has been diminished.

Of course, the costs of such regulation have usually been passed on to consumers, and there have been mistakes, excessive pettiness, and overzealous advocacy. But as one observer has pointed out: "Much of the new social regulation benefits more disadvantaged groups in society. To put it somewhat simply— but not, in my view, unfairly—those who argue, say, that OSHA should 'go soft' on its health regulations in order to spare the country the burden of additional costs, are saying that some workers should die so that consumers can pay a few bucks less for the products they purchase and stockholders can make a somewhat higher return on their investments."[16]

**Deregulation:** The idea of deregulating aspects of the economy became popular during the administration of President Jimmy Carter. The first to be deregulated, at least partially, were the railroad and airline industries, followed by the trucking, interstate bus, and banking sectors. Arguments supporting **deregulation** centered on the premise that government's heavy hand had been suppressing competition and thereby discouraging both innovation and the provision of better service to consumers.

What had been a modest movement during the Carter years became a flood of change under President Ronald Reagan. In his first six weeks in office, Reagan lifted price controls on domestic crude oil, abolished the Council on Wage and Price Stability, prevented implementation of dozens of business regulations promulgated in the last days of the Carter administration, dropped energy efficiency standards for appliances and temperature guidelines for office buildings, and urged curbs on the powers of the Federal Trade Commission, Interstate Commerce Commission, the Securities and Exchange Commission, and the Federal Communications Commission. The

catching fire. Many working people were dying from exposure to chemicals on their jobs. Firms were selling products of whose hazards consumers were ignorant. And the nation faced a legacy of racial and sexual discrimination"[15]—and there have been results. Since the establishment of OSHA, the number of accidental workplace deaths has been halved, and workers' exposure to harmful substances has been sharply reduced. Water and air pollution have been

effects of deregulation were particularly striking in the automobile industry. The Reagan administration rescinded four major regulations in this area: those mandating the installation of automatic seat belts or air bags (scheduled for 1983), the display of crash test results on window price stickers of new cars, the setting of new standards of window visibility for cars and trucks, and the development of new types of speedometers and tamper-resistant odometers. General Motors estimated that the rollback on air bag regulations alone saved it $500,000 a day in production costs. GM executives stated that compliance with all the various government regulations would have cost the company $2.2 billion a year.

The Reagan approach did not meet with universal approval. In particular, critics argued that the projected savings were largely illusory. William Nordhaus, a former member of the Council of Economic Advisers, calculated that the dropping of the air bag requirement would cost the nation $4.5 billion over the timespan 1982–85, principally in medical expenses, insurance payments, and lost wages due to deaths and injuries. Critics also pointed to new problems created by deregulation: unpredictable and less-extensive airline service, exposure of the population to hazardous foods and chemicals, sharply increased costs in basic phone service, failed banks, a chaotic transportation system.[17]

---

# Thurow's propositions on government regulation

Economist Lester Thurow set out seven basic propositions about regulation in his book *The Zero-Sum Society*. His aim was to clarify the basic facts of regulation, and thereby to eliminate much unnecessary argument. The propositions he presented, along with the reasoning behind them, were as follows.

All economies involve rules and regulations;

there is no such thing as an unregulated economy. For example, the right to own property is itself a "rule" that requires protection: that is, disputes over property require regulations and enforcement. Normal economic life is unthinkable without such rules of behavior.

There are many silly government regulations. For example, it is impossible to write universally applicable rules, for exceptional cases will always turn up. Any attempt to apply a rule uniformly in a large and diverse country is sometimes going to look silly.

In many areas, there should be fewer regulations. Many regulations remain in force only because some groups gain from them in terms of income security, while

the rest of us pay the cost.

In the United States, regulations almost invariably arise from real problems, rather than from ideology. Among these real problems were occupational health and safety, clean air, and private pension failures. It is not, therefore, very useful to be for or against regulation in the abstract.

There is no "left" versus "right" when it comes to the virtues of regulation versus deregulation. Liberals do not always support regulation, and conservatives do not always oppose it. On some issues, such as tobacco and alcohol, neither has a clear position.

There is no simple correlation between the degree of economic success and the degree of economic regulation. Many suc-

cessful economies are far more regulated than is that of the United States—for example, those of West Germany and Japan. In fact, regulation can aid economic growth.

Regulations lead to regulations. The drafting of regulations to protect one industry may lead to efforts to protect others. If you protect steel from import competition, for example, you may also have to protect autos in the same way.

Lester Thurow, *The Zero-Sum Society: Distribution and the Possibilities for Economic Change* (New York: Basic Books, 1980).

## Conclusions

Economist Herbert Kaufman has pointed out that "if there were not such a diversity of interests in our society, if we did not subscribe to such a variety of values, if we were not so intolerant of corruption and insistent on our rights, and if the governmental system were not so responsive, however imperfectly, to so many of these claims on it, we would have a great deal less red tape."[18]

Public bureaucracies are necessary because modern societies are so complex. Governmental agencies often incorporate all the functions of legislatures, executives, and judiciaries—they make rules, enforce them, judge appeals, and adjudicate controversies. Is there any other way to ensure that the disabled receive assistance, or that the stock market functions honestly, or that food and drugs are not adulterated? Is there another method of dealing with fraud in businesses, or of policing the environmental impact of new factories, dams, and housing developments? How else could we educate the young and administer social insurance schemes fairly? Or even pretend to deal with price fixing and monopolistic practices in business? Without regulation and careful supervision, society would become a paradise for those with the means and the ambition to exploit others.

Public bureaucracy, then, has not been thrust on us by a conspirational group of fools or villains—we all contribute to it. There is no way to eliminate it, once and for all. The best we can do is learn to live with it, chipping away at each individual irritant through the normal processes of politics rather than seeking a blanket solution. As for the magic formulas proposed by some critics of the bureaucracy—wholesale contraction of the federal government, devolution of authority to the states and localities, concentration of authority in administrative "czars" empowered to cut through red tape—on close inspection, each turns out to hold little promise, for they all ignore values treasured by many people.

This is not to argue that because bureaucracy is needed, that any sort of bureaucracy will do. From the standpoint of democratic theory, bureaucracies should be highly responsive, sensitive to human needs,

394

and respectful of the rights of the average person.

Unfortunately, it is very difficult to tote up a balance sheet on the U.S. bureaucracy as a whole in these regards. Some agencies have acted in highly autocratic fashion, some have diminished freedom rather than protecting it, some have harassed citizens and ignored basic rights. In contrast, many agencies have done a decent job of protecting life and limb, of helping raise the level of public information, of seeing to it that democratic rights are protected and that equality and liberty are assured. It is difficult, therefore, either to indict or to approve the bureaucracy as a whole.

## NOTES

1 Bernard Schwartz, *The Professor and the Commissions* (New York: Knopf, 1959).

2 Peter Drucker, *The Age of Discontinuity: Guidelines to Our Changing Society* (New York: Harper & Row, 1969).

3 Leonard Reed, "Bureaucrats 2, Presidents 0," *Harper's*, November 1982.

4 Charles Peters, "The Solution: A Rebirth of Patriotism," *Washington Monthly*, October 1978.

5 Charles Malek, *Washington's Hidden Tragedy: The Failure to Make Government Work* (New York: The Free Press, 1978).

6 Randall B. Ripley and Grace H. Franklin, *Congress, the Bureaucracy and Public Policy* (Homewood, Ill.: Dorsey Press, 1984), Chapter 2.

7 *Ibid.*, Chapter 3.

8 For a discussion of these problems, see Herbert Kaufman, *Red Tape* (Washington, D.C.: Brookings Institution, 1979).

9 John K. Galbraith, *The New Industrial State*, 2nd ed. (Boston: Houghton Mifflin, 1971), Chapters 2 and 3.

10 Richard E. Cohen, "Regulatory Focus: The Cut-Rate Fares Dilemma, *National Journal*, September 3, 1977, p. 1384.

11 R. Kahn, *et al.*, "Americans Love Their Bureaucrats," *Psychology Today*, June 1975, pp. 66–71.

12 Murray Weidenbaum, *The Future of Business Regulation* (New York: AMACCM, 1979) and *Prospects for Reallocating Public Resources* (Washington, D.C.: American Enterprise Institute, 1967).

13 This discussion draws on Steven Kelman, "Regulation That Works," *New Republic*, November 25, 1978, pp. 16–20.

14 *Ibid.*

15 *Ibid.*, p. 17.

16 *Ibid.*, p. 19.

17 Martin and Susan Tolchin, "The Rush to Deregulate," *The New York Times Magazine*, August 21, 1983, pp. 34–38, 70–74.

18 Herbert Kaufman, *Red Tape*, pp. 58–59.

## SELECTED READINGS

### Basic information

For basic information on the nature of bureaucracy, see Max Weber, *The Theory of Social and Economic Organization* (New York: Oxford, 1947); Michael Crozier, *The Bureaucratic Phenomenon* (Chicago: University of Chicago Press, 1967); Felix A. Nigro, *Modern Public Administration* (New York: Harper & Row, 1970); Paul Goodman, *People or Personnel* (New York: Random House, 1965).

### Current controversies

On current controversies involving bureaucratic issues and behavior, see Francis Rourke, *Bureaucracy, Politics and Public Policy* (Boston: Little, Brown, 1975); Lawrence J. White, *Reforming Regulation* (Englewood Cliffs, N.J.: Prentice-Hall, 1981); R. B. Ripley and G. A. Franklin, *Congress, The Bureaucracy and Public Policy* (Homewood, Ill.: Dorsey Press, 1984); E. Lewis, *American Politics in a Bureaucratic Age* (Cambridge, Mass.: Winthrop, 1977); R. A. Katzmann, *Regulatory Bureaucracy* (Cambridge, Mass.: Harvard University Press, 1980).

# Chapter
seventeen

# The federal judiciary

# Nonelected defenders of democracy

IN an ideal world, peopled with committed democrats, there might be little need for institutions such as the Supreme Court to decide issues involving fundamental democratic rights. Such rights would simply be observed, and the courts would concentrate exclusively on complex and abstruse aspects of litigation. But this is far from an ideal world. In our society, it is the Supreme Court, empowered to review the constitutional merits of legislation, that ensures that rights are protected, or extended, to conform with basic democratic principles. The Court can (though it does not have to) serve as the nation's conscience, the upholder of its basic democratic commitments, even in the face of hostile or reluctant majorities.

Once such an elitist institution has been created, however, it can largely go its own way. Federal judges are appointed, not elected, to a life tenure, and they are politically accountable to no one. Whatever their individual foibles, preferences, experiences, and limitations, they have the power to reshape society, and their decisions profoundly affect our political life. If these "guardians" do not rule sensibly, if they substitute their own economic and social philosophies for democratic commitments, society will be at the mercy of a judicial aristocracy.

Two brief examples will serve to show how the Supreme Court's philosophy can profoundly influence our politics and social life. Consider initially the Court's role during the early days of the New Deal in the 1930s. The nation was in a state of severe economic crisis, sweeping statutes had been passed to deal with unprecedented emergency. Enacted hurriedly, some of the New Deal legislation was poorly constructed and vague. The Court's majority seized on these aspects to declare several key statutes unconstitutional. In the eyes of many, including those of President Franklin D. Roosevelt, the Court's actions endangered the nation's economic recovery. The Court was attacked for reading its own conservative antigovernment ideology into the Constitution rather than interpreting that document as a flexible set of guidelines allowing the nation to deal with evolving circumstances.

Defenders of the Court, however, argued that it was playing an essential role by curtailing the overextension of federal power. Roosevelt's landslide reelection victory in 1936, and his threat to enlarge the Court and fill it with more liberal members, finally seemed to persuade some justices that certain New Deal legislation was legitimate. Since that confrontation in the 1930s, the Court has rarely interfered with the federal government's power to regulate economic life. Had a majority of the Court not shifted, it is hard to say how the struggle between executive and judiciary might have turned out.

A second example, which shows the Court playing a very different sort of role, was the school desegregation decision of 1954, *Brown* vs. *The Board of Education of Topeka*. In that case (discussed in detail in Chapter 5), the Court held that segregated schools were inherently unequal. This decision involved a moral and legal leap for the Court, over-

turning a precedent that had stood for fifty-eight years, and challenging head-on long-established and deeply rooted local customs. This case, just as the New Deal legislation, was attacked as being based on the philosophy of the justices rather than on a reading of the Constitution. Defenders of the Court argued, however, that it was segregation that violated the Constitution, and that the Court had simply had the courage to declare that fact.

Regardless of one's views on these matters, it is clear that the Supreme Court plays a potentially pow-

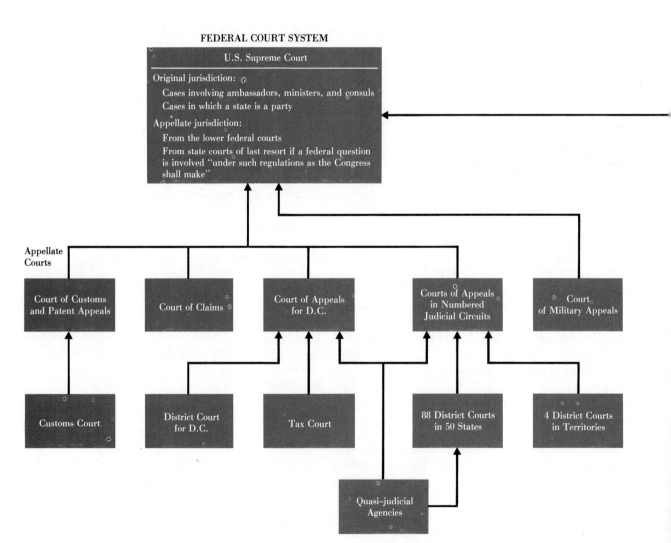

**FEDERAL COURT SYSTEM**

U.S. Supreme Court

Original jurisdiction:
Cases involving ambassadors, ministers, and consuls
Cases in which a state is a party

Appellate jurisdiction:
From the lower federal courts
From state courts of last resort if a federal question is involved "under such regulations as the Congress shall make"

Appellate Courts

Court of Customs and Patent Appeals

Court of Claims

Court of Appeals for D.C.

Courts of Appeals in Numbered Judicial Circuits

Court of Military Appeals

Customs Court

District Court for D.C.

Tax Court

88 District Courts in 50 States

4 District Courts in Territories

Quasi-judicial Agencies

erful role in our politics. The justices' views of law, morality, and of the appropriate role of the Court all contribute to the actions they will take. But how much power should the courts, particularly the United States Supreme Court, have in shaping our national life? In a democratic society, should nine nonelected individuals play a decisive role in the working out of important national issues? With these questions in mind, we will look carefully at how the national court system works, before turning to consider how the courts do or do not serve democratic principles.

## The U.S. legal system

Every court case begins with a dispute between two or more parties. These parties may be individuals, groups, corporations, or governmental bodies. Jones may sue Smith to recover damages caused by a traffic accident. Acting under the provisions of a civil rights statute, the U.S. government may sue a state government in an attempt to stop state officials from discriminating against blacks in the electoral process. The state of Nebraska may charge Adams with burglary and bring him to court to answer the charge. A group of women, dissatisfied with the abortion law in their state, may attempt to have it declared unconstitutional.

Unlike legislatures or bureaucracies, a court does not set its own agenda. Judges cannot decide unilaterally to make policy about abortions, voting rights, or racial discrimination. Rather, they must wait for others to bring matters to them for resolution. Further, in the course of resolving disputes brought before them, legal institutions may focus exclusively on the interests of the formal parties to the dispute, as is usually the case in criminal prosecutions. But they may use the **occasion for decision** provided by a particular dispute to define policies that affect broad classes of the society. As we will see later in the chapter, in the 1960s the Supreme Court often used the occasion for decision to establish rather broad policy guidelines, rather than simply to settle particular disputes.

## The dual hierarchy

The U.S. court system, as part of a federal system of government, is characterized by a dual hierarchy (see Figure 17.1). Each state has its own system of

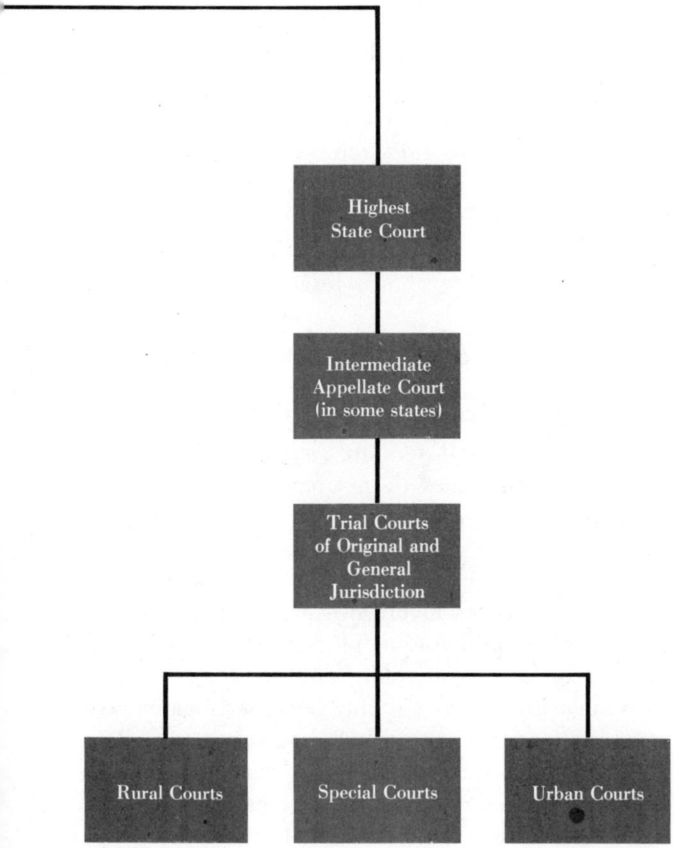

FIGURE 17.1
The State and Federal Components of the U.S.
Court System

courts, usually consisting of courts of special jurisdiction, civil and criminal trial courts, intermediate courts of appeals, and a state supreme court. The federal court system also has a pyramidal structure, divided into special-jurisdiction courts; trial courts, or district courts, that serve relatively small geographic regions (at least one for every state); circuit courts of appeal, each of which hears appeals from the district courts in a particular geographic region; and the Supreme Court of the United States. The two court systems to some extent overlap, in that certain kinds of disputes may be initiated in either system. In some cases, litigants (persons engaged in lawsuits) who lose in the state supreme courts may appeal to the Supreme Court of the United States.

In both systems, the typical case begins in a trial court—a court of general jurisdiction—or in a court of specialized jurisdiction. Most criminal and civil cases are settled at this level. The losing party, however, always has the option of appealing the trial court's decision—that is, of asking a higher court to reverse the verdict. A criminal defendant, for instance, may believe that his conviction was based on errors made by the trial judge, and file an appeal on that basis. In state court systems, appeals go to

an intermediate court of appeals, if the state has one, or to the state supreme court. If the case began in the federal district court, an appeal goes first to the circuit court of appeals for the geographic area involved. If the appeals court agrees to hear the case and renders a decision, the losing party has the option of asking the U.S. Supreme Court to review the lower court's ruling.

The Supreme Court has a large measure of control over its own docket; with certain exceptions (see Table 17.1), it can choose which cases it wishes to hear. Each year, 3,000–3,500 appellants ask the Court to review their cases. Of these appeals, about 250 are actually heard by the Court in a typical year. In the remainder, the lower-court decision is allowed to stand without a hearing. In deciding which cases to hear, the Court follows the **"rule of four"**: if four of the nine justices vote to hear a case, the case is placed on the Court's docket. From that point, briefs are filed by the opposing sides, oral arguments are heard, and a decision is rendered.

## The flow of litigation

The flow of litigation through the court system is characterized by a winnowing process. Most cases are decided at the level at which they first are heard, either because the losers are satisfied with the outcome or because they do not have the resources to mount an appeal. Appeals can be costly in both time and money. The typical Supreme Court case will have been in the court system for two or three years. The legal expenses involved—attorneys' fees for legal research, preparation of briefs, time spent in court—can be considerable.

Winnowing occurs not only because litigants give up or run out of resources, but also because appellate courts refuse to hear many cases. A case that reaches the Supreme Court typically involves issues of sufficient importance that the litigants choose to spend

TABLE 17.1
## Summary of Supreme Court jurisdiction

| Original jurisdiction | Appellate jurisdiction* |
|---|---|
| *A. Mandatory (must be heard by the Court)* | 1. Cases in which a federal court has held an act of Congress unconstitutional, if the federal government is a party; any cases in which a state supreme court has held an act of Congress to be unconstitutional |
| 1. Disputes between states | 2. Cases in which a state court has upheld a state law against a claim that it conflicts with the Constitution or federal law |
| | 3. Cases in which a federal court has overturned a state law on the grounds that it conflicts with the Constitution or federal law |
| | 4. Decisions of special three-judge federal district courts |
| *B. Discretionary (Court need not hear)* | 1. All decisions of federal courts of appeals except those in mandatory categories |
| 1. Cases brought by a state | |
| 2. Disputes between a state and the federal government | 2. All decisions of the highest state courts involving issues of federal law, except those in mandatory categories |
| 3. Cases involving foreign diplomatic personnel | |

*Some minor categories not listed.
Source: Lawrence Baum, *The Supreme Court* (Washington, D.C.: Congressional Quarterly Press, 1981), p. 11.

the time and money required and the justices of the Court feel compelled to deal with the matter. This is not to suggest that the appellate courts alone deal with important issues or that the work of lower courts is purely technical and unimportant. Lower-court decisions dealing with the enforcement of criminal statutes and traffic laws and the application of legal norms in, say, landlord-tenant relations ordinarily have a more direct impact on the daily lives of individual citizens than do decisions of the Supreme Court. Nevertheless, it is true that the development and modification of legal norms, involving important areas of social change, are more often the provinces of appellate courts.

## The decision-making process

The disputes that reach the Supreme Court often reflect basic disagreements about public policy in the society at large. As judges consider these issues, they must make choices. Judges, like other policy makers in the society, have a great deal of latitude in decision making, and the decisions they make can have significant effects on public policy. Thus, it is important to ask how a judge decides a case.

Federal appellate judges most often decide cases that involve either constitutional issues (whether or not policies being pursued by government conform to the requirements of the Constitution) or matters of **statutory construction** (interpretation of laws). There is a persistent belief that in either of these cases, judges simply apply "the law." This view of the judicial decision-making process was described by a Supreme Court justice as follows: "When an act of Congress is appropriately challenged in the courts as not conforming to the constitutional mandate, the judicial branch of the government has only one duty— to lay the article of the Constitution which is invoked beside the statute which is challenged and to decide whether the latter squares with the former."[1] This has sometimes been referred to as the "slot machine" theory of judicial decision making: feed in the statute and the Constitution, and by a mechanical process, arrive at the correct answer.

This approach seems too simple, however. The Constitution says, for example, that police may not engage in *unreasonable searches and seizures*, and that no citizen may be deprived of *equal protection of the laws* or of **due process** in the implementation of laws. How does a judge compare a statute or the behavior of a governmental official with these provisions of the Constitution? Does the stopping and frisking of a suspicious-looking individual constitute an unreasonable search and seizure? Does the racial segregation of school children deny blacks equal protection of the laws? Does a law regulating the wages and hours of employees deprive them of due process of law in the right to contract with employers for their services?

When faced with such complicated matters, judges normally consult past decisions, or precedents, on similar issues, in the hope of finding interpretations of the words of the Constitution that make its provisions less ambiguous. Yet judges have long disagreed over the answers to the questions posed above. The personal values and characteristics of the judges, their interactions with fellow judges, and the limitations placed on them by their positions all have a bearing on their decisions and opinions. The judicial decision-making process, then, often cannot be reduced to a mechanical procedure of applying the relevant law to the facts of a case.

## Recruitment of judges

One important influence on judicial decision making is the background of the person appointed to the bench.[2] In the federal judicial system, judges are nominated by the president and confirmed by the Senate. The recruitment process is quite complex and involves a variety of participants. Before making a choice public, the president normally consults with the attorney general and the senators from the state in which a proposed nominee resides. The American Bar Association's Committee on the Federal Judiciary then gives a report on the candidate to the Senate Judiciary Committee, which holds a hearing. Finally, the full Senate then votes on the nominee. Throughout this process, the participants are intensely lobbied by interest groups, as well as by

## How should judicial appointments be made?

Some experts have argued that federal justices should be appointed strictly on the basis of legal competence. Others have contended that a potential judge's political philosophy should be the primary consideration. Yet others have asserted that a specifically legal background may not be absolutely necessary for a Supreme Court Justice—that political experience, good judgment, proper temperament, and a sense of the public interest should weigh more heavily.

During the 1980 Republican convention, the platform committee passed a plank calling for the appointment of federal judges who espoused a conservative philosophy. Not surprisingly, President Ronald Reagan's judicial appointments comprised a distinctly homogeneous and conservative group. In Reagan's first term (1981–85), 98 percent of his 165 appointees to the federal bench were white, 98 percent were Republicans, 92 percent were male, and 25 percent were millionaires.* Most also were experienced judges with a proven record of judicial conservatism. President Jimmy Carter, in contrast, appointed high percentages of minorities (20 percent) and women (15 percent). Only 5 percent of Carter's judicial appointees were millionaires.

*Al Kamen, "Reagan's Judges: They're White, Male, Republican and Very Rich," *Washington Post*, national weekly edition, March 11, 1985, p. 34.

TABLE 17.2
## Selected characteristics of Supreme Court justices appointed since 1937

| Justice | Age[a] | State of residence[b] | Position at appointment[c] | Years judge | Elective office[d] | Admin. position[e] |
|---------|--------|------------------------|-----------------------------|-------------|---------------------|---------------------|
| Black | 51 | Alabama | Senator | 1 | Senate | — |
| Reed | 53 | Kentucky | Solicitor general | 0 | State leg. | Solicitor general |
| Frankfurter | 56 | Mass. | Law professor | 0 | — | Subcabinet |
| Douglas | 40 | Washington | Chairman, Fed. Regulatory Commission | 0 | — | Fed. Regulatory Commission |
| Murphy | 49 | Michigan | Attorney general | 7 | Governor | Attorney general |
| Byrnes | 62 | South Carolina | Senator | 0 | Senate | — |
| Jackson | 49 | New York | Attorney general | 0 | — | Attorney general |
| Rutledge | 48 | Iowa | U.S. ct. app. | 4 | — | — |
| Burton | 57 | Ohio | Senator | 0 | Senate | — |
| Vinson | 56 | Kentucky | Sec. of treasury | 5 | House of Rep. | Sec. of treasury |
| Clark | 49 | Texas | Attorney general | 0 | — | Attorney general |
| Minton | 58 | Indiana | U.S. ct. app. | 8 | Senate | Asst. to president |
| Warren | 62 | Calif. | Governor | 0 | Governor | — |
| Harlan | 55 | New York | U.S. ct. app. | 1 | — | Asst. U.S. attorney |
| Brennan | 50 | New Jersey | State sup. ct. | 7 | — | — |
| Whittaker | 56 | Missouri | U.S. ct. app. | 3 | — | — |
| Stewart | 43 | Ohio | U.S. ct. app. | 4 | City council | — |
| White | 44 | Colorado | Dep. atty. general | 0 | — | Dep. atty. general |
| Goldberg | 54 | Illinois | Sec. of labor | 0 | — | Sec. of labor |
| Fortas | 55 | Washington, D.C. | Private practice | 0 | — | Subcabinet |
| Marshall | 59 | New York | Solicitor general | 4 | — | Solicitor general |
| Burger | 61 | Minnesota | U.S. ct. app. | 13 | — | Asst. attorney general |
| Blackmun | 61 | Minnesota | U.S. ct. app. | 11 | — | — |
| Powell | 64 | Virginia | Private practice | 0 | — | State bd. of education |
| Rehnquist | 47 | Arizona | Asst. atty. general | 0 | — | Asst. atty. general |
| Stevens | 55 | Illinois | U.S. ct. app. | 5 | — | — |
| O'Connor | 51 | Arizona | State ct. app. | 7 | State senate | State asst. atty. general |

[a]Age at time of appointment.
[b]Primary state of residence prior to selection.
[c]In this and following columns, positions are federal except where noted.
[d]Highest office.
[e]Highest appointive administrative position; minor positions omitted.
Source: Lawrence Baum, *The Supreme Court* (Washington, D.C.: Congressional Quarterly Press, 1981), pp. 50–51.

political nominees and their friends and political allies.[3]

A large measure of politics attends federal judicial appointments: lobbying in favor of various candidates, ideological judgments about the decisions a person might make on the bench, campaign or other partisan debts owed or receivable, consideration of the symbolic effects of a judicial appointment. (The widespread notion that seats on the Supreme Court are "reserved" for various ethnic or racial groups reflects the symbolic patronage involved in Supreme Court appointments.)

Moreover, nominees to federal judgeships traditionally have been involved in political activity. Such activity is important, because it brings an individual to the attention of those who choose judges and provides an avenue for the personal relationships that lead to appointment to the bench. Political participation on the part of a potential nominee has another significant purpose: to reveal the nominee's attitudes

# Comparative perspective Court systems in Sweden and Great Britain

The court systems of other democratic countries can differ in several fundamental respects from the U.S. system. For example, jury trials, which are common in the United States, are comparatively rare in many European nations. In Sweden, juries are reserved for cases of criminal libel only. Instead of juries, the Swedes employ "lay judges," who are elected by communal assemblies to assist professional judges in their work. Stockholm, for example, has 750 lay judges; together with chief magistrates, they hear evidence and participate in court decisions. Each lay judge sits for a minimum of ten days per year in court. Lay judges and magistrates usually concur in their decisions;

should they differ, a majority on a panel of lay judges can overrule a magistrate. Lay judges are used in all criminal and almost all civil cases.

Great Britain generally reserves jury trials for more serious crimes. Overall, its judicial system is simpler and smoother in operation than is that of the United States, mainly because the British are not so concerned with the rights of the accused. For instance, the exclusionary rule, which bars the introduction in court of illegally seized evidence, was explicitly rejected in Great Britain in 1979.

The British system of justice also is not so adversarial as ours is. In the courtroom, prosecutor and defense counsel sit together, wearing identical robes. Lawyers tend to steer away from controversial tactics and often reach informal agreements outside the courtroom. In fact, British prosecutors are private lawyers who may work for the defense in another case. In the United States, public prosecutors must work only for the government.

on public policy. Because most presidents seek to appoint men or women whose philosophy of government does not radically differ from their own, they tend to pick nominees whose political views have been made known through participation in public life. President Richard Nixon, for example, sought to appoint judicial conservatives to the Court, so he nominated men whose records of public service indicated adherence to conservative values. Such predictions have often gone awry, however: three of the four justices appointed by Nixon voted to strike down abortion laws, a policy he did not support. Typically, a president will have the opportunity to appoint a justice to the Supreme Court every two years; as a result, a president who serves two terms can expect to appoint nearly half the justices. This ongoing recruitment process ties the Supreme Court into the broad currents of thought that characterize the political life of the day.

## Powers and restraints

The U.S. court system has enormous power. Many matters that in other nations are regarded as being outside the realm of legal institutions are treated as legal issues in the United States. Examination of the nature of judicial power, its development, and its limitations is necessary in order to understand the significant policy role played by the courts in this country.

### Judicial review

The extensive powers of the federal courts are rooted in the concept of **judicial review**. Under this concept, the courts are empowered to review the acts of federal and state legislatures and the actions of members of executive agencies, to determine whether they conform to the provisions of the Constitution and the laws of the land. Thus, for example, state laws dealing with abortion or the apportionment of legislatures, congressional legislation dealing with subversive activities, and police activities in investigating criminal suspects can all come under the scrutiny of the federal courts.

Judicial review is an extraordinary power, in that it enables courts to negate the activities of other branches of government. Critics have argued that judicial review is highly undemocratic, because the judges who exercise it serve for long terms or for life and thus are not accountable to the public in the way that elected officials are. The opposite point of view is that the protection of the rights of minorities by means of judicial review is a vital function in a democratic society; only the courts, in this view, have the necessary detachment to restrain the volatile and sometimes repressive will of the majority.

The concept of judicial review is not explicitly spelled out in the Constitution. The framers of the Constitution, although certainly aware that judicial review was an issue, did not expressly address the question. Lacking a clear constitutional mandate, the courts simply asserted that they had the power of review, and that power gradually became an integral part of the U.S. legal system.

The first case in which the Supreme Court asserted the power to declare federal legislation unconstitutional was *Marbury* v. *Madison* (1803),[4] in which the Court declared a provision of the Judiciary Act of 1789 to be in violation of the Constitution and thus null and void. The implications of this ruling were profound. Because many of the provisions of the Constitution are rather vague, application of them in the context of judicial review gives enormous power to the courts. Over the following two decades, the Court built slowly on the provisions of *Marbury*. In *McCulloch* v. *Maryland* (1819),[5] Chief Justice Marshall cited the supremacy of national law (Article I) in holding Maryland's attempt to tax national banks to be unconstitutional. And in the same year, the

justices held that states might not pass legislation impairing contracts.

Since the mid-nineteenth century, there has been little dispute over the question of whether or not the Supreme Court has the power of judicial review. Some Courts have been more active than others in exercising this power, however, and there is still much debate over how far the Court should go in nullifying the actions of other, more tyically democratic institutions.

## Self-restraints on power

The scope of the power conferred on the courts by judicial review is restricted by a series of self-imposed rules for restraint. The most significant of these rules is that the courts will consider only those cases in which the parties have standing to sue: that is, in which the plaintiff (the party that brings suit) can demonstrate actual injury—loss of money, prop-

Perhaps the most important of all Supreme Court Chief Justices, John Marshall, who helped shape the significant power and enduring presence of the Court as an ultimate arbiter in the American Constitutional system.

# *Marbury* v. *Madison*

Thomas Jefferson was elected to the presidency in the fall of 1800. In the period between his election and his inauguration, the lame duck president, John Adams, made a series of appointments to federal judgeships designed to ensure continued Federalist control of the judiciary.

One of those appointments, as a justice of the peace, went to William Marbury. When Jefferson was inaugurated, he refused to allow his secretary of state, James Madison, to deliver to Marbury the latter's official commission. Marbury thereupon requested that the Supreme Court issue a writ of *mandamus* (an order compelling an official to perform his duties under the law). In his suit, Marbury cited the Judiciary Act of 1789, which gave the Supreme Court original jurisdiction to issue such writs.

In writing the majority opinion for the Court in the case of *Marbury* v. *Madison*, Chief Justice Marshall, a Federalist, neatly sidestepped the central issue of the case and at the same time established the principle of judicial review. Marshall argued that although Marbury was legally entitled to the commission, the Supreme Court lacked the authority to issue the writ of *mandamus*, because the Judiciary Act of 1789 had unconstitutionally conferred on the Court original jurisdiction to issue writs of *mandamus* to federal officials. As Marshall pointed out, the

Constitution explicitly listed those areas in which the Court was to exercise original jurisdiction and left to Congress the power to specify only its appellate jurisdiction. Marshall went on to argue that because the Constitution was the supreme law of the land, binding on judges and all other government officials, Congress could not pass a law that contradicted it: "a law repugnant to the Constitution is void . . . ; courts as well as other departments are bound by that instrument."

---

erty, freedom, etc.—from the government law or action in question. For a long period of time, the Supreme Court utilized this rule to avoid suits brought by taxpayers who alleged that activities of government funded by their tax dollars were unconstitutional. An individual, the Court held, had to show a more direct interest in the matter. In the 1960s, the Court relaxed the standing rule to some extent by agreeing to hear taxpayers' suits against certain government activities, including federal aid to education.

Another rule for self-restraint rests on avoidance of political questions. The Supreme Court has often held that certain types of issues are political rather than legal in nature, and thus are more appropriately addressed by legislative bodies. For example, for a long period of time the Court refused to hear suits dealing with malapportionment of legislative districts, holding that the question of whether particular

legislators should be seated could only be addressed by a legislature. The courts have used the same doctrine to avoid becoming involved in foreign policy.

Finally, the Supreme Court can avoid many issues simply by refusing to hear particular cases. The justices need not give a reason for declining to review an appellate court ruling in matters that do not fall under the Court's original jurisdiction.

These self-imposed constraints are highly flexible: the Supreme Court, in particular, can invoke them when it wishes to avoid an issue and ignore them when it wishes to get involved. When the Court consistently ignores the restraints, it tends to become more and more involved in public policy-making. Under Chief Justice Earl Warren, the Court of the 1950s and 1960s did exactly that. Conservatives, unhappy with such activism, charged the Court with going beyond its legitimate functions in order to make law rather than merely to interpret the Constitution.

Subsequent appointments to the Court have turned it in a more conservative direction. At her confirmation hearings in 1981, Sandra Day O'Connor stated that "as a judge it is not my function to develop public policy." President Ronald Reagan, voicing the sentiments of most conservatives, praised her judicial philosophy as "one of restraint."

## Legislative reaction

Another brake on the power of the Supreme Court to participate decisively in public policy making is Congress's ability to overrule unpopular court decisions by passing new laws or constitutional amendments. Even when attempts to overturn Court rulings via the legislative process do not succeed, they provide important cues to the Court that it has gone too far and should reconsider the policy it has been pursuing.

During the 1950s, for example, strong anticommunist sentiment throughout the country triggered a great deal of governmental activity designed to ward off the perceived communist menace. In a series of decisions handed down in 1957 and 1958, the Court introduced limits on the power of congressional committees to investigate communists, on the use of criminal sanctions against members of the American Communist Party, and on the power of government agencies to dismiss employees whose loyalty was suspect. In Congress and the newspapers, opposition to these decisions grew, and legislation designed to overturn them was introduced. In addition, Congress threatened to restrict the Court's ability to hear appeals of lower-court decisions dealing with such matters as loyalty and security. Although none of this proposed legislation passed, the message to the Court was unmistakable.

During the 1959–61 period, the Court sent down a series of decisions that seemed to lift many of the restraints imposed in 1957 and 1958. What had changed was not the Constitution or the factual issues of the cases, but rather the willingness of the Court to intervene in this area. Thus, the congressional and public response provided a cue to some members of the Court that unless they wished to provoke a serious constitutional crisis, they should back off a bit in rulings that dealt with the powers of the government to restrict liberty in the name of national security.[6]

More recently, there has been intense legislative reaction to Court decisions outlawing prayer in public schools and government restrictions on abortions. Efforts to overturn the school prayer decisions have failed to produce the constitutional amendment critics have sought, even though President Reagan lent the prestige of his office to the effort. Critics of the abortion decision have had some success in complicating the process of obtaining an abortion in some states and in restricting funding for Medicaid abortions, but not in altering the Court's decision itself. In both instances, interestingly, the Court has shown little inclination to shift its position, despite the intensity of legislative and popular reactions.

## Noncompliance

Noncompliance is the most severe limitation on public policy-making faced by any branch of the federal government. Court decisions, in particular, are not self-executing. In order for them to take effect, persons or agencies outside the court must implement them. Some decisions are very narrow and require relatively simple changes in behavior: let John Smith out of prison or give him a new trial. Other decisions require changes of behavior on the part of large numbers of people if they are to be translated into changes in public policy.

Local officials and bureaucracies in both the public and the private spheres have frequently asserted their braking power on policy emanating from the courts. Local school districts, for example, used a series of evasive schemes to thwart the Supreme Court's goal of school desegregation as set forth in *Brown* v. *Board of Education* (1954). And when the

Court held in 1963 that the reading of the Bible as part of devotional services in public schools violated the First Amendment, compliance with the decision was spotty.[7] Where school prayer was most common, in the East and South, there was less compliance; in the Midwest and West, compliance with the Court's orders was better.[8] A similar record of noncompliance followed the Court's 1966 ruling that all police officers were required to give criminal suspects a series of warnings about their rights before interrogating them.[9] Nearly ten years later, however, some officers continued to interrogate suspects without giving the warnings, or to give the warnings in tones that implied that they are meaningless.[10]

There is a tendency to view these instances of noncompliance to Court decisions as manifestations of something wrong in the system. But it is also possible to view noncompliance as a defining characteristic of the U.S. political system. As already suggested, the broad policy areas that define politics in this country are recurring issues, one in which various individuals, groups, and institutions are continually involved. The court system participates in the process by deciding cases, and in so doing it sometimes announces broad policies. These policies then

reenter the arena of public affairs and are reacted to by other institutions and groups and by society at large. If the issue is one about which people in the society care strongly—as is often the case in foreign affairs, economic policy, race relations, and civil liberties—then it is unreasonable to suppose that any one policy-making institution can definitively resolve the matter.

## Major eras in Supreme Court history

It is accepted practice to view Supreme Court history in terms of a series of more-or-less distinctive "eras," most of them named after unusually influential chief justices. For example, the activist and liberal court

FIGURE 17.2
An Overview of the Workings and Effects of the Judicial Process

Source: Alice F. Bartee, *Cases Lost, Causes Won* (New York: St. Martin's, 1984), p. 8.

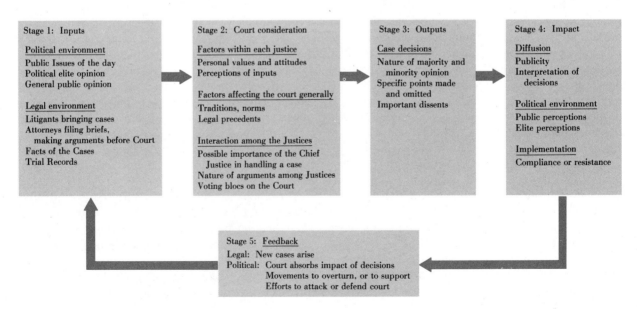

of the 1950s and 1960s is commonly referred to as the Warren Court, after Chief Justice Earl Warren.

### The Marshall Court (1801–35)

Under Chief Justice John Marshall, the Court established the principle of judicial review of both state and federal laws and activities. During this era the Court also introduced the concept that the Constitution must be flexibly interpreted to serve changing needs and established that the national government has implied powers to achieve the ends established in the Constitution. (See the discussion of the *Marbury* and *McCulloch* cases.)

### The Taney Court (1836–64)

Chief Justice Roger B. Taney (pronounced *Tawney*) was a staunch supporter of Andrew Jackson, an activist for states' rights. The most famous case decided in this era, *Dred Scott* v. *Stanford* (1857), involved the issue of whether a slave could sue for his freedom.[11] Dred Scott, a slave, sued for his freedom on the grounds that he had traveled with his owner, an army doctor, into various free territories. The case was brought in Missouri in 1846, during a period of agitation over whether states admitted to the Union would be slave states or free states. The Taney Court, weighting its decision toward the South, denied Scott's claim to freedom. In addition, it declared that under the Constitution former slaves could *never* become citizens of the United States, although they could become citizens of particular states in which they lived. Only a constitutional amendment, the Court declared, could change the national status of slaves. This ruling, widely considered the most racist position ever adopted by any branch of the national government, was rendered moot by the Civil War and formally overturned by the Fourteenth Amendment.

The *Dred Scott* decision was also the first since *Marbury* v. *Madison* in which an act of Congress was declared unconstitutional. In it, the Court held that the Missouri Compromise, which prohibited slavery in certain territories, was unconstitutional on the grounds that Congress was depriving persons of their property without due process of law.

### Enlargement of judicial power (1865–90)

Throughout this period, the Court significantly enlarged its powers. Between 1864 and 1873 alone, ten acts of Congress were held unconstitutional; in contrast, only two had been struck down in the preceding seventy-four years. The Court also overturned many state laws. Generally, the Court helped to undermine the position of freed slaves by adopting a very narrow interpretation of the 14th Amendment, which was designed to assure blacks equal protection of the laws.

### Judicial self-confidence (1890–37)

In this era of increased activism, the Court struck down many state and federal laws designed to aid workers, farmers, and others who had been hurt by rapid industrial development and the evolution of the modern corporation. Ignoring popular demands, the Court interpreted the Constitution according to the justices' own conservative political and economic philosophy. The Court also continued narrowing the interpretation of the Fourteenth Amendment and the Fifteenth Amendment (giving voting rights to blacks), eventually emasculating them completely. In *Plessy* v. *Ferguson* (1896),[12] the Court established the "separate but equal" doctrine that was not thoroughly overturned until 1954.

As we saw earlier in the chapter, the Court's economic conservatism continued well into the 1930s,

Justice Louis Dembritz Brandeis, one of the most influential of 20th-century Supreme Court justices. Brandeis helped fashion a new style of legal thinking in which contemporary political and social realities became part of the evidence under discussion.

the proposal, the Court did shift its views. During the five months the Roosevelt plan was under consideration in Congress, the Court upheld several significant pieces of New Deal legislation—including the Social Security Act, the National Labor Relations Act, and the Farm Mortgage Act—and ended a dangerous conflict with the executive and Congress.

In the area of civil liberties, the Court generally upheld convictions of dissenters convicted during and immediately after World War I while taking a somewhat stronger position in defense of free speech. (See Chapter 5 for fuller discussion.)

## The New Deal era (1937–53)

In this period, the Court was no longer so concerned with the protection of property rights and large-scale corporate enterprise. Although all levels of government undertook extensive regulation of economic life, only three minor pieces of federal legislation were held unconstitutional. It is noteworthy, however, that the formerly antagonistic relationship between business and government had by this time grown more cooperative, so conflicts were less likely to show up in the courts.

The Court also moved generally toward extending protection of civil rights and liberties at this time. There were exceptions to this trend, however: the Court upheld the evacuation of Japanese-Americans from the West Coast during World War II; and under Chief Justice Vinson (1946–53), the Court upheld prosecutions of American Communist Party members.

during the New Deal period. The first pieces of New Deal legislation came before the Court for review in 1935. Within a short time, eight of ten New Deal programs brought before the Court were declared unconstitutional, including the Railroad Pension Act, a portion of the National Industrial Recovery Act, and the Municipal Bankruptcy Act. After President Franklin Roosevelt was reelected by a wide margin in 1936, he devised a scheme to change the Court. Roosevelt's famous "court-packing" plan called for voluntary retirement of Supreme Court justices at age seventy; if a justice reached seventy and did not retire, the president would be empowered to appoint an additional justice, to a maximum number of fifteen. Roosevelt defended the plan as a way to "save our National Constitution from hardening of the judicial arteries." Although Congress did not approve

## The Warren Court (1953–69)

The Warren Court was the most controversial in modern Supreme Court history. Under Chief Justice Earl Warren, the Court decided issues that struck deep into vital, and often controversial, areas of American life. The major decisions came in the areas of school desegregation, legislative reapportionment, school prayer, pornography, and the rights of the accused. Public reaction was often negative, particularly in the cases of desegregation, school prayer, and the rights of the accused.

The Warren Court did not upset precedents in every area. It upheld Sunday closing laws, for example, and refused to expand First Amendment protections to those who burned their draft cards. Generally, however, the Court left a legacy of high ideals, representing much of the best in American liberalism.

The far-reaching decisions of the Warren Court reopened the old controversy about the role of the Supreme Court, but from a different direction. Whereas in the 1930s the Court had been attacked for its conservatism, the Warren Court was criticized for its excessive liberalism—for making rather than interpreting law. Conservatives called for the return of "strict construction" (literal interpretation) of the provisions of the Constitution. Supporters of the Court claimed that it was precisely the Court's willingness to stretch the Constitution ("loose construction") that made that document useful in the modern era. Seeing a need for far-reaching alterations in American life, supporters of the Warren Court viewed it as a key agency for initiating change.

Chief Justice Earl Warren doning his robe, while chatting with Associate Justice William O. Douglas. The Supreme Court Warren led proved to be one of the most liberal and controversial in U.S. history. Warren, a Republican and an Eisenhower appointee, surprised observers with his willingness to take on highly volatile issues such as school desegregation and the rights of the accused. Justice Douglas was one of the Warren Court's most liberal and best-known members.

## The Burger Court (1969–    )

The intense activism of the Warren years subsided during the era of Chief Justice Warren Burger, a Nixon appointee. Liberals have criticized the Burger Court for its backpedaling on civil liberties and civil rights issues. And yet even its critics have acknowledged that it has made some highly controversial decisions of a strongly liberal stamp. Most notably, the Burger Court established liberalized standards for abortion in 1973,[13] a decision that continues to stimulate major controversy and efforts to overturn the Court's ruling. The Court also found against the government in the "Pentagon papers" case (1971), permitting those photocopied government documents

to be published by *The New York Times* despite government claims that publication would adversely affect national security.[14] President Richard Nixon's effort to prevent release of his White House tapes was also thwarted by the Burger Court,[15] an action that surely sealed Nixon's downfall (see Chapter 16).

Nevertheless, most observers would agree that the activist traditions of the Warren Court have generally been discontinued in the rather conservative Burger era. In the civil rights area, the Burger Court has limited the use of school busing as a remedy for segregation[16] and held that the state of Texas did not deny its citizens equal protection of the laws by allowing considerable inequality in the financing of local school districts.[17] In the latter case, the Court majority held that only if students had experienced an "absolute deprivation" would their constitutional rights have been violated. In criminal justice matters, the Court has come close to turning the clock back to the pre-Warren era. In a series of decisions, the Court majority sharply limited the rights of sus-

pects in the streets, in interrogation rooms, in police lineups, and in the courts. The justices have also allowed far greater intrusions on the individual's rights of privacy, allowing banks to pass checkbook records on to the government and telephone companies to keep track of numbers dialed—without the consent of the bank depositor or dialer. Finally, the Court has restricted the rights of the press and permitted more police intrusions into newsrooms.

The difficulty in arriving at a firm characterization of the Burger Court was made clear by the contrast between its 1983 and 1984 terms. In 1983 the Court issued a series of rulings that represented a sharp rebuff to conservative interests; these decisions ranged from abortion to deregulation and tax exemptions for private schools that practiced racial discrimination. But in the 1984 term, the Court handed down a string of major decisions highly pleasing to the Reagan administration and other conservatives. The 1984 decisions came in civil rights (upholding seniority over affirmative action considerations), civil liberties

President Ronald Reagan and the United States Supreme Court, 1982. Front row (*left to right*): Thurgood Marshall, William Brennan, Chief Justice Warren Burger, Reagan, Byron White, Harry Blackmun; Standing (*left to right*): John Paul Stevens, Lewis Powell, William Rehnquist, and Sandra Day O'Connor. As of 1985, Reagan had made only one court appointment: Justice O'Connor. But four justices were over 75 years of age, and several were ailing. Many expected that Ronald Reagan's most enduring legacy might be a changed Supreme Court.

(upholding the government's authority to restrict travel to Cuba), religion (upholding the right of a town to include a nativity scene in an official Christmas display), and prisoners' rights (declaring that prisoners have no rights of privacy in their cells). Most strikingly, in the area of criminal law, the Court made the first exceptions to the exclusionary rule in decades. Under the exclusionary rule, first fashioned in 1914 and greatly expanded by the Warren Court, the authorities were forbidden to use illegally obtained evidence in court. The purpose of the rule was to influence police actions: if police knew they could not use illegally obtained evidence to convict, according to the theory, they would be motivated to obey legal strictures and obtain proper search warrants. In two cases, however, the Burger Court decided that evidence *could* be used in court, even when the warrants obtained were faulty in one respect or another.[18] The Court majority argued that the crucial point was whether police had acted in "good faith" in trying to stay within the requirements of the law. Purely technical issues involving warrants, the Court argued, were not sufficiently important to keep significant evidence out of court.

Many civil liberties advocates were shocked by the pattern of 1984 decisions. The legal director of the American Civil Liberties Union charged the Court had become a "cheerleader for the government." We should note, however, that in several important decisions, the Court was almost evenly divided. Of the 150 decisions made in 1984, twenty-nine were decided by one-vote margins. It seemed quite possible that, given slightly different cases, the Court majority might have shifted in another direction. And it is notable that the conservative decisions of 1984 were

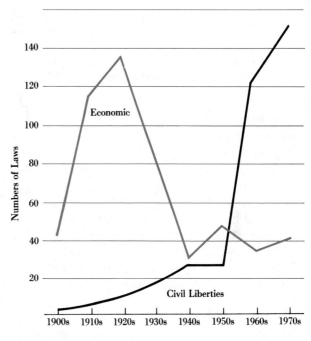

FIGURE 17.3

Numbers of Economic and Civil Liberties Laws Overturned by Supreme Court: The figure above shows the sharp shift in the sorts of laws found unconstitutional by the Supreme Court. Since the 1920s, there has been a marked decline in the Court's tendency to reject economic legislation, while, on the other hand, there has been a growing tendency to reject legislation that restricts civil liberties. In this sense, the Court has moved away from its earlier economic "conservatism" and toward a stronger defense of first amendment rights. (From Lawrence Baum, *The Supreme Court* [Washington, D.C.: Congressional Quarterly Press, 1981], p. 168.)

accompanied by rulings upholding women's rights in a case involving discrimination by the Minnesota Jaycees (an all-male organization) and declaring unconstitutional a federal law barring editorials on public radio and television stations that receive federal funds.[19]

## The dilemma of an expanded legal system

In recent decades, Americans have turned more and more to the judiciary to solve their problems. The courts have had to deal with the complexities of school integration, police behavior, environmental pollution, and standards for assistance to the poor. In the minds of many, these new and complicated issues have taxed the traditional resources and procedures of the courts.

Judicial responsibility has expanded as the government in general has extended the scope of its activity. Much of the increase in judicial activity has taken place independently of Congress and the bureaucracy—or even in opposition to their policies. In many cases, the courts, rather than play their usually passive role, have seized the initiative. The courts, many claim, have usurped some of the functions of legislatures.[20] In Alabama, for example, various federal court decisions had the effect of raising the state's annual spending for mental institutions from $14 to $58 million.

Such actions and tendencies on the part of the courts have encouraged lawsuits that seek solutions to widespread problems rather than simply rectification of specific grievances. The particular person bringing the suit has become less important, and the general problem presented has grown in significance. Some have found this new tendency distasteful, arguing that too many federal judges have come to believe they hold roving commissions as problem solvers and have a mandate to act when political institutions fail to. How did this happen?

The most influential factor in the expansion of judicial powers was probably the impact of the school desegregation decisions. The massive amount of litigation on that issue seemed to turn the courts into

an avenue for bringing about social changes. The courts, once considered conservative institutions, were taking the lead in areas in which other institutions, supposedly better designed to deal with change, were reluctant to act. In this sense, the courts became the lightning rods of our system. They took on intricate and volatile issues that legislatures and executives found too hot—too "political"—to handle. This was possible because federal judges, with life-tenure positions, are protected from waves of popular sentiment. Insulation of the judicial system from public opinion has obvious advantages and drawbacks. On the one hand, the fact that judges do not have to account for their actions is an obviously undemocratic feature of U.S. politics. On the other hand, only judges who do not have to bend before popular

sentiment can defend ideals that temporary majorities attack or neglect. Only such judges can defend the liberties of groups that a majority would rather outlaw. It even appears that, on occasion, courts may be better informed and show a clearer comprehension of complex issues than legislatures or other organs of government.[21]

In recent years, political conservatives have sought ways of limiting the powers of the courts. One way to overrule a court decision is to amend the Constitution, but in practice this route is long, cumbersome, and highly uncertain. The tactic hit upon more recently is to attempt, through congressional legislation, to limit the jurisdiction of the Court and thereby curb its powers. (Article III of the Constitution gives Congress the power to create lower federal courts and gives the Supreme Court jurisdiction over state and federal appeals "with such exceptions, and under such regulations as the Congress shall make.") Conservatives have also called for popular election of judges and the abolition of life tenure. There is some irony in this conservative attack on the courts, since the courts have traditionally been considered the most conservative of the three branches of government.

Along with growth in the powers and activism of the courts has come an epic expansion of the legal profession. The United States has three times as many lawyers per capita as Great Britain, and twenty times as many as Japan. Laws are multiplying even faster. Each year, legislative bodies at all levels pass hundreds of thousands of new laws, each of which leads to the issuance of new regulations. At the same

Its busing decisions have been among the most controversial the Supreme Court has made in recent decades. Busing arrangements have, in some places, been highly effective and have worked smoothly. In others, there has been intense conflict that has resulted in schools being less integrated than before. Busing has not, however, been a popular public policy.

## Judge Garrity and Boston harbor

In 1982 the city attorney of Quincy, Massachusetts, filed suit against state and local sewage treatment agencies, charging them with illegally polluting Boston harbor. Judge Paul Garrity of the Massachusetts Superior Court, before whom the case was brought, appointed a special master, Professor Charles M. Haar of Harvard Law School, to investigate the problem. One month later, Haar and his technical advisers produced a report that showed because treatment plants in the harbor area were drastically inadequate, 12 billion gallons of raw sewage were flowing into the harbor each year.

The lawsuit and the report startled many, since Boston harbor was still commonly used for swimming and other recreational activities. Massachusetts Governor Michael Dukakis proposed that the state legislature create a new state water and sewage authority with powers to deal with the situation, but this proposal stalled in the state house of representatives.

Late in 1984, Judge Garrity, seeing that no political action was forthcoming, issued an order stopping almost all new tie-ins to the metropolitan sewer system—a move that threatened to stop all construction in the area. A higher judge set aside the order, but Garrity proceeded with a suit brought against the main state agency involved. Pressure from public opinion, as well as from business and banking interests finally pushed the legislature to act, and the new water and sewer authority was approved in December 1984.

This was a case in which a judge acted on the best information available to protect the interests of a poorly organized and unfocused majority. Was this judicial imperialism, as some in the legislature claimed? Or was the judge acting properly as an educator and a goad to the legislature?

Source: Anthony Lewis, "Why Judges Act," *The New York Times*, December 20, 1984, p. 29.

---

time, the legal system remains far from "just." For example, the federal Legal Services Corporation, even in handling 1 million cases a year in the 1970s, met less than 15 percent of the needs for legal services among the poor. Middle-class people are also being priced out of the legal market by increasing fees.[22]

Perhaps some of this expansion of law is inevitable in a complex society in which economic competition and exploitation are common and individuals seek ways to protect their rights. As social customs, habits, and traditions break down in a more atomized and mobile society, law replaces other means of social control. As long ago as the mid-nineteenth century, however, observers were commenting on the tendency of Americans to take all their controversies into court. Perhaps we are just a law-oriented society.

How do we deal with being law-ridden? Several remedies have been suggested. One is deregulation:

if cumbersome government regulations could be eliminated and more competition substituted, it has been argued, the burdens of law could be cut back. Frequently, however, those being regulated—the trucking industry is a good example—are the last ones to favor deregulation. Also, deregulation can create new problems, as we saw in Chapter 16.

Another possible remedy is what one writer has called dejudicialization—keeping issues out of the courts. There are many good reasons for doing so. For example, a five-year wait to get a case into a federal courtroom is common, and defendants who cannot afford bail may have to wait up to six months in jail before their cases are dealt with. Despite passage of the Speedy Trial Act in 1975, which requires a trial within 125 days after arrest on most charges, the problem of delay is still cited as the most serious of all court problems. The speedy trial provisions have also been criticized as not allowing the government sufficient time to prepare a case. Many states have passed similar statutes, but so far they have had only a spotty impact on court conduct.

Dejudicialization might help in some ways. No-fault insurance—as employed in the case of auto accidents—has cut motor vehicle damage suits by as much as 87 percent in some states. An attempt to pass similar legislation nationally was narrowly defeated in 1976 in the United States Senate. The no-fault concept could also be applied to divorce suits.

The concept of dejudicialization could be expanded to include the development of neighborhood justice centers, which would resolve disputes through arbitration and mediation. Such centers, which handle family arguments, minor assaults, and controversies involving landlords and tenants, bosses and workers, consumers and stores, already exist in various cities. A Justice Department experiment in Kansas City demonstrated that hearings commonly take only two hours, and only two weeks elapse before final hearings are held. Eighty-six percent of all cases heard were successfully resolved, with the remainder going into the court system. California has voted to make arbitration mandatory in all civil cases involving less than $15,000.

Some of what needs doing will require action by Congress. For example, the Sherman Antitrust Act, which dates back to the last decade of the nineteenth century, has been very difficult to enforce. With an average charge under the act, it is eight years before a judgment is reached. Some cases go on indefinitely. Major corporations are difficult to attack in the courts: Exxon, for example, has more lawyers on retainer than are employed by the entire Department of Justice. Only clarification of the Sherman Act by Congress could place less of the burden of proof on the government and thereby make it easier to pursue antitrust violations.

## Conclusions

It seems clear that over the past 50 years, the federal courts on the whole have served important democratic purposes in extending equality, strengthening

A moment in the ritual of the American courtroom. The prosecuting attorney approaches the bench, with defendant and defense attorney in the foreground. The bailiff is seated at the far left while the witness is on the stand, court reporter keeping track at the right. The American way of conducting trials and organizing a legal system is only one method. Other democratic nations have organized their justice systems differently, though all have certain basic elements in common.

417

the protection of rights and liberties, and taking on issues that other branches of government could not or would not resolve. Lacking a legislative consensus, how could reapportionment, school desegregation, and rights of the accused have been settled in any national fashion? Imagine if those decisions had not been made. How much less would the country conform to the norms of democratic life? Yet the courts, in addressing these issues, entered that "political thicket" that many legal experts have warned against. As a result, the courts have been at the center of intense controversy in recent decades.

Policy-making by the courts obviously poses problems. In intruding into this area, courts may actively thwart majority rule, or emasculate legislation designed to protect basic rights. This is clearly what took place after the Civil War, when an interventionist court undercut the substance of the 14th Amendment and postponed for decades the achievement of a decent level of legal equality for black Americans. The same antidemocratic trend was apparent when the courts took on the role of defenders of a particular style of economic life, using their conservative views of an appropriate capitalist society to thwart unions, delay child labor legislation, and to strike down key parts of the New Deal program.

Ideally, the courts can serve as a source of power for those who are too weak to exercise much political clout. All citizens—whether they are blacks seeking school desegregation, mental patients seeking protections of their rights, or welfare mothers trying to get a fair shake—should be able to turn to the courts when the other components of the political process ignore their interests. This is precisely what has often tended to happen in recent decades. From the standpoint of democratic politics, it is, on the whole, a healthy development.

So much depends, however, on the political philosophies of the judges, their feeling for democratic life, and their willingness to risk controversy. In the end, given the power of courts in our political processes, we are perhaps more dependent than we ought to be on the instincts and opinions of the people who wear the judicial robes—our nonelected defenders of the Constitution.

## NOTES

1 *United States* v. *Butler* (297 U.S. 1), 1936.

2 Although we are dealing here with the appointment of federal judges, many of the points made are relevant to the appointment or election of state and municipal judges.

3 See Howard Ball, *Courts and Politics: The Federal Judiciary System* (Englewood Cliffs, N.J.: Prentice-Hall, 1980); and R. K. Burke, *The Path to the Court* (Ann Arbor, Mich.: University Microfilms, 1959).

4 1 Cranach 137 (1803).

5 4 Wheaton 316 (1819).

6 Walter Murphy, *Congress and the Court* (Chicago: University of Chicago Press, 1962).

7 *Abdington School District* v. *Schempp*, 374 U.S. 203.

8 Frank Sorauf, *The Wall of Separation* (Princeton, N.J.: Princeton University Press, 1976).

9 *Miranda* v. *Arizona*, 384 U.S. 436.

10 M. Wald, *et al.*, "Interrogations in New Haven: The Impact of Miranda," *Yale Law Journal*, July 1967.

11 19 Howard 393 (1857).

12 163 U.S. 537.

13 *Roe* v. *Wade*, 410 U.S. 113 (1973).

14 *New York Times Company* v. *United States*, 403 U.S. 713 (1971).

15 *United States* v. *Nixon*, 418 U.S. 683 (1974).

16 *School Board of the City of Richmond* v. *State Board of Education*, 412 U.S. 92 (1973).

17 *San Antonio Independent School District* v. *Rodriguez*, 411 U.S. 1 (1973).

18 *United States* v. *Leon*, 82-1771 (1984); *Massachusetts* v. *Sheppard*, 82-963 (1984).

19 *Roberts* v. *V. S. Jaycees*, 83-724; *FCC* v. *League of Women Voters of California*.

20 The issues are spelled out comprehensively in Donald Horowitz, *The Courts and Social Policy* (Washington, D.C.: Brookings Institution, 1977). See also Nathan Glazer, "Should Judges Administer Social Services?" *The Public Interest*, Winter 1978. For a fuller discussion, see James Duffy, *Domestic Affairs* (New York: Simon and Schuster, 1978).

21 Stephen L. Wasby, "Arrogation of Power or Accountability: 'Judicial Imperialism' Revisited," paper delivered before the American Political Science Association, New York City, September 1981.

**22** These matters are debated in Lawrence Tribe, "Too Much Law, Too Little Justice," *Atlantic Monthly*, July 1979.

## SELECTED READINGS

### Background on law and the judiciary
A. H. Kelly and W. A. Harbison, *The American Constitution* (New York: Norton, 1970); H. L. A. Hart, *The Concept of Law* (Oxford: Clarendon Press, 1961); Herbert Pacher, *The Limits of the Criminal Sanction* (Stanford, Cal.: Stanford University Press, 1968); Alexander Bickel, *The Least Dangerous Branch* (Indianapolis, Ind.: Bobbs-Merrill, 1962); Charles Black, *The People and the Court* (Englewood Cliffs, N.J.: Prentice-Hall, 1960).

### Current issues
Michael Meltsner, *Cruel and Unusual* (New York: Morrow, 1974); Richard Kluger, *Simple Justice* (New York: Random House, 1977); Anthony Lewis, *Gideon's Trumpet* (New York: Random House, 1964); Donald Horowitz, *The Courts and Social Policy* (Washington, D.C.: Brookings Institution, 1977); Frank Sorauf, *The Wall of Separation* (Princeton, N.J.: Princeton University Press, 1976); Robert Woodward and Scott Armstrong, *The Brethren* (New York: Simon and Schuster, 1979).

# Part four

# Public policy

# Chapter
eighteen

# Creating public policy | Power and agendas

THE U.S. government is a powerful force in our society. The government that was envisioned by most of the Founders—a minimum state that would protect rights and perform a limited number of governmental functions—is a thing of the past. Many Americans may still believe that "the government is best which governs least," but we are unlikely to see such a government again. And in reality, most Americans want government to perform a whole series of basic tasks, ranging from national defense to education, from regulation of the economy to provisions for the public welfare. This necessarily means that government will be a highly significant factor in our national life.

In modern times, in fact, governments are important everywhere—in rich nations and in poor, in democracies and, even more, in undemocratic nations. Today, governments rule over populations that reach into the tens of millions in societies that are enormously complex. Modern governing involves so many highly technical functions that the range of government powers and the complexity of many of its functions are often difficult to grasp. Over the past two decades, for example, the U.S. government has taken it upon itself to, among many other things, fight a war in Southeast Asia, educate handicapped children, provide Social Security to tens of millions, is-sue pamphlets on how to grow alfalfa, send men to the moon, oversee vast national forests, make rules about disposal of nuclear wastes, send registrars to protect black voters in the South, and spy on alleged domestic dissidents.

In exercising such powers, the government must set public policy priorities, and these priorities are, or should be, the focus of intense public debate. Should government focus on defense or on domestic needs? On the unemployed or on investors in the stock market? On dealing with pollution or on economic growth? Of course, such alternatives are overly simplistic. Usually the end result of policy-making is a compromise among contending priorities—yet even compromises carry priorities of their own.

In studying the complexities of modern government, we often lose human detail. We tend to think of Social Security, for example, in terms of a faceless class of tens of millions of recipients, and lose sight of the particular individuals and families involved. This is one of the hazards inherent in discussing vast institutions. We can easily forget that behind the general discussion of calculations, policy questions, and arguments, we are really dealing with the lives of human beings.

Chapters 19–23 will deal with specific policy areas: economic management, the welfare state, civil rights

and liberties, foreign and defense policies, and energy and environment. In these chapters, we will delineate some of the most significant policies of government and explore major controversies concerning them. We will also attempt to judge their success or failure and make several comparisons with similar policies in other societies.

Before jumping directly into the arenas of public policy, however, we must answer a few general questions about the study of policy: How do issues arise? How are issues "handled" or "processed"? How does policy get formulated and implemented? And most important for our purposes, Can democratic theory

help us to sort out from within the forest of policies the particular trees of greatest significance to us as democrats?

## How issues reach the political agenda

Many political scientists have said that the best guide to what government will do next year is what government does this year. In this view the work of

The core questions of politics: Whose interests will be attended to? Who will set the political agenda? Whose problems will obtain real as opposed to entirely symbolic attention? In these pictures, we see (*clockwise*) World War I veterans who walked to Washington in 1932 to get Congress to act on their bonus, which it failed to do; mothers and children in a New York City welfare office; American farmers; and people lining up for gasoline during the shortage of 1979. We should note that only some of the time do personal problems reach out for political solutions.

government most often proceeds by tiny steps, or *increments*.[1] In a sense, this process builds conservatism into policymaking. Government continues to do more or less what it has been doing—budgets go up or down slightly, policies are carried out with greater or lesser vigor—all within a well-established and -understood political framework.

Looking back over the development of the U.S. government's agenda of policy-making, we can see how governmental functions have arisen to meet social needs and to cope with the requirements of coordination, order, stability, and growth. This growth often occurs piecemeal, step by step, over time.

Sometimes government acquires new functions because of spillover effects in economic and social life. For example, when water is polluted by industrial waste and people become sick by drinking it, there usually is a call for government intervention. Occasionally, spillovers are caused by the government itself. The building of the interstate highway system in the United States helped to stimulate the growth of suburbs and the decline of central cities in the period after World War II. The decline of the cities, in turn, stimulated further government action to deal with the new problems of urban areas.

The historical record also reveals several drastic

shifts in the governmental agenda, however. The Great Depression led to one such shift, in the form of the New Deal. And as we have already noted (see Chapter 1), new groups occasionally have broken into the arena of policy-making and put their needs on the public agenda. For women and blacks, the key issue was the basic right to participate in the setting of the political agenda.

In sum, then, the term **incremental politics** provides a good description of the day-to-day business of government, but one that must be supplemented with a longer view taking into account the crises that develop in political life, the emergence of new groups with new demands and needs, and the rise and fall of issues from the policy agenda. Sometimes a potential issue can be a social reality for a considerable period without being "officially" recognized. Poverty was largely off the public agenda in the 1950s, then was rediscovered at the beginning of the 1960s by a new administration. In contrast, the issue of a nationwide prohibition of the sale of alcoholic beverages was *dropped* from the national policy agenda when the Eighteenth Amendment was repealed in 1933. Until that point, Prohibition had been high on the agenda of national issues for several decades.

The way an issue is defined, and the priority assigned to an issue in relation with those given to other issues, are questions that lay at the core of political conflict. The candidate who effectively defines the issues in a campaign usually controls that campaign. Thus, liberals and conservatives battle over whether the "real" issue is inflation or unemployment, or whether it is too much government spending or a stingy government that neglects the needy. To cite another example, How do we know whether the defense budget is large enough? To one who believes that the Soviet Union has more or better long-range missiles and thus could threaten U.S. security, defense obviously deserves a high priority. But to one who believes that we are reasonably secure and that the Soviets do not pose a serious threat, defense understandably has a considerably lower priority. This kind of issue has been fought out in several recent presidential elections.

One of the most controversial public policy issues has been the question of what types of functions government can legitimately take on. For example, whereas some Americans believe that government can legitimately set limits to the fees that doctors or hospitals charge, others believe that such action would violate appropriate limits for government action. In another policy sphere, some believe that school officials, state legislatures, or Congress can legitimately prescribe that prayers be said in public schools. Others, however, believe that the prescription of prayer in public schools violates constitutional tradition and represents wrongful interference by government in the realm of individual conscience. The focus of these controversies is not what actions government should take on the issues involved, but whether government can legitimately act at all. For some Americans, some of the time, government itself—its size, complexity, and power—is one of the major issues.

## Processing issues

Whose agenda becomes *the* agenda of politics? And how are issues dealt with once they become part of the national agenda?

### Competing agendas

We have been talking about the larger agenda of political life—the rough ordering of pressing political problems at a certain time. But there are also specific agendas held by, among others, interest groups, professional politicians, and the bureaucracy. Conflicts among these various agendas lead to struggles both in and out of government over which agenda will prevail.

The issues that comprise these competing agendas are reflected in the measures Congress acts on, the proposals made by the president, the activities of the federal bureaucracy, and the principal issues before the courts. Sometimes an issue ignored on one agenda is picked up elsewhere—as was the case with abortion, a matter that Congress left alone but was finally acted on by the courts. Official agendas also may differ or conflict. Conflicts often generate new issues that must be dealt with. Frequently, battles within the executive branch have clear and important effects on the shape of public policy. For example, the competition among the army, air force, and navy for shares of the defense budget usually results in a higher budget overall and may cause the inclusion of unnecessary weapons systems.

## Dealing with issues

Once an issue has emerged, how is it resolved? Two significant factors in the working out of issues are *who* comes to participate in dealing with an issue and how much the *scope* of the issue is enlarged, making new policy options available.[2] The first factor comes into play when new groups pick up an issue that offers them the opportunity to make successful demands for change. For example, the civil rights movement sparked the growth of ethnic consciousness and brought together new groups, such as Hispanics, women, and white ethnics, who made similar demands for attention and equality. The scope of an issue widens as the range of considerations being dealt with expands. For example, the welfare issue might be focused narrowly on one problem of the poor, such as adequate housing. Enlargement of the scope of this issue might lead to a consideration of a whole range of related matters—health, employment, even the distribution of wealth. The broader the scope, the wider the range of solutions considered—and the more complex the issue.

Many issues reach the public agenda without ever being substantially resolved. Some issues are re-solved only at a *symbolic* level. In this case, whatever action is taken on an issue is not only ineffective, it is not really meant to be effective. A symbolic action is an attempt at reassurance—a way of giving the public the impression that the issue is being handled or resolved.[3] Consider the health warnings on cigarette packages: government action to counter the hazards of smoking doesn't go much beyond this symbolic act; in fact, tobacco farmers enjoy government subsidies. Symbolic moves are extremely common in foreign policy. For years, the United States government called officially for the "liberation" of Eastern Europe from the Soviet Union, but never really contemplated pressing that issue very far.

Symbolic actions can have real consequences, however. Frequently, public quiescence results from symbolic policy-making—people feel reassured and cease to agitate. In other cases, people take the symbols seriously and expect further action to follow. Commissions established to investigate social problems, such as crime, violence, or racism, fall into this category. Their recommendations, although attended by much publicity, are frequently ignored.

Issues also can be dealt with by being displaced,

Law is one of the most significant instruments of public policy. During the energy crisis of 1973, speed limits were lowered. But law, as we know, is sometimes not honored.

Public policy sometimes grows directly out of social conflict. Who will gain, who will suffer—and who will decide?

deferred, or diverted,[4] rather than being completely resolved. **Displaced issues** are those that flare up and then quiet down, to be replaced by other issues or fragments of the original issue. An example would be the energy crisis of 1973–74, which quickly shot to the top of the public agenda, only to fade within a few years. **Deferred issues,** in contrast, are likely to return in one form or another. For many years, the civil rights issue was deferred by politicians who sought to avoid deep and potentially frightening conflicts.

**Diverted issues,** finally, are those that are handled by calling for a reevaluation of the problems involved. Sometimes the public focus is shifted from the issue itself to a debate over various governmental solutions, as has happened in the area of health policy. At other times, the issue becomes whether or not government ought to be involved in a particular area at all: Should there be federal action to deal with abortion, pornography, or ghetto unemployment? Also, particular policies spawned by the original issue may replace the latter as the focus of debate. This development characterized the policy debate over school desegregation, in which busing became the main subject of discussion.

## Policy formulation and implementation

Dealing with political issues requires specific proposals, and once an alternative is adopted, a complex implementation process begins. It is in the conceptualizing of problems and the discussion of alternative positions that ideological factors enter political debate. One group's "solution" is a mere gesture to another. Let us examine these aspects of the policy process.

428

Proposals for action

As we have seen in several chapters, proposals for public policy come from many sources. Interest groups concerned with an issue commonly have specific proposals ready to present to their allies in Congress or the administration. Governmental bureaucracies in the executive branch also may advance policy proposals; in fact, it is part of their job to do so. Privately financed research institutes, or "think tanks," can also be the source of new policy ideas. Such institutes can be liberal, conservative, or even radical in orientation. When the Reagan administration took office in 1981, for example, the Heritage Foundation, a conservative think tank, issued a whole series of policy recommendations to guide the new administration. Individual legislators and, sometimes, legislative committees or groups develop new policy proposals or refine the proposals offered by others. One of the unique features of the U.S. political system is the powerful role played by the courts in the process of policy formulation. Only through court decisions were standards elaborated for school desegregation, legislative reapportionment, criminal justice procedures, and constitutional action in many other areas. Another—and perhaps the most influential—source of policy proposals is the president, who has increasingly become the focus of governmental leadership.

The formulation of policy alternatives, however, may or may not lead to new policies. Many items have been on the public agenda for years, even decades, without being resolved. They are "nibbled at" rather than dealt with in any thoroughgoing manner. The chaotic state of health policy in the United States is an outstanding example of nonresolution. Most often, issues are not resolved when the interest groups involved are powerful enough to thwart any bold action, or when there is too much confusion or conflict to permit decisive steps to be taken. The alternatives may be there, but none can be chosen. Instead, incrementalism continues.[5]

A significant component in policy formulation is the balancing of what needs to be done with what can realistically be accomplished. Enactment of any wide-ranging piece of legislation depends on its being acceptable to diverse elements. Here the law of *anticipated reactions* applies.[6] After assessing the expected reactions, policy formulators shape proposals to fit with what is considered possible. This idea of politics as the "art of the possible" is considered a basic, realistic approach to political life. Yet it can easily be abused. It can be used as an excuse for not seeking change more seriously, or as a way of passing the buck. Sometimes it is all too easy to argue that nothing is possible at a particular time in a particular branch of the government. The real "art" in the "art of the possible" lies in sensing how far current situations can be changed by determined action. This can be a hard judgment to make—often,

only a crisis or large-scale mass action makes possible what was previously beyond the realm of possibility.

## Implementation

The process of policy implementation is a subtle and many-sided aspect of politics, and one that is often overlooked. Most citizens assume that once a bill is passed and a policy adopted, the political battles are over and the problems solved. But implementation presents difficulties of its own. For example, new policies are often phrased in very vague terms.[7] Just what do phrases such as "the public interest or convenience," or "maximum feasible participation," or "fairness" mean? When a policy is implemented, specifics have to be attached to such vague injunctions.

Another aspect of the implementation process is the need for information. Very often, policymakers simply don't know enough about the conditions in

Community effort: a recycling center on Long Island, New York. Sometimes social action precedes government action, and local action precedes national action. Democratic politics usually presupposes a good deal of initiative will remain with the citizenry.

429

which policies will be carried out. The Clean Air Act of 1970 ran into implementation problems because the scientific knowledge needed to implement the act intelligently was simply not available. Governments often look foolish when attempting to carry out ill-conceived policies. When the Kennedy administration sought to implement elaborate plans to overthrow the Cuban government of Fidel Castro by launching the Bay of Pigs invasion in 1961, the result was what one observer called "a perfect fiasco."[8] In this case, as in many others, intelligence estimates were drastically wrong. Inaccurate information can lead to disaster not only in the foreign policy area, but also in education, housing, welfare, and many other public policy sectors. Many times, government is caught by surprise by the effects of its own actions.

Another point to bear in mind is that political activity continues during the implementation process. Interest groups are still active at this stage, trying to shape the decisions of the bureaucrats who implement policy. Sometimes administrative agencies put up resistance to new policies. In 1981, for example, Congress ordered the Veterans Administration to provide free medical care to veterans for any ailment that might reasonably be assumed to result from exposure to atomic radiation or from Agent Orange, a herbicide used in Vietnam. The VA, however, refused care to all but a handful of veterans—after seventeen months only twenty-nine claims out of 2,067 had been approved—and thereby clearly violated the intent of Congress. Congress held hearings to highlight the VA's failure, and instructed agency directors to alter policy.

## Policy evaluation

In recent years, there have been many serious attempts to evaluate the effects of public policies. The potential benefits of such efforts are obvious. It is important to know, for example, whether efforts to control water pollution are really having any effect,

or whether occupational health and safety measures are achieving the intended results. Evaluation can furnish policymakers with a sense of the successes and failures of policy-making, and thereby help in the formulation of new guidelines. Systematic evaluations of public policies are often difficult, however, and frequently enmeshed in controversial judgments.

Often, policies are carried out in haphazard fashion, or once implemented, grow in an uncontrolled fashion. In a society, unlike in a laboratory, it is rarely possible to experiment and control the circumstances in order to allow for a careful assessment of the results of a specific policy. Even when rigorous methods of assessment are conscientiously applied, values and ideologies can cloud the evaluation. For example, some observers have judged the Great Society programs of the Johnson administration to have been an obvious and almost predetermined failure, whereas others have regarded them as a reasonable success.[9] This is not so much a dispute over what happened as over what perspective should be brought to bear in judging it. Objective methods of evaluation are helpful, but they cannot substitute for political judgment, which necessarily involves the weighing of ethical factors.

Much policy evaluation is still completely unsystematic. Such "seat-of-the-pants" judgments, however, often represent the best that can be done in the absence of more-objective methods. They may be heavily biased and self-serving, but they are not necessarily useless.

## Who rules, and why it matters

One of the central questions of any politics (and certainly a crucial one for comprehending policymaking) is, Who rules? Which individuals and groups exercise the most power, and why? Obviously, in a democratic system, this is sensitive and important territory.

## Elitist and pluralist views

There has been a lengthy debate in political science about who actually "runs" the United States. Proponents of the elitist point of view have argued that a relatively homogeneous group of people—similar in background, lifestyle, and most of all, political outlook—make the key decisions that shape our political and economic lives.[10] Usually included in this elite are the top officials in major corporations, leading politicians, the upper stratum of the national bureaucracy, and leading military officials. Of course, the argument goes, these people do not agree on everything, nor do they see or talk to each other constantly. Elites, in other words, are not engaged in a conspiracy of some sort. But the views and attitudes of this group do tend to coincide to a very high degree. In this view, the American people, as a whole, are largely excluded from effective political decision making. The people cast their votes once every four years, but that is about all they do. The real power rests in the hands of the elite, who have the information needed to address policy questions and who hold the strategic positions necessary to carry through on their decisions.

The alternative to the elitist view is the more popular pluralist conception of U.S. politics.[11] Adherents of this view have argued that no *one* elite group dominates our national life; rather, there are many influential groups, whose degree of influence varies according to the particular policy area involved. In defense policy, for example, an array of interest groups attempts to exercise influence over decision-making: major defense-involved corporations, legislators whose districts or states have defense interests, members of the armed forces, and so on. There are also a few groups with strong ideological interests in foreign policy and defense decisions, such as the nuclear freeze lobby, or the Committee on the Present Danger, which organized to defeat the SALT II Treaty in 1979. Turning to health policy, we find quite a different array of groups competing for influence: associations of health professionals, private insurance agencies, public health groups, and some representatives of health care consumers.

Thus, the pluralists have contended, the patterns of interest-group competition vary in different policy areas. It would be very unusual for the same groups or individuals to exert a dominant influence in a number of areas. According to one version of the pluralist argument, the U.S. political system is characterized not by majority rule, but by *minorities rule*,[12] whereby important groups exercise influence in those areas of chief concern to them. In the pluralist view, then, the U.S. political process is basically a highly subdivided arena, each portion of which has different participants and different winners and losers.

Theodore Lowi, a political scientist, coined the term **interest-group liberalism** to describe the pattern of political decision making most commonly found in recent U.S. politics.[13] In this form of politics, according to Lowi, each participant in every controversy receives something, and thus each has some impact on the decision-making process. As a result, the government rarely says no to any well-organized interest; instead, it gives some reward, some subsidy, some benefit to each interested party. This pluralistic pattern tends to minimize conflict through the buying off of the groups involved. For Lowi, the problem with such a system is that it avoids any thoroughgoing effort to determine what the public interest is in a policy area. The need to discover a "just" solution is ignored, standards of public life degenerate, and government budgets are inflated, while large public benefits go to various private groups.

Who is right, the pluralists or the elitists? Most students of U.S. politics side with the pluralists, whose view seems the most commonsensical. Obviously, different groups *do* have power in different areas. Moreover, the patterns of group success and failure do change from time to time. For example, whereas the elderly as a group once exercised little influence in U.S. politics, they have grown into a significant force that cannot easily be ignored in public policy-making.

Yet there is also a sound basis to the elitist position. Despite the bewildering array of policy arenas, and despite the incredible proliferation of groups with some sort of influence on some aspects of public policy, larger patterns of policymaking do tend to take hold over the long term. Examination of these long-term patterns reveals that some groups tend to benefit much more heavily than others, and that certain individuals have disproportionate influence over policy-making. It also shows that policy changes rather slowly in some areas and that there is a strong consensus on the limits of policymaking. Certain issues, in other words, simply do not make it onto the policy agenda in U.S. politics.

## The boundaries of policymaking

The boundaries of policymaking are clearest in three main areas. To begin with, there is no real debate over the fundamentals of the distribution of wealth and economic power in U.S. society. In the United States, there is a strong consensus that the current capitalistic society, which includes large degrees of economic inequality, is a "good" society. As was pointed out in Chapter 2, the absence of a viable political left in U.S. politics has meant that this basic issue has never appeared on the political agenda.

Another area in which political consensus sets clear boundaries is that of foreign policy. For two decades after World War II, the foreign policy consensus was very powerful. Many policy options that the United States might have pursued were never even seriously considered. The anticommunist Cold War policy of the country was virtually unchallengeable. With the Vietnam War, that foreign policy consensus broke down. For the first time, the range of debate over our future foreign policy began to widen.

The third policy area with rather clear boundaries is that represented by the Constitution. The fundamental political structure of the nation has rarely been challenged directly. But as we will see in the chapters to follow, there have been occasional challenges to aspects of that structure. For example, we will see in Chapter 19 that opponents of Supreme Court rulings on abortion have sought to make what some consider to be basic alterations in our constitutional arrangements in order to undo those decisions.

432

## Conclusions

The elitist/pluralist debate can help us orient ourselves in the bewildering arena of policymaking. In the first place, this debate tells us that we should be aware of the larger, long-term patterns of policymaking. Is there a "consensus" in some area of policymaking? And *if* there is, what sorts of questions are excluded from consideration?[14] Second, the debate directs us toward a careful look at the participants in various policy areas. Who is actually involved in influencing policy decisions? How do they exercise their influence? Who is dominant? Do some groups find it impossible to be effective?

Often these considerations can help us to evaluate policy from a democratic perspective. If decisions are made by a few, if large numbers of people are excluded or ignorant, if the interests of the many seem to play little role in decisions, then a democrat must worry about what is taking place. As we will see, since democracy in the United States is a highly imperfect matter, such problems crop up again and again in various areas of policy-making.

Democracy does not come easily. In the policy discussions to follow, the reader should remain aware of the problems of popular enlightenment involved in each of the major areas of policy conflict. How well do most people grasp the main dimensions of the issues? Are most of us reasonably well-informed? Do we *want* to know more? Are there ways citizens can make themselves more knowledgeable about the issues we face as a society? How well-informed are our leaders in these significant matters? Can we trust those in authority to have a firm grasp on what they are up to?

Knowledge, of course, is only a part of what is needed to create a democratic public and to provide an intelligent dialogue in public life. What we also hope to find is a firm commitment to democratic values, a sense of equality, a good measure of fairness, a willingness to involve the public in policy debate. In reading the policy chapters, you should ask yourself how "democratic" these debates sound. Are our leaders being guided by a clear commitment to a democratic ethic?

## NOTES

1 The term *incrementalism* was popularized by Charles E. Lindblom in *The Intelligence of Democracy* (New York: The Free Press, 1965). It has also been widely used in the literature on budgeting.

2 E. E. Schattschneider, *The Semi-Sovereign People* (New York: Holt, Rinehart and Winston, 1975).

3 Murray Edelman, *Politics as Symbolic Action* (New York: Academic Press, Institute for Research on Poverty Monographs, 1971).

4 Robert Eyestone, *From Social Issues to Public Policy* (New York: Wiley, 1978).

5 On the role of leadership in this process, see R. T. Nakamura and Frank Smallwood, *The Politics of Policy Implementation* (New York: St. Martin's, 1980), Chapter 4.

6 See E. E. Schattschneider, *The Semi-Sovereign People*, Chapters 2 and 3.

7 George C. Edwards III, *Implementing Public Policy* (Washington, D.C.: Congressional Quarterly Press, 1980), Chapters 1 and 2.

8 Irving L. Janis, *Groupthink* (Boston: Houghton Mifflin, 1982), Chapter 2.

9 On the negative side, see Peter Steinfels, *The Neoconservatives: The Men Who Are Changing America's Politics* (New York: Simon & Schuster, 1979); on the positive side, see John E. Schwartz, *America's Hidden Success* (New York: W. W. Norton, 1983).

10 For two perspectives on elitism, see C. Wright Mills, *The Power Elite* (New York: Oxford University Press, 1959); and William Domoff, *Who Rules America Now? A View for the Eighties* (Englewood Cliffs, N.J.: Prentice-Hall, 1983).

11 There are many sorts of pluralists. For a look at two very different views, both pluralist, see Robert Dahl, *Who Governs?* (New Haven, Conn.: Yale University Press, 1961); and Grant McConnell, *Private Power and American Democracy* (New York: Random House, 1970).

12 The term is from Robert Dahl, *A Preface to Democratic Theory* (Chicago: University of Chicago Press, 1963), Chapter 5.

13 Theodore S. Lowi, *The End of Liberalism* (New York: W. W. Norton, 1979), Chapter 3.

14 This is one of the views taken by Peter Bachrach and

Morton S. Baratz, "Two Faces of Power," *American Political Science Review* 56 (1962).

## SELECTED READINGS

### Basic readings in policy literature

Robert A. Dahl, *Modern Political Analysis* (Englewood Cliffs, N.J.: Prentice-Hall, 1976); Duncan MacRae, Jr., and James A. Wilde, *Policy Analysis for Public Decisions* (North Scituate, Mass.: Duxbury Press, 1979); M. H. Moore and G. T. Allison, eds., *Public Policy* (Cambridge, Mass.: Harvard University Press, 1979); Mancur Olson, *The Logic of Collective Action* (Cambridge, Mass.: Harvard University Press, 1971); J. L. Pressman and A. B. Wildavsky, *Implementation* (Berkeley, Cal.: University of California Press, 1973); Murray Edelman, *Politics as Symbolic Action: Mass Arousal and Quiescence* (New York: Academic Press, 1971); George C. Edwards III, *Implementing Public Policy* (Washington, D.C.: Congressional Quarterly Press, 1980); Ellen F. Paul and Philip A. Russo, Jr., eds., *Public Policy: Issues, Analysis and Ideology* (Chatham, N.J.: Chatham House, 1982); Robert T. Nakamura and Frank Smallwood, *The Politics of Policy Implementation* (New York: St. Martin's, 1980); and Robert A. Dahl, *Dilemmas of Pluralist Democracy: Autonomy vs. Control* (New Haven, Conn.: Yale University Press, 1982).

### Specific issues

Francis E. Rourke, *Bureaucracy, Politics and Public Policy* (Boston: Little, Brown, 1976); Daniel P. Moynihan, *Maximum Feasible Misunderstanding* (New York: The Free Press, 1970); Aaron B. Wildavsky, *The Politics of the Budgetary Process* (Boston: Little, Brown, 1964); Peter Bachrach and M. S. Baratz, *Power and Poverty: Theory and Practice* (New York: Oxford University Press, 1970); Frederick V. Malek, *Washington's Hidden Tragedy: The Failure to Make Government Work* (New York: The Free Press, 1978); Charles F. Adrian, *Politics and Economic Policy in Western Democracies* (North Scituate, Mass.: Duxbury Press, 1980); Thomas Ferguson and Joel Rogers, eds., *The Political Economy: Readings in the Politics and Economics of American Public Policy* (Armonk, N.Y.: M. E. Sharpe, 1984); Robert D. Holsworth and J. Harry Wray, *American Politics and Everyday Life* (New York: John Wiley, 1982); Randall B. Ripley and Grace A. Franklin, *Congress, the Bureaucracy, and Public Policy*, 3rd ed., (Homewood, Ill., Dorsey, 1984).

# Chapter nineteen

# Management
of the
economy

# In
whose
interest?

ECONOMICS has often been referred to as "the dismal science."[1] In part, this is a compliment, for most economists would like to think of their discipline as a science. The "dismal" part cannot please economists, however. One "dismal" aspect of economics is that it deals with scarcity—with alternative ways of allocating resources. It is also filled with numbers and calculations. Economists necessarily turn flesh-and-blood human beings and their busy social and commercial lives into dollars and cents, and into abstractions such as supply and demand. Economists ascend from the real world of people— sweating and working, haggling in the marketplace—to the airy (but usually dismal) realm of inflation and recession, money markets and gold standards.

What has economics to do with democratic concerns? The answer may well be, *everything*. It is not hard to see that economic matters are intimately intertwined with democratic aspirations. Some students of democratic evolution have advanced the theory that a certain level of economic development is a prerequisite for the establishment and maintenance of a modern democratic society.[2] Historically, they have argued, poor and economically primitive societies tend to be authoritarian, intolerant, and politically stagnant. Democratic politics usually evolves only when affluence increases, education spreads, urbanization helps widen people's horizons, communications improve, and greater sophistication fosters tolerance and the spirit of compromise. This argument is certainly not conclusive, since democracies have developed under other conditions, but it is quite persuasive.

On the other side of the coin, economic crises can precipitate the decline and destruction of democracies. There can be little doubt that the catastrophic economic conditions of the 1920s and 1930s opened the way for the success of fascist movements in many nations. It seems very unlikely that the Nazis, for example, could have come to power in Germany were it not for the drastic economic decline that preceded their political successes in the early 1930s.

History and theory aside, how do economic matters mesh with issues of democratic life in our society today? To answer that question, we must first examine the basic distributive patterns in the United States. Who gains the most and the least from the U.S. economy? Are rewards and deprivations distributed in a fair, or sensible, way? Are some people severely and unnecessarily deprived? Do some individuals and groups fall below a humanly decent standard of living? Next, we need to consider the ways in which serious economic problems affect our quality of life. Are cities, for example, in a state of decay? Are health services adequate to cope with the needs of citizens? Finally, we must look at how the U.S. economy is being managed. Does the government seek to implement a coherent economic policy? Can the economy, as presently structured, provide all Americans with a decent standard of living? Do most citizens understand economic issues, and are they able to make their views heard? All these issues are closely related to the democratic concerns voiced throughout this book.

## History of economic management

A historical perspective can help to show us how the U.S. government presently defines the task of managing the economy. In the course of U.S. history, the government has pursued three major types of economic policy: **mercantilism**, which involved direct government intervention in the economy; **laissez-faire capitalism**, in which government gave a relatively free hand to business; and today's **controlled capitalism**, in which government intervenes to some extent to regulate the economy. A mere recitation of these three policies suffices to destroy the myth that government management of the economy is a phenomenon of the twentieth century. In the broadest sense, management of the economy is as old as the nation itself.[3]

### Mercantilism

The economic theory of mercantilism evolved in seventeenth-century Europe. Operating under its tenets, the rulers of nation-states such as England and Holland established government-chartered corporations and encouraged their growth through subsidies, or financial support. The corporations were protected from competition through grants of monopoly status,

and their output, production, and distribution were extensively controlled. Colonies were formed overseas to provide wealth in the form of raw materials and markets for exports. In exchange for protection and subsidization, the semipublic corporations gave the government a share of their income. Mercantilism benefited both the government and the businessman, but profits often were made at the expense of the general public, in nation and colony alike.

The American colonies rebelled against the taxation policies and regulations imposed by the British government. In developing their own political system, however, Americans eventually resorted to many of the same mercantilist devices, which aided business growth at the expense of farmers, artisans, and laborers.[4] Operating under the Constitution, the U.S. government imposed high taxes on imported goods (protective tariffs), gave subsidies to business, and granted monopoly powers to a national bank. Although the Founders disagreed over the question of how extensive government control of economic affairs should be, there was general agreement that the protection and promotion of propertied interests was one of the vital functions of government.

### Laissez-faire and the growth of regulation

The principal tenet of laissez-faire capitalism, which by the mid-nineteenth century had replaced mercantilism as the favored economic policy of Western governments, was that national wealth would be increased if government restrictions on economic activity were kept to a minimum. In theory, this policy called for the abolition of such mercantilist strategies as government-backed corporate monopolies, detailed regulatory laws, and high protective tariffs. In practice, the laissez-faire movement "democratized" capitalism by throwing open to all comers those sectors of the economy previously restricted to the government-chartered corporations. The new, privately held corporations that emerged under the laissez-faire doctrine wanted to be free of competition from government enterprises and from the detailed regulations imposed on the previously chartered companies. President Andrew Jackson endorsed the movement and gave it impetus in his successful fight to terminate the government-chartered National Bank.

The irony of the laissez-faire period, however, was that as it progressed, business competition actually declined and monopolies returned. As the more successful corporations expanded, they either bought out their competitors or drove them out of business. As the public monopolies of the 1820s were replaced by the private monopolies of the 1880s, public protest, particularly from farmers and small businessmen, led to the passage of regulatory legislation. In the 1880s, many states, bowing to the demands of Western farmers and Eastern merchants, imposed restrictions on the rates charged by railroads. New regulatory legislation by the federal government came more slowly, because of doubts about its constitutionality. The first federal regulatory commission, the Interstate Commerce Commission, appeared in 1887. In 1890, Congress passed the Sherman Anti-trust Act, which was designed to prevent monopolies and trusts (the pooling of resources by several companies for the purpose of controlling a market). Only in a few cases, however, was the act enforced with vigor.[5]

Another area of controversy during the laissez-faire period revolved around the supply of money and credit, which fluctuated between being plentiful and being scarce. When government spending and strict banking policy made money hard to get, companies got caught short of money, business growth decreased, prices went down, and people lost jobs. (This condition is referred to today as depression if it leads to a major economic crisis and a recession if it is less severe.) In the latter part of the nineteenth century, many people contended that the solution to their money and credit problems lay in the printing of more money by the federal government. The government resisted this course of action, however. Whenever too much money is printed, the currency is debased and prices go up to compensate for the lower value of money. This condition is known as inflation; if uncontrolled, it can ruin a nation's economy.

## Controlled capitalism

The third era of U.S. economic policy, that of controlled capitalism, began around the turn of the century and is still evolving today. During this era the government, rather than dismantling large corporations or allowing them to operate unfettered, has created regulatory agencies (see Chapter 16) to oversee and control their activities. One of the chief characteristics of this period has been the transfer to the federal government of many of the regulatory and productive activities formerly handled by the states. Federal regulatory agencies multiplied first during the Progressive Era (1900–17) and again during the New Deal of the 1930s, as the nation tried to cope with the Great Depression. That economic catastrophe represented a turning point in economic management. As such, it is worth looking at in more detail.

There was no single cause for the Depression, which swept over all industrialized nations and lasted for close to a decade. Its onset usually is linked to the collapse of the U.S. stock market in October 1929. But that event was only the crystallization of many other factors that had been building for some time. During the 1920s, there had been a vast expansion of credit buying in the United States, and a "get-rich-quick" attitude had led to extensive land and stock speculation. As the decade progressed, the production of goods increased more rapidly than the incomes required to buy those goods. The distribution of income in the United States also grew increasingly unequal during the 1920s. In 1929, the richest 1 percent of the population received as much income as the bottom 42 percent. All these factors fueled the situation that developed into the Depression.

Much of American economic life operated on the faith that large profits would continue into the indefinite future. But demand could not keep up with supply. As incomes grew more unequal, even with installment buying, demand for goods began to dry up. As a result, the economy became more and more dependent on a high level of luxury spending and

# Memories of the Great Depression

### Sidney J. Weinberg

*A senior partner in Goldman-Sachs Company, a leading investment house, who served during President Franklin Roosevelt's first two administrations as an industrial adviser.*

October 29, 1929—I remember that day very

In the photographs on pp. 438-441, we see what the Depression meant in the United States. Here (*left*), we see the turmoil on Wall Street on Black Monday, Oct. 29, 1929. On p. 439 we see some of the consequences: men eating bread and soup in one of the many soup kitchens that sprang up to aid the destitute; rural children behind the wire fence of poverty.

intimately. I stayed in the office a week without going home. The [ticker] tape was running, I've forgotten how long that night. It must have been ten, eleven o'clock before we got the final reports. It was like a thunder clap. Everybody was stunned. Nobody knew what it was all about. [Wall] Street had general confusion. They didn't understand it any more than anybody else. They thought something would be announced. . . .

Pools combined to support the market, to no avail. The public got scared and sold. It was a very trying period for

me. Our investment company went up to two, three hundred, and then went down to practically nothing. As all investment companies did. . . .

I don't know anybody that jumped out of the window. But I know many who threatened to jump. They ended up in nursing homes and insane asylums and things like that. These were people who were trading in the market or in banking houses. They broke down physically, as well as financially.

Roosevelt saved the system. It's trite to say

the system would have gone out the window. But certainly a lot of institutions would have changed. We were on the verge of something. You could have had a rebellion, you could have had a civil war.

### Ben Isaacs

*A small businessman*

I was in business for myself, selling clothing on credit, house to house. . . .

All of a sudden, in the afternoon, October, 1929 . . . I was going on my

business and I heard the newspaper boys calling, running all around the streets and giving news and news: stock market crashed, stock market crashed. It came out just like lightning. . . .

We lost everything. It was the time I would collect four, five hundred dollars a week. After that, I couldn't collect fifteen, ten dollars a week. I was going around trying to collect enough money to keep my family going. It was impossible. Very few people could pay you. Maybe a dollar if they would feel sorry for you or what.

We tried to struggle along living day by day. Then I couldn't pay the rent. I had a little car, but I couldn't pay no license for it. I left it parked against the court. I sold it for $15 in order to buy some food for the family. I had three little children. . . .

I didn't want to go on relief. Believe me, when I was forced to go to the office of the relief, the tears were running out of my eyes. I couldn't bear myself to take money from anybody for nothing. If it wasn't for those kids—I tell you the truth—many a time it came to my mind to go commit suicide. Than go ask for relief. But somebody has to take care of those kids. . . .

### Cesar Chavez

*President of the
United Farm
Workers of
America.*

Oh, I remember having to move out of our house. My father had brought in a team of horses and wagon. We had always lived in that house, and we couldn't understand why we were moving out. When we got to the other house, it was a worse house, a poor house. That must have been around 1934. I was about six years old.

It's known as the North Gila Valley, about fifty miles north of Yuma. My dad was being turned out of his small plot of land. He had inherited this from his father, who had homesteaded it. I saw my two, three other uncles also moving out. And for the same reason. The bank had foreclosed on the loan.

*continued*

We all of us climbed into an old Chevy that my dad had. And then we were in California, and migratory workers. . . . We had been poor, but we knew every night there was a bed *there*, and that *this* was our room. There was a kitchen. It was sort of a settled life, and we had chickens and hogs, eggs and all those things. But that all of a sudden changed. . . .

When we moved to California, we would work after school. Sometimes we wouldn't go. "Following the crops," we missed much school. Trying to get enough money to stay alive the following winter, the whole family picking apricots, walnuts, prunes. We were pretty new, we had never been migratory workers. We were taken advantage of quite a bit by the labor contractor and the crew pusher. . . .

Labor strikes were everywhere. We were one of the strikingest families, I guess. My dad didn't like the conditions, and he began to agitate. Some families would follow, and we'd go elsewhere. Sometimes we'd come back. We couldn't find a job elsewhere, so we'd come back. Sort of beg for a job. Employers would know and they would make it very humiliating.

Oscar Heline

*A farmer who has lived his entire life on the same Iowa farm.*

The farmers became desperate. It got so a neighbor wouldn't buy from a neighbor, because the farmer didn't get any of it. It went to the creditors. And it wasn't enough to satisfy them.

. . . First, they'd take your farm, then they took your livestock, then your farm machinery. Even your household goods. And they'd move you off. The farmers were almost united. We had penny auction sales. Some neighbor would bid a penny and give it back to the owner.

Grain was being burned. It was cheaper than coal. Corn was being burned. A county just east of here, they burned corn in their courthouse all winter. '32. '33. You

couldn't hardly buy groceries for corn. It couldn't pay the transportation. In South Dakota, the county elevator listed corn as minus three cents. *Minus* three cents a bushel. If you wanted to sell 'em a bushel of corn, you had to bring in three cents. They couldn't afford to handle it. . . .

We had lots of trouble on the highway. People were determined to withhold produce from the market—livestock, cream, butter, eggs, what not. If they would dump the produce, they would force the market to a higher level. The farmers would man the highways, and cream cans were emptied in ditches and eggs dumped out. They burned the trestle bridge, so the trains wouldn't be able to haul grain. Conservatives don't like this kind of rebel attitude and aren't very sympathetic. But something had to be done. . . .

Some of the farmers with teams of horses, sometimes in trucks, tried to get through. He was trying to feed his family, trying to trade a few dozen eggs and a few pounds of cream for some groceries to feed his babies. He was desperate, too. One group tried to sell so they could live and the other group tried to keep you from selling so they could live. . . .

Through a federal program we got a farm loan. A committee of twenty-five of us drafted the first farm legislation of this kind thirty-five years ago. . . . New money was put in the farmers' hands. The Federal Government changed the whole marketing program. . . . People could now see daylight and hope. It was a whole transformation of attitude. You can just imagine. . . . (He weeps.). . . .

Source: Studs Terkel, *Hard Times, An Oral History of the Great Depression* (New York: Pantheon, 1970).

(*Left*) A Civilian Conservation Corps (CCC) camp in Lassen National Forest, California. The CCC was organized as part of the New Deal to provide jobs to young people and perform socially useful tasks, such as maintaining national parks and building highways. (*Center*) Migrants walking the road west to find work as tens of thousands lost their farms and moved elsewhere. (*Right*) President Roosevelt signs the Social Security Act of 1935 to the obvious satisfaction of those around him.

investment by the rich. In such circumstances, anything that created a loss of confidence among the wealthy in the continued expansion of the economy could lead to a catastrophic decline in investment and purchases. This is just what happened when the market crashed in October 1929. The "crash" broke the confidence that had helped create the expansion of the 1920s. After the crash, both consumption and investment declined over and over again. It was a vicious cycle of declining confidence, declining investment and incomes, from which the nation and its leaders could not escape.

Gross investment fell 35 percent from 1929 to 1930, and 35 percent more from 1930 to 1931. In the next year, it fell by 88 percent. The situation was unprecedented. From 1929 to 1933, gross national product (the value of all goods and services produced in the nation) dropped by 29 percent, construction declined by 78 percent, and unemployment rose from 3.2 percent to 24.9 percent.[6]

Until the time of the Depression the idea that government could or should serve as a basic shaping element in economic life was generally rejected. The New Deal remedies proposed by President Franklin Roosevelt's administration in the 1930s, however, involved large-scale government intervention in the economy. By reducing taxes, starting new programs, and creating new jobs, Roosevelt and his advisers hoped that new life could be infused into the economy. This idea of regulating the business cycle by deficit spending—that is, by allowing the government to spend more money than it received—was championed most brilliantly by British economist John Maynard Keynes, who had an important impact on economic policymakers after 1930. This philosophy of economics, accordingly, is generally referred to as **Keynesian economics.**

Although it was once thought that there was no way for government to help cure a depression, increased government spending in the late 1930s and during World War II did pull the nation out of economic stagnation and bring about a return to high employment levels. After the war, the idea of government manipulation of spending levels to stabilize the economy became more acceptable. This change was reflected in the passage of the Employment Act of 1946, which created the Council of Economic Advisors and authorized the president to deliver an annual economic report to Congress recommending actions to achieve high levels of employment.

The New Deal experience was a genuine watershed in U.S. history. Although some observers argued after World War II for a reduction in government involvement in and regulation of the economy, very few talked of turning back the clock to the pre–New Deal situation.

After pulling through the rigors of the Depression and World War II, the United States and Western European nations entered into a new phase of economic development. During the 1950s and much of the 1960s, industrial democracies achieved unprecedented levels of affluence. Economic growth was rapid, but prices remained stable. The techniques of economic management seemed to be equal to their tasks. The capitalist system, previously viewed as predestined to great cycles of boom and bust, now seemed to be sufficiently tamed to prove a powerful engine for growth, but not so powerful as to be beyond the control of proper manipulation.[7]

The so-called age of affluence began coming to an end in the late 1960s, however, and the problems that began developing at that time have been with us ever since. Economic fluctuations became more unpredictable and growth more erratic. Mild recessions became commonplace, unemployment grew, and inflation increased inexorably. In 1974 and 1975 came the worst downturn of economic activity since the Great Depression. Even when the Western economies pulled out of this downturn, considerable unemployment remained. Also a product of the 1970s was the new and surprising economic phenomenon of **stagflation**—a combination of high inflation and high unemployment, two problems that, according to previous economic theory, could not occur simultaneously. Most economic policies in the 1970s and the early 1980s were designed to cope with this novel situation.

The United States, along with the Western European democracies, has remained a capitalist nation characterized by private control of most of the economy. Yet in every industrial democracy the government has come to assume much responsibility for the overall management of economic life. For one thing, the public sector has grown so significantly that government has become one of the chief elements in economic life. Government is likely to be the chief purchaser of goods and services, the largest distributor of income (through income maintenance programs and the jobs it provides), and the largest single borrower of money. Given such a situation, governments can hardly avoid taking a leading role in economic management. Then, too, modern economic theory has largely encouraged increased government involvement in the economy. The experience with the Great Depression, as well as theoretical considerations, convinced many economists and politicians that capitalist economies could not function successfully without government action. Governments, it was concluded, could help stimulate employment and growth, and keep prices stable. There is no doubt that these Keynesian ideas were widely influential and conducive to the growth of a governmental responsibility for economic life. Finally, governments have become inextricably enmeshed in a set of financial relationships with the private economy—guaranteeing the safety of bank accounts, supporting home loans and payments to farmers, giving tax incentives to certain industries, and generally aiding various aspects of the economy.

For all of these reasons, it would be virtually impossible for any democratic government to detach itself from economic affairs without disastrous effects. Government involvement in economic management is here to stay. The real issues today are how government can intervene most effectively in the economy, what interventions are most important, and who should gain and lose by intervention.

## The tools of economic intervention

In the area of economic management, there is widespread agreement that democratic governments should pursue full employment, stable prices, and steady levels of economic growth. There is also a large measure of agreement on how progress toward these goals should be measured. All democratic, industrial nations keep records on unemployment levels, maintain various indices of price changes, and measure changes in the gross national product (GNP). Governments periodically (usually monthly) issue reports about the state of these various measures. In other words, most governments know what their economic goals are and how to know if progress toward them is being made.

There is a wide divergence of opinion, however, over the best means of achieving economic goals. Should government spend more or reduce taxes? Expand the money supply or contract it? Worry more about inflation or about recession? About rising prices or rising unemployment? In dealing with these difficult and complex questions, democratic governments can employ any or all of several tools of economic management, which fall into the general categories of fiscal policy and monetary policy.

## Fiscal policy

**Fiscal policies** involve the deliberate manipulation of elements of the budget to affect the economy. Since the various levels of government in the United States account for the expenditure of roughly 35 percent of the GNP, and the federal government alone accounts for 20 percent, budgetary manipulations by the government clearly will have major economic effects. The two ways in which the government can alter its budget are through spending policies and through tax policies.

**Spending policies:** When the government spends, it pumps money into, and thereby stimulates, the economy. One of the fundamental ideas of Keynesian economics is that there are times when government should *deliberately* spend more than it takes in. This will produce a budgetary deficit in the short run, but if economic growth were sufficiently stimulated, the deficit would be rectified in the long run, through increased tax revenues. In addition, the theory runs, government spending would create employment opportunities and alleviate a good deal of human suffering. The basic notion is that the government can counteract the worst effects of the usual business cycle by running a deficit when the economy is slow and then taking in a surplus when the economy is booming. This approach is known as a countercyclical policy.

A deficit can be achieved through either tax cuts or spending increases. Surpluses can be created through either tax increases or spending reductions. In actual practice, however, tinkering with the economy is not so simple. Political considerations frequently play an important part in economic decisions. For example, governments usually do not want to raise taxes, or to cut back on programs that are popularly supported. Largely as a result, the federal budget has run a surplus in only two of the last twenty years.

The dictates of fiscal policy confront government managers with some hard choices. Most basically, governments must set budget priorities. If it is decided to increase spending, will that mean more for national defense, more for highway building, more for Social Security, or more for urban reconstruction? It may not be possible to do everything at once. In the late 1960s, President Lyndon Johnson attempted to increase spending both on the Vietnam War and on domestic programs. In doing so, he probably overstimulated the economy and thus opened the way toward many of the economic problems of the 1970s. In the early 1980s, President Ronald Reagan sought to curtail federal expenditures, yet he also decided to increase spending for defense. These policy decisions necessarily entailed deep cuts in social programs. What is important to note is that the use of fiscal policy does not in itself dictate *where* to expand the budget or to contract it. Such decisions reflect the larger priorities of the particular administration in office.

In addition, there is often less room for maneuver in the federal budget than meets the eye. Up to two-thirds of the budget is fixed by past commitments, such as those to Social Security and pensions, interest on the national debt, and contractual obligations. Because the discretionary portion of the budget

is relatively small, cutting the budget is a difficult business. In fact, the three largest sources of growth in the federal budget in future years will be debt interest, Social Security, and Medicare.

**The tax system:** Policymakers also must face many difficult decisions in formulating taxation policies. Which taxes should be raised or lowered—the individual income tax, corporate taxes, excise taxes (taxes on commodities)? If taxes are being cut, who should receive the chief benefits? If raised, how should the burden be spread?

To understand the complicated U.S. tax system, we must first examine its historical roots. Prior to the American Revolution, there was widespread resentment toward the taxes imposed by the British. The colonists had no voice in how much they were taxed, or in how the money was spent. Taxation remained a highly sensitive question after independence. In the Constitution, Congress was granted power to "collect taxes, duties, imposts and excises to pay debts and provide for the common defense and general welfare." Until the Civil War, the federal government used customs and excise taxes almost exclusively. A tariff of 5 percent was imposed on all imported goods, and luxury taxes were levied on whiskey, carriages, and other items.

The first real income tax was a Civil War measure that was allowed to expire in 1872. Excise taxes on liquor and tobacco (which affected most people, and hit the poor hardest) were retained, however. In the 1890s the Populist Party campaigned for a graduated income tax. In response to Populist electoral successes, Congress in 1894 passed a 2 percent income tax on all incomes over $4,000. After the Supreme Court declared the tax unconstitutional in 1895, sentiment for a constitutional amendment sanctioning an income tax grew, and in 1913 the Sixteenth Amendment was ratified.

During World War I, only about 5.5 million people paid any income tax at all. Taxes declined in the 1920s and 1930s, and by 1939 only 4 million people—about 4 percent of the population over age fourteen—were paying federal income tax. World War II changed this picture. By 1945, 43 million Americans were paying income tax. At the same time, corporate taxes increased, and the modern system of withholding income taxes from wages and salaries was established. In 1954 there was a major overhaul of the Internal Revenue Code, and Congress began to create a host of tax loopholes and subsidies. The code was revised again in 1964, 1976, and 1981.

In its present form, the U.S. tax system reflects the complex political and economic realities of American life. Embedded in the tax system are the differences between what our society professes to value and what it actually rewards. In examining the special subsidies, tax benefits, and loopholes available to some, we can get a deeper sense of what inequality means in U.S. society, and how it persists.

Today, Americans pay a host of different taxes: sales tax, property tax, state and federal income taxes, Social Security tax, and an assortment of others. Some of these taxes are, at least in theory, *progressive*— that is, the rate of taxation is related to one's ability to pay. The federal income tax is theoretically a progressive tax, in which progressively higher rates are levied on progressively higher incomes. Actual rates paid, however, are far less progressive than the rates on paper. Other taxes are regressive in effect, meaning that they impose a higher-percentage tax on those with lower incomes. A sales tax on food is a regressive tax, because lower-income people are likely to spend a higher percentage of income on food than are higher-income people. A proportional tax is one that draws the same percentage of income from all income groups. In some ways the Social Security tax is a proportional levy; however, because it does not tax income beyond a certain point, wealthier individuals actually pay a lower pecentage than do poorer ones.

Despite the frequent complaints about taxation in the United States, our overall tax rates are considerably below those in many other societies. Among the industrial democracies, only Switzerland, Australia, and Japan have lower rates of taxation.

As Table 19.1 shows, the largest share of federal government receipts comes from the individual income tax. Next come payroll taxes (social insurance receipts), whose contribution has risen as Social Security rates have gone up. Corporate income taxes have declined steadily as a percentage of total fed-

TABLE 19.1
## Federal, state, and local taxes and other revenues, by major source, 1982

| Major source | Revenues* | |
| --- | --- | --- |
| | Amount (billions of dollars) | Percentage of total |
| *Federal* | | |
| Individual income | 296.7 | 49.1 |
| Corporation income | 46.5 | 7.7 |
| Excises | 32.4 | 5.4 |
| Estate and gift | 7.6 | 1.3 |
| Payroll | 204.5 | 33.9 |
| Other | 16.2 | 2.7 |
| Total | 603.9 | 100.0 |
| *State and local* | | |
| Individual income | 51.8 | 16.0 |
| Corporation income | 12.7 | 3.9 |
| Sales | 95.5 | 29.5 |
| Estate and gift | 2.6 | 0.8 |
| Payroll | 4.0 | 1.2 |
| Property | 86.5 | 26.7 |
| Other | 71.0 | 21.9 |
| Total | 324.1 | 100.0 |
| *All levels* | | |
| Individual income | 348.5 | 37.6 |
| Corporation income | 59.2 | 6.4 |
| Sales and excises | 127.9 | 13.8 |
| Estate and gift | 10.2 | 1.1 |
| Payroll | 208.4 | 22.5 |
| Property | 86.5 | 9.3 |
| Other | 87.3 | 9.4 |
| Total | 928.0 | 100.0 |

Source: Joseph A. Peckman, *Federal Tax Policy* (Washington, D.C.: Brookings Institution, 1983), p. 2.
*Revenues are defined as receipts in the national income accounts less contributions for social insurance other than payroll taxes. Federal grants-in-aid are not included in state and local receipts.

eral revenue in the postwar era, dropping from 34 percent of the total in 1944 to 7.7 percent in 1982. Excise taxes on gasoline, automobiles, telephone use, alcohol, tobacco, truck parts, fishing equipment, firearms, matches, gambling, and other commodities have also become less prominent in the federal budget. On the whole, excise taxes are regressive in effect, placing a heavier burden on lower-income tax pay-ers. In addition, the proportion of individual income taxes paid by average wage earners has risen, and that paid by wealthier people has dropped. Finally, enforcement of the tax laws often is not very effec-tive. It has been estimated that state governments lose up to half of all corporate taxes owed them due to careless administration.

## Monetary policy

Another major technique of economic management is monetary policy, or the regulation of the supply of money in the economy. Monetary policy has been a conflict-ridden issue for two centuries in this coun-try.

In the traditional method of money management, all paper money was backed with gold. The idea was that paper money, in order to retain its value, would have to be redeemable in that precious metal. The use of this so-called gold standard placed sharp lim-its on how quickly the money supply could grow. The gold supply, after all, depended on how much of that metal was being mined, or brought into the country from abroad. If the demand for money by borrowers and consumers exceeded the existing sup-ply of money, then interest rates on borrowed money would go up. As a result, people would take out fewer loans and investment would decline. In short, a tight money supply could drastically limit the growth of the economy. This was exactly the issue raised by the many nineteenth-century reformers who called for abandonment of the gold standard in favor of a standard based on silver or some other metal more plentiful than gold.

In 1971, President Richard Nixon officially took the United States off the international gold standard, an act prompted by the economic problems of the early 1970s. Nowadays, U.S. money is not backed by gold in any way. As one student of the subject has put it: "If you take a $1 bill to the Treasury and ask for metal, you will probably be given a Susan B. Anthony copper-and-nickel coin, worth less than 3¢ melted down."[8]

The U.S. money supply is controlled by an inde-pendent regulatory agency, the **Federal Reserve System** (the Fed)—in essence, the central bank of the United States. The president appoints the mem-bers of the Fed Board but has no formal control over them. The Federal Reserve Board oversees twelve regional Federal Reserve banks and approximately 5,500 member banks in the various states. All na-tionally chartered banks must belong to the Federal Reserve System, and many state banks voluntarily join. The member banks are required to keep a cer-tain percentage of assets in one of the reserve banks. In addition, member banks may borrow money from the reserve banks to finance lending activities.

The Federal Reserve Board can manipulate the economy in several ways. It can control the amount of money in the economy by raising or lowering the percentage of money that each member bank must keep in reserve rather than loan out or invest. More frequently, the Fed manipulates the economy by raising or lowering the interest rate charged to mem-ber banks (the prime rate); they, in turn, pass on this charge to customers. Generally, as interest rates drop, the amount of money borrowed increases, and the economy expands. To cool down an overheated economy, the Fed can boost the interest rate, thereby discouraging borrowing and slowing economic growth.

There has been considerable debate over whether the government should rely primarily on fiscal policy or monetary policy in regulating the business cycle. Proponents of monetary policy have argued that it is more direct in application, quicker to take effect, and if used properly, more effective in stabilizing the economy. As long as regulation of monetary pol-icy remains outside the direct control of the presi-dent, however, presidents will continue to prefer the fiscal tools. Most presidents have been understand-ably reluctant to leave the economic fate of the coun-try in the hands of an agency that so far has failed to do better than the White House in maintaining a stable business cycle.

Many observers have decried the Fed's lack of accountability to the larger public through the dem-ocratic process. If the Fed is accountable to anyone, it is to the banking community. The Fed has also been known to make sudden shifts linked to the political preferences of its directors, as when the money supply was expanded to help Richard Nixon avoid a more serious recession before the 1972 presidential election. At times, it also has acted under the assumption that full employment is inflationary—an attitude that some economists have labeled callous.

Defenders of the current Federal Reserve System have argued that bringing it under direct presidential control would mean the intrusion of politics into economic policy-making. However, such a move would give presidents greater freedom of action in those instances when the makers of monetary policy are reluctant to follow the lead of the White House.

## The politics of economics

If economics is a science, there remains a great deal of disagreement among its practitioners over how its tenets should be used. There are liberal economists, conservative economists, radical economists, and many shades and textures in between. Economics, in short, is hard to employ in an entirely neutral manner. When people argue economics—when they speculate about why the economy is doing well or badly, or when they argue about exactly what "well" or "badly" means—they are not just talking "science." Inevitably, they are deeply enmeshed in political debate.

As we have already seen, for many decades the dominant economic concept was that of laissez-faire capitalism, which extolled nonintervention by government in economic life and the capacity of capitalism to work as a self-regulating system. Since the Great Depression, however, more interventionist ideas have taken hold. These notions remained dominant until the economic difficulties of the 1970s began to undermine their persuasiveness. Since that time, arguments have raged among economists about the nature of the economic problems we now face.

In the real world, economic ideas must interact with political realities. Economic theory can be perverted, misused, or skillfully manipulated. Economic ideas can be employed as a form of rhetoric,

in an effort to obscure real problems, or twisted to advance political ends. Economic considerations can also be ignored, with either good or bad results. Such interactions between economic theories and the real world of U.S. politics are exemplified in the three cases presented in this section.[9]

## Fiscal policy in the Kennedy-Johnson years

The economists who came to Washington with President John Kennedy in 1961 were, without exception, Keynesians: that is, they believed in the efficacy of government intervention to strengthen the economy. They disagreed, however, over the question of how the government should seek to stimulate the economy. Some argued for increased spending on social programs, both to stimulate the lagging economy and to deal with poverty problems. Others, although not opposed to social spending, focused on tax reduction as a politically practical step, since they believed Congress was too conservative to support a major boost in spending. In 1962, President Kennedy came around to the view that a tax cut would serve useful national purposes.

In his famous 1962 Yale University commencement address, which focused on economic myths, Kennedy attacked the near-sacred concept of a balanced budget and made the Keynesian argument that judiciously formulated tax cuts could lead to increased government revenues in the long run. In proposing this course of action, Kennedy was opposing what his chief economic adviser Walter Heller called the American "Puritan ethic" in the economic sphere: "balance the budget, stay out of debt, live within your means." Kennedy attempted to persuade his audience that a government budget should not be compared with a family budget, in which income should equal expenses. Instead, he argued, the government was more like a major corporation that must borrow for future expansion. As it grows, it pays off the debt, and at all times its total indebtedness is dwarfed by its economic potential.

After Kennedy was assassinated in 1963, President Lyndon Johnson was quickly able to obtain a tax cut from Congress, totaling $14 billion for individuals and corporations. The cut worked just as the Keynesians had said it would. Economic growth spurted, the gross national product increased, unemployment dipped, and federal revenues rose. In 1965, unemployment hit a post-Depression low of 4 percent.

At that point, however, Johnson faced the opposite problem. As the economy began to overheat, his economic advisers warned him that either a tax increase or government spending cuts would be necessary. Johnson refused to sanction reductions in spending on either the Vietnam War (then already in progress) or his Great Society programs, and he sought to avoid a debate on a tax increase altogether. The results came in rather quickly. Within another year, wage and price increases spiraled upward in tandem, and inflation rose. Johnson finally asked for a tax increase in 1967, but Congress did not pass it until a year later. By then, inflationary pressures had become strongly established.

### Nixon and monetary policy

When Richard Nixon became president in 1969, inflation had become a major concern. Nixon and many of his advisers were influenced by the monetarist ideas of economist Milton Friedman, who counseled that inflation could be controlled through restrictions on the growth of the money supply. This theory suited the Nixon people, who did not want to seek a tax increase, especially after Johnson's increase had proved ineffective.

The monetarist solution seemed to work at first. By 1970, inflation had dropped from 6 percent to 4.5 percent. Unfortunately, a recession ensued, and unemployment rose from 3.5 percent to 6 percent. Nixon's advisers thereupon tried to persuade Fed chairman Arthur Burns to increase the money supply more rapidly. When Burns resisted this move, the presidential advisers were faced with an impossible

situation, given their aversion to Keynesian efforts to stimulate employment or growth. After a period of battling between the administration and Burns, Nixon unilaterally froze wages and prices in August 1971. No business could increase what it paid its employees or what it charged for its products. This step stunned the "free enterprise" economists who had been advising the president. The controls did not work very well, however, and they were later dismantled.

Later, the Gerald Ford and Jimmy Carter administrations attempted to get voluntary cooperation from business and labor in order to keep inflation within reasonable bounds, but these efforts, too, were largely unsuccessful. Of course, this failure was not entirely the fault of the government, since the economy received many unexpected jolts in the mid-1970s—most notably, the huge increase in oil prices between 1973 and 1978.

## Reagan and supply-side economics

Ronald Reagan's first major order of business as president was to propose an economic package to Congress and the country. In January 1981, he stated in his inaugural address that he did not intend to preside over the continued deterioration of the U.S. economy, and he proposed what to many people seemed a radical departure from recent government policies.

The Reagan economic package included two major elements and three secondary ones. The principal measures proposed included a series of cuts in the federal budget, totaling $41.5 billion in fiscal year 1982 and increasing thereafter; and tax reductions for businesses and individuals, to start as of July 1, 1981. The secondary features of the Reagan plan were (1) the weeding out of federal regulations and rules that allegedly raised business costs and limited competition, (2) the maintenance of slow growth in the national money supply, and (3) consolidation of federal money going to state and local governments into a series of block grants to the states. Only defense expenditures were to be exempted from budget cuts—something Reagan had pledged in his campaign. The defense budget over the period 1982–87, including increases, was projected at $1.3 trillion.

The Reagan tax package was designed to lower individual tax rates and allow businesses to assume larger deductions for capital equipment. Instead of ranging from 14 percent to 70 percent, tax rates were to drop to 10–50 percent. Overall, taxes were to fall 27 percent, on average, by 1984.

The philosophy behind the Reagan experiment rested on three key ideas. The tax and budget cuts

(*Right*) David Stockman, director of OMB (1981–85) and one of the masterminds of Reaganomics, testifies in 1984. Not everyone was happy with the consequences of Reaganomics. (*Left*) Bob Jones, an unemployed steelworker from Pennsylvania, indicates his response.

449

were based on **supply-side economics,** according to which supply, or production, is the crucial element in economic recovery.[10] Supply-side economists have argued that cuts in taxes will lead more people to invest more money, and thereby will stimulate vital new productive enterprise. Government taxation, according to the supply-siders, discourages investment and removes incentives to better one's financial state. This, in turn, leads to a fall in government revenue, since there would be less income to tax. The supply-side solution to this problem is to slash taxes, thereby increasing incentives and productivity—and, in the end, increasing government revenues, since there would be *more* income to tax. Supply-side theorists have also called for the removal of various government regulations, such as environmental requirements, that tend to raise costs of doing business and, allegedly, lower the amount of money available for investment and growth. The Reagan package of tax cuts, budget cuts, and regulation cuts, accordingly, represented a supply-side attempt to stimulate the new economic prosperity. In their emphasis on the role of the private sector, particularly the role of wealthy investors and corporations in stimulating economic recovery, the supply-siders were almost the opposite of the Keynesians, whose theories had helped pull this and other nations out of the Depression. Keynesians had emphasized the central role of government in stimulating demand and creating jobs by putting money in the hands of ordinary citizens through deficit spending, government investment, and public works projects.

A second key component of the Reagan program was the traditional conservative aversion to big government, especially the federal government. Conservatives had campaigned for decades against burgeoning federal power, and Reagan had maintained during the 1980 campaign that there was vast waste, mismanagement, and fraud in the federal budget.

Finally, the Reagan team argued that the federal government had become involved in many activities that were better left to individuals or to state and local governments. The use of block grants, which gave states greater flexibility in the use of federal funds, was designed to deal with that issue.

FIGURE 19.1
The U.S. Economic Experience, 1964–83: U.S. Industrial Production Index (1967 = 100)

Source: The New York Times, January 8, 1984.

Could such a new direction in national policy survive attack by those who might be hurt in the process of change? The basic approach taken by the administration was to stress that everyone would suffer—all programs would be subjected to careful consideration with an eye toward budget trimming. Powerful interest groups, accustomed to receiving large subsidies, would simply have to reconcile themselves to doing with less. The Reagan team also stressed the urgency and importance of taking action on the package. Congress must act, they claimed, because the health of the whole economy was at stake. Reagan gave assurances that a "safety net" of social programs would be maintained for truly needy individuals.

Did supply-side economics work? Were the Reagan programs successful? The answers to these questions are highly controversial. In his successful campaign for reelection in 1984, President Reagan asserted that his economic measures had been successful. He frequently cited the drastic lowering of the inflation rate and the modest increase in economic growth. He also argued that in terms of equity, his programs had helped everyone—not just the rich, as his critics claimed.

Those critics, however, found supply-side economics sadly lacking. For one thing, the tax cuts did not bring about the boom in economic growth and consequent increase in tax revenues that supply-siders had predicted. After four years in office, the administration found itself with the biggest budget deficit in national history, thanks largely to the tax cuts. On this matter supply-side economics had *not* delivered, though some argued that it was still too soon to reach a verdict.

Why had inflation slowed, then, and why had there been a modest economic recovery? Inflation declined, some argued, because of the very high in-

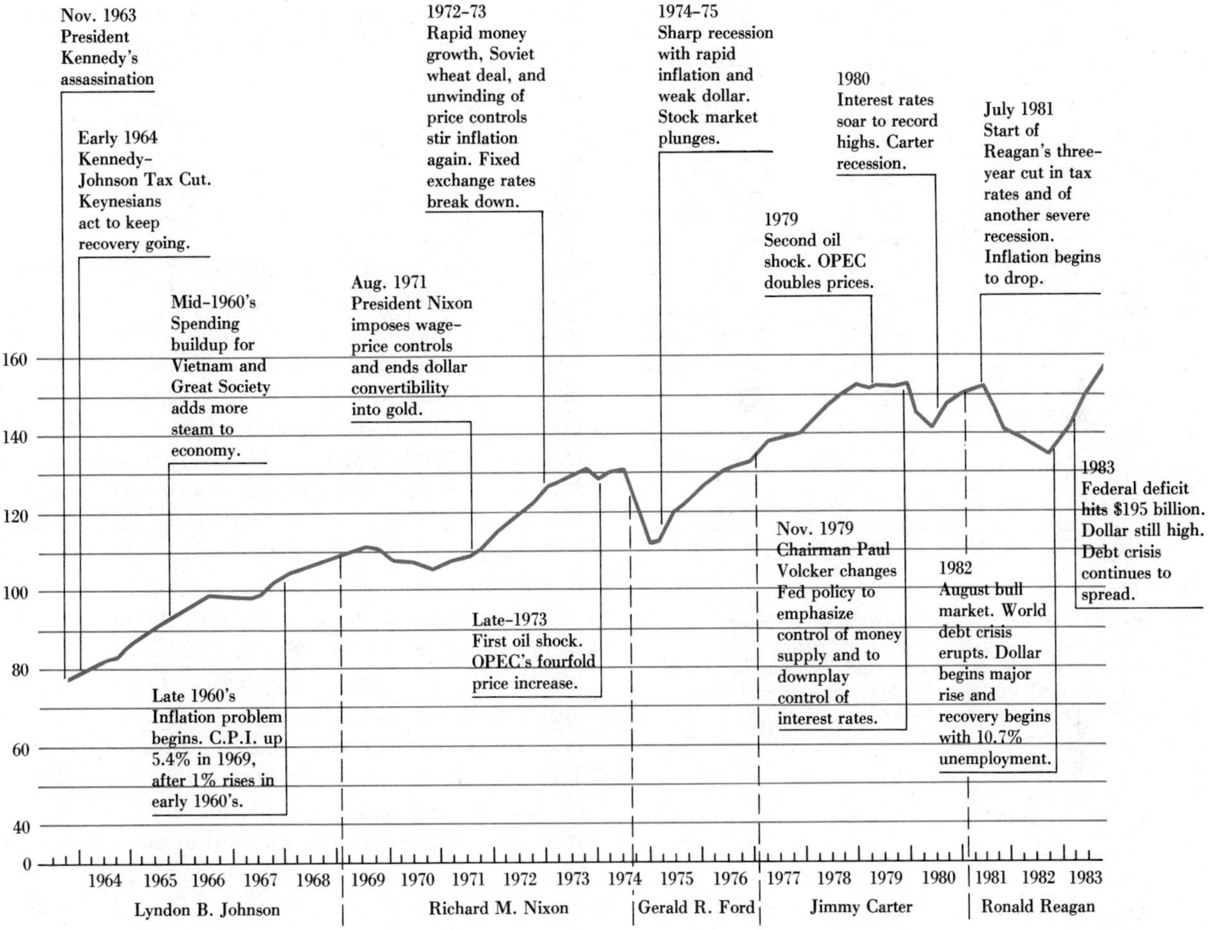
Nov. 1963
President Kennedy's assassination
Early 1964
Kennedy-Johnson Tax Cut. Keynesians act to keep recovery going.
Mid-1960's
Spending buildup for Vietnam and Great Society adds more steam to economy.
Late 1960's
Inflation problem begins. C.P.I. up 5.4% in 1969, after 1% rises in early 1960's.
Aug. 1971
President Nixon imposes wage-price controls and ends dollar convertibility into gold.
1972–73
Rapid money growth, Soviet wheat deal, and unwinding of price controls stir inflation again. Fixed exchange rates break down.
Late-1973
First oil shock. OPEC's fourfold price increase.
1974–75
Sharp recession with rapid inflation and weak dollar. Stock market plunges.
1979
Second oil shock. OPEC doubles prices.
Nov. 1979
Chairman Paul Volcker changes Fed policy to emphasize control of money supply and to downplay control of interest rates.
1980
Interest rates soar to record highs. Carter recession.
July 1981
Start of Reagan's three-year cut in tax rates and of another severe recession. Inflation begins to drop.
1982
August bull market. World debt crisis erupts. Dollar begins major rise and recovery begins with 10.7% unemployment.
1983
Federal deficit hits $195 billion. Dollar still high. Debt crisis continues to spread.
160
140
120
100
80
60
40
0
1964 1965 1966 1967 1968 1969 1970 1971 1972 1973 1974 1975 1976 1977 1978 1979 1980 1981 1982 1983
Lyndon B. Johnson
Richard M. Nixon
Gerald R. Ford
Jimmy Carter
Ronald Reagan

terest rates established by the Fed, not because of the administration program. The modest recovery, ironically, may have been due to the vast budget deficits the federal government was running—a kind of Keynesianism, stimulating demand through government spending in military areas. Finally, the Reagan administration had not had to face the economic shocks, such as the rapid rise in energy prices, that had characterized the 1970s.

Although the administration claimed its programs had not hurt the poor, the evidence seemed to say otherwise (see Figure 19.1). A 1984 study by the Congressional Budget Office found that the average family with an income under $10,000 had lost $390 as a result of the administration's combination of tax cuts and spending cuts, whereas the average family with an income over $80,000 had gained $8,270. By 1982, the percentage of Americans living in pov-

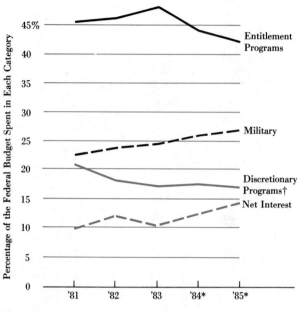

*Estimates

†Includes grants to state and local governments, including
education and highways; foreign aid; cost of Federal
government operation; energy; research and development;
services to individuals, including housing assistance, student
financial aid and veterans' medical care.

FIGURE 19.2

Government Spending in
the Reagan Years: The
figure gives some indication
of the successes and failures
of the Reagan effort to
redirect federal government
activity. Discretionary and
entitlement spending de-
clined as a percentage of the
total budget and military
spending increased, as the
administration wished. The
increase in interest pay-
ments, however, was defi-

nitely not supposed to be
part of the picture. Moreover, total federal spending
did not decline in the Reagan
years as a percentage of the
Gross National Product,
as the administration had
argued it would. Source:
*New York Times*, Oct. 23,
1984, p. 18.

erty (as officially defined) was higher than at any time
since 1967. In addition, even after the "recovery,"
unemployment remained over 7 percent.

## Interactions of politics and economics

We can draw no single conclusion from these three
cases, which reflect only broad patterns in the interaction of politics and economics. In some circumstances, economic strategies work and we think we
understand why they do. In other cases, they work
but we cannot be sure exactly why. A good deal of
luck is involved. What would have happened if the
Vietnam War had, in fact, lasted only a few months?
What would have developed if the Reagan administration had had to face another major price increase
by the oil-producing nations?

The cases we have examined do show us that economic strategies are chosen, in part, because of the
ideological implications they carry. Those who oppose extensive government involvement in the economy, for example, are less likely to be Keynesians.
The cases also demonstrate that strictly political considerations often play an important role in economic
strategies. Tax increases are hard to implement and
rarely popular; cutting popular government programs, too, is hard to accomplish, although at times,
increasing them may be even more difficult.

## Emerging problems in the U.S. political economy

Not long ago, the United States was regarded as far
and away the most powerful, productive, and successful world economy. Like all the industrial nations, however, the United States has experienced
many economic setbacks in the last decade and a
half. In this section, we will look at a set of problems
connected to our political economy. Rather than
strictly economic problems, in the narrow sense of

that term, these problems encompass a variety of issues.

## Tax equity and tax expenditures

One of the central issues usually raised about any tax system is how equitably the tax burden is allocated. One common notion of what is equitable is that those who are better able to pay should be taxed more than those less able to pay. In that way, the tax burden will not fall too heavily on the poorer sectors of the community.

In the United States, however, the less well-off pay a considerable portion of their income in taxes. One reason for this anomaly is that, as we have already mentioned, many regressive taxes are an important part of the U.S. tax system. In addition, the federal income tax structure is not as progressive in practice as it appears on paper (see Table 19.2), principally because the federal tax code is riddled with special provisions, or loopholes. A more dignified name for these loopholes is tax expenditures.

TABLE 19.2
**Effective rates of federal and of state and local taxes by population decile, 1980**

| Population (from poorest to wealthiest) | Federal tax | State and local taxes | Total taxes |
|---|---|---|---|
| First 10% (poorest) | 11.7 | 9.0 | 20.6 |
| Second | 12.8 | 7.6 | 20.4 |
| Third | 13.6 | 7.1 | 20.6 |
| Fourth | 14.8 | 7.0 | 21.9 |
| Fifth | 15.9 | 6.9 | 22.8 |
| Sixth | 16.3 | 7.0 | 23.3 |
| Seventh | 16.6 | 7.0 | 23.6 |
| Eighth | 17.8 | 7.2 | 25.0 |
| Ninth | 18.4 | 7.3 | 25.7 |
| Tenth 10% (richest) | 19.4 | 7.9 | 27.3 |
| Top 5 percent | 19.4 | 8.1 | 27.5 |
| Top 1 percent | 18.9 | 8.6 | 27.5 |

Source: 1980 Brookings MERGE file. Figures are rounded.

The term *expenditure* is used because, in effect, the government makes grants of money to various taxpayers through the tax code, rather than through the federal budget. In this sense, the various loopholes in the tax code actually constitute a hidden form of government spending.

One rather large loophole stems from the differing rates at which different sorts of income are taxed. If you earn $18,000 in wages, you will pay about 25 percent in federal taxes, but if you make $18,000 on investments in the stock market you will pay only about 12.5 percent in taxes. If you are fortunate enough to make $18,000 from tax-exempt bonds, the government won't tax you at all. A similar situation obtains for corporations: some pay up to 40 percent in corporate taxes, whereas others pay little or nothing. There are special tax breaks for particular industries, such as oil, timber, and mining. Corporations can also take advantage of complicated provisions for delaying tax payments, calculating depreciation of property, and assigning losses. Overall, many major U.S. corporations with what appear to be very large profits are able to avoid paying any federal taxes at all.[11]

Among the most controversial loopholes is the special tax rate on capital gains, the income earned through the buying and selling of stock. Why do capital gains have such a privileged position? According to defenders of this loophole, the lower tax rate on capital gains encourages investment, which benefits everyone by stimulating economic growth. In response, critics have argued that the lower tax rate is an extraordinary boondoggle for the wealthy and that its general benefits are, at the very least, debatable. Among other loopholes are those covering mortgage interest, charitable contributions, and money invested in real estate, farming, oil and gas drilling, equipment leasing, motion pictures, and sports franchises.

Some observers have called the system of tax expenditures a form of disguised welfare for the wealthy. There is a clear relationship between the size of one's income and the amount by which one benefits from special tax breaks. In general, wealthier citizens benefit far more than poorer ones. Of the total revenue lost to the government through tax expenditures, 53 percent goes to the weathiest 15 percent of taxpayers. This fact has several implications. First, as we mentioned, the actual tax system is far less progressive than it seems to be in theory. Second, the special tax status of certain forms of income means that income tax collections are significantly reduced—by an estimated $140 billion annually in recent years. Finally, tax breaks represent a relatively hidden dimension of public policy-making. Welfare payments to the poor are well known, highly publicized, and frequently investigated. But benefits conferred on the wealthy through the tax system are usually less scrutinized. For example, a person in a high tax bracket who buys an expensive house and makes a substantial mortgage interest payment each month receives a proportionately larger benefit in tax relief than that received by a person who has a lower income and buys a cheaper house. If large checks from the government went out each month to wealthy homeowners, people might begin to ask whether this was the way they wanted public policy to be made.

## Federal budget deficits

Despite its public commitment to a balanced budget and the president's often-proclaimed desire for a bal-

anced budget amendment to the U.S. Constitution, the Reagan administration quickly created the largest federal deficits in U.S. history. This was an irony savored by Democrats who had long been accused of reckless spending. Some joked that Ronald Reagan had turned out to be the biggest spender of them all, but in fact the massive Reagan tax cuts were the real basis of the giant deficits, plus the fact that supply-side economic strategies simply had not delivered the goods in terms of expected revenues. During the first months of the administration in 1981, the Office of Management and Budget had predicted a balanced budget by 1984 despite tax reductions. These predictions turned out to be drastically inaccurate.

How serious a problem is the growing deficit? Some argued, including many balanced-budget conservatives within the administration, that the deficits were not all that important. They stated that the general health of the national economy would sooner or later allow the budget to be balanced. The president himself continued to push for a balanced budget amendment, but only to be applied at some later date. But many saw dangers in the deficit. For one, there were strong prospects that government debts might grow even larger. David Stockman, a central figure in the early days of Reaganomics and the director of OMB until he left in 1985, put the issue this way: "The basic fact is that we are violating badly, even wantonly, the cardinal rule of sound public finance: Governments must extract from the people in taxes what

---

## The U.S. tax system: how progressive?

A recent study of the U.S. tax system (including federal, state, and local taxes) found it to be, at best, only mildly progressive. As Table 19.2 demonstrates, the wealthiest taxpayers (those in the top 10 percent of income earners) paid at an effective tax rate (that is, the *real*, as opposed to the *supposed*, rate) of 27.3 percent in 1980, whereas the poorest taxpayers (those in the lowest 10 percent of income earners) paid 20.6 percent. These figures are based on the most progressive assumptions about tax payments and their relation to income.

Our tax system grew less progressive in impact between 1966 and 1985 because of a decline in the importance of the corporate income tax and of property taxes at the local level, and because of increases in payroll taxes, such as Social Security. The federal tax cuts of 1981–83 also contributed to this pattern.

Source: Joseph A. Peckman, *Who Paid the Taxes, 1966–85?* (Washington, D.C.: Brookings Institution, 1985), pp. 60–61.

TABLE 19.3
## Major tax expenditures, fiscal years 1976 and 1983

|  | Cost (in billions of dollars) | |
|---|---|---|
|  | 1976 | 1983 |
| Deductibility of state and local taxes | $10.0 | $20.1 |
| Home mortgage interest | 6.5 | 25.1 |
| Property taxes | 5.3 | 8.8 |
| Charity | 5.4 | 7.9 |
| Consumer credit | 3.7 | 10.8 |
| Medical expenses | 2.6 | 3.1 |
| Depletion allowances for oil, gas, and minerals | 1.8 | 2.8 |
| Capital gains | 8.7 | 21.3 |
| Income-security transfer payments (such as social security, railroad retirements) | 8.7 | 27.4 |
| Investment tax credit | 8.8 | 28.8 |
| State and local bond interest | 4.8 | 13.7 |
| Pensions, contributions, and earnings | 6.5 | 53.4 |

Sources: 1976 figures, Brandon, et al., pp. 54–74; 1983 figures, *1984 Statistical Abstract of the United States*, Table 509, p. 321.

they dispense in benefits, services and protections. . . ."[12] Others saw rising interest rates and economic recession as an inevitable result, as interest payments on the debt rose from $53 billion in 1980 to an estimated $234 billion in 1990. There were predictions that by that time the United States would have to borrow money from foreign sources in order to pay interest on the debt owed to foreign sources. It was a depressing prospect.

Finally, some argued that the Reagan administration was using the deficit situation to turn back the clock and eliminate or diminish social programs developed since the 1930s. Because of the huge deficit,

the administration argued that social programs would have to be cut back, while it continued to champion a rising military budget. The national debt became a club with which to beat social welfare spenders. Liberals were placed in the awkward position of having to defend balanced budgets and increases in taxation as ways out of the debt problem.

## The decline in industrial power

As far back as the early 1960s, some observant critics of the American economy noted that there were problem areas in the generally rosy picture of U.S. economic achievements. Unemployment seemed always to be higher here than in many European nations. In addition, portions of U.S. industry were not being modernized. Finally, chronic areas of poverty and deprivation remained in the nation, and much of the economic infrastructure (roads, water systems, bridges, etc.) was deteriorating.

Not until the 1970s, however, did the full impact of the nation's industrial decline became clearer. At that point the United States ceased to be the world's leader in many industrial areas. Even in our own nation, there was widespread disillusion with the quality of American products. "Made in America" ceased to carry the connotation of excellence. Japanese and European cars, TVs, and electrical and electronic appliances took over a major portion of the U.S. market. Some major industries were hard hit: automakers fell on hard times, and the steel industry seemed to move into permanent decline. There were predictions of worse to come. The industrial heartland of the nation, stretching from Chicago to Boston, became an economically depressed area.

The reasons for this decline were complex. American industries had failed to innovate and invest. Capital investments had gone to countries where labor was cheaper and profits higher. The United States also was undergoing changes in the mix of employment, as more and more of the population moved into service jobs and away from jobs in production

# Reforming the tax system?

Ronald Reagan began his second term as he had his first—with a focus on changes in the American tax system. Where the emphasis of the first term had been on tax cuts (most of which were targeted for wealthier taxpayers), the second-term program emphasized tax *reform*. In May 1985 the president launched his tax reform package in a speech in which he called the tax code "complicated, un-fair, cluttered with gob-bledy-gook and loopholes designed for those with the power and influence to hire high-priced legal and tax advisers." The American people, on the whole, agreed. A 1985 survey showed 75 percent believed that the tax system was unfair to the ordinary person; 52 percent said that corporations were undertaxed; and 92 percent agreed that the rich used lawyers and accountants to escape taxation.

The White House reform proposal featured the following major elements:

Simplifying the tax brackets: the present 15 brackets would be reduced to three with tax rates of 15 percent (to $30,000), 25 percent (from $30,000 to $70,000), and 35 percent (above $70,000)

Doubling the personal exemption to $2,000

Dropping the maximum tax on corporations to 33 percent from the current 46 percent

Enacting a minimum tax rate of 20 percent on wealthy individuals and profitable corporations who now often escape paying any taxes at all

Dropping deductions for state and local taxes

Repealing the special write-offs allowed for depreciation of equipment by businesses

Reagan claimed that these reforms would reduce taxes on working people, close loopholes, and provide a simplified tax code. The Treasury Department estimated that 58 percent would pay lower taxes after reform, 21 percent higher taxes, and 21 percent would come out even. The biggest gainers from the plan would be those who made under $20,000 and over $200,000 a year. Middle-class tax-payers would get the smallest tax breaks and were most likely to pay more taxes. The plan was supposed to be "revenue neutral," meaning that it would raise neither more nor less taxes than the present system.

Though the plan met with some initial enthusiasm, there were many doubters. Various interest groups, for example, complained about specific aspects of the proposal, among them real estate interests, banks and life insurance companies, and state and local governments, all of whom

industries. Government policies that had protected particular industries (such as steel) against foreign competition had reduced incentives to innovate and compete internationally.

What could be done to revive U.S. industry and stimulate full employment? Most conservatives, including President Reagan and his advisers, argued that "market forces" would do the job. Government, they asserted, should do what it could to create spirited economic competition, which would, in turn, spark a general economic recovery. More liberal commentators assailed this approach and recommended a mix of market stimulation and closer co-operation among government, business, and labor—somewhat on the model of various European nations (see box). Such cooperation would involve sacrifices from all groups in the effort to rebuild the nation's competitive position in the world. Still other critics took the position that nothing short of a far more active government would solve our economic malaise. High on the priority list, they maintained, should be a good deal of planned social investment. The only way the United States could regain its economic edge and also supply full employment would be to rebuild its own decaying society and to target investment funds for areas needing economic recovery.

would be losers under the reform plan. In addition, there were doubts that the program really would turn out to be revenue neutral. Some predicted a further reduction in tax collections in the future, making the deficit even worse. Other critics claimed that the president had caved in to certain powerful interests between the announcement of the Treasury's plan in November and the White House proposals of May. The Treasury plan would have closed many more loopholes, including exclusions for capital gains (a main source of income for the very rich) and the depletion allowances for oil and gas. It also offered a far more thorough reform of accelerated depreciation than in the final plan. Altogether, the Treasury proposals would have netted the government an estimated additional $767 billion in revenues over five years. But the White House proposal scaled back this loophole closing in a major way.

Finally, some argued that the president's package was not enough of a reform. The three-bracket tax system looked simple and progressive, but when social security taxes and capital gains deductions were figured in, it did not look so obviously appealing to common sense. One critic of the plan calculated that when the social security tax of 14 percent was figured in, the real rates of taxes being paid were: 29 percent (below $40,000); 25 percent ($40,000–$80,000, because Social Security is no longer paid); 35 percent ($80,000–$200,000, the maximum tax on wages); and 17.5 percent (over $200,000, where most income is from capital gains, since capital gains are only 50 percent taxable under the plan). Was this a fair or thorough reform? Opinions varied on both the plan as a whole, and on specific elements of it.

Sources: Robert S. McIntyre, "Inside the Sellout," *The New Republic*, June 24, 1985, pp. 9–11; "Reagan's Tax Reform," *U.S. News and World Report*, June 10, 1985, pp. 20–32; "Tax Americana," *Public Opinion*, February/March, 1985, pp. 19–29; Robert D. Hershey, Jr., "Battle over Revising Income Tax Law Begins to Take Shape," *New York Times*, Nov. 13, 1984, p. 36; Henry J. Aaron and Harvey Galper, *Assessing Tax Reform* (Washington, D.C.: Brookings Institution, 1985).

Whichever strategy, or mix of strategies, eventually is chosen, it seems clear that in the immediate future, many sectors of U.S. society will continue to suffer from the problems of overall economic decline.

## Conclusions

According to many students of politics, successful management of the economy can mean more to a president than almost any other aspect of his administration. He may stand or fall on whether unemployment has been lowered to a reasonable level, inflation has been controlled, or public confidence in the economy has been restored. Of course, administrations are not moved by political considerations alone to pay careful attention to economic management. They are also very much influenced by ideological factors—that is, by beliefs about how an economy should be run. Ideological factors play a central role in shaping the actions that governments take or fail to take. President Herbert Hoover believed strongly enough in not interfering with the "free market" that he did not take actions that might at least have softened the worst of the Great Depression. President Ronald Reagan was sufficiently committed to the free market to push deregulation and tax reductions as top-priority items in 1981.

What should be clear is that today, economic management is invariably the centerpiece of the agenda of *any* national government we elect. This is true not only in the United States, but also in all industrial-

# Comparative perspective Industrial policy

Governments employ various forms of *direct* intervention in the economy in order to achieve the goals of growth, employment, or economic stability. In many Western European industrial

democracies, as well as in Japan, interventionist policies have become highly developed.* Forms of direct intervention include government ownership of portions of the economy; close collaboration between business and government, including fairly detailed planning of economic goals; and cooperation between government and labor to avoid strikes. These instruments of industrial policy are more highly developed in some nations than in others. France, for example, has emphasized close collaboration be-

ized nations, and probably in every other nation as well. Managing economies has become, in one form or another, a key function of government. Even governments that profess to believe that the best way to run the economy is to do *less* managing continue to perform many functions that have come to be regarded as essential: regulation of interest rates and the supply of money, the setting of rates of taxation, the formulation of spending policies, maintenance of the extensive network of regulation that affects virtually every form of economic activity, and so on.

In short, economic life has become highly politicized. Many of the battles fought in Congress, between Congress and the executive branch, and in

One of the thorniest issues any government faces is the problem of protecting or not protecting its domestic industries from foreign competition. Many U.S. industries, including tex-

tiles, shoes, steel, and autos, have been badly hit. In this photo, a garment worker in New York makes his position clear on the question of quotas.

tween business and government, with extensive use of government loans and credit arrangements to help industry achieve agreed-upon goals. Both France and Great Britain have nationalized certain major industries. Both the British and the Swedes are notable for clear, long-term relationships between labor and major political parties. In West Germany, the banking system plays an important collaborative role. In all of these cases, there has been a focused, long-term effort to link overall economic goals to specific policies aiding particular industries, though such efforts are not always successful.

It is widely agreed that a clear industrial policy is lacking in the United States. Except in time of war, the U.S. government has not sought to develop the tools for detailed intervention in particular industries and aspects of the economy. There have been occasional interventions—the government bailout of the failing Lockheed Corporation during the Nixon administration, the guaranteeing of loans to the near-bankrupt Chrysler Corporation during the Ford and Carter administrations. These instances, like many others that could be cited, were not part of an overall plan, however. Rather, they were simply cases in which particular interest groups were able to plead successfully to have their demands met.

Although some people think that this is as it should be, others believe that the U.S. economy needs precisely the forms of direct intervention that a coherent industrial policy would supply. Only such a policy, it has been argued, will provide the help needed by many ailing American industries and by those areas of the nation afflicted by chronically high unemployment.

*See A. J. Heidenheimer, Hugh Heclo, and C. T. Adams, *Comparative Public Policy*, 2nd ed. (New York: St. Martin's, 1983), pp. 141–48.

---

many of our election campaigns, now revolve around how the economy should be managed, and in whose interest it should be run. How far should government go in reshaping the workings of the marketplace? For example, should government help failing businesses to survive—and if so, which ones? Is it legitimate to assist an ailing Chrysler Corporation with special loan arrangements, but not to assist farmers about to lose their land?

Another question is, How much, if anything, should government do to reshape the distribution of income through our tax system? As we have seen, the current tax system is not particularly progressive in impact. Should it be made more so—not just in theory, but in practice? This would mean closing many tax loopholes. Recent proposals for a simplified tax code with lower maximum rates propose doing exactly this, but those who benefit from the current system typically mount powerful attacks against change. In fact, the current state of the U.S. tax system testifies to the potency of interest groups in lobbying government. Overall, there is good reason to question the fairness of the U.S. system of taxation, as well as its efficiency in raising revenue. From the perspective of democratic theory, a fair method of taxation would seem essential, since this is the way we go about paying for the government we have.

A final point, from the perspective of democratic theory, concerns economic planning. Our government does not do very much overall economic planning. Many of us associate the very term *economic planning* with communist governments that own and run the entire economy. Various sectors of the economy do benefit from planning, however. The government provides farmers with certain price supports, for example, and plans new weapons system more than a decade in advance. But we are reluctant, as a society, to engage in the kind of long-term economic planning that might enable us to cope with the most severe problems of dislocation, waste, and deprivation we face. The United States has lived with a considerable level of unemployment for decades. We have also seen central cities deteriorate and whole regions of the nation suffer prolonged economic cri-

Chrysler President Lee Iacocca speaking in 1983. Iacocca's reign at Chrysler brought considerable success to that corporation, but the company would have gone under years earlier had it not been for special credits extended by the federal government.

sis. Our distrust of government and our reverence for private property and the workings of the market have made it difficult for us at times to engage in a national effort that could remedy these difficulties.

## NOTES

1 This term was first used by British writer Thomas Carlyle (1795–1881) to describe his attitude toward economics.

2 Seymour Martin Lipset, *Political Man* (Garden City, N.Y.: Doubleday, 1960), Chapter 2.

3 W. A. Williams, *The Contours of American History* Cleveland: World, 1961); and Louis Hartz, *Economic Policy and Democratic Thought* (Cambridge, Mass.: Harvard University Press, 1948).

4 Richard Hofstadter, *The American Political Tradition* (New York: Knopf, 1948).

5 Clair Wilcox, *Public Policies Toward Business* (Irwin, Ill.: Homewood, 1971).

6 Robert S. McElvaine, *The Great Depression* (New York: Times Books, 1984), Chapters 2 and 4.

7 A. J. Heidenheimer, Hugh Heclo, and C. T. Adams, *Comparative Public Policy*, 2nd ed. (New York: St. Martin's, 1983), Chapter 5.

8 Lawrence G. Brewster, *The Public Agenda* (New York: St. Martin's, 1984), pp. 26–27.

9 Much information for these cases was derived from Lawrence Brewster, *op. cit.*, Chapter 1.

10 For two views on supply-side economics, see Frank Ackerman, *Reaganomics: Rhetoric vs. Reality* (Boston: South End Press, 1982); and Paul C. Roberts, *The Supply-Side Revolution* (Cambridge, Mass.: Harvard University Press, 1984).

11 Joseph A. Peckman, *Federal Tax Policy* (Washington, D.C.: Brookings Institution, 1983), Chapter 5.

12 Quoted in Daniel Patrick Moynihan, "Reagan's Inflate-the-Deficit Game," *New York Times*, July 21, 1985, p. E21.

## SELECTED READINGS

For basic background on modern economics and its applications, see Paul Samuelson and William Nordhaus, *Economics* (New York: McGraw-Hill, 1985); Andrew Shonfield, *Modern Capitalism* (New York: Oxford University Press, 1965); Otto Eckstein, *Public Finance* (Englewood Cliffs, N.J.: Prentice-Hall, 1964); Robert Heilbroner, *Between Capitalism and Socialism* (New York: Vintage, 1970); J. K. Galbraith, *The New Industrial State* (Boston: Houghton-Mifflin, 1967); and J. K. Galbraith and N. Salinger, *Almost Everyone's Guide to Economics* (Boston: Houghton-Mifflin, 1978).

On specific issues discussed in this chapter, see Herman Miller, *Rich Man, Poor Man* (New York: Crowell, 1971); Joseph A. Pechman, ed., *Setting National Priorities—The 1984 Budget* (Washington, D.C.: Brookings Institution, 1983); Joseph A. Pechman, *Federal Tax Policy*, 4th ed. (Washington, D.C.: Brookings Institution, 1983); Irving

Kristol, *Two Cheers for Capitalism* (New York: Basic Books, 1978); Edward R. Tufte, *Political Control of the Economy* (Princeton, N.J.: Princeton University Press, 1978); Alan Wolfe, *America's Impasse: The Rise and Fall of the Politics of Growth* (New York: Pantheon, 1981); and George Gilder, *Wealth and Poverty* (New York: Basic Books, 1981).

For intriguing studies of the interaction between politics and economics, see John F. Manley, *The Politics of Finance: The House Committee on Ways and Means* (Boston: Little, Brown, 1970); Thomas J. Reese, *The Politics of Taxation* (New York: Quorum Books, 1980); Mervyn A. King, *Public Policy and the Corporation* (London: Chapman & Hall, 1977); M. King and D. Fullerton, eds., *The Taxation of Income from Capital: A Comparative Study of the U.S., U.K., Sweden and West Germany* (Chicago: University of Chicago Press, 1984); and J. Richard Aronson, *Financing State and Local Governments*, 3rd ed. (Washington, D.C.: Brookings Institution, 1977).

# The welfare state

# Safety net or sieve?

To many people, the term **welfare state** conjures up images of unemployment lines, of needy people receiving food stamps, of public housing. Such images are accurate, but they tell only part of the story. It is too often forgotten that many welfare programs apply to all Americans and have little or no relationship to *need*. The welfare state includes provisions for education and veterans' benefits, as well as medical care for the indigent. The single largest welfare state program, Social Security, provides benefits that are virtually universal in scope: that is, they go to those with high incomes as well as to those with incomes under the poverty line. The reason the welfare state is not usually viewed in this more comprehensive fashion is that most of the controversy attending it swirls around those programs targeted at the needy, such as Aid to Families with Dependent Children and food stamps. Most of this chapter treats these more controversial aspects of the welfare state. But it is important to keep in mind that need-related programs are only that—*aspects* of the welfare state. Hence, basic information about all the programs that rightly fit into this category of public policy will also be given here.

The concept of provisions for social welfare is neither new nor, in the main, controversial. Almost all societies make provisions for care of the poor, aged, disabled, and others who need assistance. In Great Britain, welfare provisions date back to the so-called poor laws of the Elizabethan period; in the United States, assistance to the poor was a government function even before the Revolution. The modern welfare state, however, has several distinctive features. Today, government, rather than families or private charities, plays the dominant role in supplying assistance. Moreover, national, rather than local, governments now direct and fund most welfare programs. Finally, modern welfare states, unlike their predecessors, address the issue of redistribution of wealth, in that they seek to lessen the disparities that arise from social and economic systems.

The fundamental intention of the welfare state is to provide a minimum of economic security and a degree of social equality. By the end of World War II, after a century of struggle, most Western societies had arrived at a consensus that individuals should not be allowed to fall below an economic minimum and that opportunities for advancement, principally through the educational system, should be open to all. Beyond this broad agreement, however, lay many areas of controversy, particularly in the United States. To what income level should poor families be supported through public funds—and with what strings attached, if any? How low a level of unemployment can or should society tolerate? How should Social Security be funded? What should be done about high levels of youth unemployment among disadvantaged groups?

Some of the questions connected with the welfare state are practical ones, such as how best to insure that poor children receive adequate nutrition. But some involve values or beliefs—such as whether a society should foster greater equality in incomes. Often these two types of questions are intertwined, as when new welfare reform proposals are debated.

How do democratic ideals pertain to welfare state issues? Democratic commitments lead us to view the welfare state in terms of three basic issues: security, equality, and the problem of paternalism. Do all Americans have the opportunity to live reasonably secure and healthy lives? Do welfare programs foster economic equality among our citizens, especially in helping to raise the living standard of the poorest members of society? Do the methods of administration of welfare programs interfere excessively with individual freedom and democratic rights? In other words, is our government too paternalistic, and does it interfere too much in the way citizens conduct their lives?

It will not be easy to make judgments on these matters. The numerous programs that make up the welfare state are highly diverse in objectives and methods, as well as in breadth of achievement. In order to obtain an accurate view of the welfare state, we must first analyze the most important programs, and then look at the criticisms, evaluations, and suggestions for reform of the welfare state put forward by various schools of thought.

## The U.S. welfare state

Though efforts to provide security and various welfare protections were undertaken prior to the 1930s, the origins of the modern welfare state can be found in New Deal legislation of that decade. New Deal

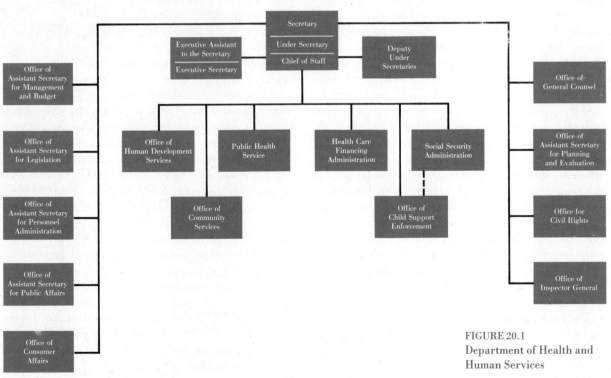

FIGURE 20.1
Department of Health and
Human Services

most estimates, was a considerable help to the American poor, but it fell far
short of abolishing severe
deprivation.

reforms laid the foundation for what might be called
the "positive state"—one in which the government
is an active partner in economic and social life. In
general, the New Deal was conceived as a response
to economic and social problems that had always
existed in the United States, but that were greatly
exacerbated by the Great Depression. With unemployment claiming 25 percent of the work force, millions of people living in destitution, and state and
local governments out of resources, national action
was required. Similar actions occurred in many other
industrialized societies.

Some New Deal programs represented efforts to
undo the economic damage of the Depression and to
prevent such a catastrophe from occurring again. Yet
even without the crisis of the Depression, some social welfare programs would have evolved in this and
other democratic nations. As societies grew more
complex and modernized, political systems inevitably were forced to take over some of the responsibilities that previously had been carried by families,
localities, and private groups. It is notable that despite
the extensive criticisms of welfarism and socialism,
the basic elements of the welfare state—including
Social Security, a degree of national responsibility

for health care, unemployment insurance, and some
forms of aid to the poor—have become permanent
features of all industrialized democratic societies.

The centerpiece of New Deal legislation was the
Social Security Act of 1935, whose main features
were unemployment compensation, aid to dependent
children and grants to states for maternal services,
old age assistance (including the common meaning
of "Social Security"), and aid to states for pensions.
The act failed to provide for uniform national standards
covering welfare provisions to the poor. Nor was any
provision made for national health coverage. In the
view of many observers, these inadequacies plague
us still.

The next significant expansion of the welfare state
occurred in the 1960s, during the administration of
Lyndon Johnson. Under the heading of the "Great
Society," new efforts were initiated to help the poor
and to provide added security for others. In 1965
alone, Congress passed legislation designed to

Provide medical care to the elderly, disabled, and indigent, through Medicare and Medicaid.

Provide aid to public schools and loans to college students.

Supplement rents for poor people.

Establish grants, loans, and training programs for health
professionals.

Provide development assistance to Appalachia (see box).

The Economic Opportunity Act, passed in 1964, was
the main vehicle for Johnson's "war on poverty." It
provided for community action programs, VISTA (a
domestic Peace Corps), legal aid to the poor, and
other services.

The Great Society programs promised a great deal—
an end to poverty, racial and ethnic equality, equal

465

Most of America's poor are white, but a far higher proportion of black Americans live in poverty. Ghetto unemployment is one of the most obvious and intractable problems.

educational opportunities, a vastly improved welfare system, adequate employment, decent housing for all, a greater sharing of the wealth. According to their critics, however, these programs were ineffectual, overly ambitious, and poorly conceived. Critics also have maintained that rather than leading to a better life for most Americans, the Great Society left a heritage of ethnic bitterness and disappointed hopes, and gave rise to an overly bureaucratic federal establishment that continues to dissipate our national resources.

No doubt many of the Great Society programs had effects that no one anticipated—for example, the vast growth in outlays for Medicaid—and poverty was certainly not eradicated. Yet many Great Society programs were quite successful and have become an accepted part of what we now think of as the U.S. welfare state. These well-established programs include, most notably, Medicare, Medicaid, and federal aid to education.

As for the Great Society's antipoverty programs—the fact is that without them, a far higher percentage of the nation's citizens would be poor. Expansion of

the private sector of the economy has not, in and of itself, been able to lift large numbers of people out of poverty. For example, between 1965 and 1972, despite substantial economic growth in the nation, almost one American in five would have been below the poverty line were it not for government welfare programs. The benefits provided by these programs reduced the percentage of poor Americans to about one in ten. One reason why economic expansion alone cannot solve the problems of poverty is that many of the poor are senior citizens or female heads of household; members of both these categories tend to find jobs at very low wages.[1]

Under President Richard Nixon, the number of new programs enacted dropped but spending on social welfare continued to increase, particularly as welfare eligibility requirements were eased and Social Security payments were tied to the rate of inflation. The explosive growth of the food stamp, Medicare, and Medicaid programs caught the government unprepared. These "open-ended" programs, designed to meet food and medical care needs, grew more quickly than anticipated.

These and other problems continue to plague the U.S. welfare state, which in some regards remains an unfinished edifice. The United States is the only Western industrial democracy without a comprehensive national health plan. The system of aid to the needy has been under attack for years, from all sides of the political spectrum; and Social Security, once a pillar of the system, has long been in need of reform. In the meantime, poverty, even destitution, remain serious problems.

Let us now look briefly at the major programs that make up the welfare system. Then we will take a more detailed look at how well some of these programs are working.

# Appalachian development: success or failure?

When John Kennedy traveled to West Virginia in 1960 to campaign in the Democratic Party primary, he was shocked by the desperate poverty he encountered. These conditions of deprivation he encountered were typical of "Appalachia"— a region that stretches from Mississippi to New York State along the spine of the Appalachian Mountains.

In 1965, Congress established the federally funded Appalachian Regional Commission to help change these conditions. Over the next fifteen years, the commission financed $15 billion in economic development and social welfare programs. Road building, which was expected to attract more industry to the area and to help end the isolation of many mountain people, accounted for more than 60 percent of all the Commission's funds. The remainder was devoted to some seven hundred projects in areas such as vocational education, community health, child development, sewer and water systems, and regional industrial parks.

Was the effort a success? By some standards, yes. Infant mortality dropped dramatically, and per capita income increased modestly. The percentage of Appalachians living under the poverty line dropped significantly until it approached the national average. Serious problems remain, however. In some pockets of extreme poverty, infant mortality remains high and per capita income barely reaches 70 percent of the national average. Conservative critics have argued that many of the big highway projects served no useful purpose and that economic development actually resulted from the revival of the coal industry. Radical critics, in contrast, have maintained that antipoverty efforts in Appalachia did not go far enough. Thousands of acres, suitable for new housing, were kept off the market by corporate owners. And coal mining companies continued to hold vast reserves of land that were not included in development efforts—a significant deprivation among a desperately land-poor people.

The Reagan administration attempted to kill the Appalachian Regional Commission in 1981, but succeeded only in cutting its budget in half. Prospects were that all Commission activities would end by 1990, when the road building program was to be phased out.*

*Sandra Sugawara, "Appalachian Sunset," *Washington Post*, national weekly edition, April 22, 1985, pp. 9–10.

## Current "welfare state" programs

It is easy to become confused about the terms of this discussion. In the United States the term *welfare* is commonly associated with severe deprivation, prolonged unemployment, lack of incentive to succeed—even lack of "moral fiber" on the part of the recipient. Many Americans think of welfare as a handout, a public form of charity. Such programs exist (although it is not necessary to think of them as "charity"), but they comprise only one segment of the welfare state. As used here, the term *welfare state* refers to the whole complex of benefits, protections,

forms of insurance, and services that provide security and a measure of equity for most citizens. Under this definition, Social Security is a part of the welfare state, and so is Medicare, even though neither of these programs is targeted at the poor.

There are two basic types of welfare state program: **social insurance programs**, such as Social Security, in which there is a link between past contributions and the benefits to be received; and **public assistance programs**, in which need is the main basis for eligibility. Each of these categories has three subdivisions, based on how benefits are distributed: **cash transfers**, such as cash payments for Social Security or the various types of public assistance to

One phase of the War on Poverty was VISTA (Volunteers in Service of America), a domestic Peace Corps.

Here a college student discusses matters with a friend in North Carolina.

the poor; services, such as education and job training; and **"in-kind" transfers**, such as food stamps or Medicaid, which supply a particular sort of help. (See Table 20.1.)

On the whole, the most controversial of these programs are those in the public assistance category. Over the last twenty years fierce arguments have raged over welfare payments to mothers in the AFDC program, job training, food stamps, Medicaid, and housing. All of these welfare programs have been criticized as inadequate and poorly organized, as well as excessively generous, destructive of motivation, and wasteful. In contrast, the social insurance programs, which are available to almost everyone, are extremely popular. According to a 1985 report by the U.S. Census Bureau, 30 percent of all households receive social insurance benefits for which they are not required to demonstrate financial need, and 19 percent of all households benefit from government programs for which financial need must be shown. In all, 47 percent of all households benefit from one or more government social programs.[2]

## Social insurance

The major social insurance programs are Social Security, unemployment compensation, and Medicare.

**Social Security:** This program, whose formal title is OASDI (Old Age, Survivors, Disability Insurance), is the nation's major cash transfer program. Currently, it pays benefits to more than 30 million persons over age sixty-five. It is financed by payroll taxes that are split equally between employer and employee. In 1981, 90 percent of all nongovernment payrolls were covered by OASDI. (Government em-

468

ployees do not participate in OASDI; instead, they are covered by a generous federal pension plan.)

A prorated share of an employee's wages is collected for Social Security, and the payments to beneficiaries are prorated in terms of their previous incomes. Benefits are adjusted for inflation. About 25 percent of Social Security recipients have incomes below the poverty line, whereas about 30 percent have outside income, such as private pensions or investments, that exceeds their Social Security income. The total cost of the OASDI program in 1984 was $179 billion.

**Federal-state unemployment compensation:** Unemployment compensation is a federal program administered by the Labor Department through various state employment agencies. It is predominantly state-funded through a tax on employers that varies from 0.6 percent to 4.6 percent of wages, depending on the state.

Benefits differ state to state, as do eligibility requirements and the length of time over which benefits can be received. Most states provide basic coverage for twenty-six weeks, and recent federal legislation has extended coverage for an additional

TABLE 20.1
## Distributions of major welfare state programs

|  | Services | Transfer payments | In-kind |
|---|---|---|---|
| 1. Social Insurance | Education | Social Security unemployment insurance | Medicare |
| 2. Public Assistance | Job training | Aid to Families with Dependent Children (AFDC) Supplemental Security Income (SSI) | Food stamps Medicaid Housing subsidies |

13–26 weeks. The average duration of benefits received is sixteen weeks. The system covers workers who have had a history of regular employment and have lost their jobs, but not those who have never held a regular job or who hold jobs not covered by the program, such as domestic work.

In the recession of the mid-1970s, the federal government provided funds to shore up the program and extended the number of weeks of eligibility. In 1977, average weekly benefits were $79; in 1982, $119 (about 37 percent of the average weekly wage). In 1984, 34 percent of the jobless received some form of unemployment compensation. Among those unemployed for six months or more, that figure was 25 percent. A total of $21 billion was paid out in 1984.

**Medicare:** Since its establishment in 1965, Medicare has become one of the mainstays of the U.S. welfare state. Medicare provides payments to all persons eligible for Social Security, to persons classified as disabled, and to almost anyone who suffers from kidney failure. The program has two parts. Part A covers hospital, nursing home, and home health services through a specified period of time; it is available to all eligible persons and is financed through a payroll tax of 2.6 percent, split between employer and employee. Part B, which covers doctors' bills, outpatient hospital services, home health services, and certain other costs, is a voluntary program based on monthly premiums.

Medicare, like private insurance, has limited benefits: that is, recipients must pay a portion of the costs out of their own pockets. Despite these limits, Medicare has come to cover an increasing share of the health care costs of the elderly. There is some concern that rising health care costs will cause serious financial problems for the Medicare system, which enrolled almost 29 million persons in 1984

The unemployed line up at an Illinois center in 1982. The U.S. unemployment insurance system was 50 years old in 1985. In 1983, $31.5 billion was spent on unemployed workers; $5 billion was spent on various programs that provide training and incentives to industry to rehire workers. U.S. benefits, however, usually run out after 26 weeks, and in 1984, only 34 percent of the unemployed were receiving benefits.

and cost a total of $61 billion. Among the various proposals put forward for remedying this anticipated problem are tighter controls on expenditures and cost limits for hospital and other services.

## Public assistance

The five principal public assistance programs are Medicaid, Supplemental Security Income (SSI), Aid to Families with Dependent Children (AFDC), food stamps, and public housing.

**Medicaid:** This state-option program extends medical assistance to the "needy." Each state establishes its own eligibility rules and compensation levels. In twenty-one states, Medicaid coverage is limited to those receiving public assistance benefits. Other states use broader definitions of the "medically indigent." Medicaid has become the largest federal "in-kind" program: more than $38 billion in benefits was paid out in 1984.

**SSI:** In 1974, Congress created the Supplemental Security Income program to provide added assistance to the aged, blind, and disabled. Unlike Social Security, SSI pays benefits on the basis of need and is entirely funded by the federal government. When the program came into existence, the number of people receiving aid nearly doubled. In 1984, SSI cost the government close to $9 billion. Individuals could receive a maximum of $314 a month; couples, $472.

**AFDC:** Aid to Families with Dependent Children is the most controversial welfare state program and the one most people cite when they speak pejoratively of "welfare." AFDC payments go only to families with a dependent child. The benefits differ from state to state. In 1981, monthly payments to a family of two (usually a mother and her dependent child) ranged from $87 in Mississippi to $447 in Alaska. A total of $15 billion in federal and state funds was paid out in 1984. AFDC and SSI are the only two welfare programs that provide cash to recipients, rather than services or in-kind benefits.

**Food stamps:** The food stamp program provides food coupons to all recipients of public assistance, as well as to those whose income falls below certain standards. It is administered jointly by state and federal governments but funded entirely by the federal government. The number of food stamp recipients rose from 2 million people in 1968 to 21 million in 1983, when the cost of the program reached $10 billion. The open-ended nature of the program, plus the fear that many recipients are not truly needy, has led to recent congressional attacks on the program.

**Public housing:** This is a program designed to provide low-cost housing for those too poor to afford adequate living space. Actual construction has lagged far behind demand, and less than 10 percent of eligible households receive help. The program has also been plagued by administrative difficulties, scandal, and the shifting political priorities of succeeding administrations. In the 1970s, the Department of Housing and Urban Development (HUD) experimented with giving out housing grants rather than funding public housing, but this form of housing aid was deemphasized under the Reagan administration. Rent supplements, interest subsidies, and housing

allowances are other avenues tried—with mixed success—by HUD.

**Other programs:** A variety of other federal programs, ordinarily less costly than those listed above, have been set up to aid the poor. WIC (Women, Infants and Children), a nutritional supplement program, served just over 2 million in 1981, at a cost to the federal government of $943 million. Other assistance measures include school breakfast and lunch programs, Head Start (preschool for poor children), various medical programs, and vocational guidance.

| Overall cost
| and extent
| of coverage

The cost of the welfare state has risen very rapidly over the last 20 years, as Figure 20.2 shows. Growth is evident in all major categories. Social Security payments, for example, grew from less than $800 million in 1950 to over $179 billion in 1984. Med-

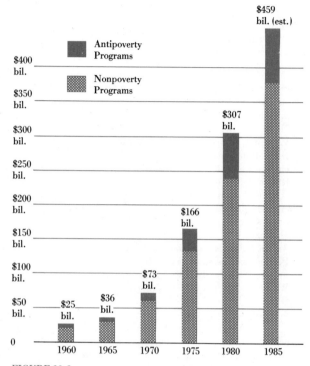

FIGURE 20.2
25 Years of Social Spending.
*Source: U.S. News & World*
*Report*, December 24,
1984, p. 39.

Public housing has sometimes been a modest success; other times, it has been spectacularly flawed. In these photos, we see tenants working at a low-income housing project in Boston, and the wreckage of St. Louis's Pruitt-Igoe complex, which was eventually demolished. Overall, spending on low-income housing falls far short of acknowledged needs.

TABLE 20.2
## A benefits breakdown

|  | Recipients | Percent of population |
|---|---|---|
| Those who received benefits from one or more program | 66,454 | 29.6% |
| Social Security | 31,710 | 14.1 |
| Medicare | 26,711 | 11.9 |
| Veterans' compensation and pensions | 4,622 | 2.1 |
| Education assistance | 3,624 | 1.6 |
| Unemployment compensation | 3,040 | 1.4 |
| Railroad retirement | 759 | 0.3 |
| Workers' compensation | 702 | 0.3 |
| Those who benefited from one or more means-tested program | 42,061 | 18.8 |
| Food stamps | 18,662 | 8.3 |
| Medicaid | 17,508 | 7.8 |
| Aid to Families with Dependent Children | 9,323 | 4.2 |
| Public or subsidized rental housing | 8,465 | 3.8 |
| Federal Supplemental Security Income | 3,205 | 1.4 |
| Women's-Infant-Children Nutrition Program | 2,429 | 1.1 |
| Other cash assistance | 2,311 | 1.0 |

Source: *The New York Times*, September 27, 1984. Almost 30 percent of the U.S. population received benefits from various federal programs in 1983 that, like Social Security, were not means-tested, that is, were not based on the proven need of the recipient but were a matter of general policy. Means-tested programs such as Medicaid and food stamps benefited close to 19 percent of the population. Some people received benefits from more than one program, the most common combination being food stamps and Medicaid.

icare and Medicaid payments make up a substantial part of the total.

A breakdown of welfare benefits received in 1983 is given in Table 20.2. In 1983, almost three out of every ten Americans received benefits of some kind, and nearly one in five benefited from programs for which low income was the major qualifying factor.

## How is the system working?

How well is the federal government handling the U.S. welfare state? A close look at four key programs—Social Security, food stamps, AFDC, and health care—reveals a decidedly mixed picture. The first two programs have been quite successful, but the latter two have been the focus of much controversy.

## Social Security: the specter of insolvency

The Social Security system has long been a stable and noncontroversial part of the U.S. welfare state. Social Security is the nation's largest income security program. For many of the approximately 35 million people who receive monthly Social Security payments, those checks represent the difference between abject poverty and being able to make do. Social Security is the major source of income for two-thirds of our elderly.

In recent years, however, several factors have worked to destabilize the Social Security system. For one thing, the population is gradually getting older. Right now, ten workers pay into the system for every three beneficiaries who draw monthly checks. But as the population ages, this ratio will shrink. By the year 2030, for example, there will be five beneficiaries for every ten workers—a ratio that will put a considerable strain on the system. A second factor is that more people are retiring early and living longer. As the number of years lived in retirement increases, Social Security has to pay out more benefits. Finally, Social Security benefits are currently indexed to inflation: that is, recipients receive automatic cost-of-living increases in each year that inflation moves upward. Although this provision has made it possible for many of the elderly to hold their own under difficult economic circumstances, it has contributed significantly to the increased costs of the system. In 1977, Congress increased the percentage of income withheld from employees' paychecks for Social Security, but the combination of increased unemployment and continuing inflation has held down the hoped-for increase in funds for the system.

How serious is the threat of insolvency? Pessimists have argued that the system is about to go bankrupt—that in the relatively near future, we could be facing enormous Social Security shortfalls. A report compiled by the Social Security Board of Trustees in 1982, however, set forth reassuring prospects for the long run. According to the report, the system may encounter funding shortfalls in the late 1980s, but after 1990 there will likely be no financial problems until 2015, when the "baby boom" generation of the 1950s reaches retirement age. A bipartisan commission appointed to evaluate the system gave a rather encouraging report in 1983 and advocated moderate reforms, including increases in the payroll tax that finances Social Security, a tax on Social Security payments when a recipient's annual income exceeds $20,000 ($25,000 for a couple), a freeze on cost-of-living increases for six months, and the inclusion of newly hired federal workers under the system (instead of under the more costly federal pension scheme).

Overall, the U.S. Social Security system can be judged a success. It has worked relatively well for fifty years, supplying a variety of benefits with a high level of efficiency. And it offers a level of income security that would otherwise be out of the financial reach of most workers. Of course, the pessimists may be right about the system running into serious trouble

down the road. It seems more likely, however, that it will continue functioning quite successfully into the distant future.

The public has remained very supportive of Social Security. Most people are willing to pay higher payroll taxes to keep the system solvent, and most prefer higher taxes now to a reduction in benefits later. Social Security addresses one of the major anxieties people experience in our society—the terrible fear of being destitute, dependent, and helpless in old age.

Still, many people have questioned the equitability of the system, in terms of both how it distributes income to the elderly and how it shifts income across the generations. As the population ages and a smaller number of nonelderly pay the benefits, the burden on the younger generations will grow heavier, and the issue of generational equity will become, in all probability, more significant.

## Food stamps: a program that works

In 1967 a group of American doctors traveled to an area where malnutrition had been reported. Their report stated: "Wherever we went and wherever we looked we saw children in significant numbers who were hungry and sick, children for whom hunger is a daily fact of life, and sickness in many forms an inevitability. The children we saw were more than just malnourished. They were hungry, weak, apathetic. Their lives are being shortened. They are visibly and predictably losing their health, their energy, their spirits."[3] Where was this tragedy taking place? In the rich and powerful United States, where, according to the doctors' report, roughly 10–15 million people suffered from hunger or malnutrition.

The food stamp program that was developed in response to that and other reports has grown from a $288 million effort serving 2.8 million people in 1968 to a $10.5 billion program serving 21 million in 1984. The program was made mandatory in every county in the country in 1975.

The program works rather simply. Each month those who qualify for the program receive food coupons redeemable at groceries and supermarkets. One can qualify on the basis of need, as determined by income plus other assets. For example, no one who owns a car worth more than $4,500 or has more than $1,500 in assets is eligible. The food stamp program is one of the few government programs open to the working poor; in other words, one need not be utterly destitute to qualify.

It is widely agreed that the food stamp program has dramatically reduced hunger and malnutrition in the United States. Because of it, many poor people at least have food to eat. Along with several other nutrition-oriented assistance programs—particularly those providing school breakfasts and lunches—the food stamp program has been one of the bright spots for the poor in recent times.

According to its critics, however, the program has grown too fast and is out of control. Some have argued that benefits should be cut back to the point where only "truly poor" families receive assistance. Others have claimed that fraud is rampant—that affluent students, for example, are able to qualify. The Reagan administration, convinced that many undeserving people were being helped, curtailed food stamp eligibility and cut several hundred thousand people from the program in the early 1980s. A commission created by President Reagan to look into the issue of hunger admitted there was hunger in the nation, but declared that it was not "rampant" or "widespread," as others had maintained. The report agreed with the administration that the states, not the federal government, should be permitted to design their own antihunger programs with federal money. Uniform national standards, it argued, were not needed.

The Physicians' Task Force on Hunger in America, in contrast, reported in 1985 that 20 million Americans were going hungry at least some of the time—a sharp increase from the hunger levels of the late 1970s.[4] This rise in hunger was traced to higher levels of unemployment and cuts in federal programs. Some families went hungry because unemployment benefits had run out and they did not qualify for welfare. This was often the case because in most states two-parent families did not fall under the

usual welfare provisions, which were designed for mothers and children alone. The presence of a husband disqualified needy families. This was a perverse element in welfare policy that some states did not follow. Congress also showed some signs in 1985 of wanting to shift policy so that intact families could qualify for assistance. In other cases, the hungry were children who were no longer receiving diet supplements and formulas through the WIC (Women-Infant-Children) program, which reached only 28 percent of those eligible in 1984.[5] Overall, economics and policy choices have sharply diminished the positive effects of a set of programs that had been working relatively well.

## AFDC: the center of controversy

Over the years, Aid to Families with Dependent Children has been the most controversial of all welfare programs. "AFDC" conjures up images of women having babies solely in order to receive increased welfare benefits, or of able-bodied men spending their girlfriends' welfare money on alcohol while they lounge away the daylight hours. AFDC, critics have argued, destroys the initiative to work and encourages the breakup of marriages so that the mothers may qualify for benefits.

AFDC, one of the older assistance programs, was created in the 1930s. Benefit levels vary widely from one state to another, since the program has never been provided with a genuinely national standard. In many states the benefits do not even bring recipients up to the federal poverty standard, and in quite a few, the level of benefits falls far below the poverty level. The program is administered locally, but most of the funds are federal- and state-supplied.

For many years, AFDC was a noncontroversial program that provided aid mainly to those widows and their families not covered by other programs. In the 1960s, however, the number of recipients more than doubled—from 4 to 10 million—and costs quadrupled, to $4 billion. A key factor in this explosive growth was increased awareness of the welfare system on the part of potential recipients. As various protest movements of the 1960s assured the poor that they had a right to public assistance, welfare became more acceptable to poor families, and less of a social stigma throughout society. Most of the new recipients were black—a circumstance that fueled the political controversy. Other factors contributed to the dramatic increase in AFDC recipients: the Supreme Court outlawed rules that required recipients to be without husbands or any other "man in the house"; state residency requirements were outlawed in 1969; and states raised benefit levels and loosened eligibility requirements, so that by 1970, 81 percent of new applicants were approved, compared with 54 percent in 1953.

Many critics of the entire welfare system have argued that it has helped to create a permanent class of dependent and disadvantaged people, particularly black people. Welfare, in their view, has contributed to the disintegration of the black family and has provided incentives for teenagers to become pregnant and go on welfare for themselves, thereby getting away from their own families. Welfare dependence, it has been maintained, can be passed on from one generation to another. When the government becomes the chief supplier of economic well-being, the role of the husband and father is diminished and his place in the family is undermined.

Do such allegations have a basis in fact? The evidence is mixed. One large-scale study found that the children of families who were brought up on welfare were no more likely to go on welfare themselves than were other people. The charge that welfare programs such as AFDC encourage illegitimate births was also challenged by statistics showing that such births also increased among whites and nonwelfare teenagers. Yet some elements in these criticisms have stuck, if only in popular attitudes about welfare.[6]

Perhaps the most difficult question of all is that of work motivation. Why should a welfare mother, for example, take a low-paying job when she could make almost as much by not working? Yet if welfare payments are lowered to create greater work incentives, children in poor families will be made to suffer. Is that fair, or wise, policy? The federal government requires all welfare recipients with children over age six to register for work. Many states have created "workfare" programs, which require welfare recipients to take low-paying jobs in order to remain eligible for assistance. To their critics, workfare often fails because welfare recipients view it as punitive— even as a form of slavery. In one successful program, developed in Massachusetts, the recipients were allowed to decide for themselves whether to seek a job, get career counseling or training, or participate at all. Many welfare recipients chose to participate. It was calculated that the program would save the state $100 million over five years, even including expenses paid by the state for day-care and job placement services.[7]

The significant growth in AFDC through the 1960s and into the 1970s was a healthy development in many ways. More of those in need found help, and thus the proportion of Americans living in poverty and destitution fell. AFDC benefits have gradually approached the poverty line and, in combination with other assistance programs, such as food stamps, have helped pull many poor families out of poverty (at least as defined by the government).

## Health care programs

Several characteristics of the U.S. health care system are almost universally acknowledged. It is beyond dispute that many Americans receive excellent health care and that American medicine is among the most advanced in the world. It is equally apparent that American health care is among the world's costliest, and that costs have been increasing very rapidly. And most observers agree that many Americans do *not* receive adequate health care, and that the distribution of care is highly related to the capacity to pay. Finally, almost everyone knowledgeable on the subject agrees that the system needs reforming. There is no agreement, however, on what sort of reforms should be instituted. Some have argued for a national health insurance scheme that would cover major medical expenses for all, others for government controls on increasing costs, and yet others for more government involvement in the distribution and planning of health care.

In the United States, unlike in almost all other democratic industrial nations, much of the average citizen's health care bill is paid for out of his or her own pocket. The U.S. health care system has two major elements: a private health care system, in which costs are paid for by consumers or through group insurance plans; and a public system, which is financed through governmental programs supplemented by consumer contributions. In general, those served only by the various publicly supplied health services—the poor and the elderly—are likely to have the lowest levels of health. Having the money to pay for services or to buy insurance makes a significant difference in the kind of health care one receives.

For the average middle-class American covered by some form of private health insurance, basic health care is more than adequately assured. Still, many insurance plans do not meet important medical needs. Catastrophic illness may boost costs beyond what insurance covers. Preventive medical steps may not fit into insurance coverage. Then, too, millions of Americans have no medical insurance at all, and so are constantly at risk. The ranks of the uninsured swell as unemployment increases, for many of the jobless are left without coverage through the insurance plans provided at the workplace. In 1983, 35 million, or 15 percent of the nation's population, lacked private insurance coverage.

President Franklin Roosevelt considered adding a national health insurance section to the Social Security Act of 1935, but did not do so because of the fear of arousing too much political opposition. The issue of a national health care plan has been politically volatile ever since. Most Americans favor some sort of national insurance, but the opposition of the American Medical Association and other interest groups has been sufficiently potent to doom specific proposals over the years.

As we have seen, the one major step toward governmental responsibility for health care was taken in 1965, when Congress, under the prodding of President Lyndon Johnson, created the Medicare/Medicaid programs. Medicare expanded rapidly after its

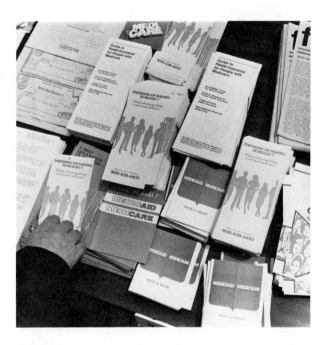

creation. The steady and sharp increase in Medicare spending since its inception has stemmed from three factors. First, the establishment of Medicare spurred millions of people to get medical care they would otherwise have done without. Second, the size of the elderly population covered by Medicare has been growing: by the year 2000, 13 percent of Americans will be over age sixty-five. Finally, and perhaps most importantly, hospital costs have soared, climbing at more than double the inflation rate. The system of federal payments has been a financial windfall to many sectors of the medical profession.

Despite the growing increase in Medicare costs, Medicare paid only 44 percent of the elderly's medical bills in 1982. It did not cover such ordinary expenses as drugs, dental care, and eyeglasses. More significantly, it did not provide sufficient coverage for nursing home care or catastrophic, long-term illness. Medicare is designed to cover most effectively short stays in the hospital. For the first sixty days, a patient pays only $304. After that, costs to the patient increase sharply, and after 150 days, Medicare pays nothing at all. Nursing home care, which

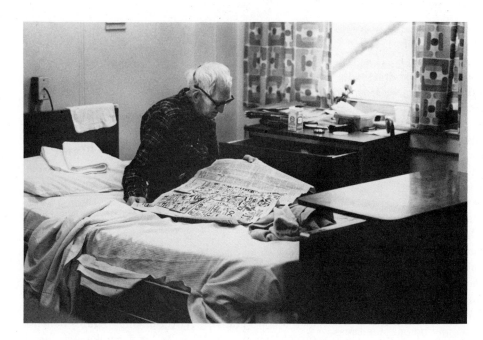

The American health system is often hard to figure out, especially for the elderly. One of the most pressing needs is for adequate nursing home care. A portion of that care is provided by government (*left*). (*Right*) a resident of a Veterans Administration nursing home in Johnson City, Tennessee.

is necessary for millions of the elderly, is barely covered by Medicare. Of the $20 billion Americans spent on nursing homes in 1982, Medicare supplied only $400 million. In 1985, approximately 6.5 million senior citizens with chronic illnesses required some kind of nonspecialized nursing care but were excluded from Medicare benefits,[8] and that number is expected to increase to 9 million by the year 2000. The average cost of nursing home care is $18,000 a year—a level of expenditure that swiftly depletes the savings of most elderly people.[9] Of course, indigent patients can receive care through the Medicaid system, which also covers the indigent elderly. But to qualify for Medicaid, a patient must demonstrate need. Middle-class persons with modest savings, accordingly, have to use up virtually all those savings before the government will step in to aid with nursing home care. Medicaid, which was originally intended to provide health care protection for the *non*elderly poor, now spends 40 percent of its money on nursing home care, mostly for the elderly.

There have been many proposals for refashioning the Medicare system. Some observers have urged

that the elderly pay more of the costs; others have recommended stricter controls on hospital costs; in one effort to force hospitals to economize, the Reagan administration in 1983 set up a fixed schedule of reimbursements for hospital costs. Still other experts have proposed that Medicare be financed out of the overall federal budget, rather than through a separate trust fund, so that the system will draw on general revenues each year.

As a reaction to skyrocketing health care costs and a Medicare budget whose growth had exceeded all expectations, a major change was made in the formula for allocating reimbursement for Medicare patients in 1983. Instead of reimbursing hospitals on a cost-plus basis (which allowed hospitals to set their own fees), the government established fixed-price reimbursement. The effects were drastic. The fixed-price scheme grouped medical procedures into 468 diagnosis-related groups. Based on this categorization, the hospital was reimbursed according to a predetermined fee regardless of the actual cost of treatment. Within a year, the average hospital stay covered by Medicare had declined 20 percent and hospital

477

occupancy rates dropped to the lowest point in twenty years. Medical inflation was cut in half.

But negative effects were also abundant. Hospitals were forced to economize, sometimes too drastically. Necessary tests were sometimes neglected. Hospital stays were sometimes shortened too greatly. In an increasing number of cases, poor patients were turned away from private hospitals and referred to public facilities that became heavily burdened. By 1985, two years after the new payment system was introduced, transfers from private to public hospitals showed startling increases in many cities, up 680 percent, for example, in the Cook County Hospital in Chicago. Many feared that in the effort to economize, the nation was creating a two-tiered medical system, with separate and unequal care for the poor.

All national health systems have some problems. In Great Britain, the popular National Health Service provides health care to all as a matter of right; costs to the individual are very low, and no one need fear the financial burdens of catastrophic illness. But the British spend little on health care, and their system needs modernization—often, people must wait months or years for elective surgery that in the United States would be performed quickly. All national health care systems must deal with rising costs, inequities, inefficiencies, and other problems. The U.S. system, however, has more bugs in it than most: it provides some of the best health care in the world, but only to some people some of the time; it is costly; and its coverage is spotty. As of 1975, the United States ranked second out of six Western nations in health spending but fifth in overall quality of health care.[10] The six nations involved in the comparison were West Germany, Great Britain, Sweden, France, the Netherlands, and the United States. West Germany ranked first in health expenditures, with the United States second. The ranking of overall health care was based on seventeen specific mortality rates. In this ranking, Sweden showed the best health care, the Netherlands came second, the United States fifth, and West Germany, the top spender, sixth. Ours is a complex system that, like much else in the U.S. welfare state, represents an uneasy compromise between the desire to meet human needs and distrust of government as an instrument for doing so.

## Evaluating the welfare state

How an individual views the welfare system depends to some extent on his or her political philosophy. Conservatives tend to cast a jaundiced eye on government intervention in the marketplace and on spending on social programs, whereas liberals generally support welfare state programs.

### The conservative attack

Conservatives have long argued that government involvement in the marketplace should be kept to a minimum—even in the labor market. According to many conservatives, government welfare benefits discourage people from seeking employment, and thereby undermine market mechanisms that would efficiently deal with unemployment. When benefits are raised too high, that is, incentives to work are reduced, and those who do work become discouraged. In areas such as health care and housing, con-

servatives have also argued that the market should do more and the government less. Private enterprise should be looked to as the main solution.

Conservative critic Charles Murray attacked the new rules of life for the poor that Great Society programs created. Like many conservatives, he saw the new welfare programs as encouraging poverty, not attacking it: "The first effect of the new rules was to make it profitable for the poor to behave in the short term in ways that were destructive in the long term. Their second effect was to mask these long-term losses—to subsidize irretrievable mistakes. We tried to provide more for the poor and produced more poor instead. We tried to remove the barriers to escape from poverty, and inadvertently built a trap."[11]

Upon taking office in 1981, President Reagan immediately sought significant reductions in many federal welfare programs. The Reagan administration planned for cuts of nearly $12 billion in programs aimed at low-income people in 1982. Food stamp and nutrition programs were to be cut by $3 billion. Legal services to the poor and the job training program were to be eliminated entirely, at a savings of $4 billion. Public housing was to be cut $595 million; Medicaid, $950 million; AFDC, $700 million.

The president assured observers that no cuts would affect the "truly needy"—a term repeated by many members of his administration. The implication was that many who were not "truly needy" were receiving benefits. The problem was determining exactly who the "truly needy" were.

The Reagan administration maintained that the poor would be supported by a basic "safety net" of programs—Social Security, Medicare, veterans' compensation and pensions, Supplemental Security Income, free school lunches, Head Start and summer jobs for youth, and AFDC. Taken together, these programs cost nearly $220 billion in fiscal 1982, and benefited about 50 million Americans. However, the three largest safety net programs—Social Security, Medicare and veterans' benefits—provide benefits for millions who do not live in poverty.

As it turned out, 23 percent of the approximately 25 million Americans with incomes below the poverty line were receiving no benefits from the safety net programs, and 60 percent were getting either nothing or no more than a free school lunch on school days for their children. Ironically, the Reagan cuts, as enacted, hit the working poor the hardest. For example, a typical working mother in New York with

The welfare system can be both frighteningly impersonal and terribly intimate. Here the unemployed form lines to apply for benefits, and a social worker assists a homebound woman in Manhattan.

two school-age children had her disposable income reduced by 15 percent, from $700 to $600 a month, as a result of the cuts.

Reagan administration policies designed to shrink allocations for entitlement and welfare programs were generally quite successful in doing so over the period 1981–85. The largest cuts in percentage terms were made in AFDC, food stamps, and Medicare. The only programs that showed an increase in percentage terms over this period were Supplemental Security Income and the feeding program for women, children, and infants (known as WIC). Both of these programs were increased by Congress contrary to the original proposals of the administration.

## The liberal response

"The 'safety net' of social programs is made of the cheapest cheesecloth designed to leak like a sieve at the lowest end," declared Senator J. James Exon (D, South Dakota) during hearings held in 1981 on Reagan budget cuts. The U.S. welfare state has been largely a liberal creation, and so liberals tend to be defensive about it. But they also have criticized its inadequacies. The main problems liberals have focused on can be summarized as *too little*, *too complicated*, and *too late*.

**Too little:** To liberals, the system provides less than it should. Many people fall through the cracks, and millions who are eligible for various welfare benefits never apply. As a result, poverty has continued to be a major problem in U.S. society. Many liberals have singled out the absence of a comprehensive national health plan as a critical failing of the welfare state. Although liberals have differed on the question of the right solutions, the need for more comprehensive health coverage is generally regarded as vital.

**Too complicated:** This criticism revolves around the absence of a genuinely *national* welfare system. Benefits vary considerably from state to state, often with little or no basis in the needs of recipients. Under the influence of Daniel Moynihan (later elected Democratic senator from New York State), President Richard Nixon proposed such a nationalization of welfare benefits in 1969, in his Family Assistance Program. It was defeated in Congress by a coalition of conservatives who found it too liberal and liberals who found its assistance provisions too stingy.

**Too late:** Many liberals have viewed the current U.S. welfare system as more of a series of Band-Aids than a comprehensive solution to poverty. The various programs, it has been argued, patch up the victims of our social and economic systems—those who fail, who fall by the wayside, who can't keep up. But the real problem is that those systems create so many needy. The proposed solution to this perceived "welfare problem" is a full-employment economy. With everyone working, the burdens and needs of welfare would be sharply reduced, although not eliminated. At the same time, more people would gain needed skills and self-respect. Liberals in Congress have introduced various bills that would provide jobs to the unemployed by making government an employer of last resort. But no such program has ever been acted upon. The Comprehensive Employment and Training Act (CETA), which provided a relatively small number of public service jobs, was not the full-scale employment program many had called for, and it has widely been viewed as a failure.

In response to the Reagan administration's assertion that the "truly needy" would not be hurt by cuts in social welfare programs, liberal critics asked why benefits (in the form of tax breaks and subsidies) should go to such "unneedy" elements of society as the oil and gas industry.

Noting that children seem to have increasingly become the victims of poverty, some liberals proposed programs specifically aimed at that problem. By 1985, 40 percent of the poor were children. One in five American children lived in poverty as officially defined, twice the rate for adults. More than half of these poor children lived in female-headed households, where mothers typically were young, unmarried, and undereducated. Between 1980 and 1985 black children particularly had lost ground.

## Reflections on policy

The picture presented by the U.S. welfare state is a mixed one. On the one hand, it has become more humane, more extensive (and more expensive) over the last twenty years. Yet, as we have seen, notable problems remain in both social insurance and public assistance programs.

Welfare state programs do make a difference, as Table 20.3 shows. Poverty is reduced very significantly through government assistance, and the combination of federal taxes and transfer payments has a significant impact on the overall distribution of income (Table 20.3). In 1982 the poorest 20 percent of the population was considerably better off after taxes and transfers.

By liberal standards, however, the U.S. welfare state remains incomplete, especially by comparison with most of the West European nations. We are without universal health coverage, millions of Americans still live in officially defined poverty, and hunger continues to be a serious problem. U.S. welfare programs simply have not eliminated real need. Although Americans spend more per capita on health

care than do the citizens of most other nations, the quality of that care is not comparable. And we spend considerably less of our national income on welfare state programs overall.[12]

The reasons for this disparity are not hard to find. Fundamentally, the forces that helped create the welfare state in Europe have been far weaker in the United States. Most notably, as mentioned in Chapter 2, left-wing political parties and trade unions have been less influential here. As a result, most of the major leaps forward in welfare state programs have come only in the face of severe crises or unusual political circumstances. Without a highly organized trade union movement or a popular labor or social democratic party, the poor and the near poor remain a politically vulnerable constituency. As pointed out in Chapter 8, the poor are less likely to vote and become politically involved.

The effectiveness of anti–welfare interest groups has also played a role in weakening the U.S. welfare state. Were the American Medical Association to alter its views on national health insurance, for example, changes in the U.S. health industry would develop very quickly.

Yet another factor that has worked against the welfare state has been the generally "conservative" ethos in U.S. politics when it comes to the welfare state. Unlike in much of Europe, there is no tradition of paternalistic concern for the poor. Our political cul-

TABLE 20.3
## Percentage of Americans in poverty

|  | Official poverty rate* | Poverty rate if food stamps and noncash benefits are counted as income** | Poverty rate without government benefits† |
|---|---|---|---|
| 1965 | 17.3% | 12.1% | 21.3% |
| 1972 | 11.9 | 6.2 | 19.2 |
| 1976 | 11.8 | 6.7 | 21.0 |
| 1979 | 11.7 | 6.1 | 20.5 |
| 1982 | 15.0 | 8.8 | 24.0 |

*U.S. Census Bureau. Includes personal income plus cash benefits from the government.
**Timothy M. Smeeding, University of Utah. Includes adjustments for underreporting and taxes.
†Sheldon Danziger, University of Wisconsin.
Source: *Washington Post*, national weekly edition, May 21, 1984.

ture, as was pointed out in Chapter 2, emphasizes independence, individualism, and economic success. The values of cooperation, community concern, and charity are supposed to be private, not public matters. As a result, "welfare" still has an emotional stigma attached to it. The percentage of national wealth devoted to welfare programs is considerably lower in the United States than in almost any European nation.[13]

Incongruities abound in our system. As one observer put it: "Today we have a system where elderly millionaires jet between their Florida condominiums and Manhattan townhouses and get generous pensions and heavily subsidized medical care; meanwhile, poor mothers with sick children are labeled freeloaders just for trying to see a doctor."[14] Programs that service the large middle class constituency—Social Security and Medicare—are difficult to touch politically. Programs that are targeted mainly toward the poor—such as food stamps, housing, AFDC, and child nutrition—are far more vulnerable politically, because their constituency is smaller, less organized, and generally weaker. In addition, as many studies have shown, programs targeted for poor people become poor programs. They stigmatize recipients and are often administered in a demeaning and uncaring way.

Many of these issues are further complicated by racial feelings. Since a larger percentage of blacks than whites are poor (although many more of the poor are white than black), many Americans have associated poverty with race. As a result, racial antagonisms have interfered with a sounder, more genuinely national policy concerning poverty and deprivation.

The U.S. welfare system is so complicated, the rules so varied, the results so difficult to gauge, that effective coordination has been difficult to achieve. Benefits levels for the needy vary considerably from state to state, and many are below any reasonable standard of assistance. Most students of welfare politics have proposed a further "nationalization" of our system, with less financial responsibility, as well as less arbitrary power, in the hands of state and local officials.

## Conclusions

Americans have long tended to view themselves as a very individualistic people, with social responsibility a personal matter. The hard times of the Great Depression demonstrated that poverty and unemployment were not solely personal issues, but integrally connected with the functioning of society as a whole—in social arrangements that no one individual could change. Yet the individualist ethic has persisted, intensifying the antigovernment attitudes so common in our nation. Oddly, however, we have been quite willing to see government step in to help people during disasters, to bail out major corporations, to aid business through tax loopholes, to keep farmers solvent.

As a result of this ambivalence, we have not been able to solve the problems of need in our midst—problems that affect almost all Americans sooner or later. We have taken some steps, but they have been hesitant, inconsistent, and often inefficient. The "safety net" continues to be riddled with major holes, and human beings keep falling through. It need not be this way.

In the matter of equality, the U.S. welfare state does do part of the job. A modest redistribution of resources does take place, and government programs do aid most of the vulnerable poor. At the same time, some Americans still fall below a minimum decent standard of living. Is this justified by the savings in money and the spur to action provided by the fears of extreme want?

Finally, there is the problem posed by the paternalism of our welfare state. Various programs have acquired the reputation of demeaning their recipients, especially when the recipients must continually prove that they are poor enough to qualify. Fortunately, the infamous welfare regulations of the past, which often involved extensive surveillance of poor people, have largely been humanized. Still, some sort of proof of need will be required as long as programs remain "mean-tested."

Is there a solution to this complex set of problems? One proposed solution to the problems of insecurity

# Comparative perspective
# The welfare state against the wall in Western Europe

The modern welfare state was invented a century ago in Germany by Chancellor Otto von Bismarck, who established a comprehensive system of health and disability insurance. Bismarck's purpose was purely utilitarian: he sought to head off an increasingly militant workers' movement and to prevent the Socialist Party from gaining political advantages by campaigning for such benefits. Other European countries followed suit over the next half-century, most for more altruistic reasons. In Great Britain, for instance, the post–World War II Labour government implemented programs that were "universalist" in scope: government-paid health care, housing subsidies, and retirement benefits were seen as rights of all citizens, not charity for the poor. By the 1950s, this view was the basis of most Western European social programs.

Today, under the combined weight of aging populations, high unemployment and general economic stagnation, the welfare dream has become a fiscal nightmare. European governments are seeking ways to stem increases in social spending. They are in large measure prevented from doing so by the same forces that prompted Bismarck's initial embrace of social welfare policy—workers' outcries, and their veto power via the ballot box. Some dimensions of the problem:

From 1974 to 1983, total government spending among Common Market (EEC) countries averaged an amount equal to 48 percent of their economies' output of goods and services. (In the United States, the figure was 34 percent.)

About 15 percent of Western Europe's population is age sixty-five or over, and disability and old-age payments take up about 20 percent of public expenditures. In the EEC, 1984 brought an average of 11.4 percent unemployment in member countries— about 12.9 million people.

Youth unemployment ran as high as 35 percent in some EEC countries in 1983. In that year, the EEC estimated that about 1.7 million people under twenty-five would spend more than a year looking for work.

Denmark typifies the welfare state. Danish welfare state benefits are literally "cradle-to-grave." The state provides free medical care and hospitalization. Day care is subsidized, as are rents and even theater tickets. A state pension comes with retirement, and about $235 towards burial expenses follows one's death. Unemployment benefits—which can last 2½ years at up to 90 percent of a laid-off worker's last salary— and basic welfare payments (about $160 a week for a single person) help compensate for hard times.

The price? For an average worker with spouse and two children who earns $13,500, a 35 percent tax rate. (Top income earners pay 75 percent.) For the state, a rate of social spending that rose from 21 percent to 29.3 percent of gross domestic product from 1972 to 1981.

But despite grumbling about high taxes, social welfare programs remain extremely popular in Denmark, as they are in the rest of Western Europe. When a conservative-led government took office in 1982 and attempted to cut back spending by requiring every Dane to pay the equivalent of $2.35 for each visit to the doctor, it brought a public outcry and the idea was killed. Medical-care benefits remain untouched. Nor could the government touch unemployment benefits to those still eligible. Even conservative politicians refused to touch the old-age pensions, and the proposed 1985 government budget contained few social service cutbacks.

and inequality is a national income security policy that would provide a minimum income adjusted to a national level of cost for food, clothing, shelter, transportation, and health care. The costs, however, would be high, especially if an effort were to be made to help the working poor as well as the unemployed or the desperately poor.[15] Such a policy would at least help settle the issue of what level of government should ultimately be responsible for dealing with poverty and need. Our federal system has, to a degree, served to confuse and tangle the issues of welfare. As we have seen, the existence of fifty separate jurisdictions has often prevented the implementation of an effective, uniformly applied national policy.

Another suggestion has been to focus our attention on children and orient many programs around their well-being. Senator Daniel P. Moynihan proposed the following child-centered rearrangements of the welfare state:[16]

Indexing of welfare aid for children: all federal entitlement programs, such as aid to veterans and Social Security, have been adjusted (indexed) for inflation, but programs affecting children have not.

Establishment of a national benefit standard for child welfare.

Support for programs with demonstrated success rates, such as Head Start.

Creation of programs aimed at preventing teenage pregnancy and abortion.

Another proposal, closer to the logic of the Reagan administration, has been to slash those social programs that assist the poor and allow economic factors, the spur of want, and fundamental economic insecurity to do the job of encouraging people to find work and to help each other. This agenda could be supplemented by programs, such as "workfare," that require welfare recipients to take some sort of employment.

In the end, basic ideological commitments shape the ways one views welfare state issues. Although we may have arrived at a mixed economy that incorporates elements of both capitalism and socialism, the old debates have continued between those

who are more and those who are less egalitarian in outlook. More-egalitarian Democrats have argued that democracy cannot function well without a substantial degree of social and economic equality. The more-inegalitarian have rejoined that too much equality dulls motivation and requires excessive government interference in the economy and in personal life. Consideration of these questions requires both a careful attention to the facts and a willingness to confront one's basic assumptions about what is good and bad for society. A few facts seem beyond debate: that a substantial government involvement in welfare state policies is here to stay; that the U.S. government does less in this regard than most other governments in industrial democracies; that we have not been able so far to develop programs that strike a reasonable balance between compassion and regulation; and finally, that the distribution of the good things of life remains, even after the activities of the welfare state, highly unequal in U.S. society.

## NOTES

1 John E. Schwarz, *America's Hidden Success* (New York: W. W. Norton, 1983), pp. 32–44.

2 Reported in *The New York Times*, April 17, 1985, p. A23.

3 Citizens' Board of Inquiry into Hunger and Malnutrition in the United States, *Hunger USA* (Washington, D.C., 1972); also see Nick Kotz, *Let Them Eat Promises: The Politics of Hunger in America* (Garden City, N.Y.: Anchor, 1971).

4 *The New York Times*, February 27, 1985, p. 8.

5 *The New York Times*, March 5, 1985, p. 26.

6 John Schwarz, *America's Hidden Success*, pp. 42–43. See also Cesar Perales, "Myths about Poverty," *The New York Times*, October 26, 1983, p. 27.

7 William Raspberry, "Choosing Work over Welfare," *Washington Post*, July 6, 1984, p. A19.

8 Andrew Stein, "Medicare's Broken Promises," *The New York Times Magazine*, February 17, 1985, p. 44.

9 *Newsweek*, May 6, 1985, p. 67.

10 A. Heidenheimer, H. Heclo, and C. T. Adams, *Comparative Public Policy*, 2nd ed. (New York: St. Martin's, 1983), p. 87.

11 Quoted in Christopher Jencks, "How Poor Are the Poor?" *New York Review of Books*, May 9, 1985, p. 41.

12 A. Heidenheimer, *et al.*, *Comparative Public Policy* (New York: St. Martin's, 1983), Chapters 3, 4, and 7.

13 *Ibid.*, p. 204.

14 Keishing, p. 43.

15 Such a policy was proposed by Democratic Governor Bruce Babbitt of Arizona. See Nick Kotz, "The Politics of Hunger," *The New Republic*, April 30, 1984, pp. 19–20.

16 *The New York Times*, April 9, 1985.

## SELECTED READINGS

For basic background on the welfare state, see H. L. Wilensky and C. N. Lebeaux, *Industrial Society and Social Welfare* (New York: The Free Press, 1965); Richard M. Titmuss, *Commitment to Welfare* (New York: Pantheon, 1968); Karl de Schweinitz, *England's Road to Social Security* (Philadelphia: University of Pennsylvania Press, 1947); Roy LuBove, *The Struggle for Social Security, 1900–1935* (Cambridge, Mass.: Harvard University Press, 1968); T. H. Marshall, *Class, Citizenship and Social Development* (New York: Doubleday, 1964); and Neil J. Smelser, *Social Change in the Industrial Revolution* (Chicago: University of Chicago Press, 1959).

On contemporary issues and evaluations, see Donald Hancock, *Sweden: The Politics of a Post-Industrial Society* (Hinsdale, Ill.: Dryden, 1972); N. Furniss and T. Tilton, *The Case for the Welfare State* (Bloomington, Ind.: Indiana University Press, 1973); Edward Banfield, *The Unheavenly City* (Boston: Little, Brown, 1974); Susan Sheehan, *A Welfare Mother* (New York: Mentor, 1976); William Ryan, *Blaming the Victim* (New York: Vintage, 1971); John E. Schwarz, *America's Hidden Success* (New York: Norton, 1983); A. Heidenheimer, *et al.*, *Comparative Public Policy* (New York: St. Martin's, 1983); and F. F. Piven and R. Cloward, *Regulating the Poor* (New York: Pantheon, 1971).

On specific issues related to the welfare state strategies of the Reagan administration, see Alan Gartner, Colin Green, and Frank Riessman, *What Reagan Is Doing to Us* (New York: Harper & Row, 1982); Charles Murray, *Losing Ground: American Social Policy, 1950–1980* (New York: Basic, 1984); F. F. Pivan and R. A. Cloward, *The New Class War* (New York: Pantheon, 1982); Michael Harrington, *The New American Poverty* (New York: Holt, Rinehart & Winston, 1984); Robert Kuttner, *The Economic Illusion: False Choices Between Prosperity and Social Justice* (Boston: Houghton Mifflin, 1984); Neil Gilbert, *Capitalism and the Welfare State: Dilemmas of Social Benevolence* (New Haven: Yale University Press, 1984); U.S. Bishops Ad Hoc Committee, *Catholic Teaching and the U.S. Economy* (New York: National Catholic News Service, 1984).

# Chapter
## twenty-one

# Civil liberties, civil and social rights

# Is justice being done?

DEMOCRATIC rights and liberties are not simply "givens"—things we have always, somehow, had, and can therefore take for granted. In fact, intense struggles over the nature of these rights and liberties have taken place throughout U.S. history. For long periods, basic democratic freedoms were denied to various groups and individuals, who obtained their rights only after sustained and bitter social conflicts. The historical perspective shows that rights and liberties come into being as part of social and political processes involving confrontation, changes in attitudes, efforts at accommodation, and, very often, personal courage.

In our own time, such struggles have continued, although their focus has changed. Because minority or disadvantaged groups for the most part have obtained the basic civil rights, the issue now is to define and implement the idea of equal protection under the laws. The evolution of our ideas of what democracy involves has led to such questions as, should a woman be free to obtain an abortion? and should adults be free to obtain any sort of pornography they wish? New concepts have developed around clusters of new issues. For example, in dealing with the abortion issue and with gay rights, the courts have been defining a "right to privacy." There has also been considerable discussion of a basic "right

to know" in matters concerning governmental policies. We will not find this right discussed in the original Bill of Rights, but many have argued that it is very closely related to the concepts of free speech and discussion and to the notion of an informed citizenry. In the area of social rights, the basic idea of government responsibility for public health and safety is now widely accepted. Still to be answered, however, are the questions, How much protection? At what cost? In what form? As the cases presented in this chapter show, these issues are thorny and important.

This chapter offers a sampling of current debates over democratic rights and liberties. In examining the controversies, we will be asking several questions: Does our politics permit an opportunity for new rights and liberties to evolve? Can the political process cope with the conflicts generated? Are all relevant groups able to make their views heard? Are important rights and liberties being ignored or inadequately protected?

We will begin with a discussion of new types of civil liberties. Then, we will turn to civil rights issues, focusing mainly on current controversies in the battles for equality being fought by blacks and women. Social rights to health and safety will be taken up in the final section of the chapter.

## The struggle for new civil liberties

Recently, two observers of the U.S. civil liberties scene commented that "The politics of unreason is at a low ebb at the start of America's third century."[1] By this they meant that extremist movements of the sort that have popped up throughout U.S. history, such as the Ku Klux Klan and McCarthyism, were now less powerful and attractive. But if no mass extremist movement currently threatens civil liberties in this country, many serious civil liberties questions remain unresolved.

The U.S. civil liberties scene has been complicated by a new set of moral issues revolving around the definition of legitimate and illegitimate life-styles. These issues, involving gay rights, abortion, pornography, and drugs, have proven difficult to resolve, since they pit largely unorganized but emotionally intense groups against one another. What is at stake in such matters often is more than the specific issue being fought over. The success or failure of a measure has become a symbolic affirmation or rejection of certain practices and individuals, and thus a judgment on the moral status of the issue involved.[2]

In contemporary U.S. society, must conservatives call for less regulation in the area of business but more extensive regulation in the area of morals. They tend to favor restrictions on drug use, pornography, the rights of gays, and abortion. Most liberals take

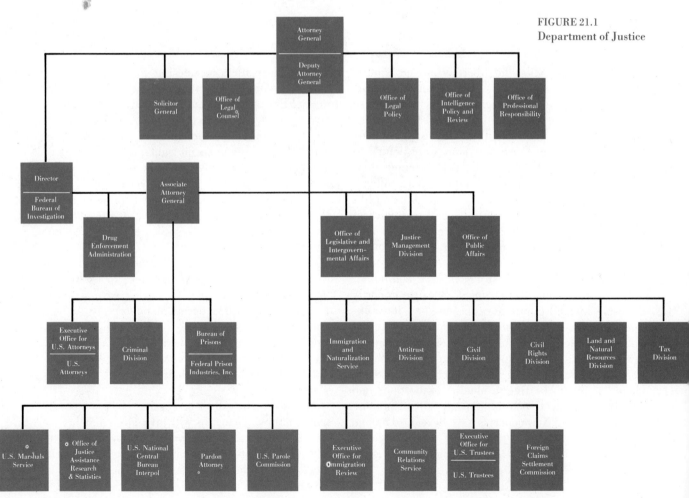

FIGURE 21.1
Department of Justice

the opposite position. They tend to favor more regulation of the economy in the name of the public welfare but less regulation in areas of morals—or "personal choice," as they are more likely to call it.

These polar positions partly arise from reasoned arguments about the actual effects of regulation and nonregulation. But they also reflect convictions about personal rights and liberties, and about which areas of life should be free from government interference. Much of the current debate over areas of morals and personal choice has been carried on in just these terms—on how the public interest is best served and when people ought to be left alone.

On the whole, U.S. society has been moving gradually in a more liberal direction, accepting more public regulation of economic matters and less regulation in the areas of morals. This is not to say that government interferes in every aspect of business life, or that regulation is always effective. (One theme of this text is that it is not.) Compared with the pre–New Deal era, however, economic regulation is extensive. Meanwhile, we have become more tolerant of moral diversity in areas such as pornography, abortion, and sexual preference. Perhaps inevitably, however, this increase in tolerance has provoked the intense reactions of the anti-obscenity, "right to life," and anti-gay movements. An enlightening example of this tolerance-and-reaction cycle is the treatment of obscenity by the courts. As a matter of both taste and tolerance, the obscenity issue raises questions about the actual consequences of greater tolerance: Will it lead to harm to others or to greater public good? Or will it have no general effects at all?

## Obscenity

For decades the Supreme Court has grappled with the complex problem of defining exactly what is "obscene." In case after case, the Court has been called upon to decide whether a specific magazine, movie, or book is really obscene. And even were society to agree that obscenity should be censored, there would remain the question, By what (or whose) standards?

Yet a deeper issue is whether there actually *is* such a thing as obscenity—and if there is, why it should not simply be viewed as a form of "speech" entitled to the protections of the First Amendment.

The first significant attempt by a court to define *obscenity* came in the landmark British case of *Hicklin* v. *Regina* (1868). The case dealt with an anti-religious tract called *The Confessional Unmasked*, which described, among other things, the seduction of women during "confessions." The judge in *Hicklin* sought to define *obscenity* as follows:

The test of obscenity is this, whether the tendency of the matter charged as obscene is to deprave and corrupt those whose minds are open to such immoral influences, and into whose hands a publication of this sort may fall.

Vague as it was, the *Hicklin* decision became the basic standard for U.S. obscenity cases for almost a century. Under *Hicklin*, even small parts of books or other materials could be taken out of context and declared obscene. In 1934, however, the Supreme Court accepted the argument of the publisher of James Joyce's *Ulysses* that a work should be considered *as a whole*. Finally, in 1957 the Court altogether rejected the Hicklin rule in the case of *Roth* v. *United States*. Although upholding the conviction of Samuel Roth himself, a New York publisher, on the charge of mailing obscene materials, the Court rejected the Hicklin rule as unconstitutional, and proposed a new standard:

The test is not whether it would arouse sexual desires or sexual impure thoughts in those comprising a particular segment of the community, the young, the immature or the highly prudish. . . . The test in each case is the effect of the book . . . considered as a whole, not upon any particular classes, but upon all those whom it is likely to reach . . . . [Y]ou determine its impact upon the average person in the community.[3]

In other words, one class of society should not be singled out in judging the effect of the material. What should count, rather, is how the material, taken as a whole, affects the "average person." This rule was loosened further in 1966, when the Court held that obscene material had to offend national standards, not just those of a small community.[4]

What followed was a liberalization of the appli-

As rules against obscenity have loosened, so have public displays of it increased. Here, women march on 42nd Street in New York City protesting pornography. They argued that pornography was not just a matter of personal taste but actually was violence against women.

cation of obscenity laws. As more sexually explicit materials became more easily obtainable, more and more of the public began to object. In *Miller* v. *California* (1973) the Court shifted ground again, voting, 5–4, to uphold a group of obscenity convictions.[5] In the majority opinion, Chief Justice Warren E. Burger argued that there *was* such a thing as "obscenity," and that it was *not* protected by the First Amendment. To be considered obscene, the Court declared, a work, taken as a whole, must appeal to "prurient interest" in sex, portray sex offensively, and "lack serious literary, artistic, political or scientific value." For such materials, the Court ruled, local standards should be used as the basis for judgment.

Many people have questioned the entire basis for subjecting obscene materials, however defined, to prosecution and censorship. What is wrong, they have asked, with appealing to what the Supreme Court has called prurient interest ("having morbid or lascivious longings")? After all, a majority on the President's Commission on Obscenity and Pornography, appointed by Lyndon Johnson, found there was no connection between exposure to pornography and any sort of crime, sexual or otherwise. If pornography does not demonstrably cause social harm, why should it be subject to legal restraints? Conservatives have contended that the widespread availability of obscene materials sooner or later will contribute to the destruction of order, civility, and various civic virtues. Is there any evidence supporting such a hypothesis?

Yes, according to an unusual coalition of feminists and conservative and religious groups such as the Moral Majority. Feminist Andrea Dworkin has maintained that "pornography is the theory and rape is the practice," and argued that pornography discriminates against women and hence is a violation of equal protection of the laws. In May 1984, Indianapolis, Indiana, passed an ordinance that declared pornography to be a violation of women's civil rights. According to the ordinance, "Pornography is central in creating and maintaining sex as a basis for discrimination."

Both sides in the debate have taken absolutist positions. Some feminists and right-wing crusaders have viewed all pornography as illegitimate, whereas free speech advocates have proclaimed a pervasive protection under the First Amendment for virtually all forms of "speech." Both arguments seem somewhat inflated. Certain types of pornography appear, at least to common sense, far more pernicious than others—child pornography, for example, or particularly degrading and brutal forms of pornography.

Some communities have sought to isolate pornographic establishments through zoning laws, and thereby to reduce the amount of pornography available and to keep it out of sight of people who do not wish to come in contact with it. The Supreme Court has upheld the right of communities to take such steps. One advocate of this sort of compromise on the pornography issue has put her case as follows:

To the extent that pornography is symptomatic of, and helps to further, social disintegration, in which the least powerful (especially children) suffer the most, it becomes an appropriate target for action, regulation, and reproof. But with this proviso: the knowledge that we cannot return to a past in which Americans harmoniously shared one set of moral values. Communities must put pornography "in its place" rather than seek to eradicate it altogether.[6]

## Abortion

In recent decades the Supreme Court has elaborated a doctrine of "personal privacy" in cases involving contraception and abortion. In 1965 the Court voided a Connecticut law forbidding the issuance of birth control information, on the grounds that the law violated the rights of marital privacy. The Court majority spoke of "zones of privacy" and cited the Ninth Amendment, which states that rights not spelled out in the Bill of Rights are retained by the people. Justice Hugo Black, in dissenting, argued that the Court was creating a new right—one that was not to be found anywhere in the Constitution.

Eight years later, in a momentous decision on abortion handed down in *Roe* v. *Wade*, the Court majority noted that "the Constitution does not explicitly mention any right of privacy . . . [but] the Court has recognized that a right of personal privacy . . . does exist under the Constitution."[7] The Court ruled that during the first trimester (three months) of pregnancy, the question of abortion was a private matter between a woman and her physician. In the second trimester, states could impose restrictions to protect

the mother's health; and in the third trimester, states could ban abortions altogether in recognition of the status of the developing fetus.

*Roe* v. *Wade* (1973) touched off a decade of intense controversy. Some hailed the decision as a decisive step forward for civil liberties and the rights of women. Some regarded it as a fundamentally immoral decision—a license for fetal murder. Opponents argued that the Court's decision failed to take into account the "right to life" of the unborn child.

Foes of abortion have taken two basic tacks in attempting to reverse or dilute the *Roe* decision. Some antiabortion advocates have sought passage of a constitutional amendment giving the states and the federal government concurrent powers to enact a "Human Life" bill. In other words, either government could pass a bill defining life as beginning at conception and thereby providing constitutional protec-

Norma McCorvey, the woman whose desire to have an abortion led to the Su-

preme Court's *Roe* v. *Wade* decision.

# Comparative perspective The politics of abortion in West Germany

In West Germany, as in the United States, the courts have played a significant role in dealing with the abortion issue. Unlike U.S. courts, however, the West German courts have played a conservative role. West German abortion politics began in the late 1960s, when existing regulations permitted abortion only in dire emergencies and severe penalties were mandated for anyone involved in illegal abortion practices. Nonetheless, an estimated two hundred thousand abortions were performed each year, and women who could afford it traveled to nations where abortions could be legally obtained.

In 1970, the governing coalition led by Chancellor Willy Brandt of the Social Democratic Party announced its intention of reforming the abortion laws. A majority of West Germans favored some reform. Interest groups had organized on both sides of the issue, and politicking was intense. Although it was generally agreed that some reform should occur, there was no agreement on just what form it should take. Catholic members of the government were particularly reluctant to vote for any extensive changes. Following the elections of 1972, with government proposals still bogged down in controversy, several members of the German parliament seized the initiative (a highly unusual development in German political life) and proposed a series of different reforms—ranging from a highly permissive law allowing abortion in the first trimester to one that would have made scarcely any changes at all. After several more months of political maneuvering, the most permissive of the abortion bills was passed.

The German Conference of Catholic Bishops then sought a constitutional test of the new legislation, and a conservative state government took the issue to the Constitutional Court. In February 1975, the Court declared the law unconstitutional, on the grounds that the law violated the spirit of the West German Basic Law (constitution) concerning the sanctity of life. The Court seemed particularly sensitive on the abortion issue because of Germany's Nazi past, during which euthanasia had been practiced on those whom the Nazis regarded as "useless." The Court did spell out more-specific criteria under which a revised abortion law would be constitutionally acceptable, and such a law was subsequently passed. A majority of Germans, according to public opinion polls, disapproved of the Court's decision.

Source: A comprehensive source of both U.S. and foreign abortion data is Christopher Tietze's *Induced Abortion: A World Review, 1983* (New York: The Population Council, 1983). See also Walter F. Murphy and Joseph Tanenhaus, *Comparative Constitutional Law: Cases and Commentaries* (New York: St. Martin's, 1977), pp. 422–429.

---

tions for the unborn fetus. In the *Roe* decision, Justice Harry Blackmun had stated that the question of the beginning of life was one that the Court could not then resolve.

Antiabortion forces have also supported restrictions on the use of federal funds for abortions. Such restrictions, commonly called the Hyde amendments (after their chief sponsor, Republican Representative Henry Hyde of Illinois) have been passed by Congress in every year beginning with 1976, and were upheld as constitutional by the Supreme Court in 1980. The Hyde restrictions have affected mainly poor women. As federally financed abortions dropped from 295,000 in 1976 to 2,400 in 1979, many private abortion clinics dropped fees for women who cannot afford to pay.

In recent years, antiabortion activists have energetically picketed abortion clinics, a few of which were attacked or fire-bombed. It seems unlikely, however, that antiabortion forces will be able to turn back the clock. Given the absence of a strong moral consensus in U.S. society on this issue, any effort to ban abortion would likely suffer a fate similar to that which befell Prohibition in the 1920s. The social costs would be very large if abortion were driven underground.

## The Freedom of Information Act

After years of discussion about making government documents and records more accessible to citizens, the **Freedom of Information Act** (FOIA) was passed in 1966. In the wake of Watergate disclosures, the act was substantially amended in 1974. Basically, the FOIA required that federal agencies compile a listing of the information they possess and reply to

requests for information within ten days; if they deny such a request, the requester may sue for release of the information. Certain categories of information were exempted from the act's provision, including classified material, personnel records, and internal agency documents.

Passage of the FOIA led to a flood of requests for information and made available to the public a vast quantity of hitherto unavailable information. Historians and investigators were able to unearth new and important material on a variety of topics, such as the FBI surveillance of Martin Luther King, Jr. Tens of thousands of citizens were able to find out if the FBI was keeping files on them and to examine much of what was in those files. The FOIA also made it possible to obtain materials vital to uncovering the effects of Agent Orange, a herbicide used in Vietnam.

Generally, the FOIA has served as a powerful tool for those seeking to expose government corruption, waste, and misuse of power. Defenders of the act have claimed that it "has been spectacularly suc-

**TABLE 21.1**
## Views on abortion

| Proposed amendment to: | Favor | Oppose | Don't know |
|---|---|---|---|
| Make all abortions illegal | 28% | 63% | 9% |
| Allow abortions only to save life of mother | 43 | 48 | 9 |

*Changes in long-term trends*

| Abortion should be legal if | Percent agreeing in: | | | | | | |
|---|---|---|---|---|---|---|---|
| | 1972 | 1974 | 1976 | 1978 | 1980 | 1982 | 1984 |
| 1 there is a strong chance of serious defect in baby | 79 | 85 | 84 | 82 | 83 | 85 | 80 |
| 2 a woman is married and doesn't want any more children | 40 | 47 | 46 | 40 | 47 | 48 | 43 |
| 3 a woman's health is endangered by the pregnancy | 87 | 92 | 91 | 91 | 90 | 92 | 90 |
| 4 the family cannot afford more children | 49 | 55 | 53 | 47 | 52 | 52 | 46 |
| 5 a woman becomes pregnant as a result of rape | 79 | 87 | 84 | 83 | 83 | 87 | 80 |
| 6 a woman becomes pregnant and does not wish to marry | 44 | 50 | 50 | 41 | 48 | 49 | 44 |

Source: Based on CBS/*New York Times* poll (Sept. 30–Oct. 5, 1984) and on polls conducted by National Opinion Research Center.

# Freedom to visit?

In 1984, Gabriel Garcia Marquez, a Colombian novelist who had won the Nobel Prize for Literature, sought an unconditional five-year visa from the U.S. State Department in order to participate in a conference in the United States. For many years Garcia Marquez had been denied any type of visa, solely because he had worked for the official Cuban news agency in the 1960s.

Later, he was granted a restricted visa requiring negotiations with the State Department. The department offered him another such visa in 1984, but he declined it "for reasons of principle and personal dignity."

The Colombian author was only one of many visa applicants—an estimated eight hundred in 1983—who have been turned down or permitted only restricted visits by the State Department. Under the McCarren-Walter Immigration Act of 1952, passed at the height of the anticommunist fervor in the United States, visas can be denied to aliens who are or were affiliated with a communist or procommunist organization, as well as to any foreigner the State Department deems undesir-

able for reasons of "the public interest."

Thousands of Communists and others enter the country every year by obtaining waivers of the exclusion rules. But such waivers are granted quite arbitrarily, and a person admitted on one occasion may be turned down the next time. No other Western democracy imposes visa restrictions on ideological grounds. Among those for whom travel to the United States was restricted, delayed, or denied by the Reagan administration, on the grounds that they sought "to engage in activities which would be prejudicial to the public interest," were

Hortensia de Allende, widow of the late president of Chile and a human rights activist.

Dennis Brutus, black South African poet.

Julio Cortazar, the late Argentine novelist.

Mahmoud Darwish, Palestinian poet.

Bernadette Devlin, Irish nationalist and former Member of the British Parliament.

Olga Finlay, Cuban feminist scholar and activist.

Gerry Adams, head of the Irish Republican Army's political wing.

Dario Fo, Italian playwright.

Ian Paisley, Irish Protestant leader.

Yves Montand, French singer and actor.

Guillermo Ungo, left-wing Salvadoran guerilla leader.

320 Japanese delegates to the June 1982 United Nations special session on Disarmament.

Roberto D'Aubuisson, right-wing Salvadoran political leader.

Source: *Harper's*, June 1984, p. 23; and *The New York Times*, April 24 and July 15, 1984.

---

cessful in curbing the routine secrecy that had traditionally surrounded the operational records of the Federal government."[8] It has also forced federal employees to keep better records and to improve classification practices.

Opponents of the FOIA have persistently endeavored to dilute its provisions. The CIA, FBI, and other national intelligence agencies initially wanted to be exempted from the act altogether, on the grounds that the act would jeopardize informants and allow vital

secrets to become public. Critics have also claimed that private business information has been revealed and that enemies of the United States have been able to avail themselves of information that should not have been made public. In addition, they have argued, the processing of answers to FOIA requests has consumed vast numbers of hours and considerable funds. The Reagan administration lent its support to efforts to amend the act and enable the government to protect more of its information.

## Defining
## "equal treatment"

The American ideal is one of equal opportunity, but many Americans continue to face discrimination and inequality. It is commonly thought that discrimination has merely been an expression of popular prejudices and that through governmental action and the power of law, the United States has steadily moved toward the ideal of equal opportunity for all. The historical record shows, however, that governmental power has often been used to increase inequality. Only in recent decades has governmental policy been directed toward achieving greater political, social, and economic equality. In this section, we look at some of the issues involved in government efforts to provide greater equality for both blacks and women.

### School
### desegregation

Despite the historic *Brown* v. *Board of Education* decision (1954), which called for the desegregation of public schools, only about one in every hundred black children in the South attended a desegregated school a decade later. During most of that period, the president and Congress were unable to decide on any effective action to implement desegregation, and so left the matter up to the courts. Using the appealing rhetorical banner of "freedom of choice," the courts had developed a legal doctrine that put the full burden of desegregation on black families. Thus, black families could challenge the racial status quo only by choosing to enroll their children in predominantly white schools, entering into long and difficult litigation, and accepting all the risks their actions entailed. The effect of this system was to inhibit desegregation.

Finally, at the urging of President Lyndon Johnson, Congress passed the **Civil Rights Act of 1964,** which gave the attorney general the power to file desegregation lawsuits and prohibited federal aid to school districts that remained segregated. For the first time, the federal bureaucracy came to play a major role in the desegregation struggle. The Department of Health, Education and Welfare (HEW) was given the authority to create a single set of national standards and to set up a procedure for forcing school districts to comply with the Constitution *before* they could receive any federal assistance. School

It took Federal troops dispatched by President Dwight D. Eisenhower to ensure the integration of the schools in Little Rock, Arkansas, in 1957. The Little Rock crisis was one of many as school desegregation was met with intense resistance.

# Highlights of civil rights progress

*Thirteenth Amendment* (1865): Prohibited slavery.

*Fourteenth Amendment* (1868): Guaranteed equal protection of the laws.

*Fifteenth Amendment* (1870): Extended the right to vote to blacks.

*Creation of the Civil Rights Commission* (1957).

*Legislation making it a federal crime to interfere with voting in a federal election* (1957).

*Attorney general given the power to appoint federal referees to investigate voting discrimination* (1960).

*Civil Rights Act* (1964): Prohibited discrimination in public accommodations, such as theaters, restaurants, gas stations, and hotels on grounds of race, color, religion, or national origin. Exception made for small rooming houses.

Prohibited discrimination in hiring, firing, and pay levels in firms employing twenty-five or more.

Efforts at social change often require courage and commitment. Both were found in abundance in the civil rights movement. Here, blacks link arms with a white volunteer at a voter registration rally in St. Francisville, Louisiana. Many white students poured into the South to aid the movement. The other photo shows a moment during the Selma to Montgomery march led by Martin Luther King, Jr., in 1965. The marchers encountered police brutality, Ku Klux Klan violence, and general hostility along the way. Although two people were murdered, 25,000 rallied at the Alabama capital to demand "Freedom Now!"

Attorney general given the power to bring suits to enforce school desegregation.

Mandated that federal money could be withheld from any project in which discrimination was found.

*Voting Rights Act* (1965): Mandated that where discrimination had been found, or where less than 50 percent of eligible voters were registered in 1964, the Civil Service Commission could appoint registrars who could require registration of all eligible voters in federal, state, and local elections. Suspended the use of literacy tests.

*Housing Act* (1968): Prohibited discrimination in the sale or rental of much housing.

*Education Amendments* (1972): Prohibited schools that receive federal aid to discriminate according to sex.

*Rehabilitation Act* (1973): Prohibited discrimination against the handicapped.

*Institutionalized Persons Act* (1980): Permitted the federal government to bring suit on behalf of inmates of prisons and mental hospitals who are being denied their civil rights.

districts that refused to comply would not only lose needed funds, but would also face the threat of litigation by the Justice Department or by civil rights groups.

President Johnson and his ranking officials committed themselves to enforcing the law. During the first year of enforcement, more desegregation occurred than had taken place during the entire preceding decade. All but a handful of Southern school districts agreed to implement desegregation plans. In the Deep South, where absolute resistance had been the rule, freedom-of-choice plans with token integration became the norm.

The Supreme Court lent the desegregation movement moral force in 1968 in the case of *Green* v. *School Board of New Kent County, Virginia.*[9] Local authorities, the Court held, must "take whatever steps might be necessary to convert to a unitary system in which racial discrimination would be eliminated root and branch." Unless freedom of choice worked extremely well in a particular community, it was not constitutionally acceptable.

The courts, HEW, and the Justice Department had finally begun to work together toward a common goal. HEW handled most of the massive administrative and political problems. The courts sustained HEW standards and moved to settle unresolved issues in school desegregation law. The Justice Department both threatened those districts tempted to defy HEW and provided important support for the courts in the development of new legal principles, which took rapid hold in the South.

**De facto/de jure:** While the schools of the South were undergoing a period of drastic change, however, schools in the rest of the nation were becoming more segregated than ever. The people of the North maintained that segregation in their schools was of a different kind from that encountered in the South— that it was not imposed by state or local officials, but rather was the unplanned result of using a neighborhood-school policy in a setting of intense housing segregation. Northerners distinguished their *de facto* ("in fact") segregation from the Southern variety of *de jure* ("under law") segregation.

Because the constitutional guarantee of equal protection of the laws applies only to officially imposed segregation, it seemed that nothing much could be done about *de facto* segregation. For a decade and a half the courts accepted this distinction and required virtually no significant urban desegregation outside the South.

In the case of *Swann* v. *Charlotte-Mecklenburg County Board of Education* (1971),[10] the Court finally faced the important question of urban segregation. The school board of Charlotte, North Carolina, attempted to justify segregation as an innocent by-product of a racially neutral neighborhood-school policy. In rejecting this argument, the Court declared that if there had *once been* official school segregation, school authorities had a positive obligation to do whatever is necessary, including busing, to achieve integration.

Once the neighborhood-school argument fell in the South, the doctrine was rapidly and successfully attacked in Northern cities. Civil rights lawyers found that the history of segregation in Northern districts almost always entailed some official involvement in racial separation, through such factors as zoning and school site decisions, real estate deals, residential convenants, and so on. Federal judges across the country took the Court's strong action in *Swann* as a mandate for rapid, comprehensive desegregation, and soon began handing down decisions requiring extensive transportation of pupils in a number of Northern cities.

**Busing:** Local reactions to school busing orders were intense. The angry protesters filling television screens were as likely to speak in the accents of Michigan or Southern California as of Louisiana or Texas. As political criticism grew, President Richard Nixon announced in August 1971 that HEW and the Justice Department would do everything possible to minimize busing and that officials who disobeyed this directive would be summarily removed. The Nixon administration then took the extraordinary step of formally asking that its own desegregation proposals be *disregarded* by the courts. Coming just weeks before schools opened, the president's new position intensified confusion and resistance.

Opposition to school busing by a majority of Americans intensified when several federal district courts ordered that students be transferred across city-suburban lines, if necessary to achieve integration. The judges felt impelled to prescribe this remedy because the schools in several of the nation's largest cities—including New York, Chicago, Detroit, Atlanta, Baltimore, Cleveland, Houston, and Richmond—already had such large enrollments of minority groups that integration *within* the cities' school systems seemed impossible. Adding to this problem was the growing tendency of white families to leave the cities for the suburbs in order to avoid enforced busing—a phenomenon known as white flight. These families were bitterly opposed to busing their children back into city schools.

Antibusing sentiment had a profound effect on Congress. With racial issues, unlike many other matters, the correlation between local attitudes and the voting behavior of legislators usually is very high. Race is such an emotional issue in U.S. society that when public attitudes are mobilized at the local level, members of Congress often feel that their political survival depends on going along with the dominant mood.[11] When asked about "busing of Negro and white schoolchildren from one school district to another" in a 1971 Gallup poll, 82 percent of the respondents opposed it or had no opinion, whereas only 18 percent supported it. Surveys taken among educators showed that three-fourths of school superintendents and teachers were opposed to busing.

The busing controversy has raised basic questions about the ability of the government to sustain civil rights law in the face of a hostile majority. The historical evidence strongly suggests that when the hostile majority remains actively opposed and the issue continues to dominate politics, the courts tend to pull back. Restraints on judicial action can come from within the court system, from new members appointed to the courts, from judicial acceptance of some form of congressional restriction, or from a constitutional amendment.

As the 1970s drew to a close, the Supreme Court, in a series of decisions, made it clear that in general it would not mandate integration between city and suburbs. Thus, one of the obvious remedies for heavily segregated urban school systems seemed to pass

Two societies or one?

out of political reach. At the same time, however, the prospects for legislative or constitutional action to limit or prevent school busing also diminished considerably. Efforts to pass such legislation failed in the House in 1979, although with the election of Ronald Reagan and a Republican Senate majority in 1980, further efforts to limit busing were made. The Reagan administration ordered the Justice Department to oppose mandatory busing in many cases.

## Affirmative action and black progress

Exactly what does *equality* mean? That the door of opportunity be opened for all through the removal of legal barriers? Or that those who actually pass through that door represent a true racial and ethnic cross-section of the population? Simply that more blacks, for example, enter the middle class, or become corporate executives and government officials? Or that blacks as a group achieve real economic parity with whites?

In exploring these questions, we will look first at the *Bakke* case, which involved many of the basic issues raised by **affirmative action**—the attempt to remedy past discrimination by favoring minorities in particular programs. We will then turn to a discussion of black progress in political, economic, and social matters—a topic that turns out to be far more complicated than it may at first appear.

The *Bakke* case: At age 31, Allan Paul Bakke became interested in pursuing a career in medicine and very determinedly set out to receive training as a physician. In his initial attempts to get into medical school, he was rejected by both the University of Southern California and Northwestern University—the latter chiefly because of his age. The following year, he sought entry into eleven medical schools, none of which admitted him. One of these schools was the University of California at Davis, which had had a special-admissions program for students who were well-qualified for medical school but who would not have been admitted through the regular competitive admissions procedures. Almost all special-ad-

TABLE 21.2
## Public attitudes on busing and integrated schools, 1981

| | Integrated schools | | |
| | All white parents | South | Rest of U.S. |
|---|---|---|---|
| Would object to sending children to schools where: | | | |
| A few children are black | 5% | 5% | 5% |
| One-half are black | 23 | 27 | 22 |
| More than one-half are black | 55 | 66 | 51 |
| No objections | 45 | 34 | 49 |

| | Busing for better racial balance | | |
| | Favor | Oppose | No opinion |
|---|---|---|---|
| NATIONAL | 22% | 72% | 6% |
| Whites | 17 | 78 | 5 |
| Blacks | 60 | 30 | 10 |
| East | 23 | 69 | 8 |
| Midwest | 18 | 76 | 6 |
| South | 25 | 71 | 4 |
| West | 24 | 70 | 6 |
| College education | 21 | 75 | 4 |
| High school | 22 | 72 | 6 |
| Grade school | 27 | 65 | 8 |
| Under 30 years | 31 | 62 | 7 |
| 30–49 years | 21 | 75 | 4 |
| 50 and older | 18 | 76 | 6 |

Source: Gallup poll, January 1981. In January 1981, a Gallup poll found Americans overwhelmingly opposed to busing in order to achieve racial balance. Of interest, white parents did not object to integrated schools as long as half or fewer of the students were black.

missions students were members of minorities. Of the one hundred places at the Davis Medical School, sixteen were reserved for special admissions. When Bakke applied yet again, and again was turned down despite scoring higher than some minority applicants who were accepted, he went to court. In a lawsuit filed in state courts, he charged that he had been the victim of discrimination, in that the affirmative action program of the Davis Medical School had unfairly reduced the number of places available for more-qualified students. Bakke's main purpose in bringing the suit was not so much to challenge racial "quotas" (as he put it) in general, as to get himself into medical school.

When the California Supreme Court upheld Bakke's position, the state appealed the case to the Supreme Court. The case involved a serious conflict between two apparently worthwhile goals: affirmative action to aid disadvantaged groups, and equal treatment for all, regardless of race, ethnicity, or sex. The dilemma was made all the more difficult because of the increased pressures on law and medical school admissions. In 1970, only 1 percent of American lawyers, and only 2 percent of doctors and 6 percent of medical students, were black.

Another factor influencing the political atmosphere surrounding the *Bakke* case was a growing disenchantment with affirmative action programs, on the grounds that they led to reverse discrimination. For example, many employers had been required to employ and promote more women and minority group members as a condition for doing business with government agencies. To avoid losing business, employers gave preference in hiring and promotion to applicants on basis of race and sex—a form of reverse discrimination against white males.

The Supreme Court decision in *Regents of the University of California* v. *Allan Bakke*, handed down in the spring of 1978, was marked by a notable lack of unanimity.[12] The Court ruled, 5–4, that Bakke should be admitted to the Davis Medical School. But the Court *really* divided 4–1–4. One block of four justices took the position that the Civil Rights Act of 1964 prohibits racial quotas such as that used by the Davis Medical School. The other group of four argued that the Davis program was permissible. The

swing vote belonged to Justice Lewis F. Powell, Jr. Powell sided with the first group on one set of issues and with the other group on another set. The end result was that whereas the Davis special-admissions program was struck down and Bakke ordered admitted, the use of race as a factor in admissions procedures was deemed acceptable so long as there were no "quotas" and the objectives of the "race-conscious" admissions procedures were "reasonable"— such as to ensure a diverse student body. Powell's "solution" had a certain appeal—it banned quotas while allowing continued preferential admissions under the banner of "student diversity." Yet it was not at all clear what standards, if any, applied to this notion of diversity. Such a vague concept could be used to establish informal quotas of any sort.

*Bakke* turned out not to be the landmark case many had expected. Because no firm majority emerged on the Court, there was no transformation of legal doctrine comparable to that achieved in the *Brown* decision in 1954. Given only limited guidance, lower courts later handed down contradictory decisions. One U.S. circuit court of appeals approved a plan requiring that blacks comprise 50 percent of those promoted to sergeant in Detroit's police force. Another appeals court, however, declared illegal a plan requiring specific minority representation on two student government boards at a state university. Further, the admissions plan at one law school was struck down, even though it contained no quotas, whereas a minority hiring program that did set quotas was approved.

In *Fullilove* v. *Klutznick* (1980), the Supreme Court clarified matters a bit.[13] Here the Court upheld federal regulations stipulating that 10 percent of federal public-works contracts be set aside for companies controlled by minority group members. But the Court limited its ruling to *Congress's* powers, leaving educational institutions, government agencies, and the states without definitive guidance on the affirmative action issues.

In a ruling that reversed earlier decisions supporting affirmative action arrangements in employment, the Supreme Court found in *Memphis Fire Department* v. *Stotts* (1984) that a court could not order an employer to protect the jobs of recently hired black employees at the expense of whites who had more seniority.[14] Some observers felt that this decision represented a serious blow to affirmative action programs, whereas others saw it as rather narrow in application, since a preexisting seniority agreement played an important role in the Court's reasoning. In the majority opinion, Justice Byron White stated that the policy of the Civil Rights Act of 1964 was "to provide make-whole relief only to those who have been actual victims of illegal discrimination." Were such a guideline to be applied in general, affirmative action programs would be in serious trouble. The question is whether an *entire group* is entitled to affirmative action to remedy discrimination without any one member having to prove that he or she was actually discriminated against.

**Black progress:** The day after the *Bakke* decision was handed down, a Harvard admissions officer sent the following letter to *The New York Times* on June 28, 1978:

To the Editor:

It is strange that on the day of the famous Bakke decision ABC televised a frightening documentary, "Youth Terror: A View from Behind the Gun," about the millions of bitter and hopelessly lost members of minorities in the urban centers of this country.

If that documentary accurately reflects the existence of these young people (I have no reason to think it does not), then debating the correctness of the Supreme Court's Bakke decision is like arguing over sun-deck chairs on the *Titanic*.

From this sobering perspective, we will consider the question of black progress over the past twenty-five years.

Obviously, much has changed. There are no more legally segregated restaurants, motels, drinking fountains, bathrooms, schools, armies. Instead of arguing about whether a black can be admitted to an all-white law school, we're now arguing about *Bakke*. Systematic attempts to keep blacks from the voting booth are a thing of the past. Indeed, blacks are voting in ever-greater numbers, and more and more black officials are being elected. Recognizing political reality, a new crop of Southern governors has buried hard-line segregationist styles. On the eco-

nomic level, poverty has been diminished, and increasing numbers of blacks are entering the middle class, as opportunities have enlarged.

Yet, just as obviously, much has not changed. There are still the black ghettos—Harlem, Bedford-Stuyvesant, Watts. There is still a great disparity between black and white income levels. The death and infant-mortality rates remain higher among blacks, as do crime and unemployment rates (Figure 21.2).

The median weekly income for all full-time work-

TABLE 21.3
## Public attitudes on preferences and quotas, 1978

*Q.* The government should see to it that people who have been discriminated against in the past get a better break in the future.

|  | Whites | Blacks |
|---|---|---|
| Agree | 63% | 88% |
| Disagree | 32 | 9 |

*Q.* Businesses should be required to hire a certain number of minority workers.

|  | Whites | Blacks |
|---|---|---|
| Agree | 35 | 64 |
| Disagree | 50 | 26 |

*Q.* Colleges and graduate schools should give special consideration to the best minority applicants, to help more of them get admitted than would otherwise be the case.

|  | Whites | Blacks |
|---|---|---|
| Agree | 59 | 83 |
| Disagree | 36 | 16 |

*Q.* Should schools reserve a number of places for qualified minority applicants if that meant that some qualified white applicants wouldn't be admitted?

|  | Whites | Blacks |
|---|---|---|
| Approve | 32 | 46 |
| Disapprove | 60 | 42 |

Popular attitudes toward the affirmative action/quota issue accord fairly well with the mix arrived at by the split Court in *Bakke*. About 60 percent of whites and 80–90 percent of blacks approve of providing some special programs or consideration for minorities. When it comes to any quota-linked arrangement, however, the white percentages reverse themselves—60 percent oppose. Among blacks, there is also less approval.

Source: S. M. Lipset and W. Schneider, "The Bakke Case: How Would It Be Decided at the Bar of Public Opinion?" *Public Opinion*, March/April 1978.

ers in 1982 was $309 a week. But for white men the median was $382; for black men, $281; and for Hispanic men, $272. White women earned $244; black women, $223; and Hispanic women, $207. In 1982, 36 percent of all blacks were officially classified as poor, compared with 12 percent of whites. The black unemployment rate has generally remained almost twice that of whites. For black youth, the jobless figures have hovered around 40 percent. It appears that a permanent black underclass has developed, and that much of this generation of ghetto youth will never actually enter the work force. Government efforts to reach this group through community development and job training programs have largely failed.

Many in and out of government have taken a more pessimistic view toward what could be done to change this situation. Since previous programs haven't worked, why continue to fund them? This argument implies an abandonment by government of the very people who most need its efforts.

**The Reagan perspective:** Many suspected that policies to assist blacks and other minorities would not be a high priority of the Reagan administration, and to critics, the actions of the administration bore out these suspicions. Along with cutting many programs of particular assistance to blacks, the administration showed considerable reluctance to endorse the extension of the Voting Rights Act and initially supported tax exemptions for segregated schools. President Reagan also took a set of positions opposed to quotas, affirmative action programs of many kinds, and court-ordered busing arrangements.

In a highly inflammatory political move, the president fired three members of the Civil Rights Commission, the federal government's civil rights watch-

FIGURE 21.2

Blacks in America: A Statistical Profile. *Source: The* *New York Times*, August 28, 1983.

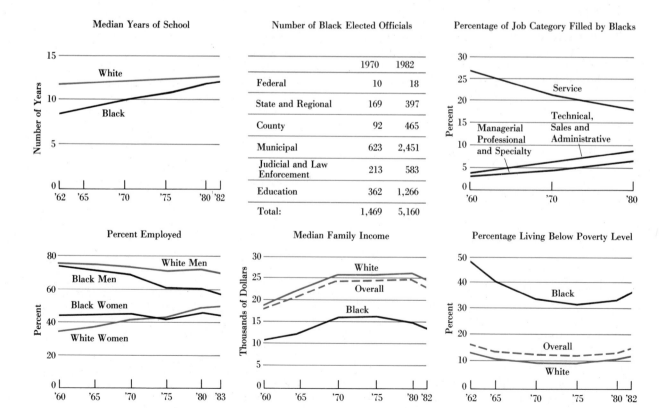

| | 1970 | 1982 |
|---|---|---|
| Federal | 10 | 18 |
| State and Regional | 169 | 397 |
| County | 92 | 465 |
| Municipal | 623 | 2,451 |
| Judicial and Law Enforcement | 213 | 583 |
| Education | 362 | 1,266 |
| Total: | 1,469 | 5,160 |

dog, and replaced them with appointees who did not favor race-based formulas to correct past discrimination.[15] One of the new Reagan appointees, John Bunzel, stated that

it is a crude oversimplification . . . to suggest that racism and discrimination are the root cause of why certain minority groups fall below the average in income and occupation. To accept this premise is to overlook better-than-average achievements of other minorities that have suffered discrimination. Differences among ethnic groups are complex and deeply anchored. This is why doubling the Equal Employment Opportunity Commission's resources or mandating preferential employment and promotion according to some race-based formula will not really help minorities at the low end of the ladder.

In defense of its positions, the administration argued that quotas constituted a denial of equal protection, both for minorities and for women; that its "free-market" economic programs would do more for the poor than social programs could accomplish; and that mandatory busing should no longer be required where past discrimination had been corrected.

## Women and equality

[The reason for high unemployment] is not as much recession as it is the great increase in the people going into the job market, and ladies, I'm not picking on anyone, but [it is] because of the increase in women who are working today and two-worker families.

President Ronald Reagan, April 1982

Once you see work as crucial to both men's and women's sense of who they are, that kind of statement is abhorrent.

Rosalind Barnett, psychologist,
Wellesley College

The issue of equality for women touches a deep nerve in our culture. Western societies in general have been strongly patriarchal. Under long-established traditions of male dominance, the particular roles charted out for women have been quite clearly distinguished from those allowed for males. For most of U.S. history, accordingly, women were relegated to the roles of child-raisers and homekeepers. They also were reared as the passive partners in life—the less aggressive, the more tender-minded and emotional, the less sexual.

Champions of equality for women have challenged such conceptions. At the minimum, they have asserted, regardless of intrinsic differences in the natures of men and women, women are entitled to be judged as individuals and to make their way in the world just as men do. In recent decades, feminists have directed their efforts chiefly at achieving equality in jobs and pay levels and in getting constitutional recognition of the issue of equality for women.

In the United States today, many more women are working than ever before. In 1950, 34 percent of all women worked outside the home; in 1982, 52 percent did so.[16] But over 80 percent of all working women hold clerical, sales, service, and light factory positions, and considerable discrimination in jobs and in pay levels has remained. A male high school dropout earns, on the average, $1,600 more than a woman with a college degree. Median yearly income for all women was $13,663 in 1982, compared with $21,655 for men—63 percent of the male total. This level of disparity has changed little since the enactment of legislation in 1963 supposedly providing for equal pay for women. Even in the federal government, women hold 75 percent of the lowest-paying jobs, and only 3 percent earn more than $40,000 a year. Of course, many women lack the education or training to compete for better positions.

Lately the number of women in managerial and professional roles has increased, and women have entered professional schools, such as in law and medicine, in record numbers. In 1982, 30 percent of law school graduates were women. By 1985, an estimated 18 percent of all professionals in the United States were women. Yet at managerial levels in industry, despite some increase in the representation of women, the average female's salary is only slightly more than 50 percent of that of a male counterpart.

In the political sector, the ranks of female state legislators rose from 301 in 1969 to 908 in 1981, and those of female elected officials from 5,765 in

In recent years many jobs previously open only to men have been opened to women. Here, a police-woman talks to a man stopped for running a red light.

1975 to 16,881 by 1982. Yet these are still very small percentages of the total number of elected officials and state legislators. In 1985, there were two women governors, five women lieutenant-governors, eleven women secretaries of state, eleven women state treasurers, and ninety women mayors of cities with more than 30,000 inhabitants.[17]

### Defeat of the ERA

The wording of the **Equal Rights Amendment** is remarkably simple: "Equality of rights under the law shall not be denied or abridged by the United States or by any state on account of sex." The constitutional amendment was first proposed in 1923 by feminist Alice Paul, and introduced into Congress that year. It was not until 1972 that Congress passed the ERA, on a crest of national feeling in support of equal rights. Congress set a seven-year deadline for passage by state legislatures.

At first, the going seemed rather easy. Twenty-two states had ratified the amendment by the end of 1972.

Then anti-ERA forces mobilized, and a backlash began. The ensuing struggle over the amendment was intense. Anti-ERA leader Phyllis Schlafly, supported by conservative groups, charged that the amendment would undermine the American family. Schlafly and her allies argued that the ERA would require women to serve in combat and would eliminate the need for men to pay alimony and to support their wives and children. They conjured up a unisex world created by the ERA, in which sex differences would be altogether erased and federal bureaucrats and judges would gain new powers over marriage, divorce, and other areas traditionally under the jurisdiction of the states.

Pro-ERA forces, led by the National Organization of Women, also demonstrated a capacity for applying sustained pressure tactics. When it seemed clear that the ERA would not pass within the seven-year deadline, proponents of the measure succeeded in gaining a three-year extension from Congress, until 1982. The pro-ERA forces stressed the significance of the amendment in supplying a national standard of equal treatment for women. They pointed out its importance in the area of job equality. In the end, however, their efforts fell short. The anti-ERA forces were better organized and better financed, and needed only to prevent ratification by thirteen out of fifty states. Of the fifteen states that never passed the ERA and the five that passed it and later rescinded passage, a majority were Southern—another testament to the enduring conservative tendencies of that region.

| Government actions
| on gender
| discrimination

Two of the most important pieces of civil rights legislation of the 1960s were the Equal Pay Act of 1963, which required that men and women receive equal remuneration for similar jobs; and Title VII of the

Civil Rights Act of 1964, which prohibited sexual discrimination in employment and by state and local governments. (The Title VII provisions were originally suggested by congressional conservatives, who thought that the addition of such controversial measures would lead to the defeat of the Civil Rights Act as a whole. They were wrong.) In 1972 the Title VII provisions were extended to educational institutions under the nomenclature of Title IX. The enactment of Title IX led to a steady stream of litigation brought by women—and even, occasionally, men— who felt they had been discriminated against in admissions procedures, financial aid, extracurricular activities, athletics, health services, sex-stereotyped courses, counseling programs, dormitory rules, and other campus regulations.

Two executive orders lent momentum to the drive to reduce discrimination based on gender. A 1967 executive order forbade discrimination in federal employment and required companies with $50,000 or more in federal contracts to submit affirmative action plans for women in addition to such plans for minorities. Another executive order, promulgated in 1969, called for equal opportunities for women throughout the federal government itself and established a program to implement this commitment.

At the same time, the courts began to play a more significant role in redefining "gender discrimination." Until 1971 the courts had largely upheld the government's authority to "classify by gender." Some court decisions prevented women from entering certain professions (such as bartending), or engaging in certain activities; other decisions were aimed at

EQUALITY OF RIGHTS UNDER THE LAW SHALL NOT BE DENIED OR ABRIDGED
BY THE UNITED STATES OR BY ANY STATE ON ACCOUNT OF SEX

The full text of the proposed Equal Rights Amendment, unfurled in a dramatic, if familiar, context. Seated is Isola Dubik, a former suffragette and a campaigner for women's rights.

"protecting" women (as in certain family issues connected with child custody and alimony). For decades the courts, reflecting the views of the society as a whole, found that a woman's appropriate place was still in the home.

As legislative and social attitudes changed, however, the courts faced many new problems. From 1974 to 1977 the Supreme Court dealt with more cases related to the rights of men and women than it had decided in all its previous history. Since that period, gender discrimination cases have constantly been on the Court's agenda. Two cases in particular marked new departures.

The first significant case concerned a young man who committed suicide at the age of nineteen. His mother, Sally Reed, applied to be the administrator of his estate; his father applied two weeks later. Both were residents of Idaho, and under Idaho law, "As between persona equally entitled to administer a decedent's estate, males must be preferred to females." The American Civil Liberties Union took the case to the Supreme Court, which unanimously ruled that the drawing of a sex line was inconsistent with the equal protection provisions of the Fourteenth Amendment.[18]

The second case was brought by Charles Moritz, a 63-year-old unmarried man who lived with and took care of his mother. Moritz had hired a nurse to look after his mother during the day. The Internal Revenue Service permitted the partial deduction of such expenses for a daughter who had never been married and was caring for a parent, but did not allow sons to make such deductions. Moritz sued, charging discrimination, and a U.S. Appeals Court overturned the IRS regulation, ruling that the distinction between dutiful sons and dutiful daughters was arbitrary.[19] After the *Moritz* case the U.S. solicitor general informed the Court that its decision called into question hundreds of laws nationwide that contained "gender-based references." The Supreme Court refused to hear the case on appeal.

Although the Court has struck down sex discrimination in a number of other cases involving both men and women, it has not been willing to exclude gender considerations completely. Most importantly,

in a 6–3 decision handed down in 1981, it upheld the all-male draft registration mandated by Congress. The Court majority argued that Congress had carefully studied the inclusion of women and had decided that for reasons of "military flexibility" women should be excluded. The Court minority argued that the all-male provision violated equal protection guarantees in the Constitution. In 1984 the Supreme Court narrowed some of the protections against gender discrimination in education in the *Grove City* case, in which it found that the government could enforce antidiscrimination requirements in federal law only in the *specific* educational "program or activity" receiving federal money, and not in all programs at the university in question.

Overall, then, the courts have failed to develop clear guidelines on exactly when the drawing of gender-linked legal lines is constitutionally legitimate. The Court has not been as hard on gender discrimination as on racial discrimination, arguing that gender discriminations are sometimes valid since men and women are not always "similarly situated." The Court has upheld, for example, statutory rape laws that punish only men, on the grounds that since only women can become pregnant, the state can legitimately punish for rape men who seduce underage girls while not punishing women who seduce underage boys.

A gender-related issue that emerged in the 1980s was that of "comparable worth." Advocates of the concept of comparable worth have argued that a long history of sex-based discrimination had created systematic pay inequalities between certain female-dominated jobs and comparable male-dominated jobs. Women were being paid less, in other words, for jobs demanding comparable skills and training. Proponents of comparable worth called for job evaluation studies, to establish equitable pay standards, and the idea caught on. By 1985, several states, including Minnesota and Iowa, had adopted comparable-worth standards for state jobs, and several others had authorized studies. Similar legislation was put before Congress, and some federal employees went to court, charging violations of the Federal Equal Pay Act of 1963.[20]

The Reagan administration opposed comparable worth. A Reagan-appointee majority in the Civil Rights Committee voted to reject the doctrine in April 1985. Chairman of the Committee, Clarence M. Pendelton, Jr., argued that comparable worth advocates were taking "a disingenuous attempt to restructure our free enterprise system into a state-controlled system under the false guise of fairness."[21]

## Social rights

Throughout the twentieth century, as we saw in Chapters 5 and 16, the federal government has played a steadily widening role in protecting citizens against various health and safety hazards. When the Reagan administration came to power in 1981, it brought with it a new approach to health and safety enforcement—or, some might say, a nonapproach. The administration deemphasized federal regulation, arguing for increased "voluntary compliance" as opposed to federal enforcement, and dropped or diluted specific standards and procedures designed to impose stricter standards on U.S. industry.[22] The Food and Drug Administration revoked a regulation requiring the manufacturers of ten classes of prescription drugs to provide package inserts containing information on proper use of drugs and their potential side effects. The secretary of transportation revoked vehicle safety standards requiring "passive restraints" (airbags) in U.S.-made cars. The secretary of agriculture relaxed standards governing the composition and labeling of mechanically processed meat products, and cut back on inspections of meat plants. The director of the Mine Safety and Health Administration cut the number of mine inspections by 8 percent, and the number of inspectors by 10 percent; as a result, citations issued by the agency fell by 15 percent.

Administration officials defended these and similar actions on a variety of grounds. They emphasized the need to lighten the burden of federal regulation on industry, in order to lessen the costs of production

and to encourage more trust between industry and government. Critics saw many dangers in this permissive regulatory approach, however. Joan Claybrook, who had been head of the National Highway Traffic Safety Administration under President Jimmy Carter, summarized the critics' position as follows:

Rather than bolster the federal health and safety regulatory agencies in their work to protect the public, the Reagan administration, animated by profound ignorance and rigid ideology, has inflicted severe damage on these unique institutions of our society. The agencies no longer respond to the needs of unorganized victims of technological hazards. Instead, they service the business executives and stockholders who are responsible for the hazards. . . . Without government regulation, a manufacturer regulates the quality, content, design and performance of products to suit *its* needs. . . . When the federal government regulates on behalf of health and safety, however, a measure of public responsibility is established for all manufacturers. . . . Contrary to the rhetoric of the Chamber of Commerce, the question is not whether there is too much regulation in the marketplace, but rather *who* is doing the regulating."[23]

Reagan supporters replied that there is a point of diminishing returns in the efforts of government to regulate industry. Part of the reason for the declining performance of U.S. industry, they maintained, was the excessive complexity of federal rules.

Are there basic rights to health and safety that transcend economic considerations? How much, after all, is a cotton industry worker's life worth (see box)? And who is empowered to place a price upon it? Can federal agencies perform their functions without interfering in business operations, or is a good deal of interference required to get results? Whose estimates of the costs of regulation, and the incidence of illness, should we believe—those set forth by industry or those put forward by industry's potential victims and their advocates? These are intricate moral, economic, and technical issues. But the longer U.S. society remains bogged down in arguments of such issues, the longer it will take to frame and implement effective regulation that actually does protect life and health. The costs of effective action can be considerable—but so can the costs of delay.

## OSHA and cotton dust

In 1970, Congress established the Occupational Safety and Health Administration (OSHA) with a mandate to issue regulations that would enhance worker safety. Early in its existence, OSHA targeted cotton dust as a major workplace health hazard. Cotton dust is a common problem in textile mills, but its consequences are a matter of controversy. Many health researchers have claimed that exposure to certain levels of cotton dust triggers the development of "brown lung" disease, which leads to lung deterioration and impaired functioning or death. OSHA estimated in 1971 that of five hundred thousand textile workers, eighty-four thousand had some degree of brown lung, and at least thirty-five thousand current and retired workers had been permanently disabled by it. Representatives of the textile industry claimed that lung impairment among workers could be traced to other causes, such as smoking.

---

## Conclusions

What insights into public policy-making can we glean from this excursion into recent rights and liberties controversies? To begin with, we can note that some problems can remain latent—on the political back burner—for years, decades, or even generations. The issues of equality raised in recent years by blacks and women had largely been ignored by public policymakers for more than a century. Only from time to time are such issues raised forcefully enough to compel change.

What makes a latent issue become a pressing policy concern? That is, how does it get on the agenda of matters that political elites *must* cope with? At least three factors are involved. For one thing the affected group must organize itself—a process that often requires a significant shift of consciousness within the group itself. Its self-image must alter: feelings of fatalism and hopelessness must give way to indignation and the belief that some change is possible. A second factor is a shift in the attitudes of political elites. This was clearly signaled in the case of blacks' rights by various actions of the Roosevelt and Truman administrations and, most importantly, by the Supreme Court's *Brown* decision of 1954. *Brown* provided a legal and constitutional argument to which supporters of equal rights could turn for support. With this shift, the law became an ally instead of an

These workers operate in a plant that is pervaded by cotton dust. One key question was whether workers should be protected by the use of individual masks, or whether a factory-wide air-cleaning system was more appropriate.

OSHA proposed a standard for cotton dust, but internal politicking within the Nixon administration kept it from being issued. When no action had been taken by the end of 1975, a suit was brought by the Textile Workers Union and the North Carolina Public Interest Research Group. The standard was finally issued in 1978.

The textile industry immediately challenged the new standard in the courts, claiming that the standard required unreasonable expenses on the part of the industry and that these costs were not proportional to the benefits that would accrue. A federal appeals court judge upheld the OSHA standard, however. He argued that Congress's mandate in creating OSHA did not require the agency to do a formal cost-benefit analysis to justify its standards. All it was required to do was propose feasible standards that were beneficial to the workers involved. (In fact, a study requested by Congress found that OSHA's standard did offer the best worker protection at the least cost.) The long struggle between the textile workers and the textile industry over brown lung seemed about to come to a close.

The advent of the Reagan administration changed that situation, however. The new director of OSHA, Thorne Auchter, announced that the agency wanted to reexamine its position and embark on a careful cost-benefit analysis of the cotton dust standard and other standards. OSHA then requested that the Supreme Court reverse the lower-court ruling upholding its own standard and return the cotton dust standard to the agency for further review. The Court denied the request, thus upholding the 1978 standard. Despite this decision, OSHA in 1983 proposed a revised cotton dust standard that would exclude over three hundred thousand workers in similar industries, such as knitting.

Source: R. Guerasci and G. Peck, "Brown Lung Settlement Lets Textile Workers Breathe Easier," *In These Times*, August 10–23, 1983.

---

opponent. The third key factor is a shift in the attitudes of the general public. Racial and sexual attitudes have been changing fairly rapidly in the United States, and these changes have helped set the stage for the movements for blacks' and women's rights.

From a democratic perspective, the United States has made enormous progress in recent decades toward achieving its own ideals. The steps taken by and for minorities and women have been major achievements. It is difficult to remember now, in the mid-1980s, that only twenty years ago millions of American blacks were systematically prevented from voting and that the battle for equal rights for women had barely begun. Of all currently democratic nations, the United States had one of the most difficult situations of inequality to come to terms with—our heritage of black slavery. Overcoming the system of legal segregation marked a definite coming of age of the democratic ideal in this country—a realization that we had lived with our own hypocrisy long enough.

Of course, these affirmative steps have not ended the matter. In place of the old, clear issues of legal rights and equal protection, we find newer, subtler, more complex issues such as affirmative action, busing, the ERA, and "comparable worth." It is sobering to reflect on the continuing economic and social problems of blacks and some other minorities in U.S. society, and to realize that these problems are not likely to be solved anytime in the near future.

To turn to other aspects of liberties and rights

issues, it is also encouraging to find new and important items on the public agenda that reflect democratic concerns. The upsurge of interest in health and safety matters reflects a broadened sense of social responsibility—an extension of the idea of community to many who were previously unprotected. This is a definite change in the public agenda—and from a democratic perspective, a salutary one. In addition, the Freedom of Information Act supplies us with a significant tool for enhancing public knowledge and better assessing whether government lives up to its responsibilities. Without getting into the arguments about the appropriate scope of that Act, we can note simply that it has greatly increased the public's understanding of what government has and has not done—vital concerns in a democratic nation.

One of the most interesting questions that arises from this chapter is the matter of *how* intensely-felt issues are dealt with in our political processes. Issues such as abortion, pornography, busing, and gay rights trigger deep and potentially explosive responses. From a democratic perspective, we would hope that the dialogue essential to a civil and respectful public life could be carried out relatively free of violence, of stereotyping, abuse, and threat. How have we done in this regard? Here the picture is mixed. We have had our share of uncivil disobedience, of raw and threatening dissent, of crude accusations and intolerance. Yet on the whole, our political processes have been able to deal with such issues, to include the many voices that clamor to be heard on these subjects, and to hammer out various compromises that, if not entirely satisfactory, are livable for most of us. We could have done considerably worse.

## NOTES

1 S. M. Lipset and Earl Raab, *The Politics of Unreason* (Chicago: University of Chicago Press, 1978).

2 Joseph Gusfield, *Symbolic Crusade* (Urbana, Ill.: University of Illinois Press, 1963).

3 354 U.S. 476 (1957).

4 *Mernous* v. *Attorney General of Massachusetts*, 383 U.S. 413 (1966).

510

5 93 S. Ct. 2607 (1973).

6 Jean B. Elshtain, "The New Porn Wars," *The New Republic*, June 25, 1984, pp. 15–20.

7 410 U.S. 113 (1973).

8 *Congressional Digest*, February 1982, p. 47.

9 391 U.S. 430 (1960).

10 402 U.S. 1 (1971).

11 Warren E. Miller and Donald E. Stokes, "Constituency Influence in Congress," *American Political Science Review* 57 (March 1963): 45–56.

12 438 U.S. 265 (1978).

13 100 S. Ct. 2758 (1980).

14 82 U.S. 229 (1984). For a discussion of the implications of the Memphis case, see "Seniority vs. Minorities—Impact of Court Ruling," *U.S. News and World Report*, June 25, 1984, pp. 22–23; and F. Barbash and K. Sawyer, "A New Era of 'Race Neutrality' in Hiring?" *Washington Post*, National Weekly Edition, June 25, 1984.

15 John H. Bunzel, "Promoting Rights," *The New York Times*, September 20, 1983.

16 See "Working Women," *U.S. News and World Report*, January 15, 1979, pp. 64–68.

17 *U.S. News and World Report*, March 4, 1985, 76–77.

18 *Reed* v. *Reed*, 404 U.S. 71 (1971).

19 Commissioner of Internal Revenue v. Moritz. U.S. Court of Appeals, 10th Circuit 72–1298.

20 William French Smith, "Comparable Worth: Flirting with Disaster," *Washington Post*, National Weekly Edition, February 11, 1985, p. 24.

21 *The New York Times*, April 12, 1985, p. 11.

22 P. Simon and K. Hughes, "OSHA: Industry's New Friend," *The New York Times*, September 5, 1983, p. 19; Christine Russell, "Government Heedless of Hazards in Food, Consumers Contend," *Washington Post*, April 6, 1983; and Ben A. Franklin, "OSHA Changes . . . ," *The New York Times*, April 9, 1984, Section II, p. 16.

23 Joan Claybrook, *et al.*, *Retreat from Safety: Reagan's Attack on America's Health* (New York: Pantheon, 1984), pp. xi and xiii.

## SELECTED READINGS

For insightful treatments of civil liberties matters, see Victor Marchetti and John D. Marks, *The CIA and the*

*Cult of Intelligence* (New York: Knopf, 1974); David M. O'Brien, *The Public's Right to Know* (New York: Praeger, 1981); and B. F. Chamberlin and C. J. Brown, eds., *The First Amendment Reconsidered* (New York: Longman's, 1982).

On a variety of civil rights issues, consider Richard Kluger, *Simple Justice* (New York: Vintage, 1977); J. H. Wilkinson, *From Brown to Bakke* (New York: Oxford University Press, 1979); James Coleman, *Equality of Educational Opportunity* (Washington, D.C.: U.S. Government Printing Office, 1966); J. Dreyfuss and C. Lawrence, *The Bakke Case* (New York: Harcourt, 1979); Thomas Sowell, *Civil Rights: Rhetoric or Reality?* (New York: Morrow, 1983); Jo Freeman, *The Politics of Woman's Liberation* (New York: Longman's, 1975); Janet K. Boles, *The Politics of the Equal Rights Amendment* (New York: Longman's, 1979); and Lois G. Forer, *Money and Justice* (New York: Norton, 1984).

On the issues involved in social rights, look at John Mendeloff, *Regulating Safety* (Cambridge, Mass.: MIT Press, 1979); Nicholas Ashford, *Crisis in the Work Place* (Cambridge, Mass.: MIT Press, 1976); E. J. Mishan, *Economics for Social Decisions* (New York: Praeger, 1973); and E. Bardach and R. A. Kagan, *Social Regulation* (San Francisco: ICS Press, 1984).

On school integration and related issues see Jennifer L. Hochschild, *The New American Dilemma: Liberal Democracy and School Desegregation* (New Haven, Conn.: Yale University Press, 1984); Raymond Wolters, *The Burden of Brown: Thirty Years of School Desegregation* (University of Tennessee Press, 1978); Tony Freyer, *The Little Rock Crisis: A Constitutional Interpretation* (Westport, Conn.: Greenwood Press, 1984). On popular prejudices and their consequences, see Jonathan Rieder, *Canarsie: The Jews and Italians of Brooklyn Against Liberalism* (Cambridge, Mass.: Harvard University Press, 1985).

# Chapter
twenty-two

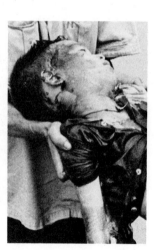

# Foreign and defense policies

# What values are we defending?

THE United States emerged from World War II a Great Power—in fact, the dominant power in the world. Since 1945, U.S. foreign policy has been marked by both successes and failures. The United States "contained" the Soviet Union, as it aimed to do, but fought frustrating and confusing wars in Korea and Vietnam. It engineered the overthrow of certain governments for dubious reasons, but often later, as in Iran, stood by while "friendly" governments fell. The issues grew more complex. In the Cold War against the Soviet Union, Americans often found themselves aiding allegedly undemocratic, or even tyrannical governments. Just what values were we defending?

Americans like to think of themselves as the chief defenders of that abstraction, "the free world." Without us, it has been said, the Soviets, and perhaps others, would dominate the globe. Democratic societies would be doomed. Such views have often led the United States to assume a very militant posture in the world—a posture involving tremendous investment in armaments and a capacity to intervene almost anywhere.

Not everyone has shared this view of our nation's mission, however. Many have called us "imperialists," citing our part in overthrowing foreign governments and the worldwide interests of U.S.-based multinational corporations. Many have resented our bigness, our ability as a great power to "throw our weight around." During the Vietnam War, many Americans came to question the wisdom of U.S. policymakers and the directions of U.S. foreign policies. Was the United States really aiding freedom?

In this chapter, we first take a look at the historical evolution of U.S. foreign policy, and then examine those who contribute to the making of U.S. foreign policy. Next, we focus on three major issues of foreign policy: the U.S.-Soviet rivalry, the arms race, and the complex problems of Third World politics. Underlying all these issues, we will find, is the question of *values:* What has the United States chosen to stand for? What values have we sought to defend? What battles have we chosen to fight, and why? As we will see, Americans have often disagreed intensely over these questions.

## A historical perspective

In order to gain a focus on America's present role in the world, we need to step back and review a bit of history. The themes of expansionism and growing power have figured heavily at certain stages of U.S. national development.

## Isolation and expansion

For most of its history, the United States was isolated from (though not unaffected by) the mainstream of international politics. Isolation was the preference of many of our political leaders. They feared, as George Washington put it, becoming involved in "entangling alliances" that would drag us into the "corrupt" maze of European rivalries and intrigue.

Although somewhat isolated from European struggles, the United States was a decidedly expansionist power within the Western Hemisphere. We continually warred with the Native Americans, driving them from their traditional lands. In 1823, President James Monroe enunciated the Monroe Doctrine, in which he warned European powers to keep out of the Western Hemisphere and declared our right to oversee developments in North and South America. From 1845 to 1848, we fought with Mexico, and acquired considerable territory as a result.

By the beginning of the twentieth century, the United States had begun to intervene further from home. U.S. forces first defeated Spanish forces in both Cuba and the Philippines and then stopped revolutions in both countries. As the United States was on the way to becoming a Pacific power, some U.S. leaders proclaimed their devotion to an "Open Door" policy—meaning that we stood for free trade with other nations. Nations that preferred a less open door, such as Japan, were coerced into changing their minds.

During the first thirty years of this century, U.S. forces intervened frequently in various Latin American countries, usually to put down revolutions. These interventions were defended as necessary to keep the peace in the hemisphere—but to their critics, they seemed motivated principally by a desire to protect U.S. business interests.

Most Americans did not see U.S. expansionism as a purely selfish endeavor. Interventions, even against the Native Americans, were often explained as part of a "mission"—to defend the rights of free trade, or the rights of self-determination.

**World War I and II:** The United States entered both world wars rather late. We stayed out of World War I until April 1917, by which time the war had

It's over! The Japanese had surrendered and U.S. servicemen celebrate. We had won a war on two fronts and suffered relatively little damage to our own society.

been raging for over two years. When we did enter, President Woodrow Wilson saw U.S. participation as a crusade to free the world from the curse of dictatorship and war—to make the world, in his words, "safe for democracy." Wilson struggled to help create the League of Nations (a forerunner of the United Nations) after World War I, but isolationist sentiment, and Wilson's own inflexibility, led the Senate to reject U.S. membership in the League. In the aftermath of the war, we returned, in part, to isolation from European affairs.

World War II had been going on in Europe for more than two years before we became involved in December 1941. President Franklin Roosevelt had been anxious to come to the aid of anti-fascist forces in the late 1930s, but antiwar and isolationist feeling was still running high. Had it not been for the Japanese attack on Pearl Harbor, we may have remained on the sidelines indefinitely.

Carter, Sadat, and Begin signing the Camp David Accords. The United States has been a staunch ally of Israel since its founding in 1948, but it has also sought to maintain influence in the Arab world. Cold War rivalries continued to influence Mideast policies, but that region offered its own rich complexity of problems. U.S. efforts to solve some of them reached a high point with Camp David.

## The making of foreign policy

Before turning to a discussion of contemporary foreign policy issues, we need to consider the process of foreign policy making—a subject that will help us understand some of the aspects of current policy.

### The president and the executive branch

Presidents are preeminent in U.S. foreign affairs. Traditionally, both the courts and Congress have deferred to presidential decision making in foreign and military policy. As commander in chief of the armed forces, the president has usually enjoyed wide latitude in military and diplomatic activity. But as we noted in Chapter 15, the president's powers in foreign affairs, although substantial, are occasionally not adequate to obtain the ends sought. Woodrow Wilson failed to obtain Senate approval of U.S. membership in the League of Nations after World War I,

and Jimmy Carter could not get the Senate to approve the SALT II arms control treaty in 1979. Franklin Roosevelt was unable to alter the temper of public sentiment and arouse support for more vigorous U.S. opposition to Nazism in the late 1930s.

The roles played by recent presidents in shaping foreign policy have varied considerably. Dwight Eisenhower and Gerald Ford turned most foreign policy matters over to their secretaries of state. John Kennedy, Richard Nixon, and Jimmy Carter were more-active participants. Every president is aided by a national security adviser, who coordinates and advises on foreign policy matters. Another coordinating device is the National Security Council, consisting of the vice-president, the secretaries of defense and of state, and other members appointed by the president—usually including the CIA director and chairman of the Joint Chiefs of Staff.

During recent presidencies, significant disagree-

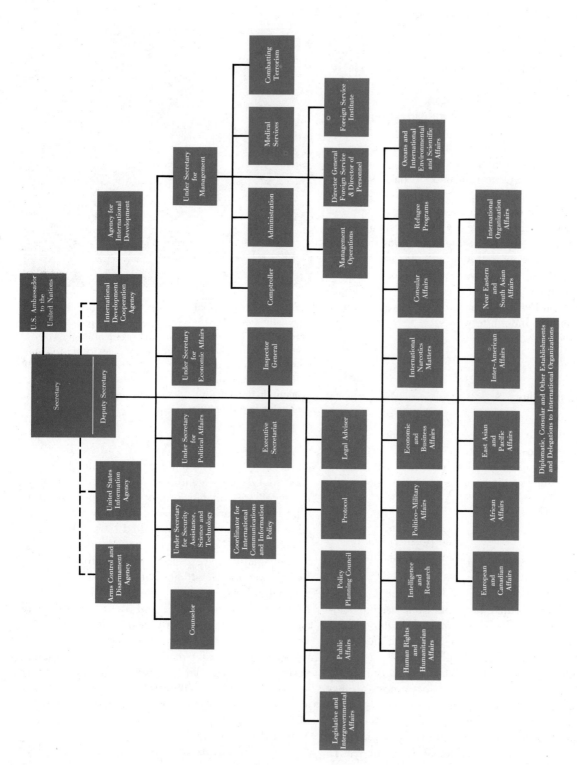

FIGURE 22.1
Department of State

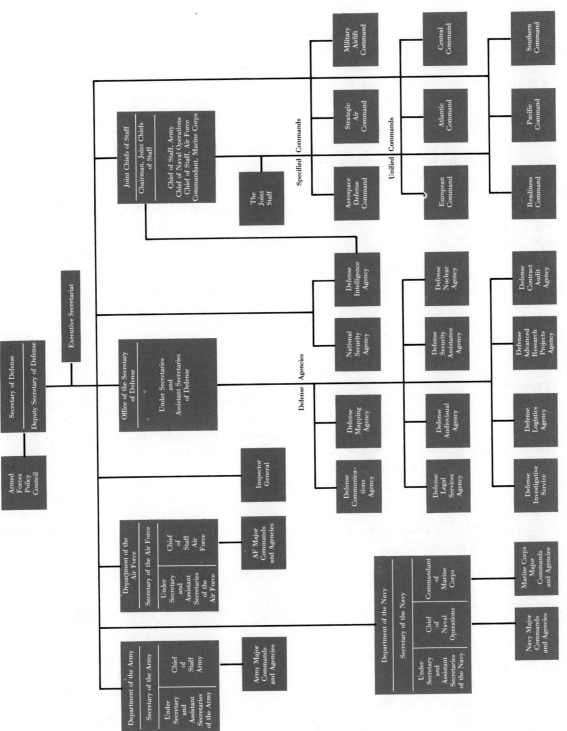

FIGURE 22.2
Department of Defense

ments have developed between secretaries of state and national security advisers. From the president's point of view, policy disagreements and struggles for influence among top advisers can sometimes serve the useful purpose of keeping options out in the open and encouraging the development of new alternatives. A serious danger, however, is that such policy disagreements will create confusion both at home and abroad.

**The State Department**, the main instrument in the foreign policy process, maintains about thirty-five hundred foreign service officers in several hundred posts. State has often been criticized for its alleged traditionalism, lack of creativity, and organizational diffuseness.

Two other significant executive agencies in the foreign policy making process are AID (Agency for International Development) and ACDA (Arms Control and Disarmament Agency). AID handles a portion of U.S. economic, technical and military assistance; the rest is administered through international bodies such as the World Bank and International Development Agency. ACDA participates in arms control negotiations, such as those that led to the Test Ban Treaty of 1963 and the SALT talks.

Defense policy is officially the province of the secretary of defense, the head of the **Defense Department**. Typically, secretaries of defense have had considerable difficulty coordinating the demands and missions of the various armed services, as interservice rivalries are often acute. The Defense Department presides over some four thousand defense installations within the United States. Almost three-quarters of the government's purchases of goods and services are defense-related.

The military services are represented by the **Joint Chiefs of Staff**, who advise the president as well as the secretary of defense. The chairman of the JCS heads a staff of four hundred and a larger organization of about two thousand. Splits among the chiefs are frequent, as each service seeks to maximize its role in defense planning. Logrolling is common in military affairs: often, chiefs endorse the various requests and ideas of other services in order simply to win support for their own.

Intelligence gathering and covert operations com-

prise another significant element in foreign policy. Many government agencies are involved in intelligence work: the FBI, the CIA, the Defense Intelligence Agency, the State Department's Bureau of Intelligence, and the National Security Agency. The Central Intelligence Agency, with a known budget of almost $1 billion annually and approximately fifteen thousand employees, has had wide-ranging interests, including sending up spy satellites and running various covert operations.

From its inception in 1947, the CIA has been charged with directly aiding the president in foreign policy planning. The agency soon developed two basic functions: classic intelligence gathering and covert action. Classic intelligence gathering refers to the assembly, verification, and analysis of information. Specifically, this means such things as reading and analyzing the foreign press, planting spies in the Kremlin, sending spy planes and satellites throughout and over the world, and bugging foreign embassies.

The legislation creating the CIA did not mention "covert action," but a 1948 directive of the National Security Council specified "propaganda, economic warfare, preventative direct action, including sabotage, anti-sabotage, demolition, evacuation measures, subversion against hostile states, including assistance to underground resistance groups and support of indigenous anti-communist elements in threatened countries of the free world." Over the next fifteen years the CIA involved itself in such actions as supplying secret subsidies to anticommunist labor unions in Western Europe, overthrowing the Mossadegh regime in Iran in 1953 and restoring the Shah to power; organizing a secret army that overthrew the government in Guatemala in 1954; planning the Bay of Pigs invasion of Cuba in 1961; sponsoring guerrilla raids against mainland China during the 1950s; supplying support for the French in Indochina; playing a key role in installing and later assassinating President Ngo Dinh Diem of South Vietnam; assassinating and attempting to assassinate various foreign leaders, including Fidel Castro of Cuba, Patrice Lumumba of the Congo, and Rafael Trujillo of the Dominican Republic. By the mid-1960s, the CIA was also keeping files on approximately three hundred thousand

Americans it regarded as actual or potential subversives, despite the fact that its charter specifically forbade it to operate within the United States.

In the 1960s and 1970s, controversies over U.S. policy in Cuba and Vietnam, along with fallout from the Watergate scandals, opened the gates to publication of more-complete information about CIA activities. These revelations showed that many CIA activities were far removed from the original purposes of the agency, and that the agency had gone so far afield that it had become difficult to tell which of the activities linked to it were genuinely independent of agency control and which were arms of the agency. Congress reevaluated the agency and, in an effort to prevent new abuses in the future, passed the Hughes-Ryan Act of 1974. This piece of legislation required that the president personally approve all important covert actions and that Congress be notified of such actions.

During the Reagan administration, however, the CIA again expanded its covert actions.[1] In 1984, an estimated fifty covert operations were conducted—half of them in Latin America and a substantial number in Africa. Covert operations remained controversial. When it was discovered in 1984 that the CIA was helping mine Nicaraguan harbors, many in Congress were shocked that there had been so little consultation. National Security Adviser Robert McFarlane defended the need for covert operations, arguing that the government needed some range of actions between total war and total peace. In this "gray area," he said, covert operations served a useful role. The alternatives, he maintained, were sending in the Marines or doing nothing. Others saw the agency again embarked on a dangerous course, with fateful policy decisions being removed from legislative and popular discussion and evaluation.

## Influences on foreign policy

**Elites:** Students of the subject have generally agreed that political elites play a more central role in foreign policy decisions than in the making of domestic policy. Underlying this phenomenon has been the lack of widespread public sophistication about foreign affairs—as well as a frequent lack of interest, although this has changed in recent years. These political elites include top politicians, corporate executives, military brass, people in media, influential academics, and people at the top of groups and institutions especially concerned with foreign policy.

Since the Vietnam war, those involved in making our foreign policies have been divided along several dimensions. For one thing, détente with the USSR and friendly relations with China have made the international scene far more complicated. But some have argued that the Cold War is still alive and well and the US should respond accordingly. Others continue to press for reduced tensions with the USSR. Some have advocated tougher American actions in connection with threats from the Third World while others believe we must compromise and come to terms with these changes. The developing debates about our foreign policy seem to revolve mainly around these issues.

**Interest groups:** Many interest groups have a great deal at stake in the way U.S. foreign policy is conducted. Business groups, organized labor, farmers, various ethnic groups, ideological interest groups, and others have attempted to influence the directions of U.S. international relations.

Business interests are, of course, pervasive. Some observers have argued that U.S. foreign policy since World War II has been largely business-oriented. Others have questioned the extent of the power of business, but none have debated the fact that U.S. policies have often been shaped by key business leaders and have generally reflected business interests in both Democratic and Republican administrations. Still, "business" is not a united interest. Businesses frequently oppose each other, as when some groups seek freer trade while others try to raise tariffs and protect their market position.

Often, major multinational corporations virtually conduct their own foreign policies. With interests all over the globe, large corporations work out their own deals with other governments. Some such deals bring satisfactory benefits for all involved. At other times, however, they have entailed illegal activities, as when

Gulf Oil gave $4.2 million in bribes to politicians in fifteen countries, or when the Lockheed Corporation set its money to work in Japanese political circles. At other times, it can mean the exploitation of Third World populations, both by their own governments and by international business interests. Some business activities can become highly controversial, as when U.S. businesses invest heavily in racially divided South Africa.

Organized labor also exercises some influence over foreign policy. Like business, labor often seeks to protect the interests of workers in industries threatened by foreign imports. The AFL-CIO has sometimes attacked government policies that encourage U.S. corporations to invest abroad, since such policies usually mean fewer jobs at home. With the decline of certain U.S. industries, such as steel, labor has had to face the problem of how to best protect its interests: Should the government be asked to aid failing U.S. companies? Should foreign companies be encouraged to invest here? Should U.S. companies be encouraged not to invest elsewhere?

Labor also takes stands on many noneconomic issues. Since the 1950s, the AFL-CIO generally has been fiercely anticommunist. The Vietnam War, however, split labor's ranks. Some labor leaders joined the antiwar movement, whereas others rallied around Presidents Nixon and Johnson and supported escalation of the conflict. At times labor, like business, has done its own foreign policy-making. When Polish workers went on strike in the summer of 1980, the AFL-CIO established a fund to assist the newly formed Polish "free trade unions."

Particular U.S. ethnic groups often take a keen interest in U.S. foreign policies. Over the past decade or so, Greek-American views on the struggle between Greeks and Turks on Cyprus have had a marked effect on U.S. actions there. American Jews have maintained a high level of interest in our relations with Israel, the Arab nations, and the Palestinians. Without doubt, the "Jewish vote" has influenced the stands many politicians have taken on Middle Eastern issues.

Ideological groups also influence our foreign policies. For two decades, the Committee of One Million campaigned to prevent U.S. diplomatic recognition of Communist China. Later, many conservative political groups campaigned vigorously against what they called the "giveaway" of the Panama Canal.

**Public opinion:** Some students of the subject have seen the public as largely passive in the area of foreign policy. In this view the public is poorly informed, well-socialized to patriotic feeling, and therefore accepting of direction from above. Within very broad limits, political decision-makers have a free hand in the making of foreign policy. Recent studies show us that about 30 percent of the American public seems to lack almost all knowledge of foreign policy. Another 45 percent are aware of most major developments but are not deeply involved or very well informed. This leaves about 25 percent who are consistently interested.

It is very difficult to ascertain exactly what constraints public opinion places on policymakers. Clearly, the general structure of opinion does have some effect. A president could not unilaterally seek to disarm the country without arousing considerable popular uproar. Still, many policies followed by political leaders in recent years could probably have been changed without disastrous political consequences for the leaders involved. It seems unlikely, for example, that President Johnson's political career would have suffered had he *not* escalated the war in Vietnam; or President Kennedy's had he canceled the Bay of Pigs invasion of Cuba; or President Nixon's had the SALT I arms control negotiations not been held. Clearly, the latitude available to political leaders is considerable, although not unlimited.

As the American public has become better educated and better acquainted with the realities of politics in the rest of the world, a larger and more sophisticated audience for foreign policy issues has developed. As a result, the media have occasionally adopted a more critical attitude in this field (as happened in Vietnam), and portions of the political elite have become disenchanted with U.S. foreign policies. We will see many of these forces—elites, public opinion, interest groups, and political institutions—at work as we examine the central aspect of American foreign policy since the end of World War II: the Cold War with the Soviet Union.

## Relations with
the Soviet Union

Of all U.S. foreign involvements since the end of World War II, clearly the most significant has been our relationship with the Soviet Union. The rivalry between the United States and the Soviet Union has not only dominated the foreign policies of both great powers; it has also dominated much of the world scene since 1945. Although many other important developments have taken place in international relations—including independence for many former colonies, the emergence of China, various processes of change and evolution among the less-developed nations—the shadow of U.S.-Soviet competition has fallen over much of what has occurred.

## Origins of
the Cold War

The Cold War surfaced at the end of World War II, but its origins lay in 1917, when V. I. Lenin and his Bolshevik colleagues seized power in Russia. These were Marxist revolutionaries—enemies of capitalism—and as such, feared and detested by most Western governments. Woodrow Wilson, like other Western leaders, sent troops to help destroy the fledgling revolution, but the intervention failed. The United States withheld diplomatic recognition of the Bolshevik regime until 1933. Subsequently, the struggle against Nazi Germany placed the United States and the Soviet Union on the same side of a wartime alliance.

As the end of the war approached, however, distrust between the two countries began to surface once more. Decisions worked out in 1945 at the Yalta and Potsdam conferences began to unravel. For example, the Red Army was allowed to occupy Eastern Europe on the understanding that free elections would be held in those countries. But the Soviets installed communist governments in Eastern Europe, and free elections were never held. As tensions and suspicions mounted, the West hardened its positions. The Russians blockaded Berlin in 1947 and a lengthy airlift was required to supply the city. A communist coup took place in Czechoslovakia. The United States sponsored a large economic aid package for Western Europe, known as the Marshall Plan. The West formed the North Atlantic Treaty Organization (NATO) to counterbalance Soviet power. The Soviets responded by forming the Warsaw Pact among Eastern European nations.

Rather quickly after World War II, then, foreign policy lines were drawn that have dominated world politics ever since. The division of Europe became permanent, and large armies were stationed at its heart.

Could the Cold War have been avoided? Whose fault was it? It was probably inevitable that some tensions and power struggles take place after World War II. It is not clear, however, that they had to escalate as far as they did. The Soviet leader Josef Stalin sought long-term security for his nation, which had just suffered an estimated 20 million casualties because of the Nazi invasion. Stalin also sought to extend communist influence. In addition, the evidence seems to show that he was an extremely suspicious person who expected the Western powers to attempt to extend their influence. Those on the Western side suspected that Stalin planned to use the Red Army to invade Western Europe—a fear that remains alive even today. President Harry Truman and his advisers also were disillusioned by the Soviets' refusal to hold elections in Eastern Europe.

## Containment

The doctrine that guided U.S. policymakers in the early years of the Cold War was spelled out by George Kennan, a State Department official. In a 1947 article, Kennan used the term **containment** to describe an appropriate policy toward the Soviets.[2] According to Kennan, the United States had to stand ready to contain the expansionist thrusts of Soviet power until such time as the Soviets learned to accommodate themselves to world realities. Kennan thought of containment as a temporary policy, designed primarily for the European situation, but others

Vietnam: The South Vietnamese national police chief executes a suspected Viet Cong officer in what is one of the most famous photos of the war. The shooting took place in the early days of the 1968 Tet offensive in which Communist forces staged surprise attacks throughout South Vietnam. In the second photo, we see what was a most common event: a civilian casualty, in this case, a child. The extensiveness of civilian casualties led many to question the morality of the war effort. As an American officer put it as he surveyed a bombed-out village: "We destroyed the village in order to save it."

saw it in a worldwide context. The United States, they felt, must stop the expansion of communism everywhere. When the Chinese communists took control of their country in 1949, many interpreted this development as another extension of Soviet power. The Communist world was seen as a monolith, completely unified and directed from the Kremlin. A communist challenge in one place was basically no different from a communist challenge anywhere else. Thus, the United States should be ready to intervene anywhere in the world where communism threatened.

Members of both political parties generally agreed that U.S. foreign policy had to be anticommunist. The real question was *how* anticommunist. The race to be more anticommunist than the next politician helped make many political careers. Senator Joseph McCarthy (R, Wisconsin), for example, made a name for himself primarily by leaping on the anticommunist bandwagon. In 1950 he charged that there were over two hundred communists in the U.S. State Department—an allegation never substantiated in a single case. McCarthy's hunt for "subversives" in and out of government became, for several years, a regular feature of U.S. political life.

But McCarthy was just the flag-waver on the tip of the iceberg. The nation became obsessed with real or imagined threats of subversion. For one thing, many Americans could not understand how the nation had lost its position of security and dominance after World War II. An explanation—or a scapegoat—was needed. Also, anticommunism was good politics—a simple, intense, and widely understood position. In this atmosphere, the discussion of U.S. foreign policy became muted. The anticommunist consensus hardened into a dogma; fear of appearing "soft" on communism pervaded political life.

## Peaceful coexistence

Dwight Eisenhower rode to the presidency in 1952 on a tide of anticommunist feeling. His secretary of state, John Foster Dulles, diligently worked to es-

competition between the Great Powers, but it was to be competition by nonmilitary means. Neither side was ready to work out ground rules for peace, however. For example, U.S. policymakers wanted the Soviets to stay out of anticolonial struggles in the Third World, but the Soviet Union viewed anticolonialism as a basic commitment under Marxist-Leninist principles. The typical U.S. response was to form alliances with any Third World leader who was sufficiently anticommunist. As we will see later in the chapter, this response led us to befriend many dictators in Latin America, Asia, and the Middle East.

**Korea and Vietnam:** The tradition of **isolationism** returned to haunt policymakers after World War II. Anxious to counteract isolationist tendencies, U.S. leaders sometimes exaggerated the threats the nation faced in order to gain public support for international military action. The perceived threat of communist expansion into Asian countries drew the United States into conflicts in Asia. We sent troops to Korea in 1950 as part of a United Nations peacekeeping force after communist North Korean forces invaded South Korea. As defeat loomed for the North Koreans, the Chinese entered the war in force. During the ensuing military stalemate, some in the United States urged extending the war to China itself. Peace talks led to a ceasefire in July 1953. Korea is still divided at the ceasefire line—close to the pre-1950 north-south boundary.

Our entry into the Vietnam conflict also came in response to a perceived communist threat. Forces in that country had fought a long war after World War II to win independence from France. When the French withdrew in 1954, they left behind a divided nation in which rival groupings vied for control. One group was the Vietminh, made up of communist nationalists based in the north of the country. For the United States, the communist part of the equation seemed more important than the nationalist one, and we took sides with noncommunist forces in the south of the country. Many U.S. leaders were concerned that the Soviet Union intended to support the Vietminh. They reasoned, as in the case of Korea, that if the communist challenge was not met in Vietnam, we would have to meet it again in other parts of Asia.

tablish a worldwide network of alliances designed to contain communism. His rhetoric indicated U.S. willingness to go to the brink of war. Eisenhower, however, showed considerable flexibility. His administration, like the Truman administration before it, intervened covertly to overthrow governments perceived as threats to U.S. interests, as in Guatemala in 1954. But in the same year, Eisenhower refused to send troops to help the French in Indochina. And in 1956, he refused to intervene in an anticommunist revolution in Hungary, despite congressional resolutions calling for the liberation of Eastern Europe. The risks of world war were too great, Eisenhower argued.

During the Eisenhower years a critical change took place in the Soviet Union: Stalin died in 1953 and was replaced by Nikita Khrushchev. To some extent, Khrushchev was more flexible than Stalin, and more interested in negotiations with the West. He coined the term **peaceful coexistence** to describe the type of relationship he preferred with the United States. Peaceful coexistence did not preclude continued

Some facts about the situation in Vietnam that were glossed over at the time must be restated here: (1) that the United States inherited a situation of conflict *within* a temporarily divided country; (2) that the communists in North Vietnam had been leaders in the revolutionary struggles against the French and were national heroes to some; (3) that the leadership in South Vietnam, which we supported, lacked a popular base; (4) that the situation in Vietnam was largely a homegrown struggle, at least at the outset, and not one imported from or directed by the Soviet Union or China.

The U.S. military presence in Vietnam escalated from a few military advisers in the early 1960s to close to half-a-million combat troops in 1968. It was a prolonged, costly, and destructive war. More than fifty thousand American troops and at least six hundred thousand North Vietnamese troops died. Much of the Vietnamese countryside was destroyed. At home, Americans divided over the question of the war, and political conflicts spilled over into the streets. President Richard Nixon, elected in 1968, pledged to end the war, but it took seven more years before the conflict ended. In the end, Congress forced the final withdrawal of U.S. troops by refusing aid to the South Vietnamese. Vietnam was the first war the United States ever lost.

The Vietnam experience became a lesson from which various conclusions were drawn. Some Americans, including President Ronald Reagan, have called it a noble cause that was lost only because we did not support it fully. Others have viewed the war as an immoral and arrogant adventure in which the United States tried to impose its power on others. Still others have argued that we had erred strategically, fighting the wrong sort of war against an aggressor.

During the war, some of its most ardent supporters predicted a "domino" effect if South Vietnam were lost. They foresaw all of Southeast Asia going communist, and perhaps other countries as well. The domino theory proved correct in part. South Vietnam, Cambodia, and Laos came under communist rule, but the rest of Southeast Asia did not. Moreover, U.S. power was not badly damaged by our withdrawal from Vietnam, as some had warned. Overall,

our position in the world did not suffer greatly. Our European allies were generally relieved by the end of the war, and normalization of relations with China became possible. The Soviet Union did not seem to gain appreciably in world affairs as a result of the war's outcome.

Peace activists who had expected a relatively benign regime in South Vietnam were also proven wrong, however. The North Vietnamese imposed a rigid dictatorship from which millions had fled by the 1980s. Far worse, the Khmer Rouge regime in Cambodia carried out a genocidal campaign of death and terror that no one had anticipated—not even the most ardent supporters of the war—and that claimed 3 million lives.

In terms of U.S. politics, the war left a legacy of distrust and confusion. Conflict over the war probably ended the presidency of Lyndon Johnson and demoralized the Democratic Party. It created new and serious tensions between president and Congress. The congressional rebellion discussed earlier was largely fueled by the fires of Vietnam. For a time, many Americans became deeply cynical about our political leaders and our values as a society. In some ways, the election of Ronald Reagan represented a reaction against the political and social legacy of the Vietnam War—an effort to restore a sense of pride in American patriotism. If nothing else, the experience of Vietnam made it clear that a nation such as ours cannot long engage in a foreign war without solid support from the public.

During the Vietnam War, the bipartisan consensus on foreign policy that had prevailed since World War II was shattered. A president can no longer expect the virtually unanimous support Lyndon Johnson obtained for the 1964 Tonkin Gulf resolution, which provided him a free hand (temporarily) in Vietnam. Both parties are divided over when, where, how, and if the United States should intervene. The debates over Central American policy discussed later in the chapter bear out the enduring quality of these new divisions.

What were the lessons of Vietnam? One was that it is dangerous to make policy by analogy. Some policymakers in the 1950s and 1960s had compared the situation in Vietnam to the 1930s, when the Western powers had an opportunity to stand up to Nazi aggression but instead gave in to their demands. In the 1980s some compared Central America to Vietnam. The roots of any conflict, however, have to be understood in their own terms. In Vietnam, American power proved to be limited. The limits encountered were not only military but moral and political. In the words of Irving Howe and Michael Walzer (*The New Republic*, April 29, 1985), "The U.S. sent its troops into Vietnam to reverse the verdict of a local struggle, which meant, in turn, imposing a ghastly death and suffering upon the Vietnamese. As it turned out, the U.S. could not reverse that verdict finally; it could only delay its culmination."

## Crises and détente

Throughout the 1960s, many serious world crises threatened to turn the Cold War into a hot one. In 1961 the East Germans constructed the Berlin Wall, which still seals off that country from the West. Cuba

underwent a revolution and the radicals who came to power developed close ties with the Soviet Union. This development set the stage for what many consider the low point in modern U.S. foreign policy— the Bay of Pigs invasion, a U.S.-sponsored attack on Cuba mounted by Cuban refugees in April 1961. The invaders were routed, but Cuba was the focus of yet another crisis a year later, when the United States discovered that the Soviet Union had placed nuclear missiles in Cuba. President Kennedy demanded that the missiles be withdrawn, and he instituted a naval blockade of the island. The Soviets backed down, after some very tense moments. President Kennedy himself had estimated the odds of war as "between 2–1 and even money."[3] The Vietnam War provided another obstacle to improved East-West relations, as did the Soviet invasion of Czechoslovakia in 1968.

Despite these crises, the process of easing tensions moved forward, with U.S. presidents and secretaries of state meeting and negotiating with their Soviet counterparts. By the early 1970s, Soviet-U.S. relations seemed to have entered a new state—one the Soviets called *razriadka* and the West knew as **détente.** Both words connote a form of relaxation, or "unwinding." Ironically, President Richard Nixon,

President Kennedy surveys U.S. aircraft during the 1962 Cuban missile crisis. Most observers agree that this was the moment when the United States and the Soviet Union came closest to war.

525

A Soviet tank in the streets of Prague, 1968. The Soviets were not exactly welcomed in Czechoslovakia. Since World War II, the Soviet Union has been extremely reluctant to allow political evolution to take its course in Eastern Europe. As a result, it has intervened repeatedly with force or the threat of force.

who had built his political career on staunch anticommunism, instigated the rapprochement with the Soviet Union. Nixon also was the first U.S. president to improve relations with Communist China—a move he had once opposed.

Nixon's security adviser and, later, secretary of state, Henry Kissinger, was highly influential in the détente process. Kissinger argued that certain basic realities had to be recognized in Soviet-U.S. relations: (1) that direct confrontation between the Great Powers would only result in mutual suicide; (2) that the growing split between the Soviet Union and China gave the Soviets an incentive to improve relations with the United States; (3) that a crusading anticommunism was no longer popular in the nation, and that "limited" wars, such as in Vietnam, were too costly and uncertain; and (4) that rivalry with the Soviet Union would continue, but at a lower level of tension.

Over a period of years, U.S. and Soviet negotiators hammered out a series of agreements that comprised

the heart of détente. The agreements covered issues ranging from the control of nuclear weapons to forms of technical cooperation. Nixon and Soviet leader Leonid Brezhnev signed the SALT I agreements in 1972 and also a statement of basic principles agreeing to consult in dangerous situations. Then, in the Helsinki agreements of 1975, East and West endorsed human rights for the citizens of all nations, called for reduced tensions in Central Europe, and pledged increased cooperation in economics, science, and technology. It seems clear that Brezhnev never intended to comply with the human rights provisions, and Soviet failure to comply occasionally has proved a source of embarrassment for the Soviet leadership.

The Carter administration pressed on with arms control talks and concluded an agreement, known as SALT II, in 1978. SALT II, however, represented the last gasp of détente. Senate approval of the treaty was doomed by the Soviet invasion of Afghanistan in December 1979.

## Return of the hard line

Opponents of détente—usually conservatives—argued that while we were negotiating, the Soviets had been making important gains in many military areas and had achieved nuclear superiority. In addition, they claimed that the Soviet Union or its proxies, Cuba and Vietnam, had gained new influence in Asia and Africa. Some saw the Afghanistan invasion as a first step toward greater Soviet involvement in the oil-rich Middle East.

Not everyone viewed the Soviet Union as in the ascendancy. In fact, many students of Soviet politics took the opposite view, citing the fact that China had definitely moved toward the West and that U.S. influence was clearly dominant in the Middle East. Further, upheavals in Poland in 1980 showed that the Soviet empire was highly vulnerable even on its doorstep.

The Reagan administration returned to a hard-line policy toward the Soviet Union—one reminiscent of the harsher anticommunism of the 1950s. This position had substantial public support in the early 1980s. Reagan sharply increased arms spending and focused on efforts to support anticommunist regimes, which the administration viewed as under attack from leftists. Talk of détente faded. In fact, Reagan did not meet with any Soviet leader until the last months of his first term.

## Current issues

The biggest question facing U.S. policymakers—and the general public—today is, Exactly what are our objectives vis-à-vis the Soviet Union? The original goal of containment implied that we were willing to learn to live with the Soviets, but not to countenance their efforts to expand their influence, particularly by military means. More militant U.S. anticommunists, however, have long hoped to diminish Soviet power, or even to undermine the dominance of the Communist Party in Russia itself. Is it our objective to live on a more-or-less equal footing with communism, or is it our aim to destroy it?

The rulers of the Soviet Union must also decide whether they prefer détente or confrontation: that is, whether they will work to undermine Western democracies or will live with the West as it is. On both sides, there are champions of the paths of détente and of confrontation.

One of the reasons that Soviet-U.S. relations matter so much is that the two Great Powers have accumulated weapons of destruction that threaten the lives of hundreds of millions. The arms race throws its shadow over all international developments. We turn now to that shadow.

## The arms race

Arms races are nothing new, but a *nuclear* arms race is something distinctly new. It is possible that the possession of nuclear weapons by both sides has actually prevented World War III from taking place. Had NATO and the Warsaw Pact countries been armed only with conventional weapons, the feared confrontation might have occurred long ago, probably in Central Europe. Nevertheless, if nuclear weapons *are* ever unleashed, it will likely mean the end of the United States, the Soviet Union, and all of Europe, with serious consequences for the rest of life on earth. The gamble of nuclear weapons is enormous. But that genie has gotten out of the bottle. Nuclear weapons exist, and we cannot turn back the clock.

## Nuclear strategy and arms calculations

The reasoning behind the building of nuclear weapons seemed quite simple at first. The United States built its atomic bombs out of fear that Nazi Germany would develop them. Once it was demonstrated that such bombs could be built, however, any nation with

527

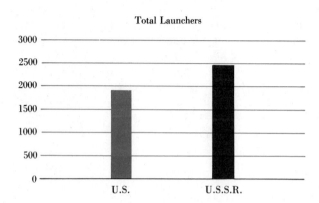

Total Launchers

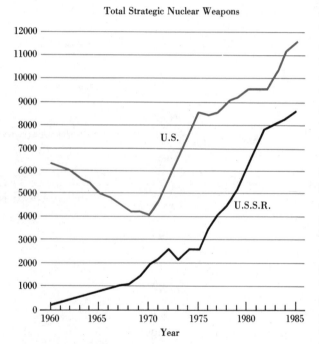

Total Strategic Nuclear Weapons

U.S.

U.S.S.R.

Year

Source: Center for Defense Info., Wash., DC., 1985

FIGURE 22.3

U.S.–Soviet Strategic Nuclear Forces (April 1985)

cordingly, nuclear weapons were viewed solely as a deterrent whose actual use would be irrational.

President Eisenhower, along with most experts of that time, took the view that a relatively small number of bombs on each side would be sufficient to ensure a "balance of terror." By the late 1950s, however, many anxieties began to surface in the United States about possible Soviet military superiority—particularly after the Soviets launched the first space satellite, in 1957. In 1960, presidential candidate John Kennedy focused on the alleged "missile gap," claiming that the Soviet Union might gain a great lead over the United States in intercontinental ballistic missiles, which could reach their targets in a matter of minutes. Once in office, the Kennedy administration embarked upon a crash program of missile building, despite the discovery that earlier estimates of Soviet missile superiority had been mistaken. As a result, the United States pulled ahead—so far ahead, in fact, that the Soviets may have begun to fear that they were in a position of severe military weakness.

At the same time, U.S. strategists argued that nuclear superiority in numbers and accuracy was required by a new and influential doctrine, called **counterforce.** Counterforce targets were military sites, such as missile silos, submarine bases, and air bases. The idea was to knock out the opponent's ability to retaliate by destroying its nuclear weapons on the ground, thus leaving the enemy defenseless. Obviously, counterforce required a powerful delivery system. Equally as obvious was that this logic applied to either side. Some observers believed that it was anxiety over the counterforce doctrine that led Soviet Premier Khrushchev to place missiles in Cuba in 1962, in an attempt to balance out U.S. missile superiority.

To ensure greater security, each side began diversifying its nuclear weapons delivery systems. By the mid-1960s both the United States and the Soviet Union maintained three distinct nuclear delivery systems: long-range ICBMs, submarine-launched ballistic missiles (SLBMs), and long-range bombers. Because neither side wished to become vulnerable to a counterforce first strike, strategists in both camps also turned their attention to possible defenses against

the requisite scientific and industrial ability could do so. In the 1950s, by which point both the United States and the Soviet Union had nuclear weapons, the Eisenhower administration explained its nuclear strategy as based on "massive retaliation." Were the Soviets to attack us with nuclear weapons, we would in turn retaliate with every nuclear warhead we possessed. Such action would mean mutual suicide. Ac-

incoming missiles. For a time in the late 1960s, both nations experimented with ABMs (antiballistic missiles), which could, theoretically, shoot down incoming missiles before the latter reached their targets.

The momentum of technology moved ever faster. To counter the perceived threat from ABMs, scientists began to experiment with increasing the power of the offensive missiles. The result was another leap in the arms race—the development of the MIRV (multiple independently-targeted delivery vehicle). Each missile could now be equipped not with a single nuclear weapon, but with three or five or ten or twenty—each of which could be programmed to hit a different target. Such a large number of warheads would serve to overwhelm any possible missile defense.

At this point, the sheer futility of the arms race began to sink in with some Soviet and American leaders. It seemed clear that simply building more and more nuclear weapons of ever-increasing sophistication would not get either side anywhere. Why not begin to slow down the arms race, to place limits on the weapons each side could amass? The idea of controlling the arms race led both countries to the negotiating table in the **Strategic Arms Limitation Talks (SALT)**.

| Arms
| control talks

The SALT talks were carried on over a period of roughly ten years. The issues were complex and often highly specialized: one important question, for example, was whether a particular Soviet bomber should be considered a long-range or a medium-range weapon. But the underlying thrust of the talks was clear from the start: that it was in the interests of both nations to set limits to the arms race, to curtail the momentum of nuclear weapons development. In this area, both superpowers shared a common interest—*survival*. They also stood to save huge amounts of money.

The talks accomplished a good deal. SALT I set overall limits to the number of missiles and bombers each side could possess. The United States was allowed an edge in bombers, the Soviets in land- and sea-based missiles. Both sides agreed not to develop antiballistic missile systems. At the same time, however, technological improvements such as MIRVs were allowed to continue unchecked. The end result was that both nations greatly increased the number of total nuclear warheads they possessed during the 1970s. SALT II came to grips with the MIRV issue by limiting the number and type of warheads as well. Yet even newer technological developments, such as the virtually undetectable cruise missile and an even more accurate ICBM called the MX missile, made it increasingly difficult to bring the arms race under control. Technological momentum was still moving faster than the ponderous process of negotiation.

Many in the United States came to believe that the Soviet Union had forged ahead in the area of land-based missiles, and even imagined that the Soviets might launch a first strike against U.S. targets. Such fears, plus the Soviet invasion of Afghanistan in 1979, doomed Senate approval of the SALT II treaty. Both sides, however, continued to limit themselves, more or less, to the guidelines of the SALT II accords.

In June of 1985, President Reagan decided to continue informal observance of the limitations established in the SALT II treaty. Further observance of the treaty (which was scheduled to expire at the end of 1985 had it been ratified) was contingent, the president argued, on questions of Soviet violations, further arms build-ups by the USSR, and progress made at the arms talks in Geneva. But the Reagan administration also responded to supposed Soviet advantages in nuclear weapons by embarking on a vast arms buildup at all levels. Over its first term in office, the administration proposed about $1.1 *trillion* dollars in defense spending.[4] Congress cut back these proposals somewhat, but military spending still accelerated dramatically.

Would the spending of such huge sums make the United States safer? Or, as the administration argued, bring the Soviets to the bargaining table? In 1985, the secretary of defense reported that the Soviets had continued to make rapid progress in various areas of nuclear weaponry. In the meantime, arms control negotiations either stalled or did not take place at all. The Reagan administration proposed to replace SALT II with START (Strategic Arms Reduction Talks), and called for a limit of five thousand ballistic missile warheads on each side. The START proposal, however, did not include any limitations on the development of new weapons or on deployment of advanced weapons already underway. The net result of Reagan's proposal would have been a reduction of warheads for the Soviets but an increase of several thousand for the United States. Not surprisingly, the Soviet Union showed little interest.

Overall, after four years of military buildup under President Reagan, the nuclear balance changed little between 1981 and 1985. If anything, the Soviets were pouring even more money and effort into building up their arsenal and were widening their advantage in some areas, such as intercontinental ballistic missiles. Both sides continued to develop new and

more sophisticated weapons, at a great cost to each society.

Another ominous development was the Reagan administration's so-called Star Wars proposal, which called for the development of space-based defenses against missile attack. Many experts argued that such a defense was not technically possible, was in any case prohibitively expensive, and would destabilize the arms race. The Soviets vigorously protested against the idea, although they, too, seemed to be entertaining such notions.

In all, the events of the early 1980s did not give much comfort to those who wished to see a slowdown of the arms race. In the first months of the Reagan administration, there was loose talk in Washington of the possibility of using nuclear weapons in a "limited" war in Europe. Others argued for the need to develop a nuclear war-fighting capacity, based on the assumption that it actually was possible to win such wars. Scientists came forward with the disturbing concept of a nuclear winter, according to which virtually all life on earth could be extinguished by the aftereffects of a nuclear war.[5]

Such developments triggered popular, if short-lived, nuclear freeze campaigns in the United States and Western Europe. Freeze advocates called for a moratorium on the testing, development, and deployment of nuclear weapons as a first step toward reducing nuclear arsenals. Although a majority of Americans favored a freeze, the concept had only a limited impact on political debate, and the arms buildup continued.

TABLE 22.1
## Basic elements in the SALT I and SALT II treaties

*SALT I (1972)*

1. Deployment of antiballistic missiles was limited to one site apiece, with strict controls on numbers installed. An ABM race was thereby avoided.

2. The numbers of land-based ICBM and SLBM launchers was frozen for five years at the numbers operational or under construction in 1972. At that time the United States had 1,054 ICBMs and 656 SLBMs, and the Soviets had 1,607 ICBMs and 740 SLBMs. The United States was permitted to maintain its advantage in heavy bombers and in total numbers of warheads.

*SALT II (1978)*

1. Each side was limited to a *total* of 2,250 strategic nuclear delivery vehicles of all types, including ICBMs, SLBMs, air-to-surface missiles, and heavy bombers.

2. Sublimits were established for various types of launchers carrying MIRVs—for example, only 820 MIRVed ICBMs were permitted.

3. Bans on various technical developments were imposed, including increases in the number of warheads and the "throwweight" (carrying capacity) of ballistic missiles of all types.

| Tactical and
medium-range
nuclear weapons

Both the United States and the Soviet Union possess thousands of smaller nuclear weapons designed for battlefield use, called tactical weapons. Both sides also possess medium-range nuclear missiles that cannot travel as far as ICBMs but are equally destructive. Both superpowers have deployed most of their tactical and medium-range weapons in Europe.

# Nuclear war: no place to hide

A single one-megaton nuclear weapon detonated over a major city would produce the following effects.

A fireball over 1 mile in diameter if the bomb were detonated above ground. A crater 1,000 feet in diameter and 300 feet deep if it were detonated on the ground.

Fifty square miles of total destruction by blast and fire; in a 600-square-mile area, all unprotected people would be killed.

Close to five hundred thousand fatalities; total casualties of over seven hundred and fifty thousand.

In a 1,000-square-mile area—about the size of Rhode Island—all persons looking at the fireball would be permanently blinded. A 4,000-square-mile area—the size of Connecticut—would be blanketed with deadly radioactive contamination.

In a full-scale nuclear war between the United States and the Soviet Union,

As many as fifty thousand nuclear weapons would be detonated.

In excess of 100 million Soviet citizens and a comparable number of Americans would be killed outright, and at least another 50 million in each country would die of injuries.

Deadly fallout would blanket large portions of the United States and the Soviet Union; air, water, and land would be contaminated; livestock and crops would suffer enormous destruction.

In both nations, medical facilities would be largely destroyed; little help of any kind would come to the survivors, many of whom would die from starvation and epidemics.

Industry, agriculture, and communications would be destroyed in

both countries, which would be unable to recover for an indefinite period. Widespread death and destruction would hit many bystander nations.

Smoke and dust from blast and fire, along with destruction of ozone in the atmosphere, might severely damage the global environment and the biosphere.

Source: Union of Concerned Scientists, 1982.

---

NATO strategy apparently has called for use of tactical nuclear weapons in the event that Warsaw Pact forces break into Western Europe using only conventional (nonnuclear) weapons. Should NATO initiate the use of even tactical nuclear weapons—some of which are as powerful as the Hiroshima bomb? Early in his first term, President Reagan indicated that he believed a "limited" nuclear war could be fought in Europe. When the Europeans reacted strongly to this statement, Reagan tried to clarify his position by saying that he had meant only that *if* a nuclear war broke out, perhaps it could be kept limited in some way.

To strengthen its nuclear capabilities, NATO decided in December 1979 to place new land-based medium range missiles in Western Europe. The plan was to deploy more than one hundred Pershing 2 missiles (each carrying an explosive power of about 1½ Hiroshima bombs) and 464 ground-launched cruise missiles. From Western Europe the Pershing, a new, highly sophisticated weapon, could reach targets in the Soviet Union in six minutes—giving the Soviets almost no warning time at all. The plan to deploy these missiles in Europe stirred tremendous controversy within NATO countries and raised a strong protest from the Soviets. Not until 1984 were the first missiles put in place—amid many protest demonstrations, particularly in West Germany.

## Crisis planning

Some experts have argued that advance planning for emergency situations is crucial to the avoidance of nuclear war. For example, what would happen if a low-flying aircraft with U.S. markings were to drop

TABLE 22.2
## Cost equivalents of selected military items

| Outlay | Civilian equivalent |
|--------|---------------------|
| 1. 7% of military outlays from 1981–86—$100 billion | Cost of rehabilitating the U.S. steel industry |
| 2. 63% of the cost overruns, to 1981, of 50 major weapons systems—$110 billion | 20-year cost of solar devices for energy conservation in commercial buildings, saving 3.7 million barrels of oil per day |
| 3. Two B-1 bombers—$400 million | Cost of rebuilding Cleveland's water-supply system |
| 4. Two nuclear-power carriers—$5.8 billion | Cost of converting 77 oil-using power plants to coal, saving 350,000 barrels of oil per day |
| 5. Three AH-64 helicopters—$82 million | 100 top-quality, energy-efficient electric trolleys |
| 6. Reactivation of two WW II battleships—$376 million | Reagan 1981 and 1982 cuts in energy-conservation investment |
| 7. Cost overrun, to 1981, of the army's UH-60A helicopter program—$4.7 billion | Annual capital investment for restoring New York City's roads, bridges, aqueducts, subways, and buses |
| 8. One A-6E Intruder (attack plane)—$23 million | Annual cost of staff of 200 to plan reversal of the arms race and conversion of military economy to civilian use |

Source: Seymour Melman, "Looting the Means of Production," *The New York Times*, July 26, 1981.

a nuclear bomb on a Soviet city? How could it be determined whether this plane actually were from the United States? Would Soviet reaction be automatic? Generally, could some third party trigger nuclear war? Could someone down the chain of command, such as a submarine commander, fire weapons without authorization? Could a computer mistakenly warn that an attack was approaching? In the near future, many other nations may possess nuclear weapons. Terrorist possession of nuclear weapons has also become increasingly likely. Some members of Congress have called for the pooling of information by U.S. and Soviet authorities and the establishment of a crisis center to monitor and contain nuclear incidents.

## Costs

It is hard to overestimate the cost burden of the arms race. The burden on the U.S. economy is serious; on the Soviet economy, staggering. Several scholars have traced the decline of the United States as an industrial power to the concentration of technical and scientific manpower in the defense industries. Defense dollars, if diverted for civilian use, also could go very far toward solving major social inadequacies in areas such as transport, health, and housing (see Table 22.2).

Spending on defense in the period 1981–85 exceeded that of the previous four-year period by one-third. In the view of many critics, we did not get our money's worth. There were spectacular examples of waste in procurement by the Pentagon—a hammer costing $435, a coffee brewer costing $7,622, an ashtray costing $659. The Pentagon's procurement procedures have been under attack for years. Defense contractors always seemed to make very handsome profits, regardless of design problems and cost overruns. Weapons were purchased with very little competitive bidding, which led to an excessively cozy relationship between Pentagon bureaucrats and defense contractors. The whole system, critics have charged, is woefully inefficient and in need of wholesale reform.

By 1985, bipartisan support for defense increases had begun to disappear. Whereas in 1981 Congress had debated only fifteen minutes before approving the goal of a 600-ship navy, by 1985 it appeared ready to freeze the defense budget altogether. The public, too, had become disillusioned, and support for more defense spending dropped drastically. Many maintained that before spending more money, the Pentagon should reform the way it went about its business and U.S. military strategy should be reassessed.

## The Third World

The nations of the so-called Third World—those not aligned with either the industrial democracies or the Soviet bloc—have come to loom large in discussions of the future of the international system. Most people on earth live under conditions that vary from serious economic privation to absolute poverty. In most of Africa and much of Asia, as well as in substantial portions of Latin America, poverty is endemic. Of course, Third World nations vary greatly in wealth, ranging from the oil-rich Arab states of the Middle East to nations in which most people live under conditions of extreme deprivation, such as Bangladesh.

The United States' foreign policy toward the Third World has combined self-interest with humanitarianism, and fear of communism with concern for human rights—a decidedly mixed picture. We must now examine the U.S. response to social change and economic deprivation in the Third World.

### Movements for social change

World War II unleashed anticolonial sentiments in many parts of the Third World. Prior to 1950, the British withdrew from the Indian subcontinent, the Dutch from Indonesia. France lingered in Indochina, fighting a losing battle. Most African nations gained independence in the 1950s and 1960s. The whole structure of world power seemed up for grabs, and social change inevitable. But who would control the change, who would direct the energies released?

Those in charge of U.S. foreign policy have found themselves facing a dilemma in this regard. Officially, the United States has long identified itself with popular aspirations for a "better life," as well as for democracy and national independence. But how should we respond to an independence movement inspired or directed by communists, threatening U.S. interests or violating our ideas of normalcy? Very often, the answer was to oppose the movement for social and political change. Out of fear of communist or other left-wing revolutions, the United States has often supported military or right-wing governments that, to our leaders, looked like a safer alternative. Of course, many of our leaders have hoped for some choice between these two alternatives, but in reality, such a moderately progressive, democratic alternative frequently did not exist. Over the years, the United States trained and lent significant military aid to many a police state. Through covert CIA operations, we also managed to help overthrow several left-leaning governments, including some that had significant popular support, as in Chile in 1973.

The U.S. dilemma in dealing with movements of social change was highlighted by developments in two countries in 1979. In that year, two right-wing leaders long supported by the United States were overthrown by popular uprisings: the Shah of Iran and Anastasio Somoza of Nicaragua. In both cases, there was convincing evidence that the regime had been widely unpopular and had engaged in extensive repression. Although both rulers had been in power for a long time, the forces of change eventually became too powerful.

In the Iranian case, the United States had aided and supported the Shah, either openly or behind the scenes, for several decades. Our presidents had regarded the Shah as a key element in U.S. efforts to ensure stability in the Middle East. Hence, there was a strong tendency on the part of U.S. policymakers to ignore the negative side of the Shah's policies and to lavish praise on his achievements—a tendency that led to incorrect assessments of the stability of the Shah's regime. When street demonstra-

Iran: before and after. First, we see President and Mrs. Nixon visiting the Shah of Iran and his wife in 1972. Then we see blindfolded American captives during the first day of the occupation of the U.S. embassy in Tehran in 1979. U.S. policy was closely identified with the person of the Shah; his overthrow led to violent anti-American actions.

tions escalated and the regime fell in a short period of time, U.S. policymakers were taken by surprise.

Iran's new rulers were sharply anti-American, though certainly not pro-Soviet. In fact, many elements were mixed in the Iranian revolution, ranging from an ultra-orthodox Islamic revival built around the Ayatollah Khomeini to left-wing revolutionaries, and including many groups in between. Later, U.S. efforts to deal with the new government were complicated by a year-long hostage crisis that ended on the day of Ronald Reagan's inauguration.

In Nicaragua, administrations prior to President Carter's had had generally cordial relations with the Somoza regime, despite its repressive and corrupt character. When revolutionary efforts began to undermine the regime's stability, the Carter administration did not rush to Somoza's support. In fact, the United States pressured Somoza to give up the presidency, which he refused to do. A popular revolution led by the Sandinista guerrillas overthrew Somoza in the summer of 1979. In many ways, U.S. influence in Nicaragua had sunk to its lowest point.[6] By failing to intervene to protect Somoza, we had alienated the

534

military and the right wing, while the leftist revolutionaries remained suspicious and hostile. The moderate forces preferred by the United States, such as Christian Democratic and Social Democratic political groups, seemed to be losing ground as conflicts became more and more polarized.

The more conservative Reagan administration then moved back toward policies characteristic of the 1950s, when the U.S. government had extended support to most right-wing regimes, including many that violated human rights. Within weeks of his inauguration, Ronald Reagan highlighted "communist subversion" in Central America as a key focus of U.S. foreign policy. The Reagan administration went on to support efforts by groups of guerrilla rebels ("contras") to overthrow the Sandinista government in Nicaragua. The administration argued that the Sandinistas were basically a Marxist government in the process of suppressing civil liberties and private enterprise in Nicaragua and transporting arms to revolutionaries in El Salvador. Many people disagreed with this assessment. It was pointed out that various freedoms in Nicaragua had been maintained to some

degree, that political debate continued on many issues, and that although some of Nicaragua's leaders were probably hard-line communists, the political situation there was fluid.

In 1984, it was discovered that the Central Intelligence Agency had assisted the contras in mining Nicaraguan harbors. Nicaragua took the United States to the World Court, which pronounced the American government guilty of a violation of international law. The United States rejected the court's jurisdiction but halted the mining. In 1985, President Reagan declared an embargo on trade with Nicaragua and compared the contras to the American founding fathers. Critics of Reagan's policy argued that the contras were not popular, that Nicaragua was no threat, and that the United States was pushing the regime into the arms of the USSR and into more authoritarian practices. After some hesitation, Congress approved nonmilitary aid to the contras.

What would have happened had the United States taken a less belligerent stance? Could the Sandinistas have been persuaded to maintain a pluralistic society? In 1984 the Sandinistas held elections, which

were won by Daniel Ortega, the Sandinista candidate. The U.S. government condemned the elections as fraudulent; other observers argued that the elections had been substantially open and that Ortega had real popular support.[7] Was this another case of U.S. unwillingness to live with a leftist revolution, whether entirely Marxist-Leninist or not? Or was the Sandinista government likely to jell into a Cuban mold, regardless of what the U.S. government might attempt to do? In either case, was U.S. intervention justified?

The Reagan administration also focused attention on events in El Salvador, alleging that an insurgency in that country was being assisted heavily by various communist countries, including Cuba and Vietnam. A memorandum issued by the State Department in February 1981 argued that "the insurgency in El Salvador has been progressively transformed into a textbook case of indirect armed aggression by Communist powers."[8] Critics of this interpretation argued that the State Department's case was full of factual errors, misleading statements, and ambiguities, and that its conclusion about the insurgency being inspired by external forces was far too sweeping. Even the Salvadoran government itself saw the war as primarily an internal struggle. Perhaps most important, critics declared, the Reagan administration's view simply ignored the many moderate elements connected with the insurgency—democratic leftists who had despaired of bringing change to El Salvador in any other fashion.

By 1985 there was evidence that a democratic center might be emerging in El Salvador. Jose Napoleon Duarte was able to fashion several electoral victories. The Reagan administration hailed Duarte as the sort of alternative they sought between right-wing and left-wing terrorism. Whether Duarte would survive or prevail was not clear. In the meantime, the administration said little and did less in regard to other human rights violators in South and Central America. Guatemala, where mass killings had taken place, and Chile, where political repression remained in force, were on the periphery of the Reagan administration's interest.[9] What small gestures of censure were taken toward Chile, for example, were ineffectual, and administration spokesmen seemed

535

# Human rights policy

Human rights is at the core of our foreign policy because it is central to what America is and stands for. "Human rights" is not something we tack on to our foreign policy but its very purpose: the defense and promotion of freedom in the world. . . . Our human rights policy is not a decoration.

*President Jimmy Carter*

Concern for human rights as an explicit element in U.S. foreign policy was a unique feature of the Carter administration. Addressing the United Nations in 1977, Carter described a commitment to basic human rights that included condemnation of all torture and mistreatment of political prisoners. He also established a State Department office for human rights enforcement, and endowed it with significant powers. During the Carter years, sanctions were imposed on many alleged human rights violators, including Argentina, the Philippines, South Korea, Ethiopia, Zaire, Guinea, Haiti, Brazil, Guatemala, Chile, Paraguay, and Uruguay. U.S. economic aid, loans, and military sales to these nations were sometimes stopped or limited. Carter's human rights policies also had the effect of increasing concern with human rights internationally.

Were Carter's policies successful or sensible? On the plus side, the United States dissociated itself from some very unsavory regimes and exerted pressure in a direction most Americans regard as a moral one. In addition, the policy occasionally had concrete results: some political prisoners were released, and some regimes did show more respect for human rights. Critics made three chief arguments against the policy. They maintained that little attention had been paid to human rights violations in communist countries, such as China and the Soviet Union. Further, they attacked Carter for a general lack of consistency and for allegedly making enemies needlessly. Finally, critics took the position that the United States should aid its friends, whether those friends were human rights violators or not.

---

to indicate that the military dictatorship there was not entirely unsatisfactory to them.[10]

## Economics: rich and poor

Approximately 1 billion people throughout the world live in desperate poverty—including 750 million in the poorest of conditions. About 10 million die every year of diseases related to malnutrition, and half of those are children. Most of the abject poor, who comprise nearly one-fifth of humanity, live in what are referred to as less-developed countries, or LDCs.

The U.S. government has often sounded a strongly humanitarian note in its proclamations about the problems of Third World poverty. President Carter, for example, stated in 1978 that "we cannot have a peaceful and prosperous world if a large part of the world's people are at or near the edge of hunger." The United States has often been in the vanguard of relief efforts in emergency situations such as the Ethiopian famine of 1984–85. Also, American volunteers and relief agencies often have played important roles in such crises, and the Peace Corps has helped with development projects in many poor nations.

Clearly, such activities are in our own best interests. Fear of the dominance of anti-American regimes in such countries is a crucial factor, as is the fact that the poor nations are now among our more important trading partners. The United States sells more of its goods to LDCs than to Europe and the Soviet Union combined. And the developing countries supply us with many critical raw materials and low-cost consumer goods.

What policies has the U.S. government followed

President Reagan sharply deemphasized human rights in foreign relations. Close relations were resumed with many sanctioned countries. Vice-President George Bush spoke of the "wonderful democracy" of the Philippines led by Ferdinand Marcos, whom most observers considered to be a virtual dictator. Efforts were abandoned to withhold loans and military aid from Argentina, Chile, and Uruguay. In its broad foreign policy initiatives, the Reagan administration chose to emphasize terrorism rather than human rights issues. But with violations of human rights becoming increasingly common, it is unlikely that the issues involved will disappear entirely from the foreign policy debate. In regard to perhaps the worst human rights offender of all, South Africa, many critics maintained that the Reagan administration had taken a far too friendly approach. They called for a much tougher stand against the South African regime and its racist policies—a stand that would reflect a renewed concern with human rights.

velopment. Second, more aid was focused on fewer nations. The chief recipients in 1984, for example, were Israel, Egypt, South Korea, Turkey, Pakistan, Greece, Spain, and El Salvador. Third, the aid was more likely to be *bilateral:* that is, given directly to the recipient nation. This procedure gave the U.S. government greater control over the use of the aid. These new policies were defended on the pragmatic grounds that they better served our immediate interests in various world trouble spots. We should also note that U.S. aid programs have given a big boost to U.S. multinational corporations. About 75 percent of total development assistance money is spent on purchases in the United States itself.

Foreign aid, in whatever form, has never been very popular with the American people, many of whom have regarded it as a kind of international handout. For most of the 1960s and all of the 1970s, foreign aid expenditures declined. By 1980 the United States ranked close to the bottom of all the rich nations in terms of nonmilitary foreign aid as a percentage of GNP (see Table 22.3). In the early 1980s, the levels of foreign aid dropped drastically in all the more advanced industrial nations, in response to their own economic problems. In addition, less and less aid was going to the poorest countries, who needed it most. Whereas in 1970, 48 percent of foreign aid from all nations went to the lowest-income nations, by 1980 only 35 percent was going to those countries. The income gap between the "Fourth World" of poorest nations and the rest of the world was widening rapidly.

What would the poor nations like from the rich? They want new terms of trade, to aid them in selling their goods, and worldwide stabilization of the prices of the raw materials they export. The many poor nations that are energy-short have called for the creation of an energy affiliate of the World Bank that would provide credits to developing nations. On a loftier plane, the LDCs would like to see the gradual creation of a new world economic order—one in which they could gain a larger slice of the world's economic pie.

In response, President Reagan called for poor nations to pull themselves up by their bootstraps. He

in dealing with the precarious economic conditions of the Third World? Since the end of World War II, America has regularly extended economic assistance to poorer nations.

During much of the 1970s, U.S. foreign aid efforts were focused on alleviating poverty and bringing poorer nations into the mainstream of the world economy. The theory behind this effort was that such aid would help prevent economic failure and social disruption, and thereby assure more-stable politics as well as ameliorate suffering. U.S. aid in the 1970s was often *multilateral:* that is, it was channeled through international organizations such as the World Bank and International Monetary Fund, where it was pooled with the contributions from other countries.

The Reagan administration, while pushing for increases in foreign aid, also shifted the priorities of that aid. First, a larger percentage of aid was given for "security" purposes, as opposed to economic de-

TABLE 22.3

## Development assistance* as a percentage of GNP, 1980

| | Percent of GNP | Total assistance in millions, 1975–80 |
|---|---|---|
| Switzerland | 2.6% | $2,698 |
| United Kingdom | 2.4 | 12,795 |
| France | 1.8 | 11,522 |
| Sweden | 1.5 | 1,837 |
| West Germany | 1.3 | 10,584 |
| Canada | 1.1 | 2,755 |
| Japan | 0.7 | 6,766 |
| United States | 0.5 | 13,852 |
| Finland | 0.4 | 196 |

*The United Nations defines development assistance as "financial aid from developed economies (or donor countries) to developing countries expressly intended for the economic and social development of the latter." At least 25 percent of the aid must be in the form of grants (as opposed to loans).
Sources: G. T. Kurian, *The New Book of World Rankings* (New York: Facts on File, 1984), p. 73; International Bank for Reconstruction and Development, *World Development Report, 1982* (New York: Oxford University Press, 1982).

maintained that the magic of the free market would work for Third World nations as it had for the United States. Not many LDCs were convinced by this argument, particularly because most were at least partially socialist in economic organization. Because of the international economic power wielded by the United States, however, it would be virtually impossible to revise world economics without U.S. participation.

Why should the United States care about the problems of people in other nations when we have our own problems to deal with? Senator John Danforth (D, Missouri) reasoned as follows: "The answer, I think, has to do with who we are and how we perceive ourselves as a country. America is more than a place to hang your hat. It does represent a value system most of us believe in very strongly. That value system has to do with the worth of human beings, whoever they are, wherever they are. We believe that lives are worth saving, that our fellow humans must be fed. But it is not enough to profess this belief. We must act on it."[11]

## Conclusions

Democratic concerns are clearly related to U.S. foreign policy objectives, even if such relationships are often controversial. To begin with, most U.S. leaders have maintained that the question of democracy is at the core of our conflict with the Soviet Union: we defend the "free world," whereas the communists stand for tyranny. This justification seemed persuasive in the early Cold War days, but it has grown increasingly hazy and complicated of late.

A whole series of issues have come to complicate the simple relationship between U.S. foreign policy and the defense of democracy:

1 Should the United States seek to destabilize governments that our current policymakers dislike, but that are relatively popular with their own people?

2 Should we ally ourselves with dictatorial governments simply because they are anticommunist? Conversely, should we oppose any government that calls itself communist, Marxist, or radical?

3 Does détente with the Soviet Union help the cause of human rights relaxation within the communist world, or is it a naive policy that permits the Soviets to gain global advantages?

4 Since democracy rests on the basic possibility of survival, what path should the United States follow in the nuclear arms race? Should we seek superiority over the Soviets, hoping that will prevent them from a first strike? Or should we seek to reduce the threat of nuclear war through arms limitation or reduction?

5 What role should the United States play in assisting the development of the poorer nations? How much of our own wealth should we be willing to share? Should direct economic aid play a major role? Should the United States support only capitalistic development in these nations, or

A Peruvian Indian carries a U.S. food aid bundle to a village in the Andes. Despite considerable donations of surplus food, underlying problems of underdevelopment persist. These cannot be remedied by emergency efforts.

should it assist other types of economic systems? Is there anything we can do to further democratic development in LDCs?

On the question of foreign policy and democratic consent, some practitioners of U.S. politics once argued that foreign affairs generally were far less important in deciding elections than were domestic politics. In 1960, for example, the governor of Illinois told his party's presidential nominee, Richard Nixon, that "what is really important is the price of hogs in Chicago." How ironic this remark now seems in the light of twenty-five years' additional experience! Foreign policy issues have loomed extraordinarily large in recent presidential elections, and assuredly will continue to do so in the near future.

Much has changed in U.S. politics. Since the Vietnam War, a far larger "attentive public" has become involved in foreign policy debates. In addition, the old bipartisan foreign policy consensus has broken down, apparently for good. In such a situation, the range of debate on foreign policy has grown broader and deeper. Although such conflict can lead to paralysis or contradictory actions, it can also lead to a much-needed clarification of our goals as a nation and to a reassessment of the means we should employ to reach those goals.

Many observers have wondered, however, whether it makes any sense for a large electorate to actively debate foreign policy issues or such technical questions as arise, for instance, in negotiations related to nuclear weapons. Yet foreign policy and defense matters affect us all—sometimes drastically. The making of such policies is too important to be left to a few elected officials and their advisers. Inevitably, certain issues will require a high level of knowledge and expertise. But many others can be understood and assessed by almost any democratic citizen. The process of gaining informed consent from citizens is a vital element in keeping democracy alive in the area of foreign and defense policies. If leaders believe they can simply do whatever they think best in these areas, we will all be less safe—and we will lose part of the essence of democracy.

As the political philosopher Michael Walzer once noted in regard to the issue of nuclear weapons strategy: "The day-to-day drift is always toward specialized, secret, technically complex, and esoteric doctrine. But real political leaders, *if they can hear the clamor of their constituents*, can stop the drift. Nuclear deterrence will defend democracy only if it is democratically constrained."[12] This point applies to all the areas of foreign policy we have discussed in this chapter.

## NOTES

1 *U.S. News and World Report*, "Inside the CIA," June 25, 1984.

2 George F. Kennan, "The Sources of Soviet Conduct," *Foreign Affairs* 25 (July 1947): 566–82.

3 On the missile crisis, see Robert Kennedy, *Thirteen Days* (New York: New American Library, 1969); and Irving Janis, *Groupthink* (Boston: Houghton Mifflin, 1982), Chapter 6.

4 Mark Rovner, *Defense Dollars and Sense* (Washington, D.C.: Common Cause, 1983), p. 14.

5 Paul R. Ehrlich, Carl Sagan, Donald Kennedy, and Walter O. Roberts, *The Cold and the Dark: The World After Nuclear War* (New York: W. W. Norton, 1985).

6 Richard Millett, "Central American Paralysis," *Foreign Policy*, Summer 1980, pp. 99–117.

7 John B. Oakes, " 'Fraud' in Nicaragua," *The New York Times*, November 15, 1984, p. 31. See also *Report of the Latin American Studies Association Delegation to Observe the Nicaraguan General Election of November 4, 1984*.

8 U.S. Department of State, *Communist Interference in El Salvador*, Special Report #80 (Washington, D.C.: U.S. Government Printing Office, February 23, 1981).

9 Piero Gleijeses, "The Guatemalan Silence," *The New Republic*, June 10, 1985, pp. 20–23.

10 Jackson Diehl, "U.S. Policy in Chile: How to Please Nobody," *Washington Post*, national weekly edition, June 10, 1985, p. 18.

11 John C. Danforth, "Africa: Does Anybody Really Care?" *Washington Post*, national weekly edition, February 13, 1984, p. 29.

12 Michael Walzer, "Deterrence and Democracy," *The New Republic*, July 2, 1984, p. 21.

## SELECTED READINGS

For historical perspectives on U.S. foreign policy, see F. Mark, *Manifest Destiny and Mission in American History* (New York: Vintage, 1963); Samuel P. Huntington, *The Soldier and the State* (New York: Vintage, 1964); William A. Williams, *The Tragedy of America Diplomacy* (New York: Delta, 1962); John W. Spanier, *American Foreign Policy since World War II* (New York: Praeger, 1973); and John L. Gaddis, *The United States and the Origins of the Cold War* (New York: Columbia University Press, 1972).

On Vietnam and other recent episodes in U.S. foreign policy, see David Halberstam, *The Best and the Brightest* (New York: Fawcett, 1973); Frances FitzGerald, *Fire in the Lake* (New York: Vintage, 1967); R. W. Gregg and C. W. Kegley, Jr., *After Vietnam* (New York: Anchor, 1971); K. A. Oye, *et al.*, *Eagle Entangled* (New York: Longman's, 1979); and Richard E. Feinberg, *The Intemperate Zone: The Third World Challenge to U.S. Foreign Policy* (New York: Norton, 1983).

On the U.S.-Soviet rivalry and the arms race, consider Richard Barnet, *The Giants* (New York: Simon & Schuster, 1977); Anatol Rapoport, *The Big Two* (New York: Pegasus, 1971); R. J. Pranger, *Six U.S. Perspectives on Soviet Foreign Affairs* (Washington, D.C.: American Enterprise Institute, 1979); R. Falk and R. J. Lifton, *Indefensible Weapons* (New York: Basic Books, 1982); Elie Abel, *The Missile Crisis* (Philadelphia: Lippincott, 1966);

A. George and R. Smoke, *Deterrence in American Foreign Policy: Theory and Practice* (New York: Columbia University Press, 1974); Thomas Powers, *Thinking about the Next War* (New York: Mentor, 1982); John Newhouse, *Cold Dawn: The Story of SALT* (New York: Holt, 1973); Alva Myrdal, *The Game of Disarmament* (New York: Pantheon, 1976); Jonathan Schell, *The Fate of the Earth* (New York: Knopf, 1982), and *The Abolition* (New York: Knopf, 1984); Freeman Dyson, *Weapons and Hope* (New York: Harper & Row, 1984); G. Allison, A. Carnesale, and J. S. Nye, Jr., *Hawks, Doves, and Owls: An Agenda for Avoiding Nuclear War* (New York: Norton, 1985); and Daniel Ford, *The Button: The Pentagon's Strategic Com-* *mand and Control System* (New York: Simon & Schuster, 1985).

On Central American matters, see J. L. Fied, *et al.*, *Guatemala in Rebellion* (New York: Grove, 1983); M. E. Gettleman, *et al.*, *El Salvador* (New York: Grove, 1981); Raymond Bonner, *Weakness and Deceit: U.S. Policy and El Salvador* (New York: Times Books, 1983); R. A. White, *The Morass: United States Intervention in Central America* (New York: Harper & Row, 1983); and H. J. Wiarda, ed., *Rift and Revolution: The Central American Imbroglio* (New York: American Enterprise Institute, 1984).

# Chapter
twenty-three

# Energy and environment

# Fulfilling or polluting the American dream?

A host of new terms and names entered the common language in the 1970s. There was talk of "synfuels," "photovoltaics," and "passive solar." We heard about "radioactive waste," "carrying capacity," "fossil fuels," "breeder reactors," "meltdowns," and "Agent Orange." "Environmental impact statements" became matters of controversy. Places and groups imprinted themselves on popular consciousness: Three Mile Island, Love Canal, the Clamshell Alliance, OPEC. A completely new set of issues suddenly entered our national consciousness and our politics.

In texts on U.S. politics written fifteen years ago, few of these terms appeared. Only in the last two decades has the complex set of issues connected with energy and the environment emerged with full force in U.S. society. Only since the early 1970s have our political processes begun to come to grips with these issues in any sustained—not to say successful—way.

What are the main dimensions of these problems? They can be divided into two "shocks" and a "realization":

*Shock 1:* We discovered (are still discovering) that we have been poisoning and degrading our environment. Environmental degradation has taken the form of air pollution, water pollution, the widespread and uncontrolled use of toxic chemicals, and many other activities.

*Shock 2:* When the Arab nations embargoed their oil exports in 1973–74, Americans very sharply and suddenly realized that energy was a problem. We could no longer take for granted a continuous, unlimited, and relatively cheap supply of fuel. As it became clear that even were the Organization of Petroleum Exporting Countries (OPEC) to continue producing oil at peak capacity, sooner or later the world supply of fossil fuels would run short.

*Realization:* Resources are not infinite, and neither is the carrying capacity of the environment. We have the ability to use up our resources, pollute our environment, destroy the fertility of the land, kill off other species, and create serious dangers to ourselves. We can, through neglect or even deliberate planning, create vast pollution and resource depletion problems for future generations—who may or may not be able to cope with them.

Having experienced these shocks and come to this realization, where do we go from here? A whole series of difficult and highly political questions must be answered. How much pollution, if any, can we live with? Should we continue to destroy other species through pollution or alteration of natural habitats? How much economic growth are we willing to sacrifice for a cleaner environment? Are there viable

543

Ahmed Zaki Yamani, Saudi Arabia's oil minister, and members of his delegation at an OPEC conference in 1980. Saudi Arabia is the world's major oil producer and as such plays a central role in OPEC's policy-making. By the mid-1980's, OPEC's unity had weakened as oil prices dropped and controversies broke out about the pricing of crude oil.

energy alternatives that might prove less polluting? Do we have to change our lifestyle? Who will bear the costs of needed changes? What role should government play?

To complicate the picture further, U.S. society has failed to reach a national consensus on just how serious these issues are. Many Americans, including many politicians and political activists, do not believe that either environmental or energy problems are all that severe. Definition of the problems, therefore, has become a political battleground.

Another complicating factor is that many of these issues are interrelated. For example, solutions to energy problems are likely to have serious consequences for the environment: coal is a major polluter; nuclear power has safety and waste disposal problems. Whatever course we pursue, there will be a price to pay. Both energy and environmental issues are tied closely to economic questions. Stiff environmental rules, for example, tend to add new costs to the production of goods. In times of economic difficulties, many people demand that environmental restrictions be relaxed.

Energy issues also have important international dimensions. As the nations of OPEC bargained and compromised among themselves about oil prices and supplies, their impact on the international economy became increasingly important. A new actor appeared on the international political scene—one whom U.S. policymakers had to take into account. U.S. dependence on Middle East oil even led President Jimmy Carter to announce that we would take whatever steps were needed to protect our supplies from the Persian Gulf area. One of the objectives of the Nixon, Ford, Carter, and Reagan administrations was to extricate the United States from dependence on imported oil. This proved impossible in the short run—and perhaps even in the long run. As long as imported oil looms large in the energy picture, the OPEC nations and Persian Gulf stability will remain critical elements of U.S. foreign policy.

In this chapter, we will set out the major issues involving energy and environment and examine our choices and governmental policies. The first step in doing so will be to look at the distinctly American context of these issues.

544

## The environment: from exploitation to protection

Alexis de Tocqueville, a young Frenchman, visited the United States in the 1840s. He, like many other foreign observers, was awed by the bountifulness of the American continent, noting "Fortune's immense booty to the Americans." Many students of U.S. history have noted the important effects of this abundance on the national psychology and political culture of the United States. Abundance has influenced the way we think about (or fail to think about) our political, social, and economic problems. We long ago accepted a philosophy of growth—of "more" and "bigger"—as our national ethos. We were to be a nation of producers and consumers—enjoying the fruits of our good fortune.

In taking maximum advantage of these immense resources, we have radically transformed this land. Unlike the Indians, European settlers were not content to live in harmony with nature, using only small pieces of the environment for their purposes. Instead, Americans sought to make *the most* of resources, to transform nature and make her serve our needs.

Government's role in this process of developing the continent has been, historically, to facilitate growth. The U.S. water system and the energy resources related to it, for example, have been developed through the work of the Federal Bureau of Reclamation and the Army Corps of Engineers. Much of the work of these agencies undoubtedly was beneficial on the whole, but critics have objected to the large numbers of fish killed, the immense tracts of land flooded, and the numerous wildlife habitats destroyed. Government policies have also played essential roles in land development, railroad growth, and the creation of suburbia via the vast network of superhighways. All these developments have had serious effects on our environment, on the ways we employ energy, and the amount of energy we use.

In the 1960s, this picture began to change. Now, at least officially, federal, state, and local governments are committed to greater environmental concern and to energy consciousness. Government now works in two directions instead of one. One result has been frequent battles within the government between advocates of different environmental and energy positions.

Concern for the environment was not solely a product of the 1960s, however. Its roots extend back into the nineteenth century, when nature lovers and

One of the major symbols of environmentalism, the giant sequoias of California. Some regarded these trees with a special reverence; others quipped that if you'd seen one redwood you'd seen them all.

545

French soldiers help clean up an oil spill that swept onto the coast of Brittany. Oil spills like this one played a key role in focusing popular consciousness on environmental problems.

sportsmen sought protection of park areas. In 1872, Yellowstone was designated as the first national park. President Theodore Roosevelt, working with aide Gifford Pinchot, expanded the national forest reserves to 190 million acres. Additional conservation measures were passed in the 1960s, including the Wilderness Act (1964), Land and Water Conservation Act (1965), and the Wild and Scenic Rivers Act (1968).

Pollution had also been a concern for several decades. A few cities began treating their sewage in the nineteenth century. But not until 1948 was the first federal water pollution legislation passed by Congress. Air pollution, too, had been on the agenda of U.S. localities for several decades. Cincinnati and Chicago passed smoke control ordinances in 1881. California made efforts to control smog and industrial pollution, and added auto emission controls in the 1960s. The first federal air pollution law came into effect in 1955.

Federal legislation of the late 1960s and early 1970s added a new dimension to efforts to deal with the problems of the environment. These new, tougher laws ushered in a great wave of change, reflecting a suddenly deepened public awareness of the issues. Growing numbers of people began to take environmental issues seriously. In 1966 the Sierra Club staged

its first major political battle, running ads that opposed a federal Bureau of Reclamation plan to place a dam on the Colorado River to provide electricity for Los Angeles. (One ad headline: "SHOULD WE ALSO FLOOD THE SISTINE CHAPEL SO THE TOURISTS CAN GET NEARER THE CEILING?") Sierra Club membership doubled over the next two years. In May 1970, several environmental groups staged the first Earth Day celebration, which was aimed at heightening public consciousness of environmental problems. Later came Sun Day, focused on solar energy as an alternative to fossil fuels.

In part, the environmental movement grew out of the social activism of the 1960s, which had taught citizens that grass-roots action was often required to focus government's attention on pressing issues. But the environmental movement also drew on popular dissatisfactions with the insensitivities of business, government, and others to the quality of life. Many Americans had decided that *more* was not necessarily *better*, especially if "more" meant polluted air, fish kills, dying lakes, a landscape strewn with unsightly waste, and crowded, sprawling, and unplanned urban and suburban developments.

By the mid-1960s, environmentalists were busy launching attacks on federal policy, or the lack of it. They called for giving environmental considerations a higher priority. In 1969, Congress responded to the new wave of public concern by passing the National Environmental Policy Act. The act, passed overwhelmingly, constituted a pledge by the federal government to protect and renew the environment. It established the basis for creation of the **Environmental Protection Agency (EPA)** to coordinate efforts in this policy field, and provided for the creation of the President's Council on Environmental Quality. The CEQ reviews federal programs, recommends legislation, and sponsors independent studies. NEPA also required that **environmental impact statements** be prepared whenever proposals for legislation or other major federal actions may significantly affect the quality of the environment.

EPA took authority over much of the then-fragmented federal environmental programs. For example, it acquired control over water pollution from the Department of the Interior, over air pollution and solid-waste management matters from HEW, and over regulation of pesticides from the Department of Agriculture. EPA soon became the government's largest regulatory agency in terms of budget and number of employees.

NEPA passed Congress without much controversy, but once it became law, it set off sparks. Many federal agencies had to reappraise their normal way of conducting business. Billions of dollars worth of programs had to be reassessed. Thousands of hours were spent considering environmental impacts. The law

Hoover Dam with Lake Mead behind it, and power generators below. Built in the 1930s, the dam (and many others like it) provided immense new sources of power. In addition, they created areas for recreation and were useful in flood control. At the time they were built, there was little attention paid to the question of any negative effect the dams might have on fish or the natural environment.

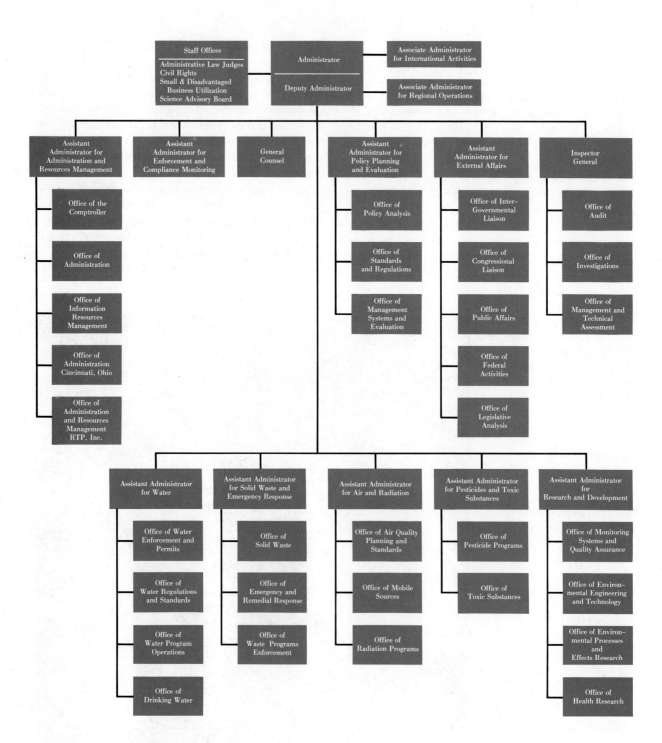

FIGURE 23.1
Environmental Protection Agency

# The Tellico Dam: a triumph of bad sense

In June 1979, Jimmy Carter signed the Energy and Water Development Appropriations Act. Attached to the act was a rider, added at the last moment in a slick parliamentary maneuver, that authorized the Tennessee Valley Authority to complete the controversial Tellico Dam project "notwithstanding the Endangered Species Act or any other law." It was an extraordinary step to take—placing a federal building project beyond the reach of the law. Carter signed "with regret," not wanting to involve himself any further in a battle with those members of Congress for whom the Tellico project had become a personal battle.

Most Americans knew very little about the meaning of the Tellico struggle. For the ones who did know, the conflict seemed to be between those who wanted to save the last remaining habitat of a three-inch minnow known as the snail darter and those who wanted to complete a major hydroelectric and flood control dam and not waste the $120 million already spent. Seen in this light, the whole struggle had a touch of absurdity about it—was it really sensible to stop a vast project for the sake of a few tiny fish?

Yet the reality of the situation differed considerably from the public image of a fish-versus-dam battle. In fact, the Tellico Dam was only a small part of a much larger project involving the creation of a 38,000-acre lake. Very few Americans realized that the figure of $120 million usually mentioned was largely spent not on the dam itself, but on road development and acquisition of land, including 22,000 acres that were not to be flooded. Supporters of the dam argued that the dam and the lake it would create were needed for recreation and electric power, but it turned out that there were already twenty-four major dams and lakes within 60 miles of Tellico. Many of these had undeveloped shores. Moreover, Tellico would produce only 23 megawatts of electricity within a regional capacity of 27,000 megawatts. Even the TVA was willing to admit in 1978 that the lake to be created when the dam was closed was not necessary, and that the farmland to be flooded exceeded in value the benefits to be obtained from the dam project. In 1977, a General Accounting Office study argued that the dam was uneconomic and that only 1 percent of the claims of future benefits were justified. In addition, archeologists discovered a Cherokee Indian burial site of worldwide significance in the area.

Faced with mounting opposition, Republican Senator Howard Baker, a Tennessean, called for a special cabinet level review committee to consider the project. A unanimous committee found the project unsound on economic, not just ecological, grounds. Baker and his allies, however, wouldn't give up. On June 18, 1979, in a virtually empty House of Representatives, the rider was attached to the appropriations bill—a process that took 43 seconds. It squeezed by the Senate by four votes.

Sources: On the Tellico Dam project, see L. J. Carter, "Lessons from the Snail Darter Saga," *Science*, February 23, 1979; "TVA's Bitter Victory," *Newsweek*, November 26, 1979; and "Snail Darter vs. Dam: Pork Barrelers Win," *Science News*, October 6, 1979.

---

also spawned a considerable body of litigation in the courts. Industry and conservative politicians joined forces to resist the regulatory requirements set forth by EPA.

Let us now look at some particular environmental problems and the specific ways government has responded to them. Later, we will take a closer look at the political conflicts involved.

## Environmental problems and governmental responses

The environment, we have learned, involves an extremely complicated net of relationships. Poisons poured into the waters can come back to haunt us through fish we eat or the liquid that comes out of the tap. Pollution spewed into the air affects not only our lungs, but also rivers, lakes, and trees. How we handle the spaces we live in determines the visual and auditory sensations we subject ourselves to. The environment also includes other living things—plants, insects, animals, fish—some of which may perish because of human choices. We are only beginning to understand that we are ourselves part of various ecological systems. Whether those systems operate in a healthy fashion or not has important consequences for us, and for nature itself.

Today's environmental problems run a gamut of issues: air pollution, water pollution, toxic waste, solid-waste management, natural resource use, coastal ecology, land use, and noise. In this section we will focus on the first three of these issues, which are generally acknowledged to be the most significant.

## Air pollution

The main sources of air pollution are factories, cars and trucks, and electric generating plants. Every one of the country's major manufacturers is a major air polluter; on average, U.S. industry turns out an average of 300 pounds of air pollution per year per citizen. The more than 3,400 plants that generate electricity produce tons of sulfur oxides, nitrogen oxides, and ashes. Nevertheless, vehicles comprise the major source of air pollution, producing about 60 percent of the total.

A by-product of the emissions of industrial pollutants into the air has been the development of "acid rain" throughout the industrial world. Some rain now falling on the eastern United States has an acidity about equal to lemon juice. Although there is disagreement about the causes and effects of acid rain, it is known to kill fish life and vegetation and to erode stone and steel structures. It may also be introducing dangerous elements into drinking water.

The other effects of air pollution are fairly well documented. The famous Los Angeles smog, for example, leads doctors to advise thousands to leave

the area every year for their health. Studies suggested that in New York City in 1977 a nonsmoker involuntarily ingested the equivalent of half a pack of cigarettes a day from the air. The National Academy of Science has estimated that fifteen thousand deaths a year and 7 million sick days are traceable to air pollution. According to EPA figures, we spend about $9 billion per year on health costs incurred from air-related ailments, such as lung cancer and emphysema. The EPA has also estimated that air pollution annually causes $8 billion in property losses and $7.6 billion in destruction of vegetation.[1] Finally, the release of carbon dioxide and heat into the atmosphere has been linked by some scientists to a "greenhouse effect," which may lead to a gradual and dangerous increase in the Earth's temperature.

In 1963, Congress passed the **Clean Air Act**, establishing national air quality standards; amendments in 1970 put some teeth in the act. The EPA was to set standards for five specific pollutants that posed proven health hazards: sulfur dioxide, nitrogen dioxide, particulates, carbon monoxide, and photochemical oxidants. Later, hydrocarbons were added to the list. The EPA has adopted various strategies for achieving cleaner air: the adoption of standards limiting emissions of pollutants from power plants, for example, and the issuance of a requirement that cars be equipped with emission-control devices and that unleaded fuel be used in most new vehicles.

Over the years, the EPA has relaxed some of its standards in the face of severe political pressures, as well as disagreements among experts. Some of EPA's strategies to reduce pollution from autos—such as banning cars from high pollution areas, raising tolls on access routes, and imposing parking taxes—have encountered fierce opposition. Congress legislated against some of these strategies explicitly in the Clean Air amendments of 1977, which also postponed until 1987 the date for achieving a satisfactory level of air quality nationwide.

The EPA's efforts have encountered opposition on several grounds: that they impose excessive costs, particularly on industries that must install new equipment; that they require excessive changes in people's usual habits, such as driving their cars into urban areas; and that they require too much federal interference with local governments and industry. On the other side, environmentalists have argued that pressures on EPA to delay implementation of clean air standards or to loosen them up have only meant additional long-range health costs for society as a whole.

By some measurements, air quality has shown a startling and rapid improvement. In the 1970s, particulate matter in the air and carbon dioxide emissions declined. By 1975 the Council on Environmental Quality was able to report that the steady increase in air pollution since 1940 had been halted. In 1983 the Council on Environmental Quality reported that over the previous twelve years, sulfur dioxide emissions had declined by almost 25 percent, particulate emissions by 58 percent, carbon monoxide by 27 percent, and oxidants by 28 percent. Nitrogen oxide emissions, however, had *increased* by 12 percent in the same period.[2] Clearly, considerable progress had been made in regard to most of the major sources of polluted air.

Not everyone has agreed, however, that progress has gone far enough or fast enough. Some conservationist groups have argued, for example, that smog remained a problem in 25 percent of the nation's counties. Also, the problem of acid rain has not yet been handled. Even when faced with powerful pressures to take vigorous action to reduce those industrial emissions that appear to be the major source of acid rain, the Reagan administration refused to act, claiming that more research was necessary. Industries that burned high-sulfur coal claimed that the costs of installing the necessary antipollution equipment would raise utility rates 20 to 50 percent. The United Mine Workers estimated that as many as eighty thousand mining jobs might be lost if the use of such coal were curtailed. Environmentalists countered by pointing out that unless acid rain were curtailed, large numbers of lakes and vast areas of forest would be killed entirely. **Acid rain** was also found to have highly corrosive effects on buildings and other structures, with estimates of damage ranging well up into the billions.

Another bleak development was the release in 1985 of the first systematic study of toxic chemicals emitted into the air. The study, ordered by Congressman Henry A. Waxman, chairman of the House Subcommittee on Health and the Environment, found hazardous materials at far higher levels in many more locations than previously estimated, and concluded that thousands of tons of potentially carcinogenic agents were being released into the air from hundreds of factories. Waxman pointed out that there were no national standards regarding emissions of most of the chemicals involved.[3]

## Water pollution

Many of the nation's rivers, bays, and lakes have become seriously degraded. The chief source of water pollution is industry, which accounts for approximately 80 percent of the pollutants that deprive water of oxygen. The volume of water used in industrial production is staggering. The steel industry alone uses close to 4 trillion gallons a year, and steel production generates suspended solids, oils, acids, and poisonous gases that mix with the wastewater. Another source of water pollution is the waste released by cities into nearby waterways.

Agricultural producers generate over 20 billion tons of waste per year, principally in the form of manure from feed lots. In the Missouri River basin, an area noted for cattle production, commercial feed lots secrete organic wastes into the surrounding water system equivalent to the untreated sewage of a city of 37.5 million inhabitants. In addition, agricultural pesticides that find their way into the water supply have been responsible for large kills of shellfish, birds, and aquatic animals. The fact that ingested pesticides are passed up the food chain further increases the health risks for animals.

In 1972, Congress passed amendments to the Federal Water Pollution Control Act that were aimed at restoring and maintaining the "chemical, physical, and biological integrity of the Nation's waters." The new law set a target date of 1983 for achieving fishable, swimmable waters. Subsequent laws extended these protections to oceans and to drinking-water supplies.

The basic thrust of the 1972 amendments was an effort to control **effluent,** the polluted water released by cities and industries. Technological standards were set and timetables for cleanups were established. Also, large federal grants were provided to induce cooperation; in particular, Congress appropriated huge federal expenditures for waste treatment plants. This cleanup effort proved to be the largest public works program in U.S. history. By the early 1980s, much had been done. Between 1970 and 1982, the number of people served by municipal wastewater treatment systems almost doubled, to 150 million. The volume of some pollutants entering waterways largely from industrial sources was drastically reduced—oil and grease by 71 percent, dissolved solids by 52 percent, phosphates by 74 percent, and heavy metals by 78 percent.[4]

A 1985 report (cited in *The New York Times* on May 13, 1985) prepared by the Association of State and Interstate Water Pollution Control Administrators found that since 1972, 296,000 miles of streams had maintained their water quality, 47,000 miles had improved, and 11,000 were degraded. As for lakes, 10.1 acres had maintained their quality, 390,000 acres had improved, but 1.6 million acres had become degraded, while an additional 4.1 million acres were of unknown status. The study also found that 12 percent of municipal sewage systems were in significant noncompliance with rules for control of pollutants, as were 5 percent of industrial discharges. Overall, six key pollutants in the water had been reduced 52 percent since 1972. A study of trends in forty-four major cities showed increases in pollution in 28 percent, decreases in 46 percent, and no change in 26 percent.

The Great Lakes present a special environmental problem. The repository of approximately 20 percent of the world's supply of fresh water, they once were regarded as an inexhaustible source of high-quality water. By the 1960s, however, Lakes Erie and Ontario had become seriously degraded, and the other three lakes seemed to be in trouble. Costly efforts to limit polluting discharges into the Great Lakes were necessary to bring some improvement in water quality in the 1970s and 1980s. Less fortunate have been the many East Coast estuaries and coastal areas cur-

rently suffering the most serious pollution problems in the nation. The problem areas run down the coast from New England to Virginia, and include Narragansett Bay, Long Island Sound, Raritan Bay, New York harbor, coastal New Jersey, and Chesapeake Bay.[5]

There have also been some successes in cleaning up waterways. Under the Clean Lakes program, federal money has been used to restore several biologically dead lakes, such as Lake Washington, east of Seattle. In the East, fishermen have returned to the Connecticut and Penobscot rivers. Moreover, the steps taken to restore these bodies of water have not been economically destructive to the industries involved. One continuing problem has been that state and local governments have not taken an active enough role in the process, and their lack of commitment has slowed implementation.

Many sources of water pollution still remain: runoff from farms and construction projects, storm-sewer runoffs from urban areas, airborne wastes and wastes disposed of on land that eventually seep into soil and water. All these problems involve serious technical and political issues, and expenditures of money alone will not deal with them effectively. Moreover, even as surface water quality has improved, there has been growing concern about the pollution of ground water supplies in many parts of the nation.

## Toxic chemicals

The EPA has classified some thirty-five thousand chemicals as either definitely or potentially hazardous to human health. The growing evidence that such chemicals pose serious health problems has often been highly dramatic in nature. Perhaps the most publicized case involved the Love Canal area in upstate New York. In 1979, toxic chemicals were found to have seeped from a Love Canal landfill site into a nearby area containing twelve hundred homes and a school. Love Canal residents were found to suffer from abnormally high incidences of cancer, birth defects, and respiratory and neurological problems.[6]

The world's worst toxic leak took place in Bhopal, India, in 1985. Over 2,000 people were killed when vapors from a Union Carbide plant escaped in the night. In this photo, victims of the accident receive medicine at an emergency clinic opened near the plant site. The accident called attention to the safety of such plants, many of which were in the United States.

The EPA has estimated that toxic chemicals have been dumped at up to fifty thousand sites nationwide, at least twenty-five hundred of which pose serious health hazards. Others place the number far higher. The Office of Technology Assessment in 1985 estimated there were ten thousand priority waste sites and that costs of cleanup would be closer to $100 billion than to the $16–$22 billion EPA had estimated.[7] Toxic spills became commonplace in America in the 1980s. Texas alone had over 400 reported leaks of toxic chemicals between 1983 and mid-1985, with many other states reporting spills in the hundreds. America, of course, was far from alone in this regard. The dangers of leaks and spills of toxic chemicals were worldwide. Several European nations suffered serious accidents. Perhaps the most terrifying of all accidents, however, took place in Bhopal, India, in 1985, when the leakage of a toxic chemical from a Union Carbide plant there killed 2,500 people and seriously injured tens of thousands. The Bhopal tragedy made clear just how devastating a large-scale toxic leak could be. Many feared that there would

be other tragedies in developing nations where controls and inspection might be less effective. A study reported in *The New York Times* on August 19, 1985, estimated that there were thousands of U.S. chemical plants without effective safety equipment in case of a major toxic leak.

There are other aspects to the toxic-waste problem. In industry, for example, workers are exposed to toxics during production. We are just starting to learn about toxic-induced illnesses—asbestos and lung cancer, benzene and leukemia, Kepone and sterility, vinyl chloride and cancer of the liver—for the symptoms of such diseases usually do not show up for years. Some health experts have speculated that a substantial percentage of all cancers may be environmentally induced—from exposure at the workplace, from toxic dumps, from chemicals that have seeped into water supplies, from food additives, radiation, and other sources.

In November 1980, the EPA put into effect new rules designed to prevent the haphazard dumping of toxic chemicals. The rules mandated that hazardous wastes be carried only by government-approved transporters and be disposed of only at approved disposal sites. In addition, companies that use and manufacture dangerous substances were made responsible for disposing of them legally. Violations of the new procedures were punishable by stiff penalties, such as $1 million fines and five-year prison terms. Subsequently, however, the EPA moved very slowly toward detailing acceptable disposal techniques. Since proper disposal techniques often are very costly, many companies have made it a practice to find cheap and unsafe methods, such as dumping wastes in the oceans or depositing them in unprotected sites.

As of the beginning of the 1980s, the problems of dealing effectively with toxic substances remained

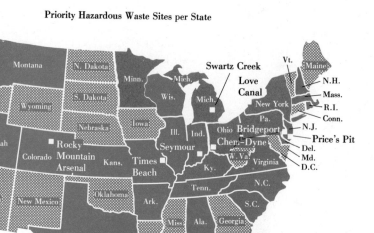

Priority Hazardous Waste Sites per State

Alaska: 0
Hawaii: 6
Outlying U.S. Areas: 12

26–95      7–25      Below 7

Numbers are Actual and Proposed Sites
on the Environmental Protection Agency's
National Priorities List as of October 1984.

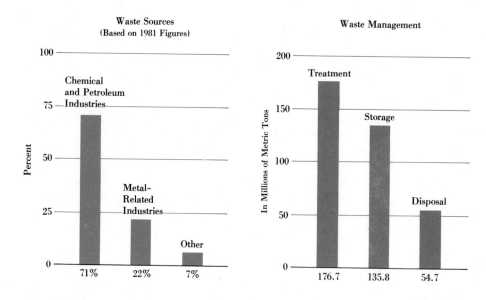

Waste Sources
(Based on 1981 Figures)

Waste Management

FIGURE 23.2
EPA Waste Cleanup Priorities, by State.
Source: National Geographic, March
1985.

formidable. The Carter administration had set up a "Superfund" to assist state and local governments in cleaning up hazardous toxic dumps. Enforcing the tough new rules about future disposal of toxic materials did not prove to be easy, however, despite the penalties provided. Illegal dumping practices were hard to keep track of, much less to stop.

The EPA's approach to the toxic dumping issue took an entirely new turn under the Reagan administration, which moved at a glacial pace on the toxic waste issue. In 1981 and 1982, the EPA allocated less than one-third of the Superfund, and by 1985, only 538 sites were being cleaned up. EPA's budget for enforcing toxic waste control in 1985 was 25 percent below that in 1981, and the agency's director of the Office of Solid Waste admitted that 60 percent of major disposal facilities were not in compliance with new federal laws.[8]

In early 1983 a major scandal hit the EPA. Investigations showed that top EPA officials had refused to press chemical companies on dumping procedures. This development came as no surprise to critics, especially since many Reagan appointees to the EPA had come from the very businesses to be regulated or had established strong anti-environmentalist reputations. The scandal forced the resignations of the EPA director and the assistant in charge of the Superfund.

Efforts by some in Congress to reform the use of the Superfund focused on creating mandatory deadlines for cleanups, mandatory standards for the thoroughness of cleanups, and on providing for a citizen's right to sue when health and environment are threatened. As of mid-1985, EPA estimated it would only be able to clean up 130 dump sites per year, at which pace, more than 100 years would be required to deal with all major toxic dumps, even by the most optimistic estimates.

## Costs and benefits of pollution control

By the mid-1970s, there was already considerable controversy about the costs and benefits of pollution control. Industry representatives tended to emphasize the costs of antipollution equipment and the unemployment caused by shutdowns of plants that did not meet federal standards. Supporters of the measures to clean up pollution emphasized the benefits from such efforts. According to some studies, the number of jobs actually lost due to pollution expenditures by industry has been far lower than industry's own predictions. Moreover, the new environmental regulations have created an estimated 1 million jobs con-

A Flint, Michigan, auto worker decorates his hard hat with warnings about toxic waste. For many workers, there was nothing amusing about the matter, as tens of thousands were exposed daily to chemicals that were potentially hazardous.

## Comparative perspective the Europeans deal with toxic wastes

Like the United States, the industrial democracies of Europe began to face the problem of dealing with toxic chemicals in the 1970s. Their responses to this issue have varied considerably. The European trendsetter in toxic waste disposal has been Denmark, which was the first country to introduce a centralized system for dealing with waste disposal. The Danish railroads transport toxic chemicals in specially designed cars that are loaded at designated collection points around the country and unloaded at a central treatment plant. That plant either destroys the wastes or recycles and stores them.

Italy, in contrast, has not devised a national plan to deal with toxics, and the Italian parliament has passed no legislation pertaining to waste materials. As a result, Italy has been plagued with more and bigger scandals involving toxic materials than has any other European country. In a controversial incident in 1976, a plant explosion sent a cloud of highly lethal materials over the surrounding countryside, causing many animal deaths and the evacuation of five hundred people.

A West German waste disposal law passed in 1972 closed down fifty thousand illegal dump sites and opened up five thousand new, regulated ones. New factories built in West Germany must show that they have made adequate plans to deal with the waste materials they produce. Although German business executives are relatively happy with the prevailing laws, many German environmentalists regard U.S. toxic waste laws as more comprehensive. They note that German laws exclude many potentially dangerous chemical products and worry that the safe dumping areas in the nation are rapidly being filled up.

Great Britain has, on paper, an effective and comprehensive system for dealing with the 5.5 million tons of toxic waste generated annually. The basic responsibility for dealing with the issue, however, lies with 165 local councils, each of which must draw up a plan and license dumping sites. Although the national legislation was passed in 1976, by 1981 only twelve of the local councils had completed their tasks.

Source: *The New York Times*, February 20, 1983.

---

nected with the labor-intensive work of cleaning up the environment.[9]

Industry estimates on costs also were at odds with estimates of the Council on Environmental Quality. Industry maintained that expenditures for environmental purposes would be an intolerable economic burden. The CEQ, however, estimated in 1980 that such costs average only 3 percent of plant and equipment expenditures each year. And in response to the argument that the costs of cleaning up the environment would spell increased inflation, the CEQ estimated that environmental costs would mean only a 1 percent inflation increase a year.

Ultimately, however, the main conflict stirred by environmental measures was that with energy production. Conflicts between environmental standards and energy production were already evident during the Carter administration. In 1979, President Carter announced a national synthetic fuels program and signed into law a bill directing that the controversial Tellico Dam in Tennessee be completed—two measures opposed by environmentalists. As Carter put it in his discussion of energy needs: "We will protect the environment. But if the nation needs to build a pipeline or a refinery—we will build them." It was this point that Ronald Reagan and his supporters stressed in the 1980 presidential campaign. Environmental restrictions would have to give way to greater emphasis on the production of energy—the nation's overriding concern, in their eyes.

Environmentalists have pointed out that the costs of pollution controls should be borne by the producers, who had previously escaped paying their share of the environmental bill. As an ex-director of the Sierra Club put it: "With controls, the producer of the pollution pays the cost, rather than the downwind breather who pays extra doctor bills to cope with emphysema, or the downstream municipality that must pay extra to clean up a polluted water supply; or the downwind farmer or forest owner whose crops grow too slowly because of acid rainfall; or the factory worker who finds the paint job on his house ruined by factory fumes. The market costs of pollution are very real and somebody pays them."[10]

It has been suggested that polluters pay a graduated series of fines comparable to the costs their pollution causes. Companies willing to pay the fines can continue to pollute; those who are not must alter their production methods. Such a system would build economic incentives directly into the cost calculations of producers. In this way, the "real" costs to society of pollution could be made part of industry's calculations. Theoretically, such a system should prove efficient. Much would depend, however, on how accurately the fines were scaled. How, after all, does one measure the "costs" of one thousand additional cases of emphysema, or one thousand more birth defects? Some costs. in other words, simply can't be measured in monetary terms.

The Environmental Protection Agency has commonly found establishing the rules to be easier than enforcing them. Big industries have the money and legal talent to wage lengthy court battles over just what "compliance" with EPA rules entails. Moreover, EPA enforcement efforts have often been hindered by forces within the government, as when inflation fighters in both the Carter and the Reagan administrations opposed EPA standards on the grounds that some cheaper methods might be discovered. When EPA had to give ground on some compliance issues, environmental groups brought legal action to force more efforts at enforcing the law. Finally, EPA has frequently found itself in the embarrassing position of seeking enforcement figures from the companies themselves, which monitor the equipment that keeps track of pollution levels. Many EPA administrators have concluded that the pollution problems facing the nation will take decades to solve.

## The politics of environmental issues

Despite their often highly technical nature, environmental issues have stirred quite intensive political conflict. Groups have struggled to define the issues and resolve them in accord with their own views of the meaning of what is at stake.

### Group strategies

In the early days of the environmental movement, many groups followed the pattern set earlier by the civil rights and peace movements: marches, symbolic protests, and personal commitment. Later, with the creation of new federal and state environmental agencies, political action moved into more traditional channels, such as lawsuits, lobbying, education, and campaign activity. Only in the area of nuclear power did 1960s-style activism remain a major tactic. Some of the new environmental laws encouraged citizen activism, particularly of the legal variety: for example, certain NEPA provisions provide citizens with standing to sue, a prerequisite for legal action. Frequently, environmental groups have differed over priorities and strategies. Some have taken a "hard line"—insisting on a relatively pure preservation of wilderness areas, for example—whereas others have been willing to allow for multiple uses, including recreation and commercial development.

Arrayed on the other side of environmental issues are corporate interests. Business is a major producer, consumer, and polluter. Many businesses are directly affected by government environmental decisions. For example, the lumber industry harvests over one-third of its commercial softwood from federal forests, and tens of millions of federally owned acres are leased for mineral development. Although U.S. business is highly diverse (11 million corporations and three thousand trade associations), the strategies used in dealing with the new environmental standards and attitudes have not varied much

TABLE 23.1
# The decline in EPA spending over four years (in millions of dollars)

|      | Air | Drinking water | Water quality | Noise | Pesticides | Radi-ation | Hazardous waste | Interdis-ciplinary | Toxic substances | Energy | Management and support | Total outlays |
|------|-----|----------------|---------------|-------|------------|------------|-----------------|--------------------|------------------|--------|------------------------|---------------|
| 1980 | $266.5 | $69.3 | $362.5 | $11.8 | $67.7 | $11.6 | $ 77.5 | $27.5 | $59.2 | $137.4 | $160.2 | $1,251.2 |
| 1981 | 224.5 | 79.8 | 312.1 | 12.0 | 52.8 | 11.8 | 142.9 | 13.3 | 88.3 | 101.5 | 190.7 | 1,229.7 |
| 1982 | 198.1 | 65.0 | 253.3 | 5.3 | 49.5 | 9.9 | 99.6 | 11.6 | 66.3 | 73.1 | 170.6 | 1,002.3 |
| 1983 | 147.2 | 57.7 | 191.8 | 1.3 | 39.9 | 9.4 | 87.0 | 17.3 | 60.2 | 42.4 | 172.1 | 826.3 |

Source: *The New York Times*, March 6, 1984.

from industry to industry.[11] Businesses typically have argued that the problem is exaggerated, that regulation is or will be too strict and unreasonable, that economic growth is threatened, and that evidence about the alleged problem is scanty and controversial. When the Oregon legislature passed strict environmental legislation, for example, an Oregon labor lobby argued: "As a result of overzealous, erroneous governmental regulations and actions, that segment which produces jobs and profits has been rendered a serious economic blow."[12] Business interests have spent many millions of dollars on advertising campaigns designed to convey their point of view to the public, have lobbied extensively in Congress and state legislatures, and have utilized political action committees (see Chapter 10) to gain access to candidates.

## The Reagan administration and the environment

There was little love lost between Ronald Reagan and environmentalists when the former assumed the presidency in 1981. Reagan had alienated proenvironment people for years with his disdain for conservation projects. Also, he and his aides strongly favored United States economic growth—which, to them, meant a drastic curtailing of environmental rules. Before taking office, Reagan announced that he regarded the nation's environmental problems as more-or-less solved. These typical business com-

munity attitudes came to dominate the approaches of the Reagan administration.

Shortly after taking office, the administration moved to delay the imposition of many new environmental standards. The entire staff of the President's Council on Environmental Quality, whose views were distinctly proenvironment, was fired. There were deep cuts in outlays for environmental protection, and several thousand EPA employees were fired. Many key career officials, particularly lawyers trained in environmental law, were lost. The appointment of many inexperienced people led to a sharp dip in agency morale. Sweeping powers were delegated to the states, which lacked the resources to handle them. In 1983, Reagan appointed as EPA head William Ruckelshaus, a respected figure who had headed the agency under President Nixon. Still, many observers believed it would take years to repair the damage done to environmental programs.

Reagan's first secretary of the interior, James Watt, also took a generally antienvironment stance. Watt moved to open up coastal areas for oil drilling, proposed the sale of millions of acres of federal land for development, and sought to eviscerate strip-mining

TABLE 23.2
# The Superfund (in millions of dollars)

|  | 1981 | 1982 | 1983 |
|--|------|------|------|
| Congressional appropriation | $78.0 | $169.6 | $196.4 |
| Money spent | 8.0 | 71.1 | 165.4 |

Source: *The New York Times*, March 6, 1984.

laws. Watt's main backers were the oil and gas industries and business interests engaged in off-shore development.

It was widely agreed that certain Reagan administration moves made sense. Some strip-mining rules needed to be relaxed, for instance, and also certain government-owned lands could reasonably be sold. In addition, it seemed legitimate to give business a voice in shaping regulations that affected the economy and were so closely tied to prospects for economic growth. The major problem was that instead of representing another side of the debate about balancing environment and economy, the Reagan administration seemed committed to ignoring environmental hazards and to furthering the needs and ideas of business.

Toward the middle of 1984, with the presidential election approaching, President Reagan sought to shift his negative image among environmentalists. He claimed that his administration's record in improving the environment was one of the country's "best kept secrets." He held well-publicized meetings with environmental organizations and claimed that his administration had tripled expenditures for the cleanup of hazardous waste dumps and doubled outlays for research into acid rain. But critics pointed out that the administration had held back funds for use in toxic waste cleanups. In addition, the administration continued to reject any *action*, as opposed to *research*, on acid rain. Critics also pointed out that the administration, despite its growing moderation on some environmental issues, continued to drag its feet. Although James Watt had resigned as secretary of the interior in 1983, many environmentalists found little change under his replacement, William Clark. The view of the administration continued to be that public lands must be opened up for rapid exploitation by oil, gas, timber, and mining interests.

## Energy: its sources and problems

Energy issues are universal in impact and complex in nature. A large assortment of questions are interconnected in the energy area. What are the available supplies of natural gas, coal, or petroleum? Estimates of energy reserves are absolutely vital to any sensible consideration of our energy situation, yet few experts agree on the correct numbers. Other issues require that we weigh some gains against some losses. Should we mine more coal, despite the erosion and destruction of the land that will likely result? Should we proceed with nuclear development, despite the safety risks? Many important interests—both organized and unorganized—are involved in the energy area: producers, such as the major oil companies; trade unions, such as the United Mine Workers or United Auto Workers; consumers; and others. Questions of power—who decides, who benefits, and who pays—invariably arise. Finally, some issues involve basic questions of values. Should we change our lifestyles in order to conserve resources for ourselves and others?

The United States has the reputation of being an energy guzzler. Heavy energy consumption is necessary to turn out the vast quantities of consumer

TABLE 23.3
## Comparative energy/output relationships, 1980

| Country | Gross National Product per capita (dollars) | Energy consumption per capita (tons of coal equivalent) |
|---|---|---|
| United States | 11,500 | 10.4 |
| Britain | 9,100 | 4.9 |
| Canada | 10,300 | 10.1 |
| France | 12,300 | 4.8 |
| Japan | 9,400 | 3.9 |
| Mexico | 2,400 | 1.8 |
| Spain | 5,500 | 3.0 |
| Sweden | 14,300 | 6.3 |
| Venezuela | 4,000 | 3.1 |
| U.S.S.R. | 5,200 | 6.0 |
| West Germany | 13,400 | 6.4 |

Source: Stobaugh and Yergin, *Energy Future*, p. 181.

goods available in the United States. Americans use considerably more energy than people in other developed nations. The Swedes, West Germans, and Swiss use only about 60 percent of the energy we do, per person.

Governments at all levels can no longer avoid making energy policy. The question remains, What sort of policies will be made? Regardless of what governments do or do not do, those choices will affect not just Americans, but the rest of the world as well.

Let us now take a closer look at the U.S. energy situation. We will first outline the current status of U.S. energy use and production, and then consider several proposed alternatives and the problems posed by each. Finally, we will look at the politics of energy, weighing the priorities of the Carter and Reagan administrations.

## Energy production and consumption

Three nonrenewable fuels account for the vast majority of our energy supply: crude oil, natural gas, and coal. Coal and natural gas supplies are still drawn almost entirely from our own resources, whereas about half of our supplies of crude oil are tied to foreign sources. Nuclear power accounted for a little over 1.4 percent of all U.S. energy use in 1981. Nuclear plants do produce about 13 percent of our electricity, but electricity accounts for only about 10 percent of overall energy usage.

About 37 percent of the energy consumed in the United States goes for heating, air conditioning, lighting, and the like, in residential and commercial establishments. Industrial usage accounts for about an equal amount, with transport consuming the remaining 25 percent or so.

Oil:  Oil is a very special fuel—the basis of modern transport. As the key fuel in international trade, it is highly vulnerable to disruptions of supply, as the 1973–74 Arab oil embargo demonstrated. Without the peculiar problems associated with oil, one wonders if we would yet be discussing the energy crisis

at all. If we could easily substitute coal or natural gas for oil, our energy problems would immediately undergo a spectacular change. Such a change is unlikely to come about very soon, although it is one of the main alternatives under discussion.

At the moment, oil is vital, vulnerable, and over the long haul, expensive. The supply of oil is subject to wide fluctuations, however. After the squeeze in oil supplies and sharp increase in oil prices during the 1970s, an oil glut developed in the early 1980s as a result of increases in the supply of oil and the conservation measures taken in the industrial countries, such as the production of more fuel-efficient vehicles. The glut lowered prices and produced significant strains within the OPEC countries. In the United States oil imports declined after 1980.

Natural gas:  The United States has large supplies of natural gas. Use of this fuel increased steadily after World War II, peaking at 40 percent of total energy consumed in 1971. Natural gas has two clear advantages over other fossil fuels: it burns cleanly and it is easily transported. Gas can be substituted for oil in many situations, and such substitutions have become increasingly common in recent years. Industry currently accounts for the bulk of natural gas usage—about two-thirds. [13]

The extent of natural gas reserves in the United States has been a matter of dispute. Another complication in the natural gas picture has been competition for it among domestic users—specifically, households, industries, and utilities. In past years, shortages of natural gas have forced closings of schools and factories in some parts of the country. Allocation by region and use remains an important issue.

Coal:  Through the nineteenth century, coal fueled the vast expansion of industrial societies in Europe and the United States. Oil, cheaper and cleaner, replaced coal as the dominant fuel in industrialized societies in this century, but now many look to coal as the "black hope" of the U.S. energy future. The United States is the Saudi Arabia of coal—the repository of an estimated one-third of the total world reserves. [14] Appalachia, the Midwest, and relatively unexploited areas of the West are the main sources

This scene could be from any one of a number of nations: the United States, Sweden, France, or the Soviet Union, among the most likely. In fact, it is from Yorkshire, in Great Britain. A crucial question is raised: Would you want a nuclear plant in your backyard?

to tens of billions of dollars, safety and other concerns have upped the costs to the point where the cheap possibilities of nuclear power no longer exist.

The accident at the nuclear power plant on Three Mile Island in 1979 underlined many of these issues and produced greater public skepticism about the benefits of nuclear power. Nevertheless, President Carter insisted that nuclear plants could be safe and beneficial, and President Reagan also took a pro-nuclear stand. How valuable a contribution nuclear power can make to future energy supplies remains very much in doubt.

of these reserves. Although coal supplies account for only about 20 percent of current U.S. energy consumption, it accounts for about 90 percent of our remaining fossil fuel resources. Most of our coal is consumed by utilities to produce electricity.

**Nuclear power:** In the 1950s, when scientists first began describing the possibilities of the peaceful uses of the atom, many expected that energy generated through nuclear power would be so cheap and abundant we would no longer even need electric meters to keep track of its use. The United States, Britain, France, and the Soviet Union all moved quickly to harness atomic power. By 1983, 282 commercial reactors in the world were generating 176,000 megawatts of electricity, and 227 more plants had been ordered or were under construction.[15]

By some estimates, nuclear power has turned out to be slightly cheaper than oil or coal in producing electricity—although those estimates have been contested. By the late 1970s, the nuclear power industry itself had begun to entertain doubts on the cost issue. Despite very heavy government subsidies, amounting

## Alternative solutions

Proposed solutions to the country's energy problems have revolved around either increasing the supply of energy or diminishing energy demands. Obviously, these two alternatives are potentially compatible.

**Increasing the supply:** The nation's remaining oil reserves lie principally in Alaska and in offshore settings along the continental shelf. Eventually, according to some estimates, we may be able to locate as much as 200 billion barrels—about twice what has been discovered since the 1960s. Much domestic natural gas also remains to be exploited, although there has been considerable disagreement over just how much.

The task of increasing domestic production of these two fuels presents two major problems. To begin with, no one really knows how much oil and natural gas actually remains to be discovered. Given this uncertainty, we cannot depend on such supplies as the basis for future energy planning. The second prob-

Here comes the oil! We see part of a pipeline carrying oil the 780 miles from Prudhoe Bay to Valdez, in Alaska. The pipeline is made with bends in order to slow the movement of the oil. The Alaskan find was one of the major new U.S. domestic oil discoveries.

lem is providing incentives to find and exploit potential resources. Since additional supplies will not be easy to locate, exploration will be costly.

What are the possibilities for increasing coal production? Known coal reserves, according to Stobaugh and Yergin, could supply us with fifty years' worth of energy at a rate equal to more than all present energy used each year. If we include the additional supplies of coal that could be exploited were coal prices to increase, many additional years' energy could also be obtained.

The Carter administration threw its support behind a synthetic fuel program that involved the conversion of coal, tar sands, and oil shale to gas and oil. Even with a substantial investment, however, a synfuels alternative would only have become productive in significant quantities after about a decade. It also represented an enormous financial gamble. Plants would have to be built on a vast scale, rivaling nuclear power facilities, at a cost estimated at $5–6

billion. These questions became moot, however, when the Reagan administration dropped the synfuels idea. In line with its emphasis on increased production from already available resources, the new administration found the synfuels idea far less attractive.

Increased use of coal presents serious environmental problems. Coal burning increases air pollution, unless costly antipollution equipment is used. Also, mining for coal requires the defacing of land through strip-mining, as has already occurred in much of Appalachia. Strip-mined land can be restored to some degree—but again, only at significant cost.

Nuclear power also has drawbacks, of which ominous safety issues loom the largest. As pronuclear power proponents point out, however, nuclear power is the only energy technology not known to have killed a single member of the public. Given appropriate safety in design and operation, they have claimed, nuclear power can be surprisingly safe. But other problems have surfaced as well: disposal of nuclear wastes remains a sensitive and unresolved matter, and increasing costs have made nuclear plants less economically attractive. Even nuclear power optimists have seen nuclear energy as serving a relatively minor role in the future—supplying 20–25 percent of electric power and perhaps 10 percent of overall U.S. energy needs. Whether such a minor contribution would be worth the risk and cost involved is dubious.

Two other nuclear possibilities are offered by the liquid metal fast breeder reactor (LMFBR) and by fusion power.[16] The LMFBR would be far more efficient than current nuclear plants, but also more dangerous in terms of radiation emitted. Fusion reactors would be far safer than the fission reactors now being used, but fusion technology is still in its infancy. A working fusion reactor might not be built until the year 2000, and the costs involved might be enormous.

An attractive alternative boosted by many observers is solar power—a category that includes a variety of renewable energy sources, such as the sun itself, wind, water, and plants. For many people, solar power has seemed uniquely attractive, since dependence on solar energy would minimize pollution problems, ultimately reduce energy costs significantly, and provide greater independence from foreign sources.

How practical is the use of solar power? The answer to this question depends on many factors, since solar has several major elements. In the Netherlands, for example, wind power has long been employed. In other countries, houses have long been constructed so as to make use of the sun for heating. In the United States, solar hot water collectors were widely used in Florida several decades ago. New breakthroughs in the solar area seem possible, even likely. For example, photovoltaic cells, which transform sunlight directly into electricity, already exist,

although production costs are still too high for common use.

Another solar energy alternative that deserves specific mention is the use of biomass, since it touches on the nation's oil dependence. *Biomass* refers to all organic waste materials, such as animal and poultry manure, garbage, rotting plants and trees, and, particularly, crops raised for the purpose of supplying fuel. These materials can either be burned or converted into a gas or liquid fuel. Instead of being a major disposal problem, they can be changed into a major energy source. Use of biomass has already begun on a modest scale in the United States, especially in some municipal power plants. Some of the potential of biomass is indicated by the fact that our forests and municipal waste, if converted to alcohol

For a time in the 1970s it appeared that gasoline prices would go so high and supplies would run out so quickly that alternatives would have to be found. That urgency had diminished by the mid-1980s, but the long-term issues were still there.

Scene from a major solar project in New Mexico, 1984. Although there was some experimentation with deployment of large-scale solar devices, the real breakthroughs in terms of solar energy still awaited the extensive investment that nuclear power had once obtained from government and other sources.

or methane gas, could together furnish the equivalent of 4.5 million barrels of oil a day.

The major problem with solar alternatives is a deep-seated unwillingness to shift to radically different ways of creating energy. Since U.S. society now runs largely on fossil fuels, the extent of the changeover necessary would be considerable, and it could not be accomplished overnight. Most solar advocates have argued that solar could become the major source of energy by perhaps the year 2025, and supply about 25 percent of our energy needs by the year 2000—but only if we turn emphatically in that direction now. Critics of solar alternatives have argued that they are technologically uncertain and unlikely to meet the full energy needs of U.S. society.

The Reagan administration made drastic cuts in programs to encourage renewable energy (see Figure 23.4). In addition, Congress allowed renewable energy tax credits to expire in 1985. At the same time many hundreds of millions of dollars in subsidies still went to oil and utility industries. Many critics regarded these steps as precisely the opposite of what the United States ought to be doing—learning to conserve and develop its renewable resources. Despite increased investment in various forms of solar power, most observers have agreed that it will take a public-private partnership to make renewable resources competitive with fossil fuels.

**Conservation:** Another way of dealing with our energy needs would be to reduce them. More than half of all the energy used in the United States is wasted. We waste more fuel than the poorest half of humanity uses. Aside from the obvious need to reduce such large-scale wastage, serious efforts at conservation would buy us precious time as petroleum supplies begin to dwindle. The idea of conservation has too-

often been confused with the curtailing of important uses. But as conservationist Denis Hayes has pointed out, there are sharp differences: "Curtailment means giving up automobiles, conservation means trading a seven-mile-per-gallon status symbol for a 40-mile-per-gallon commuter vehicle. Curtailment means a cold house; conservation means a well-insulated house with an efficient heating system."[17]

Hayes maintained that we could save significant amounts of energy in the areas of transport, heating and cooling, the food system, electrical generation, industrial efficiency, waste recovery, recycling and lighting. Energy-saving measures would include tripling the gasoline mileage of vehicles, decreasing vehicle size, increasing the use of trains and buses, imposing strict standards of building insulation, boosting the use of solar power, increasing the efficiency of electrical power generation, and using waste heat from power generation.

With these and other measures, Hayes estimated, we could halve our energy consumption without altering our standard of living. Plainly, the achievement of such goals cannot take place without extensive government involvement and more clearly defined public policy.

It should be pointed out, however, that about 40

percent of the difference between U.S. and European rates of energy use is rooted in factors that are not easily changed, such as greater distances between cities and industrial specialization. The other 60 percent of our excess energy use arises from various inefficiencies, on which pricing levels surely have a marked effect. Historically, relatively cheap petroleum and natural gas have led Americans to be less concerned with fuel economy. Also, politicians have been loath to burden the United States public with heavier taxes on energy supplies. Taxes on gasoline are significantly higher in Western Europe than in the United States. In 1984, the British taxed gas at $1.20 per gallon, the French at $1.36, and the Italians at $1.86, whereas the U.S. gasoline tax was only $0.20.

TABLE 23.4
## U.S. energy supply, actual 1981 and prudent estimate for 1991 (millions of barrels daily of oil equivalent)

|  | 1981 Actual | 1991 Prudent estimate |
|---|---|---|
| *Domestic* (excluding U.S. exports) |  |  |
| Oil | 9.6 | 7.0 |
| Natural Gas | 9.2 | 7.7 |
| Coal | 7.4 | 10.4 |
| Nuclear | 1.4 | 2.5 |
| *Subtotal*, Non-renewables | 27.6 | 27.6 |
| Renewables | 2.4 | 3.2 |
| **Total Domestic** | 30.0 | 30.8 |
| *Imports* |  |  |
| Oil | 6.0 | 5.0 |
| Gas | 0.4 | 0.8 |
| *Subtotal* | 6.4 | 5.8 |
| TOTAL | 36.4 | 36.6 |
| Conservation Needed | — | 5.4 |
| TOTAL | 36.4 | 42.0 |

*Sources:* 1981, from Department of Energy, Energy Information Administration, *Monthly Energy Report* (Washington, D.C.: Government Printing Office), expect renewables which are from *Securing America's Energy Future: The National Energy Policy Plan* (Washington, D.C.: Government Printing Office, July 1981), p. 22.
*Source:* R. Stobaugh and D. Yergin, eds., *Energy Future*, 3rd ed. (New York: Random House, 1983), p. 305.

## The politics of energy issues

For decades, in one way or another, governmental policies (or the absence of such policies) have affected energy supplies and prices. Generally the government has tended to consider each energy area separately. The United States has not had a national, unified energy policy. Instead, separate policies in different areas have been developed to meet needs and satisfy interests in those respective areas. Coal, for example, was a relatively unregulated energy source until very recently. In contrast, the production, distribution, and pricing of the prosperous oil and gas industries have been highly political matters. Most recent political battles, thus, have focused on these two fuels.

The main issue in these battles has been decontrol—the abolition or weakening of government controls on the pricing of gas or oil. Advocates of decontrol have argued that market forces alone should determine prices. Only in this way, they have contended, can the "real" price of a resource be ascertained. When prices rise, people will conserve or switch to cheaper energy sources. Critics of decontrol have argued that such higher prices would cause severe hardships on the poor and lead to monopolistic profits for energy companies.

**Decontrol of oil:** When the price of imported oil rose sharply in the early 1970s, domestically produced oil became relatively cheaper, because its price was regulated under the Nixon administration's wage and price controls. By 1974, a domestic barrel of crude oil was being held at $6.87, whereas the world market price had reached $10.77. Not surprisingly, U.S. oil companies lobbied hard for decontrol of domestic oil prices: were controls to be lifted, the price of domestic oil would rise to world market levels, and the companies would enjoy higher profits. Price controls were relaxed somewhat under President Gerald Ford, but the issue was fully addressed only by President Jimmy Carter, who favored gradual decontrol.

All U.S.-produced oil was effectively decontrolled as of October 1, 1981, but at the same time the oil companies were assessed a special "windfall profits" tax designed to reduce the financial bonanza accorded them by decontrol. Without such a tax, decontrol of oil would have been politically unacceptable, in view of public and congressional outrage over the immense profits oil companies were making at the time. As legislated, the windfall profits tax was expected to lead to increased federal revenues of $227 billion during the 1980s. Congress mandated that these revenues were to be used in the following ways: approximately 25 percent ($57 billion) for assistance to lower-income persons, to help them cope with increased energy costs; 60 percent ($136 billion) for tax reductions to individuals and businesses; and 15 percent ($34 billion) for energy development and mass transport.

The windfall tax issue illustrates some important aspects of energy policy-making. In this case, public opinion served as a constraining force, since decontrol of oil prices without a tax would have been politically unwise at a time when oil company profits were already so high. Accordingly, the oil companies, once virtually unchallenged within their own domain, had to yield, at least to some degree, to countervailing political forces. Another significant point was that the newly created Department of En-

ergy played an important role in the decontrol process. The DOE was a staunch advocate of decontrol, and its lobbying within the government was instrumental in bringing the process about.

**Decontrol of natural gas:** Natural gas prices had long been regulated on two levels: in the interstate market, which was regulated by the Federal Power Commission; and in the fifty intrastate markets, which were largely uncontrolled, although nominally under the control of state utility commissions. This dual system originated in the Natural Gas Act of 1938, a measure aimed at protecting consumers from excessive prices. When gas supplies started falling behind demand for gas in the 1970s, the two levels began to diverge. By 1975, natural gas was averaging $0.34 per 1,000 cubic feet in interstate commerce and $1.40 in intrastate markets.

President Jimmy Carter favored decontrol of natural gas for two reasons: because it would lead to conservation through higher prices, and because higher profits would give the industry incentive to explore for more gas. Opponents argued that, as with oil, current profits were high enough and that conservation would be very difficult for many. The natural gas decontrol legislation that passed Congress in 1978 was a complicated piece of work. Controls were not to be removed entirely until 1986, but prices were to be allowed to increase 10 percent annually in the meantime. Moreover, natural gas was divided into three different types—"old," "new," and "deep" (i.e., harder-to-reach deposits)—each of which was treated differently.

**Energy independence and presidential policies:** Presidents Nixon and Ford both sought greater U.S. energy independence—which meant lower oil imports. As of 1980, however, we were importing twice as much OPEC oil as in the early 1970s. President Carter's policies were aimed at several aspects of the energy issue. He sought support for conservation measures and for solar energy, favored gradual gas decontrol, and proposed an increase in the federal gasoline tax and a heavy tax on gas-guzzling autos. In the latter portion of his administration, Carter also sought large-scale financial subsidies for a synfuels effort. In the end, he got much of what he wanted: the gasoline tax was defeated except for emergency situations, and the gas-guzzler provisions were watered down; but synfuels, conservation measures, and gas decontrol were approved.

Ronald Reagan came to the presidency determined to increase U.S. production of fossil fuels in particular. He allowed greater exploration for oil and gas on federal lands, while cutting back drastically federal energy investment in other areas, such as solar energy. During his first term, the United States was able to reduce its dependence on Middle East oil by greatly increasing imports of oil from Mexico and Venezuela.[18] This was certainly one of the reasons that the Reagan administration came to regard Central America and the Caribbean as increasingly vital to U.S. concerns. Many energy specialists argued that the Reagan approach would not sufficiently ensure future petroleum supplies. They proposed more work on the development of synthetic fuels and greater conservation efforts.

## Conclusions

Energy and environmental issues are new and very complicated. Can democratic theory tell us anything useful about these matters? Three issues seem most significant. First, who decides how energy/environment issues are resolved? Is the process democratic or even semi-democratic? Second, who benefits and who pays for the ways in which we deal with energy/environment questions? Are some being victimized to make life easier for others? Are basic human rights being neglected? Finally, democratic concerns should lead us to wonder about the long-term significance of energy/environment issues. What are the consequences of our decisions in these areas for future generations? How will our decisions affect the heritage we leave?[19]

None of these questions is easy to answer, but a few points can be made. Until quite recently, energy/environment decision making has not been a prominent part of the U.S. political process. Up to around 1973, most key decisions in this area were made or shaped by those interests most heavily involved. Oil interests had a large hand in shaping the politics of oil; companies with a strong interest in nuclear power had a large say in obtaining government subsidies for their efforts. As for environmental concerns, few decisions were made by anyone. Air and water pollution and the dumping of toxic wastes took place without interference from democratic politics.

Now that energy/environment issues *have* become part of our political agenda, many experts have argued that the intricacies of these issues, like the complex problems involved in foreign policy, are simply too difficult for ordinary citizens to comprehend. In some ways, this argument is correct: very few of us have the time or the inclination to explore the problems of waste disposal or the various ways of dealing with air pollution. Still, the developments of the last fifteen years demonstrate that the public can learn quickly—and learn a great deal—about the issues of energy and environment, and can play a significant role in bringing about more-democratic policies in these areas. In general, the public has taken a resolutely proenvironment stance. As for energy, the mass public is no more confused than are the political elites in terms of finding a way out of coming energy dilemmas. It seems likely, therefore, that popular sentiment can play a constructive role in shaping future energy and environment policy.

In considering the costs and benefits of energy/environment policy, basic human rights come into play. If air pollution is taking years off our lives, if toxic dumps increase health risks for millions, if carcinogens in the workplace mean that many will die years early, then basic issues of democratic politics are at stake. The actual applications may not be simple, but the basic guideline of democratic commitment is that the life and health of some should not be sacrificed to the ease and convenience of others. This means that an aroused public must make clear that environmental hazards require serious, sustained action by the political leadership. Without such action, the sheer technological momentum of industrial society will take its toll on many of us.

Finally, democratic commitments should lead us to show concern for the long-term effects of current actions. Should we aim at the maximum feasible production now, even if that means downgrading our concern for preserving the environment? How vigorously should we press our cleanup of the environment in the immediate future, as opposed to leaving the job to the next generation?

Democratic theory can take us only so far, however. It cannot tell us whether to prefer a high-energy, high-consumption lifestyle, or something simpler and more conservation-oriented. It cannot tell us whether the investment in solar options will be worthwhile or not. It cannot tell us how strict we should be about toxic dumping. Nevertheless, it does remind us that no person's life is more important than any other's, and that the profits or comforts of a few are not so important as the well-being of the many.

Finally, we must recognize that Americans have always wanted to "develop" their nation. Historically, we have wanted more and better, bigger and richer. Now the complex issues of energy and environment seem to threaten this hallowed American dream. Americans believe in capitalism—but in this area, capitalistic styles of doing things have obvious shortcomings. Energy markets are often uncompetitive. Making a short-term profit may not be in the public interest. Externalities, such as the toxic wastes produced by industry, seem cheaper to deal with if someone else pays the costs, like the people who live downstream from the plant that produces the toxic wastes. Capitalism, in this area, does not force those who should be paying the real costs of doing business to actually pay those costs. Therefore, government has a particularly important role to play in energy/environment issues. But what should that role be? Can we arrange to have our cake and eat it too—to preserve the environment and still generate the energy for an "American" lifestyle? And if this proves impossible, who will have the political courage to say so?

## NOTES

1 Council on Environmental Quality, *Environmental Quality* (Washington, D.C.: U.S. Government Printing Office, 1979), Chapter 3.

568

2 Council on Environmental Quality Report, December 1983, p. 3.

3 *The New York Times*, March 26, 1985, p. 18.

4 CEQ, *Environmental Quality, 1983* (Washington, D.C.: U.S. Government Printing Office, 1983), p. 4.

5 *Ibid.*, pp. 106–14.

6 Michael Brown, *Laying Waste: The Poisoning of America by Toxic Chemicals* (New York: Washington Square Press, 1981).

7 *The New York Times*, March 10, 1985, p. 1.

8 *National Geographic*, March 1985, p. 332.

9 CEQ, 1983, *op. cit.*, Chapter 12.

10 Michael McClosky, quoted in *Earth, Energy Environment* (Washington, D.C.: CQ Press, 1977), pp. 176–77.

11 Quoted in Walter A. Rosenbaum, *The Politics of Environmental Concern* (New York: Holt, Rinehart, 1977), pp. 81–87.

12 *Ibid.*, pp. 83–84.

13 David Howard Davis, *Energy Politics* (New York: St. Martin's, 1982), Chapter 4.

14 *Ibid.*, Chapter 2.

15 Lester R. Brown, *et al.*, *State of the World 1984* (New York: Norton, 1985), p. 118.

16 CEQ, 1979, *op. cit.*, pp. 364–69; and D. H. Davis, *Energy Politics*, pp. 239–40.

17 Denis Hayes, *Rays of Hope* (New York: Norton, 1977).

18 Leslie H. Gelb, "Oil = X in a Strategic Equation," *The New York Times*, October 7, 1983.

19 These questions were suggested by the insightful work of David Orr. See his articles, "Leviathan, the Open Society and the Crisis of Ecology" (with Stuart Hill), *Western Political Quarterly*, December 1978, pp. 457–69; and "Perspectives on Energy," *Dissent*, Summer 1979, pp. 280–84.

## SELECTED READINGS

For various perspectives on environmental issues, see Walter A. Rosenbaum, *The Politics of Environmental Concern* (New York: Holt, Rinehart, 1977); Cynthia H. Enloe, *The Politics of Pollution in a Comparative Perspective* (New York: McKay, 1975); Gerald O. Barney, *et al.*, *The Global 2000 Report to the President* (Charlottesville, Va.: Blue Angel Press, 1981); Wendell Berry, *Un-*

*settling of America* (San Francisco: Sierra Club, 1977); Lester Brown, *The Twenty-Ninth Day* (New York: Norton, 1978); Garrett Hardin and John Baden, eds., *Managing the Commons* (San Francisco: W. H. Freeman, 1977); Barry Commoner, *The Closing Circle* (New York: Knopf, 1971); E. F. Schumacher, *Small Is Beautiful* (New York: Harper & Row, 1973); and F. Capra and C. Spretnak, *Green Politics* (New York: Dutton, 1984).

On the energy debate, consult D. H. Davis, *Energy Politics* (New York: St. Martin's, 1982); R. Stobaugh and D. Yergin, *Energy Future* (New York: Random House, 1983); H. H. Landsberg, *et al.*, *Energy: The Next Twenty Years* (Cambridge, Mass.: Ballinger, 1979); C. D. Goodwin, ed., *Energy Policy in Perspective* (Washington, D.C.: Brookings Institution, 1981); Amory B. Lovins, *World Energy Strategies* (New York: Harper & Row, 1980); J. L. Simon and H. Kahn, *The Resourceful Earth* (London: Blackwell, 1984); Walter C. Patterson, *Nuclear Power*, 2nd ed. (New York: Penguin, 1983); and Daniel F. Ford, *Three Mile Island* (New York: Penguin, 1982).

# Epilogue

IN one of his famous pithy aphorisms, the young Karl Marx wrote: "The philosophers have only interpreted the world: the task however is to change it." He might also have said "preserve it" (as some environmentalists do these days), but such an observation on the part of a 26-year-old would not have impressed anyone except the authoritarian heads-of-state Marx opposed.

Textbooks, of course, also only "interpret" the world—and do *that* only at their best, since many texts hardly even reach the level of interpretation. Many, perhaps most, American government texts conclude with a paean of praise to our democratic system and offer a strong recommendation that the reader get out there and participate (the magic word). Instead of throwing the usual ritualistic phrases at you, I want to attempt, in this last section of the book, to offer a few specific recommendations for improving democratic life in America. My purpose is to stimulate your thinking, to give you something to focus on.

First, the matter of our electoral system. One of the most glaring problems in our polity is the relatively low levels of electoral participation. A related issue is the complexity and expense of campaigns. There have been many suggestions for possible improvements. In my opinion, we should make voting easier through automatic registration of high school graduates and the creation of a national election holiday to coincide with presidential and congressional elections. The United States is currently one of the few democratic nations that does not make election day a national holiday or hold it on a Sunday, when people are not working. There is nothing sacred about the first Tuesday after the first Monday in November as the time to hold most elections. As for campaigns, public financing of Congressional elections deserves to be tried, and in addition, free TV and radio time should be made available. The media operate on what are publicly controlled airwaves. It is certainly not asking very much to see to it that elections not be made another source of profit. These are hardly revolutionary suggestions, but taken together, they *might* raise the quality of involvement at the electoral level of our politics.

Second, we need to take democratic education more seriously. Most American children do not learn thoroughly about democratic political issues, such as civil liberties, civil rights, or social rights. They acquire little solid background about the historical struggles of democracy and so bring little perspective to current issues. Some form of "democratic curricula," to start in the elementary school and continue with increasing complexity through high school and college, seems an appropriate addition to what we already learn about government and how it works—a subject far too dry in itself to enlist our emotions.

Third, democratic reforms should extend to remedying the serious deprivations in our midst. Severe poverty and powerlessness touch tens of millions in our society, yet it is part of the American ethic that such conditions are basically an individual responsibility. This perspective is, in some sense, correct and will always remain so, but a democrat cannot be unconcerned when so many fellow citizens lack the basics of a decent life. More freedom and security for the least free and least secure should be a high priority. This means better housing, health care, and jobs.

Fourth, we should experiment with increasing democracy in the workplace. The workplace can become an environment for the practice of democratic attitudes rather than for attitudes of superiority and subordination. Reformers have discussed such possibilities for a century and a half, but we in America have not done much to achieve them. Many factors in modern society push us toward bigger and bigger organizations—government among them—in which the ordinary worker has little to say about overall management and conduct of business. More democratic decision-making at the workplace might help counteract these hierarchical, bureaucratic tendencies and thereby strengthen the democratic character of our people.

Finally, we need to reassess the meaning of democracy as it applies to the conduct of our foreign policy. The United States has often operated as if only our version of democracy were the appropriate one, as if we could not imagine other forms of democracy that combined political rights with a "leftist" economy. We saw such attitudes in our opposition to the Allende government in Chile in the early 1970s. American political leaders, generally speaking, have equated democracy and capitalism, with little room for experimentation with other forms of democratic life. It is entirely appropriate for us to be concerned about the totalitarian practices of left-wing governments such as the Sandinistas in Nicaragua. But we also need to recognize the possibility that left-wing regimes can be induced to become more democratic in the same way we have attempted to move right-wing regimes toward greater respect for human rights. Such a policy would provide greater flexibility than the one we often pursue, equating revolution from the left with anti-Americanism and pro-Soviet policies. But it is not a simple policy either to think through or to implement.

Textbooks seem to try to include everything. Textbook authors sometimes have the feeling that they must assimilate whole libraries of information, wolfing down enormous volumes of data and interpretations at each sitting. And yet no textbook really does include *everything*, despite appearances to the contrary. Every author has to do a good deal of selecting, and in that process of selection the biases, sensitivities, and judgments of the author show quite clearly. One interesting question about a text, therefore: What does it omit, what subjects are neglected? This question is difficult for students to answer, for they often know too little about a subject to pass judgment on omissions and selectivity. Because of this reality, I want to point out some of the most glaring problems concerning omissions.

What would this book have included if there had been more space? Most significant, I would have included more in the area of foreign and defense policy. For one, the subject of our policy toward South Africa deserves a place in a book concerned with democratic values. In that tormented nation, we see a profound drama being played out whose conclusion is not now foreseeable, except that change is likely at some point in the future. The United States and other western nations are deeply implicated in that drama because we are economically and politically enmeshed in South African life. It is appropriate therefore that American students have again begun to debate issues related to this involvement, such as the investment of university funds in corporations which in turn do business in South Africa.

There are other foreign policy topics I would like to have discussed that are significant in our policymaking. These include the various Israeli-Arab disputes, energy supplies, relations with China, and the prospects of nuclear proliferation.

Outside the foreign policy area, there are other subjects that the book has had to omit or touch on only lightly. These include the criminal justice system—including the working of the courts, prisons, the overall question of why crime occurs and how effectively we deal with it. We did not have much chance to discuss federal housing policy or federal investments in education or to what degree we should finance artistic endeavors through governmental sources. Although there is some mention of questions of secrecy and freedom of information, here, too, there is a good deal more to talk about. Access to important information is one of the essential elements in democratic life, yet this ingredient often conflicts with various rationales for secrecy. How are such issues to be evaluated?

Larger questions of the world environment—questions that could take up an entire complex text in themselves—deserve far more attention than my brief references. World resource supplies, pollution, endangered species, land erosion, and the adequacy of food supplies all loom large on the agenda of future politics.

Finally, we did not discuss in sufficient detail either the structures of power in America or the philosophies of politics that we find on the current American scene. How is power exercised in America? Which groups tend to have it, and which do not? There are more than glimpses of the answers in this book—especially in Chapter 6 and the various policy chapters—but there is a great deal more that needs to be debated. It is also important to note that *ideas* do matter in politics. Since the late 1960s, for example, American liberals have found themselves confused and divided, despite the fact that liberalism met with many great successes. On the other hand, various forms of conservatism have become ideologically powerful, ranging from the Christian Right of Jerry Falwell to the sophisticated neoconservatism of Jeane Kirkpatrick and other intellectuals. Why is liberalism in disarray and conservatism dominant? Does this reflect the worth of conservative ideas and the uselessness of liberal ones? And what has happened to the streak of radicalism in America? Is the American left politically dead, even after its tremendous effectiveness in the 1960s? A whole chapter on topics like these would have been easily worthwhile. My hope is that students will pursue such subjects

on their own or in other courses. And I have supplied the beginnings of a bibliography to help them on their way.

Democracy in the abstract is not our only concern. We might feel ambivalence toward a democratic society, for example, because of the way it conducted itself in world affairs. Many Americans felt such conflict about the United States during the Vietnam War. Some critics of that involvement believed our conduct in the war delegitimized the democratic process itself.

But that event was unusual. Generally, we Americans have had a strong tendency toward self-righteousness and missionary zeal, toward high self-regard. We are better than other nations, we think, and sometimes along with that comes the feeling that whatever we do or did, it cannot basically have been very wrong. We also don't like to be losers. "Losing" the Vietnam War was a deep humiliation. We know we could have won. We know we were right. A failure of leadership or too much self-criticism must have made us self-destruct. But such attitudes are not much help in getting a clear picture of the world, or of ourselves. The first requirement of a healthy, skeptical patriotism is objectivity. We need to know ourselves and to see the world clearly, and this is not easy. We Americans also like to consider ourselves first in everything. This too presents problems. If the Soviet Union has more land-based missiles than we do, does that mean we must catch up and build more to finally get ahead, or do such comparisons matter at all? As we saw in Chapter 22, it makes little sense to make comparisons of each category of strategic weapons since the arsenals of the United States and the Soviet Union are quite different. In the end, the basic destructive meaning of those arsenals is the same. Nonetheless, such logic will not appeal to people who see that big Soviet lead in ICBMs and worry that the United States is no longer first in that category. Our obsession with being on top may blind us to deeper, long-term issues.

In America, there is great unease on the subject of patriotism, and for good reason. We are a very great power in the world. What we do and don't do influences the lives of so many. We can destroy and create, can nurture and cut down in a manner that few other nations are able to conceive. Yet at times our great power seems impotent. We rage inside our boundaries. We don't know whether to seek revenge, to employ all of our vast power, or to be patient. Was Jimmy Carter right to try to rescue the hostages in Iran in 1980, or would he have been right to wait the situation out? Should we have used nuclear weapons or burned up North Vietnamese cities during the Vietnam War, or should we even have been militarily involved in the first place? There is a long, long list of such painful questions, and as a society, we are not sure of the answers.

Yet America is not in a position to withdraw from the world, and so it is important to think through our participation and our ideas of patriotism. We have talked some in this book about foreign policy commitments but what about loyalty? What should patriotism mean? There seem to be three leading conceptions. One form of patriotism is the sense of gut loyalty—the sort of thing one feels toward the flag, toward national symbols. It is the unreflective patriotism that says: "My country right or wrong." A second form calls attention to the "meaning" of the na-

tion, to its historic commitments, its heritage, its higher values. This sort of patriotism can criticize as well as affirm; can be expressed in dissent as well as allegiance. A third sort of patriotism arises out of a concern for national security and the "vital interests" of the nation. This sort of patriotism is highly pragmatic, hardnosed, concerned with an assessment of our capabilities and the balances of power in the world.

It is my hope that this book will nurture the second sort of patriotism, the loyalty based on principle and an ethic of thoughtful involvement. If citizens become more skeptical and morally concerned, leaders are also likely to consider the ethical side of their policies more fully. Politics is and will always be about power, but power takes many forms. It can grow, as Mao Tse-tung and many others have argued and practiced, out of the barrel of a gun, or it can be shaped by the ethical concerns of citizens. If the world as we know it is not to end in various paroxysms of violence, engulfing democracies and tyrannies alike, it may be that citizens who are skeptical patriots will be required to save it from the abyss.

# Glossary

**acid rain:** A term used to describe rain containing high acidic content believed caused by certain industrial emissions and which damages bodies of water, forests, and buildings. Acid rain problems were recognized throughout the industrial world in the 1970s and 1980s.

**affirmative action:** A policy of providing special preferences and consideration to groups previously discriminated against such as blacks, women, or Hispanics.

**Aid to Families with Dependent Children (AFDC):** A welfare program begun during the Great Depression to provide assistance to mothers raising children by themselves. It has proven, in recent decades, to be the most controversial of U.S. welfare programs.

**alienation:** A variety of negative attitudes including powerlessness and meaninglessness which frequently lead to withdrawal or cynicism.

**Antifederalists:** A political group opposed to the ratification of the Constitution, who stressed protection of individual liberties, the powers of the states, and keeping government closer to the people.

**Articles of Confederation:** Ratified on March 1, 1781, the Articles were the first Constitution of the United States. It is generally agreed they were a failure, in particular because the national government created was far too weak to govern interstate relations and rivalries.

**basic rights:** Fundamental claims that are believed to inhere in individuals as individuals and that government and society should honor, such as the right to decent and equal treatment, and freedoms of expression and lifestyle.

**bicameral legislature:** A two-house or two-chamber lawmaking body, such as the U.S. Congress.

**bill of attainder:** A law designed to declare as criminal the acts of a specific individual or group.

**Bill of Rights:** The first ten amendments to the Constitution, which supporters of the document agreed to add in response to criticisms, and to ensure protection of various basic rights and liberties.

**Brown v. Board of Education of Topeka:** The 1954 Supreme Court decision which ruled that segregated schools were inherently unequal, thereby overturning the *Plessy* decision of 1896. The *Brown* decision also ordered that schools be desegregated.

**bureaucracy:** A complex, hierarchically arranged organization composed of many small subdivisions with specialized functions. Such a form of organization is typical of modern governments and corporations.

**cabinet:** The heads of the thirteen executive departments such as the Secretaries of State, Defense, Treasury, Health and Human Services and so on, and also the U.S. representative to the United Nations, who meet at the pleasure of the president to discuss administration policy questions.

**cabinet departments:** The sections of the executive branch represented in the cabinet, including such departments as Transportation, Health and Human Services, Defense, State, and Treasury.

**capitalism:** An economic system based on supply and demand as determined by market forces rather than government planning; which is also characterized by private ownership of most of the economy and competition among firms and individuals.

**cash transfers:** Welfare programs that provide money to those who qualify, such as Aid to Families with Dependent Children (AFDC).

575

**caucus:** The meeting of a group, such as a political party, to select leadership, choose potential candidates, or to decide the group's position on strategically important issues.

**Central Intelligence Agency (CIA):** The chief intelligence gathering agency of the U.S. government, created after World War II. Much about the CIA is secret, including the size of its budget. Its most controversial function is covert activity such as espionage and the overthrowing or destabilizing of foreign governments.

**checks and balances:** The political idea embodied in the separation of powers, whereby each government branch has powers which are distinct from those of the other branches and where one branch may limit or check the power of another in various ways.

**civil disobedience:** The deliberate and open breaking of a particular law or rule, nonviolently, for the sake of protesting that law or some other related matter. Those who commit civil disobedience, at least in the classic manner, are willing to accept punishment for their lawbreaking.

**civil liberties:** Basic freedoms such as freedom of speech, press, or assembly which are protected from interference by governments or others.

**civil rights:** Basic social and political capacities such as the right to vote, or to be treated equally under the law, which are protected from interference by the actions of governments or others.

**Civil Rights Act of 1964:** Legislation which prohibited, among other things, segregation in public accommodations on the grounds of race and discrimination in hiring, firing, and pay levels in firms of twenty-five or more on the basis of race, religion, color, sex, or national origin.

**civil service system:** In contrast to the spoils system, a method of filling government posts based on "merit" as determined through competitive examinations overseen by a Civil Service Commission.

**Clean Air Act:** Legislation passed in 1963 and updated by amendments in 1970 to provide standards and deadlines for dealing with various sorts of air pollution.

**clear and present danger:** An interpretation of the conflict between free speech and public order elaborated by Justice Oliver Wendell Holmes in the 1920s. The clear and present danger doctrine argues that only that speech can be limited which creates a "clear and present danger" as when someone shouts "fire" in a crowded theater.

**cloture:** The vote to end debate in a legislative body, as when the U.S. Senate votes to end a filibuster.

**Cold War:** A global conflict carried on without overt military attack between the United States and the Soviet Union for much of the period since 1945.

**Common Cause:** A public interest lobby formed in 1970 which has focused on the need to create more honest and open government.

**concurrent powers:** Powers constitutionally granted to both state and national governments, such as the power to tax, to borrow money, to charter corporations, and to exercise the right of eminent domain.

**Congressional Budget Office (CBO):** A research arm of Congress created in 1974 to provide the Congress with independent information in connection with the annual budget and related matters, so that Congress does not have to depend entirely on information supplied by the executive.

**Connecticut Compromise:** The great compromise of the Constitutional Convention whereby Congress would be bicameral, consisting of the Senate, in which each state has two representatives; and the House of Representatives, in which representation is based on population.

**conservative:** An advocate of a political approach based on gradual change, traditional stability, and established institutions and practices, and which opposes government interference in business or in lifestyles.

**containment:** A U.S. policy developed in 1947 by George Kennan to cope with Soviet expansion in Europe. Its chief idea was the containment of the Soviet Union with the hope that its leadership would prove amenable to negotiation in the future.

**controlled capitalism:** A form of political economy in which government plays a substantial role in regulating and shaping the workings of a capitalistic economic process.

**Council of Economic Advisors (CEA):** An advisory board of economists who provide advice to the president on matters such as long-term economic predictions, inflation, recession, unemployment, taxes, and overall governmental policy as it affects the economy.

**counterforce:** A military doctrine which targets nuclear weapons on the weapons of the other side, as opposed to targetting population centers.

**Defense Department:** That portion of the executive branch whose function is to deal with national defense and military issues. The armed services are all located within the Department of Defense.

**delegated powers:** Specific constitutional authorizations to act held by each level or branch of government.

**democracy:** A system of government based on popular consent and majority rule. There are differing interpretations of its precise content.

**Democratic-Republicans:** A political party that emerged in the early 1820s from the split within the Republican party. In 1824 and 1828, the party nominated Andrew Jackson for the presidency. By the late 1820s the party began using the term Democrats to describe itself.

**democratic socialist parties:** Political parties which support both socialism and democratic procedures, such as the British Labour Party, or the French Socialist Party.

**deferred issues:** Issues, often highly controversial, that are postponed by politicians to avoid intense conflicts. These issues are likely to return in one form or another.

**deregulation:** The concept of lessening government regulation in various areas of economic life, as, for example, in trucking, air transport, banking, and communications.

**detente:** A systematic policy of improving U.S.-Soviet relations, undertaken by both sides in the late 1960s and 1970s, which involved arms control and other treaties, as well as generally warmer relations.

**direct legislation:** The use of the referendum or initiative in order to pass laws; hence, legislation derived directly from the people, as opposed to from the legislature.

**direct socialization:** The deliberate inculcation of certain political attitudes, values, and behaviors.

**displaced issues:** Issues that flare up, quiet down, and are often replaced by fragments of the original issues or other issues.

**diverted issues:** Issues handled by calling for a reconsideration of the demands made by the groups involved, for example, by arguing that meeting such demands will have various negative consequences.

**dual federalism:** The doctrine developed by the Supreme Court after the Civil War under which it clearly charted separate spheres of regulation for federal and state laws. For example, in the regulation of commerce, the states were supreme in the sphere of *intra*state commerce, while the national government was supreme in its sphere, of *inter*state commerce, and the Supreme Court could draw the line between them.

**due process of law:** Constitutional guarantees that the national government (Fifth Amendment) and the state governments (Fourteenth Amendment) cannot deprive individuals of life, liberty, or property without acting in accordance with established rules and procedures. This is a protection against arbitrary use of governmental power.

**egalitarian democracy:** Rule by the people based on the principle of equality, including not just political equality but also social and economic equality.

**electoral college:** A complex and indirect method of electing the president originally agreed to as a compromise at the Constitutional Convention. Electors from each state, chosen by methods designated by each state legislature and equal to the number of that state's senators and representatives, assemble to officially elect the president and vice-president.

**environmental impact statement (EIS):** An assessment, required by law under the National Environmental Policy Act, specifying the environmental consequences of governmental actions, such as the building of dams or highways. An EIS is required before such projects can be begun.

**Environmental Protection Agency (EPA):** An executive agency created by the National Environmental Policy Act (NEPA), passed in 1969, which oversees the implementation of environmental legislation and makes recommendations to Congress and the president on environmental issues.

**equal protection of the laws:** A standard embodied in the Fourteenth Amendment that prohibits national and state governments from discriminating against individuals or groups. In recent decades, the standard has been applied to issues of race, gender, age, and ethnicity.

**Equal Rights Amendment:** The proposal designed to guarantee equal rights to women by adding an amendment to the U.S. Constitution. Originally proposed in the 1920s, the amendment was passed by Congress in 1972, but failed to receive support from three-fourths of the states by the deadline of June 30, 1982.

**establishment clause:** A portion of the First Amendment which forbids Congress to make any law with regard to an establishment of religion.

**ex post facto law:** Any law that declares as criminal an act which was not a crime when it was committed.

**executive agreements:** Arrangements reached between the U.S. president and other nations which, unlike treaties, do not have to be submitted for Senate approval.

**Executive Office of the President:** The complex of auxiliary services, including staff support, research, and high level consultative bodies that provide the president with assistance.

**executive privilege:** The doctrine that the president can refuse cooperation of various sorts with investigations conducted by Congress or the courts on the grounds that such cooperation would be detrimental to the work of the executive branch. The issue of executive privilege played a prominent role in the Watergate affair.

**extraordinary politics:** A large variety of political tactics, employed by both citizens and governments, that transcend the usual patterns of day-to-day political life. These include forms of protest, civil disobedience, mass involvement, legal harassment, rebellion, and counterviolence.

**Federal Reserve System (the FED):** An independent government agency that regulates banks, controls the supply of currency, and regulates the amount of credit available. The system is centrally supervised by a seven-member, presidentially appointed Federal Reserve Board of Governors.

**federal system:** A form of government characterized by a constitutional division of power between national and constituent governments, such as states or provinces, in which each has independent powers.

**Federalist Papers:** A series of essays, written by John Jay, Alexander Hamilton, and James Madison in 1787–88, which stressed the need for a strengthened central government and defended the new Constitutional arrangements. Many consider the Papers among the finest examples of American political thought.

577

**federalists:** A political group, led by Alexander Hamilton and others, who supported the ratification of the Constitution and favored a strengthened central government.

**filibuster:** The tactic of delaying a vote on legislation pending in the U.S. Senate by engaging in extraordinarily lengthy debate; an attempt to talk a bill to death. In the Senate, until recently, debate could only be stopped by a two-thirds vote of that chamber, which often proved difficult to obtain. The vote now required is 60 votes, or a three-fifths vote of the whole Senate.

**First Amendment:** The initial amendment to the U.S. Constitution which provides for freedoms of speech, assembly, and press; the right to petition government to redress grievances; the protection of religious freedom; and calls for the separation of church and state.

**fiscal policy:** Economic policy related to matters of raising revenue through taxation and patterns of government expenditures.

**food stamps:** A program begun in the early 1960s to remedy problems of malnutrition and hunger in the United States by providing those who qualify with "stamps" that can be used for the purchase of food.

**free enterprise:** A competitive economic system based on private ownership in which government intervention is to be kept minimal.

**Freedom of Information Act (FOIA):** Legislation first passed by Congress in 1966 and amended in 1974 which provided new processes through which citizens could have greater access to government information, including classified documents.

**full faith and credit:** A clause of the Constitution requiring states to accept as valid the decisions of other states' civil courts.

**House Rules Committee:** A committee of the House of Representatives which establishes the conditions under which a bill will be discussed and when it will be brought to the floor of the House. The "rule" given to each bill can determine, for example, whether it can be amended by floor action. The Rules Committee can also try to stop a bill by refusing to grant it a "rule."

**human rights:** Basic rights which are believed to belong to all human beings—such as the right to decent treatment, to be free from torture, and to have a voice in the shaping of government.

**ideology:** A highly structured and coherent set of political and social ideas.

**implied powers:** Powers not specifically enumerated in the Constitution which are useful to Congress in carrying out its delegated powers.

**impoundment:** The president's refusal to spend funds allocated by Congress—often used to thwart programs opposed by the president.

**incremental politics:** The process of political change through very small steps ("increments").

**indirect socialization:** The inculcation of politically relevant attitudes and behavior in an indirect fashion.

**inherent powers:** Powers of the national government to act in foreign affairs and other areas which have been found by the courts to inhere in the very nature of national governmental power; such powers need not be based on specific enumeration in the Constitution.

**initiative:** A law proposed by a petition of citizens and then submitted to popular vote.

**in-kind transfers:** Welfare programs that provide services to those who qualify, such as Medicaid or housing, as opposed to providing cash.

**interest group:** An organization unified by common attitudes or goals which seeks to influence public policy formation and implementation. Interest groups, unlike political parties, do not run candidates for office.

**interest-group liberalism:** A term coined by political scientist Theodore Lowi to describe the workings of much of America's political process as of the early 1970s. It is a process in which every interest group recognized as legitimate is successfully able to make its claim felt in the political process and gain a certain measure of satisfaction. Lowi is critical of this process as one in which claims of "justice" and the public interest take second place to the appeasing of organized groups.

**isolationism:** The policy of keeping the United States separate from and uninvolved in European conflicts. Sometimes applied more generally to any reluctance to commit the United States to overseas involvements.

**item veto:** The selective rejection, by the president, of specific items in a larger piece of legislation passed by Congress, especially specific budget items. The American president does not possess the power of an item veto, but some have favored its adoption.

**Joint Chiefs of Staff:** A committee made up of the heads of the armed services, with a chief appointed by the president, which oversees military policy matters and reports to Congress and the president.

**judicial review:** The power of the judicial branch to review the actions of the executive and legislative branches of the federal and state governments and judge them in accord with the standard of constitutionality.

**Keynesian economics:** Economic practices based on the theories of the twentieth century British economist John Maynard Keynes. Keynes argued that government could employ tax policy and expenditures to counteract the problems created by the trade cycle. His views became influential particularly during the Great Depression of the 1930s and thereafter.

**laissez-faire:** An economic philosophy which argues for nonintervention by government in the workings of economic life.

**legislative veto:** A provision written into certain legislation by which Congress can override actions taken by executive agencies to implement these laws. The Supreme Court ruled in 1983 that such veto provisions violate the constitutional separation of powers.

**liberal:** In its modern usage, someone who favors strong protections for civil rights and liberties while favoring government action to remedy economic problems and injustices.

**liberal democracy:** A form of democratic government that combines majority rule with respect for civil liberties and protection of individual rights such as free speech, freedom of conscience, protections for property, and due process of law.

**liberalism:** An approach to politics based on a belief in the essential importance of the individual, in equality among citizens, and in the protection of civil liberties and individual rights by the government.

**majoritarian democracy:** Rule by the people based on preferences of more than 50 percent of voters. Pure majoritarianism might ignore the protections afforded to individuals in a liberal democracy.

**majority leader:** The chief floor spokesperson of the majority party in either the House or the Senate, who directs much of that party's business, and has considerable power over the conduct of that house.

**majority rule:** Decision making by more than 50 percent of the voters.

**Marbury v. Madison:** The 1803 Supreme Court case in which the Court for the first time set forth its power to declare acts of Congress unconstitutional.

**McCulloch v. Maryland:** The 1819 Supreme Court decision which established a broad interpretation of the powers of the national government and established the supremacy of the national government.

**Medicaid:** Welfare program begun during the Johnson administration to help pay medical costs for the indigent.

**Medicare:** Welfare program begun during the Johnson administration to help pay health care costs for the elderly and the disabled.

**mercantilism:** An economic philosophy that developed in the seventeenth century and which advocated strong protectionist measures which would strengthen the nation's economy and lead to a favorable balance of trade.

**minority leader:** The chief floor spokesperson for the minority party in either house who looks after the interests of his (or her) party.

**minority rights:** Protections against potential abuses by a majority that might be inflicted on a minority in a democratic political process. Minority rights such as the right to vote, to protest, and to express political views, are designed to prevent majority tyranny.

**mixed system:** An economic, social, and political system which has characteristics of both socialism and capitalism.

**Moral Majority:** A religiously based fundamentalist group led by the Reverend Jerry Falwell which champions a variety of conservative causes, including a staunchly anticommunist foreign policy, the return of prayer to public schools, and opposition to the 1973 Supreme Court abortion decision. The Moral Majority exercised considerable influence in U.S. politics, especially within the Republican Party, in the late 1970s and 1980s.

**national committee:** A coordinating group at the top levels of both Democratic and Republican political parties which attempts to establish basic party policy and develop plans for national activities. National committees have varied considerably in their success at coordination.

**National Security Council (NSC):** A body that provides the president with advice on defense and foreign policy matters, often functioning in important ways during severe crises.

**natural rights:** Inalienable rights of the individual to life, liberty, and property believed to be in accord with divine will or basic ethical principles.

**necessary and proper clause:** A constitutional clause empowering Congress to enact all measures needed for carrying out its mandate.

**New Deal:** President Franklin D. Roosevelt's administrative and legislative program of the 1930s designed to promote reform and economic recovery during the Depression. It involved development of welfare state programs such as Social Security and extensive government regulation and stimulation of the economy.

**New Deal coalition:** The political base of support for the policies pursued by Franklin Roosevelt in the 1930s. This coalition included Southern whites who were traditionally Democrats, Catholics, blacks, immigrants, Jews, and other minorities. This coalition continued to be an important force in American politics for decades.

**New Jersey Plan:** A proposal introduced at the Constitutional Convention which would have limited each state to one representative in a unicameral legislature, and would have greatly strengthened the state.

**nuclear freeze:** A proposal that the United States and the Soviet Union agree to halt the production, testing, and deployment of more nuclear weapons, pending further negotiations between the two countries.

**occasion for decision:** Courts using the decision in a particular case as an opportunity for establishing policy to deal with broader issues than those in the case itself.

**Office of Management and Budget (OMB):** The largest component in the Executive Office of the President. It deals with the preparation of the federal budget and thereby plays a significant role in shaping and overseeing governmental policy-making and the choice of its priorities.

**oligarchy:** Rule by a small group, usually self-appointed.

**one-party district:** An electoral area which chooses a member of the House of Representatives and which is dominated by one political party over a considerable period of time.

**parliamentary democracy:** A form of government in which parliament (the legislature) is the supreme governing body. In parliamentary democracies, executive leadership (the Cabinet) grows directly out of the parliament and there are not separate elections for an executive as in the United States.

**peaceful coexistence:** A view articulated by Soviet Premier Nikita Khruschev in the 1950s that the United States and the Soviet Union should engage in peaceful competition and coexist, as opposed to threatening each other's fundamental interests.

**Plessy v. Ferguson:** The 1896 Supreme Court decision declaring that "separate but equal" treatment of the races was legitimate under the Constitution. It established the legal basis for an elaborate system of segregation and was not overruled until 1954.

**pocket veto:** The president's ability to veto a piece of legislation by failing to sign it within a specified period after Congress adjourns.

**political action committee (PAC):** A special organization designed to use money and persuasion to influence elections and various political battles. PACs frequently represent particular interests, such as a Realtors PAC, or an Auto Workers PAC, but can also reflect a general ideological position, such as a Conservative PAC. PACs grew very rapidly as an effort to circumvent legislation to control the financing of elections.

**political culture:** Shared ways of thinking that relate to questions of the organization of government, the distribution of power, and other aspects of political life.

**political economy:** The complex interrelations between politics and economics—each affecting and being affected by the other. Also, the study of these interrelations.

**political efficacy:** The sense that one's opinions and behavior will count in politics. The opposite of efficacy is inefficacy, or alienation.

**political party:** A group of people organized on the basis of common political objectives who seek to gain control of government.

**political machine:** A tightly run, well-organized political operation run by a political boss and his lieutenants which offers various services to its constituents in return for their steady support in elections.

**political socialization:** The processes through which an individual acquires the political attitudes and behavior common in a particular culture.

**populism:** Political sentiments that defend the interests of the common person against institutions and power elites, such as big business and big government.

**Populist Party:** American political party of the 1880s and 1890s, with its core support in the rural south, midwest, and southwest, which campaigned for social reform and against the interests of big business.

**president pro tem:** The presiding officer of the Senate, usually the senior member of the majority party, who serves as president of the Senate in the absence of the vice-president.

**prerogative powers:** Powers held by some to be inherent in the office of president and which allow the president a very wide latitude in dealing with crisis situations.

**primary election:** An election in which voters choose their party's candidates for the general election which follows.

**proportional representation:** Representation assigned on the basis of the percentage of the total votes received by each party, rather than through geographical districts.

**public assistance:** A general term which refers to programs which aid those who are in need; frequently used to describe aid given to those who have not received assistance under a more specific program.

**public interest groups:** Interest groups whose announced purpose is to serve the "public interest" as opposed to a particular private interest. Public interest groups often focus on issues such as honest government, public safety, consumer protection, and the right of the public to be accurately informed.

**public opinion:** The patterns of opinion on various subjects to be found among the citizens in a society; occasionally contrasted with the opinions of top decision makers.

**Regents of the University of California v. Allan Bakke:** A 1978 Supreme Court case in which the Court held that Bakke had been unconstitutionally deprived of his rights due to a quota system favoring minority admissions at Davis Medical School. The Court banned "quotas" but allowed continued use of race in admissions procedures to ensure a diverse student body.

**realignment:** A change in the pattern of voter preferences, reflecting a shift in the coalitions that support each party, especially as revealed in presidential elections.

**reapportionment:** Alteration of the pattern of representation among different electoral districts, as, for example, between rural and urban districts, in accordance with changes over time in population in those areas.

**referendum:** A legislative proposal, or initiative, which is submitted to popular vote.

**regulatory commissions:** A form of government organization established to regulate some specific area of social or economic life such as the Interstate Commerce Commission, the Federal Trade Commission, or the Federal Communication Commission. These agencies exercise some executive, legislative, and judicial functions and are relatively independent of control by Congress or the president.

**Reserved Powers:** Powers not specifically enumerated in the Constitution which are assumed to be reserved to the states or to the people. Such reserved powers are referred to in the Tenth Amendment and there is controversy about exactly what powers are involved.

**revenue sharing:** A program of federal allotment of funds to state governments, begun during the Nixon administration which provides the state with considerable flexibility in the use of those funds.

**rider:** A special section attached to an already existing piece of legislation, often having little to do with the main content of that legislation.

**Roe v. Wade:** The 1973 Supreme Court decision that legalized abortion throughout the nation and placed decision-making power in the hands of the mother.

**"rule of four":** The Supreme Court practice of accepting a case for consideration if at least four of the nine justices wish to hear it.

**seniority rule:** The informal but powerful rule that grants congressional committee appointments and chairmanships on the basis of the length of time the member has served in that house.

**separation of powers:** The distribution of various powers among the three branches of the federal government, so that no one branch can entirely control the others; also the division of powers between state level and national level governments.

**Seven Years' War:** The war from 1756–63 between Great Britain and France for control of Canada and Spain for Florida, won by the British. Sometimes referred to as the French and Indian War.

**Shays' Rebellion:** A rural revolt led by Daniel Shays in 1786 to protest mortgage foreclosures in western Massachusetts. The rebellion led to anxieties which convinced political leaders of the need for a new constitution.

**single-issue group:** A type of interest group focused exclusively on a particular issue or set of issues, such as abortion, the environment, or consumer interests.

**single-member district:** A geographical area from which a single representative is chosen. Usually, as opposed to proportional representation.

**Speaker of the House:** The presiding officer in the House of Representatives. The speaker chairs and directs meetings of the House according to parliamentary procedures. The Speaker is elected by majority vote of the House and this, in effect, means the Speaker is selected by the party with a majority in the House.

**social classes:** Societal groups whose status and power are related to such matters as ownership of property, occupational prestige, income, and traditional respect. Such groups might include: the middle class, white collar workers, or blue collar workers.

**social insurance programs:** Welfare state programs, such as Social Security, in which workers make contributions (i.e. taxes) and are then entitled to receive benefits upon retiring or being disabled.

**Social Security:** The largest of all U.S. welfare state programs, Social Security is designed primarily to provide payments to the disabled, the elderly, or to their survivors or dependents.

**socialism:** A political philosophy advocating the deliberate creation of greater economic equality, public ownership of major means of production, and considerable economic planning by government.

**Socialist Party:** A political party that developed in the late nineteenth century and reached its electoral peak in the second decade of the twentieth century. Led by Eugene Debs, the party, like the European democratic socialists, favored greater equality, the welfare state, and government ownership and control of major portions of the economy.

**spoils system:** A form of political reward in which the winners in an election fill many government posts with their followers. From the expression: "To the victor belongs the spoils."

**stagflation:** An economic situation characterized by both high inflation and high unemployment—common in many industrialized nations in the 1970s.

**State Department:** That portion of the executive branch whose function is to deal with foreign policy matters, including diplomacy, treaty-making, and advising on policy.

**statuatory construction:** The interpretation of a law by courts in terms of their conception of the intentions of the legislature when the law was passed.

**Strategic Arms Limitation Talks (SALT):** A process of arms control negotiations between the United States and the Soviet Union begun in the late 1960s and continuing into the late 1970s, from which the SALT I and SALT II treaties evolved.

**strict construction:** The concept that courts should stick as close as possible to the "intentions" of the writers of the Constitution; hence to be strict in their construction of the legal situation.

**Superfund:** A special federal allocation for the purpos of cleaning up toxic waste sites, begun during the Carter administration.

**Supplemental Security Income (SSI):** A current welfare program that provides cash benefits to the aged, blind, and disabled on the basis of need.

**supply-side economics:** An economic strategy popular in the early 1980s that focused on stimulating economic growth through cuts in governmental taxes. The theory, adopted in the early days of the Reagan Administration, argued that stimulating the productive sectors of the economy would create growth throughout the system, which would in turn "trickle down" to the general population.

**Taft-Hartley Act:** A labor law passed in 1947 and opposed by organized labor which gave the president power to seek to halt a strike for 80 days when in his judgment a national emergency would be created. The law also bans "closed shops" and secondary boycotts.

**third party government:** A process in which certain federal government functions are carried out by state and local governments and organizations in the private sector through contracts with the government.

**unicameral legislature:** A lawmaking body composed of only one house. In the United States, only Nebraska has such a legislature.

**unitary system:** A form of government characterized by a constitutional concentration of power in the central government with constituent governments lacking independent powers.

**Virginia Plan:** A proposal introduced at the Constitutional Convention which advocated a bicameral legislature in which representation would be apportioned on the basis of population.

**War Powers Resolution:** Legislation passed by Congress in 1973 (over President Nixon's veto) requiring that the president consult with Congress before sending U.S. armed forces into combat. In case of emergency, the president is required to consult with Congress within forty-eight hours, and Congress must approve involvement within sixty days or the troop commitment is ended.

**Watergate:** The name of an apartment and office complex in Washington, D.C., where burglars were caught in the offices of the Democratic National Committee in June 1972. This burglary led step-by-step to a series of revelations of wrongdoing—including illegal campaign financing, other burglaries, campaign dirty tricks, and other improprieties—which, in the end, led directly to the White House staff, the Committee to Re-elect the President, and finally, President Nixon himself. Eventually, many close advisors to the president were sentenced to prison, including the Attorney General of the United States, and, for the first time in U.S. history, a president resigned his office.

**welfare state:** A set of social policies including pensions, unemployment insurance, provisions for health care, and various other benefits that are indicative of society's accepting a collective responsibility for the overall well-being of individuals.

**Whig Party:** A political party formed in 1828 from a faction of the Republican Party and remnants of the Federalists. It continued in existence until 1854 and nominated two successful presidential candidates, William Henry Harrison and Zachary Taylor. The Whigs splintered over the issue of slavery.

**whip:** A subleader of either party in either house who acts as a liaison between the party leader and the members of that party.

**yuppies:** A term used to designate young urban professionals, who, as of the mid-1980s, appeared to be a major new force in U.S. society and potentially in U.S. poltics.

# The Declaration of Independence

When in the Course of human events, it becomes necessary for one people to dissolve the political bands which have connected them with another, and to assume among the Powers of the earth, the separate and equal station to which the Laws of Nature and of Nature's God entitle them, a decent respect to the opinions of mankind requires that they should declare the causes which impel them to the separation.

We hold these truths to be self-evident, that all men are created equal, that they are endowed by their Creator with certain unalienable Rights, that among these are Life, Liberty and the pursuit of Happiness. That to secure these rights, Governments are instituted among Men, deriving their just powers from the consent of the governed. That whenever any Form of Government becomes destructive of these ends, it is the Right of the People to alter or to abolish it, and to institute new Government, laying its foundation on such principles and organizing its powers in such form, as to them shall seem most likely to effect their Safety and Happiness. Prudence, indeed, will dictate that Governments long established should not be changed for light and transient causes; and accordingly all experience hath shown, that mankind are more disposed to suffer, while evils are sufferable, than to right themselves by abolishing the forms to which they are accustomed. But when a long train of abuses and usurpations, pursuing invariably the same Object evinces a design to reduce them under absolute Despotism, it is their right, it is their duty, to throw off such Government, and to provide new Guards for their future security.—Such has been the patient sufferance of these Colonies; and such is now

the necessity which constrains them to alter their former Systems of Government. The history of the present King of Great Britain is a history of repeated injuries and usurpations, all having in direct object the establishment of an absolute Tyranny over these States. To prove this, let Facts be submitted to a candid world.

He has refused his Assent to Laws, the most wholesome and necessary for the public good.

He has forbidden his Governors to pass Laws of immediate and pressing importance, unless suspended in their operation till his Assent should be obtained; and when so suspended, he has utterly neglected to attend to them.

He has refused to pass other Laws for the accommodation of large districts of people, unless those people would relinquish the right of Representation in the Legislature, a right inestimable to them and formidable to tyrants only.

He has called together legislative bodies at places unusual, uncomfortable, and distant from the depository of their public Records, for the sole purpose of fatiguing them into compliance with his measures.

He has dissolved Representative Houses repeatedly, for opposing with manly firmness his invasions on the rights of the people.

He has refused for a long time, after such dissolutions, to cause others to be elected; whereby the Legislative Powers, incapable of Annihilation, have returned to the People at large for their exercise; the State remaining in the mean time exposed to all the dangers of invasion from without, and convulsions within.

He has endeavoured to prevent the population of

these States; for that purpose obstructing the Laws of Naturalization of Foreigners; refusing to pass others to encourage their migration hither, and raising the conditions of new Appropriations of Lands.

He has obstructed the Administration of Justice, by refusing his Assent to Laws for establishing Judiciary powers.

He has made Judges dependent on his Will alone, for the tenure of their offices, and the amount and payment of their salaries.

He has erected a multitude of New Offices, and sent hither swarms of Officers to harass our People, and eat out their substance.

He has kept among us in times of peace, Standing Armies without the Consent of our legislature.

He has affected to render the Military independent of and superior to the Civil power.

He has combined with others to subject us to a jurisdiction foreign to our constitution, and unacknowledged by our laws; giving his Assent to their acts of pretended Legislation.

For quartering large bodies of armed troops among us:

For protecting them, by a mock Trial, from punishment for any Murders which they should commit on the inhabitants of these States:

For cutting off our Trade with all parts of the world.

For imposing taxes on us without our Consent:

For depriving us in many cases, of the benefits of Trial by Jury:

For transporting us beyond Seas to be tried for pretended offences:

For abolishing the free System of English Laws in a neighbouring Province, establishing therein an Arbitrary government, and enlarging its Boundaries so as to render it at once an example and fit instrument for introducing the same absolute rule into these Colonies.

For taking away our Charters, abolishing our most valuable Laws, and altering fundamentally the Forms of our Governments:

For suspending our own Legislature, and declaring themselves invested with Power to legislate for us in all cases whatsoever.

He has abdicated Government here, by declaring us out of his Protection and waging War against us.

He has plundered our seas, ravaged our Coasts, burnt our towns, and destroyed the lives of our people.

He is at this time transporting large Armies of foreign Mercenaries to compleat the works of death, desolation and tyranny, already begun with circumstances of Cru-

elty & perfidy scarcely paralleled in the most barbarous ages, and totally unworthy the Head of a civilized nation.

He has constrained our fellow Citizens taken Captive on the high Seas to bear Arms against their Country, to become the executioners of their friends and Brethren, or to fall themselves by their Hands.

He has excited domestic insurrections amongst us, and has endeavoured to bring on the inhabitants of our frontiers, the merciless Indian Savages, whose known rule of warfare, is an undistinguished destruction of all ages, sexes and conditions.

In every stage of these Oppressions We have Petitioned for Redress in the most humble terms: Our repeated Petitions have been answered only by repeated injury. A Prince, whose character is thus marked by every act which may define a Tyrant, is unfit to be the ruler of a free People.

Nor have We been wanting in attention to our British brethren. We have warned them from time to time of attempts by their legislature to extend an unwarrantable jurisdiction over us. We have reminded them of the circumstances of our emigration and settlement here. We have appealed to their native justice and magnanimity, and we have conjured them by the ties of our common kindred to disavow these usurpations, which, would inevitably interrupt our connections and correspondence. They too have been deaf to the voice of justice and of consanguinity. We must, therefore, acquiesce in the necessity, which denounces our Separation, and hold them, as we hold the rest of mankind, Enemies in War, in Peace Friends.

We, therefore, the Representatives of the United States of America, in General Congress, Assembled, appealing to the Supreme Judge of the world for the rectitude of our intentions, do, in the Name, and by Authority of the good People of these Colonies, solemnly publish and declare, That these United Colonies are, and of Right ought to be Free and Independent States; that they are Absolved from all Allegiance to the British Crown, and that all political connection between them and the State of Great Britain, is and ought to be totally dissolved; and that as Free and Independent States, they have full Power to levy War, conclude Peace, contract Alliances, establish Commerce, and to do all other Acts and Things which Independent States may of right do. And for the support of this Declaration, with a firm reliance on the protection of divine Providence, we mutually pledge to each other our Lives, our Fortunes and our sacred Honor.

# The Constitution of the United States of America

We the People of the United States, in Order to form a more perfect Union, establish Justice, insure domestic Tranquility, provide for the common defence, promote the general Welfare, and secure the Blessings of Liberty to ourselves and our Posterity, do ordain and establish this Constitution for the United States of America.

## Article I

Section. 1. All legislative Powers herein granted shall be vested in a Congress of the United States, which shall consist of a Senate and House of Representatives.

Section. 2. The House of Representatives shall be composed of Members chosen every second Year by the People of the several States, and the Electors in each State shall have the Qualifications requisite for Electors of the most numerous Branch of the State Legislature.

No Person shall be a Representative who shall not have attained to the age of twenty-five Years, and been seven Years a Citizen of the United States, and who shall not, when elected, be an Inhabitant of that State in which he shall be chosen.

Representatives and direct Taxes shall be apportioned among the several States which may be included within this Union, according to their respective Numbers, *which shall be determined by adding to the whole Number of free Persons, including those bound to Service for a Term of Years,* and excluding Indians not taxed, *three fifths of all other persons.*[1] The actual Enumeration shall be made within three Years after the first Meeting of the Congress of the United States, and within every subsequent Term of ten Years, in such Manner as they shall by Law direct. The Number of Representatives shall not exceed one for every thirty Thousand, but each State shall have at Least one Representative; and until such enumeration shall be made, the State of New Hampshire shall be entitled to chuse three, Massachusetts eight, Rhode-Island and Providence Plantations one, Connecticut five, New-York six, New Jersey four, Pennsylvania eight, Delaware one, Maryland six, Virginia ten, North Carolina five, South Carolina five, and Georgia three.

When vacancies happen in the Representation from any State, the Executive Authority thereof shall issue Writs of Election to fill such Vacancies.

The House of Representatives shall chuse their Speaker and other Officers; and shall have the sole Power of Impeachment.

Section. 3. The Senate of the United States shall be composed of two Senators from each State, *chosen by the Legislature thereof,*[2] for six Years; and each Senator shall have one Vote.

---

[1]Italics are used throughout to indicate passages that have been altered by subsequent amendments. In this case, see Amendment XIV.

[2]See Amendment XVII.

Immediately after they shall be assembled in Consequence of the first Election, they shall be divided as equally as may be into three Classes. The Seats of the Senators of the first Class shall be vacated at the Expiration of the second Year, of the second Class at the Expiration of the fourth Year, and of the third Class at the Expiration of the sixth Year, so that one third may be chosen every second Year; *and if Vacancies happen by Resignation, or otherwise, during the Recess of the Legislature of any State, the Executive thereof may make temporary Appointments until the next Meeting of the Legislature, which shall then fill such Vacancies.*[3]

No Person shall be a Senator who shall not have attained to the Age of thirty Years, and been nine Years a Citizen of the United States, and who shall not, when elected, be an Inhabitant of that State for which he shall be chosen.

The Vice President of the United States shall be President of the Senate, but shall have no Vote, unless they be equally divided.

The Senate shall choose their other Officers, and also a President pro tempore, in the Absence of the Vice President, or when he shall exercise the Office of President of the United States.

The Senate shall have the sole Power to try all Impeachments. When sitting for that Purpose, they shall be on Oath or Affirmation. When the President of the United States is tried, the Chief Justice shall preside: And no Person shall be convicted without the Concurrence of two thirds of the Members present.

Judgment in Cases of Impeachment shall not extend further than to removal from Office, and disqualification to hold and enjoy any Office of honor, Trust or Profit under the United States: but the Party convicted shall nevertheless be liable and subject to Indictment, Trial, Judgment and Punishment, according to Law.

Section. 4. The Times, Places and Manner of holding Elections for Senators, and Representatives, shall be prescribed in each State by the Legislature thereof; but the Congress may at any time by Law make or alter such Regulations, except as to the Places of chusing Senators.

*The Congress shall assemble at least once in a Year, and such Meeting shall be on the first Monday in December, unless they shall by Law appoint a different Day.*[4]

Section. 5. Each House shall be the Judge of the

Elections, Returns and Qualifications of its own Members, and a Majority of each shall constitute a Quorum to do Business; but a smaller Number may adjourn from day to day, and may be authorized to compel the Attendance of absent Members, in such Manner, and under such Penalties as each House may provide.

Each House may determine the Rules of its Proceedings, punish its Members for disorderly Behavior, and, with the Concurrence of two thirds, expel a Member.

Each House shall keep a Journal of its Proceedings, and from time to time publish the same, excepting such Parts as may in their Judgment require Secrecy; and the Yeas and Nays of the Members of either House on any question shall, at the Desire of one fifth of those Present, be entered on the Journal.

Neither House, during the Session of Congress, shall, without the Consent of the other, adjourn for more than three days, nor to any other Place than that in which the two Houses shall be sitting.

Section. 6. The Senators and Representatives shall receive a Compensation for their Services, to be ascertained by Law, and paid out of the Treasury of the United States. They shall in all Cases, except Treason, Felony and Breach of the Peace, be privileged from Arrest during their Attendance at the Session of their respective Houses, and in going to and returning from the same; and for any Speech or Debate in either House, they shall not be questioned in any other Place.

No Senator or Representative shall, during the Time for which he was elected, be appointed to any civil Office under the Authority of the United States, which shall have been created, or the Emoluments whereof shall have been encreased during such time; and no Person holding any Office under the United States, shall be a Member of either House during his Continuance in Office.

Section. 7. All Bills for raising Revenue shall originate in the House of Representatives; but the Senate may propose or concur with Amendments as on other Bills.

Every Bill which shall have passed the House of Representatives and the Senate, shall, before it become a Law, be presented to the President of the United States; if he approve he shall sign it, but if not he shall return it, with his Objections to that House in which it shall have originated, who shall enter the Objections at large on their Journal, and proceed to reconsider it. If after such Reconsideration two thirds of that House shall agree to pass the Bill, it shall be sent, together with the Objections, to the other House, by which it

[3]Ibid.

[4]See Amendment XX.

shall likewise be reconsidered, and if approved by two thirds of that House, it shall become a Law. But in all such Cases the Votes of both Houses shall be determined by Yeas and Nays, and the Names of the Persons voting for and against the Bill shall be entered on the Journal of each House respectively. If any Bill shall not be returned by the President within ten Days (Sundays excepted) after it shall have been presented to him, the Same shall be a Law, in like Manner as if he had signed it, unless Congress by their Adjournment prevent its Return, in which Case it shall not be a Law.

Every Order, Resolution, or Vote to which the Concurrence of the Senate and House of Representatives may be necessary (except on a question of Adjournment) shall be presented to the President of the United States; and before the Same shall take Effect, shall be approved by him, or being disapproved by him, shall be repassed by two thirds of the Senate and House of Representatives, according to the Rules and Limitations prescribed in the Case of a Bill.

Section. 8. The Congress shall have Power to lay and collect Taxes, Duties, Imposts, and Excises, to pay the Debts and provide for the common Defence and general Welfare of the United States; but all Duties, Imposts and Excises shall be uniform throughout the United States;

To borrow Money on the credit of the United States;

To regulate Commerce with foreign Nations, and among the several States, and with the Indian Tribes;

To establish an uniform Rule of Naturalization, and uniform Laws on the subject of Bankruptcies throughout the United States;

To coin Money, regulate the Value thereof, and of foreign Coin, and fix the Standard of Weights and Measures;

To provide for the Punishment of counterfeiting the Securities and Current Coin of the United States;

To establish Post Offices and post Roads;

To promote the Progress of Science and useful Arts, by securing for limited Times to Authors and Inventors the exclusive Right to their respective Writings and Discoveries:

To constitute Tribunals inferior to the Supreme Court;

To define and punish Piracies and Felonies committed on the high Seas and Offences against the Law of Nations;

To declare War, grant letters of Marque, and Reprisal, and make Rules concerning Captures on Land and Water;

To raise and support Armies, but no Appropriation of

Money to that Use shall be for a longer Term than two Years;

To provide and maintain a Navy;

To make Rules for the Government and Regulation of the land and naval Forces;

To provide for calling forth the Militia to execute the Laws of the Union, suppress Insurrections and repel Invasions;

To provide for organizing, arming, and disciplining, the Militia, and for governing such Part of them as may be employed in the Service of the United States, reserving to the States respectively, the Appointment of the Officers, and the Authority of training the Militia according to the discipline prescribed by Congress;

To exercise exclusive Legislation in all Cases whatsoever, over such District (not exceeding ten Miles square) as may, by Cession of particular States, and the Acceptance of Congress, become the Seat of the Government of the United States, and to exercise like Authority over all Places purchased by the Consent of the Legislature of the State in which the Same shall be, for the Erection of Forts, Magazines, Arsenals, dock-Yards, and other needful Buildings;—And

To make all Laws which shall be necessary and proper for carrying into Execution the foregoing Powers, and all other Powers vested by this Constitution in the Government of the United States, or in any Department or Officer thereof.

Section. 9. The Migration or Importation of such Persons as any of the States now existing shall think proper to admit, shall not be prohibited by the Congress prior to the Year one thousand eight hundred and eight, but a Tax or duty may be imposed on such Importation, not exceeding ten dollars for each Person.

The Privilege of the Writ of Habeas Corpus shall not be suspended, unless when in Cases of Rebellion or Invasion the public Safety may require it.

No Bill of Attainder or ex post facto Law shall be passed.

No Capitation, or other direct, Tax shall be laid, unless in Proportion to the Census or Enumeration herein before directed to be taken.

No Tax or Duty shall be laid on Articles exported from any State.

No Preference shall be given by any Regulation of Commerce or Revenue to the Ports of one State over those of another: nor shall Vessels bound to, or from, one State, be obliged to enter, clear, or pay Duties in another.

No Money shall be drawn from the Treasury, but in

Consequence of Appropriations made by Law; and a regular Statement and Account of the Receipts and Expenditures of all public Money shall be published from time to time.

No title of Nobility shall be granted by the United States: And no Person holding any Office of Profit or Trust under them, shall, without the Consent of the Congress, accept of any present, Emolument, Office, or Title, of any kind whatever, from any King, Prince, or foreign State.

Section. 10. No State shall enter into any Treaty, Alliance, or Confederation; grant Letters of Marque and Reprisal; coin Money; emit Bills of Credit; make any Thing but gold and silver Coin a Tender in Payment of Debts; pass any Bill of Attainder, ex post facto Law, or Law impairing the Obligation of Contracts, or Grant any Title of Nobility.

No State shall, without the Consent of the Congress, lay any Imposts or Duties on Imports or Exports, except what may be absolutely necessary for executing its inspection Laws: and the net Produce of all Duties and Imposts, laid by any State on Imports or Exports, shall be for the Use of the Treasury of the United States; and all such Laws be subject to the Revision and Control of the Congress.

No State shall, without the Consent of Congress, lay any Duty of Tonnage, keep Troops, or Ships of War in time of Peace, enter into any Agreement or Compact with another State, or with a foreign Power, or engage in War, unless actually invaded, or in such imminent Danger as will not admit of delay.

## Article II

Section. 1. The executive Power shall be vested in a President of the United States of America. He shall hold his Office during the Term of four Years, and, together with the Vice President, chosen for the same Term be elected as follows:

Each State shall appoint, in such Manner as the Legislature thereof may direct, a Number of Electors, equal to the whole Number of Senators and Representatives to which the State may be entitled in the Congress; but no Senator or Representative, or Person holding an Office of Trust or Profit under the United States, shall be appointed an Elector.

*The Electors shall meet in their respective States, and vote by Ballot for two Persons, of whom one at least shall not be an Inhabitant of the same State with themselves. And they shall make a List of all the Persons voted for, and of the Number of Votes for each; which*

*List they shall sign and certify, and transmit sealed to the Seat of the Government of the United States, directed to the President of the Senate. The President of the Senate shall, in the Presence of the Senate and House of Representatives, open all the Certificates, and the Votes shall then be counted. The Person having the greatest Number of Votes shall be the President, if such Number be a Majority of the whole Number of Electors appointed; and if there be more than one who have such Majority, and have an equal Number of Votes, then the House of Representatives shall immediately chuse by Ballot one of them for President; and if no Person have a Majority, then from the five highest on the List the said House shall in like Manner chuse the President. But in chusing the President, the votes shall be taken by States, the Representation from each State having one Vote; A quorum for this purpose shall consist of a Member or Members from two thirds of the States, and a majority of all the States shall be necessary to a Choice. In every Case, after the Choice of the President, the Person having the Greatest Number of Votes of the Electors shall be the Vice President. But if there should remain two or more who have equal Votes, the Senate shall chuse from them by Ballot the Vice President.*[5]

The Congress may determine the Time of chusing the Electors, and the Day on which they shall give their Votes; which Day shall be the same throughout the United States.

No Person except a natural born Citizen, or a Citizen of the United States, at the time of the Adoption of this Constitution, shall be eligible to the Office of President; neither shall any Person be eligible to that Office who shall not have attained to the Age of thirty-five Years, and been fourteen Years a Resident within the United States.

The Case of the Removal of the President from Office, or of his Death, Resignation, or Inability to discharge the Powers and Duties of the said Office, the Same shall devolve on the Vice President, and the Congress may by Law provide for the Case of Removal, Death, Resignation, or Inability, both of the President and Vice President, declaring what Officer shall then act as President, and such Officer shall act accordingly, until the Disability be removed, or a President shall be elected.

The President shall, at stated Times, receive for his Services, a Compensation which shall neither be encreased nor diminished during the Period for which he

[5]See Amendment XII.

shall have been elected, and he shall not receive within that Period any other Emolument from the United States, or any of them.

Before he enter on the Execution of his Office, he shall take the following Oath or Affirmation:—"I do solemnly swear (or affirm) that I will faithfully execute the Office of President of the United States, and will to the best of my Ability, preserve, protect, and defend the Constitution of the United States."

Section. 2. The President shall be Commander in Chief of the Army and Navy of the United States; and of the Militia of the several States, when called into the actual service of the United States; he may require the Opinion, in writing, of the principal Officer in each of the executive Departments, upon any Subject relating to the Duties of their respective Offices, and he shall have Power to grant Reprieves and Pardons for Offences against the United States, except in Case of Impeachment.

He shall have Power, by and with the Advice and Consent of the Senate, to make Treaties, provided two thirds of the Senators present concur; and he shall nominate, and by and with the Advice and Consent of the Senate, shall appoint Ambassadors, and other public Ministers and Consuls, Judges of the supreme Court, and all other Officers of the United States, whose Appointments are not herein otherwise provided for, and which shall be established by Law; but the Congress may by Law vest the Appointment of such inferior Officers, as they think proper, in the President alone, in the Courts of Law, or in the Heads of Departments.

The President shall have Power to fill up all Vacancies that may happen during the Recess of the Senate, by granting Commissions which shall expire at the End of their next Session.

Section. 3. He shall from time to time give to the Congress Information of the State of the Union, and recommend to their Consideration such Measures as he shall judge necessary and expedient; he may, on extraordinary Occasions, convene both Houses, or either of them, and in Case of Disagreement between them, with Respect to the Time of Adjournment, he may adjourn them to such Time as he shall think proper; he shall receive Ambassadors and other public Ministers, he shall take Care that the Laws be faithfully executed, and shall Commission all the Officers of the United States.

Section. 4. The President, Vice President, and all civil Officers of the United States, shall be removed from Office on Impeachment for, and Conviction of, Treason, Bribery, or other High Crimes and Misdemeanors.

## Article III

Section. 1. The judicial Power of the United States, shall be vested in one supreme Court and in such inferior Courts as the Congress may from time to time ordain and establish. The Judges, both of the supreme and inferior Courts, shall hold their Offices during good Behavior, and shall, at stated Times, receive for their Services, a Compensation, which shall not be diminished during their Continuance in Office.

Section. 2. The Judicial Power shall extend to all Cases, in Law and Equity, arising under this Constitution, the Laws of the United States, and Treaties made, or which shall be made, under their Authority;—to all Cases affecting Ambassadors, other public Ministers and Consuls;—to all Cases of admiralty and maritime Jurisdiction;—to Controversies to which the United States shall be a Party;—to Controversies between two or more States;—*between a State and Citizens of another State*;[6]—between Citizens of different States;—between Citizens of the same State claming Lands under Grants of different states, *and between a State, or the Citizens thereof, and foreign States, Citizens, or Subjects*.[7]

In all cases affecting Ambassadors, other public Ministers and Consuls, and those in which a State shall be Party, the supreme Court shall have original Jurisdiction. In all the other Cases before mentioned, the supreme Court shall have appellate Jurisdiction, both as to Law and Fact, with such Exceptions, and under such Regulations as the Congress shall make.

The Trial of all Crimes, except in Cases of Impeachment, shall be by Jury; and such Trial shall be held in the State where the said Crimes shall have been committed; but when not committed within any State, the Trial shall be at such Place or Places as the Congress may by Law have directed.

Section. 3. Treason against the United States, shall consist only in levying War against them, or in adhering to their Enemies, giving them Aid and Comfort. No person shall be convicted of Treason unless on the Testimony of two Witnesses to the same overt Act, or on Confession in open Court.

The Congress shall have Power to declare the Punishment of Treason, but no Attainder of Treason shall work

[6]See Amendment XI.

[7]*Ibid.*

Corruption of Blood, or Forfeiture except during the Life of the Person attainted.

## Article IV

Section. 1. Full Faith and Credit shall be given in each State to the public Acts, Records, and judicial Proceedings of every other State. And the Congress may by general Laws prescribe the Manner in which such Acts, Records, and Proceedings shall be proved, and the Effect thereof.

Section. 2. The Citizens of each State shall be entitled to all Privileges and Immunities of Citizens in the several States.

A Person charged in any State with Treason, Felony, or other Crime, who shall flee from Justice, and be found in another State, shall on Demand of the executive Authority of the State from which he fled, be delivered up, to be removed to the State having Jurisdiction of the Crime.

*No Person held to Service or Labour in one State, under the Laws thereof, escaping into another, shall, in Consequence of any Law or Regulation therein, be discharged from such Service or Labour, but shall be delivered up on Claim of the Party to whom such Service or Labour may be due.*[8]

Section 3. New States may be admitted by the Congress into this Union; but no new State shall be formed or erected within the Jurisdiction of any other State; nor any State be formed by the Junction of two or more States, or Parts of States, without the Consent of the Legislatures of the States concerned as well as of the Congress.

The Congress shall have Power to dispose of and make all needful Rules and Regulations respecting the Territory or other Property belonging to the United States; and nothing in this Constitution shall be so construed as to Prejudice any claims of the United States, or of any particular State.

Section. 4. The United States shall guarantee to every State in this Union a Republican Form of Government, and shall protect each of them against Invasion; and on Application of the Legislature, or of the Executive (when the Legislature cannot be convened) against domestic Violence.

## Article V

The Congress, whenever two thirds of both Houses shall deem it necessary, shall propose Amendments to this Constitution, or, on the Application of the Legislatures of two thirds of the several States, shall call a Convention for proposing Amendments, which, in either Case, shall be valid to all Intents and Purposes, as Part of this Constitution, when ratified by the Legislatures of three fourths of the several States, or by Conventions in three fourths thereof, as the one or the other Mode of Ratification may be proposed by the Congress; Provided that no Amendment which may be made prior to the Year One thousand eight hundred and eight shall in any Manner affect the first and fourth Clauses in the Ninth Section of the first Article; and that no State, without its Consent, shall be deprived of its equal Suffrage in the Senate.

## Article VI

All Debts contracted and Engagements entered into, before the Adoption of this Constitution, shall be as valid against the United States under this Constitution, as under the Confederation.

This Constitution, and the Laws of the United States which shall be made in Pursuance thereof; and all Treaties made, or which shall be made, under the Authority of the United States, shall be the supreme Law of the Land; and the Judges in every State shall be bound thereby, any Thing in the Constitution or Laws of any State to the Contrary notwithstanding.

The Senators and Representatives before mentioned, and the Members of the several State Legislatures, and all executive and judicial Officers, both of the United States and of the several States, shall be bound by Oath or Affirmation, to support this Constitution; but no religious Test shall ever be required as a Qualification to any Office or public Trust under the United States.

## Article VII

The Ratification of the Conventions of nine States, shall be sufficient for the Establishment of this Constitution between the States so ratifying the Same.

Done in Convention by the Unanimous Consent of the States present the Seventeenth Day of September in the Year of our Lord one thousand seven hundred and eighty seven and of the Independence of the United States of America the twelfth. In witness whereof We have hereunto subscribed our Names.

\* \* \*

Articles in addition to, and amendment of, the Constitution of the United States of America, proposed by Con-

[8]See Amendment XIII.

gress, and ratified by the several States, pursuant to the Fifth Article of the original Constitution.

## Amendment I[9]

Congress shall make no law respecting an establishment of religion, or prohibiting the free exercise thereof; or abridging the freedom of speech, or of the press; or the right of the people peaceably to assemble, and to petition the Government for a redress of grievances.

## Amendment II

A well regulated Militia, being necessary to the security of a free State, the right of the people to keep and bear Arms, shall not be infringed.

## Amendment III

No Soldier shall, in time of peace be quartered in any house, without the consent of the Owner, nor in time of war, but in a manner to be prescribed by law.

## Amendment IV

The right of the people to be secure in their persons, houses, papers, and effects, against unreasonable searches and seizures, shall not be violated, and no Warrants shall issue, but upon probable cause, supported by Oath or affirmation, and particularly describing the place to be searched, and the persons or things to be seized.

## Amendment V

No person shall be held to answer for a capital, or otherwise infamous crime, unless on a presentment or indictment of a Grand Jury, except in cases arising in the land or naval forces, or in the Militia, when an actual service in time of War or public danger; nor shall any person be subject for the same offence to be twice put in jeopardy of life or limb; nor shall be compelled in any criminal case to be a witness against himself, nor be deprived of life, liberty, or property, without due process of law; nor shall private property be taken for public use, without just compensation.

## Amendment VI

In all criminal prosecutions, the accused shall enjoy the right to a speedy and public trial, by an impartial jury of the State and district wherein the crime shall have

[9]Ratification of the first two amendments was completed December 15, 1791.

been committed, which district shall have been previously ascertained by law, and to be informed of the nature and cause of the accusation; to be confronted with the witness against him; to have compulsory process for obtaining witness in his favor, and to have the Assistance of Counsel for his defence.

## Amendment VII

In Suits at common law, where the value in controversy shall exceed twenty dollars, the right of trial by jury shall be preserved, and no fact tried by a jury, shall be otherwise re-examined in any Court of the United States, than according to the rules of the common law.

## Amendment VIII

Excessive bail shall not be required, nor excessive fines imposed, nor cruel and unusual punishments inflicted.

## Amendment IX

The enumeration in the Constitution, of certain rights, shall not be construed to deny or disparage others retained by the people.

## Amendment X

The powers not delegated to the United States by the Constitution, nor prohibited by it to the States, are reserved to the States respectively, or to the people.

## Amendment XI   [January 8, 1798]

The Judicial power of the United States shall not be construed to extend to any suit in law or equity, commenced or prosecuted against one of the United States by Citizens of another State, or by Citizens or Subjects of any Foreign State.

## Amendment XII   [September 25, 1804]

The Electors shall meet in their respective states and vote by ballot for President and Vice President, one of whom, at least, shall not be an inhabitant of the same state with themselves; they shall name in their ballots the person voted for as President, and in distinct ballots the person voted for as Vice President, and they shall make distinct lists of all persons voted for as President, and of all persons voted for as Vice President, and of the number of votes for each, which lists they shall sign and certify, and transmit sealed to the seat of the government of the United States, directed to the President of the Senate:—The President of the Senate shall, in the presence of the Senate and House of Representatives, open all the certificates and the votes shall then be counted;—The person having the greatest number of votes for President, shall be the President, if such number be a majority of the whole number of Electors appointed; and if no person have such majority, then from the persons having the highest numbers not exceeding three on the list of those voted for as President, the House of Representatives shall choose immediately, by ballot, the President. But in choosing the President, the votes shall be taken by states, the representation from each state having one vote; a quorum for this purpose shall consist of a member or members from two thirds of the states, and a majority of all the states shall be necessary to a choice. And if the House of Representatives shall not choose a President whenever the right of choice shall devolve upon them, *before the fourth day of March next following,*[10] then the Vice President shall act as President as in the case of the death or other constitutional disability of the President.—The person having the greatest number of votes as Vice President, shall be the Vice President, if such number be a majority of the whole number of Electors appointed, and if no person have a majority, then from the two highest numbers on the list, the Senate shall choose the Vice President; a quorum for the purpose shall consist of two-thirds of the whole number of Senators, and a majority of the whole number shall be necessary to a choice. But no person constitutionally ineligible to the office of President shall be eligible to that of Vice President of the United States.

## Amendment XIII   [December 18, 1865]

Section 1. Neither slavery nor involuntary servitude, except as a punishment for crime whereof the party shall have been duly convicted, shall exist within the United States, or any place subject to their jurisdiction.

Section 2. Congress shall have power to enforce this article by appropriate legislation.

## Amendment XIV   [July 28,1868]

Section 1. All persons born or naturalized in the United States, and subject to the jurisdiction thereof, are citizens of the United States and of the State wherein they reside. No state shall make or enforce any law which shall abridge the privileges or immunities of citizens of the United States; nor shall any state deprive any per-

son of life, liberty, or property, without due process of law; nor deny to any person within its jurisdiction the equal protection of the laws.

Section 2. Representatives shall be apportioned among the several States according to their respective numbers, counting the whole number of persons in each State, excluding Indians not taxed. But when the right to vote at any election for the choice of electors for President and Vice President of the United States, Representatives in Congress, the Executive and Judicial officers of a State, or the members of the Legislature thereof, is denied to any of the male inhabitants of such State, being twenty one years of age, and citizens of the United States, or in any way abridged, except for participation in rebellion, or other crime, the basis of representation therein shall be reduced in the proportion which the number of such male citizens shall bear to the whole number of male citizens twenty one years of age in such State.

Section 3. No person shall be a Senator or Representative in Congress, or elector of President and Vice President, or hold any office, civil or military, under the United States, or under any State who having previously taken an oath, as a member of Congress, or as an officer of the United States, or as a member of any State legislature, or as an executive or judicial officer of any State, to support the Constitution of the United States, shall have engaged in insurrection or rebellion against the same, or given aid or comfort to the enemies thereof. But Congress may by a vote of two thirds of each House remove such disability.

Section 4. The validity of the public debt of the United States authorized by law, including debts incurred for payment of pensions and bounties for services in suppressing insurrection or rebellion shall not be questioned. But neither the United States nor any State shall assume or pay any debt or obligation incurred in aid of insurrection or rebellion against the United States, or any claim for the loss or emancipation of any slave; but all such debts, obligations, and claims shall be held illegal and void.

Section 5. The Congress shall have power to enforce, by appropriate legislation, the provisions of this article.

## Amendment XV   [March 30, 1870]

Section 1. The right of citizens of the United States to vote shall not be denied or abridged by the United States or by any State on account of race, color, or previous condition of servitude.

---

[10]See Amendment XX.

Section 2. The Congress shall have power to enforce this article by appropriate legislation.

## Amendment XVI   [February 25, 1913]

The Congress shall have power to lay and collect taxes on incomes, from whatever source derived, without apportionment among the several States, and without regard to any census or enumeration.

## Amendment XVII   [May 31, 1913]

The Senate of the United States shall be composed of two Senators from each State, elected by the people thereof, for six years; and each Senator shall have one vote. The electors in each State shall have the qualifications requisite for electors of the most numerous branch of the State legislatures.

When vacancies happen in the representation of any State in the Senate, the executive authority of such State shall issue writs of election to fill such vacancies: *Provided,* That the legislature of any State may empower the executive thereof to make temporary appointments until the people fill the vacancies by election as the legislature may direct.

This amendment shall not be so construed as to affect the election or term of any Senator chosen before it becomes valid as part of the Constitution.

## Amendment XVIII   [January 29, 1919]

Section 1. *After one year from the ratification of this article the manufacture, sale, or transportation of intoxicating liquors within, the importation thereof into, or the exportation thereof from the United States and all territory subject to the jurisdiction thereof for beverage purposes is hereby prohibited.*

Section 2. *The Congress and the several States shall have concurrent power to enforce this article by appropriate legislation.*

Section 3. *This article shall be inoperative unless it shall have been ratified as an amendment to the Constitution by the legislatures of the several States, as provided in the Constitution, within seven years from the date of submission hereof to the States by the Congress.*[11]

[11]Repealed by Amendment XXI.

## Amendment XIX   [August 26, 1920]

The right of citizens of the United States to vote shall not be denied or abridged by the United States or by any State on account of sex.

Congress shall have power to enforce this article by appropriate legislation.

## Amendment XX   [February 6, 1933]

Section 1. The terms of the President and Vice President shall end at noon on the 20th day of January, and the terms of Senators and Representatives at noon on the 3rd day of January, of the years in which such terms would have ended if this article had not been ratified; and the terms of their successors shall then begin.

Section 2. The Congress shall assemble at least once in every year, and such meeting shall begin at noon on the 3rd day of January unless they shall by law appoint a different day.

Section 3. If, at the time fixed for the beginning of the term of the President, the President elect shall have died, the Vice President elect shall become President. If a President shall not have been chosen before the time fixed for the beginning of his term, or if the President elect shall have failed to qualify, then the Vice President elect shall act as President until a President shall have qualified; and the Congress may by law provide for the case wherein neither a President elect nor a Vice President elect shall have qualified, declaring who shall then act as President, or the manner in which one who is to act shall be selected, and such person shall act accordingly until a President or Vice President shall have qualified.

Section 4. The Congress may by law provide for the case of the death of any of the persons from whom the House of Representatives may choose a President whenever the right of choice shall have devolved upon them, and for the case of the death of any of the persons from whom the Senate may choose a Vice President whenever the right of choice shall have devolved upon them.

Section 5. Sections 1 and 2 shall take effect on the 15th day of October following the ratification of this article.

Section 6. This article shall be inoperative unless it shall have been ratified as an amendment to the Constitution by the legislatures of three fourths of the several States within seven years from the date of its submission.

## Amendment XXI   [December 5, 1933]

Section 1. The eighteenth article of amendment to the Constitution of the United States is hereby repealed.

Section 2. The transportation or importation into any State, Territory, or possession of the United States for delivery or use therein of intoxicating liquors, in violation of the laws thereof, is hereby prohibited.

Section 3. This article shall be inoperative unless it shall have been ratified as an amendment to the Constitution by conventions in the several States, as provided in the Constitution, within seven years from the date of the submission hereof to the States by the Congress.

## Amendment XXII   [February 26, 1951]

Section 1. No person shall be elected to the office of the President more than twice, and no person who has held the office of President, or acted as President, for more than two years of a term to which some other person was elected President shall be elected to the office of President more than once. But this Article shall not apply to any person holding the office of President when this Article was proposed by the Congress, and shall not prevent any person who may be holding the office of President, or acting as President, during the term within which this Article becomes operative from holding the office of President or acting as President during the remainder of such term.

Section 2. This article shall be inoperative unless it shall have been ratified as an amendment to the Constitution by the legislatures of three fourths of the several States within seven years from the date of its submission to the States by the Congress.

## Amendment XXIII   [March 29, 1961]

Section 1. The District constituting the seat of Government of the United States shall appoint in such manner as the Congress may direct:

A number of electors of President and Vice President equal to the whole number of Senators and Representatives in Congress to which the District would be entitled if it were a State, but in no event more than the least populous State; they shall be in addition to those appointed by the States, but they shall be considered, for the purposes of the election of President and Vice President, to be electors appointed by a State; and they shall meet in the District and perform such duties as provided by the twelfth article of amendment.

Section 2. The Congress shall have power to enforce this article by appropriate legislation.

## Amendment XXIV   [January 23, 1964]

Section 1. The rights of citizens of the United States to vote in any primary or other election for President or Vice President, for electors for President or Vice President, or for Senator or Representative in Congress, shall not be denied or abridged by the United States or any state by reason of failure to pay any poll tax or other tax.

Section 2. The Congress shall have power to enforce this article by appropriate legislation.

## Amendment XXV   [February 10, 1967)

Section 1. In case of the removal of the President from office or of his death or resignation, the Vice President shall become President.

Section 2. Whenever there is a vacancy in the office of the Vice President, the President shall nominate a Vice President who shall take office upon confirmation by a majority vote of both Houses of Congress.

Section 3. Whenever the President transmits to the President pro tempore of the Senate and the Speaker of the House of Representatives his written declaration that he is unable to discharge the powers and duties of his office, and until he transmits to them a written declaration to the contrary, such powers and duties shall be discharged by the Vice President as Acting President.

Section 4. Whenever the Vice President and a majority of either the principal officers of the executive departments or of such other body as Congress may by law provide, transmit to the President pro tempore of the Senate and the Speaker of the House of Representatives their written declaration that the President is unable to discharge the powers and duties of his office, the Vice President shall immediately assume the powers and duties of the office as Acting President.

Thereafter, when the President transmits to the President pro tempore of the Senate and the Speaker of the House of Representatives his written declaration that no inability exists, he shall resume the powers and duties of his office unless the Vice President and a majority of either the principal officers of the executive department[s] or of such other body as Congress may by law provide, transmit within four days to the President pro tempore of the Senate and the Speaker of the House of Representatives their written declaration that the President is unable to discharge the powers and duties of his office. Thereupon Congress shall decide the issue, assembling within forty-eight hours for that purpose if not in session. If the Congress, within twenty-one days after receipt of the latter written declaration, or, if Congress is not in session, within twenty-one days after Congress is required to assemble, determines by two-thirds vote of both Houses that the President is unable to discharge the powers and duties of his office, the Vice President shall continue to discharge the same as Acting President; otherwise, the President shall resume the powers and duties of his office.

**Amendment XXVI**   [June 30, 1971]

Section 1. The right of citizens of the United States, who are 18 years of age or older, to vote shall not be denied or abridged by the United States or by any state on account of age.

Section 2. The Congress shall have power to enforce this article by appropriate legislation.

# ACKNOWLEDGMENTS *(continued)*

William E. Schmitt: "The TVA has Come to a Bend in the River," *The New York Times*, May 20, 1984, Section E, p. 5. Copyright © 1984 by The New York Times Company. Reprinted by permission.

Lester R. Brown: "Reshaping Economic Policies," in Lester R. Brown, et al.: *State of the World, 1984* (New York: Norton, 1984). Copyright © 1984 by Worldwatch Institute. Reprinted by permission of the publisher.

Tables from Stichting European Value Systems Study Group, Tilburg, Netherlands, 1982. Reprinted by permission.

Table 7.2 from M. Kent Jennings and Richard G. Niemi: *The Political Character of Adolescence: The Influence of Families and Schools*, at p. 41. Copyright © 1974 by Princeton University Press. Reprinted by permission of Princeton University Press.

Table 7.3 adapted from John L. Sullivan, James Pierson and George E. Marcus: *Political Tolerance in American Democracy* (Chicago: University of Chicago Press, 1978) at p. 198. Reprinted by permission.

Table 7.4 from Michael Corbett: *Political Tolerance in America*. Copyright © 1982 by Longman Inc. Reprinted by permission. 1954 data results are from Samuel Stouffer: *Communism, Conformity, and Civil Liberties* (New York: Doubleday, 1955); 1977 data results are from the National Opinion Research Center, University of Chicago.

Figure 8.1 from Everett Ladd: "The New Lines are Drawn: Class and Ideology in America," *Public Opinion*, July/August 1978, at p. 52. Reprinted by permission. Data from 1974 Harris-Chicago Council on Foreign Relations Survey, and 1972–1977 General Social Surveys, National Opinion Research Center (NORC).

Table 8.1 from Louis Harris: *The Harris Survey*, October 24, 1985.

Copyright © 1985 The Tribune Media Service, Inc., Orlando, Florida. Reprinted by permission.

N.H. Nie and K. Anderson: "Mass Belief Systems Revisited: Political Change and Attitude Structure" in R.G. Niemi and H.F. Weisberg (eds.): *Controversies in American Voting Behavior*. W.H. Freeman and Company. Copyright © 1976. Reprinted by permission.

Table 8.2 from D. Glass, P. Squire and R. Wolfinger: "Voter Turnout: An International Comparison," *Public Opinion*, December/January 1984. Reprinted by permission.

Richard Rose: "Citizen Participation in the Presidential Process" published by permission of Transaction, Inc. From *Society*, Vol. 11, No. 1, copyright © 1978 by Transaction, Inc.

Table 8.6 from Sidney Verba and Norman H. Nie: "Political Participation" in Fred I. Greenstein and Nelson W. Polsby (eds.): *Handbook of Political Science* (Reading, Mass.: Addison-Wesley, 1975). Reprinted by permission.

Leon D. Epstein: *Political Parties in Western Democracies*. Copyright © 1967 by Frederick A. Praeger, Inc. Reprinted by permission of CBS College Publishing.

Table 9.1 adapted from David M. Wood: *Power and Policy in Western European Democracies*, 2nd ed. Copyright © 1982 by John Wiley and Sons, Inc. Reprinted by permission.

Table 9.2 and Figure 9.1 from David Price: *Bringing Back the Parties* (Washington, D.C.: Congressional Quarterly Press, 1984). Reprinted by permission.

Figure 9.3 from *The Gallup Poll*, 1985. Reprinted by permission.

Tables 10.1 and 10.2 from Herbert E. Alexander: *Financing Politics*, 3d ed. (Washington, D.C.: Congressional Quarterly Press, 1984). Reprinted by permission.

Martin Schran: *Running for President 1976: The Carter Campaign*. Copyright © 1977 by Martin Schran. Reprinted with permission of Stein and Day Publishers.

Richard Joslyn: *Mass Media and Elections*. Copyright © 1984 by Addison-Wesley Publishing Co., Inc. Reprinted by permission of Random House, Inc.

Table 10.3 adapted from Richard Joslyn: "The Content of Political Spot Ads," *Journalism Quarterly* 57 (Spring 1980). Reprinted by permission.

Table 10.4 from Gary C. Jacobson: "The Republican Advantage in Campaign Finance" in John E. Chubb and Paul E. Peterson (eds.): *The New Direction in American Politics* (Washington, D.C.: Brookings, 1985). Reprinted by permission.

Figure 10.1 from Thomas B. Edsall: "The Ins and Outs of the American Money Machine," *The Washington Post*, National Weekly Edition, December 12, 1983. © The Washington Post 1983. Reprinted by permission.

Norman J. Orenstein and Shirley Elder: *Interest Groups, Lobbying and Policymaking* (Washington, D.C.: Congressional Quarterly Press, 1978). Reprinted by permission.

R.J. Samuelson: "The Campaign Reform Failure" reprinted by permission of *The New Republic*, © 1983, The New Republic, Inc.

Martin Luther King, Jr.: *Why We Can't Wait* (New York: Signet, 1984). Reprinted by permission of New American Library, Inc.

Figure 13.1 from John Clements: *Taylor's Encyclopedia of Governmental Officials: Federal and State*, Vol. 9 (Dallas: Political Research, Inc., 1983). Reprinted by permission.

Figure 13.2 from *Guide to Congress*, November 1976 (Washington, D.C.: Congressional Quarterly, Inc.) Reprinted by permission.

Tables 13.1 and 13.3 from Walter Oleszek: *Congressional

Procedures and the Policy Process* (Washington, D.C.: Congressional Quarterly Press, 1978). Reprinted by permission.

Table 13.2 from *Congressional Quarterly Weekly Report*, January 26, 1985. Reprinted by permission.

Table 14.1 from *U.S. News and World Report*, January 14, 1985. Reprinted by permission.

Tables 14.2, 14.3 and 14.6 from Roger Davidson and Walter Oleszek: *Congress and Its Members* (Washington, D.C.: Congressional Quarterly Press, 1981). Reprinted by permission.

Table 14.5 from *Congressional Quarterly Weekly Report*, November 10, 1984. Reprinted by permission.

"TRB," *The New Republic*, May 3, 1980, reprinted by permission of *The New Republic*, © 1980, The New Republic, Inc.

Steven Kelman: "Regulation that Works," *The New Republic*, November 25, 1978, reprinted by permission of *The New Republic*, © 1978, The New Republic, Inc.

Tables 17.1, 17.2 and Figure 17.3 from Lawrence Baum: *The Supreme Court* (Washington, D.C.: Congressional Quarterly Press, 1981). Reprinted by permission.

Figure 17.2 adapted from Alice Fleetwood Bartee: *Cases Lost, Causes Won*. Copyright © 1984 by St. Martin's Press, Inc., and used with the publisher's permission.

Studs Terkel: *Hard Times: An Oral History of the Great Depression*. Copyright © 1970 by Studs Terkel. Reprinted by permission of Pantheon Books, a Division of Random House, Inc.

Table 19.1 from Joseph Peckman: *Federal Tax Policy* (Washington, D.C.: Brookings, 1983). Reprinted by permission.

Table 19.2 from 1980 Brookings MERGE File, Washington, D.C. Reprinted by permission.

Figure 19.1 from Leonard Silk: "Recovering from the Era of Shocks," *The New York Times*,

January 8, 1984, Section III, p. 1. Copyright © 1984 by The New York Times Company. Reprinted by permission.

Figure 19.2 from *The New York Times*, October 23, 1984. Copyright © 1984 by The New York Times Company. Reprinted by permission.

Table 20.2 from Robert D. Hershey, Jr.: "U.S. Study Finds Nearly 3 out of 10 Get Benefits," *The New York Times*, September 27, 1984, Section B, p. 10. Copyright © 1984 by The New York Times Company. Reprinted by permission.

Table 20.3 from *The Washington Post*, National Weekly Edition, May 21, 1984. © The Washington Post 1984. Reprinted by permission.

Christopher Jenks: "How Poor Are the Poor?" in *The New York Review of Books*, May 9, 1983. Reprinted with permission from *The New York Review of Books*. Copyright © 1983 Nyrev, Inc.

Figure 20.2 from *U.S. News and World Report*, December 24, 1984. Reprinted by permission.

Jean B. Elshtain: "The New Porn Wars," *The New Republic*, June 25, 1984. Reprinted by permission of *The New Republic*, © 1984, The New Republic, Inc.

Table 21.2 from *The Gallup Poll*, January 1981. Reprinted by permission.

Table 21.3 adapted from S.M. Lipset and W. Schneider: "The Bakke Case: How Would It Be Decided at the Bar of Public Opinion?" *Public Opinion*, March/April 1978. Reprinted by permission. Data from *The New York Times*/CBS News Poll, October 1977.

John H. Bunzel: "Promoting Rights," *The New York Times*, September 20, 1983. Copyright © 1983 by The New York Times Company. Reprinted by permission.

Joan Claybrook and the Staff of Public Citizen: *Retreat from Safety: Reagan's Attack on America's Health*. Copyright © 1984 by Pantheon Books. Reprinted by permission of

Pantheon Books, a Division of Random House, Inc.

Figure 21.2 adapted from David Shribman: "A Generation Later, Youths Join in March," *The New York Times*, August 28, 1983, p. 30. Copyright © 1983 by The New York Times Company. Reprinted by permission.

Table 22.2 from Seymour Melman: "Looting the Means of Production," *The New York Times*, July 26, 1981. Copyright © 1981 by The New York Times Company. Reprinted by permission.

Table 22.3 adapted from G.T. Kurian: *The New York Book of World Rankings* (New York: Facts on File, 1984) and from International Bank for Reconstruction and Development: *World Development Report, 1982* (New York: Oxford University Press, 1982). Reprinted by permission of the publishers.

Congressional Quarterly, Inc.: *Earth, Energy, Environment* (Washington, D.C.: Congressional Quarterly Press, 1977). Reprinted by permission.

Tables 23.1 and 23.2 from *The New York Times*, March 6, 1984. Copyright © 1984 by The New York Times Company. Reprinted by permission.

Tables 23.3 and 23.4 from Robert Stobaugh and Daniel Yergin (eds.): *Energy Future: Report of the Energy Project at the Harvard Business School*, Rev. ed. Copyright © 1983 by Random House, Inc. Reprinted by permission of the publisher.

Figure 23.2 from Allen A. Boraiko: Storing Up Trouble . . . Hazardous Waste," *National Geographic*, March 1985, p. 322. Reprinted with permission.

## PICTURE CREDITS

Chapter 1
*Page 10:* James Nachtwey/Black Star; *page 13:* Eugene Richards/Magnum; *page 13:* Herman Kokojan/Black Star; *page 15:* National Archives; *page 19:* The Bettmann Archive; *page 21:* Raymond Depardon/Magnum; *page 23:* The Bettmann Archive; *page 24:* The Bettmann Archive;

*page 26:* Alan Copeland/Black Star.

Chapter 2
*Page 32:* National Archives; *page 36:* The Bettmann Archive; *page 37:* Mathew Naythons/Black Star; *page 40:* UPI/Bettmann Newsphotos; *page 40:* Sy Seidman/National Archives; *page 41:* James Nachtwey/Black Star; *page 42:* Dorothea Lange/National Archives; *page 43:* National Archives; *page 46:* Stephen Ferry/Gamma-Liaison; *page 47:* National Archives; *page 48:* Mathew Naythons/Black Star; *page 51:* Library of Congress/Photo Researchers.

Chapter 3
*Page 58:* Library of Congress; *page 59:* The Bettmann Archive; *page 60:* The Bettmann Archive; *page 61:* Library of Congress; *page 62:* The Bettmann Archive; *page 63:* The Bettmann Archive; *page 68:* The Bettmann Archive; *page 72:* The Bettmann Archive; *page 74:* The Bettmann Archive; *page 76:* The Bettmann Archive.

Chapter 4
*Page 83:* The Bettmann Archive; *page 84:* The Brady Collection/National Archives; *page 84:* The Bettmann Archive; *page 85:* Library of Congress; *page 91:* Michal Heron/Woodfin Camp & Associates; *page 92:* Leif Skoogfors/Woodfin Camp & Associates; *page 96:* Raymond Depardon/Magnum; *page 96:* S. Greenwood/Gamma-Liaison; *page 99:* UPI/Bettmann Newsphotos; *page 99:* Eve Arnold/Magnum.

Chapter 5
*Page 104:* P.P./Magnum; *page 108:* Martin A. Levick/Black Star; *page 109:* Martin A. Levick/Black Star; *page 113:* AP/Wide World Photos; *page 117:* Bryce Flynn/Picture Group; *page 122:* The Bettmann Archive; *page 124:* National Archives; *page 125:* Library of Congress; *page 126:* Marc Pokempner/Black Star; *page 129:* Robert Phillips/Black Star; *page 130:* Leonard Lessin/Black Star.

Chapter 6
*Page 139:* The Bettmann Archive; *page 140:* Jean Gaumy/

Gamma-Liaison; *page 142:* Georg Gerster/Photo Researchers; *page 144:* National Archives; *page 146:* Sepp Seitz/Woodfin Camp & Associates; *page 147:* Sepp Seitz/Woodfin Camp & Associates; *page 148:* Catherine Noren/Photo Researchers; *page 149:* Bob Adelman/Magnum; *page 150:* Dorothea Lange/National Archives; *page 151:* Jan Halaska/Photo Researchers.

Chapter 7
*Page 164:* Burk Uzzle/Woodfin Camp & Associates; *page 167:* Chuck Fishman/Contact Press; *page 168:* Danny Lyon/Magnum; *page 169:* Jeffrey D. Smith/Woodfin Camp & Associates; *page 171:* Bobbie Kingsley/Photo Researchers; *page 173:* National Archives; *page 179:* Chip Hires/Gamma-Liaison; *page 179:* Gaby Sommer/Gamma-Liaison.

Chapter 8
*Page 190:* Steve Shapiro/Black Star; *page 191:* Bob Adelman/Magnum; *page 191:* John Crispin/Woodfin Camp & Associates; *page 192:* Martin A. Levick/Black Star; *page 192:* Bettye Lane/Photo Researchers; *page 193:* John Lopinot/Black Star; *page 194:* Black Star; *page 196:* David Burnett/Contact Press; *page 197:* Martin A. Levick/Black Star.

Chapter 9
*Page 211:* Alon Reininger/Contact Press; *page 215:* The Bettmann Archive; *page 216:* FDR Library, Hyde Park/Photo Researchers; *page 218:* The Bettmann Archive; *page 218:* Kubota/Magnum; *page 219:* UPI/Bettmann Newsphotos; *page 223:* Jacob Sutton/Gamma-Liaison; *page 226:* Bettye Lane/Photo Researchers.

Chapter 10
*Page 237:* AP/Wide World Photos; *page 238:* Burt Glinn/Magnum; *page 239:* Joan Liftin/Archive; *page 247:* Library of Congress/Photo Researchers; *page 249:* David Burnett/Contact Press; *page 251:* Burt Glinn/Magnum; *page 253:* AP/Wide World Photos; *page 257:* Steve Shapiro/Black Star; *page 257:*

Flint Journal Photo by Michael Hayman/Photo Researchers.

Chapter 11
*Page 264:* John Troha/Black Star; *page 265:* Jim Anderson/ Black Star; *page 266:* Bill Owens/Archive; *page 269:* Olivier Rebbot/Woodfin Camp & Associates; *page 272:* Dennis Brack/Black Star; *page 274:* Judy Sloan/Gamma-Liaison; *page 275:* UPI/Bettmann Newsphotos; *page 276:* Teri Leigh Stratford/Photo Researchers; *page 277:* Janet Fries/Black Star.

Chapter 12
*Page 288:* Bruce Roberts/Photo Researchers; *page 289:* Leif Skoogfors/Woodfin Camp & Associates; *page 290:* Danny Lyon/Magnum; *page 291:* Danny Lyon/Magnum; *page 293:* Howard E. Ruffner/Black Star; *page 295:* Henri Cartier-Bresson/ Magnum; *page 296:* Bruce Davidson/Magnum; *page 297:* Bob Fitch/Black Star; *page 298:* Dan Budnik/Woodfin Camp & Associates; *page 301:* Gene Daniels/Black Star; *page 303:* AP/Wide World Photos.

Chapter 13
*Page 310:* Fritz Henle/Photo Researchers; *page 311:* Art Stein/Photo Researchers; *page 315:* Dennis Brack/Black Star; *page 319:* Art Stein/Photo Researchers; *page 319:* Art Stein/Photo Researchers; *page 322:* AP/Wide World Photos.

Chapter 14
*Page 330:* AP/Wide World Photos; *page 331:* Art Stein/

Photo Researchers; *page 332:* AP/Wide World Photos; *page 334:* Art Stein/Photo Researchers; *page 336:* AP/Wide World Photos; *page 346:* AP/ Wide World Photos.

Chapter 15
*Page 352:* National Archives/ Photo Researchers; *page 352:* AP/Wide World Photos; *page 355:* Brady Collection/National Archives; *page 356:* Library of Congress/Photo Researchers; *page 356:* UPI/Bettmann Newsphotos; *page 357:* Art Stein/ Photo Researchers; *page 360:* Jaques Lowe/Woodfin Camp & Associates; *page 366:* Marc Riboud/Magnum; *page 366:* Marc Riboud/Magnum; *page 367:* UPI/ Bettmann Newsphotos; *page 367:* Owen/Black Star; *page 369:* Dan McCoy/Black Star; *page 371:* Robert Cohen/Black Star.

Chapter 16
*Page 376:* Paul Sequiera/Photo Researchers; *page 377:* David Burnett/Contact Press; *page 378:* Leif Skoogfors/Woodfin Camp & Associates; *page 384:* UPI/ Bettmann Newsphotos; *page 388:* Frank Muller-May/Woodfin Camp & Associates; *page 389:* Olivier Rebbot/Woodfin Camp & Associates; *page 392:* John Marmaras/Woodfin Camp & Associates.

Chapter 17
*Page 400:* Fred Ward/Black Star; *page 405:* UPI/Bettmann Newsphotos; *page 410:* Fred Ward/Black Star; *page 411:* UPI/ Bettmann Newsphotos; *page 412:* UPI/Bettmann Newsphotos; *page*

*414:* Alon Reininger/Contact Press; *page 415:* Arthur Tress/ Photo Researchers; *page 417:* Bill Bachman/Photo Researchers.

Chapter 18
*Page 424:* The Bettmann Archive; (*top center*): Bonnie Freer/Photo Researchers; (*bottom center*): Jim Pozarik/Gamma-Liaison; *Page 425:* Michal Heron/Woodfin Camp & Associates; *page 427:* Sepp Seitz/ Woodfin Camp & Associates; *page 428:* Katrina Thomas/Photo Researchers; *page 429:* Martin A. Levick/Black Star.

Chapter 19
*Page 438:* UPI/Bettmann Newsphotos; *page 439 (left):* The Bettmann Archive; (*right*): Ronny Jacques/Photo Researchers; *page 440:* N.A.S./Photo Researchers; (*right*): Dorothea Lange/Library of Congress from Photo Researchers; *page 441:* NYT Pictures; *page 448:* Earl Dotter/ Archive; *page 449:* Art Stein/ Photo Researchers; *page 458:* Leif Skoogfors/Woodfin Camp & Associates; *page 460:* Dan Ford Connolly/Gamma-Liaison.

Chapter 20
*Page 465:* UPI/Bettmann Newsphotos; *page 466:* Chester Higgins, Jr./Photo Researchers; *page 468:* Bruce Roberts/Photo Researchers; *page 469:* Marc Pokempner/Black Star; *page 470:* AP/Wide World Photos; *page 471:* AP/Wide World Photos; *page 476:* Arthur Tress/Photo Researchers; *page 477:* Kenneth Murray/Photo Researchers; *page 478:* Doug Wilson/Black Star;

*page 479:* David M. Grossman/ Photo Researchers.

Chapter 21
*Page 490:* Jim Anderson/Black Star; *page 491:* AP/Wide World Photos; *page 495:* UPI/Bettmann Newsphotos; *page 496 (top):*Bob Adelman/Magnum, *page 496 (bottom):* Bruce Davidson/ Magnum; *page 498:* Bruce Davidson/Magnum; *page 504:* Sepp Seitz/Woodfin Camp & Associates; *page 505:* Bettye Lane/Photo Researchers; *page 508:* Bruce Roberts/Photo Researchers.

Chapter 22
*Page 514:* National Archives; *page 515:* Owen/Black Star; *page 522:* AP/Wide World Photos; *page 523:* Philip J. Griffiths/ Magnum; *page 525:* Flip Schulke/Black Star; *page 526:* Sonja Bullaty and Angelo Lometo/Photo Researchers; *page 534:* UPI/Bettmann Newsphotos; *page 535:* UPI/Bettmann Newsphotos; *page 539:* Carl Frank/Photo Researchers.

Chapter 23
*Page 544:* UPI/Bettmann Newsphotos; *page 545:* Alexander Lowry/Photo Researchers; *page 546:* Pavlovs Kyrap/Photo Researchers; *page 547:* Joe Munroe/Photo Researchers; *page 533:* Reuters/ Bettmann Newsphotos; *page 555:* Photo Researchers; *page 561:* Martine Franck/Magnum; *page 562:* James M. McCann/Photo Researchers; *page 563:* Photo Researchers; *page 564:* Fred Ward/Black Star.

# Index